# Exploring Business Ecosystems and Innovation Capacity Building in Global Economics

Mihir Joshi
*Banasthali Vidyapith University, India*

Mohsen Brahmi
*University of Sfax, Tunisia*

Luigi Aldieri
*University of Salerno, Italy*

Concetto Paolo Vinci
*University of Salerno, Italy*

A volume in the Advances in Finance, Accounting, and Economics (AFAE) Book Series

IGI Global
PUBLISHER of TIMELY KNOWLEDGE

Published in the United States of America by
IGI Global
Business Science Reference (an imprint of IGI Global)
701 E. Chocolate Avenue
Hershey PA, USA 17033
Tel: 717-533-8845
Fax: 717-533-8661
E-mail: cust@igi-global.com
Web site: http://www.igi-global.com



Library of Congress Cataloging-in-Publication Data

Names: Joshi, Mihir, editor.
Title: Exploring business ecosystems and innovation capacity building in global economics / Mihir Joshi, Mohsen Brahmi, Luigi Aldieri, and Concetto Paolo Vinci, editor.
Description: Hershey, PA : Business Science Reference, [2023] | Includes bibliographical references and index. | Summary: "As per Gartner there are eight major dimensions of Business Ecosystems namely Openness, Strategy, Participants, Relationships, Value Exchange, Industries, Complexity and Technology. However, Business Ecosystems are much more complex than the interactions of these dimensions. Innovative Capacity Building is not a newly formed construct but lacks a standard explanation. Jensen and Krogstrup (2017) define capacity building as: [...] the continuous enhancement of capabilities, but [capacity building] also concerns the building of the capacity to identify the need for further development as well as the need for new competences which may enable the formulation and achievement of own goals. Another definition that explicitly encompasses the individual and the organizational levels of analysis is provided by Ku and Yuen-Tsang (2013). They define capacity building as: Activities that strengthen the knowledge, abilities, skills and behaviour of individuals, and improve institutional structure and processes, so that the organization can efficiently meet its goals in a sustainable way (Ku and Yuen-Tsang, 2013). This study takes into context the current Pandemic issue and the changes occurring in the businesses around the globe. All nations are pressing the need to become self reliant and as such the need to analyse the concept and terminologies associated to Business Ecosystems and Social Innovation Ecosystems is required"-- Provided by publisher.
Identifiers: LCCN 2022039737 (print) | LCCN 2022039738 (ebook) | ISBN 9781668467664 (hardcover) | ISBN 9781668467671 (paperback) | ISBN 9781668467688 (ebook)
Subjects: LCSH: Business networks--India. | Organizational change--India. | Strategic planning--India.
Classification: LCC HD69.S8 E86 2023 (print) | LCC HD69.S8 (ebook) | DDC 650.1/30954--dc23/eng/20220930
LC record available at https://lccn.loc.gov/2022039737
LC ebook record available at https://lccn.loc.gov/2022039738

This book is published in the IGI Global book series Advances in Finance, Accounting, and Economics (AFAE) (ISSN: 2327-5677; eISSN: 2327-5685)

British Cataloguing in Publication Data
A Cataloguing in Publication record for this book is available from the British Library.

# Advances in Finance, Accounting, and Economics (AFAE) Book Series

Ahmed Driouchi
Al Akhawayn University, Morocco

ISSN:2327-5677
EISSN:2327-5685

## Mission

In our changing economic and business environment, it is important to consider the financial changes occurring internationally as well as within individual organizations and business environments. Understanding these changes as well as the factors that influence them is crucial in preparing for our financial future and ensuring economic sustainability and growth.

The **Advances in Finance, Accounting, and Economics (AFAE)** book series aims to publish comprehensive and informative titles in all areas of economics and economic theory, finance, and accounting to assist in advancing the available knowledge and providing for further research development in these dynamic fields.

## Coverage

- Corporate Finance
- Comparative Accounting Systems
- Finance
- Statistical Analysis
- International Trade
- Microfinance
- E-Finance
- Applied economics
- Behavioral Economics
- Economics of Intellectual Property Rights

IGI Global is currently accepting manuscripts for publication within this series. To submit a proposal for a volume in this series, please contact our Acquisition Editors at Acquisitions@igi-global.com or visit: http://www.igi-global.com/publish/.

The Advances in Finance, Accounting, and Economics (AFAE) Book Series (ISSN 2327-5677) is published by IGI Global, 701 E. Chocolate Avenue, Hershey, PA 17033-1240, USA, www.igi-global.com. This series is composed of titles available for purchase individually; each title is edited to be contextually exclusive from any other title within the series. For pricing and ordering information please visit http://www.igi-global.com/book-series/advances-finance-accounting-economics/73685. Postmaster: Send all address changes to above address. 

## Titles in this Series

*For a list of additional titles in this series, please visit: www.igi-global.com/book-series*

***Handbook of Research on Changing World Economic Order in the Post-Pandemic Period***
Sushanta Kumar Mahapatra (IBS Hyderabad, The ICFAI Foundation for Higher Education, India) and Vishal Sarin (Lovely Professional University, ndia)
Business Science Reference • © 2023 • 470pp • H/C (ISBN: 9781799868965) • US $325.00

***Concepts, Cases, and Regulations in Financial Fraud and Corruption***
Abdul Rafay (University of Management and Technology, Pakistan)
Business Science Reference • © 2023 • 419pp • H/C (ISBN: 9781668450079) • US $250.00

***Exploring the Dark Side of FinTech and Implications of Monetary Policy***
Sheraz Ahmed (LUT University, Finland) John Agyekum Addae (LUT University, Finland & Ghana Communication Technology University, Ghana) and Kwame Simpe Ofori (International University of Grand-Bassam, Côte d'Ivoire & University of Electronic Science and Technology of China, China)
Business Science Reference • © 2023 • 281pp • H/C (ISBN: 9781668463819) • US $250.00

***Tax Audit and Taxation in the Paradigm of Sustainable Development***
Bistra Svetlozarova Nikolova (University of Economics, Varna, Bulgaria)
Business Science Reference • © 2023 • 300pp • H/C (ISBN: 9781799890676) • US $215.00

***Emerging Insights on the Relationship Between Cryptocurrencies and Decentralized Economic Models***
Dhanapal Kesavan (SRM Institute of Science and Technology, India) and N. Mari Anand (SRM Institute of Science and Technology, India)
Business Science Reference • © 2023 • 300pp • H/C (ISBN: 9781668456910) • US $250.00

***Future Outlooks on Corporate Finance and Opportunities for Robust Economic Planning***
Siraj Kariyilaparambu Kunjumuhammed (Modern College of Business and Science, Oman) and Nithya Ramachandran (University of Technology and Applied Science, Oman)
Business Science Reference • © 2023 • 278pp • H/C (ISBN: 9781668453421) • US $240.00

***Considerations of Territorial Planning, Space, and Economic Activity in the Global Economy***
Helmuth Yesid Arias Gomez (Masaryk Institute of Advanced Studies (MIAS), Czech Technical University in Prague, Czech Republic) and Gabriela Antošová (Institute of Education and Communication, Czech University of Life Sciences in Prague, Czech Republic)
Business Science Reference • © 2023 • 356pp • H/C (ISBN: 9781668459768) • US $250.00

IGI Global
PUBLISHER of TIMELY KNOWLEDGE

701 East Chocolate Avenue, Hershey, PA 17033, USA
Tel: 717-533-8845 x100 • Fax: 717-533-8661
E-Mail: cust@igi-global.com • www.igi-global.com

## Editorial Advisory Board



## List of Reviewers

# Table of Contents

# Detailed Table of Contents

*Alireza Rajabipoor Meybodi, Yazd University, Iran*
*Elahe Hosseini, Yazd University, Iran*
*Joma Khan Kazimi, Yazd University, Iran*
*Ahsanullah Sazawar, Yazd University, Iran*

Despite of a vast amount of research about the significance effects of entrepreneurship on different economic and social aspects in developed and developing countries, there are limited studies about entrepreneurship barriers in developing countries; but in Afghanistan, due to unfavourable situations, this shortcoming is more serious. To the best of the authors' knowledge, still this important topic is not addressed in Afghanistan. This study aims to identify entrepreneurship barriers in Afghanistan. In this exploratory study, in a targeted sampling approach using chain-referral method, data collected through semi structured interviews and 11 participants, including defacto- entrepreneurs, potential entrepreneurs and one academic professional, were interviewed. Sample size depend on data saturation that happened in 8th and 9th. For data analysis, the authors use thematic analysis to investigate the research question.


*Amit Banerji, Maulana Azad National Institute of Technology, India*
*Nirbhay Mahor, Maulana Azad National Institute of Technology, India*

The study aims to improve understanding of knowledge dissemination on performance determinants in the Indian pharmaceutical industry. Panel data analyses have been used to describe R&D spillover mediated through fixed assets act as a knowledge diffusion pathway, along with five other factors that affect profitability. R&D spillover mediated through physical capital points to knowledge diffusion, albeit in a small way, indicating that such things can take a permanent shape all across the industry. Fixed assets' negative relationship with profitability results from a directional shift in the last two decades.


*Sabrina Schneider, Management Center Innsbruck, Austria*

Business ecosystems have emerged as an increasingly popular and powerful mode of inter-firm collaborations. As such, business ecosystems are highly complex forms of joint value creation and capture activities between actors who, while partly loosely connected, depend on one another. Building on a combination of stakeholder and paradox theories, this chapter provides insights into two emerging paradox tensions: (1) The ecosystem engagement paradox (balancing the diverging interests of the focal firm and the overall ecosystem); and (2) the ecosystem coopetition paradox (balancing competition and cooperation with other ecosystem actors). This view allows displaying the complementary nature of both theoretical perspectives and their joint contribution to the ecosystem context. Further, by identifying two paradox tensions inherent to the business ecosystem context, this chapter offers insights for managers on how to engage in business ecosystem and how to deal with ecosystem competitiveness.

With the widespread use of the Internet, social networks have become an important tool for online marketing. The authors designed and tested various social media platforms to enrich the literature on the effectiveness of multiple types of posts with web links. In this article, researchers investigated the impact of social media marketing campaigns on continued intentions and purchase intentions. For data analysis, this study performed an online survey of 100 social media users, which was examined using SEM analysis. It was concluded that continuance intention has more influence on social media marketing as comparison to purchase intention.



The study aims to explore the continuous usage intention of ride-hailing apps by millennials utilizing the TAM model with the mediation role of service quality. Purposive sampling was employed to collect primary data from 277 Indian millennials, and structural equation modeling was utilized to analyze the data. The findings showed that perceived ease of use boosted perceived usefulness, attitude, and hedonic value, while perceived usefulness substantially affected utilitarian value and perspective. It was shown that utilitarian and hedonic values strongly impacted millennials' opinions and continued the desire to use ride-hailing applications. Service quality seems to significantly moderate impact attitudes, utilitarian and hedonic values, and ride-hailing applications' continuous intention.



Technological disruptions, hyper innovation, and a more globalized world has changed the way businesses were done. Competitive pressure in today's world is ever increasing; one of the most effective ways of staying competitive in these challenging times is through building efficient business ecosystems. This economic community leverages the services of its members to offer value to customers. Over time, they co-evolve their capabilities and roles and tend to align themselves with the directions set by one or more central companies. With growing concern towards environment safety more and more companies are putting effort to include element of sustainability in their business ecosystem. This chapter will be structured around how to build sustainable business ecosystem through circular business model.

Innovation has become in recent years a tool to promote and allow the creation of value, that is, the ability of a company or a company to generate utility, wealth, and growth. In this chapter, the contribution of innovation in decarbonization and in combating the climate crisis is illustrated, paying particular attention to the role of renewable energy communities. They are classified as a means capable of guaranteeing environmentally friendly wealth that aims not only at maximizing profit but also at creating economically sustainable models. Currently, digitalization allows a connection to nodes, peer to peer, while initially, the model was based on one-to-many transmissions, which did not allow the decentralization that are the basis of renewable energy communities; they also have a strong social impact, aiming to increase the production and consumption of energy by renewable sources, with the aim of achieving high levels of energy efficiency within society.

# Foreword

न हि ज्ञानेन सदृशं पवित्रमिह विद्यते। तत्स्वयं योगसंसिद्धः कालेनात्मनि विन्दति॥*4.38*॥ *Bhagwad Gita: Karma Yoga*

*There is no purifier as great as knowledge on this earth and the one who has attained purity of heart through prolonged practice of karmayoga ultimately achieves wisdom and truth in self and soul in due course of time.*

In this era of artificial intelligence when businesses are dealing with constant changes in industry, knowledge and information has emerged as the most powerful tool. Industries are transforming into ecosystems where they are working similar as the natural biological systems. The whole structure of business firms are transforming and cross cultural relationships are developing to sustain themselves in the market.

Post pandemic several new firms have emerged and are working on value creation, social innovation, developing platforms for entrepreneurs and forming symbiotic associations to magnify diversity. The openness of firms is augmenting to face unidentified challenges and entry of rivals in the market. Besides digital platforms are giving opportunities to new business ideas by nurturing their thoughts and taking advantage of the core services despite of different goals and targets. Business and products are incomplete without customer involvement. Addressing the basic necessity of consumers and increasing the value proposition amplifies the purpose fulfillment of a firm.

*Exploring Business Ecosystems and Innovation Capacity Building in Global Economics* book by Dr. Mihir Joshi (Banasthali Vidyapith, India), Prof Mohsen Brahmi (Sfax University Tunisia), Luigi Aldieri (University of Salerno, Italy), and Concetto Paolo Vinci (University of Salerno, Italy) explores the application of different theories and frameworks that contribute to the business ecosystem through empirical and conceptual research. Ongoing through the book each chapter covers an important dimension for the business organizations such as Interorganization structures, Symbiotic ecosystem, Dynamic and complex business environments, virtual reality tourism, knowledge diffusion, circular economy and other relevant topics that give this book an edge to modern business management books. The authors have made a dedicated effort to address diverse aspects of workforce diversity at practitioner-envisioned businesses. It is commendable that reading the entire book would yield valuable insights.

I congratulate the editors, authors, and publisher on this amazing academic initiative and wish this book every success. I believe it will be a helpful resource for academics, researchers, and policymakers in this subject.

*Pankaj Mittal*
*Association of Indian Universities, New Delhi, India*

# Preface

James Moore comprehended the ecosystem in the world of business during early 1990s. Similarly, several ecological terminologies have established themselves as the insignia. Several decades later the cataclysmic pandemic enforced several organizations to establish bonds, alliances and even mergers not just to sustain their business but for existence. The business ecosystem involves a trajectory of profit composition besides the organizational ecosystem addresses the structures and interconnections between and within the organizations.

According to Gartner, business ecosystems include eight primary dimensions: openness, strategy, participants, relationships, value exchange, industries, complexity, and technology. Business ecosystems, on the other hand, are far more complicated than the interconnections of these variables. Innovative Capacity Development is not a new concept, but it does not have a conventional explanation. Jensen and Krogstrup (2017) define capacity building as "The continuous enhancement of capabilities, but [capacity building] also includes the capacity to identify the need for further development as well as the need for new competencies that may enable the formulation and achievement of one's own goals." Ku and Yuen-Tsang (2011) propose another definition that explicitly includes the individual and organisational levels of analysis. They describe capacity development as "activities that increase individuals' knowledge, talents, skills, and behaviour, as well as improve institutional structure and procedures, so that the organisation can fulfil its goals effectively and sustainably." Individual skill development and organisational changes are examples of capacity building measures. Internationally, firms have also established inter-organizational networks to provide resources that aid in the exploration of uncharted territory, therefore establishing future markets and new enterprises (Aldrich & Pfeffer, 1976). Using notions from graph theory, social network theory aids in the investigation of several organisational phenomena at both the micro and macro levels (Freeman, 1978).

While micro level contains factors within the organization such as leadership, team building, power, trust, labor relations, the macro level states the interfirm or inter-organizational, intra organizational, alliances, joint ventures and network governance and others(Granovetter, 1973). Social exchange theory aids in the development of transactions and exchanges among organisations (Blau, 1955, 1964). According to this notion, each party exchanges what they consider to be the most valuable to the other. These transfers might be physical, such as money, or intangible, such as technology. Trust is a crucial component of social exchange theory since there is always a risk associated with identical reciprocations from parties. Individualistic and collectivistic methods are used in the study of social exchange theory (Makoba, 1993).

Researchers, academics, rising entrepreneurs, and managers who are unfamiliar with business and innovation ecosystems or who aim to establish business and innovation platforms would undoubtedly benefit from the book. This book provides a venue for prospective uses and settings for research, scholarship, study, and academic inquiry in the domain of innovation and social capital in organisational ecosystems, as well as for policymakers and practitioners. This book consists of 17 chapters and each chapter covers a significant theme for the book.

Chapter 1 is a qualitative assessment of Inter-Organizational Networks, Organizational Ecosystems and Joint Venture associations. Initially in this chapter through literature review several variables were identified that contribute to the Interorganizational Networks, Organizational Ecosystems, Social Exchange Theory and Joint Ventures. The study argues following assertions: 1) The formation and necessity of understanding IONs in ever changing business eras. 2) The association of Interorganizational networks, Organizational Ecosystems and constituents of Social Exchange Theory 3) The failures of JV associations and IONs.

covers a comprehensive framework for the strategic analysis of dynamic and complex environments at micro/macro levels with a subjective/objective approach is presented. The research method used in this paper incorporated the epistemological foundations of critical realism and complexity theory with an inductive-deductive approach and the research has been done quantitatively-qualitatively using Delphi panel and network of experts and AHP method for selecting dimensions.

Chapter 3 assembles latest literature review on Corporate social responsibility. In this regard, 317 papers on corporate social responsibility were selected which their theoretical frameworks, methodologies, theoretical gaps have been reviewed. The results indicate that CSR has been recognized and widely used in companies or organizations. Ethical, environmental, economic and psychological concerns have not been taken into account individually in this study. Further it also states the future direction for researchers and policy makers.

Chapter 4 is an empirical investigation of student e-trust and enrollment intention in online paid Hult Prize through application of partial least squares. Data analysis shows that the Hult Prize Certificate Program Digital Brand Image, E-WOM and Perceived Price have an impact on the students' Online Trust. The latter has a strong and significant influence on the students' Enrollment Intention. Followed by the moderating effect of Perceived Benefits of COVID-19 social distancing on the link between Online Learning and e-trust which is rejected. This chapter can help budding researchers and scholars to utilize such platforms. Besides policy makers can draw out conclusions on parameters of improvement in online based enrollments.

Chapter 5 examines the virtual tourism sector where tourist experience the world of augmented reality. Virtual tourism presents an opportunity to tourism industry for safeguarding their interests from business uncertainties like pandemic. This chapter analyses the relationships between enjoyment, emotional involvement, flow, positive emotions and VR experience besides also represents the linkages between VR experience and attitudes towards tourism destination. It also discusses the managerial implications and provides insights to future researchers and managers.

Chapter 6 explains the impact of digital transformation across the developing and developed nations. The chapter explores different facets of digital impacts across different nations. Electronic content, cultural diplomacy, values, communication, and interactions, as well as the preservation of culture, were all topics of discussion in industrialised countries over how digital technology impacted them. In this study the distribution of indigenous knowledge, expansion of education, boom in tourism, smart government services, and value systems in cultural communities were all examined for developing countries.

This study will help researchers identify the impacts on social life that digital footprint has left upon numerous individuals while business organizations can seek for better implementation of digital systems across different platforms.

Chapter 7 is a study on 18 different software tools from research and practice where the authors provide a comprehensive taxonomy that identifies five novel categories of software-based business model development tools and a new generation of tools using the AI for Business Model that can give explanations in order to increase trust in suggested solutions. The chapter also addresses the future challenges in developing the business data tools that require AI implementation.

Chapter 8 is a study on entrepreneurship barriers in autocracy effected Afghanistan that discourses some serious issues. The study employs a targeted sampling approach using chain-referral method and conduct interviews to assess and understand the barriers which is quite significant for the current course of changes happening in this developing country.

Chapter 9 based on panel analyses provides a better comprehension of knowledge diffusion in context to the Indian pharmaceutical industry. R&D spillover mediated through physical capital points to knowledge diffusion, albeit in a small way, indicating that such things can take a permanent shape all across the industry. Fixed assets' negative relationship with profitability results from a directional shift in the last two decades. This study will be useful to future researchers working on knowledge dissemination and for policy makers in pharma industry.

Chapter 10 provides insights into two emerging paradox tensions: (1) The ecosystem engagement paradox (balancing the diverging interests of the focal firm and the overall ecosystem); and (2) the ecosystem coopetition paradox (balancing competition and cooperation with other ecosystem actors). This chapter studies the complexities of business ecosystem which are interconnected and interdependent. Business ecosystems are inter-firm collaborations that are essential to business development and sustenance. Further, by identifying two paradox tensions inherent to the business ecosystem context, this chapter offers insights for managers on how to engage in business ecosystem and how to deal with ecosystem competitiveness.

Chapter 11 researchers investigated the impact of social media marketing campaigns on continued intentions and purchase intentions. This chapter explores the emergence of social media platforms as business platform that influences consumer intent. This study performed an online survey of 100 social media users was examined using SEM analysis. It was concluded that continuance intention has more influence on social media marketing as comparison to purchase intention.

Chapter 12 focuses on millennials and their usage of ride hailing apps. This study conducted survey on 277 millennials and employed TAM to study the continued desire of millennials to use such application platforms. The findings showed that perceived ease of use boosted perceived usefulness, attitude, and hedonic value, while perceived usefulness substantially affected utilitarian value and perspective. Service quality seems to significantly moderate impact attitudes, utilitarian and hedonic values, and ride-hailing applications' continuous intention. This chapter is useful for researchers, academicians and practitioners working on developing business models with a focus on millennials.

Chapter 13 is structured around how to build Sustainable Business Ecosystem through circular business model. In the current scenario, circular models are much sought to enhance sustainable systems across different modules in manufacturing, IT, energy and others. With growing concern towards environment safety more and more companies are putting effort to include element of sustainability in their business ecosystem.

Chapter 14 aims to investigate the impact of the use of financial technology (FINTECH) on the profitability of banks, indicate the impact of using FINTECH to increase the quality of bank's services to provided customers, and clarify the impact of using on raising the operational efficiency of banks. The results of the study found that the use of financial technology in banks facilitates the procedures for securing the necessary financing for customers, and activating electronic services such as credit card payments, mobile phone technology and other electronic services.

Chapter 15 strives to provide a concise and comprehensive picture of the importance of innovation in the renewable energy sector, as well as the role of their deployment in ensuring climate change mitigation and sustainable growth. The chapter starts from the environmental Kuznets curve (EKC) and then examine the metabolism of current societies, focusing on the trend of the diffusion of technological innovation and its contribution to the energy transition.

Chapter 16 is study on the relationship between Total Quality Management (TQM) practices and product innovation. This paper aims to investigate the link between TQM practices and product innovation in Tunisian ISO 9001-certified industries. The current study tested ten hypotheses related to TQM practices and product innovation using a self-administered survey of ISO9001-certified industries. supports the existence of significant and positive relationships between TQM practices. This study is useful for the managers involved in quality improvement and firms emphasizing on innovation practices.

Chapter 17 studies the contribution of innovation in de-carbonization and in combating the climate crisis is illustrated, paying particular attention to the role of renewable energy communities. The study emphases on developing necessity of innovation to promote and develop value. Further the study explores the implementation of renewable power plants in Europe and takes into account various technological configurations.

*Mihir Joshi*
*Banasthali Vidyapith University, India*

*Mohsen Brahmi*
*University of Sfax, Tunisia*

*Luigi Aldieri*
*University of Salerno, Italy*

*Concetto Paolo Vinci*
*University of Salerno, Italy*

## REFERENCES

Aldrich, H. E., & Pfeffer, J. (1976). Environments of organizations. *Annual Review of Sociology*, *2*(1), 79–105. doi:10.1146/annurev.so.02.080176.000455

Blau, P. M. (1955). *The Dynamics of Bureaucracy*. University of Chicago Press.

Blau, P. M. (1964). *Exchange and Power in Social Life*. Wiley.

Freeman, L. C. (1978/1979). Centrality in social networks conceptual clarification. *Social Networks*, *1*(3), 215–239. doi:10.1016/0378-8733(78)90021-7

Granovetter, M. S. (1973). The strength of weak ties. *American Journal of Sociology*, *78*(6), 1360–1380. doi:10.1086/225469

Jensen, J. B., & Krogstrup, H. K. (2017). Fra new public management til new public governance. In *Samskabelse og capacity building i den offentlige sektor* (pp. 33–55). Hans Reitzels Forlag.

Ku, B. K., & Yuen-Tsang, E. W. K. (2011). *Capacity Building. I: The Sage Handbook of Governance*. Sage. doi:10.4135/9781446200964.n30

Makoba, J. W. (1993). Toward a general theory of social exchange. *Social Behavior and Personality*, *21*(3), 227–239. doi:10.2224bp.1993.21.3.227

# Acknowledgment

We are thankful to the authors, editorial board members, IGI Global's editorial team, and reviewers who were involved in this book production. This book would not have been possible without their generous assistance.

Most importantly, we are grateful to all chapter contributors without them this book would only be an abstraction. All chapter titles in the book were essential components without which the book wouldn't have completed. We are also grateful to all of our editorial board members and chapter reviewers for their diligent work and valuable time in assisting us in improving the quality of the content featured in the book. We are thankful to all authors who also contributed as reviewers during the course of book editing. Foremost we are thankful to our families for their constant support, patience, and encouragement in composing the book on time.

# Chapter 1
# A Qualitative Assessment of Inter-Organizational Networks, Organizational Ecosystems, and Joint Venture Associations

**Mihir Joshi**
https://orcid.org/0000-0001-6922-3489
*Banasthali Vidyapith University, India*

## ABSTRACT

*Inter-organizational networks are fundamental in propelling the relationships within the organizations. ION are also important for those organizations that are involved in establishing a cross cultural association. However, such relations are affected by several factors, like social climate and economic environment. Initially through literature review, several variables were identified that contribute to the interorganizational networks, organizational ecosystems, social exchange theory and joint ventures. In the next step, qualitative data analysis was performed using RQDA. Text analytics was employed to study various correlations among the variables. The study argues following assertions: 1) The formation and necessity of understanding IONs in ever changing business eras; 2) The association of interorganizational networks, organizational ecosystems, and constituents of social exchange theory; 3) The failures of JV associations and IONs.*

## 1. INTRODUCTION

Inter-Organizational networks do not possess any customary explanation (Bergenholtz & Waldstrom, 2011). It is however, defined by the formation of associations, alliances or ventures (Kilduff & Tsai, 2003). Organizations move strategically so as to explore new opportunities in domestic or foreign markets by establishing alliances that possesses risk and uncertainty (Gulati & Gargiulo, 1999). The term network helps to deduce the basic purpose of the association of organizations that could be unexplored market, partner trust and reliability (Mayer, Davis &, Schoorman, 1995; Powell, Koput,& Smith Doerr,

DOI: 10.4018/978-1-6684-6766-4.ch001

1996; Zaheer, McEvily, & Perrone, 1998). Past studies show that the inter-organizational purposes are well served through information sharing (Dawes, 1996; Yang & Maxwell, 2011; Pardo et al.,2004,), technology sharing that can improve the collective work (Pfeffer & Salanick, 1978; Zhang and Dawes, 2006; Yang & Maxwell,2011),mutual interdependence (Hill & Hellriegel, 1994; Gulati & Gargiulo, 1999; Pardo et.al.,2004), shared interests (Ring & Van de Ven, 1994), co-existence(Idea & Vodafone merger, 2017). Researchers in the past have assessed the importance of networks that are essential for organizations in order to establish ventures which are quite complex type of association (Yan & Lou, 2016). Studies have shown that organizations establish ventures to elude the unknown risks and utilize each other's competence and resources (Gulati & Singh, 1999; Yan & Lou, 2016). A new venture formation not only gives new resources and chances but is also followed by confrontational situations like changing market conditions (Ozmel, Reuer, & Gulati, 2013).

Further, Innovation or creativity application to resolve specific problems, enhancing performance is vital for a business venture. Innovative activities performed in a business environment internal or external to the organizations creates an ecosystem of such ventures. Past studies have been central to stating and restating the set of several terminologies that define organizational ecosystem (Valkokari, 2015; Shipilov & Gawer., 2020) including innovation ecosystem (Adner, 2006), open innovation ecosystem (Chesbrough et al., 2014;Gomes et al., 2016; Xie & Wang, 2020), regional innovation ecosystem (Zmiyak, Ugnich, & Taranov,2020), hub ecosystem (Nambisan & Baron., 2013; Gomes et al., 2016), business ecosystems (Moore, 1993; Jacobides et al., 2018), social innovation ecosystems (Murray, Caulier-Grice, & Mulgan.,2010; Purtik & Arenas, 2019). Innovation ecosystem constitutes of actors and set of actors that progress and transform with time along with the changes in activities and objects that are related to institutional transformations together with complementarities and substitution (Jacobides et al., 2018; Granstrand & Holgresson, 2020). In successful application of advance technology for new product development not only private sector but the government initiatives also play a pivotal role. The formation of Inter-Organizational networks such as JV is dependent on several factors that include total cost of ownership, productivity, profitability, comparative productivity, performance, preservation, formal or real authority and network connectivity. While establishing the inter-organizational relations, firms involve in social structural interactions (Wasserman & Faust, 1994).

Although for the purpose of this study the researchers utilize qualitative approach past studies show the application of sociometric tools that explain the arrangements of organizational connections (Burt, 1992; Watts, 1999; Shipilov, & Gawer, 2020). Initially the study discusses following assertions 1) The formation and necessity of understanding IONs in ever changing business eras. 2) The interlinkages of inter-organizational networks, organizational ecosystems, and constituents of social exchange theory 3) The failures of JV associations and IONs. The initial part of the paper extensively reviews the literature over Inter-organizational networks, organizational ecosystems with a broad focus on Innovation Ecosystem and Social Innovation ecosystem. The study proposes the concept of Innovation Capacity fulfillment that is concerned with innovation from end user prospective. In the second part study analyzes the failure of ION by taking case of TATA-DOCOMO joint venture failure in Indian market. In the third step the research proposes a conceptual model on the basis of qualitative data analysis using RQDA that shows interlinkages among various systems related to IONs. The researcher also draws out the implications and conclusion over the factors that are briefly discussed in the review section.

## 2. LITERATURE REVIEW

### 2.1 Inter-Organizational Networks

IONs are created to explore the available sources of innovation, new technological breakthroughs, resources that were previously unavailable, not in knowledge of the existing enterprises or were way ahead of the existing era (Wievel and Hunter, 1985). Further, in order to access the scarce resources and unmapped markets organizations create Interorganizational networks. These associations may exist under perilous conditions where resources may create future markets and openings to the competitors (Aldrich and Pfeffer, 1976; Aldrich, 1979). Successively, a new niche market appears where several firms are beneficiaries and require each other for their existence. To some firms this may mean amassing a large number of new entrants into the market but become an essential part of a much larger symbiotic relationship (DiMaggio & Powell, 1983; Wievel & Hunter, 1985). ION also exerts symbiotic relation vital for existence and business sustainability. Joint Ventures, Strategic Collaboration and Alliances are a result of ION establishment(Podonly & Page, 1998). Past studies have defined Inter-organizational networks as "a set of nodes explaining the existing inter relations among nodes besides clarifying the nature or non-existence of association," Brass et al. (2004).

Studies in past encompass the different levels of analysis of organizational network. These levels are stated as Interorganizational, Interunits and Interpersonal Networks. Further it explains the network factors that act as antecedents and consequences in social networks at different levels (Brass et al., 2004). Joint ventures, strategic alliances, collaborations and consortia are considered as types of assistance that form an inclusive explanation of Interorganizational network (Podolny & Page, 1998; Podonly, 2001). The sources over which organizations are dependent may be internal or external. Success of organizations are dependent on optimal management of these external sources and so is the failure. Being an open system Organizations and Networks work coaxially (Pfeffer & Salancik, 1978; Astley & Fombrun, 1983).

Early Literature explains the difference in three segmentations Market, Ecosystem and Organizational Networks. Markets synchronize on the basis of prices where one firm buys a product (finished or unfinished good) from a supplier to derive a utility or sell it further. Organizational Networks represent a formal or informal association including non-generic complementarities between organizations. Past studies have reconnoitered the necessity of social factor that contribute to the mutual cooperation among associated organizations (Granovetter, 1985). Sharing of information, mutuality, joint training, and learning are important aspects of organization network form which is adds value to network. It also increases the coordination and teamwork, mutual understanding at different levels within the organization (Powell, 1990; Nohria & Eccles, 1992; Shipilov & Gawer, 2020).

### 2.2 Organizational Ecosystem

Organizational Ecosystem is loosely based on the concept of biology that states a collective interaction among the abiotic and biotic components (Valkokari, 2015; Gomez et. al., 2016). Similarly, in business organizations the concept of ecosystem denotes an interrelation among the firms where there is moderate to no hierarchical control but offers non-generic complementarities. Research by Valkokari (2015) speculates that global economy is an ecosystem where organizations and customers are the components of this ecosystem(Gomes et al., 2016). The study by Adner and Kapoor (2010) recommended that ecosystems offer unambiguous interdependency to the organizations. Past research consider the concept of ecosystems to be beneficial for value generation, capturing value and firm strategic issues (Priem et al., 2013). Ecosystem is also considered as a system of networks that consists of several actors, nodes and objects interlinked together (Basole and Karla, 2011).

### 2.2.1 Business Ecosystem

Extant research work on organization ecosystem categorizes the ecosystem into three segments. The first category "business ecosystem" focuses on firm and its internal-external environment. The term engineered by Moore (1993) explains that concepts related to strategic alliance and virtual organization offer little support to the managers in solving organizational problems. The study further suggests that managers should consider organizations as a constituent of ecosystem which has several interlinked actors that evolve themselves through creativity, skill enhancement, knowledge sharing, coordination and cooperation (Gomes et al., 2016).

As per the study by, Iansiti and Levien (2004) who were the fundamental creators of the concept, the business ecosystem consists of suppliers, original equipment manufacturers, outsource companies, distributors and other organizations that influence the firm and get affected by the firm activities. Studies concerning the business ecosystem suggest their relation to the Interorganizational networks and strategic alliance (Overholm, 2015; Gomes et al., 2016). The business ecosystem concept observes different firms, organizations, institutions even individuals as the constituents of ecosystem. These constituents or 'actors' influence the activities of each other above and apart from within the organization. Hence, designated as a community these constituents or actors affect competences of the firm besides influencing the customers and suppliers of the organization. The overall ecosystem performance influences the individual performance (Iansiti & Levien, 2004; Teece, 2007; Jacobides et al, 2018). Conversely, the explanation of mutual adaptations of firms remain unexplained.

### 2.2.2 Innovation Ecosystem

"Innovation Ecosystem" which centers around new innovative and creative ideas. Gomes et al., 2016 suggest Innovation Ecosystem to be associated with creating value while the business ecosystem seizes the value. Several authors consider Business Ecosystem tantamount to Innovation Ecosystem closely correlated (Overholm, 2015, Gawer & Cusumano, 2014, Nambisan & Baron, 2013). It is by far the most important ecosystem variable in the organizational ecosystem construct. As per the study by Adner (2006) Innovation ecosystems are customer centric and offer solutions to meet the customer requirement. The focus is on components and complements that provide support to the ecosystems. Additionally, if the cooperation within the organizations is poor or insufficient then it may lead to failure of the system. It is therefore necessary to increase value addition to customer needs and prominently innovate and materialize the gains. As the customer gains, firms associated will benefit and so will the ecosystem sustain(Adner, 2012; Adner & Kapoor, 2010; Kapoor & Lee, 2013; Jacobides et al,2018). Authors also consider the congruency between business ecosystems and innovation ecosystems(Zahra and Nambisan, 2012). The similarity between both the systems is poised by the customer needs. Innovation Ecosystem group of companies that includes several objects and individuals. These objects in the ecosystem share several aspects such as advancements in technology, goods and services development (Zahra and Nambisan,2012;Gomes et al.,2016). In Innovation ecosystem, instead of firms it is the end customer who uses the finished product. It is the end user who affixes the firm and the innovation systems so that rapid improvisations are possible in the end product. Innovation system is also addressed as a link shared between organizations and universities (Carayannis & Campbell, 2009).

The existing studies on Innovation systems consider them as a collective group of well-coordinated networks (Russell and Smorodinskaya, 2018;Benitez et al., 2020). Innovation systems concept has been elemental to the studies focused on industry 4.0 (Benitez et al., 2020), in entrepreneurial ecosystem studies (Pustovrh et al., 2020) besides in education sector studies (Zmiyak et al., 2020). The importance of Innovation system concept should be observed from the micro level where identification of set of entities is required to create value in the structure. This structure arrangement consists of multidimensional partners engaged in one or several activities with a focus to develop creative products or services (Lusch & Vargo, 2014; Adner, 2017; Benitez et al., 2020). The innovative product or service creation is, therefore, the only outcome that is co-created through multiple actors involved that may follow a hierarchical structure or self-coordinate the activities (Tsujimoto et al. 2018). The prolix technological abilities of the companies could be associated to different creative platforms with in the innovation ecosystems (Gawer & Cusumano, 2014; Benitez et al., 2020). An fsQCA analysis by Xie and Wang, 2020 gives six dimensions to the open innovation system 'firm university institute cooperation', 'interfirm cooperation', 'firm-intermediary cooperation', 'firm-user cooperation', 'asset divestiture' and 'technology transfer'. Further, they segregate the dimensions into 'inbound mode' and 'outbound mode'(Xie and Wang, 2020). Studies concerning the dimensions of innovation ecosystem have gained considerable interest among the researchers.

## 2.3 Social Innovation

The creative activities and amenities carried out in order to fulfill a social necessity which is principally dispersed from the organizations to the society and driven by social need fulfillment is stated as *Social Innovation.* It is thought provoking to bring a transformation to the very system that created the societal issues such as global warming, financial inequality, escalation in poverty and others (Antadze & Westley, 2010). The concept of Social Innovation (SI) has become a protruding topic with in the field of societal relations and social entrepreneurship as an allied area (Pel et al.,2020; Ayob, Teasdale, and Fagan 2016; Ziegler 2017). SI revolves around the axis of fostering new ways of knowing, constructing, refining and performing for the significant societal or individual development (Avelino et al. 2019).

The concept of SI can be elucidated through various examples from history such as *"All India Spinners Association"* established by the efforts of Mahatama Gandhi. Post-Independence Khadi and Village Industries Commission (KVIC), 1957 financially aided several individual spinners and institutions for promoting the use and export of Khadi (hand woven cotton cloth). Moreover, SI covers broader prospects through progressions in technology, rural and urban development, institutional innovation platforms, sharing schemes, makerspaces and sustainable practices (Haxeltine et al., 2017).

In a study by Phills, Deiglmeier and Miller, 2008 social innovation is stated as a unique, sustainable, proficient and effective method to resolve a problem that have primitive or inefficient existing solutions. Additionally, social innovation can be an ideology, a norm, interpolation of ideas, societal movement, and technological advancement, a new regulation, new product, re-engineered process or amalgamation of these factors. Further, social innovation is defined as "recognizing and conveying of new services so that individual as well as community lifestyle is improved, incorporation of novel labor market processes, improvised skills and competence, job creation, new partaking forms and several such diverse components that contribute to social problem solving agendas besides improving the workforce". Social innovation is created by the motivation to resolve social problems that have been previously ignored or neglected by the state or have been poorly attended to by the private or public services through orthodox methods. Such innovations can be created by individual or community, public, private or other section of the society. The goal SI lies in it's explanation that is to provide a "novel solution to a social problem which is more effective, efficient and sustainable" (Phills, Deiglmeier, & Miller, 2008; Gasparin et al., 2020). Additionally, the objective of SI is to generate social value above and beyond the present system through new ideas, approaches and tools (Dawson & Daniel, 2010; Adams & Hess, 2010; Gasparin et al., 2020) which makes it one of the most vital dimension in the inter-organizational network creation.

Furthermore, Murray, Caulier-Grice and Mulgan, (2009) give six stages of social innovation process that include *Prompts, inspirations and diagnoses, proposals, and ideas, prototyping and pilots, sustaining, scaling and diffusion and systematic change. Prompts, inspirations, and diagnoses* stage consists of all those factors that generate the need for innovation such as inspiration, performance, crisis (pandemics like Covid-19 or natural disasters), creativity and aspiration. This can be called as *"root cause level"* since an innovator or creator identifies the problem. The innovator or a believer (one who believes that can handle the societal issue, extracts social value) is prompted to idea generation where the core problem factor is diagnosed. In the *proposals and ideas* stage new ideas are created and can also be referred to as *idea origination phase*. It includes creativity, design generation and innovative orientation which expands the number of existing options. From a wide variety of sources available different methods can assist in enticing acumens. The third stage of social innovation process is *prototyping and pilots* which involves the evaluation of ideas generated by trying them on field. These trials can be carried out through, prototype building, short term projects, mini studies or implementation through qualitative methods. Additionally, randomized controlled trial methodology can also be applied as implementation of this technique has diversified from medicine research to economics (Banerjee & Duflo, 2009). For a successful implementation of an idea, it is necessary for it to be tested for related errors and issues. Testing and retesting strengthens the association with end user. *Sustaining* is the fourth stage where the idea is restructured and rationalized; options for financial stability and sustainability are analyzed besides refinement of the idea still continues at this stage. Every innovation requires financial plan either charity based or firm based. The fifth stage is *Scaling and diffusion* concerning the growth and expansion of the innovation. The extension of innovation happens either through franchising or licensing of venture or through inspiration and imitation. Diffusion elucidates the free mobility of the idea in the market with modulation of the demand through legislators and administrators. The last stage of social innovation is the eventual objective of the social innovation which is called as *Systematic change.* Once the innovation is executed through platform(s) it brings with it a stream of transformations in laws, regulations, databases, infrastructures, business models and societal movements.

Past studies have specified risks that are closely associated with the innovation and target market. Adner (2006), adds three elemental risks that concern Innovation ecosystems namely *Initiative risks* which involve qualms related to project. Initiative risks involve evaluation of product viability, end user benefit, and market competition, timely completion of project, team coordination and maintaining supply chain. Additionally, the qualms created among the innovators lead to interdependence risk which is linked to synchronizing with complementors.

## 2.4 Innovation-Capacity- Fulfillment

The concept of *Innovation-Capacity-Fulfillment* requires the organizations to nurture *Individual Innovation, End User Involvement, Capacity Building (Individual and Organizational) and Purpose Fulfillment. Individual innovation* is the application of creativity at assigned job role, introduction of reformed and novel ideas that benefits role performance, team, and organization in a broad prospect (Janssen, 2000). Individual innovation boosts firm performance, assists the individual from socio-psychological aspect and increases job satisfaction (Wu, Parker, & Jong, 2014). The individual innovation is a proactive work behavior that is self-originated and motivated. Such ideas bring transformation in organizational systems after their implementation. Moreover, creating a positive work environment for innovation systems is a major factor that differentiates organizational performance and effects the performance outcomes (Cooper, 2019). This requires a constant support from top management and senior officials of the organization who can motivate the individuals and encourage intrapreneurial intent. However, studies suggest the addition of customer voice in ideation process is most effective in recognizing the change required in the product (Cooper and Edgett, 2008; Cooper, 2019). Additionally, at every stage of product development the *End user involvement* is considered necessary to understand the consumer requirement. Cooper, (2017) suggests that voice of customer is to be considered in Idea generation, product viability, product creation, product trial and after product launch. It can done by collecting customer feedback, customer team visits, design thinking, taking an ethnographic approach and carrying out focus group (Cooper, 2019). *Capacity Building* is the process involving learning(adaptive and generative learning) that improves individual skills, provides strength to ability and knowledge. It also improvises the institutional framework and fortifies firm performance (Ku & Yuen Tsang, 2013). Further, literature considers Capacity building as an outcome since improvements in current individual skills and knowledge is an output of all the factors that contributed to its development (Brix, 2018; Brix, 2019). Additionally, capacity building also involves recognizing market attractiveness. The two basic aspects of market attractiveness are market potential and market competition. Firms should prepare for the market competition and analyze the market potential (Cooper, 2019).

*Purpose Fulfillment* comprises of information provided by the customer or end user, for redefining existing services or series of conveniences and end user influence on developmental decisions (Kujala, 2008). Having no generally accepted explanation to purpose fulfillment this study introduces the concept in milieu to end user necessity fulfillment. Therefore, *purpose fulfillment* is an outcome generated after the product development and consumer satisfaction which completes the consumer requirement when all other aspects of development vis-à-vis Innovation and Capacity are completed. Past studies have pointed out that customer centric innovation has become the focal point of businesses to develop products by involving customers in the process. The customer involvement helps product developers to increase efficiency and gain knowledge from open forums. The third category "Platform Ecosystem" is based on the organization of different players (Jacobides et al., 2018).

## 2.5 Symbiotic Ecosystem

The present study suggests another form of Ecosystem based on only "symbiotic association" that can be observed in contracting and sub-contracting. In a "symbiotic ecosystem" firms manage to not only adapt to the existing vulnerabilities for them in the market but also devise structures that create sustainability to sharing firms. Additionally, firms in such type of association jointly perform activities that are beneficial to associated actors, forming an ecosystem. In order to transform their processes and bring refinement to work companies can take up symbiotic arrangement. It is a viable strategy for developing core competence as both the interdependent firms gain through this relation. However, researchers are of the view that symbiotic associations are even beyond interdependencies (D'Amato et al., 2019; Diaz Lopez et al., 2019; Domenech et al., 2019; Shaikh et al., 2022; Domenech and Bahn-Walkowiak, 2017; European Commission, 2015; Fraccascia, 2020; Fraccascia et al.,2020). A constant contribution is necessary from the firms for maintaining competence since a proper symbiotic association is dependent on mutual support (Eternid, Wright, & Dana, 2001). Till present no study designates "symbiotic ecosystem" as its characteristics match to that of the existing forms of ecosystem but are different in modus operandi and is included within the concept of business ecosystem (Jacobides et al., 2018). For example, X firm offers e-commerce services in remote locations where the infrastructure to setup its own logistic operations may be higher or regulated by local government/authorities in such a case existence of Y is beneficial to X. With more and more orders for X incoming, Y shall certainly make benefits. The services of Y shall also affect the goodwill of X, since its business is dependent on timely delivery.

Similarly, from customer value enhancement prospect companies today exert a symbiotic association. Xiaomi a mobile manufacturing firm founded by Lei Jun who in the past worked closely with cellphone giants Nokia and Motorola applies a symbiotic relation with the customers. The product managers of Xiaomi spend a lot of time looking for innovative solutions on their company's mobile community. Likewise, several social media corporations follow the same and connect to their customers through online communities or application platforms on playstore. From the B2B context the investments by venture capitalists into creative entrepreneurs displays a "symbiotic association". A relevant example is Flipkart which prior to its sale out to world's largest brick and mortar store, Walmart, received constant investments from Tiger Global Investments, Accel partners, Naspers and others. The initial investment of $US 5600 by the founders turned into US$5billion by 2017. However, observing a steep rise in acceptance of e-commerce in India and extreme market goodwill of Flipkart, Walmart purchased 77% stake in Flipkart. Hence, the symbiotic association is the most important feature for the growth of modern economy and businesses across the globe.

## 2.6 Social Exchange Theory

SET has been pronounced as an activity exchanging system based on rewards processes for transfer of value by Blau (1986) and Emerson (1976). This theory takes into account the players' immediate social interactions. Such interactions are founded on mutual confidence, reciprocity, and the expectation of advantages from the voluntary transactions of value, which establish commitments between the parties concerned (Tanskanen et al., 2015). Consequently, SET is the alternative of transaction costs economics, which emphasises contractual trades instead of social interactions (Cropanzano & Mitchell, 2005). Further, social exchange theory has also been articulated on the basis of five principles namely: success, stimulus, value proposition, deprivation- satiation and the aggression proposition (Homans, 1961). An individual learns from the past experiences attempts to create constructive mechanisms and tries to reduce the negative constraints. Prior alliances of the actor and the reputation gained, future vision and present relations tend to develop the JVs.

Besides, individuals who give much to others therefore attempt to obtain much from them, while those who get much from others are compelled to give much to them (Homans, 1961). However, the social interactions have exchangeable value (Blau, 1986, Emerson, 1976). Emerson stated that the ability of one actor to control or influence other actor or individual lies in that actor's control over elements that other actor values. In Joint venture associations SET is highly important to create valuable exchanges between those who are involved in a constructive-progressive system. For this the actors involved in JV need to build trust and start association on the basis of trust as it acts as a bond between cohorts (Khalid & Ali, 2017).

## 2.7 Joint Venture

Joint Ventures(JV) or sometimes referred to as joint subsidiary (Pfeffer & Nowak, 1976) arise out of organizational growth and expansion, risk sharing, reducing investment costs (Kogut, 1991; Tayeb, 2005; Bingol & Begec, 2020), expand or create marketing strategies (Tayeb, 2005; Bingol & Begec, 2020) strategic importance for international business (Geringer,1991) intensify competition, profit stabilization, changes in vertical integration (Harrigan, 1988), acquire local complementary assets for international JV (Hennart, 2009), penetrate new and potentially profitable markets, share monetary risks with partner firms, avert confiscation risks and political instabilities, attain common goals and maintain collaboration and share knowledge (Datta, 1988). The extant literature also asserts that the purpose of creating international joint ventures(IJVs) includes product substantiation and economies of scale, flabbergast or dismantle competition, technological augmentation and procreation, roadmap to foreign market business, location procurement, product positioning, market progression and developing large projects (Tayeb, 2005; Bingol & Begec,2020). The pioneer of the concept of transaction cost theory, Williamson (1991) states that organizations establish alliances and try to engage the transactions in businesses that are different in several characteristics parallel with the governance procedure distinct in capacities so as to control the business costs and control production (Williamson,1981; Chattopadhyay & Bhawsar, 2016).

Joint ventures exhibit joint ownership of a new subsidiary that is created by the involvement of two or more established firms with complementary resources that need aid for product or service from both partners (Harrigan, 1988; Levi et al., 2020). Moreover, under substitutable resources a new product or service is developed by this association (Levi et al., 2020). The new formed entity could be an outcome of JV between two domestic firms or between an MNC and a local firm or between two MNCs (Harrigan, 1988). The International joint ventures may also arise after a part of domestic business is purchased by a foreign firm. Past studies also state a spider's web of joint ventures or joint alliance where a firm creates several alliances with distinct partners for a different purpose (Harrigan, 1988) such as Reliance-Aramco (a business deal in making where profitability aspect is a major factor), Wanda Group and Reliance MediaWorks Ltd., Reliance Jio with Google, Microsoft and Facebook(Economic Times, July2020); NTT-TATA(TATADocmo, however a failed venture), TATA-Starbucks, TATA-AIG Insurance, AirAsia ltd(TATA and AirAsia JV),Vistara(TATA Singapore Airlines JV) are few examples of International joint ventures. TATA group in India has domestic JV with TIDCO forming an entity named Titan Industries involved in watchmaking besides an IJV based in Canada named VSNL International Canada. As per Walters and Helman (2020),the basis of joint venture creation and stability depends on partnership building, JV performance, profitability, productivity, producibility and network connectivity. JVs essentially allows partner firms employ and manage resources of each other besides having control on outsourcing and open platforms for innovation (Beamish,1999; Richter, Jackson, & Schildhauer, 2018). The open innovation channels contribute to *'corporate accelerators'* that fast-track the company businesses by achieving desired outcome through other firms or insourcing(Richter, Jackson, & Schildhauer, 2018). The major influencers of business are the aware and demanding consumers, incessantly changing global market equilibrium, local and global economic collaborations, fastened technological growth, artificial intelligence and increased business risks require JVs now more than ever(Sahebi et al., 2015; Bamel, Dhir, & Sushil, 2018).

### 2.7.1 Joint Ventures and Coopetition During Covid-19

Moreover, the recent pandemic covid-19 has made *'coopetition'* emerge as a necessity to curb the business and situational crisis. As per the present literature "Co-opetition is a contradictory concept to existing business practices where rival firms collaborate with each other irrespective of their vertical or horizontal convolution." (Bengtsson & Kock, 2014; Kraus et al.,2018; Crick & Crick, 2020). There are examples from pharmaceutical industry, technological businesses, retail industry and others where coopetition has seemed to be swift and instant (Crick and Crick, 2020). This form of business collaboration has led many practitioners and thinkers to recalibrate the business models. Additionally, in order to deal with the lingering adversities in business due to covid-19 a large number of Forbes listings have transformed their business models which is focused on value proposition, customer engagement, value demonstration, product diversification, producing personal protective equipment (PPE kits)including face masks, hand sanitizers and hand gloves (Forbes, 2020; DRDO, 2020). Furthermore, prior to the pandemic JVs were in works such as Reliance BP Mobility Ltd RBML (a JV between world's oil and gas major Reliance and British Petroleum). It shall function under the title Jio-bp in which RIL holds 51% stake while BP holds 49%. As aforementioned RIL has diversified to telecom and now retail with JioMart focusing on Kirana stores (mom and pop stores) in which Amazon eyes to buy out 9.9% stake that will further strengthen Amazon's India operations as well as RIL's long term planning. RIL is expanding and diversifying by building both JVs and coopetition associations (ET, 2020A,2020B).

As per the existing literature and because of the complex characteristics of interorganizational network and business ecosystems, the study attempts to understand following assertions:

A1: The necessity of understanding IONs in ever changing business eras.
A2: The failures of JV associations and IONs.
A3: The association of Interorganizational networks and organizational ecosystems.

## 3. METHODOLOGY

Extensive literature was collected from online libraries and only Scopus indexed papers were considered for the purpose of this study. Research papers so collected had high number of citations. Using RQDA package first the researcher performed a thematic analysis where codes were created through the relevant literature review. Further codes were categorized on the basis of the factors pertaining to the variable for thematic analysis. The variables were organizational ecosystem (business ecosystem, innovative eco-system or creative ecosystem, platform ecosystem, symbiotic ecosystem), interorganizational networks, joint venture. In the current study the researcher adds a social innovation dimension to the innovation ecosystem with innovation capacity fulfillment as the sub-dimension. Additionally, one case is discussed that displayed business and innovation ecosystem using unique complementarity. The study analyzed the case through the concepts of Organizational ecosystem and ION. Another case explains the mobility of essential goods through Kirana ecosystem(mom and pop stores), a smaller form of business ecosystems, during covid-19 pandemic that sufficed the basic needs of people under lockdown and quarantine. The model of Kirana stores (mom and pop stores) during pandemic in India became lifeline for the citizens.

## 3.1 Case 1

TATA-DOCOMO JV

### Most Innovative Idea

In January of 2003 the Indian mobile consumers read warm sunny news by the then chairman of COAI (Cellular operators Association of India) Rajeev Chandrasekhran who announced that incoming calls will hence be free. Subsequently, the up-gradation of billing systems and mobile networks started. The 10.5 million cellular services users were offered packages that reduced the cost of outgoing calls. 2003 is the turning point for the mobile service providers in India who kept on introducing new tarrif vouchers, scratch cards etc but that happened because they were afraid of the giants like Reliance and TATA who were in the run for bringing WLL(Wireless Local Loop) revolution (Telegeography, 2004).

Understanding the billion consumer market can take generations and could be hostile. An alliance or venture is the best move that any foreign investor has to begin Indian business journey. The 1980's success of Suzuki Automakers with Indian Maruti Udyog Ltd. led more Japanese firms into Indian business territory. Chiyoda, Tokyo(Japan) based NTT DoComo (Nippon Telegraph and Telephone Do Communications over the Mobile Network) knew that Indian consumer market is a obfuscated cognitive network which can either build super giants (Maruti Suzuki) or is popular for acquisitions (Daichi Sankyo-Ranbaxy 485.4 billion Yen) with bitter experiences. Year 2008 showed highest direct investments by Japanese firms in India that peaked at 542.9 billion in Yen (Masanori, 2012). Japanese firms started late investments in Indian market as compared to the South Korean firms who saw an early opportunity immediately after the liberalization in 90's.

Therefore, being utterly cautious and conscious of all the facts and figures NTT Docomo decide to invest a huge sum of 2.7 billion$ (Rs 13,070 crores) in the Indian market by entering into a venture with TATA sons. In more than 150 years of history TATAs have not just valued new ventures, ideas but their customers and stakeholders. The values and goodwill measure attracted NTT DoComo to venture with TATAs at 26% stake in the TATA Docomo venture. NTT DoComo new that TATAs are risk takers as they have always focused on fulfilling the very basic necessity of Indian consumer like introducing TATA Nano besides incurring heavy losses. Therefore, they induced a clause in venture stating that if TTSL(Tata Tele services Limited) couldn't achieve the specific performance targets in five-year time period or perform below par, TATAs will have to find a buyer for TATA DoComo or will have to buy the shares of ailing organization at 50 percent discounted. However, TATAs were in a hurry to start revolution based on seconds (TOI, 2008).

### One Paisa per Second

Indian Telecom market is segmented into a huge number of major cities or circles (22) of which TTSL covered 16 major circles. In 2009 the Indian Telecom market was going through a transition phase what was later designated as *"Paradigm Shift"*. Until the June of 2009 the mobile phone subscribers were paying for a minute of call even if it lasted only a second.

TATA Indicom brand was re-branded to TATA Docomo with a subscriber base of 90 million. TATA group was highly optimistic with this new venture as they grew swiftly and consequently became sixth largest teleservices provider. Their GSM (Global System for Mobile Communication) offered a complete customer delight with offers such as full talk time plans, special tariffs, night plans etc besides per second plan. The company management studied the global GSM plans offering seconds-based pricing policy and was inspired by the *DU* brand which applied similar concept. The company targeted customer through "*Second is the new minute*" which attracted a wider proportion of consumers. The seconds plan skyrocketed the number of mobile phone subscribers and in one year, the internet penetration in India grew substantially from 29% to 43% (DOT, 2009; TRAI, 2008-09). The private telecom network also grew from 3401.79 to 4628.88 (in Lakhs) from March 2009 to December 2009 and the wireless phone user base from 391.76 in March'09 to 525.15 in december'09 (DOT, 2009).

TTSL was on cloud nine with unilateral growth in Indian telecom sector. Between August'09 to Dec'09 TTTSL venture TATA DoComo added 3.3 mn subscribers (ET, 2010) . "It was an aspiration to make TATA DoComo the light-house brand" as per the marketing head of TTSL operations. The seconds plan of TATAs made every other service provider to bring the tarrifs down and in 5 months(August '09 to Dec'09) the pricing war made TATA DoComo a star category firm. The predatory pricing policy created a lot of challenge for the existing competitors and due to which telecom law had to be amended (Ganesan & Sridhar, 2016).

### The Fall-Out

A number of reasons exist that explain why JVs are short lived like inter-management conflicts, re-organization of firm structure (Killing, 1983; Lee & Beamish, 1995; Kogut, 1988b). Failure often occurs in younger organizations due to several reasons. The JV between Japanese technology provider NTT Docomo and TATA showed Unique Complementarity that 'A cannot work without B'. But even after proper coordination the Joint Venture failed to sustain business.

## 3.2 Case 2

The Rise of Kirana Ecosystem

As per the data by Nielsen there are around 12 million Kirana stores (mom and pop stores) that govern the retail market in India. About 15% of the GDP (gross domestic product) gets its contribution from Indian retail sector (Bharucha, 2019), as per the AT Kearney's global ranking (2017) of growing retail markets in developing economies India stands second to none. With more than 1.2 billion population around 91% of the retail sector in India is dominated by unorganized retailing. In comparison to developing and developed nations the percentage of organized retail sector is extremely low. In USA organized retailing stands at 85% while in developing nations such as Thailand, Malaysia and Philippines organized retail holds 40%,55% and 35% respectively. In the pre-liberalization(before 1990) period there were few Indian retailers such as Bombay Dyeing, Raymond etc., that made the organized retail sector. The unorganized retail sector in India comprises of Kirana stores (mom and pop stores) selling all essential commodities. Further, it also includes pan and beedi shops(cigarette and beetle leaves),chemist or pharmaceutical shop, confectionery and bakery shops, vegetable and fruit vendors, general stores etc. As per the PWC statistics India has the highest number of Kirana stores or (mom and pop stores) format of American retail market (Singh, 2009; Bharucha, 2019). Kirana stores are small outlets that cover less than or equal to 500 sq.ft. or even less than 300-400 sq.ft. These stores often considered as self-sustaining retail houses (Srinivasan, 2015; Bharucha, 2019) selling products of similar kind such as aerated drinks, tea and coffee,spices, biscuits and salty snacks, potato chips and all kinds of different products belonging to different brands. Wholesalers timely (weekly or monthly) send their employees for inventory fulfillment since these kirana store owners work on low budgets (Sitaraman, 2018; Ray, Clark, & Waley, 2020).

After agriculture, the retail sector employs highest number, 8% of Indian population. This ecosystem is extremely vast and mostly unorganized which offers huge untapped market potential to the organized retailers. The retail market in India was growing at 16.7% CAGR (IBEF, 2017)while the online retailing was growing at a rapid pace of 63%CAGR (PWC,2019). Moreover, every Kirana store act as an accumulation zone for cash to hand customers and are very prevalent in societies, colonies, or narrow street settlements. Studies in the recent past expressed grave concern that whether the Kirana stores (mom and pop stores) will be able to survive the online market waves (Kumar et al., 2008; Bharucha, 2019). However, the tables turned during the lockdown situation and these Kirana stores not only emerged as the lifeline for citizens but also a medium for online business sustenance (The Hindu, 2020). All stores, supermarkets, shopping malls or brick and mortar based retail stores were forbidden to open and function during covid-19 except for the Kirana stores who were allowed by the administration to remain open for some hours under strict observation from authorities. Kirana regained the attention by the public and government. In whole of the urban as well as the rural Indian areas Kirana stores simplified the payment process by using online financial transactions as access to cash was typical during lockdown. For Kirana store owners the business is simple, get the products from wholesalers or stockists on credit or full payment and sell it to the end user or consumer. The supply chain had remained disrupted due to limited movement of transport and absence of migrant workers has added to the woes of the retailers and manufacturers. Several companies such as Metro cash and carry have been assisting these Kirana store owners in digitizing their financial transactions.

In the beginning of January 2020, Amazon founder Jeff Bezos announced their partnership with thousands of Kirana stores in Mumbai. Amazon realized the importance of building a strong association with mom and pop stores (Kirana Stores) as the E-commerce makes only 3% share in the Indian retail market. Connecting with these neighborhood stores deepens the Amazon association with Indian consumer. Besides Amazon also has a program called *Amazon Easy* that facilitates the use of technology. Walmart owned Flipkart invested 60 million US$ in december 2019 in *Shadowfax*, a logistics company that works directly with the Kirana stores in 500 cities. Shadowfax provides mobility to several companies through crowdsourcing and IOT. Reliance owned Jio, which revolutionized the Indian telecom sector by providing inexpensive data and low-priced mobile phones launched JioMart that would connect small shop owners nationwide and promote the use of technology. More than 75% of the regional, national and international brands get direct access to the end consumer with the help of Kirana stores (Bharucha, 2019; Sinha et al., 2015). The inventories of Kirana stores averages to about 1000-10000 stock keeping units or even smaller and is dependent on daily consumer demands. The main factor of their business is goodwill among the neighborhood customers. They even offer rations on credit to their frequent or monthly customers and free home delivery in time of need. Kirana store owners have limited clientele which relies on customer relationship management. Kirana store owners have unique ways to develop and maintain customer relationship which greatly relies on bargaining, credit sales, seeking advice on personal matters such as education trends for children, discussions on political matters, health, and wellness.

With the reformation in laws related to FDI post 2006 rapid strides were recorded in retail stores. Moreover, with 100 percent FDI in single brand retail and 51% in multi brands retail post 2011, hypermarkets such as reliance retail and V-mart etc. started segmenting for Indian consumers. It appeared to the Kirana ecosystem that the days of prospective prosperity due to organized retail and e-commerce are over but then came the covid-19 and saved many small family businesses. In several interviews conducted by media with the local Kirana store owners amid lockdown maximum owners felt blessed and saw a ray of hope for business sustenance in near future. In a report (ET, April 2020) the Kirana store owners mentioned that in one month of lockdown (March – April, 2020) sales figures have doubled and that their inventories require reordering on daily basis as compared to pre-covid-19 when reordering needed a month or more. Additionally, the store owners saw footfall of consumers from all walks of life including millennials and generation Y who prefer online shopping.

SnapBizz, a Benagluru based IT company provides business solutions to the Kirana store owners. Their bill payment services recorded a steep rise of 40% in Kirana businesses during the covid-19 lockdown which is highest spike in recent years. E-commerce companies have understood that for sustaining businesses and increasing their presence, Kirana ecosystem needs to be digitized and brought into the mainstream. As soon as the Kirana stores are modernized maximum reach to customers can be established. The Kirana shopkeepers are quick to learn and understand the consumer needs and behavior.. However, following a U-shaped or L shaped model of stores or increasing foot space is not possible for a majority of Kirana owners but sufficient infrastructure could be provided by the organized retailers. Additionally, studies show that Indian consumers are highly price sensitive and are mostly influenced by discounted products(Koul and Mishra, 2013). Figure 1 represents a conceptual Kirana ecosystem model 1 where the Kirana owners collaborate with the e-commerce companies, manufacturers and hypermarkets. Alternatively, some Kirana store owners can strategically compete with the retailers if they opt to stay out of any venture association with the e-commerce enterprises.

*Figure 1. Kirana ecosystem model 1*
**Source:** *Author* **Note***: This diagram was developed using an open source website for diagram creation diagrams.net.*

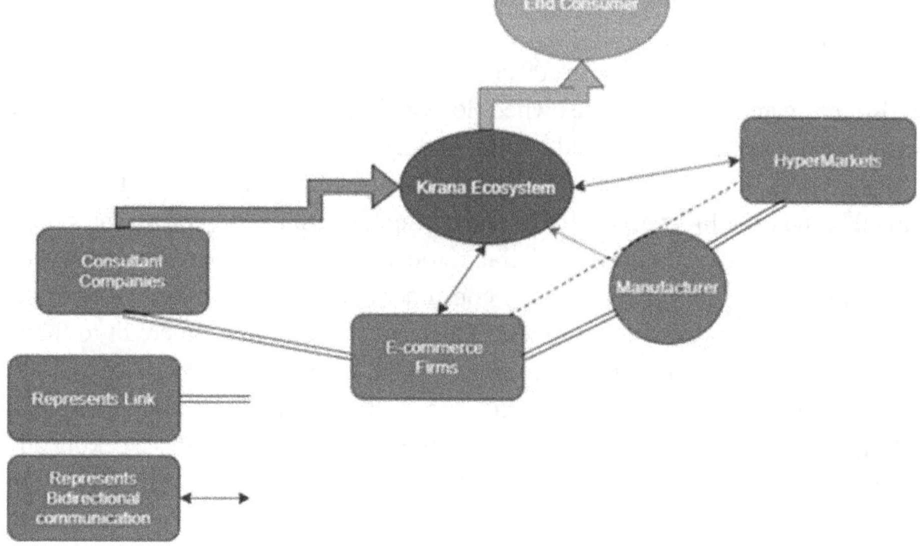

*Figure 2. Open Kirana ecosystem model 2*
**Source:** *Author* **Note***: This diagram was developed using an open source website for diagram creation diagrams.net.*

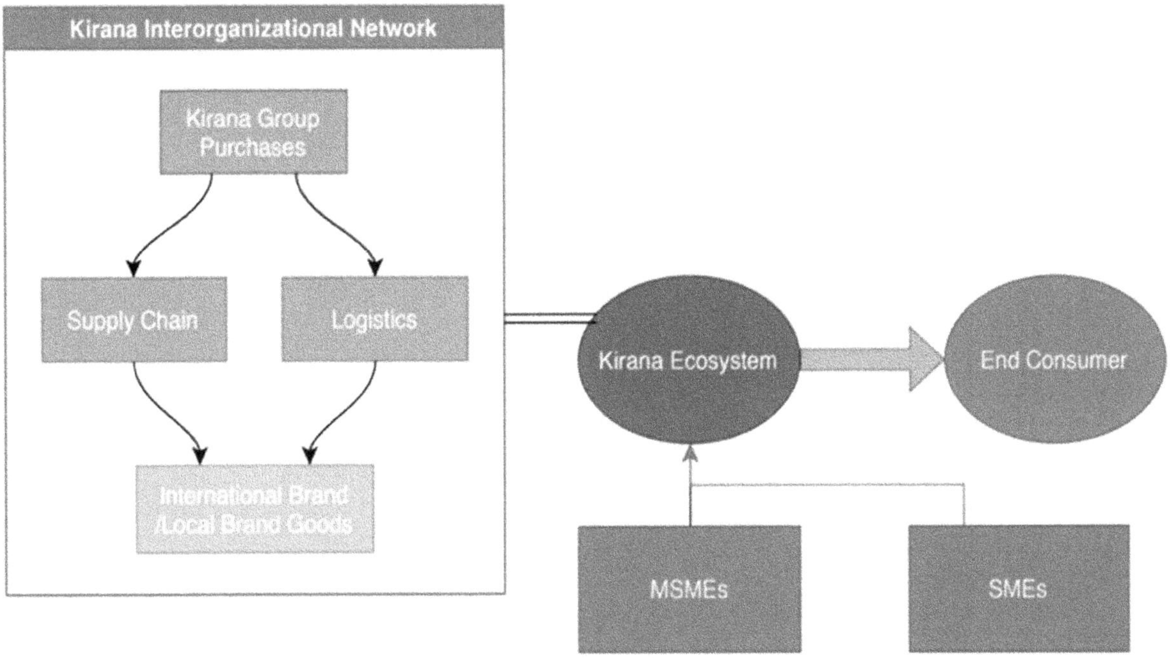


As shown in Figure 2 the open Kirana ecosystem model that follows the concept of traditional shop management. The Kirana owner stocks the goods from brands, wholesalers or stockists and sells to the end consumer. However, the figure 1 shows model ecosystem that Kirana's followed since the lockdown and has been efficient not only from delivery prospective but has added to the revenue generation. Kirana ecosystem model 1 also exhibits the adaptive behavior of businesses during crisis management. This model shows a perfect example for the firms to improvise associations with parallel organizations swiftly.

## 3.3 Thematic Analysis and Constructivist Approach

There are some softwares for performing computer assisted qualitative data analysis (CAQDAS) such as ATLAS.ti, NVivo and very recently RQDA. RQDA is an open source software that runs on R platform (Ihaka & Gentleman, 1996; Chandra & Shang, 2017).

The researcher applied RQDA (qualitative data analysis using R) for performing Thematic Analysis through specific steps. The researcher collected the relevant literature and discussions on academic portals regarding the development of inter-organizational structures, business ecosystems, joint ventures, and social exchange theory. The collected files were converted into .txt format and loaded in the RQDA which accepts files in .txt format. The thematic analysis was performed in consequent steps that included installation and setup of RQDA developed by Huang Ronggui as an open source CAQDAS application (Huang, 2014). In the next step the inductive and deductive coding was applied using the RQDA interface. Inductive coding in constructivist approach is open coding method through which the user codes a part of text (paragraph or sentence) that highlights a theory or concept. In deductive coding or positivistic approach codes are framed in the basis of established variable or factor. To apply this step all the converted files in .txt format are loaded in the environment, the user then marks the text in paragraph or the section that they want to code and also add code categories. Further the code categories can also be totaled second level code categories or abstraction. (Woods et al., 2015; Chandra & Shang, 2017). Although the coding procedure consumes time while comparing the codes and codes categories to the text during labeling but with different color combinations it becomes clear about the text theme.

*Figure 3. RQDA Sample of the coded themes*

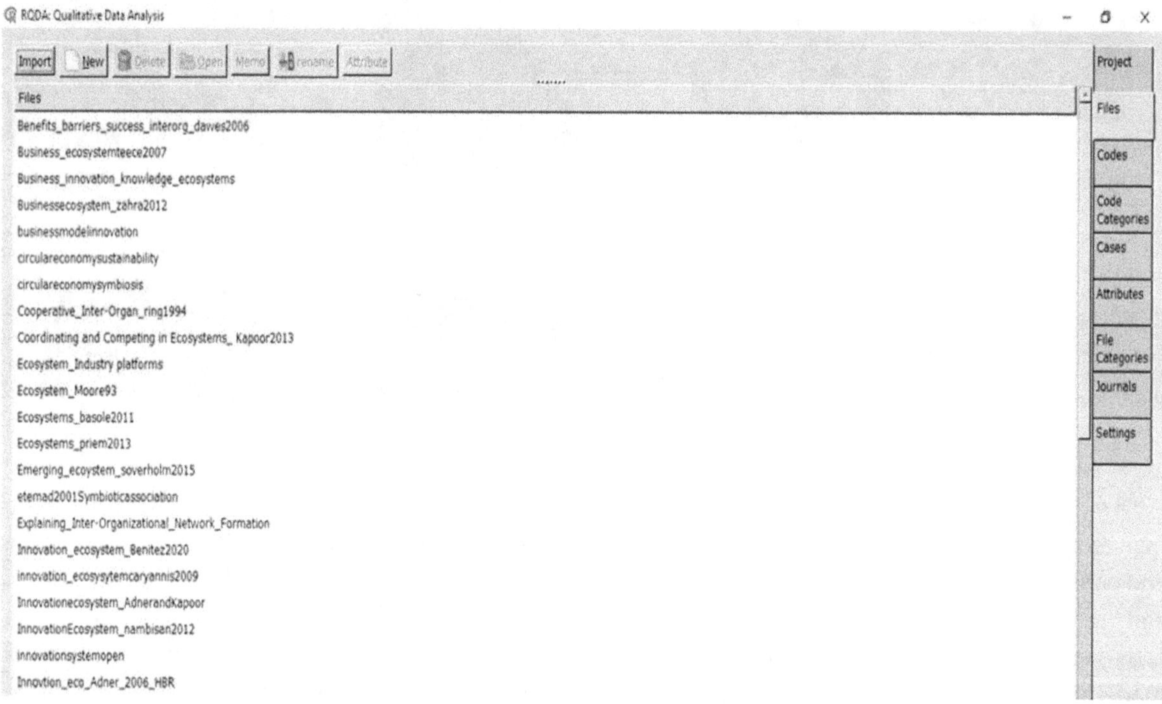

*Figure 4. RQDA code and code categories block*

*Figure 5. The coding process in RQDA which displays trust and IJV as codes*

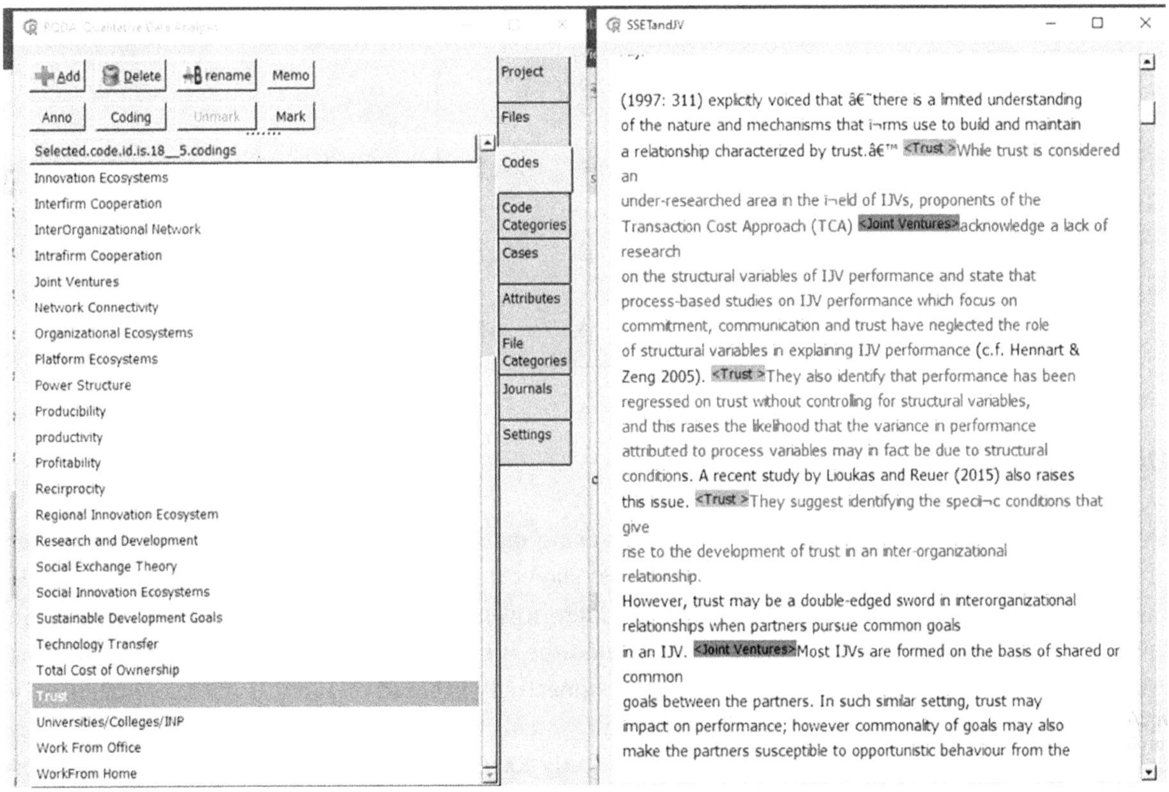

## 3.4 Conceptual Model

*Figure 6. Interorganizational Network*
**Source**: *Author* **Note**: *This diagram was developed using an open source website for diagram creation diagrams.net.*

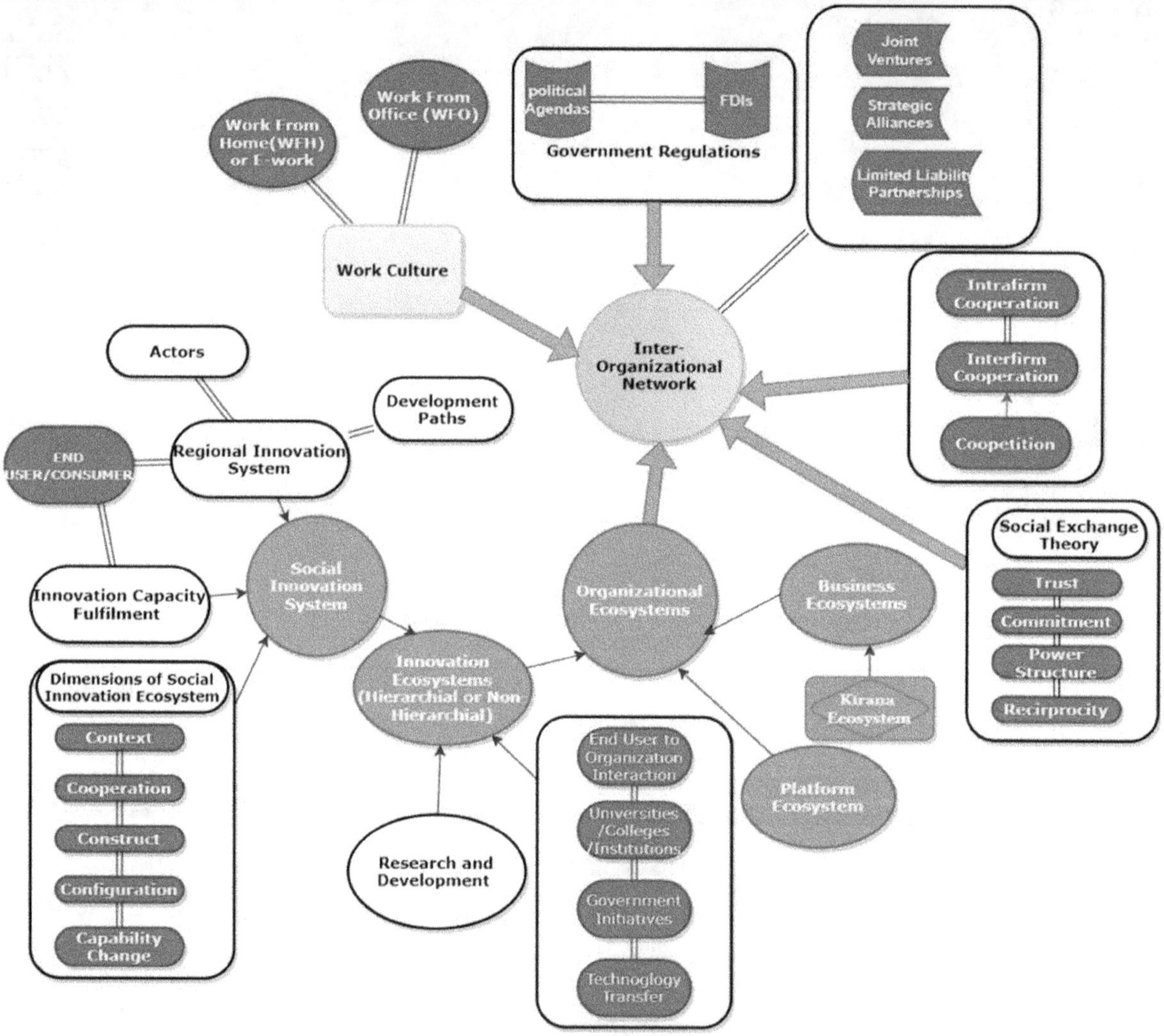


## DISCUSSION AND CONCLUSION

On the basis of the codes generated in the study using the codes and code categories the researcher presents a comprehensive business framework that shows a fusion of multiple ecosystems in a single multipurpose ecosystem. This ecosystem and the inter-organizational structure can prevent a failure in the business ecosystems which is robust and at the time it nears to failure it can elementally support other systems and sustain the business. This interconnectivity is based on the trust factor which is very necessary for the business legacies. In this model all systems government and non-government modules act and establish a balanced interconnection. The study focused on the necessity of understanding the

IONs where technology, trust and innovation help to establish a symbiotic system the one that supports other in a natural manner. A significant change in one can lead to enormous divergence in the other. Lose in trust benefits the competitor ventures and while several of them fall due to the trust and as long as they follow similar thoughts related to firm future and share same cultural beliefs.

## REFERENCES

Adams, D., & Hess, M. (2010). Social innovation and why it has policy significance. London, UK. *Sage (Atlanta, Ga.)*. doi:10.1177/103530461002100209

Adner, R. (2006). Match your innovation strategy to your innovation ecosystem. *Harvard Business Review*, *84*(4), 98–107. PMID:16579417

Adner, R. (2012). The wide lens: A new strategy for innovation. London, England: Penguin. Adner, R. (2017). Ecosystem as structure: An actionable construct for strategy. *Journal of Management*, *43*(1), 39–58. doi:10.1177/0149206316678451

Adner, R., & Kapoor, R. (2010). Value creation in innovation ecosystems: How the structure of technological interdependence affects firm performance in new technology generations. *Strategic Management Journal*, *31*(3), 306–333. doi:10.1002mj.821

Aldrich, H. E. (1979). Organizations and Environment. Englewood cliffs. NJ, NewJersey: Prentice Hall.

Avram, E. & Avasilcai, S. (2014). Symbiosis Process in Business Ecosystem. *Advanced Materials Research (vol. 1036)*. Trans Tech Publications. doi:10.4028/www.scientific.net/AMR.1036.1066

Bamel, N., & Dhir, S. Sushil, (2019) "Inter-partner dynamics and joint venture competitiveness: A fuzzy TISM approach. *Benchmarking*. doi:10.1108/ BIJ-02-2018-0041

Basole, R. C., & Karla, J. (2011). On the evolution of mobile platform ecosystem structure and strategy. *Business & Information Systems Engineering*, *3*(5), 313–322. doi:10.100712599-011-0174-4

Beamish, P. W. (1999). The role of alliances in international entrepreneurship, pp. 43-61. Research in Global Strategic Management, Emerald Group Publishing Limited. doi:10.1016/S1064-4857(99)07056-4

Bengtsson, M., & Kock, S. (2014). Coopetition - quo vadis? Past accomplishments and future challenges. *Industrial Marketing Management*, *43*(2), 180–188. doi:10.1016/j.indmarman.2014.02.015

Bergenholtz, C., & Waldstrøm, C. (2011). Inter-organizational network studies—A literature review. *Industry and Innovation*, *18*(6), 539–562. doi:10.1080/13662716.2011.591966

Bharucha, J. (2019). Sustainability of kirana stores in India: Reengineering physical with some digital. *World Review of Entrepreneurship, Management and Sustainable Development*, *15*(6), 751–764. doi:10.1504/WREMSD.2019.104866

Bingöl, D., & Begeç, S. (2020). Managing International Alliances: Joint Ventures: A Case Study. *Open Journal of Social Sciences*, *8*(04), 538–552. doi:10.4236/jss.2020.84039

Brass, D. J., Galaskiewicz, J., Greve, H. R., & Tsai, W. (2004). Taking stock of networks and organizations: A multilevel perspective. *Academy of Management Journal, 47*(6), 795–817. doi:10.2307/20159624

Brix, J. (2019). Innovation capacity building: An approach to maintaining balance between exploration and exploitation in organizational learning. *The Learning Organization, 26*(1), 12–26. doi:10.1108/TLO-08-2018-0143

Burt, R. (1992). *Structural Holes: The Social Structure of Competition*. Cambridge, MA: Carayannis, E.G., Campbell, D.F.J., 2009. 'mode 3' and 'quadruple helix': toward a 21st century fractal innovation ecosystem. *International Journal of Technology Management, 46*(3–4), 201–234.

Chandra, Y., & Shang, L. (2017). An RQDA-based constructivist methodology for qualitative research. *Qualitative Market Research, 20*(1), 90–112. doi:10.1108/QMR-02-2016-0014

Connor, T. (2003). Managing for competitiveness: A proposed model for managerial focus. *Strategic Change, 12*(4), 195–207. doi:10.1002/jsc.633

Cooper, R. G. (2019). The drivers of success in new-product development. *Industrial Marketing Management, 76*, 36–47. doi:10.1016/j.indmarman.2018.07.005

Crick, J. M., & Crick, D. (2020). Coopetition and COVID-19: Collaborative business-to-business marketing strategies in a pandemic crisis. *Industrial Marketing Management.*

D'Amato, D., Korhonen, J., & Toppinen, A. (2019). Circular, Green, and Bio Economy: How Do Companies in Land-Use Intensive Sectors Align with Sustainability Concepts? *Ecological Economics, 158*, 116–133. doi:10.1016/j.ecolecon.2018.12.026

Dacin, M. T., Dacin, P. A., & Tracey, P. (2011). Social entrepreneurship: A critique and future directions. *Organization Science, 22*(5), 1203–1213. doi:.1100.0620 doi:10.1287/orsc

Dawes, S. S. (1996). Interagency information sharing: Expected benefits, manageable risks. *Journal of Policy Analysis and Management, 15*(3), 377–394. doi:10.1002/(SICI)1520-6688(199622)15:3<377::AID-PAM3>3.0.CO;2-F

Dawson, P., & Daniel, L. (2010). Understanding social innovation: A provisional framework. *International Journal of Technology Management, 51*(1), 9–21. doi:10.1504/IJTM.2010.033125

de Vasconcelos Gomes, L. A., Facin, A. L. F., Salerno, M. S., & Ikenami, R. K. (2018). Unpacking the innovation ecosystem construct: Evolution, gaps and trends. *Technological Forecasting and Social Change, 136*, 30–48. doi:10.1016/j.techfore.2016.11.009

Diaz Lopez, F. J., Bastein, T., & Tukker, A. (2019). Business Model Innovation for Resource-efficiency, Circularity and Cleaner Production: What 143 Cases Tell Us. *Ecological Economics, 155*, 20–35. doi:10.1016/j.ecolecon.2018.03.009

DiMaggio, P. J., & Powell, W. W. (1983). The iron cage revisited: Institutional isomorphism and collective rationality in organizational fields. *American Sociological Review, 48*(2), 147–160. doi:10.2307/2095101

Domenech, T., & Bahn-Walkowiak, B. (2017). Transition Towards a Resource Efficient Circular Economy in Europe: Policy Lessons From the EU and the Member States. *Ecological Economics*. doi:10.1016/J. ECOLECON.2017.11.001

Domenech, T., Bleischwitz, R., Doranova, A., Panayotopoulos, D., & Roman, L. (2019). Mapping Industrial Symbiosis Development in Europe_ typologies of networks, characteristics, 728 performance and contribution to the Circular Economy. *Resources, Conservation and Recycling*, *141*, 76–98. doi:10.1016/j. resconrec.2018.09.016

Granovetter, M. (1985). Embeddedness. *American Journal of Sociology*, *91*, 481–510.

Etemad, H., Wright, R. W., & Dana, L. P. (2001). Symbiotic international business networks: Collaboration between small and large firms. *Thunderbird International Business Review*, *43*(4), 481–499. doi:10.1002/tie.1009

European Commission. (2015). *Closing the loop - An EU action plan for the Circular Economy*. COM.

Fraccascia, L. (2020). Quantifying the direct network effect for online platforms supporting industrial symbiosis: An agent-based simulation study. *Ecological Economics*, *170*, 106587. doi:10.1016/j.ecolecon.2019.106587

Gasparin, M., Green, W., Lilley, S., Quinn, M., Saren, M., & Schinckus, C. (2020). Business as unusual: A business model for social innovation. *Journal of Business Research*.

Gawer, A., & Cusumano, M. A. (2014). Industry platforms and ecosystem innovation. *Journal of Product Innovation Management*, *31*(3), 417–433. doi:10.1111/jpim.12105

Granovetter, M. S. (1985). Economic action and social structure: The problem of Granstrand, O., & Holgersson, M. (2020). Innovation ecosystems: A conceptual review and a new definition. *Technovation*, *90*, 102098.

Greenway, J. M., & Weiland, J. P. (2000). *Building capacity for innovation as a source of individual and organizational fulfillment* [Doctoral dissertation, Massachusetts Institute of Technology].

Gulati, R., & Gargiulo, M. (1999). Where do interorganizational networks come from? *American Journal of Sociology*, *104*(5), 1439–1493. doi:10.1086/210179

Gulati, R., & Singh, H. (1999). The architecture of cooperation: Managing coordination costs and appropriation concerns in strategic alliances. *Administrative Science Quarterly*, *43*(4), 781–814. doi:10.2307/2393616

Hill, R. C., & Hellriegel, D. (1994). Critical contingencies in joint venture management: Some lessons from managers. *Organization Science*, *5*(4), 594–607. doi:10.1287/orsc.5.4.594

Iansiti, M., & Levien, R. (2004). *The keystone advantage: What the new dynamics of business ecosystems mean for strategy, innovation, and sustainability*. Harvard Business School Press.

Kapoor, R., & Lee, J. M. (2013). Coordinating and competing in ecosystems: How organizational forms shape new technology investments. *Strategic Management Journal*, *34*(3), 274–296. doi:10.1002mj.2010

Kilduff, M., & Tsai, W. (2003). Social networks and organizations. *Sage (Atlanta, Ga.)*.

Killing, J. P. (1983). *Strategies for joint venture success*. Praeger.

Kogut, B. (1988a). A Study of the Life Cycle of Joint Ventures. In F. J. Contractor & P. Lorange (Eds.), *Cooperative strategies in international business*. D.C. Heath.

Koul, S., & Mishra, H. G. (2013). Customer perceptions for store attributes: A study of traditional retail stores in India. *Journal of Business and Economics*, *5*(1), 79–103.

Kujala, S. I. (2008). Effective user involvement in product development by improving the analysis of user needs. *Behaviour & Information Technology*, *27*(6), 457–473. doi:10.1080/01449290601111051

Kumar, V., Patwari, Y., & Ayush, H. (2008). Organised food retailing: A blessing or a curse? *Economic and Political Weekly*, *43*(20), 67–75.

Levi, R., Perakis, G., Shi, C., & Sun, W. (2020). Strategic Capacity Planning Problems in Revenue-Sharing Joint Ventures. *Production and Operations Management*, *29*(3), 664–687. doi:10.1111/poms.13128

Moore, J. F. (1993). Predators and prey: A new ecology of competition. *Harvard Business Review*, *71*(3), 75–86. PMID:10126156

Murray, R., Caulier-Grice, J., & Mulgan, G. (2010). The open book of social innovation (p. 2). London: National endowment for science, technology and the art.

Nambisan, S., & Baron, R. A. (2013). Entrepreneurship in innovation ecosystems: Entrepreneurs' self-regulatory processes and their implications for new venture success. *Entrepreneurship Theory and Practice*, *37*(5), 1071–1097. doi:10.1111/j.1540-6520.2012.00519.x

Nohria, N., & Eccles, R. (1992). *Networks and Organizations: Structure, Form and Action*. Harvard University Press.

Overholm, H. (2015). Collectively created opportunities in emerging ecosystems: The case of solar service ventures. *Technovation*, *39-40*, 14–25. doi:10.1016/j.technovation.2014.01.008

Ozmel, U., Reuer, J. J., & Gulati, R. (2013). Signals across multiple networks: How venture capital and alliance networks affect interorganizational collaboration. *Academy of Management Journal*, *56*(3), 852–866. doi:10.5465/amj.2009.0549

Ozmel, U., Reuer, J. J., & Gulati, R. (2013). Signals across multiple networks: How venture capital and alliance networks affect interorganizational collaboration. *Academy of Management Journal*, *56*(3), 852–866. doi:10.5465/amj.2009.0549

Pardo, T. A., Cresswell, A. M., Dawes, S. S., & Burke, G. B. (2004). *Modeling the social & technical processes of interorganizational information integration.* Paper presented at the Hawaii International Conference on System Sciences (HICSS-37), Hawaii 10.1109/HICSS.2004.1265307

Pfeffer, J., & G, R. Salancik. (1978). The External Control of Organizations. *Resource (Saint Joseph, Mich.)*.

Pfeffer, J., & Salancik, G. (1978). *The external con-trol of organizations. A Resource Dependence Approach.* Harp-er and Row Publishers.

Pfeffer, J. & Salancik, G. (1981). *Dependence Perspective.* New York: Harper and Row.

Phills, J. A., Deiglmeier, K., & Miller, D. T. (2008). Rediscovering social innovation. *Stanford Social Innovation Review*, *6*(4), 34–43.

Podolny, J. (2001). Networks as the pipes and prisms of the Market. *American Journal of Sociology*, *1*(1), 33–60. doi:10.1086/323038

Podolny, J. M., & Page, K. L. (1998). Network forms of organization. *Annual Review of Sociology*, *24*(1), 57–76. doi:10.1146/annurev.soc.24.1.57

Powell, W. W. (1990). Neither market nor hierarchy: Network forms of organizations. In B. Staw & L. L. Cummings (Eds.), *Research in Organizational Behavior.* JAI Press.

Powell, W. W., Koput, K. W., & Smith-Doerr, L. (1996). Interorganizational collaboration and the locus of innovation: Networks of learning in biotechnology. *Administrative Science Quarterly*, *41*(1), 116–145. doi:10.2307/2393988

Priem, R. L., Butler, J. E., & Li, S. (2013). Toward reimagining strategy research: Retrospection and prospection on the 2011 AMR decade award article. *Academy of Management Review*, *38*(4), 471–489. doi:10.5465/amr.2013.0097

Purtik, H., & Arenas, D. (2019). Embedding social innovation: Shaping societal norms and behaviors throughout the innovation process. *Business & Society*, *58*(5), 963–1002. doi:10.1177/0007650317726523

Pustovrh, A., Rangus, K., & Drnovšek, M. (2020). The role of open innovation in developing an entrepreneurial support ecosystem. *Technological Forecasting and Social Change*, *152*, 119892. doi:10.1016/j.techfore.2019.119892

Ray, N., Clarke, G., & Waley, P. (2020). The rise of corporate retailing and the impacts on small-scale retailing: The survival strategies of Kirana stores and informal street vendors in Durgapur, India. *Singapore Journal of Tropical Geography*, *41*(2), 269–283. doi:10.1111jtg.12312

Richter, N., Jackson, P., & Schildhauer, T. (2018). Outsourcing creativity: An abductive study of open innovation using corporate accelerators. *Creativity and Innovation Management*, *27*(1), 69–78. doi:10.1111/caim.12252

Ring, P. S., & Van de Ven, A. H. (1994). Developmental processes of cooperative interorganizational relationships. *Academy of Management Review*, *19*(1), 90–118. doi:10.2307/258836

Shaikh, E, Brahmi, M, Thang, PC, Watto, WA, Trang, TTN, & Loan, NT. Should I Stay or Should I Go? Explaining the Turnover Intentions with Corporate Social Responsibility (CSR), Organizational Identification and Organizational Commitment.2022. *Sustainability*, *14*(10):6030. https://doi.org/doi:10.3390u14106030

Sahebi, H., Nickel, S., & Ashayeri, J. (2015). Joint venture formation and partner selection in upstream crude oil section: Goal programming application. *International Journal of Production Research, 53*(10), 3047–3061. doi:10.1080/00207543.2014.970708

Shipilov, A., & Gawer, A. (2020). Integrating Research on Interorganizational Networks and Ecosystems. *The Academy of Management Annals, 14*(1), 92–121. doi:10.5465/annals.2018.0121

Singh, H. (2009). *Retail Management – A Global Perspective: Text and Cases, S.* Chand Publishing.

Sinha, P., Gokhale, S., & Rawal, S. (2015). Online retailing paired with kirana: A formidable combination for emerging markets. *Customer Needs and Solutions, 2*(4), 317–324. doi:10.100740547-015-0057-9

Sitaraman, K. (2018). Traditional trade in India: The resilient retailer and implications for POS (point of sale) strategies. *Journal of Indian Business Research, 10*(4), 337–344. doi:10.1108/JIBR-12-2017-0247

Srinivisan, S.R. (2015) Lessons from local self sustained retailers. *Free Press Journal, 12.*

Teece, D. J. (2007). Explicating dynamic capabilities: The nature and microfoundations of (sustainable) enterprise performance. *Strategic Management Journal, 28*(13), 1319–1350. doi:10.1002mj.640

Valkokari, K. (2015). Business, innovation, and knowledge ecosystems: How they differ and how to survive and thrive within them. *Technol. Innov. Manage. Rev., 8*(5), 17–24. doi:10.22215/timreview/919

Walters, D., & Helman, D. (2020). *Strategic Capability Response Analysis*. Springer Books. doi:10.1007/978-3-030-22944-3

Wasserman, S., & Faust, K. (1994). *Social network analysis: Methods and applications* (Vol. 8). Cambridge university press. doi:10.1017/CBO9780511815478

Watts, D. (1999). Networks, dynamics and the small world phenomenon. *American Journal of Sociology, 105*(2), 493–527. doi:10.1086/210318

Wiewel, W., & Hunter, A. (1985). The interorganizational network as a resource: A comparative case study on organizational genesis. *Administrative Science Quarterly, 30*(4), 482–496. doi:10.2307/2392693

Wu, C. H., Parker, S. K., & De Jong, J. P. (2014). Need for cognition as an antecedent of individual innovation behavior. *Journal of Management, 40*(6), 1511–1534. doi:10.1177/0149206311429862

Yan, A., & Luo, Y. (2016). *International Joint Ventures: Theory and Practice: Theory and Practice.* Routledge. doi:10.4324/9781315501338

Yang, T. M., & Maxwell, T. A. (2011). Information-sharing in public organizations: A literature review of interpersonal, intra-organizational and inter-organizational success factors. *Government Information Quarterly, 28*(2), 164–175. doi:10.1016/j.giq.2010.06.008

Zaheer, A., McEvily, B., & Perrone, V. (1998). Does trust matter? Exploring the effects of interorganizational and interpersonal trust on performance. *Organization Science, 9*(2), 141–159. doi:10.1287/orsc.9.2.141

Zahra, S. A., & Nambisan, S. (2012). Entrepreneurship and strategic thinking in business ecosystems. *Business Horizons*, *55*(3), 219–229. doi:10.1016/j.bushor.2011.12.004

Zhang, J., & Dawes, S. S. (2006). Expectations and perceptions of benefits, barriers, and success in public sector knowledge networks. *Public Performance & Management Review*, *29*(4), 433–466.

Zmiyak, S. S., Ugnich, E. A., & Taranov, P. M. (2020). Development of a Regional Innovation Ecosystem: The Role of a Pillar University. In *Growth Poles of the Global Economy: Emergence, Changes and Future Perspectives* (pp. 567–576). Springer. doi:10.1007/978-3-030-15160-7_57

# Chapter 2
# A Framework for Strategic Analysis in Dynamic and Complex Environments

**Abolghasem Arabiun**
*Independent Researcher, Iran*

**Ali Mobini Dehkordi**
*Independent Researcher, Iran*

**Elahe Hosseini**
https://orcid.org/0000-0003-3478-5320
*Yazd University, Iran*

**Mohsen Brahmi**
https://orcid.org/0000-0002-0995-0761
*University of Sfax, Tunisia*

## ABSTRACT

*In the present paper, a comprehensive framework for the strategic analysis of dynamic and complex environments at micro/macro levels with a subjective/objective approach is presented. The research method used in this chapter incorporated the epistemological foundations of critical realism and complexity theory with an inductive-deductive approach. The research has been done quantitatively-qualitatively using Delphi panel and network of experts (n = 241) and AHP method for selecting dimensions. Based on the results extracted, this framework has been obtained from the two "micro-macro" and "objective-subjective" levels and the four fragmented dimensions of micro-objective, micro-subjective, macro-objective, and macro-subjective, with three levels of analysis, so that strategic issues and key challenges can be better recognized and the integrated scanning can be performed purposefully and intelligently by professional organizations consisting of multidisciplinary specialties.*

DOI: 10.4018/978-1-6684-6766-4.ch002

## INTRODUCTION

The strategic environment is characterized by features such as uncertainty, complexity, and rapid change (Alperen, 2017). Success, survival, and competition in these environments depend on the ability to scan and adapt to the environmental conditions, which requires obtaining insights to neutralize threats and use the opportunities (Sawyer et al., 2022). This purpose cannot be achieved except by simultaneous use of quantitative and qualitative analysis methods, challenging old assumptions, and encouraging new approaches (Clapper, 2014). Environmental scanning is a method that is in the position of foresight and strategy. By creating the necessary criteria, it allows prepared human minds to discern information, knowledge, and insight from the multitude of "signals" that occur daily (YahiaMarzouk & Jin, 2022). In most cases, the starting point for environmental scanning is the design of a scanning framework which helps practitioners decide what to look at and how to judge the usefulness of the information(Slaughter, 1999). In the external or objective world, where most of the frameworks of environmental scanning are considered, the world appears only as a great interlocking order of sensory levels, empirical forms (Kamoun-Chouk, 2022; Walker et al., 2014). The current environment is full of uncertainties and global challenges (Tajpour et al.,2022). Some phenomena are not observable and measurable by experimental methods and the predominant methods which are commonly used cause them to be neglected and ignored (Sawyerr & Ebrahimi, 2022). These statements stand as an enduring critique of approaches to environmental scanning that focus primarily on the empirical data from the external world and the achievement of objective facts (Patrick, 2022). Accordingly, Slaughter (1999) criticizes these objective frameworks and presents a new framework for environmental scanning using Wilber's integral model for recognizing phenomena that focuses on the internal aspects of the environment which have been ignored so far (Slaughter, 1999).

Our worldview of a phenomenon can limit some of the strongest options for understanding the unfavorable global situation and responding to it. Reflecting on all the frameworks of environmental scanning shows that foundations and underlying assumptions of recognition and having a worldview can lead to a deeper understanding and help to obtain a framework for strategic analysis of the dynamic environment. These foundations and assumptions have varied at different times with the advancement of science. In the classical sciences, most philosophical assumptions belonged to a traditional worldview (TWV) including the underlying assumptions of "reductionism, objective observation, linear causation, entity as the unit of analysis, determinism, and objective reality"(Dent, 1999) . Then, during the early twentieth century, not many scientists have been able to describe some of the complex phenomena and happenings by "order, reductionism, predictability, and determinism." The order in the phenomena is not certain, the causes and effects are not linked, the emergent properties often appear seemingly out of the blue, and the related processes do not steer the systems to inevitable and distinct ends(Geyer, 2003). A complex whole exhibits properties that cannot be readily explained by understanding the parts (Holman, 2015) . Therefore, when it is not possible to understand all interactions, the known implicit variables must be increased, and the worldview should evolve into a random worldview with a weak cause-and-effect relationship. In the first case, we work in a deterministic environment with strong laws of causality(Elena Olmedo, 2016). However, in the latter case, the environment is unclear and the principle of causality of laws is weak (the duality of determinism-randomness)(Gulson et al., 2017).

Ken Wilber's critique has been that the traditional worldview ignores the internal world of sensations, perceptions, impulses, emotions, images, symbols, and other phenomena that constitute an important part of life(Dent, 1999) As complexity of science and dissatisfaction with the traditional worldview increase, we need to have a new worldview that complements previous worldviews and eliminates duality ("The new complex perspective in economic analysis and business management," 2002; Olmedo, 2016). The philosophical assumptions of this emerging worldview include holism, perspectival observation, mutual causation, relationship as the unit of analysis, indeterminism, and others(van der Wal et al., 2021). Perhaps the most useful mental model for thinking about the traditional worldview and emerging worldview is the model of polarity(Gentili, 2021). Polarities are sets of opposites that cannot function well independently and the two sides of a polarity are interdependent, so one side cannot be right at the expense of the other. Therefore, properties such as determinism or indeterminism and objectivity or subjectivity constitute a bipolarity (Braithwaite, 2022).

Environments may change from one type to another. Therefore, it is important to know the factors and assumptions that provide the grounds for environmental change (Haefner et al., 2021). The key question is how one can obtain a comprehensive understanding of the environment. The purpose of the present study is to present a method for recognizing complex and dynamic environment with uncertainty and to present a comprehensive framework for environmental scanning with a wide application at different levels using a qualitative-quantitative method (panel and network of experts) and the epistemological foundations of critical realism and theories of complexity and chaos. The study aims to complete the understanding of the uncertain environment with a bipolar approach in a continuum through recognizing the important dimensions of environmental scanning in different levels and put them together as a whole in a framework, both fragmentally and integrally.

## LITERATURE REVIEW AND THE EXTRACTION OF EFFECTIVE ENVIRONMENTAL FACTORS

In this section, a variety of environmental classifications have been considered to extract factors. Prominent models of organizational environments include the stable or uncertain organizational environments presented by the Paul Lawrence and Jay Lorsch and the classification presented by Bronze and Stacker(Lawrence & Lorsch, 2015). Robert Duncan also discussed simple, complex, and static-dynamic models of the organizational environment (Duncan, 1971). The key dimensions of environmental classification are first briefly discussed below.

### Objective and Subjective

The environment consists of a set of external conditions, forces, factors, and components that affect the performance of organizations and the organization has little control over them. The environment of organizations has two aspects: subjective and objective (*Advanced analysis of strategic environment( Uncertainty, complexity and intelligence)(*Nobari et al., 2020) .The subjective environment includes perceptions, images, impulses, emotions and the objective environment includes the obvious things, facts, and the observables around the organization.

### Static and Dynamic

The definition of a static or dynamic environment is related to the rate of change or displacement of the elements and factors constituting the environment(Huang et al., 2022). In fact, when the rate of change in environmental factors is small, the environment is considered static and when the rate of change in environmental factors is high, it is considered dynamic. It is called environmental sustainability(Winter et al., 2022). Each aspect (social, economic, political, legal, and technological) of the organization's environment can be static or dynamic. It is possible for an environment to be static for a long period of time and then undergo severe instability.("Environments of organizations.," 1976). In 1972, Robert Duncan introduced a model with the stable-dynamic and simple-complex dimensions for the organizational environments(Zee, 2022). Duncan's model refers to how organizations can better respond to and deal with uncertainty. Duncan points out that different types of environments create different types of uncertainty(Litschert & Bonham, 1978). The static-dynamic dimension is considered as the degree to which decision factors or variables remain stable or change over time.

## COMPLEXITY

### Order and Disorder

Complexity has recently had a strong presence in organizational science and literature (Smith, 2005). The simple-complex dimension is viewed as the number of factors that affect the decision-making process (Duncan, 1972), ("Introduction to Complex Systems and Agent Based Modeling, s.l.," 2014). In simple systems, the behavior of the system is simple in time and space, and the rules are known. However, in complex systems, the behavior of the system is complex in time and space and there is little information about how they function. Many variables are involved in complex systems and it is difficult to understand the overall performance of the system (Strogatz, 2012). Complexity exists when there is a significant degree of dependence, diversity, relevance, and adaptability between the parts of the system (Page, 2009).

In this regard, the Cynefin framework was first introduced in 2003 by Kurtz and Snowden in a paper entitled "The new dynamics of strategy: Sense-making in a complex and complicated world" in the IBM Systems Journal. Kurtz and Snowden proposed their framework by challenging the three assumptions of order, rational choice, and intent, which are usually assumed in strategic management and organizational decision-making (Hamrouni et al., 2021). This framework provides better and more accurate recognition of the environment by classifying the environment to ordered and unordered one ("The new dynamics of strategy: Sense-making in a complex and complicated world.," 2003). Ordered environments include recognizable and recognized environments, and unordered environments include chaotic and complex environments. These four categories are not opposite and the boundaries between the categories can be removed, leading to the transition between them ("Improving decision making in complexity environment. " 2014). It is possible to change a system from the recognized one to the recognizable, to complex, and then to chaotic one and vice versa ("The new dynamics of strategy: Sense-making in a complex and complicated world.," 2003).

### Micro and Macro

The environment is a complex whole consisting of smaller economic, social, cultural, and political systems, while these systems themselves are composed of subsystems (Agha & Rascher, 2016). Therefore, a hierarchy of the environment is conceivable. In addition, the functions of environmental systems and subsystems can be distinguished based on their specialization and constituent parts. There are also various ways to achieve a result.

## Individual-Collective

Wilber's framework was proposed in response to the critique of approaches to environmental scanning that are primarily on empirically based data from the external world (Slaughter, 1999; Triandis, 2018). In the external or objective world where environmental scanning was considered, the world appeared only as a great interlocking order of sensory surfaces, empirical forms ("sustainable supply chains; aframework for environmental scanning practices," 2014). Using "four quadrants", this framework provides a comprehensive and systematic basis for environmental scanning based on the ingenious division between "interior" and "exterior" on one axis and "individualism" and "collectivism" on the other. Thus, there are four parallel processes, each of which is linked with the other: interior-individual development; exterior-individual development, interior-social development, and exterior-social development. These four quadrants represent the dimensions of reality and include different ways of recognition. Wilber uses the term "holons" to indicate entities embedded in systems.(Slaughter, 1999). A Holon has four dimensions or quadrants. The interior dimension or the intent and consciousness of the holon is expressed by the "I", and it is the interior-collective dimension of the consciousness or the culture of the holon, which is expressed by the "We". The exterior dimension and the activity of the holon are expressed by "It", and the exterior-collective dimension of activities or the social dimension of the holon is expressed by "Its". The interaction between these dimensions prevents the holon from disintegrating. A healthy holon has an evolution or transcendence course on the one hand and an involution or inclusive course on the other hand (Giret & Botti, 2004; Wilber, 2000).

The dimensions of the environment can be categorized both geographically and thematically. Based on David Hanger's model (1999), the general environment of the organization along with its operational environment forms the external environment of the organization, which is composed of a set of forces, conditions, and factors that operate beyond the scope of work of a company or organization. These forces can be classified into five economic, social, political, legal, and technological dimensions. The economic dimension of the distant environment shows how resources are distributed and used within the environment. The social dimension of the distant environment describes the demographic conditions and characteristics of the communities living in the world. The political dimension is one of the elements related to governmental affairs, such as the type of government, the government's attitude towards various industries, the principles, and ideas of political parties, etc., which can play a limiting or encouraging role in the organization's activities (Tunio, et al., 2021). The legal dimension also indicates the rules and regulations governing all members of a society, organization, etc., and finally, the technological dimension of the public environment includes new attitudes toward the production of goods and services, such as new methods and equipment. All companies in dynamic and growing environments must try to understand technological advances and their effects on their products and to evaluate and analyze current and future trends and events (Daft, 2006).

## THE FRAMEWORK GUIDING THE RESEARCH

The conceptual framework is the researcher's idea of how to study the research problem with a combination of concepts, perspectives, assumptions, and principles collected from many sources. The conceptual framework includes the ontological, epistemological, and methodological foundations, with each concept playing an ontological or epistemological role in this framework. It is the epistemological foundations that make our understanding of the realities around us more accurate.

A part of the epistemological foundations of this research has been based on critical realism. Critical realists believe that there is a reality independent of human understanding that is multi-layered. Bhaskar (2014), one of the most prominent scholars in the field of critical realism, believes that the reality of existence (environment) is based on three empirical, actual, and real layers. The empirical layer is the realm of the events that we experience. In this layer, events can be explained empirically or with common sense, but the filter of human experience and interpretation acts always as an intermediary. The actual layer includes phenomena and events that occur at specific times and places. In the actual layer, there is no filter of human experience. Events occur, whether we experience and interpret them or not, and these events are often different from what we have seen experimentally. In the real layer, there are causal structures or mechanisms that include the requirements and forces from which observable environmental phenomena and events arise (Fletcher, 2017). Given the three layers of the critical realism paradigm and both objective and subjective views in this paradigm, we will have to look deeper into the parts of the world to understand the relationship between them to gain accurate knowledge and introduce two other dimensions of the environment. In the most general view of the environment, the three parts of existence can be distinguished from each other: God, man, and nature. God, as the creator of the system of existence, has created man and the world purposefully and oriented (Cruickshank, 2003).

Therefore, the world has principles, the most important of which are becoming, movement, order, and purposefulness (Wilber, 2000). Some scholars also consider a ground for the emergence of a new worldview called the second Copernican revolution(Helfrich, 2000) . The major paradigm shift in this revolution occurs in beliefs, awareness, and consciousness of the primary source of everything (Helfrich, 2000; Wilber, 2000). The creation including the processes of consciousness and movement evolves, and its potential talents become actual so that the evolution course is constantly continuing. The physical world as one of the uncertain frameworks of consciousness includes a wide range of different disciplines of consciousness and human consciousness as a unique type. Thus, the emerging new worldview is a multidimensional view of the mind (psyche) that exists in non-physical domains that are freely available through shifted or unusual states of consciousness. We are biologically equipped to experience more than five physical senses through a set of inner senses that have been understood by mystics, sages, and oracles to this day. This includes the use of direct mental experience with deep thoughts and feelings, along with intelligence and wisdom (Helfrich, 2000). On the other hand, the human as one of the variable dimensions of the environment has been given the talent of recognition so that he can achieve the recognition corresponding to reality by contemplation in the universe (nature) and by intuition, intellect, and experience. Of course, it should be noted that recognizing and choosing are two different complementary categories and can be prior or posterior to each other. The stage of exploring and recognizing environmental factors, currents, and conditions is considered to be the observation of the out-of-mind realities (what is present is seen and understood) and the recognition takes place regardless of the values and norms of the decision-maker. In the next step, this recognition helps to act, that is, to make decisions. In the choice stage, besides recognizing and understanding out-of-mind realities, the decision-makers norms and values are also involved, which affect the type of choice. Therefore, if these two stages are separated and are then combined in the final stage, they may have a better and more appropriate effect on correct recognition and stable decision (Mobini Dehkordi & Heydari, 2014) . Accordingly, it can be inferred that the creation including consciousness and constant movement forms the certain things of the environment, and the other things are uncertain or unstable. Stable realities do not change, and they are the source from which everything emerges while the uncertain or conditional realities may undergo the changes and are manifested in the light of the certain realities that form the structural layers of the environment. Given the complexity of today's world, these changing phenomena must be analyzed and recognized in the light of certain things and the conscious world of creation.

Many scholars consider a strong link between critical realism as a philosophy of social science and the foundations of complexity theory (Jörg, 2011) . Today, the simple idea of the world has been replaced by a complex and paradoxical idea (Yadolahi Farsi et al.,2021). One of the necessities of paying attention to complexity is the increasing complexity of the environment, and the drivers of increasing complexity are diversity, communication, interdependence, and acceleration in reaction time. Complex systems can produce large events. The emergence is also a feature of complex systems where the whole is both in scale and in type different from the sum of the parts. Accordingly, the universe is considered as a complex layer-by-layer system.(*Advanced analysis of strategic environment(Uncertainty, complexity and intelligence*, 2020) . Therefore, the surrounding environment is also composed of various layers and levels in which different people and parts are related and interacting, including the dimensions of order and disorder(Mobini-Dehkordi et al.,2021). Therefore, both the nature of the environment and the human perception are emerging and dynamic, and the environment is self-organizing, sensitive to the primary conditions, nonlinear, and influenced by a set of rules.

Considering the paradigm of critical realism and with a special approach to the relations between the parts of existence, the present research has a holistic view and pays attention to both the objective and subjective dimensions so that the realities are not only recognized at the micro or macro levels, but also recognized accurately by the three-stage method of fragmentation of each dimension to four parallel processes, in which the focus of the first stage is on the internal relations in each dimension, and the relations between two poles of an axis is focused at the second stage. Finally, at the third stage, using the simultaneous integration of the four dimensions, accurate and basic knowledge is provided for monitoring based on the internal and external relations and interactions between these four dimensions. It is the degree of dynamism, change, and speed and the trend and direction of the relations that shows the mechanism of the environmental dynamics. Reality is formed by the relations between phenomena. Therefore, full recognition is achieved by synthesizing four dimensions in an integrated way with a focus of relations at the macro level and their effects on the micro level, in which the triple layers of the structure of reality are considered. All of these relations are moving towards the evolution of consciousness in the system of creation that is purposeful, ordered, certain, and stable. The environmental dynamics of these relations cause a variety of recognitions of the environment at different times and levels. The assumptions of the proposed framework are shown in the Table 1.

*Table 1. Assumptions of Strategic Analysis Framework of dynamic and complex environments*

| | | |
|---|---|---|
| **Paradigm** | Critical realism and consciousness | Multilayer reality, both objective and subjective approach, both stable and unstable approach, becoming, movement, order, purposefulness |
| **Theory** | Complexity and chaos | Self-organization, sensitive to primary conditions, non-linear, dimensions of order and disorder, the emergence |
| **Approach** | Inductive-deductive | Bipolar approach to phenomena; parallel multidimensional processes; fragmentation; and processes of synthesis, interaction, and integration of the dynamics of realties |
| **Method** | Prospective reasoning, analytical and descriptive, composite and interactive | Layered and present-oriented reasoning; interactive and prospective reasoning |

## METHODOLOGY

To achieve the strategic environmental analysis framework, we first selected the paradigm and the ontological and epistemological foundations that determine the dimensions governing the framework. The two main assumptions underlying this framework have been the critical realism with a deeper look at the parts of existence and the theory of complexity and chaos as theories governing the framework. The approach used in this research to achieve the framework has been the inductive-deductive approach. The framework was designed by an inductive approach and it has been validated using a deductive approach, and the dimensions and levels of analysis were synthesized. The method used to design the framework is discussed below.

In the first step, a Delphi panel was formed consisted of 15 experts with at least 15 years of top universities of iran of Sharif, Shahid Beheshti, Tehran, Tarbiat Modares Universities in Tehran as associate or full professors, who were teaching courses related to the STEEP fields of the environment and were working on the recognition of the environment at the corporate or strategic levels and had papers published in scientific journals. The experts had different specialties and executive backgrounds in each of the social, cultural, technological, economic, political, and environmental fields, and the priority of their presence varied depending on the subject matter of recognition and the expertise of individuals. The details of the samples selected as the members of the panel are presented in Table 2.

*Table 2. The statistical population selected for the panel of experts*

| **Top-ranked universities of Tehran** | **The number of qualified professors** | **The number of selected samples** |
|---|---|---|
| Faculties of Social Sciences | 10 | 2 |
| Faculties of Economics and Management | 31 | 3 |
| Faculties of Strategic Management | 20 | 4 |
| Faculties of Geography and Environment | 13 | 1 |
| Technical and Engineering Faculties | 25 | 3 |
| Faculties of Political and International Science | 23 | 2 |
| Total | 121 | 15 |

Environmental bipolar axes extracted from the review of literature include variability (static/dynamic), geographical dimension, thematic dimension (STEEP), complexity (order/ disorder), type of view (objective/subjective), size (micro/macro), and level (individual/collective) that are commonly used to recognize the environment. They were provided to the panel members to extract the questions needed to form the Delphi network. The questions extracted were arranged in the form of a questionnaire based on a 5-point Likert scale.

In the next step, following the formation of the Delphi network, the statistical population consisting of academics and professionals in various academic and research sectors were identified (N = 646). Due to the limitations of the statistical population and the complexities involved in identifying people specifically for the statistical population and considering that the present research seeks to obtain the opinion of scholars and experts and the generalization of research results from the sample to the statistical population is not relevant, the nonlinear snowball sampling as a non-probability sampling method was used. In the nonlinear snowball sampling method, following the identification of the first samples based on the STEEP dimensions of the environment that include experts with different specialties in the field of political, economic, social, technological, and cultural sciences, they help to identify and select other experts. Using stratified random sampling and Cochran's formula with a coefficient of $\alpha = 0.05$, the sample size of n = 241 was obtained as shown in Table 3.

*Table 3. The statistical population and the samples constituting the members of Delphi network(Source: Organization for Administrative and Employment Affairs-2018- Number of faculty members of the centers)*

| Type | Research centers and target faculties | Number of members with a doctoral degree | Number of members selected as the sample |
|---|---|---|---|
| Professional | Public research and policy-making center of the government | 48 | 12 |
| | Office of national planning and development studies of the government | 16 | 4 |
| | Supreme center for national planning development and research | 22 | 8 |
| | Center for the strategic research development of the Ministry of Foreign Affairs | 38 | 10 |
| Academic | Engineering faculty of Tehran University | 136 | 37 |
| | Geography and environment faculty of Tarbiat Modares University | 39 | 10 |
| | Strategic sciences faculty of Islamic Azad University, Science and Research Branch | 25 | 7 |
| | Entrepreneurship-business faculty of Tehran University | 39 | 11 |
| | Faculty of social sciences and social sciences research center of Tehran University | 68 | 17 |
| | Management and economics faculty of Sharif University | 80 | 21 |
| | Management and commerce faculty of Isfahan University | 34 | 9 |
| | Strategic management faculty of Tehran University | 61 | 15 |
| | Political and international science faculty of Tehran University | 40 | 10 |
| | Total | 646 | 241 |

According to the statistical population, 270 members were contacted and the questionnaire was sent to them electronically and they were asked to evaluate the effect of each factor on the environmental scanning based on the 5-point Likert scale. To increase the return rate of the questionnaires, one or two people were selected as research partners in each of the research centers to distribute and collect the questionnaires. The questionnaire was emailed to research colleagues at academic and professional centers based on the output of the Delphi panel, and 241 questionnaires were collected. After analyzing the answers in the first round, the preliminary results were sent again to each member of the network of experts, and when the answers reached the correlation of 95%, the process of analyzing the data and extracting the results began using SPSS software in the second round.

By selecting the four main effective dimensions based on the collected data, the analytic hierarchy process (AHP) was used to form the framework for environmental scanning. This method is one of the most widely used decision-making methods, especially in ranking and determining the importance of dimensions and factors, which is based on pairwise comparison and allows managers and planners to evaluate different scenarios. Criterion selection is the first stage of AHP, which has been based on the review of the literature and the opinion of the experts in this paper. AHP model used in the present paper included the determination of target, weighting the studied criteria, and prioritization of them. The scale used in the AHP method included 1-5 points in cases where the number of criteria was low and 1-9 points in cases where the number of criteria was more than 5 to better differentiate between the criteria. Number 1 indicated the weakest criterion and number 5 (or 9) indicated the strongest or most appropriate criterion. Additionally, the values inside the matrix of pairwise comparisons were in the form of a fraction, in which the numerator indicated the degree of importance of the criterion in the matrix row and the denominator indicated the degree of importance of the criterion in the matrix column.

## Results

By comparing and analyzing the results obtained from the Delphi network using SPSS software and calculating the frequency and cumulative frequency of each dimension, the four main dimensions were selected based on the highest frequency for designing the framework, which have been discussed below.

### The First Dimension: Type of Factors (Objective and Subjective)

There are factors in the environment that are manifested in the form of physical realities, for example, technologies or political structures that are currently present in the world. These factors are considered as the objective part of the environment. However, those environmental currents and entities that have not yet been manifested objectively and are just in the form of ideas, thoughts, and so on are considered as subjective environmental factors. It should be noted that this part of the environment, like the objective part, may be effective and lead to changes. Thus, they should also be considered in the process of the recognition of the environment. In other words, it must be acknowledged that the external and visible part of the iceberg forms a superficial recognition, which is the same objective dimension of the environment. However, the lower layers of the iceberg that are under water indicate the depth of environmental recognition that must also be considered because the interconnection of the (objective) surface and the (subjective) depth forms the complete recognition. In fact, as Wilbur argues, the environment is formed by intertwined whole/parts (holons) so that the internal and external dimensions of the holons must be considered simultaneously to achieve recognition. Neglecting any of these dimensions would mean ignoring some of the facts, losing a set of signs of environmental change, and the imperfection of recognition. As can be seen in the following Table 4, 84.1% of the experts who were members of Delphi network considered the role of the objective dimension in environmental scanning to be very high and high, and 16.4% of them considered it to be moderate and low and very low, while 79.7% of experts considered the role of the subjective dimension in the environmental scanning to be very high and high, and 20.3% of them considered it to be moderate, low, and very low.

*Table 4. Results obtained from Delphi network; the role of objective and subjective dimensions in the environmental scanning*

| | Objective dimension | | | Subjective dimension | | |
|---|---|---|---|---|---|---|
| | **Frequency** | **%** | **Cumulative frequency** | **Frequency** | **%** | **Cumulative frequency** |
| Very high | 124 | 51.4 | 51.4 | 103 | 43.2 | 43.2 |
| High | 79 | 32.7 | 84.1 | 87 | 36.5 | 79.7 |
| Moderate | 24 | 9.9 | 94 | 34 | 14.2 | 93.9 |
| Low | 9 | 3.7 | 97.7 | 9 | 3.78 | 97.6 |
| Very Low | 5 | 2 | 100 | 5 | 2 | 100 |
| Total | 241 | 100 | | 238 | 100 | |

## The Second Dimension (Micro and Macro)

The layers of reality and the layers of the sensations, behaviors, and experiences of actors as micro-subsystems as well as the facts, factors, structures that are composed of a combination of subsystems as an integrated and macro-system include different levels and there are usually complex cause-effect relations between these levels. Events and factors observed at the micro level are highly dependent on events and trends at higher and macro levels, while they themselves form other events at lower levels. The factors vary at micro and macro levels. At the micro level, such issues as power actors and their behavior are considered, and at the macro level, such issues as trends, macro trends, intellectual and historical currents, and environmental models are considered. Paying attention to the levels of factors can make our knowledge of the environment and facts more accurate. Considering the reality as a holon, Wilber also points out that each holon itself constructs micro levels and includes macro levels or belongs to a larger holon. While being a part, a holon still has the property of being a whole (holism along with reductionism).

As can be seen in the following Table 5, 137 of 156 participants, i.e. 83.9% of experts, considered the role of micro dimension in environmental scanning to be very high and very high, and only 16.16% of them considered it to be moderate, low, and very low, while 76.9% of experts considered the role of the macro dimension in environmental scanning to be high and very high.

*Table 5. Results obtained from Delphi network; the role of macro and micro dimensions in the environmental scanning*

| | Micro Dimension | | | Maco Dimension | | |
|---|---|---|---|---|---|---|
| | Frequency | % | Cumulative Frequency | Frequency | % | Cumulative Frequency |
| Very High | 117 | 48.5 | 48.5 | 98 | 41 | 41 |
| High | 85 | 35.4 | 83.9 | 86 | 35.9 | 76.9 |
| Moderate | 26 | 10.8 | 94.7 | 38 | 15.8 | 92.7 |
| Low | 8 | 3.3 | 98.2 | 10 | 4.1 | 96.8 |
| Very Low | 4 | 1.7 | 100 | 7 | 2.9 | 100 |
| Total | 240 | 100 | | 239 | 100 | |

## Third Dimension: Geographical (National, Regional and International Environments)

According to the systems theory, the environment can be divided into global and international systems (environments), regional systems, and domestic or national systems. A national (domestic) environment refers to the environment within the geographical territory of a state, which includes various economic, geographical, territorial, social, cultural, political, technological, environmental, and many other dimensions that can be limited within the political borders. In other words, the national environment refers to all the facilities, resources, as well as the material, non-material, hardware, and software constraints that a state faces within its political boundaries. The regional environment is defined as the regions and parts of the world that are geographically formed from several neighboring countries that have mutual interactions in foreign affairs. The international environment refers to aspects of the environment that cross national borders or are organized on a global scale. This part of the environment affects and is affected by both the national and regional environment.

241 experts, i.e. 64.8%, considered the role of geographical dimension at the national, regional, and international levels to be very high and high, while 35.2% of experts considered it to be moderate, low, and very low.

## Fourth Dimension: Thematic (Social, Cultural, Technological, Economic, Environmental, and Political Factors)

To better recognize the environment, it is necessary to first thematically classify environmental factors and variables, including events and trends. For this purpose, the past, present, and future information of the six domains of social and cultural (anthropological issues, culture, lifestyles, etc.), technological (access to technology, innovations, inventions, etc.), economic (economic power, unemployment and inflation, the main areas of work, production and distribution of wealth, and the structure of the economy), environmental (air pollution, disasters, etc.), political (political system, parties, regulations, etc.), military and security (military capabilities, military, trade, and scientific complexes, military technologies, conflict zones, etc.) should be considered. 240 experts, i.e. 61.8%, considered the role of thematic dimension in STEEP domains to be very high and high, and 38.2% of them considered it to be moderate, low, and very low.

Among other dimensions of the environment, the role of the individual dimension was considered by 239 experts, i.e. 80%, to be moderate, low, and very low. 15% of experts considered it to be high and 5% very high. The role of the collective dimension was considered by 67% of the total 241 respondents to be moderate, low, and very low, and 20% and 13% of them considered it to be high and very high, respectively.

72% of the 240 respondents considered the role of order (dimension of order) in the environmental scanning to be very high, high, and moderate, 14% as low, and 14% as very low. 88% of 157 respondents considered the role of disorder to be high and moderate, and only 10% considered it to be very high and 2% as low and very low, indicating that this dimension was considered as a factor in the uncertainty, and this result has been used somehow in the framework. The role of the certainty dimension indicating the consciousness, purposefulness, and order of the creation was considered by 94% of respondents to be high and very high, while the role of the uncertainty dimension was considered by 78% of them to be high and very high. As human has an inherent cognitive limitation, the dimension of stability and certainty of the world was considered as an obvious principle beyond the human mind, and the strategic environmental analysis framework was formed in two continuums of "micro-macro" and "objective-subjective" for the uncertain things of the world in the light of the purposefulness and the inherent consciousness of certain things.

The purpose of the AHP technique used in this paper has been firstly to investigate the interconnectedness of the most effective dimensions (obtained from the results of the Delphi network) of the environmental scanning. The results of the pairwise comparisons of the dimensions using the opinions of the panel of experts in related fields are presented in Table 6.

*Table 6. The pairwise comparison matrix for prioritization of the criteria of the objective-subjective and the micro/macro dimensions*

| Criteria | Objective | Subjective | Objective-subjective |
|---|---|---|---|
| Objective | ////// | 2/4 | 2/5 |
| Subjective | | ////// | 4/5 |
| Objective-subjective | | | ////// |
| **Criteria** | **Micro** | **Macro** | **Micro-Macro** |
| Micro | ////// | 1/3 | 1/5 |
| Macro | | ////// | 3/5 |
| Micro-Macro | | | ////// |

Now, using the above pairwise comparison matrix, on which the experts reached a consensus, the weight of each of the criteria was obtained according to Table 7 (total weight is equal to one, and higher weight means more importance of the criterion)

According to the above results, the objective-subjective and micro-macro criterions has the highest importance. Therefore, the interconnection of objective and subjective dimensions and micro and macro dimensions was approved by the experts of the panel.

*Table 7. The degree of importance of objective-subjective criteria*

| Composite Criteria | Micro-Objective | Macro-Objective | Micro-Subjective | Macro-Subjective | Objective-Subjective | Micro-Macro |
|---|---|---|---|---|---|---|
| Micro-Objective | ////// | 2/5 | 2/4 | 2/7 | 2/8 | 2/7 |
| Macro-Objective | | ////// | 5/4 | 5/7 | 5/8 | 5/7 |
| Micro-Subjective | | | ////// | 4/7 | 4/8 | 4/7 |
| Macro-Subjective | | | | ////// | 7/8 | 7/7 |
| Objective-Subjective | | | | | ////// | 8/7 |
| Micro-Macro | | | | | | ////// |

Then, to achieve the dimensions and continuums of the strategic environmental analysis framework, the second stage of AHP analysis was performed to find the optimal combination of the effective dimensions (obtained from the results of the first stage of AHP analysis) of environmental scanning. Using the opinions of the experts in related fields, the results of the second stage of pairwise comparisons are as follows.

*Table 8. The pairwise comparison matrix for the prioritization of the composite criteria*

| Composite Criteria | Micro-Objective | Macro-Objective | Micro-Subjective | Macro-Subjective | Objective-Subjective | Micro-Macro |
|---|---|---|---|---|---|---|
| Micro-Objective | ////// | 2/5 | 2/4 | 2/7 | 2/8 | 2/7 |
| Macro-Objective | | ////// | 5/4 | 5/7 | 5/8 | 5/7 |
| Micro-Subjective | | | ////// | 4/7 | 4/8 | 4/7 |
| Macro-Subjective | | | | ////// | 7/8 | 7/7 |
| Objective-Subjective | | | | | ////// | 8/7 |
| Micro-Macro | | | | | | ////// |

Now, using the above pairwise comparison matrix, on which the experts reached a consensus, the weight of each of the criteria was obtained as follows (total weight is equal to one, and the higher weight means more importance of the criterion)

*Table 9. The degree of importance of composite criteria*

| Priority | Dimension | Degree of Importance (weight) |
|---|---|---|
| 1 | Objective- subjective | 0.242 |
| 2 | Micro-macro | 0.212 |
| 3 | Macro-subjective | 0.212 |
| 4 | Macro-objective | 0.152 |
| 5 | Micro-subjective | 0.121 |
| 6 | Micro-objective | 0.061 |

According to the above results, the total importance (weight) of the composite dimensions of macro-subjective, macro-objective, micro-subjective, and micro-objective (equal to 0.546) has been more than the total importance of the dimensions of objective-subjective and micro-macro (equal to 0.454). These results lead us to design the framework of strategic environmental analysis as a combination of all the effective factors determined than to design it based on only objective-subjective and micro-macro dimensions separately.

## THE EXPLANATION OF THE STRATEGIC ENVIRONMENTAL ANALYSIS FRAMEWORK (SUN FRAMEWORK)

This framework has been based on the epistemological foundations of critical realism and the theory of complexity and chaos and indicates that the sensory, experimental, and environmental realities (uncertain things) can be recognized in the light of the certain structures of the conscious system of creation and the correct understanding of the environmental scanning is achieved when the limitations of human rationality are analyzed in the light of the real layers of consciousness, orderliness, and purposefulness of the system of creation (stable things). This obvious principle which has been considered is that the human can recognize the unstable things that the system of the creation includes by his empirical and intuitive knowledge and he can follow the certain principles of the system of creation to complete his understanding. Thus, there is an order in the system of creation and the disorder is specific to human behavior with the surrounding environment, which has been called uncertain things in this framework. In fact, the two continuums considered in this framework include the micro-macro continuum (which are not opposite but are distinguished to achieve precise recognition and they are borderless) and the objective-subjective continuum that included the highest percentage of frequency and cumulative frequency in the results of the research. The order and disorder in each dimension of this framework have been considered based on the theory of complexity and they have been available in all four dimensions of the framework. STEEP factors and geographical levels are present in each dimension, forming diverse environments with different levels. For example, when the strategic analysis is conducted in the "micro-objective" dimension and at the national level, the social, economic, political, cultural, scientific and technological behaviors of the national subsystem are studied, but when the strategic analysis is conducted in the "macro-objective" dimension and at the national level, power structures and power levels in the STEEP domains are studied. Additionally, when the strategic analysis is conducted in the "micro-subjective" dimension and at the national level, the system of beliefs in a society, the culture, fundamental values, norms, rules and myths, and the intellectual patterns at the micro level are considered. However, when the analysis is done in the "macro-subjective" dimension and at the national level, the intellectual paradigms, schools, dominant social ideas and cultural currents, their role in creating power, the approach to other societies, and the worldview are considered. Thus, at the micro level, different individual identities may be examined that are collectively side by side and in relation to each other, but at the macro level, the relations between these micro things, their internal nature, and behavioral and external functions that are formed in the light of the intellectual-mental system are considered. When a connection is established between the behavioral surface and the depth formed by thought, a deeper understanding of the causes and consequences of environmental realities is obtained. Therefore, in this strategic environmental analysis framework (Sun framework), the four dimensions of "objective-subjective" and "micro-macro" in unstable things that are unordered, complex, and chaotic are considered. All four quadrants are studied in an integrated manner in the light of certain and stable things that have an order. This framework has been shown in Figure 1.

*Figure 1. Strategic analysis framework of dynamic and complex environments-sun framework*

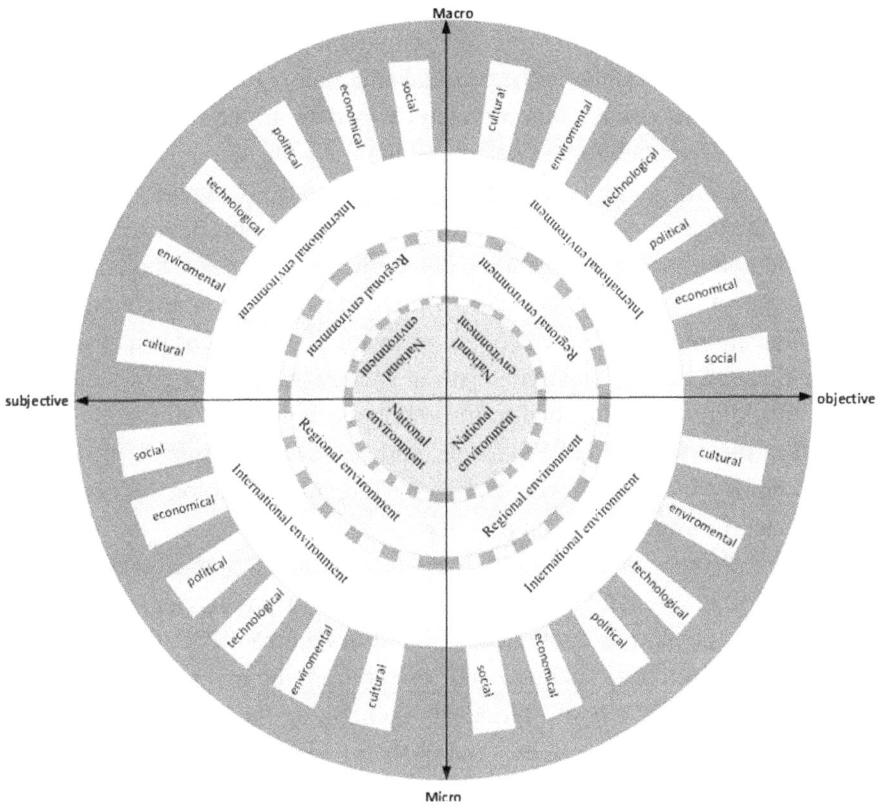


## IMPLICATIONS FOR THEORY AND PRACTICE

**The First Level of Strategic Environmental Analysis:** This level of strategic environmental analysis, i.e. subsystems, has been in the form of four fragmented and parallel processes so that different key stimuli are recognized in each of the sections which are discussed below:

*A. Macro-Objective Section:* All the factors, conditions, and currents that the human face in the light of the order of the system of creation are analyzed. Thus, the behavior of actors who have power in the macro-objective domain at the national, regional, and international levels are studied. In other words, resources, power structure, institutions, actors, and stakeholders in the political, economic, cultural, scientific, technological, and environmental domains, the governing rules and regulations, behavioral changes, alliances, exchanges, positive and negative relations, national, regional, and international conflicts, how their dynamics change, economic and political inequalities, and how international institutions and globalization currents function are studied to scrutinize the challenges of this sector for each system and business. The political, economic, ecological, and sociological sciences, history, and civilization are used in this field and recognizing the relations between environmental objective things at a macro level is emphasized.

*B. Micro-Objective Section:* In the micro-objective domain, the emphasis is on the behavior of individuals, parties, stakeholders in the social, political, technological, economic, environmental, and cultural arenas, and the behavioral characteristics, the relations and interactions, the methods of competition, cooperation, coevolution, comprehension, and conflict at the three national, regional, and international levels are studied (Aldieri et al., 2021). In this section, social and individual psychology, behavioral sociology of groups, economic variables at the national and regional level, the growth rate of countries' economies, the competition and cooperation between the parties of one country or other countries, the behavioral economics of different classes of societies, and the game theory are emphasized.

*C. Micro-Objective Section:* In this section, the system of beliefs, behaviors, values, cultures, ideals, thoughts, and ideas of the classes and individuals of societies and countries are considered as an intellectual subsystem. Under investigation is the issue of whether extremism or moderation and democracy based on the public rights of people or individualism are used as a tool to maintain the power of intellectual networks, whether culture forms the behavior of individuals and groups in a desired and compatible direction, how is intellectual fluidity and dynamism in society and among different social classes, and ultimately what are the dominant intellectual frameworks in a country. Additionally, the cooperation or conflicts in the light of the system of beliefs, ideals, and values are examined, in which such sciences as management, psychology, culture, worldview, history, literature, sociology of power, intellectual and artistic initiatives and innovations, and so on are used.

*D. Macro-Subjective Section:* Issues related to the intellectual system, worldviews, values system, dominant intellectual currents, political order, stability or instability, dynamism and staticness of governing thoughts such as geopolitical, geo-ecological, geo-cultural currents, geology, technology, thoughts forming media and the intellectual system and their orientation, the nature of power and economy, the intellectual contributions, thought schools, the ideals dominating the world, the intellectual and theoretical convergences and divergences, and the trend of the intellectual and theoretical evolution of vital organizations and large corporations dominating the advanced and leading industries in the fields that drive the future of the science and technology are studied.

**The Second Level Of Strategic Environmental Analysis:** In the second level, the two dimensions of "micro/macro-objective" or "micro and macro- subjective" are scanned as two parallel processes that are in a composite form.

The micro/macro-objective dimension: This dimension includes a composite approach to objective things at both micro and macro levels. While the beliefs are considered, the values and how beliefs and values are transformed into the culture are studied so that interdisciplinary sciences such as cognitive psychology, power sociology, behavioral psychology, cognitive sciences, and history are used, and the literary and historical documents and texts, myths, and so on are analyzed.

The micro/ macro subjective dimension: This dimension includes a composite approach to subjective things at both micro and macro levels. The behavior of subsystems and the structure of the system are scanned simultaneously and the interdisciplinary sciences that emphasize the understanding of the behavior-structure subjectivity, such as behavioral economics, culturology, and theories of complexity and dynamism of the systems are used to explore the relations between intellectual issues, micro-level beliefs and schools, and macro-level approaches and theories.

**The Third Level of Strategic Environmental Analysis:** The third level is conducted by an integrated and simultaneous look at the four subsystems, leading to a general system that includes an integrated surface and depth of micro/ macro-objective and subjective things. To improve the quality of recognition, it is necessary to use mental abilities and interdisciplinary and multispecialty teams. This level is used for complex, dynamic, and chaotic environments where there is high uncertainty, the causes of realities are not certain, and there are successive orders and disorders. In addition to the factors in each surface, the depth of relations, and the rate of their changes are investigated in an integrated form.

## DISCUSSION AND CONCLUSION

In today's world, decision-makers and experts in countries, organizations, businesses, and governments need inevitably to systematically recognize the environment. Environments are facing dynamic changes and multifaceted and multidimensional complexities in all social, political, cultural, value, scientific, and technological fields. The prospective reasoning is needed to understand the conditions of the environment when there is uncertainty. Presenting a framework of strategic environmental analysis based on the epistemological foundations of critical realism and the consciousness of the system of existence, the present paper has considered two continuums, including "micro-macro" and "objective-subjective", as the basic principles so that the unstable and uncertain things in the environment have been scanned in the light of certain things and the order of the system of creation.

The sun framework of the strategic environmental analysis includes two interconnected continuums of the "micro-macro" and the "objective-subjective", the two interactive and composite methods of scanning (fragmentation-integration), and the three levels of analysis. The first level of analysis includes four fragmented parallel processes (four dimensions). The second level focuses on two composite parallel processes of "micro-objective/subjective" and "macro-objective/subjective." Finally, at the third level, using the integration approach, the four dimensions are combined as a multi-dimensional, multi-faceted, and interdisciplinary system by considering the constant connection between the surface and depth so that the cognitive ambidexterity is applied and the dynamism and change of the dimensions of the framework (subsystems) are considered. The integration of subsystems leads to the formation of a general system in which there are simultaneously fragmentation and integration, and the surface and depth are constantly emphasized. This framework unites individualism and collectivism to provide a complete understanding of the environment. These parallel, composite, and integrated processes make it possible to use a variety of quantitative techniques. There is continuously a rotation from the micro dimensions to macro ones and from the objective dimensions to the subjective ones and vice versa when doing the analysis.

Compared to the Cynefin framework that identifies three domains of order, unorder, and disorder, the presented sun framework divides the things into certain and uncertain ones based on the underlying assumptions of it. It has been considered that certain things such as the conscious world of existence are ordered, purposeful, and stable, while uncertain things are unordered. Therefore, the framework assumes the disorder in uncertain things and the order in certain things that are manifested by the conscious world. Accordingly, order and disorder are replaced by the micro and macro levels in this framework, and it is believed that disorders should be recognized in the light of the macro-order and they are merely the realization of uncertainties in the relationship between the human and other creatures of the system of creation.

The sun framework of the strategic environmental analysis is similar to Wilber's framework in objective-subjective dimensions. However, there is a difference between the individual-collective dimensions of Wilber's framework and the micro-macro dimensions of the sun framework because Wilber's individual-collective dimensions can be examined at any micro and macro level of the sun framework and they cannot be used as two poles of a continuum for the analysis because the micro-systems (subsystems consisting of individuals-collections) can be analyzed at an integrated level and the larger system. When the subsystem is placed in a larger system (macro-system), it finds a different nature in terms of its relations, interactions, affecting, and being affected. Another difference is that the STEEP dimensions have been considered objectively, behaviorally, functionally, and subjectively with special attention to beliefs, thoughts, attitudes, and approaches. Attention to the surface (objective dimensions) along with the depth (subjective dimensions) completes our understanding of the environment. When the micro-macro level is scanned with the objective-subjective approach in an integrated way and then the dimension of time is added to it, a connection is created between scanning and monitoring so that the dynamics of interactions, relations, changes, and complexities can be monitored.

Obviously, in this new framework, different scientific disciplines can be used in each dimension because superficial layers of the environment such as experiences and realities and deeper layers of it such as intellectual structures, worldviews, and major local and global theories must be scanned and analyzed in an interdisciplinary, multidimensional, and multi-faceted way.

## REFERENCES

*Advanced analysis of strategic environment (Uncertainty, complexity and intelligence)*. (2020). University of Tehran Publications.

Agha, N., & Rascher, D. A. (2016). An explanation of economic impact: Why positive impacts can exist for smaller sports. *Sport, Business and Management*, *6*(2), 182–204. doi:10.1108/SBM-07-2013-0020

Aldieri, L., Brahmi, M., Bruno, B., & Vinci, C. P. (2021). Circular Economy Business Models: The Complementarities with Sharing Economy and Eco-Innovations Investments. *Sustainability*, *13*(22), 12438. doi:10.3390u132212438

Allen, Donald M. (2020). "Don Allen: Grove's First Editor." Interview with SE Gontarski. *Writing Into the Future: New American Poetries from" the Dial" to the Digital, 10*(3), 297.

Alperen, M. J. (2017). *Foundations of homeland security: Law and policy*. John Wiley & Sons. doi:10.1002/9781119289142

Braithwaite, J. (2022). Complexity science. In *Implementation Science* (pp. 7–12). Routledge. doi:10.4324/9781003109945-3

Clapper, J. R. (2014). *The national intelligence strategy of the United States of America*. Office of the Director of National Intelligence.

Cruickshank, J. (2003). *Critical realism: The difference it makes* (Vol. 6). Routledge. doi:10.4324/9780203512302

Daft, R. (2006). Cengage learning. *Organization theory and design.*

Dent, E. B. (1999). Complexity science. *A worldview shift. Emergence*, *1*(4), 5–19. doi:10.120715327000em0104_2

Duncan, R. B. (1971). *The effects of perceived environmental uncertainty on organizational decision unit structure: A cybernetic model.* Yale University.

Duncan, R. B. (1972). Characteristics of organizational environments and perceived environmental uncertainty. *Administrative Science Quarterly*, *17*(3), 313–327. doi:10.2307/2392145

Environments of organizations. (1976). *Annual review of sociology*, 79-105. EOO.

Gentili, P. L. (2021). Why is Complexity Science valuable for reaching the goals of the UN 2030 Agenda? *Rendiconti Lincei. Scienze Fisiche e Naturali*, *32*(1), 117–134. doi:10.100712210-020-00972-0 PMID:33527036

Geyer, R. (2003). Europeanisation, Complexity and the British Welfare State. In *Unspecified, Sheffield, UK*. Unspecified.

Giret, A., & Botti, V. (2004). Holons and agents. *Journal of Intelligent Manufacturing*, *15*(5), 645–659. doi:10.1023/B:JIMS.0000037714.56201.a3

Gulson, K. N., Lewis, S., Lingard, B., Lubienski, C., Takayama, K., & Webb, P. T. (2017). Policy mobilities and methodology: A proposition for inventive methods in education policy studies. *Critical Studies in Education*, *58*(2), 224–241. doi:10.1080/17508487.2017.1288150

Haefner, N., Wincent, J., Parida, V., & Gassmann, O. (2021). Artificial intelligence and innovation management: A review, framework, and research agenda. *Technological Forecasting and Social Change*, *162*, 120392. doi:10.1016/j.techfore.2020.120392

Hamrouni, B., Bourouis, A., Korichi, A., & Brahmi, M. (2021). Explainable Ontology-Based Intelligent Decision Support System for Business Model Design and Sustainability. *Sustainability*, *13*(17), 9819. doi:10.3390u13179819

Helfrich, P. (2000). *The emerging new worldview: An introduction and overview.* [*Unpublished* manuscript, Helfrich]. http://www. paulhelfrich. com/library/Helfrich_P_The_Emerging_New_Worldview. pdf

Holman, P. (2015). *Complexity, self-organization, and emergence. Dialogic organization development.* Berrett-Koehler.

Huang, H., Chau, K. Y., Iqbal, W., & Fatima, A. (2022). Assessing the role of financing in sustainable business environment. *Environmental Science and Pollution Research International*, *29*(5), 7889–7906. doi:10.100711356-021-16118-0 PMID:34480700

Improving decision making in complexity environment. (2014). *Procedia Economics and Finance, 16*, 402-409.

Introduction to Complex Systems and Agent Based Modeling, s.l. (2014). *Awarness: Self-Awarness in Autonomic systems.*

Jörg, T. (2011). *New thinking in complexity for the social sciences and humanities: A generative, transdisciplinary approach.* Springer Science & Business Media. doi:10.1007/978-94-007-1303-1

Kamoun-Chouk, S. (2022). How Digital Literacy, Could Impact Environmental Scanning, Business Intelligence and Knowledge Management? *International Conference on Knowledge Management in Organizations* 10.1007/978-3-031-07920-7_8

Lawrence, P., & Lorsch, J. (2015). Contingency Theory of Organizations—Differentiation and Integration. In *Organizational Behavior 2* (pp. 244–270). Routledge.

Litschert, R. J., & Bonham, T. (1978). A conceptual model of strategy formation. *Academy of Management Review*, *3*(2), 211–219. doi:10.2307/257662

Marzouk, Y. & Jin, J. (2022). Linking environmental scanning and organizational innovation with competitive advantage: evidence from Egyptian SMEs. *Management & Sustainability: An Arab Review.*

Mobini Dehkordi, A., & Heydari, H. (2014). *Fundamentals of Strategic Environmental Knowledge.* Concepts, Theories, Techniques and Applications.

Mobini-Dehkordi, A., Yadolai-Farsi, J., Arabiun, A., & Keshavarz-Turk, M. (2021). Identifying Applied Aspects, Medical Fields, and Technological Trends in Developing Future Entrepreneurial Opportunities in Telemedicine. *Health Information Management*, *17*(6), 260–267.

Nobari, N., Dehkordi, A. M., Akbari, M., & Padash, H. (2020). Innovation intelligence and its role in environmental uncertainty management: A conceptual framework. *VINE Journal of Information and Knowledge Management Systems.*

Olmedo, E. (2016). Implications of complexity in strategic management. *International Journal of Complexity in Leadership and Management*, *3*(1-2), 101–114. doi:10.1504/IJCLM.2016.075047

Page, S. E. (2009). Understanding Complexity. The Teching Company. chantilly, VA.

Patrick, O. P. (2022). Assessment of the Impact of Environmental Scanning Intensity on Innovation among SMEs Owners in Oyo State Nigeria. *JSMR.*

Sawyer, S. J., Eubanks, M. D., Beasley, J. C., Barton, B. T., Puckett, R. T., Tomeček, J. M., & Tomberlin, J. K. (2022). Vertebrate and invertebrate competition for carrion in human-impacted environments depends on abiotic factors. *Ecosphere*, *13*(7), e4151. doi:10.1002/ecs2.4151

Sawyerr, O. O., & Ebrahimi, B. P. (2022). Executive environmental scanning and strategic uncertainty: The impact of institutional context. *International Studies of Management & Organization*, *52*(1), 7–24. doi:10.1080/00208825.2021.2023442

Slaughter, R. A. (1999). A new framework for environmental scanning. *Foresight-The journal of future studies, strategic thinking and policy*, *1*(5), 441-451.

Smith, A. C. (2005). Complexity theory for organizational futures studies. *Foresight.*

Strogatz, S. H. (2012). *Sync: How order emerges from chaos in the universe, nature, and daily life.* . sustainable supply chains; a framework for environmental scanning practices. (2014). *International Journal of Operation & Production Managment.*

Tajpour, M., Hosseini, E., Mohammadi, M., & Bahman-Zangi, B. (2022). The effect of knowledge management on the sustainability of technology-driven businesses in emerging markets: The mediating role of social media. *Sustainability, 14*(14), 8602. doi:10.3390u14148602

The new complex perspective in economic analysis and business management. . (2002). *Emergence, 4(1-2)*, 147-163.

The new dynamics of strategy: Sense-making in a complex and complicated world. (2003). *IBM systems journal, 42*(3), 462-483.

Tunio, M. N., Jariko, M. A., Børsen, T., Shaikh, S., Mushtaque, T., & Brahmi, M. (2021). How Entrepreneurship Sustains Barriers in the Entrepreneurial Process—A Lesson from a Developing Nation. *Sustainability, 13*(20), 11419. doi:10.3390u132011419

van der Wal, J. M., van Borkulo, C. D., Deserno, M. K., Breedvelt, J. J., Lees, M., Lokman, J. C., Borsboom, D., Denys, D., van Holst, R. J., Smidt, M. P., Stronks, K., Lucassen, P. J., van Weert, J. C. M., Sloot, P. M. A., Bockting, C. L., & Wiers, R. W. (2021). Advancing urban mental health research: From complexity science to actionable targets for intervention. *The Lancet. Psychiatry, 8*(11), 991–1000. doi:10.1016/S2215-0366(21)00047-X PMID:34627532

Walker, H., Seuring, S., Sarkis, J., & Klassen, R. (2014). Sustainable operations management: Recent trends and future directions. *International Journal of Operations & Production Management, 34*(5). doi:10.1108/IJOPM-12-2013-0557

Wilber, K. (2000). Waves, streams, states and self. Further considerations for an integral theory of consciousness. *Journal of Consciousness Studies, 7*(11-12), 145–176.

Winter, J., Zhai, J., & Cotton, D. (2022). Teaching environmental sustainability in China: Opportunities and challenges for business and economics faculty in higher education. *Environmental Education Research, 28*(2), 318–332. doi:10.1080/13504622.2021.2012560

Yadolahi Farsi, J., Arabiun, A., & Akbar Farjadian, A.(2021). Reconceptualizing opportunity construct: An answer to a theoretical dilemma through a systematic literature review.

# Chapter 3
# A Review of Corporate Social Responsibility Literature and Future Directions

**Mehdi Tajpour**
*University of Tehran, Iran*

**Jahangir Yadollahi Farsi**
*University of Tehran, Iran*

**Brahmi Mohsen**
*University of Sfax, Tunisia*

## ABSTRACT

*Corporate social responsibility is deemed as a component that influences a company or survival of the organization. Although it has drawn considerable attention, whether a comprehensive model has been presented is a key question that has yet remained unanswered. The present chapter aims to propose an inclusive model of corporate social responsibility based on the definitions and concepts developed by another researcher. This paper expresses a different perspective on using literature review to extract corporate social responsibility dimensions and measures that make this research different from previous studies. In this regard, 317 papers on corporate social responsibility were selected which their theoretical frameworks, methodologies, theoretical gaps have been reviewed. The results indicate that CSR has been recognized and widely used in companies or organizations. Since ethical, environmental, economic, and psychological concerns have not been taken into account individually. The direction of future research is presented.*

DOI: 10.4018/978-1-6684-6766-4.ch003

## 1. INTRODUCTION

Since the nature of corporate social responsibility (CSR, henceforth) is considered dynamic, there is no inclusive definition (Gond, 2017). Since 1930, while a number of authors have carried out important research on CSR, most of them have been focused on various aspects of CSR. According to Hodkin (2002), researchers have represented a definition on the matter based on what they perceived: e.g., philanthropy, benevolence, ethics, social entrepreneurship (Chell et al. 2016), environment, deriving, evaluation, responses (Gond et al, 2017), entrepreneurial business, sustainable development, awareness (Tai & Chuang, 2014). Additionally, companies need to invest in a domestic and international competitive market in order to achieve success, which fulfilling this goal requires to use an important element and an effective factor influencing on this success. Hodkin (2002) defines CSR as respected and protecting the environment, aiming to improve the quality and opportunities of life, enabling individuals and investing in societies where companies operate in. In fact, CSR aims to support consumers (Hancock et al., 2008). Chen et al. (2018) also suggest that the integration of CSR with different strategies such as operational and managerial as well as corporate governance policies boosts the value of a company. Also, CSR programs have become an integral part of the public relations strategy in many companies. Lii and Lee (2012) also identified the consumer companies and reputation, respectively. In addition, the increased customer loyalty, higher earnings, willingness to pay premium and flexibility to the negative press about the company were recognized by Du et al. (2007) Firstly, since there is no comprehensive definition of CSR, according to the researchers (Gond, 2017). We definite CSR as turning the idea into reality, respecting for the environment, compatibility, support, innovation, benevolence and humanitarian entrepreneurship as well as company reputation, which all of these factors improve the performance of a company or organization and lead to outperform its rivals. While in the earlier research, the definition of CSR was solely limited to the used dimensions, the definition presented in this study is based on different dimensions. This definition considers CSR as a process and outcome at the individual, organizational, and institutional level whereas the previous studies had been studied on one- or two-dimensional level. Also, the numbers of papers published in conferences and journals have highlighted the importance of CSR in recent years. Sue et al. (2016) studied the emerging markets and concluded that those who participate in the CSR activities have acquired more reputation and credibility that brings about increasing the performance and revenue of the company. Moreover, Yadav et al. (2016) found that a positive CSR report would lead to positive returns in stock portfolios. Although they analyzed CSR literature such as CSR reports, financial and social performance, and even corporate reputation, they could not find any significant relationship between CSR practices and corporate reputation as a medium. After studying previous studies, it can be noted that each study has examined CSR dimensions from a different point of views, but they have not provided a comprehensive and effective model.

## 2. LITERATURE REVIEW

The managerial approaches to implementing social responsibility by companies were introduced by a researcher at classic Management in 1975. The business social commitment approach primarily focuses on economic issues and restricts social responsibility to the existing laws, including commitments that anticipate future social problems. Companies that are organized according to behaviors and activities are consistent with the social sensitivity approach in which they are socially more sensitive (Sethi, 1975). It was complicated to define the range that should be revised by one due to the interdisciplinary nature of the CSR (Bansal & Song, 2017). Corporate social responsibility investigates sub-dimensions of CSR such as behaviors supporting environment at a micro level (Gond et al., 2017). To what extent an operational structure depends on social responsibility is related to several demographic and psychological dimensions (Peterson et al., 2009). The concept of corporate social responsibility which has been evolving is an approach that companies integrates social, environmental, and economic concerns into values, cultures, strategies, and operations in a way that are enabled to respond demands; hence corporations are able to develop a sound practice that provides society with prosperity and welfare.

*Table 1. Concepts and definitions of CSR*

| Number | Author and year | Concepts and definitions |
|---|---|---|
| 1 | Chen et al. 2019 | Companies adopting CSR give better performance and therefore their risk will reduce. |
| 2 | Singh, Majumdar, & Saini, 2017 | Social entrepreneurship can support corporate social responsibility and effectively fill the gap between business and society. |
| 3 | Chell et al. 2016 | Social entrepreneurs' motivations are "altruism" and "benevolence", and social entrepreneurs concern about ethics. |
| 4 | Siltaoja et al, 2015 | Corporate social responsibility has provided employees with accountability in the corporate environment. |
| 5 | Tai & Chuang, 2014 | Large corporations with legal personality in the global structure need to go beyond the standards so that they can pursue goals for sustainable development. |
| 6 | Verma & Singh, 2014 | Corporate social responsibility is associated with achieving economic success, respecting to the moral values of individuals, communities and the natural environment. |
| 7 | Forte, 2013 | Corporate social responsibility today plays a vital role in companies in the United States, and American citizens, therefore, are reaching profitability and business success. |
| 8 | Vohra et al, 2012 | Corporate Social Responsibility (CSR) has been drawing attention to academics and business organizations over the last decade. |
| 9 | Visser, 2011 | Corporate social responsibility has turned from an idea to reality and is treated as an important dimension for contemporary business practices. |
| 10 | Chomvilailuk & Butcher, 2010 | Corporate social responsibility is considered to be a variety of factors that affect branding. |

## 2.1 Conceptual Models of Corporate Social Responsibility

In general, there are two conceptual models of corporate social responsibility:

### 2.1.1 Carol's Conceptual Model (1991-1979)

Carol's Model of Corporate Social Responsibility falls into four categories: economic responsibility, legal responsibility, ethical responsibility, and philanthropy responsibility. The economic responsibility includes opening up an investment horizon for owners and shareholders, creating jobs, fairly paying for workers, discovering new resources, promoting advanced technology, innovating, and providing new services and products. The next category, which is a legal responsibility, consists of compliance with rules and role-playing, along with following the rules of the game, although rules and regulations may lead some opportunities for companies to be lost and place some restrictions on business. Ethical responsibility is able to overcome the constraints created by laws with shaping an ethical character by which companies can survive. The last one is philanthropy responsibility where companies have a broad range of humanitarian judgment and choices while decision-making for specific activities or humanitarian partnerships assist the community. This type of responsibility is of the most controversial issues and puts many limitations. Furthermore, its application appears to contradict in commercial firms that tend to seek out economic benefits (Carroll, 1991). See figure 1.

*Figure 1. Corporate Social Responsibility Model (Carroll, 1979)*

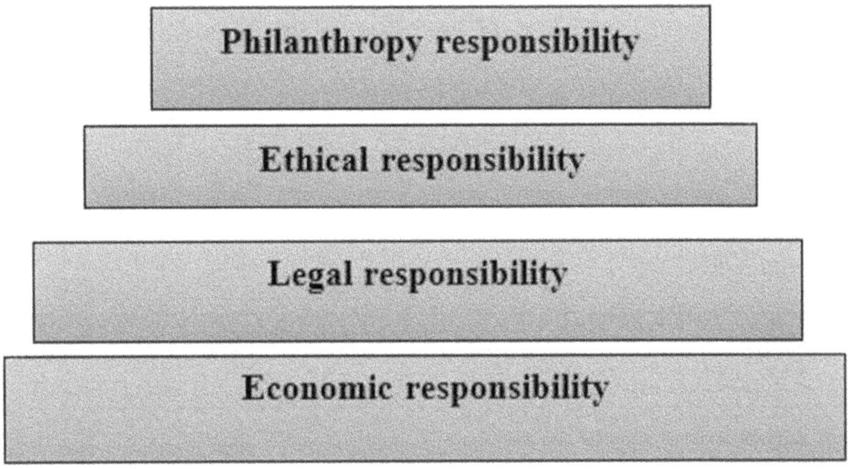


### 2.1.2 Wood's Model (1991)

According to Wood's Model, responsibility is a practical dimension (Jamali et al., 2007). A researcher who uses Wood's Model takes three levels of analysis (institutional, organizational, and individual) into an account that triggers a company to engage with CSR. Therefore, the motivations behind taking social responsibility in companies are likely to be due to the principle of legitimacy (organizational level), and it is the desire to maintain credibility and reputation. In addition, motivations, especially for the consequences associated with the primary and secondary contexts that the company is involved in, may come from an organizational sense of public responsibility. It is also likely that two or more principles interact with each other to motivate the company's social performance (Wood, 1991). Carole's and Wood's models are complementary. Both models can be efficiently adopted and integrated. Carroll groups social responsibility so that it can be represented as a scope in which the principles of CSR, processes, and outcomes are included (Jamali et al, 2007). See figure 2.

## 2.2 CSR-Related Theories

Theories and codes related to the topic in the background are as follows: See table 1.

*Figure 2. Wood conceptual framework, set (Wood, 1991)*

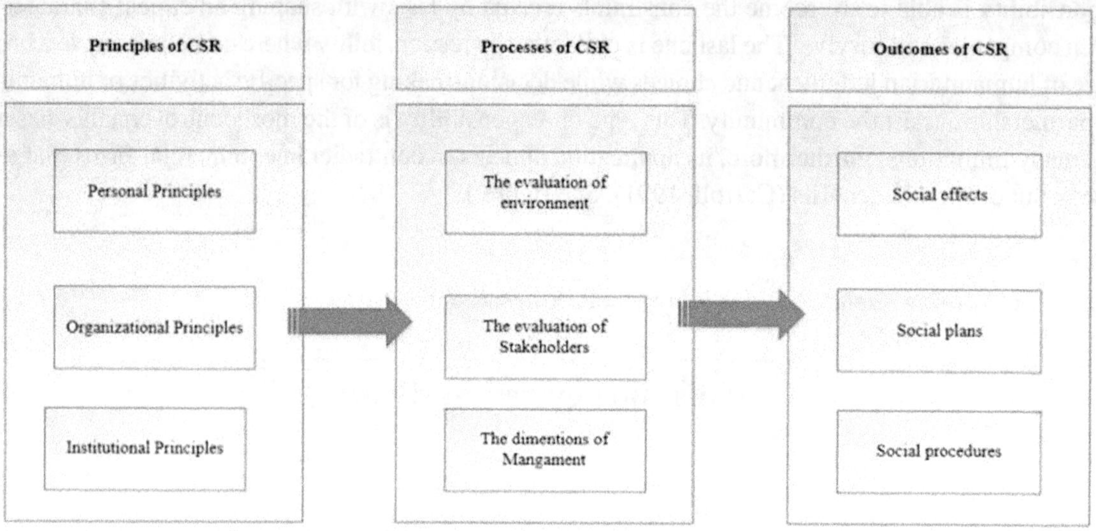


*Table 2. Theories and codes*

| Theories | The codes extracted from the background |
|---|---|
| **Stakeholders Theory** | Social commitment of business (Setti, 1975)<br>Corporate citizen (Mattin & Cran, 2005)<br>Keeping satisfied employees (Sarasvathy et al., 2010)<br>Ethical commitment (Pae & Chui, 2011)<br>Voluntary Commitment and Public Welfare (Arvalo & Arind, 2011)<br>Paying attention to the people (Carroll 1991)<br>Altruism and benevolence (Chell et al., 2016)<br>Interacting with stakeholders voluntarily (European Commission, 2001)<br>Entrepreneurial philanthropy (Shaw et al., 2013)<br>The Attention of Entrepreneurs to Social Problems (Peterson & John, 2009)<br>The positive feedback of the stakeholders (Hinson, 2011)<br>The limited private owners (Aurovalo & Arvin, 2011)<br>Meeting the needs of customers, stakeholders and employees(Aurovalo & Arvin, 2011)<br>The nature of business (Jenkins, 2009)<br>Increasing Business Profit (Mohr & Webb, 2005)<br>Explaining the Turnover Intentions (Shaikh et al., 2022) |
| **Resource-based Theory** | Customer loyalty and satisfaction (Dave et al., 2007)<br>Supporting Consumer (Hancock et al., 2008)<br>Employee safety and well-being (Lee et al., 2008)<br>Corporate Survival and Success (Visser, 2011)<br>Focusing on Short-Term Goals by Entrepreneurs ((ValMohammadi, 2011)<br>Searching for resources through innovation and acceptance of risk (Chrisan, 2012).<br>Not paying attention to the general knowledge ((ValMohammadi, 2011)<br>Discovering new resources (Jamali et al., 2007)<br>Leading the community towards the advancement of industry and technology (Rana, 2012)<br>Sustainable development in the long run (Tai and Tea, 2014)<br>Increasing environmental awareness (Jamali et al., 2007) |
| **Allocation Theory** | Attention to suitable opportunities of living (Hodkin, 2002)<br>Costs in the private and public sectors (Sarasvathy et al., 2010)<br>Humanitarian innovations (Rana, 2012)<br>The strong orientation of social responsibility (Peterson & John, 2009)<br>Strengthening market position (Chrisan, 2012)<br>Creating new products and services (Jamali et al., 2007)<br>Catching Business Opportunities (Jenkins, 2009)<br>Creating Market Opportunities (Green & Ploza, 2011)<br>Understanding entrepreneur motivation (Peterson and John, 2009) |

### 2.2.1 Allocative Theory

Efficient allocation can be made in pure or perfect competition market where the buyer and seller are not individually able to influence prices. Arrow (1962) suggests that there are three reasons why perfect competition market can lead to inefficient resource allocation to invent: lack of accessibility (inaccessibility), indivisibility, and uncertainty. Hence, allocation efficiency may be put at risk if these three reasons are not met (Sarasvathy et al., 2010). In this research, an allocative theory is used to explore an entrepreneur motivation for social partnership. In addition, it can be used to assess commitment to social responsibility, and the results will be reliable (Peterson & John, 2009). Kamien and Schwartz (1962) studied the relationship between market structure and innovation and concluded that few economists perceived the perfect competition market that is effectively allocated resources for technical progress (Kamien & Schwartz, 1975).

### 2.2.2 Resource-Based Theory (RBT)

RBT is referred to adopt and private and social value of companies that are strategically aligned with CSR. The strategic CSR is "responsible manner that enables a company to achieve sustainable competitive advantage, without taking into account incentive." (McWilliams & Siegel, 2011). Kraaijenbrink et al. (2010) have recently addressed the criticisms raised on RBT and concluded that it needs to be developed theoretically. McWilliams and Siegel (2011) states that RBT does not present any tools to determine external alternatives, but CSR creates a special asset to increase the value of the company. In fact, it provides companies with reputation and great value in comparison with the others (McWilliams & Siegel, 2011).

### 2.2.3 Stakeholder Theory

Friedman and Miles (2006) suggest that the term "stakeholder" has developed over the two past decades and it has become popular among traders, governments, NGOs and even media (Friedman & Miles, 2006). Stakeholder theory considers the shareholders' satisfaction as the measure of performance. Shareholders may be customers, suppliers, and shareholders (Peterson & John, 2009). The majority of entrepreneurs and stakeholders hold similar views on issues of social responsibility that can lead entrepreneurs to make constant and collaborative efforts to address specific social problems. (Peterson & John, 2009). A corporate social activity implies that CSR presents a discovery view over social responsibility. The CSR framework has developed based on stakeholder theory. The company's stakeholders include shareholders, creditors, employees, customers, and suppliers as the customer of reference groups and government bodies (Freeman et al., 2006).

## 2.3 Conceptual Model of CSR

Charitable changes occur when charitable institutions can head charitable goals to commercial and technological developments. Therefore, benevolent innovation refers to a phenomenon that aims to achieve benevolent goals of a firm through developing and implementing ideas that are successful in the marketplace (Rana, 2012). The question raised here is whether or not the importance of CSR has influenced changing customer behavior (Mohr & Webb, 2005). Depending on consumers' perceptions and attitudes, CSR can create value for customers or undermine the value (Green & Peloza, 2011). In fact, CSR plays a supportive role for consumers (Hancock et al., 2008). Besides, the activities of CSR reduce business risk, secure company reputation or increase the net profits of the company (Kakabadse et al., 2009). Also, entrepreneurs have gone beyond the legal requirements associated with corporate social responsibility in their interactions with their stakeholders and benefit from their growth, size, and position in society. A company should view the activities undertaken in the context of CSR and their implementation as a major factor, so that they contribute to economic benefits (Ebo Hinson, 2011). Entrepreneurial businesses are considered as a profit-making tool in different sectors. Entrepreneurship multinational companies creatively and innovatively respond to the needs of their shareholders, including social responsibility, meeting suppliers' needs, long-term sustainability of companies, investors, and employees (Tai & Chuang, 2014). Entrepreneurial philanthropy has drawn little attention to the scientific direction (Shou et al., 2013). There are few studies that focused on benevolent actions in the UK and the United States (Desai& Acs, 2008; Shaw et al., 2013). The authors show that engagement in philanthropy may not only be realized by economic capital (wealth), but it is provided with other forms of capital (cultural, social, and symbolic). It can be concluded that it is so difficult to involve in charitable activities. (Desai& Acs, 2008). Moreover, it noted that CSR has appeared in ancient India. The basic concept of CSR was driven based on specific virtues and values such as honesty, love, and trust. Such values turned into the golden rule (Freeman et al., 2006). It has also been argued that companies can treat this golden rule as accountability to stakeholders and the public (Muniapan & Dass, 2008). Depending on the circumstances, the concept of CSR in different countries has different meanings. Globalization will also affect CSR. The structure of internal business systems is the backbone of multinational corporations in CSR. Family businesses and sociological theories on CSR have been criticized from political, social, economic, and ethical perspectives (Van Oosterhout & Heugens, 2008). Papers that concentrates upon institutional analysis represent one of the three main pillars of the institutions. Papers that consider laws and standards as legal elements were analyzed CSRs at the institutional level (Scherer & Palazzo, 2011). Similarly, papers that present components created by consumers, stakeholders, and society are among normative and cultural-cognitive elements, and made an analysis at the institutional level. Researchers who study CSR at an institutional level usually consider the institutional theory as a basis. Most CSR articles focused on the organizational level of analysis. The organizational level involves those who conceptually stand at the macro level. For example, teams of senior management are evaluated at a macro theory (Arevalo et al., 2011). Therefore, the incentives to social responsibility in companies may be due to the principle of legitimacy (organizational level), i.e. the desire to maintain credibility as a responsible social actor in a community (Jamali et al., 2007). The individual level of analysis is made based on psychological theories and center upon normative motivations, such as alignment with personal values, commitment, and awareness of CSR (Scherer & Palazzo, 2011). See figure 3.

## 3. RESEARCH METHODOLOGY

This study was carried out based on a systematic approach and statistical population included previous research (articles, book) on CSR. 102 papers were selected as the most relevant studies using a targeted approach in which CSR and other variables were discussed. A qualitative approach was used to analyze the data, and software Atlas T was used for coding the research as an analytical instrument. The following steps have been taken to systematically review the papers:

*Figure 3. Conceptual Model of CSR*

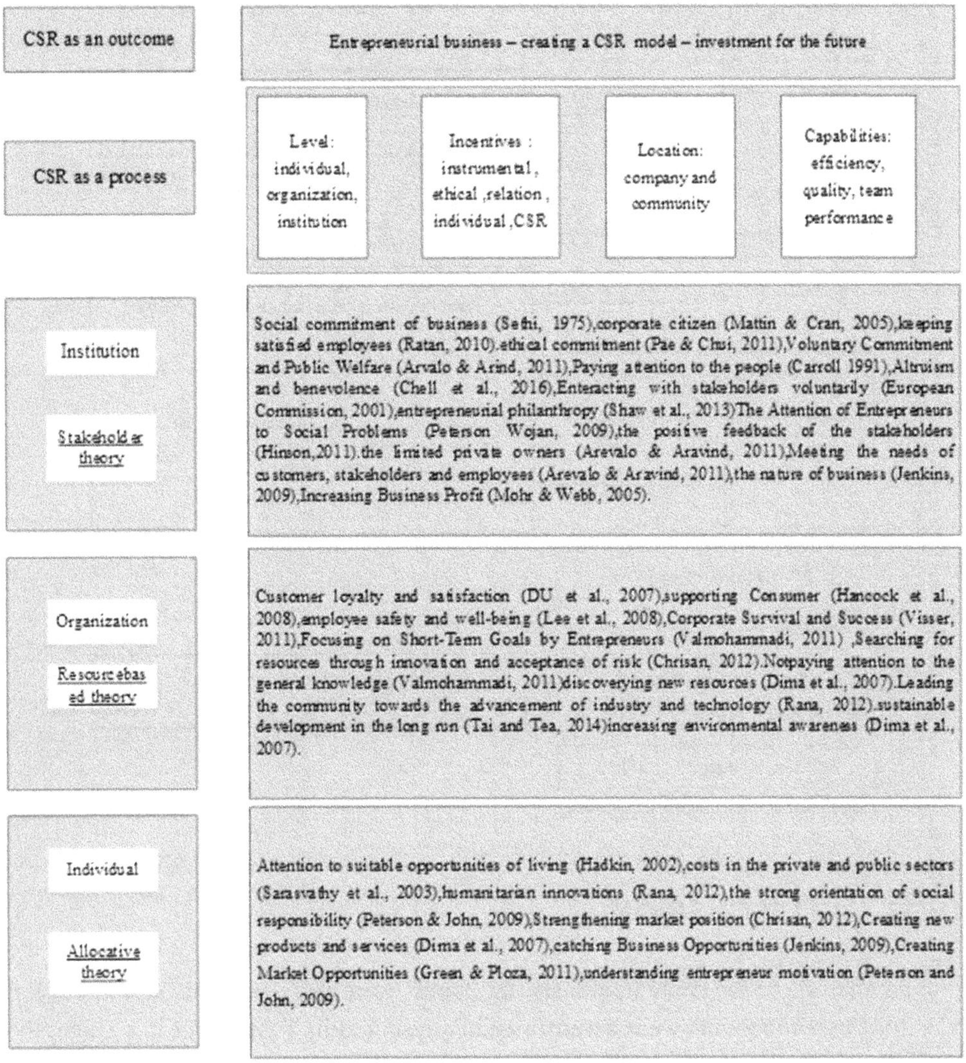


The steps are briefly described as follows. The first step begins with developing the research parameters based on research questions, according to Wetton's framework, which includes What, How, Why, What, Who, and Where. The second step is followed by the statistical population consisted of all scientific documents, databases, and foreign publications on CSR from 1930 to 2021. Key terms are corporate social responsibility, social entrepreneurship, social opportunities, and charitable entrepreneurship at Academy of Management Review, Business & Society, the Journal of Business, Ethics-Science Direct, Emerald, and so forth. Therefore, once the search finished, a list of various documents, including 317 CSR articles and books, was extracted. The targeted papers were selected based on the algorithm shown in Figure 4.

**Step 2:** The codes related to CSR were extracted based on previous studies. Once the concept of each code was recognized, they were categorized in a similar concept, and then categories related to CSR were identified. Coding has been done at all three levels in terms of open, axial and selective approach.

*Figure 4. The process of selecting papers*

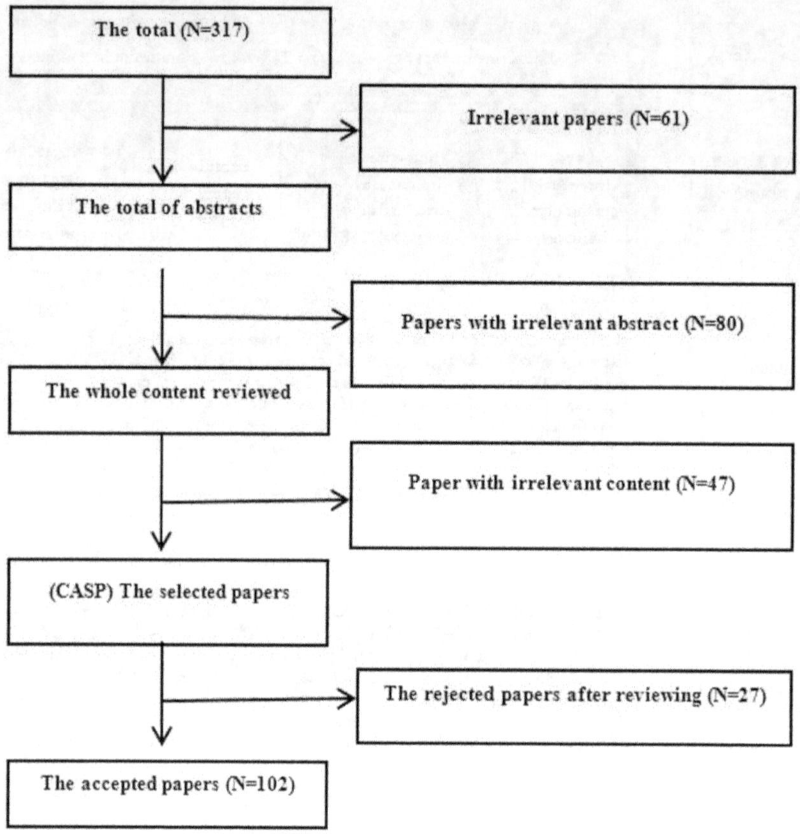


## 4. FINDINGS AND DISCUSSION

According to an analysis of the content, at last, 102 papers were selected, which a total of 9 categories and 51 codes for the components were determined as presented in Table 3. In this stage, the findings showed that previous studies had not carried out such a systematic study and only concentrated on a specific aspect of the identification and implementation of corporate social responsibility, and none of the research had been studied coherently and systematically. Table 3 represents the codes pertaining to research background with each major category of CSR. See table 3.

*Table 3. The preferred elements and codes*

| Elements | The respective code in the research background |
|---|---|
| **Social Responsibility** | Focusing on the social commitment of business (Sethi, 1975).<br>Focusing on corporate citizen. (Mattin & Cran, 2005).<br>Focusing on better living opportunities (Hodkin, 2002).<br>Focusing on the survival and success of companies (Visser, 2011).<br>Focusing on staff satisfaction (Sarasvathy et al., 2010). |

*continues on following page*

*Table 3. Continued*

| Elements | The respective code in the research background |
|---|---|
| **Customer's attitude** | Centering on the security and welfare of employees (Lee et al., 2008).<br>Centering on emotional value (Green and Plula, 2011).<br>Centering on social value (Tajpour et al., 2021).<br>Centering on intercultural differences (Mohr & Webb, 2005).<br>Centering on consumer protection (Hancock et al., 2008).<br>Centering on increasing business profits (Mohr & Webb, 2005). |
| **Ethics** | Concentrating on overcoming legal constraints (Jamali et al., 2008).<br>Concentrating on Voluntary Commitment and Public Welfare (Arvalo & Arind, 2011).<br>Paying attention to the people (Carroll 1991).<br>Having a moral commitment (Choi and Pae, 2011). |
| **Social Entrepreneurship** | Focusing on Short-Term Goals by Entrepreneurs (Salamzadeh et al., 2022).<br>Organizational Culture and Business Performance in SMEs (Arabeche et al., 2022)<br>Paying attention to costs in the private and public sectors (Sarasvathy et al., 2010).<br>Concentrating on ethical ethics (Verma & Singh, 2013).<br>Determinants of the Sustainable Entrepreneurial Engagement of Youth (Tunio et al., 2021)<br>Concentrating on the approaches in International Activities (Val Mohammad, 2011).<br>The lacking of attention to the general knowledge ((ValMohammadi, 2011).<br>Altruism and benevolence (Chell et al., 2016).<br>Search for resources through innovation and acceptance of risk (Chrisan, 2012). |
| **Benevolence** | Interacting with stakeholders voluntarily (European Commission, 2001).<br>The confidentiality of charity actions ((ValMohammadi, 2011).<br>Entrepreneurial philanthropy (Shaw et al., 2013).<br>Humanitarian innovations (Rana, 2012).<br>Leading the community towards the advancement of industry and technology (Tajpour et al., 2021). |
| **Entrepreneurial business** | Strong orientation towards social responsibility (Peterson and John, 2009).<br>The Attention of Entrepreneurs to Social Problems (Tai and Tea, 2014).<br>Business Model Design and Sustainability (Hamrouni et al., 2021)<br>The trend towards sustainable development in the long run. (Tajpour, 2021; Tajpour et al., 2022).<br>Entrepreneurial University (Mobarki et al., 2021).<br>Entrepreneurship Sustains Barriers in the Entrepreneurial Process (Tunio, et al., 2021) |
| **Corporate Social Responsibility Privileges** | Effectively filling the gap between society and business (Singh et al., 2017).<br>Strengthening the market position (Chrisan, 2012).<br>Increasing creativity (Greek, 2017).<br>Increasing Organizational Citizenship Behaviors and Improving employees Relationships (Hosseini et al, 2021).<br>Customer loyalty and satisfaction (Dave et al., 2007).<br>Sustainable development and growth in the market (Hodkin, 2002).<br>The positive feedback of the stakeholders (Hinson, 2011).<br>Increasing environmental awareness (Jamali et al., 2007).<br>Discovering new Resources (Jamali et al., 2007).<br>Improving maintenance and organizational commitment (Hosseini et al, 2021). |
| **Economic** | The limited private owners (Aurovalo & Arvin, 2011).<br>Meeting the needs of the stakeholders, customers, staff (Auroulou & Arvin, 2011).<br>Sharing Economy and Eco-Innovations Investments (Aldieri et al., 2021)<br>Increasing social and environmental performance along with focusing on the economic dimensions and business strategy of the company (McKinley, 2008).<br>Fostering innovation (Ziyae et al., 2021).<br>Geotourism Hazards and Carrying Capacity (Sunkar et al., 2022) |
| **Opportunity** | Identifying Business Opportunities (Jones Kinds, 2009).<br>The nature of business (Tajpour et al., 2021).<br>Creating Opportunities in Market (Tajpour et al., 2021).<br>Understanding entrepreneur motivation (Peterson and John, 2009). |

Concerning social entrepreneurship and social responsibility, Singh and Saiani (2017) suggest that financial, social, and environmental parameters have a strong impact on the sustainability of companies. Therefore, the innovative models of CSR need to be designed in a way that they incorporate business and social benefits (Singh, Majumdar, & Saini, 2017). El Abedin et al. (2018) pointed out that cooperation between businesses and NGO is imbalanced, and this gap and individual characteristics are likely to affect shaping the behavior of corporate executives (Al-Abdin, Roy & Nicholson, 2018). Social responsibility which comes up against this view has been formed by traders and businessmen (Muniapan & Das, 2008). While there is a different view about CSR taken by researchers regarding at different levels, they make an effort to study in detail at multilevel aimed at integrating a variety of theoretical framework as to create a roadmap for future research. Individual-level sheds light on the psychological and ethical features and respective theories. Given that various organizations understand CSR differently, the researcher is looking for a process to carry out this research at an organizational level with the characteristics of psychology and related theories such as Resource-Base-Theory. On the other hand, while understanding CSR at an organizational level is obtained based on the existing situation and conditions, the third level of institutional analysis is established upon psychological characteristics and theories related to this level, such as stakeholder theory. Papers that deal with the institutional analytical level represent at least one of the three pillars of the institutions. Papers it examines the rules and standards of legal elements that are categorized as CSR at the institutional level of analysis (Scherer & Palazzo, 2011). CSR is considered to be an important element for a person, organization, institution, but CSR goes beyond this point because it includes dimensions that have clear and comprehensive definitions. Therefore, considering the existing literature, a comprehensive definition of it should be provided by taking into account the knowledge and existing gaps. In this research, we have tried to provide a comprehensive model of CSR because there is no broad model for understanding CSR. For this reason, the papers ranged 2000-2021 have systematically interpreted and reviewed various models, but no comprehensive model has ever been developed for individuals, organizations, and institutions to gain a better understanding. Sharp and Zaidman (2010) suggest that research should be conducted on how CSR strategy can be implemented over time. Zhou et al. (2016) argued that government can have a huge impact on adopting CSR by companies in developing countries, and it is suggested that the government's impact on implementing CSR have to be investigated. This division will be changed by using a different theoretical framework. Researchers who analyze CSR studies at an organizational level usually use institutional theory as a basis. In contrast, researchers who focus on the organizational level of analysis consider a variety of theoretical frameworks, such as the resource-based view. Finally, CSR researchers at the individual level analyze a different set of theoretical frameworks, such as strong positioning in the market as well as increasing business profits. CSR is the area that was initially examined at institutional level. While the institutional level was studied based on business system theories, stakeholder theory, and reasoned action theory, at the institutional level, the theory of logical action has been considered entrepreneurial and ethical approaches. Over the past decades, the focus has widely been on the organizational level, and researchers have conducted different theories in different research. According to research done since 1930, although various research has been conducted at the institutional and organizational level, the individual level has not been studied comprehensively. It should be noted that research at the individual level account for less than institutional and organizational one do, and theories of exchange and planned behavior have not inclusively been studied.

## 5. Managerial And Practical Implication

A few important lessons for improvement in practices can be garnered from the results in this study. Firstly, most papers associated with CSR focus on an institutional level. The individual level is analyzed based on psychological theories and centers on normative motivations, such as aligning with personal values, commitment, and awareness of CSR. Secondly, CSR can create value for customers or undermine value. The activities of CSR reduce business risk, secure company reputation or increase the net profits of the company. Also, entrepreneurship multinational companies creatively and innovatively respond to the needs of their shareholders. Thirdly, the CSR of the researchers turn the idea into reality, and, in addition, it is related to the environment, compatibility, support, innovation, benevolence, and humanitarian entrepreneurship as well as company reputation, which improve the performance of a company or organization.

## 6. CONCLUSION

The results of coding textual data revealed that 9 categories were totally identified about the concept of CSR at the individual, organizational and institutional levels, including social responsibility, ethics, benevolence, customer attitudes, economics, social entrepreneurship, social responsibility privileges, entrepreneurial businesses, and opportunities existing in different theories. We found that CSR plays a crucial role in changing customers' attitude and supporting consumers. CSR plays a role of leverage in supporting social entrepreneurship. We consider actions and policies taken for CSR as primary or internal results, suggesting that whether these measures influence internal or external stakeholders. That is to say, the external results are corporate reputation, targeted customers or product. CSR is an area that initially focuses on the institutional level, whereas it has emphasized on the organizational level over the past decades. The lack of micro-level research on CSR was recognized as a gap. Chen et al. (2018) suggest that management systems should be equipped with sufficient experience and knowledge. Companies should strengthen their relationship with the stakeholders and integrate the strategies used in their business. Although uncertainty is caused by market changes, companies tend to minimize individual risks (Chen, Hung & Lee, 2018). How CSR is effective depends on organizational environments and the needs of stakeholders in different countries. It will also improve the reputation of the company. Competitive advantage, customer satisfaction, and main intermediaries are related to CSR and performance of the company (Al-Abdin, Roy & Nicholson, 2018). Companies with different sizes may have different needs in order to implement CSR (Lau et al., 2018). While responses to CSR are not same among individuals, situational features may inspire employees to be more sensitive towards the positive effects of CSR. It is argued that business characteristics will have a considerable impact on employee motivation and performance (Marquis & Qian, 2013). Most research on CSR institutional level has been conducted upon corporate reputation, consumer evaluation, financial performance, and company capabilities (Aguilera, Rupp, Williams & Ganapathi, 2007). At the end, all of these factor lead to outperform other rivals of the company. This study has several limitations. First, philanthropy and ethics in CSR need to be studied carefully. With regard to environmental and economic factors, the development of the subject could also be challenging.

## 7. FUTURE RESEARCH DIRECTION

It is recommended that researchers theoretically consider the individual level in different approaches rather than the gaps. In this research, the existing restrictions open up new opportunities for future research. Ong, Mayer, Tost, and Wellman (2018) argue that people might not only pay little attention to CSR, but they also would not be aware of. Future research should include developing countries so that the impact of CSR on beneficiaries and create socio-economic value through CSR could be examined (Al-Abdin, Roy & Nicholson, 2018). Companies should consider CSR as a corporate strategy while developing. Future research may focus on a single industry to provide industry-specific insights (Lau et al., 2018). Although there is a direct relationship between different patterns of CSR and outcomes of performance, future researchers should be focused on how the internationalization of companies will affect CSR activities (Attig et al., 2016). Future studies may continue to deep address the reliability of the present research model the unsolved puzzle among these factors in other industries, and compare the impact of CSR with different industries from the consumer perspective.

## 8. REFERENCES

Aguilera, R. V., Rupp, D. E., Williams, C. A., & Ganapathi, J. (2007). Putting the S back in corporate social responsibility: A multilevel theory of social change in organizations. *Academy of Management Review*, *32*(3), 836–863. doi:10.5465/amr.2007.25275678

Al-Abdin, A., Roy, T., & Nicholson, J. D. (2018). Researching corporate social responsibility in the Middle East: The current state and future directions. *Corporate Social Responsibility and Environmental Management*, *25*(1), 47–65. doi:10.1002/csr.1439

Aldieri, L., Brahmi, M., Bruno, B., & Vinci, C. P. (2021). Circular Economy Business Models: The Complementarities with Sharing Economy and Eco-Innovations Investments. *Sustainability*, *13*(22), 12438. https://doi.org/10.3390/su132212438

Arabeche, Z., Soudani, A., Brahmi, M., Aldieri, L., Vinci, C. P., & Abdelli, M. E. A. (2022). Entrepreneurial Orientation, Organizational Culture and Business Performance in SMEs: Evidence from Emerging Economy. *Sustainability*, *14*(9), 5160. doi:10.3390u14095160

Arevalo, Jorge A, & Aravind, Deepa. (2011). Corporate social responsibility practices in India: approach, drivers, and barriers. *Corporate Governance: The international journal of business in society, 11*(4), 399-414.

Attig, N., Boubakri, N., Ghoul, S. E., & Guedhami, O. (2016). Firm internationalization and corporate social responsibility. *Journal of Business Ethics*, *134*(2), 171–197. doi:10.100710551-014-2410-6

Bansal, P., & Song, H.-C. (2017). Similar but not the same: Differentiating corporate sustainability from corporate responsibility. *The Academy of Management Annals*, *11*(1), 105–149. doi:10.5465/annals.2015.0095

Carroll, A. B. (1979). A three-dimensional conceptual model of corporate performance. *Academy of Management Review*, *4*(4), 497–505. doi:10.2307/257850

Carroll, A. B. (1991). Corporate social responsibility: Evolution of a definitional construct. *Business & Society*, *38*(3), 268–295. doi:10.1177/000765039903800303

Chell, E., Spence, L. J., Perrini, F., & Harris, J. D. (2016). Social entrepreneurship and business ethics: Does social equal ethical? *Journal of Business Ethics*, *133*(4), 619–625. doi:10.100710551-014-2439-6

Chen, Roger CY, Hung, Shih-Wei, & Lee, Chen-Hsun. (2018). Corporate Social Responsibility and Firm Idiosyncratic Risk in Different Market States. *Corporate Social Responsibility and Environmental Management.*

Choi, T. H., & Pae, J. (2011). Business ethics and financial reporting quality: Evidence from Korea. *Journal of Business Ethics*, *109*(3), 403–427. doi:10.100710551-011-0871-4

Chomvilailuk, R., & Butcher, K. (2010). Enhancing brand preference through corporate social responsibility initiatives in the Thai banking sector. *Asia Pacific Journal of Marketing and Logistics*, *22*(3), 397–418. doi:10.1108/13555851011062296

Desai, S., & Acs, Z. J. (2008). *Democratic capitalism and philanthropy in a global economy Public policy in an entrepreneurial economy*. Springer.

Du, S., Bhattacharya, C. B., & Sen, S. (2007). Reaping relational rewards from corporate social responsibility: The role of competitive positioning. *International Journal of Research in Marketing*, *24*(3), 224–241. doi:10.1016/j.ijresmar.2007.01.001

Employment, European Commission. Directorate-General for. (2001). *Promoting a European Framework for Corporate Social Responsibility: Green Paper*: Office for Official Publications of the European Communities.

Forte, A. (2013). Corporate Social Responsibility in The United States and Europe: How Important Is It? The Future of Corporate Social Responsibility, International Business &. *Economic Research Journal*, *12*(7), N-7. doi:10.19030/iber.v12i7.7970

Freeman, R. & Velamuri, S. (2006). A new approach to CSR: Company stakeholder responsibility Corporate social responsibility (pp. 9-23): Springer.

Friedman, A. L., & Miles, S. (2006). *Stakeholders: Theory and practice*. Oxford University Press on Demand.

Gond, J.-P., El Akremi, A., Swaen, V., & Babu, N. (2017). The psychological microfoundations of corporate social responsibility: A person-centric systematic review. *Journal of Organizational Behavior*, *38*(2), 225–246. doi:10.1002/job.2170

Green, T., & Peloza, J. (2011). How does corporate social responsibility create value for consumers? *Journal of Consumer Marketing*, *28*(1), 48–56. doi:10.1108/07363761111101949

Hamrouni, B., Bourouis, A., Korichi, A., & Brahmi, M. (2021). Explainable Ontology-Based Intelligent Decision Support System for Business Model Design and Sustainability. *Sustainability*, *13*(17), 9819. doi:10.3390u13179819

Hancock, L., Schellinck, T., & Schrans, T. (2008). Gambling and corporate social responsibility (CSR): Re-defining industry and state roles on duty of care, host responsibility and risk management. *Policy and Society*, *27*(1), 55–68. doi:10.1016/j.polsoc.2008.07.005

Hinson, E. (2011). Online CSR reportage of award-winning versus non award-winning banks in Ghana. *Journal of Information. Communication and Ethics in Society*, *9*(2), 102–115. doi:10.1108/14779961111148622

Hosseini, E., Tajpour, M., Salamzadeh, A., Demiryurek, K., & Kawamorita, H. (2021). Resilience and Knowledge-Based Firms' Performance: The Mediating Role of Entrepreneurial Thinking. *Journal of Entrepreneurship and Business Resilience*, *4*(2), 7–29.

Jamali, J., & Mirshak, R. (2007). Corporate social responsibility (CSR): Theory and practice in a developing country context. *Journal of Business Ethics*, *72*(3), 243–262. doi:10.100710551-006-9168-4

Jenkins, H. (2009). A 'business opportunity' model of corporate social responsibility for small-and medium-sized enterprises. *Business Ethics (Oxford, England)*, *18*(1), 21–36. doi:10.1111/j.1467-8608.2009.01546.x

Kakabadse, Nada K, Kakabadse, Andrew P, & Lee-Davies, Linda. (2009). CSR leaders road-map. *Corporate Governance: The international journal of business in society*, *9*(1), 50-57.

Kamien, M. I., & Schwartz, N. L. (1975). Market structure and innovation: A survey. *Journal of Economic Literature*, *13*(1), 1–37.

Kraaijenbrink, J., Spender, J. C., & Groen, A. J. (2010). The resource-based view: A review and assessment of its critiques. *Journal of Management*, *36*(1), 349–372. doi:10.1177/0149206309350775

Lau, A., Lee, P., & Cheng, T. (2018). An empirical taxonomy of corporate social responsibility in china's manufacturing industries. *Journal of Cleaner Production*.

Lii, Y.-S., & Lee, M. (2012). Doing right leads to doing well: When the type of CSR and reputation interact to affect consumer evaluations of the firm. *Journal of Business Ethics*, *105*(1), 69–81. doi:10.100710551-011-0948-0

Marquis, C., & Qian, C. (2013). Corporate social responsibility reporting in China: Symbol or substance. *Organization Science*, *25*(1), 127–148. doi:10.1287/orsc.2013.0837

McWilliams, A., & Siegel, D. S. (2011). Creating and capturing value: Strategic corporate social responsibility, resource-based theory, and sustainable competitive advantage. *Journal of Management*, *37*(5), 1480–1495. doi:10.1177/0149206310385696

Mobarki, M., Ziyae, B., Rezvani, M., Tajpour, M. (2021). Conceptual Model of Internationalization of the Entrepreneurial University with an Interpretive Structural Modeling Approach. *Journal of Research on Management of Teaching in Marine Sciences*. doi:10.22034/rmt.2021.530319.1841

Mohr, L. A., & Webb, D. J. (2005). The effects of corporate social responsibility and price on consumer responses. *The Journal of Consumer Affairs*, *39*(1), 121–147. doi:10.1111/j.1745-6606.2005.00006.x

Muniapan, B., & Dass, M. (2008). Corporate social responsibility: A philosophical approach from an ancient Indian perspective. *International Journal of Indian Culture and Business Management*, *1*(4), 408–420. doi:10.1504/IJICBM.2008.018622

Ong, M., Mayer, D. M., Tost, L. P., & Wellman, N. (2018). When corporate social responsibility motivates employee citizenship behavior: The sensitizing role of task significance. *Organizational Behavior and Human Decision Processes*, *144*, 44–59. doi:10.1016/j.obhdp.2017.09.006

Peterson, R. T., & Jun, M. (2009). Perceptions on social responsibility: The entrepreneurial vision. *Business & Society*, *48*(3), 385–405. doi:10.1177/0007650307305758

Rana, S. (2012). Philanthropic innovation and creative capitalism: A historical and comparative perspective on social entrepreneurship and corporate social responsibility. *Alabama Law Review*, *64*, 1121.

Salamzadeh, A., Tajpour, M., Hosseini, E., & Salamzadeh, Y. (2022). Geotourism and Destination Brand Selection: Does Social Media Matter? In *Economics and Management of Geotourism* (pp. 105–124). Springer. doi:10.1007/978-3-030-89839-7_6

Sarasvathy, S. D., & Dew, N. Velamuri, S Ramakrishna, & Venkataraman, Sankaran. (2010). Three views of entrepreneurial opportunity Handbook of entrepreneurship research (pp. 77-96): Springer.

Scherer, A. G., & Palazzo, G. (2011). The new political role of business in a globalized world: A review of a new perspective on CSR and its implications for the firm, governance, and democracy. *Journal of Management Studies*, *48*(4), 899–931. doi:10.1111/j.1467-6486.2010.00950.x

Sethi, S. (1975). Dimensions of corporate social performance: An analytical framework. *California Management Review*, *17*(3), 58–64. doi:10.2307/41162149

Sharp, Z., & Zaidman, N. (2010). Strategization of CSR. *Journal of Business Ethics*, *93*(1), 51–71. doi:10.100710551-009-0181-2

Shaw, E., Gordon, J., Harvey, C., & Maclean, M. (2013). Exploring contemporary entrepreneurial philanthropy. *International Small Business Journal*, *31*(5), 580–599. doi:10.1177/0266242611429164

Shaikh, E., Brahmi, M., Thang, P. C., Watto, W. A., Trang, T. T. N., & Loan, N. T. (2022). Should I Stay or Should I Go? Explaining the Turnover Intentions with Corporate Social Responsibility (CSR), Organizational Identification and Organizational Commitment. *Sustainability*, *14*(10), 6030. doi:10.3390u14106030

Singh, A., Majumdar, S., & Saini, G. K. (2017). Corporate Social Responsibility and Social Entrepreneurship: An Indian Context. *Journal of Entrepreneurship and Innovation in Emerging Economies*, *3*(1), 71–76. doi:10.1177/2393957516684451

Singh, A., Verma, P. (2014). A New Model of Corporate Social Responsibility in India. *International Journal of Academic Research in Business and Social Sciences,N-10.*

Su, W., Peng, M. W., Tan, W., & Cheung, Y.-L. (2016). The signaling effect of corporate social responsibility in emerging economies. *Journal of Business Ethics*, *134*(3), 479–491. doi:10.100710551-014-2404-4

Sunkar, A., Lakspriyanti, A. P., Haryono, E., Brahmi, M., Setiawan, P., & Jaya, A. F. (2022). Geotourism Hazards and Carrying Capacity in Geosites of Sangkulirang-Mangkalihat Karst, Indonesia. *Sustainability, 14*(3), 1704. doi:10.3390u14031704

Tai, F.-M., & Chuang, S.-H. (2014). Corporate social responsibility. *Ibusiness, 6*(03), 117–130. doi:10.4236/ib.2014.63013

Tajpour, M. (2021). towards the entrepreneurial university. *Journal of Organizational Culture Communications and Conflict, 25*(3), 4–5.

Tajpour, M., Demiryurek, K., & Abaci, N. I. (2021). Design the pattern of increasing satisfaction for international students: A qualitative study with the grounded theory approach. *International Journal of Management Education, 15*(5), 458–476.

Tajpour, M., Hosseini, E., & Brahmi, M. (2022). Effect of international entrepreneurship indicators on innovative performance: The mediating role of motivation. *International Journal of Technology Transfer and Commercialisation, 19*(1), 142–162. doi:10.1504/IJTTC.2022.123090

Tajpour, M., Salamzadeh, A., Ramadani, Y., Palalić, R., & Hosseini, E. (2021). *Knowledge Sharing and Achieving Competitive Advantage in International Environments: Case of Iranian Digital Startups. International Entrepreneurship in Emerging Markets: Contexts, Behaviours, and Successful Entry*. Routledge.

Tajpour, M., Salamzadeh, A., Salamzadeh, Y., & Braga, V. (2021). Investigating social capital, trust, and commitment in family business: case of media firms. *Journal of Family Business Management*.

Tunio, M. N., Chaudhry, I. S., Shaikh, S., Jariko, M. A., & Brahmi, M. (2021). Determinants of the Sustainable Entrepreneurial Engagement of Youth in Developing Country—An Empirical Evidence from Pakistan. *Sustainability, 13*(14), 7764. https://doi.org/10.3390/su13147764

Tunio, M. N., Jariko, M. A., Børsen, T., Shaikh, S., Mushtaque, T., & Brahmi, M. (2021). How Entrepreneurship Sustains Barriers in the Entrepreneurial Process—A Lesson from a Developing Nation. *Sustainability, 13*(20), 11419. doi:10.3390u132011419

Valmohammadi, C. (2011). Investigating corporate social responsibility practices in Iranian organizations: An ISO 26000 perspective. *Business Strategy Series, 12*(5), 257–263. doi:10.1108/17515631111166898

Van Oosterhout, J., & Heugens, P. (2008). Much ado about nothing: A conceptual critique of corporate social responsibility. In D. S. Siegel, D. Matten, A. McWilliams, & A. Crane (Eds.), *The Oxford handbook of corporate social responsibility* (pp. 197–223). Oxford University Press. doi:10.1093/oxfordhb/9780199211593.003.0009

Visser, W. (2011). *The age of responsibility: CSR 2.0 and the new DNA of business*. John Wiley & Sons.

Wood, D. J. (1991). Corporate social performance revisited. *Academy of Management Review, 16*(4), 691–718. doi:10.2307/258977

Yadav, P. L., Han, S. H., & Rho, J. J. (2016). Impact of environmental performance on firm value for sustainable investment: Evidence from large US firms. *Business Strategy and the Environment, 25*(6), 402–420. doi:10.1002/bse.1883

Zhu, Q., Liu, J., & Lai, K. (2016). Corporate social responsibility practices and performance improvement among Chinese national state-owned enterprises. *International Journal of Production Economics*, *171*, 417–426. doi:10.1016/j.ijpe.2015.08.005

Ziyae, B., Sadeghi, H., Shahamat Nejad, M., & Tajpour, M. (2021). A framework of urban entrepreneurship for women breadwinners. *Foresight*, *23*(5), 597–609. doi:10.1108/FS-12-2020-0137

# Chapter 4
# An Empirical Investigation of Student E-Trust and Enrolment Intention in an Online Paid Hult Prize Certificate Program:
## A COVID-19 Study

**Amal Ben Cheikh**
https://orcid.org/0000-0003-0413-0235
*ARBRE Laboratory, ISG Tunis, Tunisia*

**Ghada Ferchichi**
*APBS Tunis, Tunisia*

## ABSTRACT

*In a fast-growing online learning environment, the purpose of this research is to investigate the factors that influence the students' enrollment intention toward the Hult Prize Certificate Program. Accordingly, a quantitative approach is chosen. A survey was conducted with 105 respondents. The partial least squares method was used. Data analysis shows that the Hult Prize Certificate Program Digital Brand Image, E-WOM, and perceived price have an impact on the students' online trust. The latter has a strong and significant influence on the students' enrollment intention. Followed by the moderating effect of perceived benefits of COVID-19 social distancing on the link between online learning and e-trust which is rejected. However, Hult Prize brand credibility moderator role on the link between students' Online trust and intention to enroll is confirmed. Managerial recommendations are drawn to help decision makers in increasing the level of enrollment intention leading to high business performance.*

DOI: 10.4018/978-1-6684-6766-4.ch004

## 1. INTRODUCTION

Online learning is becoming an essential area of educational research due to the COVID-19 pandemic. Current research on e-learning considers the following problems: lack of an effective e-learning atmosphere, insufficient interactivity in virtual classrooms, undiversified teaching methods, lack of resources for online courses. The issues listed above are more likely to affect the effectiveness and quality of online teaching and learning. Studies today focus primarily on the limits of online learning, such as satisfaction, attitude, adoption, acceptance, sustainable use, motivation, behavior of use and sharing of information and knowledge. The success of online learning largely depends on many conditions, including the learning environment, teaching methods, teaching resources and learning expectations. The adoption of new technologies, such as artificial intelligence, big data and cloud computing, has fostered the rapid development of intelligent learning environments, which provides more competent learning conditions for online learning. An intelligent learning environment is a place or space that identifies characteristics of students to help them use the most appropriate tools and resources using data logging and automated assessment of the entire process in order to promote student learning effectively. Smart mobile devices, digital learning materials and smart educational environments improve student achievement and learning outcomes. Creating an intelligent learning environment based on the most advanced technologies provides better support to meet the special needs of students, increases student-learning satisfaction and improves their educational outcomes. Intelligent interaction is an important dimension that affects the quality of online courses and is closely related to student satisfaction and learning effectiveness. Therefore, an intelligent learning environment is essential to help develop e-learning skills and achieve outstanding learning outcomes. However, research rarely focuses on a learning environment in such a digital age. The active participation of students in their distance education is one of the most important factors influencing their academic performance.

The purpose of this paper is to investigate the determinants that impact students' online trust and enrollment intention toward the Online Paid Hult Prize Certificate Program during the COVID19 pandemic. The moderating variables of perceived benefits of COVID19 social distancing and brand credibility during this pandemic crisis may influence students' online trust and the lean toward online learning. Nevertheless, the direct effect of variables on students' enrolment intention will also be surveyed. Numerous studies of online learning have been conducted that examine students' satisfaction, acceptance of online learning, distance learning success factors, and the quality of learning. The main research question is:

What are the variables that will impact students' online trust and enrollment intention in the Hult Prize Certificate Program during the Pandemic of COVID-19?

## 2. LITERATURE REVIEW

### 2.1. Theoretical Foundations:

#### a. Digital Brand Image

Digital branding is the general consumer perception and sentiment for brands and influences consumer behavior (Zheng et al, 2022). Huang et al (2022) stated that brand image is the two-way communication process between brand stimulation and consumer perception. Wu and Chen (2019) argued that branding arises from consumers' assessment of the brand and that branding in the consumer's memory will become an important consideration for purchasing decisions of consumers. According to research, digital branding strengthens the purchase intention of customers (Ho et al, 2022). Additionally, companies can improve brand value through branding, and brand value can be accumulated to create intangibles (Ho et al, 2022).

Designing a successful branding image can turn ordinary or customer's boring worries into surprising or enjoyable experiences. Therefore, a positive brand image distinguishes products for consumers (Tan et al, 2008).

## b. E-WOM (Electronic Word of Mouth)

Word of mouth (WOM) is a marketing strategy and an effective tool used by companies to convey a certain message about the product and / or services to consumers face to face with other users by providing reviews and recommendations in order to increase the level of credibility as indicated by Weiss et al (2021) and Kim and Hwang (2022). Electronic word of mouth (E-WOM) has grown over the past two decades through the development of technology and is the most widely used technique today. According to Abbas et al (2022), E-WOM has developed a significant impact over the years due to the gradual growth of digitization as traditional marketing methods have evolved to meet recent consumer needs.

## c. Perceived Price

Perceived price is the customer's perception of a sales transaction and the outcome is fair, acceptable and reasonable (Bolton et al., 2022). It is documented in several studies such as the one of Win (2022) that a consumer's perception of price fairness influences his perceived value, his satisfaction and thus produces different emotions and behavioral responses from customers. This implies that a positive perception will lead to a positive response and similar behavior; a negative perception of perceived price fairness will also lead to negative behavior. In addition, Hallikainen et al (2022) assessed the impact of perceived price fairness as it affects customer satisfaction, loyalty and long-term profitability of the business. In most studies, two factors were found to influence the customer's perception of price fairness. These two factors are the reference price or the reference transaction and the principle of double entitlement (Kimes and Wirtz, 2003).

## d. Online Learning

With the growth of technology and the Internet, online learning has grown. It is assured a good position in academia. Indeed, online learning has many advantages, especially in modern times, but conversely, there are concerns that lead to exhaustion among online students and ultimately prevent online courses from progressing.

Lack of interest or motivation is one of the main obstacles to the growth of online learning and in doing so also increases the extent of dropouts from online courses (Aragon and Johnson, 2008). Researchers, educators, and other professionals are very keen on whether online learning can provide better academic outcomes and results than traditional learning. The answer can only be found by looking at student satisfaction and motivation. To prove this point, many comparative studies have been conducted to examine whether face-to-face or traditional teaching methods are the most effective, or whether online or blended learning is the best (González et al, 2016). According to Borokhovski et al (2016), online learning students do much better than traditional learning, and this is seen through the increase in course completion rates, satisfaction of students and their level of motivation in order to acquire more knowledge from online learning. The COVID-19 pandemic has pushed all educational institutions towards online learning, despite the fact that nobody was prepared for this change.

## e. E-Trust

Trust was frequently discussed in universities and the common definition from Moorman et al (1992), which was the willingness to believe in a business partner. Barney and Hansen (1994) defined trust as the mutual trust that no one exploits the other's weaknesses. According to Jarvenpaa et al (2000), trust was the relationship between uncertainty, sensitivity and commitment. In addition, trust could also be defined as an individual's trust in others that can be ruled by their honesty, generosity and competency (Lin, 2008; McKnight et al, 2002). Followed by Pavlou and Fygenson (2006), trust has been described as the buyer's confidence that the seller should behave with generosity, professionalism and ethics.

Oh et al (2012) defined trust as a feeling of expectation formed by individuals or groups that could lead to a tendency to believe in business partners whom they trust and value. Online trust is created by positive reviews on the website (Jarvenpaa et al., 2000). Online trust has an essential role in determining the customer's attitude or purchase intention (Gefen et al, 2003; Gefen and Straub, 2003; Hassanein and Head, 2007; Limbu et al, 2012; Wang and Emurian, 2005).

## f. Enrolment Intention

Intention is viewed as one of the main components in marketing research. Ray et al (2021) argued that this idea is lined up with the buying conduct of customers where intentions are the expectation of the results of things to come. They are additionally markers that show the level of buyers' ability to buy which could be because of new online experience or adequate information to make a the choice, the undertone of purchase intention can be decided as a part connected to cognitive behavior of buyers which suggests their buy intention for specific products or services. Furthermore, this idea shows that clients will take on their encounters, gather significant data and assess the most fascinating choices based on certain standards to make the last step which is the purchasing decision. Interestingly, Chen et al (2021) saw that advertisers utilize customers' buy intention as a sort of metric to make forecasts of market share or deals for items that are available in the market or for launching new ones when in fact the date is primordial for Marketing decisions related to strategies of promotion and market-segment.

## g. Perceived Benefits of COVID-19 Social Distancing

It is fundamental to assess the effect of distance learning on the parts of schooling and the social outcomes of dealing with this sort of training. Numerous analysts have widely concentrated on the effect of distance learning on education and found that distance instruction has various benefits, for example, guaranteeing the coherence of schooling, providing life-long learning and decreasing the significant expenses related with in-person instruction. There are impediments like teaching strategies, schedules, and the time the educator and students were in various areas. Hebebci et al. (2020) directed a review in Turkey to discover what educators and students' opinions about distance applications from the CO-

VID-19 pandemic (Erum et al., 2022). Sadeghi (2019) clarified exhaustively the benefits and drawbacks of distance learning; argued that distance learning provides the benefit of studying from any place and whenever, saving enormous money, social distancing, picking the learning course and saving time.

### h. Brand Credibility

In an online surface, trust is defined as the foundation between two parties, the brand and the customer. Weiss et al. (2021) stated that building trust by building personal relationships with customers is imperative and crucial for successful marketing in the digital world. Lee and Koo (2012) also claimed that consumers are more likely to trust consumer recommendations from their peers than the organization, and that they are more likely to act if other consumers have offered information about a particular product or service. In addition, the results disclosed by Lu et al. (2014) reveal that strong brand awareness will develop positive attitudes towards a product. Thus, as carried out by Laroche et al (1996), strong brand awareness also increases the level of trust and consumer confidence subsequently increases.

## 2.2. Conceptual Framework

### a. Digital Brand Image and E-Trust

Brand image was made up of a sequence of brand associations, divided into functional concept, symbol concept and empirical branding concept based on the personal value of the product or service by consumers.

According to Wilis and Nurwulandari (2020), brand is the concept of consumers that exists in the memory network and influences consumer decision making and that brand's potential preferred feelings (such as brand trust). Therefore, branding and consumer confidence in the brand are linked and the reason is that branding is seen as a perceived impact of consumers for the tangible and intangible association of the brand. Thus, the brand image will affect the confidence of consumers in the brand (Pratiwi et al, 2021; Madjid and Hermawan, 2022).

The Hult Prize Foundation has a strong brand image that can positively impact its community and therefore vital to capturing a larger proportion of students. This factor can allow the students to trust the Hult Prize Certificate Program and the quality of the courses it can deliver since they view it positively and therefore trust it can deliver what is promised.

H1: Digital Brand Image has a positive and significant impact on E-Trust

### b. Digital Brand Image and Intention

Digital Branding is a visual interpretation or impression of a specific brand in the psyche of the customer. Digital Branding can likewise be viewed as a feature of a brand that can be perceived however not articulated, like images, letters or colors, or the buyer's impression of an item or service that it addresses (Surachman, 2008). Digital Branding is an abstract idea made by the customer and their own feelings (Ferrinadewi, 2008).

Experimental examination on branding has been displayed to impact buyers' behaviour, like their loyalty and contentment (Zhang, 2015). A positive image of a brand is known to be all the more effectively recollected and acknowledged by purchasers. A positive brand image towards a brand has been displayed to impact shoppers when buying products.

H1': Digital Brand Image has a positive and significant impact on Intention

## c. E-WOM and E-Trust

Wandoko (2020) indicated that E-WOM is known as an incredible method for communication and an instrument utilized in marketing methods and to gather data about clients and their web-based experiences. On account of E-WOM, the customer can portray every one of the positive or negative experiences identified with a product or service. In view of this experience, the customer will then, at that point, give a proposal to different customers (Solikhah, 2022).

The better the suggestions given, the higher the online trust produced in a web based business. If a customer gets a suggestion on other individuals' experiences, it will influence their degree of confidence in the site or the seller. E-WOM is a powerful tool for the Hult Prize Certificate Program, because its community finds it an unbiased and trustworthy source of product information. Potential students can search for alumni reviews that are specifically relevant to them which helps in their evaluation of the online course and positively influences their trust to enroll.

H2: E-WOM has a positive and significant impact on E-Trust

## d. E-WOM and Intention

Ramadhan et al (2022) argued that E-WOM provides positive or negative data because consumers can suggest or warn others about products based on their experiences. Positive E-WOM has a more influence on consumers than a negative E-WOM because it increases the positive view of brands and products. E-WOM has also been found to affect product purchasing decisions.

The origin of the Word of Mouth comes from the comments of people and customers more inclined to believe the information generated/published by marketing or corporate sources (Hussain et al., 2017 and Chen et al., 2016). Daugherty and Hoffman (2014) found that online communication includes Social Media networks such as Facebook, YouTube and Twitter. Therefore, customers engage in E-WOM by researching correct information before making a purchasing decision.

H2': E-WOM has a positive and significant impact on Intention

## e. Perceived Price and E-Trust

Intrinsic and extrinsic signals are used by consumers to get a feel for the quality and price of a product. Intrinsic cues, such as a product's physical makeup and design, and extrinsic cues, like advertising, brand name, presentation and seller, have shown to influence price and quality (Miao et al, 2022).

The results of a study by Dimoka and Pavlou (2006) discovered that for online transactions, consumers were willing to pay a higher perceived price for sellers they could trust more. It demonstrated that a consumer's confidence in the goodwill and credibility of a business is the direct factor of perceived price (Fatikah and Albanna, 2022).

The Hult Prize Foundation is known for delivering high quality programs along the years. This can allow the Hult Prize Certificate Program to charge premium prices for its courses, which students will actually be willing to pay since potentially they view the Hult Prize Certificate Program positively and therefore trust the online courses it can deliver.

H3: Perceived Price has a positive and significant impact on E-Trust

## f. Perceived Price and Intention

Price is the sum that should be traded by the customer to acquire a product or service (Kotler and Armstrong, 2018). Price assumes a significant part in buyers' final buying choice. The manner in which the business and customers view price is not the same as one another.

Price perception can be characterized as how customers view the price of a product as high, low or reasonable and impacts their abilities to purchase (Suhaily and Darmoyo, 2017). How customers see the cost of a product can impact their evaluations of the worth and nature of the product. More costly products might be seen as better quality as well as the other way around, yet this isn't relevant in all cases (Setiawan and Achyar, 2012). Perceived price has been displayed to impact purchase intention positively for different sorts of products and services (Li, 2017; Wang and Chen, 2016, Pitchay et al, 2022).

H3': Perceived Price has a positive and significant impact on Intention

## g. Online Learning and E-Trust

Several evidence suggests that the quality of online learning effectively affects trust (Sharma et al., 2020). In web services, the role of trust is also increasingly important. McKnight and Chervany (2001) stated that the quality of the website will positively affect user confidence.

Especially in an increasingly competitive online environment, e-learning service providers can undoubtedly change, so to improve this situation, organizations must keep the overall quality stable to make customers trustworthy (Eisingerich and Bell, 2008). Likewise, Albelbisi et al. (2022) proposed that the quality of online learning has a practical influence on learner confidence in an online learning environment.

As the shift to using online platforms due to the pandemic of COVID-19, the Hult Prize Foundation managed to continue delivering its top-notch global programs digitally (Hamrouni et al., 2021). Its community is constantly satisfied with the online learning environment and the top quality of programs delivered by the Hult Prize which can help in building and sustaining students' trust in the Hult Prize Certificate Program online courses.

H4: Online Learning has a positive and significant impact on E-Trust

## h. Online Learning and Intention

Zhu et al (2020) Online learning is portrayed by the detachment of instructors and students in space and/or time, self-control of learning by students as opposed to the educator at a distance, and non-in-person interaction between students and teacher, interceded by specialized devices and Web innovation. The

Technology Acceptance Model (TAM) clarifies that the students' acceptance of the technology used depends on the users' convictions about the results of such use (Davis et al, 2002).

In particular, users embrace new advancements when their usability and perceived convenience are positive. Lin et al (2008) inspected students' motivation and the reception of technology in internet-based courses. The outcome shows that students' goal to utilize technology influences learning results in the online study atmosphere. Additionally to perceived usability and utility elements, different measures identified with acceptance or ability to acknowledge e-learning frameworks are perceived likability (Lee et al, 2005), perceived credibility, PC self-usability and social support (Thatcher et al, 2007), and intellectual absorption (Saadé and Bahli, 2005).

H4': Online Learning has a positive and significant impact on Intention

## i. E-Trust and Intention

Intention plays an essential part in the behavior of people. The term "purchase intention" comes from intention and is primarily used to understand the consumer's intention in the purchase decision-making. The purchase intention of customers can be defined as the consumer's self-instruction to buy the brand (or to take other relevant purchasing action) (Chen et al, 2021).

In the trust literature, Li and Miniard (2006) found that consumers tend to have greater purchase intention when they can trust a business than when they cannot (Tunio et al., 2021). According to Bhattacherjee (2002) such beliefs often lead to corresponding trust intentions such as intention to buy.

The Hult Prize Foundation is constantly providing an online platform that gives its community the opportunity to pursue their academic goals in a supportive environment and at an appropriate pace for their learning style. This consistent delivery can facilitate the online trust of students and intention to enroll in the Hult Prize Certificate Program for a variety of reasons, including advanced learning, the attractiveness of the course quality as well as the access of high-caliber experts.

H5: E-Trust has a positive and significant impact on Intention

## j. Perceived Benefits of COVID-19 Social Distancing and Online Learning

As the advantages of online learning have been talked about widely in different previous research, it is currently more critical to more readily comprehend the degree of students' motivation, particularly as keeping social distancing has turned into another standard in the world during this time of pandemic. Online learning is the sort of education or training that utilizes electronic means or data technology to get to the educational programs outside an in-person classroom (Sangrà et al., 2012). Online courses and programs are all the more generally used to replace traditional learning systems (Zhang et al., 2012).

The current COVID-19 pandemic and the fundamental objective of keeping up with social distancing has driven the Hult Prize Foundation at all levels to fully change to online learning. The capacity to appropriately survey the nature of the Hult Prize Certificate Program online course is vital to the success of the program.

H6: Perceived Benefits of COVID-19 social distancing moderates the relationship between Online Learning and E-trust.

## k. Brand Credibility and E-Trust

As indicated by Erdem and Swait (2004), brand credibility is a three-term dimension based on reliability, capacity and attractiveness. Reliability means that it is convinced that a brand will keep its promises, capacity means that the brand is able to deliver the promise and attractiveness, which also means that the brand also fulfills the promise it made regarding its good appearance. Brand managers are firmly on the lookout for motivations such as perceived authenticity and uniqueness that can remarkably help build brand credibility. Maathuis et al (2004) and Swait and Erdem (2007) focused on the impact of brand credibility on consumers' purchasing decision making and their selection model. Brand credibility results in both minimizing the risk perceived by customers and reducing the time to find information when deciding to use the product and thus increases the E-trust of the brand. As noted by Shugan (1980), a credible brand leads to higher levels of consumer trust. As the Hult Prize is constantly perceived as credible, it can enjoy increased chances of building loyal relationships and long term trust, and especially for the Hult Prize Certificate Program to benefit from less price-sensitive students thanks to this favourable perception.

H7: Brand Credibility moderates the relationship between E-Trust and enrollment intention.

Figure 1 presents the conceptual model related to this research paper.

*Figure 1. Conceptual model*

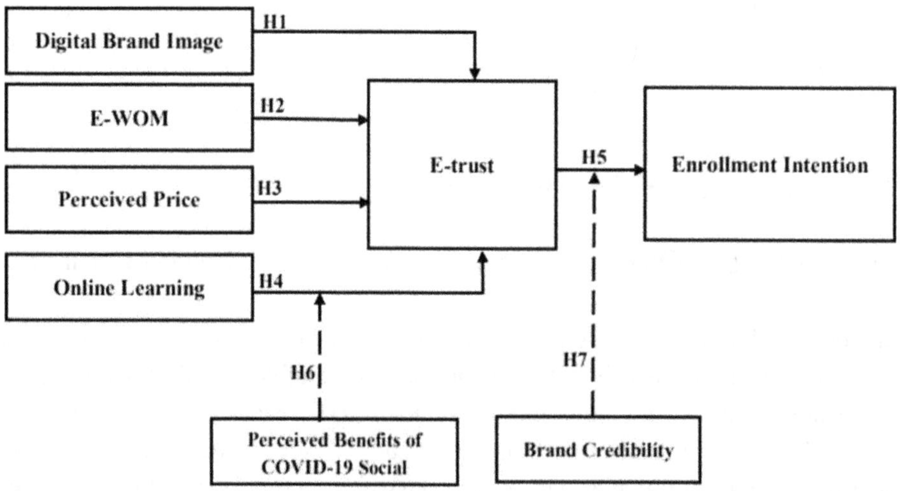

## 3. METHODOLOGY

### 3.1. Sampling, Data Collection and Analysis

#### a. Sampling

The study relies on a convenience sample that matches certain criteria. Etikan et al (2016) stated that *"Convenience sampling (also known as Haphazard Sampling or Accidental Sampling) is a type of non-probability or nonrandom sampling where members of the target population that meet certain practical criteria, such as easy accessibility, geographical proximity, availability at a given time, or the willingness to participate are included for the purpose of the study"*. In addition, this sampling technique is considered as affordable and easy to implement due to the availability of respondents.

A survey was sent through the Hult Prize Emailing account and Social Media platforms to potential students database of the Hult Prize Certificate Program.

#### b. Data Collection

A self-administered survey was used in this investigation. Within this regard, Gnambs and Kaspar (2015) claimed that one of its advantages is the capacity to introduce both the study subject and the motive of the respondents in order to guarantee the delivery of genuine, concrete, and honest responses. At the same time, data collection is less time consuming, less expensive, and does not need any expertise. The study model includes a total of 8 latent variables, and all measure items were derived or contextually adapted from existing literature to ensure content validity. A 5-point Likert scales, ranging from 1 to 5 on a scale of strongly disagree to strongly agree was used.

#### c. Data Analysis

According to Henseler et al (2009), Smart PLS is a valuable technique in management science for measuring, creating, and validating models. SmartPLS is used in several studies and it emphasizes the causal process, confirms the theoretical empirical assumptions, and uses forecast-oriented measures. The data analysis is divided into two stages: exploratory data analysis and confirmatory data analysis. As reported by Hair et al. (2014), exploratory and confirmatory factor analyses are performed to evaluate hypotheses using the structural partial least squares equation model (PLS-SEM) with SmartPLS 3.2.

## 4. FINDINGS AND DISCUSSIONS

### 4.1. Findings

#### a. Sample Characteristics

We have numerous age groupings distribution with the ages of 18 to 22 years old having the largest proportion with 39 percent. Throughout this study, only 19% of adults aged 26 to 30 are assessed. Another 7% of the total number of responders is over the age of 30. There are an almost equal number of percentages between female and male gender when it comes to the Hult Prize Certificate Program enrollment intention.

*Figure 2. Reliability and outer loadings*

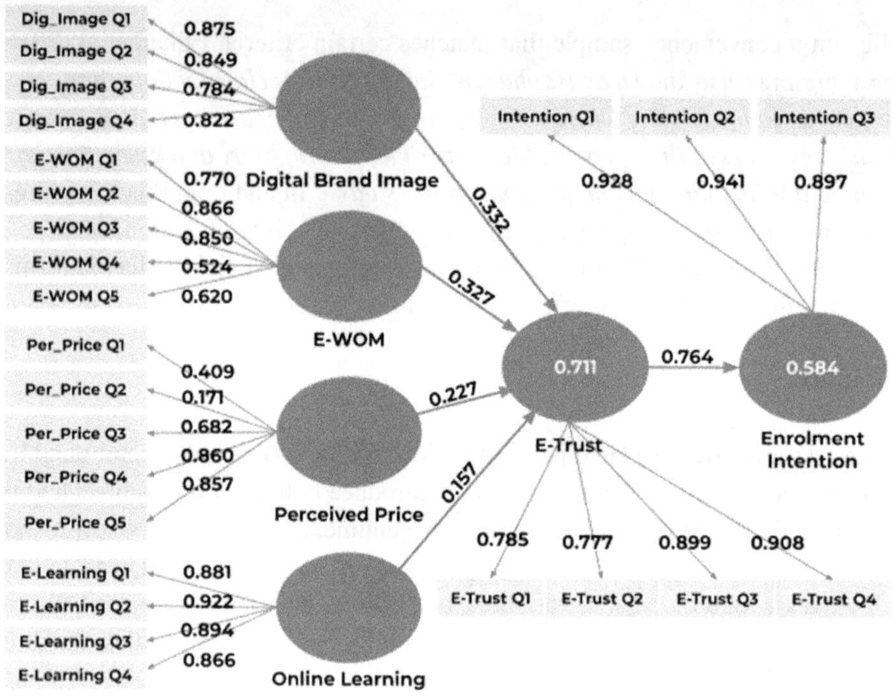


## b. The Measurement Model

Figure 2 shows the reliability of different indicators after the first algorithm.

The indicators showing low Indicator Reliability (0.50) or Outer loadings (0.7) were removed. These indicators are presented in the following list (E-WOm Q4 = 0.620: E-WOM Q5 = 0.524: Perceived Price Q1 = 0.409; Perceived Price Q2 = 0.171; Perceived Price Q3= 0,628). For the results of Cronbach's Alpha, the value of the perceived price variable is 0.314 which is less than 0.7, which means that this variable could not be taken as a reliable construct for our study if we keep the items with low loadings.

The similar conclusion may be drawn (Shaikh et al., 2022) from the Composite Reliability value for the perceived price variable, which is 0.536, which is less than 0.7. As a result, this result can be considered. Lastly, for the Average Variance Extracted (AVE), we obtain a perceived price value of 0.427, which is less than 0.5 and hence unreliable. After running the first algorithm and eliminating the items that were considered unreliable, a second algorithm as shown in figure 3 is then built that only shows the variables with their adequate indicators as it is introduced in the outer loadings of Algorithm 2. As mentioned above and based on the rule of thumb, the outer loadings should be at least 0.7 or more.

After dropping the items that were considered inadequate, the results reveal that all of the elements are having more than 0.7. Thus, to conclude, it is now safe to say that all indicators are considered as reliable to measure the latent variables.

*Figure 3. Reliability and outer loadings*

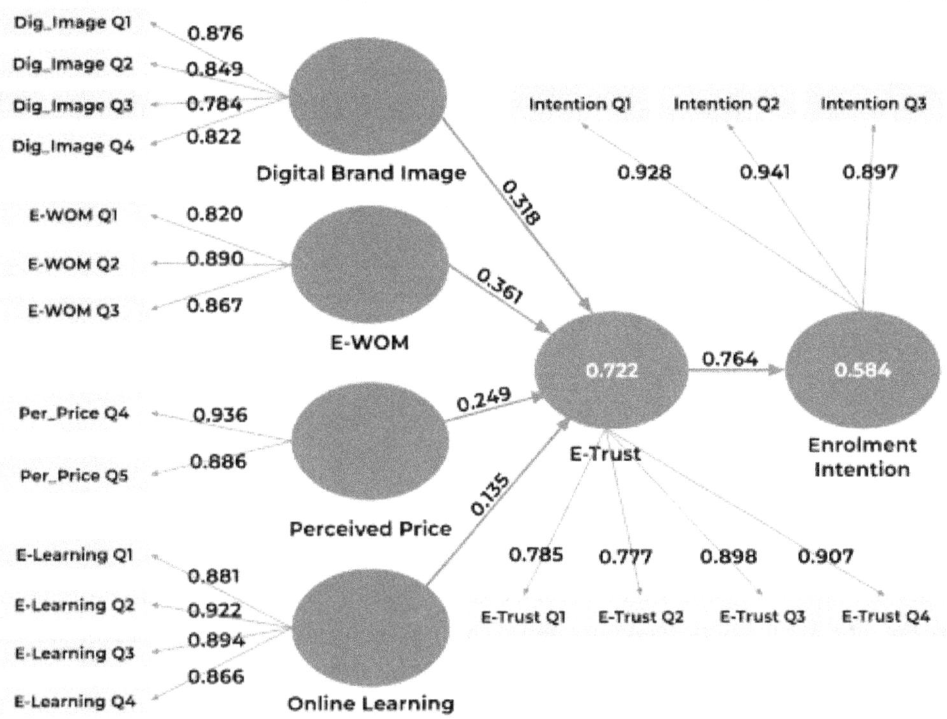


Table 1 describes the output of Algorithm 2 with its four indicators: Composite reliability (CR), internal consistency reliability (Cronbach's alpha), convergent validity (Individual indicator reliability) and Average Variance Extracted.

After dropping the unreliable items, we can notice the huge difference between the first results and these ones shown in table 1. Generally, the values of both the Cronbach's Alpha and Composite Reliability must be greater than 0.7. As presented, both the variables value of Cronbach's Alpha and Composite Reliability are greater than 0.7 which leads to conclude the validity, the reliability of the test as well as the internal consistency reliability. As a rule of thumb, this indicates that the AVE value must be greater than 0.50 All AVE values were greater than 0.50 for the variables latent accounts explain more than half of the variance of their indicators.

*Table 1. Construct reliability and validity of algorithm 2*

| | Alpha | rho_A | CR | AVE |
|---|---|---|---|---|
| Enrolment Intention | 0.912 | 0.917 | 0.945 | 0.850 |
| Online Learning | 0.913 | 0.914 | 0.939 | 0.794 |
| E-Trust | 0.866 | 0.892 | 0.908 | 0.713 |
| Digital Brand Image | 0.854 | 0.864 | 0.901 | 0.695 |
| E-WOM | 0.823 | 0.8282 | 0.894 | 0.738 |
| Perceived Price | 0.800 | 0.844 | 0.907 | 0.831 |

The coefficient of determination, R2 combines the correlation coefficient R. It measures the strength of the link between two variables.

As shown in table 2, $R^2$ of enrollment intention is equal to 0.584, implying that 58 percent of the variation of enrollment intention is accounted by prospective students' online trust, hence, prospective students online trust with the percentage of 72% contribute to the overall enrollment intention of interested students.

*Table 2. R Square of Algorithm 2*

| | R Square | R Square Adjusted |
|---|---|---|
| E-Trust | 0.722 | 0.710 |
| Enrolment Intention | 0.584 | 0.579 |

## c. Structural Model

The structural path modeling confirmed the hypotheses. Following the examination of the moderation hypotheses, the direct impacts were investigated. The statistically significant correlation was determined using the bootstrap method with a sample size of 5000 subsamples.

Direct effects of the path coefficients (β, [1, 1]) describes the links between the factors (Hair et al. 2014). Multiple motivations were found to have a significant effect on students' enrollment intention. In our case, the overall path coefficient presented are positive. Thus, the strongest and most positive linkage is between E-Trust and enrollment intention ($\beta = 0.764$, $p < 0.01$), followed by the link between E-WOM and E-Trust ($\beta = 0.361$, $p < 0.01$), the correlation between digital brand image and E-Trust ($\beta = 0.318$, $p < 0.01$) is also strong and quite valuable and the positive correlation between perceived price and E-Trust ($\beta = 0.249$, $p < 0.01$. Lastly only the correlation between online learning and E-Trust is showing a weak yet positive value ($\beta = 0.135$, $p < 0.01$).

When the T statistic is greater than the critical value (1.65, 1.96, and 2.57), the coefficient is important for a specified likelihood of error (respectively 10%, 5%, and 1%) (Hair et al., 2014). According to this assertion, and on the results of our analysis, all of our T statistic values are greater than 1.96. Thus, all of our hypotheses are confirmed and their coefficients are significant to a 5% probability of error. Except for the T statistics value of online learning and E-Trust which is (t=1,863< 1, 96) and so this hypothesis is not supported and automatically dropped. The value of T statistics' E-Trust and enrollment intention path coefficient is (t=13.421>1, 96), so as shown above the coefficient is significant to a 5% probability of error. Similar for the T statistics value of both the E-WOM and E-Trust path coefficient that is (t=3.876>1.96), the T statistics value of digital brand image and E-trust path coefficient (t=3.658>1.96) as well as the T statistics value of the perceived price and E-Trust path coefficient which is (t=3.710> 1.96). The higher the T, the more proof you have that your findings are genuine and have a low probability of error. This is precisely what our findings suggest. According to our database, the p-values of all the path coefficients analyzed are less than 0.05, indicating that the null hypothesis is unlikely to be true, with the exception of the p-value of the online learning and E-Trust path coefficient, which is 0.062> 0.05, indicating that the null hypothesis is likely to be true in this case. Table 3 summarizes the results of the structural model and illustrates the two indicators t of student and p value.

*Table 3. Path coefficients bootstrapping*

| | T Statistics | P Values |
|---|---|---|
| DBI -> E-Trust | 3.658 | 0.000 |
| E-Trust -> Enrolment Intention | 13.421 | 0.000 |
| E-WOM -> E-Trust | 3.876 | 0.000 |
| Online Learning -> E-Trust | 1.863 | 0.062 |
| Perceived Price -> E-Trust | 3.710 | 0.000 |

## d. Moderating Effects

When we have a moderation effect, a third variable can change the level of strength or even the direction of a relationship between two constructs. It means that the nature of the relationship can differ depending on the values of the third variable.

### *Perceived Benefits of COVID-19 Social Distancing Moderating Effect:*

Perceived Benefits of COVID-19 social distancing moderating effect is presented in figure 4 and 5. Figure 4 describes the linkage without the moderator variable and figure 5 shows the link when including perceived benefits of covid-19 social distancing.

The bootstrapping without the perceived benefits of COVID-19 social distancing moderation resulted to T Statistics of online learning and E-Trust Path coefficient equal to (t=9.121) and P Values equal to (p=0,000).

After adding the perceived benefits of COVID-19 social distancing moderation, we conducted a second bootstrapping to compare between the previous results without and with the moderating effect on students' E-Trust. Figure 5 presents the results after adding the moderator.

The T Statistics of the moderating Effect 1 on E-Trust is equal to (t=4.331), as for the P Values, it is equal to (p=0,000). Based on the analysis, the moderation hypothesis between perceived benefits of COVID-19 social distancing and E-Trust is rejected. T1= 9.121 is higher than T2= 5.661 and as the rule states that if T1> T2: The moderation hypothesis is then not supported, hence, perceived benefits of COVID-19 social distancing is not a moderator variable. It does not strengthen or neither reduce the intensity of the relationship between online learning and E-Trust.

### *Brand credibility moderating effect:*

A first bootstrapping without the credibility moderation as shown in figure 6 has resulted in a T Statistics equal to (t=1,556) and P Values equal to (p=0,120).

To demonstrate the moderating effect estimation, we need to first extend the original model by including the moderator variable as shown in figure 7.

The Path coefficient with the brand credibility moderation has presented the T Statistics of the Moderating Effect 1 on enrollment intention equal to (t=2.208) and P Values equal to (p=O,027).

*Figure 4. Moderating effect before adding Perceived benefits of covid-19 social distancing*

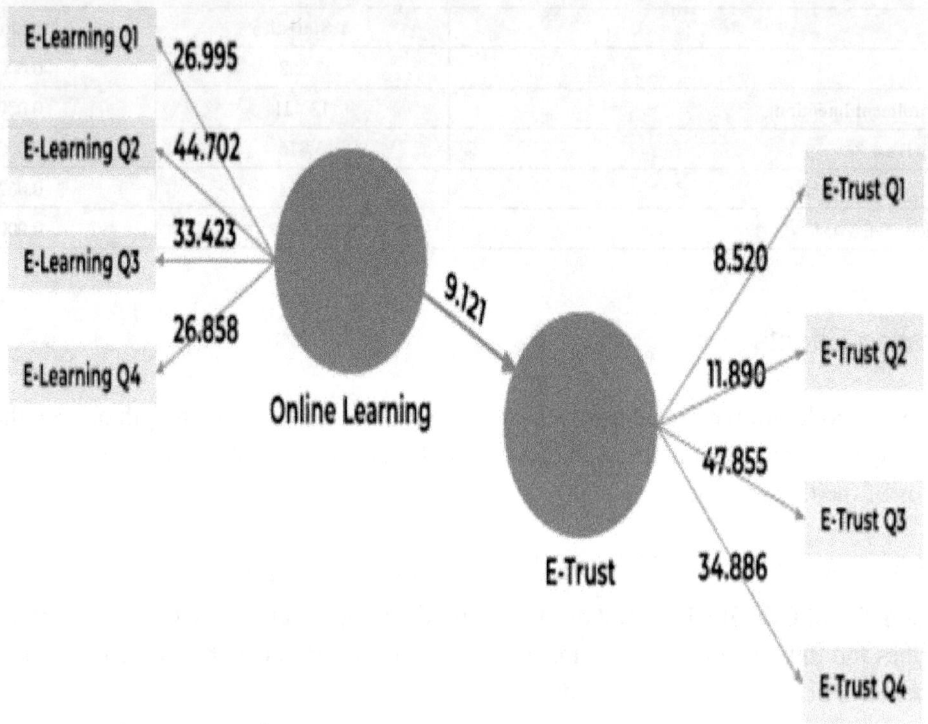


*Figure 5. Moderating effect after adding Perceived benefits of covid-19 social distancing*

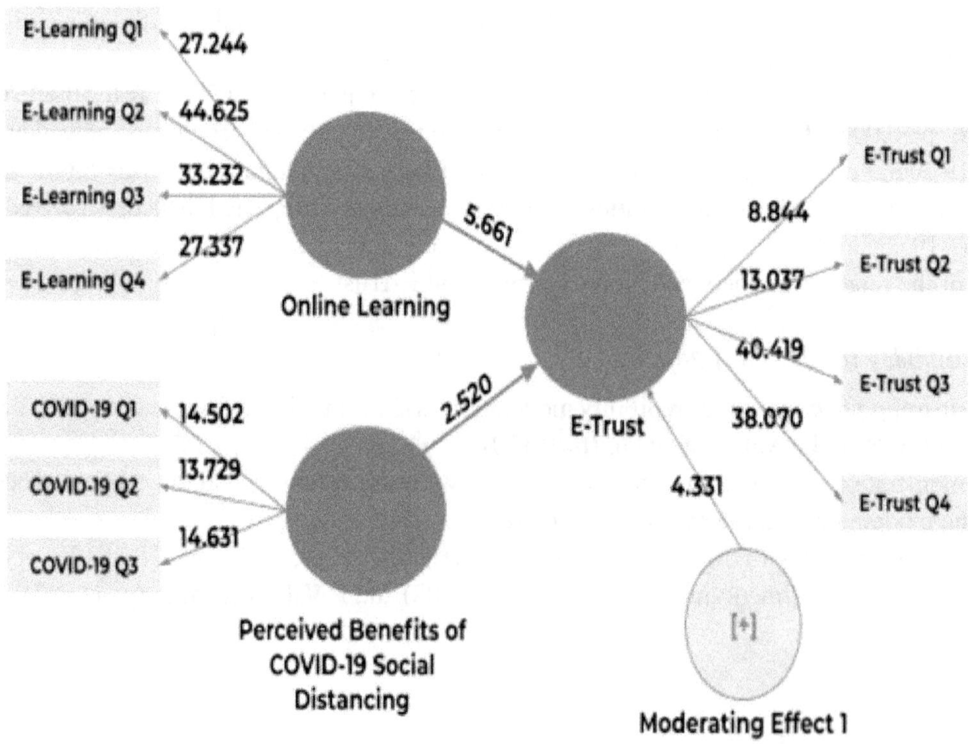

*Figure 6. Moderating effect before adding brand credibility*

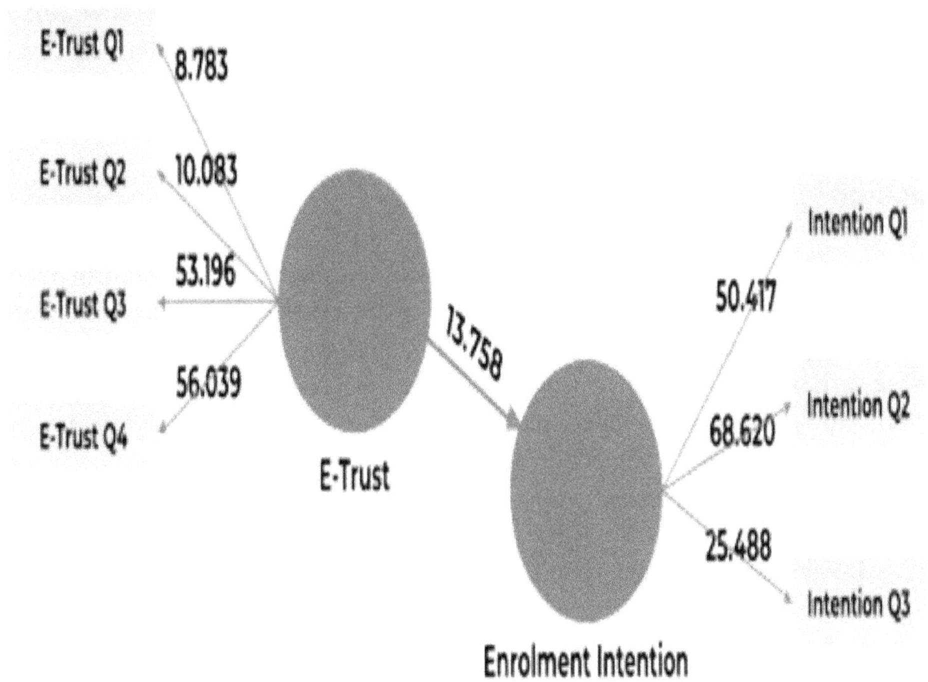


*Figure 7. Moderating effect after adding brand credibility*

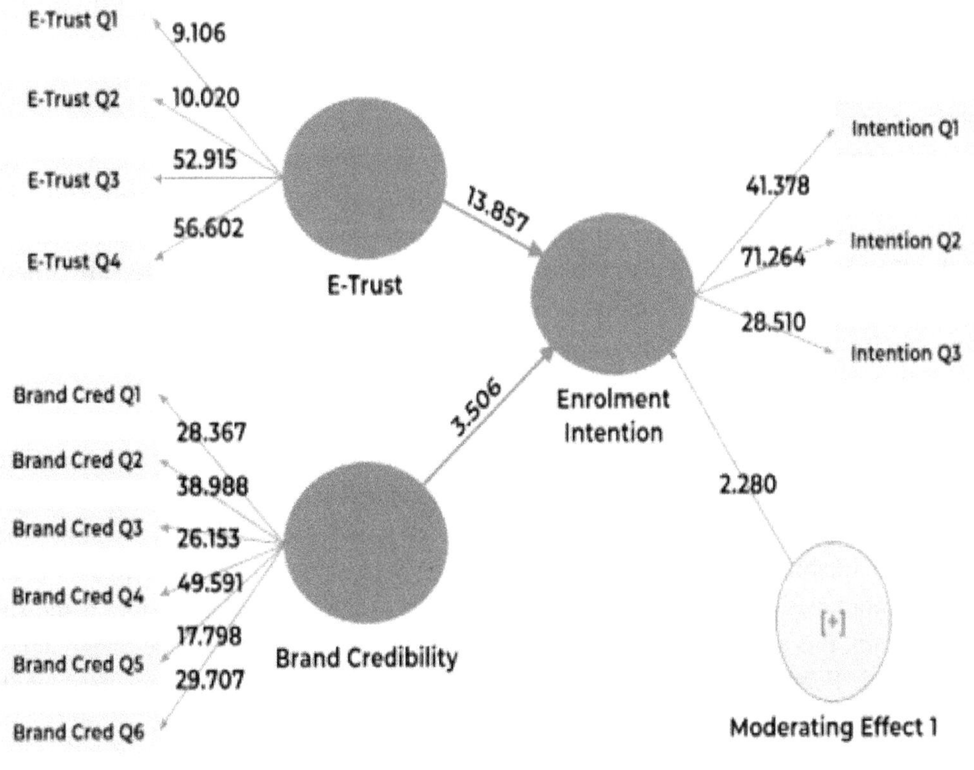

As examined above the hypothesis of the brand credibility effect on students' E-Trust is accepted. T1 is equal to 13,758 and T2 is equal to 13.857. Since T1 < T2 and if we apply the same rule used previously, we conclude that the brand credibility does moderate the students' enrollment intention. Hence, the hypothesis is supported and the overall brand credibility has an impact on students' online trust in the Hult Prize Certificate Program that will lead to the increase of their enrollment intention.

## 4.2. Discussions

From the majority of respondents' answers, the link between the electronic word of mouth and the students' enrollment intention was confirmed. The results demonstrated that electronic word of mouth positively and strongly impacts the student when they intend to enroll in the Hult Prize Certificate Program. There are various known reasons for individuals desire to share information online. Firstly, they want to network and talk about their experiences to make it easier for others to find information. Secondly, they want to be perceived as someone who has solid knowledge and experience about a product or brand and also to be seen as someone with a range of connections. Furthermore, this study reveals that E-WOM significantly affects the Students' Online Trust toward the Hult Prize Certificate Program. Usually, E-WOM plays as an informal system of advertising for online-based businesses. Supportive and effective E-WOMs can influence customer decisions and boost the buying interest and online trust of digital businesses.

Due to the growing number of For-Profit E-learning programs, the effective use of E-WOM can support and encourage the growth of such programs. Therefore, it is suggested that the promoters organize E-WOM to increase the program rate experience of its products/services, which would ultimately affect the expectations of potential students.Digital Brand Image appears to have a positive and strong relationship with Students' Online Trust. The Hult Prize Foundation already has quite good Brand Awareness from the prestigious programs it delivers. The data collected also shows that the Hult Prize Certificate Program also has a good Brand Image as well.

The positive and meaningful relationship between Digital Brand Image and students E-Trust is consistent with former studies conducted by (Alhaddad, 2015; Chinomona, 2016). A positive brand image is essential when building the trust of prospective online students. Price perception has also been demonstrated to have a strong positive relationship with students' online trust. Respondents perceive the fee of the Hult Prize Introduction to Pitching Course online course quite differently; they believe that higher prices are associated with a higher and better course quality provided. They also feel that a high-priced online course gives them a sense of pride. Not to mention the respondents who most sought out the benefits and incentives offered by the Hult Prize Certificate program. The results are consistent with findings from other previous research where price is well-known to have a positive impact on the trust of customers (Suhaily and Darmoyo, 2017). Other research also conveys that the sensitivity of the price can influence trust in brands (Sihite et al, 2015), showing that the pricing of e-learning programs are important because they influence their online trust in the brand. Individuals' E-trust in the brand has a positive and remarkable influence on purchase intention. People believe that trustworthy brands can make them feel more credible when deciding to purchase. As the subject of this paper is the Hult Prize Certificate program, this shows that its digital brand image is quite favorable. The construction of this E-Trust of an online For-Profit program must be properly designed to make students more confident in their final decision.

Brand image and price perception remarkably influence purchase/enrollment intention. These two variables must be properly carried on by the Hult Prize Certificate Program to increase the likelihood of enrolling potential students. Former studies also demonstrated the same results, where Digital Brand image influences purchase intention (Fianto et al., 2014; Wang and Tsai, 2014). The same is correct for the perceived price influencing purchase intention (Setiawan and Achyar, 2012). Interestingly, the influence of Digital Brand Image and Price Perception is much more impactful than expected on students' enrollment intention. The questionnaire results showed that most of the respondents consider the Hult Prize Certificate Program alumni who make recommendations about the course are perceived to be more dependable. Personal reviews have a major impact on prospective students' trust hence; they will feel self-confident when enrolling in the Hult Prize Introduction to Pitching course recommended by an alumnus. Consequently, it makes more sense that honest reviews are much recognized by the students, as it can facilitate for them the enrolment decision in the course. This study discovered that communicating with them has a more important impact on online trust.

This research also revealed the respondents' belief in the Hult Prize Certificate Program's commitment to tell the truth about the benefits and incentives it is promising to deliver. The results show that potential students' belief in the Hult Prize's honesty increases his/her confidence in enrolling in the recommended course. The analysis of the moderator effect was essential to be able to make a difference between the direct effects and the indirect effects on the students' enrollment intention. Between the Online Learning and Students' E-Trust, Perceived Benefits of COVID 19 Social Distancing did not play a role in boosting the students online trust and enhancing the positive impact on their enrollment intention in the Hult Prize Certificate Program.

Students might feel frustrated by the social distancing, and unexpected changes toward online learning, that is why, the content of learning might be optional to the nature of learning. The content of online learning platforms ought to be not difficult to explore and give useful and needed information during the pandemic, as this is the main interface between the students and the mentor at the time of the pandemic.

However, Brand Credibility did play an important role as a moderator variable to strengthen the Students' E-Trust towards the dependent variable that is Students' Enrollment Intention.

A positive and highly remarkable link between online trust and brand credibility shows that really trusted organizations such as the Hult Prize Foundation are building their credibility seen by students. This offers an instruction guide for managers (Arabeche et al., 2022), which means they must adopt strategies that build on the brand trustworthiness. Advertisements and policies must include the real perceptions and image of the product, hence increasing the credibility of the brand. Therefore, the findings of the research are reliable with past examinations by Erdem and Swait (2004), which presumed that high credibility will impact customers and improve the probability of a product being selected in the arrangement of a decision. Wang and Yang (2010) additionally found that brand credibility affects the buying intentions of customers (Sunkar et al., 2022). Brand credibility assumes a significant part in students' enrolment intentions and found that it has a positive and solid impact. The more credible a brand is the more there are chances that it will be remembered for the decision choices and will be chosen (Erdem and Swait, 2004).

## 5. CONCLUSION, MANAGERIAL IMPLICATIONS AND FUTURE RESEARCH SUGGESTIONS

It is imperative to understand the needs and wants of today's students and what drives them to adopt and not to adopt certain services in online learning. The present study offers answers to these important questions which may help online learning programs to make appropriate strategies out of it.

In theory, research has demonstrated the online trust and brand credibility that influence enrollment intention. When a brand is highly credible, highly trustful, and highly reliable, it will increase online trust. This supports the results of previous studies by Lee (2005), Zeithaml et al. (2000), Al-Nasser et al. Research has also contributed to the integration of digital brand image that influences online trust. As well as the perceived price of the course and the honest electronic word of mouth that will increase the trust of students. The analysis explained that these variables were significant for students' enrollment intention which concludes that if these variables be kept in mind while preparing strategies, a positive outcome in terms of high enrolment of students can be seen in the near future.

### Managerial Implications

In practice, the considerable move in the learning systems and Impact Education towards online learning has been acknowledged as the new system in this era of internet-based technology. Online learning is now regarded as an interactive network for online learning programs to communicate with their students, as well as obtaining valuable and effective feedback to help in improving and upgrading their courses.

In this research, it was found that Digital Brand Image, E-WOM, Perceived Price and Students' E-trust play important roles to interact and influence the students' enrollment intention. The Hult Prize Certificate Program with effective Social Media platforms should be concerned about the students while developing Digital Brand Image and online Trust.

The rapid growth of social media may become the most essential element to influence marketing in the coming years which could enable and improve the Hult Prize Certificate Program practices to persuade future students. It may also help it to connect with future students.

Creating discussion threads by posting posts on Social Media platforms has the ability to be spread all throughout the world and reach individuals in the blink of an eye. The Hult Prize Certificate Program must provide its community on Social Media platforms with reasons to interface with their content for different reasons, for example, the access to High-Caliber of experts, the excellent student services, the enriching personalized experiences and Alumni testimonials that prospective students would be excited to hear about.

The advantage conceded to future students will expand the discussions and the reviews shared inside the different circles of the community and subsequently will influence numerous others.

Thereafter, this will increase online trust and confidence in the Hult Prize Certificate Program, which will ultimately lead to more students enrolling and intending to re-enroll.

Besides, the search of information was likewise displayed to significantly affect the students' online trust. Circling back to this outcome, the Hult Prize Certificate Program ought to advance and refresh the content identified with the courses they offer on the web, so students can get all the information needed about the available programs.

## Future Research Suggestions

Future studies can enrich the research question by applying a qualitative approach to dig deep into the participants' enrollment intention. Furthermore, it is crucial to test the model in a context which is different technologically, culturally and economically (Aldieri et al., 2021). Increasing the sample size will be important to ensure the generalizability of the results. Additionally, other determinants of the enrollment intention can be added.

## REFERENCES

Abbas, A. F., Jusoh, A., Mas'od, A., Alsharif, A. H., & Ali, J. (2022). Effect of intrinsic and extrinsic motivations on cyber-market mavenism: Their role in information-sharing behavior. *Innovative Marketing, 18*(2), 198–211. doi:10.21511/im.18(2).2022.17

Albelbisi, N. A., Al-Adwan, A. S., Habibi, A., & Rasool, S. (2022). The relationship between students' attitudes toward online homework and mathematics anxiety. *International Journal of Mathematical Education in Science and Technology*, 1–19. doi:10.1080/0020739X.2021.2023769

Aldieri, L., Brahmi, M., Bruno, B., & Vinci, C. P. (2021). Circular Economy Business Models: The Complementarities with Sharing Economy and Eco-Innovations Investments. *Sustainability, 13*(22), 12438. doi:10.3390u132212438

Alhaddad, A. (2015). Perceived quality, brand image and brand trust as determinants of brand loyalty. *Journal of Research in Business and Management, 3*(4), 01-08.

Allah Pitchay, A., Ganesan, Y., Zulkifli, N. S., & Khaliq, A. (2022). Determinants of customers' intention to use online food delivery application through smartphone in Malaysia. *British Food Journal, 124*(3), 732–753. doi:10.1108/BFJ-01-2021-0075

Aragon, S. R., & Johnson, E. S. (2008). Factors influencing completion and noncompletion of community college online courses. *American Journal of Distance Education, 22*(3), 146–158. doi:10.1080/08923640802239962

Arabeche, Z., Soudani, A., Brahmi, M., Aldieri, L., Vinci, C. P., & Abdelli, M. E. A. (2022). Entrepreneurial Orientation, Organizational Culture and Business Performance in SMEs: Evidence from Emerging Economy. *Sustainability, 14*(9), 5160. doi:10.3390u14095160

Barney, J. B., & Hansen, M. H. (1994). Trustworthiness as a source of competitive advantage. *Strategic Management Journal, 15*(S1), 175–190. doi:10.1002mj.4250150912

Bhattacherjee, A. (2002). Individual trust in online firms: Scale development and initial test. *Journal of Management Information Systems, 19*(1), 211–241. doi:10.1080/07421222.2002.11045715

Bolton, R. N., Gustafsson, A., Tarasi, C. O., & Witell, L. (2022). Designing satisfying service encounters: Website versus store touchpoints. *Journal of the Academy of Marketing Science, 50*(1), 1–23. doi:10.100711747-021-00808-9 PMID:34608342

Borokhovski, E., Bernard, R. M., Tamim, R. M., Schmid, R. F., & Sokolovskaya, A. (2016). Technology-supported student interaction in post-secondary education: A meta-analysis of designed versus contextual treatments. *Computers & Education, 96*, 15–28. doi:10.1016/j.compedu.2015.11.004

Chen, Y., Ding, D., Meng, L., Li, X., & Zhang, S. (2021). Understanding consumers' purchase intention towards online paid courses. *Information Development*, 02666669211027206.

Chen, Y., Yang, S., & Wang, Z. (2016). Service cooperation and marketing strategies of infomediary and online retailer with eWOM effect. *Information Technology Management, 17*(2), 109–118. doi:10.100710799-015-0237-1

Chinomona, R. (2016). Brand communication, brand image and brand trust as antecedents of brand loyalty in Gauteng Province of South Africa. *African Journal of Economic and Management Studies, 7*(1), 124–139. doi:10.1108/AJEMS-03-2013-0031

Daugherty, T., & Hoffman, E. (2014). eWOM and the importance of capturing consumer attention within social media. *Journal of Marketing Communications, 20*(1-2), 82–102. doi:10.1080/13527266.2013.797764

Davis, F. D., Bagozzi, R. P., & Warshaw, P. R. (2002). X: User Acceptance of Computer Technology: A Comparison of Two Theoretical Models. *Management Science, 35*(8), 10–1287.

Eisingerich, A. B., & Bell, S. J. (2008). Perceived service quality and customer trust: Does enhancing customers' service knowledge matter? *Journal of Service Research, 10*(3), 256–268. doi:10.1177/1094670507310769

Erdem, T., & Swait, J. (2004). Brand credibility, brand consideration, and choice. *The Journal of Consumer Research, 31*(1), 191–198. doi:10.1086/383434

Erum, S.; Muhammad, N T.; Wali Muhammad, K.; Mohsen, B.; & Shahid, R., Chapter 16: The COVID-19 Pandemic Overlaps Entrepreneurial Activities and Triggered New Challenges: A Review Study, Book chapter: Managing Human Resources in SMEs and Start-ups, August 2022, 388 p. https://doi.org/doi:10.1142/9789811239212_0008

Etikan, I., Musa, S. A., & Alkassim, R. S. (2016). Comparison of convenience sampling and purposive sampling. *American Journal of Theoretical and Applied Statistics, 5*(1), 1–4. doi:10.11648/j.ajtas.20160501.11

Fatikah, B. H., & Albanna, H. (2022). The Influence of E-Servqual and E-Trust on E-Loyalty: The Role of E-Satisfaction as an Intervening on Islamic Mobile Banking Customer. *Journal of Business Management and Islamic Banking, 1*(1), 119–130. doi:10.14421/jbmib.2022.011-08

Fianto, A. Y. A., Hadiwidjojo, D., & Aisjah, S. (2014). The influence of brand image on purchase behaviour through brand trust. *Business Management and Strategy, 5*(2), 58. doi:10.5296/bms.v5i2.6003

Gefen, D., Karahanna, E., & Straub, D. W. (2003). Trust and TAM in online shopping: An integrated model. *Management Information Systems Quarterly, 27*(1), 51–90. doi:10.2307/30036519

Gefen, D., & Straub, D. (2003). Managing user trust in B2C e-services. *e-Service, 2*(2), 7-24.

Gnambs, T., & Kaspar, K. (2015). Disclosure of sensitive behaviors across self-administered survey modes: A meta-analysis. *Behavior Research Methods*, *47*(4), 1237–1259. doi:10.375813428-014-0533-4 PMID:25410404

González-Gómez, D., Jeong, J. S., Airado Rodríguez, D., & Cañada-Cañada, F. (2016). Performance and perception in the flipped learning model: An initial approach to evaluate the effectiveness of a new teaching methodology in a general science classroom. *Journal of Science Education and Technology*, *25*(3), 450–459. doi:10.100710956-016-9605-9

Hair, F. Jr, J., Sarstedt, M., Hopkins, L., & G. Kuppelwieser, V. (. (2014). Partial least squares structural equation modeling (PLS-SEM) An emerging tool in business research. *European Business Review*, *26*(2), 106–121. doi:10.1108/EBR-10-2013-0128

Hallikainen, H., Luongo, M., Dhir, A., & Laukkanen, T. (2022). Consequences of personalized product recommendations and price promotions in online grocery shopping. *Journal of Retailing and Consumer Services*, *69*, 103088. doi:10.1016/j.jretconser.2022.103088

Hamrouni, B., Bourouis, A., Korichi, A., & Brahmi, M. (2021). Explainable Ontology-Based Intelligent Decision Support System for Business Model Design and Sustainability. *Sustainability*, *13*(17), 9819. doi:10.3390u13179819

Hassanein, K., & Head, M. (2007). Manipulating perceived social presence through the web interface and its impact on attitude towards online shopping. *International Journal of Human-Computer Studies*, *65*(8), 689–708. doi:10.1016/j.ijhcs.2006.11.018

Hebebci, M. T., Bertiz, Y., & Alan, S. (2020). Investigation of views of students and teachers on distance education practices during the Coronavirus (COVID-19) Pandemic. *International Journal of Technology in Education and Science*, *4*(4), 267–282. doi:10.46328/ijtes.v4i4.113

Henseler, J., Ringle, C. M., & Sinkovics, R. R. (2009). The use of partial least squares path modeling in international marketing. In *New challenges to international marketing*. Emerald Group Publishing Limited. doi:10.1108/S1474-7979(2009)0000020014

Ho, J. L., Chen, K. Y., Wang, L. H., Yeh, S. S., & Huan, T. C. (2022). Exploring the impact of social media platform image on hotel customers' visit intention. *International Journal of Contemporary Hospitality Management*.

Huang, T. K., Wang, Y. T., & Lin, K. Y. (2022). Enhancing brand loyalty through online brand communities: The role of community benefits. *Journal of Product and Brand Management*, *31*(5), 823–838. doi:10.1108/JPBM-08-2020-3027

Hussain, S., Ahmed, W., Jafar, R. M. S., Rabnawaz, A., & Jianzhou, Y. (2017). eWOM source credibility, perceived risk and food product customer's information adoption. *Computers in Human Behavior*, *66*, 96–102. doi:10.1016/j.chb.2016.09.034

Jarvenpaa, S. L., Tractinsky, N., & Vitale, M. (2000). Consumer trust in an Internet store. *Information Technology and Management*, *1*(1/2), 45–71. doi:10.1023/A:1019104520776

Joshi, M. (2018). "Burnout and Stressors as influencers on Work engagement among law enforcement agents in selected cities. In Chaudhary, N. Sharma, & M. Singh (eds.) Management Techniques for Employee Engagement in Contemporary Organizations. IGI Global USA.

Joshi, M (February, 2018). Workforce trends and challenges: a peek into future In N. Sharma, *Management Techniques for a Diverse and Cross-Cultural Workforce*, IGI Global USA.

Joshi, M., Joshi, G., & Pathak, S. (2020). *Awareness, entrepreneurial event theory and theory of planned behavior as antecedents of student entrepreneurial intentions: an Indian perspective. International Journal of Business and Globalisation*. Inderscience Publishers.

Joshi, M., Tyagi, S., Ansari, N., & Singh, V. K. (2019). Impact of IoT to accomplish a vision of digital transformation of the cities. In *A handbook of IOT and Big Data*. CRC Press, Taylor and Francis.

Kim, J. Y., & Hwang, J. (2022). Who is an evangelist? Food tourists' positive and negative eWOM behavior. *International Journal of Contemporary Hospitality Management*, *34*(2), 555–577. doi:10.1108/IJCHM-06-2021-0707

Kimes, S. E., & Wirtz, J. (2003). Has revenue management become acceptable? Findings from an international study on the perceived fairness of rate fences. *Journal of Service Research*, *6*(2), 125–135. doi:10.1177/1094670503257038

Kotler, P., & Armstrong, G. M. (2018). *Marketing Mix: Selected Chapters From: Principles of Marketing, Philip Kotler and Gary Armstrong*. Pearson.

Laroche, M., Kim, C., & Zhou, L. (1996). Brand familiarity and confidence as determinants of purchase intention: An empirical test in a multiple brand context. *Journal of Business Research*, *37*(2), 115–120. doi:10.1016/0148-2963(96)00056-2

Lee, K. T., & Koo, D. M. (2012). Effects of attribute and valence of e-WOM on message adoption: Moderating roles of subjective knowledge and regulatory focus. *Computers in Human Behavior*, *28*(5), 1974–1984. doi:10.1016/j.chb.2012.05.018

Lee, M. K., Cheung, C. M., & Chen, Z. (2005). Acceptance of Internet-based learning medium: The role of extrinsic and intrinsic motivation. *Information & Management*, *42*(8), 1095–1104. doi:10.1016/j.im.2003.10.007

Li, F., & Miniard, P. W. (2006). On the potential for advertising to facilitate trust in the advertised brand. *Journal of Advertising*, *35*(4), 101–112. doi:10.2753/JOA0091-3367350407

Limbu, Y. B., Wolf, M., & Lunsford, D. (2012). Perceived ethics of online retailers and consumer behavioral intentions: The mediating roles of trust and attitude. *Journal of Research in Interactive Marketing*, *6*(2), 133–154. doi:10.1108/17505931211265435

Lin, Y. M., Lin, G. Y., & Laffey, J. M. (2008). Building a social and motivational framework for understanding satisfaction in online learning. *Journal of Educational Computing Research*, *38*(1), 1–27. doi:10.2190/EC.38.1.a

Lu, L. C., Chang, W. P., & Chang, H. H. (2014). Consumer attitudes toward blogger's sponsored recommendations and purchase intention: The effect of sponsorship type, product type, and brand awareness. *Computers in Human Behavior*, *34*, 258–266. doi:10.1016/j.chb.2014.02.007

Madjid, C. N. I. F., & Hermawan, A. (2022). The Influence of Viral Marketing and Brand Image on Purchase Decisions through E-Trust: Study on Avoskin Skincare Customers. *International journal of economics, management, business, and social science (ijembis)*, *2*(2), 315-321.

McKnight, D. H., & Chervany, N. L. (2001). What trust means in e-commerce customer relationships: An interdisciplinary conceptual typology. *International Journal of Electronic Commerce*, *6*(2), 35–59. doi:10.1080/10864415.2001.11044235

McKnight, D. H., Choudhury, V., & Kacmar, C. (2002). Developing and validating trust measures for e-commerce: An integrative typology. *Information Systems Research*, *13*(3), 334–359. doi:10.1287/isre.13.3.334.81

Miao, M., Jalees, T., Zaman, S. I., Khan, S., Hanif, N. U. A., & Javed, M. K. (2022). The influence of e-customer satisfaction, e-trust and perceived value on consumer's repurchase intention in B2C e-commerce segment. *Asia Pacific Journal of Marketing and Logistics*, *34*(10), 2184–2206. doi:10.1108/APJML-03-2021-0221

Moorman, C., Zaltman, G., & Deshpande, R. (1992). Relationships between providers and users of market research: The dynamics of trust within and between organizations. *JMR, Journal of Marketing Research*, *29*(3), 314–328. doi:10.1177/002224379202900303

Oh, J. C., Yoon, S. J., & Park, B. I. (2012). A structural approach to examine the quality attributes of e-shopping malls using the Kano model. *Asia Pacific Journal of Marketing and Logistics*, *24*(2), 305–327. doi:10.1108/13555851211218075

Pavlou, P. A., & Dimoka, A. (2006). The nature and role of feedback text comments in online marketplaces: Implications for trust building, price premiums, and seller differentiation. *Information Systems Research*, *17*(4), 392–414. doi:10.1287/isre.1060.0106

Pratiwi, L., Sunaryo, S., & Mugiono, M. (2021). The effect of e-service quality on e-loyalty mediated by e-trust and brand image variables: A study on OVO E-Wallet application users in Malang City. *International Journal of Research in Business and Social Science (2147-4478)*, *10*(6), 56-62.

Ramadhan, A., Hidayanto, A. N., Evik, C. S., Rizkiandini, N., Rahimullah, N. A., Muthiah, R. H., Anggreainy, M. S., & Phusavat, K. (2022). Factors affecting the continuation to use and e-WOM intention of online library resources by university students: A study in Indonesia. *Journal of Academic Librarianship*, *48*(6), 102592. doi:10.1016/j.acalib.2022.102592

Ray, A., Bala, P. K., Chakraborty, S., & Dasgupta, S. A. (2021). Exploring the impact of different factors on brand equity and intention to take up online courses from e-Learning platforms. *Journal of Retailing and Consumer Services*, *59*, 102351. doi:10.1016/j.jretconser.2020.102351

Saadé, R., & Bahli, B. (2005). The impact of cognitive absorption on perceived usefulness and perceived ease of use in on-line learning: An extension of the technology acceptance model. *Information & Management*, *42*(2), 317–327. doi:10.1016/j.im.2003.12.013

Sadeghi, M. (2019). A shift from classroom to distance learning: Advantages and limitations. *International Journal of Research in English Education*, *4*(1), 80–88. doi:10.29252/ijree.4.1.80

Setiawan, R., & Achyar, A. (2012). *Effects of Perceived Trust and Perceived Price on Customers' Intention to Buy in Online Store in Indonesia*. Asean Marketing Journal.

Sharma, S., Singh, S., Kujur, F., & Das, G. (2020). Social media activities and its influence on customer-brand relationship: An empirical study of apparel retailers' activity in India. *Journal of Theoretical and Applied Electronic Commerce Research*, *16*(4), 602–617. doi:10.3390/jtaer16040036

Shaikh, E., Brahmi, M., Thang, P. C., Watto, W. A., Trang, T. T. N., & Loan, N. T. (2022). Should I Stay or Should I Go? Explaining the Turnover Intentions with Corporate Social Responsibility (CSR), Organizational Identification and Organizational Commitment. *Sustainability*, *14*(10), 6030. doi:10.3390u14106030

Sihite, J., Harun, T. W., & Nugroho, A. (2016). The Low Cost Airline Consumer Price Sensitivity: An Investigation on the Mediating Role of Promotion and Trust in Brand. *International Research Journal of Business Studies*, *7*(3).

Solikhah, E. W. (2022). The Effect E-Wom Website Attractiveness E-Trust and Innovation on Purchase Decision Online Sales. *(JDS)*, *20*(11), 61-69.

Suhaily, L., & Darmoyo, S. (2017). Effect Of Product Quality, Perceived Priceand Brand Image On Purchase Decision Mediated By Customer Trust (Study On Japanese Brandelectronic Product). *Jurnal Manajemen*, *21*(2), 179–194. doi:10.24912/jm.v21i2.230

Swait, J., & Erdem, T. (2007). Brand effects on choice and choice set formation under uncertainty. *Marketing Science*, *26*(5), 679–697. doi:10.1287/mksc.1060.0260

Tan, Z., Sadiq, B., Bashir, T., Mahmood, H., & Rasool, Y. (2022). Investigating the Impact of Green Marketing Components on Purchase Intention: The Mediating Role of Brand Image and Brand Trust. *Sustainability*, *14*(10), 5939. doi:10.3390u14105939

Thatcher, J. B., Loughry, M. L., Lim, J., & McKnight, D. H. (2007). Internet anxiety: An empirical study of the effects of personality, beliefs, and social support. *Information & Management*, *44*(4), 353–363. doi:10.1016/j.im.2006.11.007

Tunio, M. N., Jariko, M. A., Børsen, T., Shaikh, S., Mushtaque, T., & Brahmi, M. (2021). How Entrepreneurship Sustains Barriers in the Entrepreneurial Process—A Lesson from a Developing Nation. *Sustainability*, *13*(20), 11419. doi:10.3390u132011419

Wandoko, W., Panggati, I. E., & Sukmaningsih, D. W. (2020, August). Developing e-loyalty toward Online Retailer from e-WOM, Reputation, Information Quality and e-trust. In *2020 International Conference on Information Management and Technology (ICIMTech)* (pp. 238-243). IEEE. 10.1109/ICIMTech50083.2020.9211251

Wang, Y. D., & Emurian, H. H. (2005). An overview of online trust: Concepts, elements, and implications. *Computers in Human Behavior*, *21*(1), 105–125. doi:10.1016/j.chb.2003.11.008

Wang, Y. H., & Tsai, C. F. (2014). The relationship between brand image and purchase intention: Evidence from award winning mutual funds. *The international journal of business and finance research, 8*(2), 27-40.

Wang, Y. H., and Tsai, C. F. (2014). The relationship between brand image and purchase intention: Evidence from award winning mutual funds. *The international journal of business and finance research, 8*(2), 27-40.

Weiss, A., Michels, C., Burgmer, P., Mussweiler, T., Ockenfels, A., & Hofmann, W. (2021). Trust in everyday life. *Journal of Personality and Social Psychology, 121*(1), 95–114. doi:10.1037/pspi0000334 PMID:32816511

Wilis, R. A., & Nurwulandari, A. (2020). The effect of E-Service Quality, E-Trust, Price and Brand Image Towards E-Satisfaction and Its Impact on E-Loyalty of Traveloka's Customer. *Jurnal Ilmiah MEA (Manajemen, Ekonomi, & Akuntansi), 4*(3), 1061-1099.

Win, K. S. (2022). *Factors Influencing Patient Satisfaction and Loyatly Toward Aye Thitsar Specialist Clinic* (Doctoral dissertation, MERAL Portal).

Wu, C. S., & Chen, T. T. (2019). Building brand's value: Research on brand image, personality and identification. *International Journal of Management* [IJMESS]. *Economics and Social Sciences, 8*(4), 299–318.

Zeithaml, V. A., Parasuraman, A., & Malhotra, A. (2000). *A conceptual framework for understanding e-service quality: implications for future research and managerial practice* (Vol. 115). Marketing Science Institute.

Zheng, R., Li, Z., & Na, S. (2022). How customer engagement in the live-streaming affects purchase intention and customer acquisition, E-tailer's perspective. *Journal of Retailing and Consumer Services, 68*, 103015. doi:10.1016/j.jretconser.2022.103015

Zhu, Y., Zhang, J. H., Au, W., & Yates, G. (2020). University students' online learning attitudes and continuous intention to undertake online courses: A self-regulated learning perspective. *Educational Technology Research and Development, 68*(3), 1485–1519. doi:10.100711423-020-09753-w

# Chapter 5
# An Empirical Investigation of the Antecedents and Consequences of Virtual Reality Tourism Experiences in Tunisia

**Amal Ben Cheikh**
https://orcid.org/0000-0003-0413-0235
*ARBRE Laboratory, ISG Tunis, Tunisia*

**Hajer Hadj Salem**
*ARBRE Laboratory, ISET Nabeul, Tunisia*

**Amir Kotersi**
*APBS Tunis, Tunisia*

## ABSTRACT

*Virtual tourism is related to the use of extended reality technologies, such as augmented reality and virtual reality, in order to generate a travel experience without the need to move from one place. Virtual reality represents one of the most interesting and promising digital technologies that offers significant benefits in numerous areas such as medicine, entertainment, training, and tourism. This research paper aims at examining the relationships between enjoyment, emotional involvement, flow, positive emotions, and VR experience on one hand. On the other hand, it investigates the linkage between VR experience and attitudes towards tourism destination. A quantitative approach is used to test the hypotheses. Simple linear regression shows that all hypotheses are accepted except for the flow state VR tourist experience that is rejected. Managerial implications will be drawn.*

DOI: 10.4018/978-1-6684-6766-4.ch005

## 1. INTRODUCTION

Technology is being used more and more every day to make informed decisions. It has gone a step further to make virtual technology "real" by showcasing places just the way they are (Huang et al., 2013).

Virtual Reality (VR) is a topic that is improving at a very quick speed. It is significant to stay up-to- date and accumulate knowledge about the technology if one plans to grab hold in this fast-paced industry. According to statista website, virtual tourism is considered as an increasing global industry. In fact, the market size of this industry was forecasted at 5 billion U.S. dollars in 2021. And, it is estimated to grow continuously in the next years "*totaling over 24 billion U.S. dollars by 2027*" (www.statista.com)

Numerous industry leaders in VR are growing such as Oculus and HTC. The global VR report showed that "*The global virtual reality devices market is expected grow from $9.48 billion in 2021 to $10.15 billion in 2022*" (www.globenewswire.com).

As an example for the rapid development of VR, Guttentag (2010) wrote that sites can be re-formed with great responsiveness to point out that our hearing and visual senses can be well stimulated in a virtual experience. However, from a technical standpoint, there was still a lack of technology development regarding real-time movements and accurate sound simulation. In a virtual tourism experience, the importance of the senses is highlighted.

As VR gear becomes more accessible and less expensive, along with improvements in software technology, VR and AR show commercial benefits, from supporting to boost productivity to interacting with consumers and target markets in original, fresh and innovative ways, and ensuring that organizations are hiring the appropriate people with the necessary capabilities and competences. Additionally, VR and AR may lower expenses and boost a company's environmental reputation.

Businesses start by determining how immersive technology could be effectively implemented to transform your organization is to understand the potential impact of VR and how they operate.

Our consumer behaviors are evolving in the digital era, from how and where we get information to how we view and associate with companies (Shaikh et al., 2022). This change in behavior is having a significant impact on marketing and advertising efforts, both in terms of bringing in new audiences and keeping hold of existing clientele. By embracing VR and AR, companies can differentiate themselves from the competition and engage with customers in novel and interesting ways. Strong customer relationships may be developed by firms via experiential marketing. Customers may physically interact with brands through it, increasing brand engagement and eliciting an emotional reaction. (Fan et al, 2022)

The travel industry has made extensive use of the immersive technologies of augmented reality and virtual reality. Although effective AR/VR applications in tourism have been individually investigated in the past from numerous angles and situations, no comprehensive empirical study has come to any conclusions about the virtual tourism experience. (Fan et al, 2022)

The Covid19 pandemic contributes to make human technology interactions so frequent and repeated. People were searching for safe transactions and online atmospheres and VR devises responded to this need. According to Vardomatski (2021) Consumers bought more than 50% of VR and augmented reality devises. This shows the extent to which consumers are assigning value to virtual and innovative experiences.

Recently, VR studies have shown that VR technologies can change the way tourists perceive their tourism and hospitality experience (Godovykh & Fyall, 2022). Destinations managers adopt VR technologies to increase awareness about specific attractions and to generate positive emotions regarding them.

Numerous studies have attempted to explain the impact of these tools on intention to visit (Godovykh & Fyall, 2022)

A number of authors have reported analyses of trends in VR that demonstrated that the pandemic is considered as a strong and powerful factor to utilize VR tourism, to ensure their safety tourists' intention to use VR devises was high because these devises are safe and affordable (Lee and Kim, 2021).

Tourism decision makers tried to develop new and adapted solutions during the pandemic so they can continue to satisfy their audiences and loyal visitors. The aim was to create a virtual experience that not only fits tourists 'expectations during and after the pandemic but also ensures their safety (Lu et al., 2021; Merkx & Nawijn, 2021).

Additionally, VR technologies are designed to face overtourism challenges and its negative influences on tourism attractions (Godovykh & Fyall, 2022).

The aim of the paper is to provide a conceptual theoretical framework based on virtual tourism experience, its antecedents and its impact on tourists 'attitudes towards destinations.

VR experiences in tourism may serve a variety of purposes and provide different advantages. Visitors can use VR programs made for accessibility, education, marketing, entertainment, and heritage preservation. The majority of the existing research on VR tourism experiences exclusively views VR tourism experiences as a means to regulate or mediate the visitor experience in a positive way (Wei et al, 2019).

Scholars differentiate between hedonic and eudaimonic experiences in tourism. Hedonic experiences aim to provide as many happy feelings as they can in a limited amount of time. Unless they are accompanied by pleasant ones, this also implies avoiding negative feelings (Merkx & Nawijn, 2021).

According to Merkx and Nawijn (2021), eudaimonic experiences are seen to be more meaningfully engaged and often feature a closer connection to attractions and destinations. The amount of research on VR and tourist experiences now available uses one of two approaches: either a conceptual model built on a variety of concepts is created, or particular theories are utilized to evaluate VR applications. These studies generally conclude that VR applications in tourism may influence the visitor experience favorably. Therefore, VR can be employed as an effective and efficient marketing tool in the tourism industry.

Accordingly, the purpose of this study is to investigate the impact of enjoyment, emotional involvement, flow, positive emotions on VR experience and the influence of the latter on attitudes towards tourism destination.

## 2. LITERATURE REVIEW

### 2.1 Context of This Study

Virtual worlds and virtual reality technology have been in use since the 1960s. And if we concentrate on the area and scope of the virtual reality technology and the beginning of this technology, we may feel the presence of this technology years ago. For a long period, constant study was taking place, but without major advances in virtual reality enhancements. In 1988 the team around Andy Lippmann created the Tron Movie Map. It involved a three sixty view street vision to the area (Guttentag, 1965). Users can interact and see the direction with only head mounted Display, which is considered a principal component and major enhancement in the creation of interactive screens. The package can be attributed as the creator of Google's Street view service, which tracks the same concept.

In 1968, Ivan Sutherland created and described the first technology of ultimate displays aspect and concept that could stimulate virtual reality environments in a simple way. This virtual reality technology viewed head mounted displays and appeared realistic via three dimension augmented sound and touch.

In 1990, they created the technology that is called the cave system providing a four dimensional visual response to all the parts of the body that interacts and uses visual and hearing senses of the human.

Recent years have seen huge integration and enhancements of this technology, computer technology and high quality smart phones that have powerful processors, while the prices started to decline. New and up- to- date smartphones that support virtual worlds especially in the gaming sections and Smartphones that enable 3 dimensions graphics with high density displays are now available. Companies like Oculus have released their virtual reality head mounted displays product to compete the old 360 version of google cardboard. Companies also like Samsung have also lunched in the market their new HMD the Samsung gear VR.

The concept behind virtual reality technology is based on several theories and human desire to escape the boundaries and to live in virtual world rather than real world. Once we can visualize and interact within the virtual worlds in more nomadistic visions which will help to have new form of human machine interactions.

Beyond the regular devices such as mouses and keyboards. TheVR technology as Guttentag (2020) stated in his research that the concept aims to go beyond these traditional devices that we are using in daily purposes.

## 2.2 VR and Tourism

Enhancing visitor experience is at the heart of decisions 'makers' efforts. Managers of travel destinations try to include complete designs of the journeys.

Virtual Reality is a simulation of the virtual world and surroundings, or sometimes a fictional world. In the tourism situation, the simulation of apparent virtual environments and this can visualize multiple dimensions of human senses. Especially the sense of sight that is very important in tourism. The virtual tourism industry and the virtual characteristics of the tourism attraction may send positive feelings to the travelers before formulating an attitude towards a specific destination.

Various businesses in tourism have already chosen the virtual Reality aspect and have applied virtual tours. Though, these, to the most part, many panoramic images and looks as well as entitling the street view google improving and managing to provide in the street which provide a virtual tour in the area. These applications deliver the tourists with multifunction tourism service.

Williams and Hobson (1995) were looking to improve interactive ways that may help to visualize the world and travel destinations in different and unique ways, and designed an immersive fashion that has a great impact on tourists' planning attitudes.

Williams (2006) stated that most of the tourists are using media to well visualize and obtain information about prospect destinations. However, VR can provide accurate and pertinent data about the attraction features.

One of the core benefits of providing and applying virtual reality systems is the fact that clients can test, examine and interact with the destination in advance. Destinations can provide some previews for customers to enjoy and help tourists think about visiting a place. Even though the tourist might not have decided yet, a virtual tour of the observed destination can be memorized by tourists.

Vogt (2006) argued that this technology has the ability to show a unique and perceived look about the destination before the tourist may think to visit it. It is a way to help tourists collect information. Before visiting a destination, tourists build a picture or an imprint of a journey's end that is made up of preceding knowledges, word of mouth, different ads or actions (Buhalis, 2000).

Sussmann and Vanhegan (2000) stated in their work that *"people appreciate to use virtual device and knowhow the destinations before they think to ravel to it"*. This is established on the sample of parks, which are fundamentally completely simulated environments. The pros for consumers are several, for example, they are easy, quite cheap, ostentatious fun for the whole family. In addition to that, virtual worlds provide the unique advantage that the experiences can be shaped according to tourists' wishes in a way that is attractive to them.

Guttentag (2010) examined and questioned how revenues retained from this technology will be obtained and got in the fact that the market is using many innovative technologies.

During the pandemic, governments all around the world implemented sanitary control measures that prohibited traveling and tourism, which led people to seek out travel experiences using VR technology. The need for social distance to feel safe and secure against contamination, according to scholars, has affected people's demand for contactless travelling in a constructive light since the beginning of the epidemic. (Talwar et al, 2022).

VR displays have been used to advertise travel and hospitality related services (Wei et al., 2019). Recently, the tourism and hospitality industries have seen a rise in the usage of virtual reality travel, which is now becoming increasingly popular.

The COVID-19 outbreak has increased the significance and usefulness of virtual reality tourism even though it has been successfully employed as a marketing tool (Chinazzi et al., 2020).

The World Travel and Tourism Council (WTTC, 2020) asserts that for tourism to successfully recover in the post-pandemic world, it must align with several elements such as safety and technology (Talwar et al, 2022).

As a result, it is important to explore and evaluate consumer attitudes and behaviors toward VR tourism during and after the pandemic period. In the midst of the COVID-19 pandemic (Erum et al.,2022), VR tourism is a technological advancement that allays travelers' safety and their health-related worries. This is in line with the literature which has considered VR tourism as an effective and efficient way of travelling and hospitality (Talwar et al, 2022; Schiopu et al., 2021)

## 3. CONCEPTUAL FRAMEWORK

### 3.1 Research Justification

This study is concerned with the basis that individuals will respond to the virtual world by taking actions such as requesting extra information or conveying an interest in visiting the virtual or real destination in the future. In addition, individuals may look for information related to functional aspects such as obtaining more information about a destination to use in their decision making.

Studies propose that there is a link between virtual worlds and people's attitudes and intentions to visit a destination. Thus, attitudes towards destinations are a research variable that was included in this study.

An extensive review of the literature finds that the notions of pleasure and enjoyment, positive feelings, and flow are important in comprehending the communication among the virtual experience of virtual tourists. These constructs were also chosen for this paper that studies the virtual tourist experience in the context of a three dimensional virtual world. Moreover, the attitudes of virtual tourists as preparatory steps for the travel decision phase and they are significant to tourism marketers.

## VR and Customer Attitudes

Montinho (1987) indicated that in the travel decision-making process, positive attitudes toward a tourism product or destination is predisposed by ads and media communication. Virtual worlds can provide travelers with chances to search for travel information, to book accommodations, and to make purchases via the Internet, thus reducing some of the risks associated with trip planning (Buhalis, and Law, 2008). Moreover, surfing tourism destinations in the virtual worlds provides potential tourists with mediated experiences plus idea that can be used to make travel arrangements (Crott, 1999). Because virtual reality technology can provide modified information for travelers in various phases of planning for their journey, as stated by Gretzel and Fesenmaier (2009), tourists can benefit from the relating of internet and virtual reality technology in their travel decision making. Meanwhile, VR technology will help more people to have a higher level of satisfaction with their VR travel experiences than those who did not use such devises.

Sturken and Cartwright (2009) revealed that in addition to the use of VR technology by tourists to search for travel information and to make travel arrangements, virtual reality can be used to enhance their awareness of a particular culture in a tourist destination.

According to Aho (2001), emotional involvements are a vital part of the tourist experience. Lately, academics have absorbed and comprehended the experiential and emotive aspects of traveler feelings. Bruwer and Alant (2009) investigated the consumptive experience in the context of virtual tourism. The consequences of their study advised the crucial role of enjoyment and make traveler feel and have positive feeling toward the place.

Emotions are connected to the hedonic behavior of tourists. Several hedonic concepts have started to receive a special attention from scholars. These hedonic concepts include Enjoyment, Flow, Positive Emotions and Emotional involvement. The next part details the following factors:

### *a. Enjoyment*

According to Hew et al (2018) and Wu and Lai (2021) the concept of enjoyment is considered as one of the intrinsic motivation. Venkatesh (2000) defined enjoyment as “the extent to which the activity of using a specific system is perceived to be enjoyed in its own right aside from any performance consequence resulting from system use”.

According to research on virtual reality technology and experiences, which regarded the degree of perceived enjoyment as a crucial component of the entire VR tourist experience, enjoyment is defined as the sensation of joy received from an experience using technological devises (Atzeni et al, 2022). More recently, pleasure was suggested as a factor in the explanation of visitor satisfaction and it was discovered that it mediated the relationship between visit intention and the destination (Jang & Park, 2019; Atzeni et al, 2022).

When watching a virtual tourism destination, customers may enjoy the virtual tourism experience and their level of enjoyment can contribute to shape not only their memorable experience but also their intentions and behaviors to visit the destination or to continue the use of VR devises (Wu and Lai, 2021).

Yang et al (2021), Kim and ko (2019) and Bogicevic et al (2019) stated that enjoyment is considered as a driver to amplify users' experiences with VR devises. Therefore, enjoyment is a determinant of intention use of VR devises. Lee et al (2020) demonstrated the same result. Furthermore, Rahimishian et al (2020) revealed the critical role of enjoyment as a predictor of satisfaction with 360 virtual tours.

The concept enjoyment is crucial in order to understand virtual experiences. Huang et al (2013) argued that enjoyment is fundamental to understand virtual tourism experiences. Meanwhile, Goh and Yoon (2011) highlighted the virtual devises acceptance and showed that enjoyment is needed to understand people's experiences in a virtual world.

In the same context, Huang et al (2013) stated that enjoyment is related to technological entertainment which consequently reflects its motivational nature to experience the VR devise and to develop users' intentions and behaviors. Additionally, several studies have suggested that enjoyment in the virtual world may be considered as behavioral intention determinants. Barnes (2011) and Huang et al (2013) indicated that in a virtual world enjoyment is an antecedent of users' experience, their attitudes, use intention and behavior.

In line with previous studies on the relationship between enjoyment, intentions and behaviors, the following hypothesis is proposed:

H1: enjoyment has a positive and significant impact on virtual tourist experience.

### *b. Emotional Involvement*

Poria, Reichel, and Biran (2006) stated that emotional participation plays an important role in the relationship among the general incentive to visit new destinations.

The concept of emotional involvement has gained important attention in recent papers trying to recognize user experience in virtual environments.

Emotional involvement has been considered as a vital aspect for enjoyable virtual experience. Consequently, the construct of emotional involvement was involved in this paper.

Wu and Lai (2021) pointed out the importance of emotional involvement. The research explained emotional involvement as the extent to which a customer, tourist or user is engaged emotionally in a specific behavior, for example the VR devise use. Accordingly, Holsapple and Wu (2007) defined the concept emotional involvement as "the degree to which an individual is emotionally engaged in a behavior".

The construct of emotional involvement attracted the attention of several scholars due to its role in understanding user experience. It translates the understanding of interactivity levels between humans and VR devises. From the same perspective, Saeed et al (2009) and Huang et al (2013) asserted that one of the main variables of hedonic consumption theory is emotional involvement. It is helpful to recognize tourists' experiences in VR environments and consequently to discern their attitudes towards VR tourism. In the same study, Saeed et al (2009) illustrated the concept emotional involvement as a factor influencing individuals' intentions and behaviors with regard to educational context. Yang et al (2021) found a positive and significant relationship between emotional involvement and 360þ virtual tour experience.

Emotional involvement is considered as an experience leading to profound feelings and consequently retaining consumers 'attention and their engagement to a specific technology. Emotional involvement plays a crucial role to examine tourists' interactions with VR devises and to evaluate their experiences (Atzeni et al, 2022; Kim, Lee, et al., 2020).

Scholars revealed that the variable emotional involvement directly and positively influences VR tourists experiences, while Yang et al (2021) study stated that the more emotional involvement in generated by the virtual experience, the more users of VR devises are willing to visit the destination. Moreover, existing literature has established that emotional involvement due to the use of VR is a key element to understand how tourists attitudes will be influences by such experiences.

Therefore, based on previous literature on the relationship between emotional involvement and virtual tourism experience, it is possible to suggest the following hypothesis:

H2: Emotional involvement has a positive and significant impact on virtual tourist experience.

### c. Flow

Scholars have pointed out that the notion of flow is major for understanding tourist experience (Filep, 2007; Jones, Hollenhorst, Perna, and Selin, 2000; Ritchie and Hudson 2009), as tourists attempt to draw their essential for best experience with suitable tourist activities.

Atzeni et al (2022) defined flow as the level of immersion and psychological state of a person who is fully engaged in a particular activity. It describes the way VR users are immersed in visiting a specific attraction virtually. This state has been measured as a determinant of virtual perceptions (Atzeni et al, 2022), especially in VR environments that demand the user's sense of immersing. Recently, flow has been used to understand and assess tourist virtual experiences. It is recognized as a crucial sensory factor in influencing how satisfied and devoted virtual visitors are (Zhang et al., 2019).

Flow can be used to comprehend tourism experience; individual experience and investigation into human and technology interaction.

Wu and Lai (2021) define flow state as "the process of optimal experience". Hence, Csikszentmihalyi (1975) explained it as "The holistic sensation that people feel when they act with total involvement"

A large and growing body of literature has investigated flow state in relation to virtual tourism and has described it as a deep involved and immersed state when using a specific technology (Wu and Lai, 2021; Kim et al, 2017). When individuals feel a flow state, they experience a fast evaluation of time.

Wu and Lai (2021) stated that a flow state reflects the organism phase in the context of VR tourism. When using a VR devise to watch an attraction, users who have a flow state may experience a memorable a positive virtual tourism experience.

Numerous studies have attempted to explain flow state as a determinant for users' experiences and behaviors in virtual worlds (Wu and Lai, 2021; Hamrouni et al., 2021). In a similar vein, Hooker et al (2009) investigated the concept of flow and they demonstrated its relevance in explaining virtual experience. Moreover, Nah et al (2010) found that flow can be used effectively in understanding virtual experiences and in understanding it.

Chang and Wang (2008) pointed to some of the ways in which flow is a determinant factor for consumer behavior and their online repurchase intention. Besides, flow is found to have a significant and positive impact on users' learning about tourism attractions and their intentions to select them. Thus, we believe that flow state will positively associate with the virtual tourism experience. Therefore, the following hypothesis is developed:

H3: Flow has a positive and significant impact on virtual tourist experience.

### *d. Positive Emotions*

In order to strengthen the understanding of virtual experiences, researchers shed lights on the role of hedonic concepts such as positive emotions (Huang et al., 2013).

O'Regan (2003) stressed the significance of positive emotions and how they affect customers' experiences in virtual worlds. Accordingly, Huang et al (2013) stipulated that the construct positive emotion is considered very pivotal to understand the intentions and behaviors behind using virtual devises in different contexts like tourism and hospitality services. It shows a better description of the users 'experience in a virtual environment.

Perlusz's (2004) developed a technology affect scale and demonstrated the critical aspect of positive emotions when analyzing the human technology interactions (Aldieri et al., 2021). Thus, this research will therefore examine the relationship between positive emotions and virtual tourism experience. Hence, the following hypothesis:

H4: Positive emotions have a positive and significant impact on virtual tourist experience.

### *e. Attitudes Towards Virtual Attraction*

Alyahya and McLean (2022) demonstrated the crucial role of virtual reality experience to share and communicate information about a specific destination. It is a way to enhance the level of consumer involvement and consequently their attitudes towards destinations.

Li and Chen (2019) focused on the relationship between VR experience and customers attitudes towards tourism attractions. Their research stressed the significance of this linkage between VR experience and consumer attitudes and behaviors.

Alyahya and McLean (2022) stated, "From a marketing perspective, VR has the potential to influence tourism consumers across the customer journey. For example, VR can be used to communicate inspirational content to consumers at the pretravel (prepurchase) phase to entice consumers to visit a destination, considered a "try before you buy experience."

Customers 'attitudes towards a specific destination can be influenced by the VR experience a customer tried. Due to its benefits, VR contributes to deliver valuable and relevant content about the tourism attraction which facilitates the decision-making process.

According to Tussyadiah et al. (2017), virtual reality (VR) offers a space where users may access information via a variety of sensory modalities and experience a realistic depiction of the environment (Tunio et al., 2021) it depicts. Therefore, it has been shown that the immersive character of VR experiences may help consumers learn about products, boost brand recognition, product recall, and recollection of events, as well as produce favorable attitude and behavioral reactions. Importantly, an immersive VR experience enables users to feel as though they are physically there in the virtual world, which is essential for the success of compelling VR material (Tussyadiah et al., 2017).

A deeper understanding of presence in VR experiences that feature virtual representations of real places where available activities mirror overall consumption and a conception of the function of the VR experience in forming attitudes toward actual consumption will be provided through research on VR experiences with genuine tourist sites.

Understanding how travelers react to diverse VR stimuli is crucial from a management perspective as destinations must make strategic decisions regarding investments in various VR platforms and applications.

The purpose of this study is to ascertain how VR experiences affect users' attitudes towards tourism destinations.

Thus, this research will therefore examine the relationship between VR experience and attitudes towards tourism destination. Hence, the following hypothesis:

H5: Virtual tourist experience has a positive and significant impact on attitudes towards tourism destination.

Figure 1 presents the conceptual framework (see figure 1)

*Figure 1. Conceptual model*

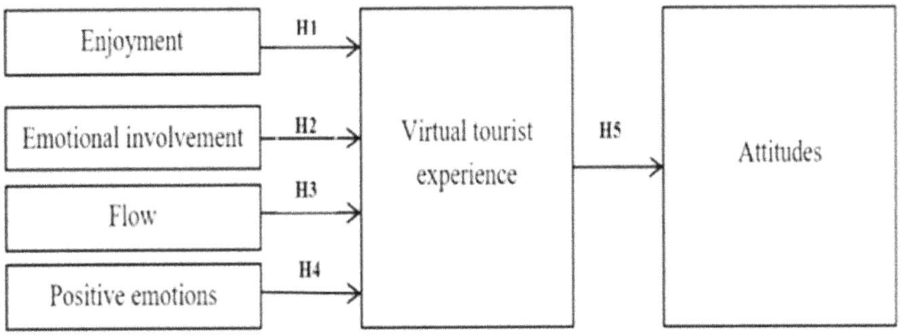


## 4. METHODOLOGY

### 4.1 Sampling, Data Collection and Measurements

#### Population and Sampling

We have numerous sampling techniques, this research paper relied on international and domesrtic tourists who tried at least once VR devices.

The data obtained from participants will be analyzed using the SPSS software.

122 tourists answered to the questionnaire. The sample size is considered as sufficient to examine the hypotheses and prove the validity of the results. The next table (see table 1) describes the respondents' profile.

#### Measurement Scales

The measurement scales of different variables included in the conceptual model are described in the next table (see table 2).

*Table 1. Respondents profile*

| Distribution based on Gender | |
|---|---|
| Male | 74.8% |
| Female | 25.2% |
| Distribution based on marital status | |
| Single | 48.8% |
| Married | 39.8% |
| Widowed | 6.5% |
| Distribution based on age group | |
| 18 – 25 years old | 38.2% |
| 26 – 35 years old | 52% |
| 36– 50 years old | 6.5% |
| > 50 years old | 2.1% |
| Distribution based on monthly income | |
| Less than 1000 TND | 39.6% |
| Between 1000 TND and 2000 TND | 33.6% |
| Between 2000 TND and 3000 TND | 0.5% |
| Between 3000 TND and 4000 TND | 23.6% |
| More than 4000 TND | 0% |
| Distribution based on nationality | |
| Tunisian customers | 68% |
| Foreign customers | 32% |

# 5. FINDINGS, DISCUSSIONS AND MANAGERIAL IMPLICATIONS

## 5.1 Data Analysis

SPSS software contributes to build predictive models efficiently. To purify constructs, it is necessary to examine three indicators, which are Cronbach's alpha coefficient, Kaiser-Meyer-Oklin indicator and Bartlett test of sphericity.

It is argued that Cronbach's alpha is a measure of internal consistency between items, that is, how closely related a set of items are as a group. When alpha is higher, we can conclude that the items measure a latent construct (Andy Field, 2005).

It is suggested that a reliability coefficient of .70 or higher is considered as acceptable and reflect a good consistency between items (Andy Field, 2005).

Bartlett's test of sphericity is a statistical test used to examine the hypothesis that the variables are uncorrelated in the population. In other words, the population correlation matrix is an identity matrix; each variable correlates perfectly with itself but has no correlation with the other variables (Arabeche et al., 2022). The Bartlett's test of sphericity should be significant (Andy Field, 2005).

Bartlett's test is significant when the significance value is less than 0.05 (5%) and it is highly significant when $p<0.001$ (Andy Field, 2005).

*Table 2. Measurement scales*

| Variables and authors | items |
|---|---|
| Enjoyment | Experiencing virtual world create relaxed and increase comfort very much. |
| | I believe sensation in three dimension virtual world was somewhat pleasant. |
| | I can say that the motion of virtual reality as exciting |
| | The involvement in VR tour was fun. |
| Positive emotions | Experiencing virtual reality make you feel pride |
| | Engaging yourself in virtual reality world provide you with joy |
| | Virtual reality games make you cheerful |
| | Delight is feeling you experience after using virtual headset |
| Flow | When experiencing virtual reality visit, my attention is totally |
| | Experiencing virtual worlds excite my curiosity. |
| | Experiencing virtual destinations is interesting. |
| | When experiencing virtual world, I feel in confident. |
| Emotional involvement | When I am using virtual helmets, I feel "connected off" in three dimension virtual world. |
| | When I am using VR product, I feel that I am in three visual worlds. |
| | When I am using virtual reality tech, I feel deeply about the three dimension virtual worlds. |
| Virtual tourist experience | I was satisfied with the authentic experience from the virtual devise. |
| | I was satisfied with the genuine experience from the virtual devise. |
| | I was satisfied with the unique experience from the virtual devise. |
| Attitudes towards virtual experience | Unappealing/appealing |
| | Bad/good |
| | Unpleasant/Pleasant |
| | Unfavorable/favorable |
| | Unlikeable/likeable |

The Kaiser-Meyer-Oklin (KMO) measures the sampling adequacy and it should be above 0.5 (Andy Field, 2005). The next table (see table 3) shows the output of the purification stage.

For enjoyment, we retain one component with a Cronbach's alpha of about .830; this indicator is above 0.7, which brings us to confirm the consistency of the scale.

*Table 3. Variables purification*

| | enjoyment | E.involvement | Flow | P.emotions | V.experience | Attitudes |
|---|---|---|---|---|---|---|
| alpha | .830 | .792 | .895 | .967 | .816 | .819 |
| KMO | .598 | .680 | .689 | .630 | .620 | .602 |
| Bartlett | .000 | .000 | .000 | .000 | .000 | .000 |
| % of V | 85.599 | 89.291 | 86.148 | 70.165 | 79.334 | 73.304 |

Progressive purification allowed us to exclude successively items that are not sufficiently correlated to the selected factor. To eliminate a number of items, a new ACP is done. This has not allowed us to eliminate items.

Thus, the factor analysis applied to the whole 4 items has allowed the extraction of a single factor which recuperates 85.60% of the initial information. The KMO's is equal to .598; this measure is above 0.5, which indicates a good integrity between the 6 items, Bartlett's test was statistically significant. It was statistically significant: $p = 0.000 < 0.05$

For emotional involvement, we retain one component with a Cronbach's alpha of about 0.792; this indicator is above 0.7, which brings us to confirm the consistency of the scale.

The factor analysis applied to the whole 3 items has allowed the extraction of a single factor which recuperates 89.291% of the initial information. The KMO's is equal to.680; this measure is above 0.5, which indicates a good integrity between the 3 items, Bartlett's test is significant.

For flow, we retain one component with a Cronbach's alpha of about .895; this indicator is above 0.7, which confirm the consistency of the scale.

The factor analysis applied to the 4 items has allowed the extraction of a single factor which recuperates 86.148% of the initial information. The KMO's is equal to .689; this measure is above 0.5, which indicates a good integrity between the 4 items, Bartlett's test was statistically significant: $p = .000 < 0.05$.

For positive emotions, we retain one component with a Cronbach's alpha of about .967; this indicator is above 0.7, which confirm the consistency of the scale.

The purification of this scale allowed us to retain all the four items because they are sufficiently correlated to the selected factor.

The factor analysis applied to the 4 items has allowed the extraction of a single factor which recuperates 70.165% of the initial information. The KMO's is equal to .630; this measure is above 0.5, which indicates a good integrity between the 4 items, Bartlett's test was statistically significant: $p = .000 < 0.05$.

For Virtual tourist experience, we retain one component with a Cronbach's alpha of about .816; this indicator is above 0.7, which confirm the consistency of the scale.

The purification of this scale allowed us to retain all the three items because they are sufficiently correlated to the selected factor.

The factor analysis applied to the 3 items has allowed the extraction of a single factor which recuperates 79.33% of the initial information. The KMO's is equal to .620; this measure is above 0.5, which indicates a good integrity between the 3 items, Bartlett's test was statistically significant: $p = .000 < 0.05$.

For Attitudes, weretain one component with a Cronbach's alpha of about .819; this indicator is above 0.7, which confirm the consistency of the scale.

The purification of this scale allowed us to retain all the five items because they are sufficiently correlated to the selected factor.

The factor analysis applied to the 5 items has allowed the extraction of a single factor which recuperates 73.304% of the initial information. The KMO's is equal to. 602; this measure is above 0.5, which indicates a good integrity between the 4 items, Bartlett's test was statistically significant: $p = .000 < 0.05$.

## 5.2 Validation of Research Hypotheses

We use the method of simple linear regression. We relied on simple linear regression in order to estimate the relationship between two quantitative variables. The objective of this research pape ris to know how strong the relationship is between the selected variables of this study. Besides, it shows the value of the dependent variable at a certain value of the independent variables: attitudes and experience, enjoyment and experience, flow and experience, emotional involvement and experience, positive emotions and experience. Regression allows estimating how a dependent variable changes as the independent variable(s) change. Thus, it is used in this research. We considered improving the analysis by using structural equation modelling or partial least squares analysis.

The next table (see table 4) shows the results related to the validation of the first hypothesis:

*Table 4. Hypotheses results*

| Index | H1 | H2 | H3 | H4 | H5 |
|---|---|---|---|---|---|
| R | .714 | .863 | .718 | .932 | .835 |
| $R^2$ | .682 | .812 | .211 | .819 | .792 |
| B | .246 | .558 | .415 | .193 | .184 |
| P | 0.003 | .000 | .08 | .002 | .000 |
| T | 2.900 | 7.846 | 5.712 | 2.122 | 2.132 |

For the first hypothesis, the R value is .714, which represents the simple correlation. It indicates a high degree of correlation. The $R^2$ value indicates how much of the dependent variable, "virtual experience", can be explained by the independent variable, "enjoyment". In this case, 68.2% can be explained, which is very large. This is to say that 68, 2% of the virtual tourist experience variation is predicted by enjoyment.

The table of coefficients provides us with information on each predictor variable. This gives us the information we need to predict enjoyment from experience. We can see that enjoyment contributes significantly to the model $p=0.003<5\%$.

Regression analysis shows that enjoyment significantly and positively influences the virtual tourist experience since the value of Student's t (2.900) is greater than 1.96 the tabulated value of t.

For the second hypothesis, R value is 0.863, which represents the simple correlation. It indicates a high degree of correlation. The $R^2$ value indicates how much of the dependent variable, "virtual experience", can be explained by the independent variable, "enjoyment". In this case, 81.2% can be explained, which is very large. This is to say that 81.2% of the virtual tourist experience variation is predicted by emotional involvement. We can see that emotional involvement contributes significantly to the model $p=0.000<5\%$.

Regression analysis shows that enjoyment significantly and positively influences the virtual tourist experience since the value of Student's t (7.846) is greater than 1.96.

For the third hypothesis, R value is 0.718, which represents the simple correlation. It indicates a high degree of correlation. The $R^2$ value indicates how much of the dependent variable, "virtual experience", can be explained by the independent variable, "flow". In this case, 21.1% can be explained, which is very large. This is to say that 21.1% of the virtual tourist experience variation is predicted by flow.

Regression analysis shows that flow does not significantly and positively influence the virtual tourist experience since the value of Student's t (5.712) is greater than 1.96 and p (0.08) is superior to 5%.

For the fourth hypothesis, the R value is 0.932, which represents the simple correlation. It indicates a high degree of correlation. The $R^2$ value indicates how much of the dependent variable, "virtual experience", can be explained by the independent variable, "positive emotions". This is to say that 81.9% of the virtual tourist experience variation is predicted by positive emotions. The latter contributes significantly to the model p=0.002<5%.

Positive emotion significantly and positively influences the virtual tourist experience since the value of Student's t (2.122) is greater than 1.96.

For the fifth hypothesis, the R value is .835, which represents the simple correlation. It indicates a high degree of correlation. The $R^2$ value indicates how much of the dependent variable, "attitude", can be explained by the independent variable, "virtual tourist experience". This is to say that 79.2% of the attitudes variation is predicted by virtual tourist experience. Virtual tourist experience contributes significantly to the model p=0.000<5%.

Regression analysis shows that enjoyment significantly and positively influences the virtual tourist experience since the value of Student's t (2.132) is greater than 1.96.

All hypotheses were accepted except the one related to the relationship between flow state and virtual tourism experience.

## 5.3 Discussions

Examining the relationship between virtual reality experience, emotional aspects and attitudes towards destinations was the aim of this research paper. Four hypotheses over five were accepted. The accepted ones are in line with previous research about the linkages between emotional involvement, positive emotions, enjoyment and virtual tourism experience. The same when it comes to experience attitude relationship.

When we see the evaluation of the variable of emotional involvements in the area of tourism, we can see that emotions play a crucial role when it comes to building the virtual tourism experience.

The answers given by this study confirmed the sense of positive emotions when engaging a tourist for virtual environment experience. A big engagements will be visualized when testing the consumers effects on the perceptions of design and provide the travelers possible effects of elective and reliable techniques of travel information.

The regression analysis confirmed a perfect vision of the tourist acceptance for this new technology.

For the first hypothesis it showed a positive influence on enjoyment that was determined in the analysis. This finding is in line with the previous research of Yang et al (2021), Kim and ko (2019) and Bogicevic et al (2019).

Second and fourth hypotheses showed also significant and positivelinksbetween emotional involvement, positive emotions and virtual tourism experience. This result is consistent with the research of Saeed et al (2009), Huang et al (2013), Yang et al (2021) and O'Regan (2003).

## 6. CONCLUSION

As with the introduction of any new travel product, it is envisioned that virtual reality travel would initially attract the more adventurous and trendy market segments, those consumers who are drawn to the novel things in life. Given time, as virtual reality technology proliferates and permeates the society, many more consumers will appreciate and use this technology. Although still a relatively novel concept, virtual reality has already demonstrated its capabilities and potential in many industrial and scientific fields. The unique features of virtual reality provide a revolutionary way to visualize and interact with computer data and images. Virtual reality can serve as a tool to enhance the planning and marketing of a tourist destination. With its ability to recreate any tourist destination, many believe that virtual reality could eventually provide a substitute for the travel and tourism product. Virtual reality is able to offer a wide range of travel options in a controlled and safe environment. Besides, virtual travel is more convenient.

## Managerial Implications

This study will help decision makers to consider VR alternatives in order to influence tourists' attitudes. It is a cost effective tool to help target markets collect relevant and reliable content about a specific attraction.

Marketing decisions start by a deep understanding of the determinants of their experience. This paper showed that it is crucial to consider enjoyment levels and emotional aspects when designing the VR user experience.

## Limitations

Future research can enlarge the model by adding other variables that sound valuable in explaining the VR experience. Additionally, a qualitative research may be effective in understanding and exploring in depth users' opinions and decisions to use the VR devises. Scholars can also test this model in another context which is different geographically and culturally (Tunio et al., 2021). Future studies can use structural equation modeling to test the hypotheses.

## REFERENCES

Alyahya, M., & McLean, G. (2022). Examining tourism consumers' attitudes and the role of sensory information in virtual reality experiences of a tourist destination. *Journal of Travel Research, 61*(7), 1666–1681. doi:10.1177/00472875211037745

Aldieri, L., Brahmi, M., Bruno, B., & Vinci, C. P. (2021). Circular Economy Business Models: The Complementarities with Sharing Economy and Eco-Innovations Investments. *Sustainability, 13*(22), 12438. https://doi.org/10.3390/su132212438

Arabeche, Z., Soudani, A., Brahmi, M., Aldieri, L., Vinci, C. P., & Abdelli, M. E. A. (2022). Entrepreneurial Orientation, Organizational Culture and Business Performance in SMEs: Evidence from Emerging Economy. *Sustainability, 14*(9), 5160. doi:10.3390u14095160

Argyropoulou, A., Dionyssopoulou, P., & Miaoulis, G. (2011). Tourist Destination Marketing and Management Using Advanced ICTs Technologies. *Advances on Information Processing and Management, 365*, 369.

Atzeni, M., Del Chiappa, G., & Mei Pung, J. (2022). Enhancing visit intention in heritage tourism: The role of object-based and existential authenticity in non-immersive virtual reality heritage experiences. *International Journal of Tourism Research, 24*(2), 240–255. doi:10.1002/jtr.2497

Barnes, S. J. (2011). Understanding use continuance in virtual worlds: Empirical test of a research model. *Information & Management*, *48*(8), 313–319. doi:10.1016/j.im.2011.08.004

Bogicevic, V., Seo, S., Kandampully, J. A., Liu, S. Q., & Rudd, N. A. (2019). Virtual reality presence as a preamble of tourism experience: The role of mental imagery. *Tourism Management*, *74*, 55–64. doi:10.1016/j.tourman.2019.02.009

Chinazzi, M., Davis, J. T., Ajelli, M., Gioannini, C., Litvinova, M., Merler, S., Pastore y Piontti, A., Mu, K., Rossi, L., Sun, K., Viboud, C., Xiong, X., Yu, H., Halloran, M. E., Longini, I. M. Jr, & Vespignani, A. (2020). The effect of travel restrictions on the spread of the 2019 novel coronavirus (COVID-19) outbreak. *Science*, *368*(6489), 395–400. doi:10.1126cience.aba9757 PMID:32144116

Csikszentmihalyi, M. (1975). *Beyond Boredom and Anxiety*. Jossey-Bass San Francisco.

Destination, B. C. (2014). Destination BC creates the wild within VR experience. *Tratto il giorno agosto, 11*, 2015.

Erum, S.; Muhammad, N T.; Wali Muhammad, K.; Mohsen, B.; & Shahid, R., Chapter 16: The COVID-19 Pandemic Overlaps Entrepreneurial Activities and Triggered New Challenges: A Review Study, Book chapter: Managing Human Resources in SMEs and Start-ups, August 2022, 388 p. https://doi.org/doi:10.1142/9789811239212_0008

Fan, X., Jiang, X., & Deng, N. (2022). Immersive technology: A meta-analysis of augmented/virtual reality applications and their impact on tourism experience. *Tourism Management*, *91*, 104534. doi:10.1016/j.tourman.2022.104534

Godovykh, M., Baker, C., & Fyall, A. (2022). VR in Tourism: A New Call for Virtual Tourism Experience amid and after the COVID-19 Pandemic. *Tourism and Hospitality*, *3*(1), 265–275. doi:10.3390/tourhosp3010018

Goh, S., & Yoon, T. (2011, January). If you build it will they come? An empirical investigation of facilitators and inhibitors of hedonic virtual world acceptance. In *2011 44th Hawaii International Conference on System Sciences* (pp. 1-9). IEEE. 10.1109/HICSS.2011.233

Gutiérrez, M. A. A., Vexo, F., & Thalmann, D. (2008). *Stepping into Virtual Reality*. Springer London. doi:10.1007/978-1-84800-117-6

Guttentag, D. A. (2010). Virtual reality: Applications and implications for tourism. *Tourism Management*, *31*(5), 637–651. doi:10.1016/j.tourman.2009.07.003

Hamrouni, B., Bourouis, A., Korichi, A., & Brahmi, M. (2021). Explainable Ontology-Based Intelligent Decision Support System for Business Model Design and Sustainability. *Sustainability*, *13*(17), 9819. doi:10.3390u13179819

Hew, J. J., Leong, L. Y., Tan, G. W. H., Lee, V. H., & Ooi, K. B. (2018). Mobile social tourism shopping: A dual-stage analysis of a multi-mediation model. *Tourism Management*, *66*, 121–139. doi:10.1016/j.tourman.2017.10.005

Holsapple, C. W., & Wu, J. (2007). User acceptance of virtual worlds: The hedonic framework. *ACM SIGMIS Database: The DATABASE for Advances in Information Systems*, *38*(4), 86–89. doi:10.1145/1314234.1314250

Hooker, R., Wasko, M., & Paradice, D. (2009). *Linking flow, brand attitudes and purchase intent in virtual worlds*. In Proceedings of The Thirtieth International Conference on Information Systems(ICIS 2009), Phoenix, Arizona.

Huang, Y. C., Backman, S. J., Backman, K. F., & Moore, D. (2013). Exploring user acceptance of 3D virtual worlds in travel and tourism marketing. *Tourism Management*, *36*, 490–501. doi:10.1016/j.tourman.2012.09.009

Jang, Y., & Park, E. (2019). An adoption model for virtual reality games: The roles of presence and enjoyment. *Telematics and Informatics*, *42*, 101239. doi:10.1016/j.tele.2019.101239

Kim, D., & Ko, Y. J. (2019). The impact of virtual reality (VR) technology on sport spectators' flow experience and satisfaction. *Computers in Human Behavior*, *93*, 346–356. doi:10.1016/j.chb.2018.12.040

Lee, H., Jung, T. H., tom Dieck, M. C., & Chung, N. (2020). Experiencing immersive virtual reality in museums. *Information & Management*, *57*(5), 103229. doi:10.1016/j.im.2019.103229

Lee, W. J., & Kim, Y. H. (2021). Does VR Tourism Enhance Users Experience? *Sustainability*, *13*(2), 806. doi:10.3390u13020806

Li, T., & Chen, Y. (2019). Will Virtual Reality Be a Double-Edged Sword? Exploring the Moderation Effects of the Expected Enjoyment of a Destination on Travel Intention. *Journal of Destination Marketing & Management*, *12*, 15–26. doi:10.1016/j.jdmm.2019.02.003

Lu, J., Xiao, X., Xu, Z., Wang, C., Zhang, M., & Zhou, Y. (2022). The potential of virtual tourism in the recovery of tourism industry during the COVID-19 pandemic. *Current Issues in Tourism*, *2021*(25), 441–457. doi:10.1080/13683500.2021.1959526

Merkx, C., & Nawijn, J. (2021). Virtual reality tourism experiences: Addiction and isolation. *Tourism Management*, *87*, 104394. doi:10.1016/j.tourman.2021.104394

Nah, F. F. H., Eschenbrenner, B., DeWester, D., & Park, S. R. (2012). Impact of flow and brand equity in 3D virtual worlds. In *Cross-disciplinary models and applications of database management: advancing approaches* (pp. 277–297). IGI Global. doi:10.4018/978-1-61350-471-0.ch011

O'regan, K. (2003). Emotion and e-learning. *Journal of Asynchronous Learning Networks*, *7*(3), 78–92.

Parker, J. (2015). *How Oculus and Cardboard Are Going to Rock the Travel Industry*. Bloomberg. https://www.bloomberg.com/news/articles/2015-06-19/how-oculus-and-cardboard-are-going-to-rock-the-travel-industry

Perlusz, S. (2004, October). Emotions and technology acceptance: development and validation of a technology affect scale. In *2004 IEEE International Engineering Management Conference* (IEEE Cat. No. 04CH37574) (Vol. 2, pp. 845-847). IEEE. 10.1109/IEMC.2004.1407500

Rahimizhian, S., Ozturen, A., & Ilkan, M. (2020). Emerging realm of 360-degree technology to promote tourism destination. *Technology in Society*, *63*, 101411. doi:10.1016/j.techsoc.2020.101411

Saeed, N., Yang, Y., & Sinnappan, S. (2009). Emerging web technologies in higher education: A case of incorporating blogs, podcasts and social bookmarks in a web programming course based on students' learning styles and technology preferences. *Journal of Educational Technology & Society*, *12*(4), 98–109.

Schiopu, A. F., Hornoiu, R. I., Padurean, M. A., & Nica, A. M. (2021). Virus tinged? Exploring the facets of virtual reality use in tourism as a result of the COVID-19 pandemic. *Telematics and Informatics*, *60*, 101575. doi:10.1016/j.tele.2021.101575 PMID:36569994

Shaikh, E., Brahmi, M., Thang, P. C., Watto, W. A., Trang, T. T. N., & Loan, N. T. (2022). Should I Stay or Should I Go? Explaining the Turnover Intentions with Corporate Social Responsibility (CSR), Organizational Identification and Organizational Commitment. *Sustainability*, *14*(10), 6030. doi:10.3390u14106030

Sussmann, S., & Vanhegan, H. (2000). Virtual Reality and the Tourism Product Substitution or Complement? *In Proceedings of the Eighth European Conference on Information Systems* (ECIS) (pp. 1077–1083). Vienna, Austria: Wirtschaftsuniversität Wien.

Talwar, S., Kaur, P., Nunkoo, R., & Dhir, A. (2022). Digitalization and sustainability: Virtual reality tourism in a post pandemic world. *Journal of Sustainable Tourism*, 1–28. doi:10.1080/09669582.2022.2029870

Tunio, M. N., Jariko, M. A., Børsen, T., Shaikh, S., Mushtaque, T., & Brahmi, M. (2021). How Entrepreneurship Sustains Barriers in the Entrepreneurial Process—A Lesson from a Developing Nation. *Sustainability*, *13*(20), 11419. doi:10.3390u132011419

Tussyadiah, I. P., Wang, D., & Jia, C. (2017). Virtual reality and attitudes toward tourism destinations. In *Information and Communication Technologies in Tourism 2017: Proceedings of the International Conference in Rome*, (pp. 229-239). Springer International Publishing. 10.1007/978-3-319-51168-9_17

Vardomatski, S. (2021, September 14). Augmented and virtual reality after COVID-19. *Forbes*. https://www. forbes.com/sites/forbestechcouncil/2021/09/14/augmented-and-virtual-reality-after-covid-19/?sh=bc07d852d97c

Venkatesh, V. (2000). Determinants of perceived ease of use: Integrating control, intrinsic motivation, and emotion into the technology acceptance model. *Information Systems Research*, *11*(4), 342–365. doi:10.1287/isre.11.4.342.11872

Wei, W., Qi, R., & Zhang, L. (2019). Effects of virtual reality on theme park visitors' experience and behaviors: A presence perspective. *Tourism Management*, *71*, 282–293. doi:10.1016/j.tourman.2018.10.024

Wu, X., & Lai, I. K. W. (2022). The use of 360-degree virtual tours to promote mountain walking tourism: Stimulus–organism–response model. *Information Technology & Tourism*, *24*(1), 85–107. doi:10.100740558-021-00218-1

Yang, T., Lai, I. K. W., Fan, Z. B., & Mo, Q. M. (2021). The impact of a 360 virtual tour on the reduction of psychological stress caused by COVID-19. *Technology in Society*, *64*, 101514. doi:10.1016/j.techsoc.2020.101514 PMID:33424061

Zhang, S. N., Li, Y. Q., Liu, C. H., & Ruan, W. Q. (2019). How does authenticity enhance flow experience through perceived value and involvement: The moderating roles of innovation and cultural identity. *Journal of Travel & Tourism Marketing*, *36*(6), 710–728. doi:10.1080/10548408.2019.1625846

# Chapter 6
# An Investigation of the Socio-Cultural Impacts of the Digital Transformation in Developed, Developing, and Middle:
## Africa and Asia Pacific

**Abolghasem Arabiun**
*Uiversity of Tehran, Iran*

**Kiandokht Mahmoodi**
*Independent Researcher, Iran*

**Elahe Hosseini**
https://orcid.org/0000-0003-3478-5320
*Yazd University, Iran*

**Brahmi Mohsen**
https://orcid.org/0000-0002-0995-0761
*University of Sfax, Tunisia*

## ABSTRACT

*The fact that the emergence, popularity, widespread accessibility, and extensive utilization of digital technologies has revolutionized life in the early third millennium goes without saying. It is also not news to anyone that digitalization has managed to sneak into each and every aspect of modern life, and in one way or another, influence it. Admittedly, society and culture are no exception to this, and given these two components cover various aspects of individuals' lives, probing the whats, whys, and hows of digitalization impacts on the seems to be genuinely crucial. To this end, the present study explored different layers and facets of these impacts in three classes of nations. In developed nations, how digital technologies shadowed tourism, cultural diplomacy, values, communication and interactions, digital media, and preservation of culture were discussed. For developing nations, smart technologies and government services, expansion of education, booming of tourism, delivery of indigenous knowledge, and value system in cultural communities were probed.*

DOI: 10.4018/978-1-6684-6766-4.ch006

## INTRODUCTION

Of the many impacts that human activities exert, the one that truly stands out is the global changes that (Feola, 2015) and in a large scale, these changes are highly likely to result in social transformations. Although sociology scholars have all reached a consensus regarding the general idea of transformation as a major, fundamental change, there is little agreement over the marginal features that makes social changes social transformation(O'Brien, 2012).

Rabie(2013) and Gerards et al.(2021) defined social transformation as a means of restructuring all facets of life, from culture to social relations, from politics to economy, and from the way humans think to the way they live (Gerards et al., 2021; Rabie, 2013). Mina (2014) added that social transformation refers to a fundamental change in society, which happens to be deeply-rooted and more rapid than gradual(Mina, 2014). Social change and social transformation have always been a heated subject of research from the time these concepts were introduced by the prominent Islamic scholar Ibn Khaldun in the fourteenth century up until the most recent paradigms of it were proposed by Immanuel Wallerstein in the twenty-first century (Ashraf et al., 2022).

Todd (2005) proposed that some core facets of social transformation – namely identity change, institutional change, and change in modes of practice – tend to be highly complicated phenomena to explore (Todd, 2005). In Schuerkens' (2004) spectacles, social changes should be probed via two fundamental elements: First, the original factor that triggered and fueled the change; and second, the original and final situation as well as how they are characterized, in a before-after-comparison manner(Schuerkens, 2004). Hegmon and Peeples (2018) remarked that in pursuit of explaining social transformations, focus should be concentrated on the changes that shadows people's life experiences, like economy and socio-political atmosphere These changes could occur either gradually and steadily, or radically rapidly (Hegmon et al., 2018).

In the post-industrial age, Rabie (2013) believed, social changes became more dynamic and faster paced in the light of revolutions in information, technology, telecommunication, societal advents, economy, and above all, with the march of globalization. It is, then, evident that at the turn of the third millennium, with the uprise of affordable user-friendly personal computers, smartphones, the Internet, and digitalization of sales and services, social transformation is coming to the stage at a far swifter pace: The age of digital transformation(Maseno & Wanyoike, 2022).

Digital transformation could be recognized as a tremendous paradigm shift (Perez, 2010). Also labeled "digitalization", or "digitization"(Demlehner & Laumer, 2019), being interchangeably employed in research (Hausberg et al., 2019), digital transformation could be basically defined as shifting from analog information to zero-one codes for the purpose of storing it in, processing it with, and transmitting it by computers(Bloomberg, 2018). In a similar definition, Legner et al. (2017) remarked that digital transformation referred to the technical process of converting analog signals to digital ones. These two definitions tend to be rather technical, nevertheless(Legner et al., 2017).

Mahraz et al.(2019) and Henriette et al. (2015) seemed to agree that, requiring the alignment of strategy and other factors – including individuals, culture, mindsets, talent development, and leadership(Goran et al., 2017; Henriette et al., 2015; Mahraz et al., 2019). Digitalization has brought about countless productive impacts in diverse facets – namely fostering decision-making (Roedder et al., 2016), creating customer value such as the optimization of customer needs and experiences(Rogers, 2016), generating novel forms of organizing such as platform organizations(Teece, 2018), giving rise to competitive advantage(Korhonen

& Halén, 2017), and promoting participation, for example, in open government (Mergel et al., 2014). The presence of digitalization and its impacts on all aspects of lives of twenty-first century dwellers got more colorful with the emergence of COVID-19 pandemic, which proved how technology could be employed to trigger social innovation and tackle the problems (Gegenhuber & Tollkuhn, 2020).

The fact that digitalization is a change of paradigm and a technological revolution in real terms has already been established(Perez, 2010). This process is the natural course of development in the new age, when businesses have no way other than implementing it in order to stay competitive and to offer the best that they can to their customers and clients. Digitalization paves the way for enterprises to boost their customizability and automation through standardization (Andal-Ancion et al., 2003). Digitalization has created a new mode of value, which lies in connecting people together; and with the proliferation of smart products, it has enabled businesses to maintain processes which they failed to maintain earlier (Porter & Heppelmann, 2015).

Not only private-sector enterprises are impacted by digitalization but also government bodies are immensely impacted. As a case in point, in "Tallinn Declaration on eGovernment" (Kassim et al., 2017), European Union governments made themselves committed to employ digitalization in designing and delivering their services in pursuit of maintaining increased transparency, interoperability, and citizen satisfaction. Digitalization has also massively influenced art, education, communication, transportation, and social relationships as well.

Amidst all the facets of the lives in the third millennium that have been transformed thoroughly by digitalization, admittedly, society and culture have not remained in wilderness. Abbasi et al. (2021) proposed that culture could be intentionally arranged and shaped; and most certainly, digitalization could be named as a powerful shaper in this regard (Mahmoudi et al., 2022). The impact of digitalization on culture is so intense that some scholars such as Roper et al.(2017) have proposed an independent category of culture called digital culture(Roper & Chaudhari, 2017). Forbach and Wähler (2021) added that digitalization has shadowed culture in various facets: digital leadership has emerged; technology and processes have been digitalized; working conditions have become autonomous; agility, entrepreneurship and collaboration have been emphasized; innovation and learning have been placed in the spotlight of attention, and customer orientation has turned to the main approach of many businesses(Fleischmann et al., 2020).

Nadkarni & Prügl (2021) remarked that digital transformation is not merely a matter of technology-driven challenge; it rather requires deep cultural change (Sadowski, 2022). Gurbaxani & Dunkle(2019) continued that digital transformation involved a whole reinvention of all concepts – visions, strategies, structures, processes, capabilities, and culture. Indeed, our entire cultural experience is being altered by digitalization, not just in terms of new technology-based access, production and dissemination, but in terms of participation and creation, and learning and partaking in a knowledge society(Gurbaxani & Dunkle, 2019). In Mamychev et al. (2021) view, the shadows of digitalization on each of these areas is prone to exert positive and negative effects on the sustainable development of the socio-cultural integrity of society (Mamychev et al., 2021). Digitalization has gone into culture so profoundly that even in the course of the COVID-19 pandemic, cultural centers – such as movie theaters and concert auditoriums – were delivering their cultural products virtually and through digital channels(Wismar, 2021). *cultural centers were presenting themselves virtually in pandemics. This matter must have been accurately predicted by* Hadžić (2004), who introduced the idea of digitization of cultural heritage one and a half decades earlier(Hadžić, 2020).

In short, Digitalization is an unstoppable power that will fall upon us, and will affect the way we think, the way we behave, the way we decide and act,, and in one word, our entire culture (FEIGE, 2019). Despite this massive impact that digital transformation has had on the global culture as well as on the culture of individual countries, very few academic studies have targeted its cultural impact, causing various aspects of this significant change in mankind to lurk in the dark. The majority of the studies who have investigated the march of digitalization and the change that it brought about with it have focused on business, organizational management, marketing, education, and communication. Therefore, a serious gap could be observed both in the digitalization literature and in the cultural studies literature in addressing how, why, and to what extent the new digital life has revolutionized human culture.

In order to address this gap, the present study attempted to probe the socio-cultural impacts of the digital revolution on societal level, and to ease the process of investigating these impacts, global discussions were avoided; rather, the nations were broken down into three major clusters. In pursuit of fulfilling the objectives of the present study, the following research questions were devised and delineated.

$\mathbf{RQ_{01}}$: What are the socio-cultural impacts of the digital transformation in developed nations?
$\mathbf{RQ_{02}}$: What are the socio-cultural impacts of the digital transformation in developing nations?
$\mathbf{RQ_{03}}$: What are the socio-cultural impacts of the digital transformation in MENAPA nations?

As it was discussed earlier, in the course of the past two decades, the attention of scholars was on a steady rise in addressing different technological and organizational aspects of digital transformation (Nadkarni & Prügl, 2021). Nonetheless, only a small portion of this attention has been directed toward scrutinizing the sociocultural impacts of this transformation. The present study, thus, gains significance as it has placed societal (Shaikh et al., 2022) and cultural effects of digitalization in the spotlight.

Besides, this study is significant given that it discusses the sociocultural impacts of the advent of digitalization in different nations based on the degree to which they are developed. As developed, developing and MENAPA nations share diverse features in common, digitalization affects their sociocultural components similarly within their category, and differently from other categories. Employing such a classification of nations has led to more accurate and detailed results.

The findings of this study could be efficiently utilized by cultural policy makers, men of pen and vision such as sociologists and journalists, and government officials whose area of authority falls in the realm of culture, granting to them a deep-seated and functional understanding of what they are facing and what they are yet to face in the culture of their nation in the new digital age. Business tycoons, media planners, education policy makers, curriculum developers, and art critics could also get benefits from the findings of this study, as leaning how digital world has impacted culture can enlighten their prospects and assist them in decision making.

## CASE OF DEVELOPED NATIONS

In response to the first research question, targeting the socio-cultural impacts of the digital transformation in developed nations, the argument must begin by a piece of statistics. According to the statistics published by Global Digital (2018) in *We Are Social and Hoot suite*, the Internet is not distributed evenly around the world. The highest rate of internalization is observed in Northern Europe (94%), with Western Europe (90%) and North America (88%) standing in the second and the third rank respectively.

In percentage terms, however, the largest penetration of the Internet could be observed in developed countries (81%) whereas this figure is almost half as big (40%) in developing countries and only(15%) in underdeveloped nations.

*Figure 1. Using internet*

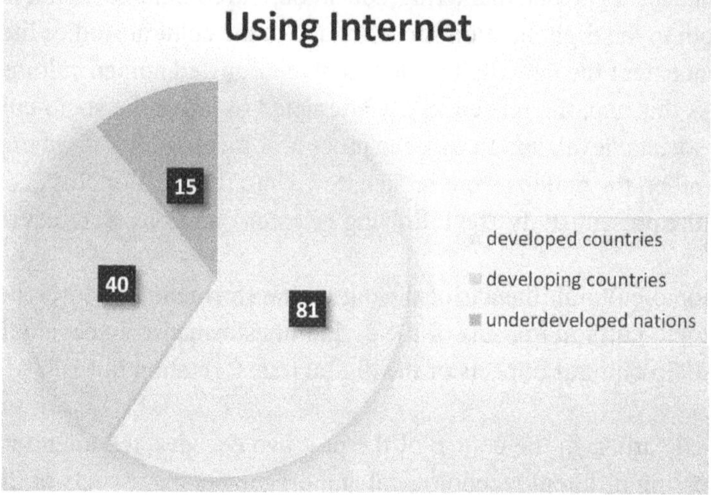


In the light of this extended coverage of the Internet in developed nations, almost all cultural values have either fully undergone or are currently undergoing massive transformation in the course of the past three decades (Saiko et al., 2020). The young generation in these nations is embracing life in its digital rather than physical format. They tend to perceive the format of traditional culture with the established system of values via the spectacles of numbers and emerging consequences: such as clip culture, screen culture, the culture of computer games, and the like.

On the top of that, a new set of cultural values are emerging in industrial nations, which seems to be an inevitable outcome of the digital age. One factor that has a lot of say in this is digital media, regardless of their strengths or weaknesses(Sokolova, 2021). According to Sokolova, with the spread of the digital media, new cultural hierarchies have been introduced into people's lives and they are experiencing various alterations in the way through which they interact with each other and the world around them.

Viktorovna et al. (2021) believed that technological progresses in developed nations has vastly impacted social processes and social institutions. It has changed social groups in different levels of families, circle of friends, communities, nations, peoples, and estates with diverse socioeconomic status (Viktorovna et al., 2021). Other than the living fabric of public life, one other societal area affected by digitalization in developed nations, Yurjevna added, is social institutions and the legal system supporting innovation processes. In these countries, the governing system of the society is mostly democratic, ensuring the optimally free introduction of new technologies, and this provides an excellent ground for the introduction of various digital technologies. Adding reliable legal basis to these technologies has boosted the quality of citizens' lives; both for the providers of these technologies since they know the intellectual property rights for their digital inventions are protected, and for the users as they see a legal and affordable way to start an innovation business.

Gumenyuk et al. (2021) asserted that digitalization in developed nations could be deemed as the third industrial revolution seeing that it has managed to boost national economy, social progress and industrial development. They proposed that European institutions of cultural diplomacy (British Council, French Institute, Polish Institute, Goethe-Institute, and Czech Center) have utilized digital technologies to get ahead in their missions. These missions include providing comprehensive state support; submitting reports to the Ministries of Foreign Affairs; establishing a network structure of operation; and promoting their language. Digital technologies have enabled them to devise and develop cultural content which is more elaborate, more effective, and more diverse (Gumenyuk et al., 2021).

Indeed, in Gumenyuk (2021) point of view, it is almost impossible to trigger cultural innovations without information and info-communication support. Such supports in developed nations have caused transformation of cultural spaces, and led to the formulation of vision and value system, and boosted collaboration and interaction(Gumenyuk, 2021).

Vujadinović and Jaksic-Stojanovic (2022) discussed the impact of digitalization on tourism in developed nations. Not only has ICT promoted touristy spots of these countries and has attracted more tourists to these areas than ever, resulting in a boom in tourism industry, but it has also enables tour operators to offer more creative services, and attain a higher degree of customer satisfaction(Vujadinović & Jaksic-Stojanovic, 2022).

In another view, Kondakov et al. (2019) ascertained that Internet-based technologies have revolutionized sports in developed countries. They remarked that sports and physical education have become more interactive, and further educational material in the field of sports is available to the common public(Kondakov et al., 2019).

Oguamanam (2009) investigated the impact of digitalization in Western nations in terms of preserving cultural heritage. He asserted that cultural heritage was vulnerable to extinction to a large extent before the emergence of the Internet, particularly in case of indigenous and local cultures that did not have any room in mainstream media and movies. Nevertheless, countless websites and social media pages now are dedicated to reflect the ins and outs of such cultures to the common public(Oguamanam, 2009).

According to Gasmi and Prlja (2020), European countries are putting in pertinacious effort to regulate and direct the process of digitization of cultural heritage so as to accomplish the most optimal results in this area. The European Union (EU) has called the digitization of cultural heritage a crucial tool of ensuring greater access(Gasmi & PRLJA, 2020). Gasmi et al. (2019) added that in certain cases, digitalization is the sheer means to provide for the availability of valuable material to future generations(Gasmi et al., 2019).

Nikolaevich et al. (2020) proposed that information technology has enhanced the accumulation of the new knowledge in a wide array of fields in developed nations, and this opened up room for new opportunities at all management levels (state, region, local level). Hence, the management culture has been revolutionized in the Western world as well. In the juncture of digital transformation and economic/social changes, however, there is always need for the permanent search of more effective methods of management in order to achieve positive results(Nikolaevich, 2020).

*Table 1. The impact of digitalization in developed nations*

| Authors/Years | The Subject Under Review |
|---|---|
| Viktorovna et al. (2021) | Social processes and social institutions |
| Gumenyuk et al. (2021) | National economy, social progress and industrial development |
| Nikolaevich et al. (2020) | Enhancing the accumulation of the new knowledge |
| Vujadinović and Jaksic-Stojanovic (2022) | Impacting of digitalization on tourism |
| Kondakov et al. (2019) | Internet-based technologies have revolutionized sports in developed countries |
| Oguamanam (2009) | Preserving cultural heritage. |

## CASE OF DEVELOPING NATIONS

The second research question of the present study dealt with the socio-cultural impacts of the digital transformation in developing nations. Wandaogoa (2022) reported a study that was conducted in 138 countries between 2006 and 2016. The study focused on exploring the application of information and communication technologies by governments, and encompassed both developing and developed countries. He reported that the effectiveness of ICT utilization was more colorfully observed in developed than in developing countries. Through several tests – including reverse causality, dynamic effect, sensitivity analysis, heterogeneities, and alternative measurements – the study highlighted that governments could fully benefit from digitalization by adopting policies that promote access to and use of ICT at all levels of the economy, that is, the government itself, businesses, and individuals. Although these benefits were not as great in developing countries as in developed ones, still, forwarding nations received valuable contributions in their government management and business structures from IT-based services.

In case of education, Sokolovskaya (2020) stated that digital technologies made valuable contributions to this area in developing countries. These innovations made distance learning, and that in high quality, available to students in rural and distant areas; and as well, it greatly assisted the education systems to keep school and university classes up and running in the course of the COVID-19 pandemic(Sokolovskaya, 2020). However, Sokolovskaya (2020) asserted that virtual education gave rise to a number of problems, both organizational and psychological because both educators and learners in these regions were not fully prepared for such radical changes. These issues came about in both teaching methodology and the methods of obtaining knowledge. For these issues to be resolved, effort is required on the side of all men of science involved, including philosophers, sociologists, cultural scientists, and psychologists. Along with that, theoretical justifications and empirical studies are required to cater to the psychological adaptability of young people learning in new conditions.

Yatsenko and Starovoytova (2020) pointed out the erosion of the value system of certain developing-nation cultural communities in the face of digital age as one of its demerits. Some demographic groups in these countries, they added, are vulnerable against valuable changes, and these rise as a result of the contradictory nature of the digitalization of social management. The confrontation between artificial intelligence and national culture is a real challenge in the context of nations which have not reached the developed stage yet. Yatsenko and Starovoytova (2020) added that preserving national culture and cultural values in the face of globalization that digitalization brings is yet another challenge that authorities and cultural policy makers need to address in these countries(Yatsenko & Starovoytova, 2020).

Lypak et al. (2020) delved into the digitalization and tourism in developing nations. They referred to the fact that many museums in third world countries are delivering their exhibits online, and this has been a rich source of attracting tourists for economically depressed regions. The reason is fairly obvious: They have managed to utilized online platforms as a means of spreading their historical and cultural heritage to the masses of people who were unfamiliar with them, in the hope that familiarity draws them to their touristy spots. A hope that yielded prosperously(Lypak et al., 2020).

Through a totally different vantage point, Vlasov et al. (2022) put forward the insights of the prominent German philosopher and cultural critic F. G. Junger, who proposed that machines had caused fear in people since ancient times and why the use of machines transforms society. They generalize and extend Junger's view to digitalization and remarked that the dominance of digitalization in developing is a threat to their self–determination in this world, resulting in the loss of the identity and culture of people(Vlasov et al., 2022).

Lodhi and Mikulecky (2010) placed the issue of indigenous knowledge on the table. Indigenous knowledge is a practical concept, which could be employed to smoothen the grounds for communication among people with different backgrounds such as researchers, development practitioners and beneficiaries. This type of knowledge, according to Lodhi and Mikulecky (2010) is commonly shared among local communities and transferred from one generation to the next. Up until the late 20th century, indigenous knowledge used to be transferred chest to chest through traditional means such as oral traditions and storytelling. Nevertheless, in developing nations, technology, in its minimalistic ways, has added value to the traditional systems and has made them more resilient. ICT has more than well managed to preserve indigenous knowledge and placed it at the disposal of a larger range and number of audiences(Lodhi & Mikulecky, 2010).

The main contribution of digital technologies to the preservation and broadcasting of indigenous knowledge in developing countries has been to "capture, store and disseminate IK so that traditional knowledge is preserved for the future generation; promote cost-effective dissemination of IK; create easily accessible IK information systems; promote integration of IK into formal and non-formal training and education; and provide a platform for advocating improving and gets benefits from IK systems to the poor" (Lodhi & Mikulecky, 2010, p. 96).

*Table 2. The impact of digitalization in developing countries*

| Authors/Years | Conclusions |
|---|---|
| (Yatsenko & Starovoytova, 2020). | Preserving national culture and cultural values in the face of globalization that digitalization brings is another challenge. |
| Sokolovskaya (2020) | Making valuable contributions like distance learning available to students in rural and distant areas; |
| Lypak et al., (2020) | Attracting tourists by utilizing online platforms as a means of spreading their historical and cultural heritage to the masses of people |
| Vlasov et al., (2022). | A threat to self–determination in developing countries, resulting in the loss of the identity and culture of people |
| Lodhi and Mikulecky (2010) | Preserving the traditional and indigenous knowledge for the future generation |
| Effah and Nuhu, (2017) | Need to align e-business to local contexts |

In the business view, Effah (2017) asserted that in developing countries, culture has always been a major barrier lying in the way of digital economy and ecommerce. He reported various studies conducted in African developing nations, and their results highlighted that although businesses are turning online and services are being sold over the Internet in these countries, the pace at which this shift is happened tends to be rather slow. The reason is that people still have not fully invested their trust in online businesses, and still, traditional means of reaching out to customers and clients seems to have the main value there. He believed that online businesses have a long way to succeed and prosper in these countries, and they need to seek ways to align e-business to local contexts(Effah & Nuhu, 2017).

## CASE OF MIDDLE-EAST-NORTH-AFRICA-PAKISTAN-AFGHANISTAN

The third research question of this study explored the socio-cultural impacts of the digital transformation in Middle-East-North-Africa-Pakistan-Afghanistan nations. According to Yurjevna (2018), digital media have promoted the development of culture and intercultural communication all throughout the globe, and they are responsible for the drastic transformation of cultural values in every corner of our home planet. In his view point, in the third millennium, countries could be divided into three categories of first, second, third world based on the level at which information technologies are accessible and widely used(Yuryevna, 2022). Developed countries, also knowns as first world nations, are the ones where these technologies are available and accessible to just any one, and ample Internet-based infrastructures (Hamrouni et al., 2021) have already been provided. Second world countries are the ones in which these technologies are insufficient and limited by an economic structure, meaning that the richer and the more privileged a strata are, the wider access they have to these technologies. Third world nations, however, are the ones that practically do not use information technologies and the ones where digital amenities and services are accessible to a narrow layer of privileged people(Ali, 2022).

It is conspicuously evident that in the majority of Middle Eastern nations – such as Pakistan, Afghanistan, Iran, Iraq, and some Arabic nations with the exception of Emirates – digital services have not become a trend yet, and the implementation of such innovative business means have a long way to go. As Yurjevna (2018) stated, the major underlying reason for backwardness in this area in Middle Eastern countries is the closed and highly confined governing system in these countries. Due to different layers of limitation of liberty as well as the poor sense of welcoming the new on the side of government decision-makers, optimally free introduction of new technologies to the society cannot be ensured(Yuryevna, 2022).

Even with the limited delivery of digitalization in MENAPA nations, the cultural impacts of IT-based technologies in this region have been noticeable. According to Olkhovikov et al. (2021), digital transformation has conferred tolerance of diversity in terms of religion, race, and faith, and the like. People have started to appreciate diversity in such areas more welcomingly that the days before the digital media. It has also brought comfort, convenience, and security(Olkhovikov et al., 2021).

Ghali et al. (2022) explored the impact of culture on digital innovation within the framework of workplace in the context of Middle Eastern and North African culture features(Ghali-Zinoubi, 2022). They discovered that Middle Eastern culture exerted an immense impact on how the employees adapt to the changes within the workplace. In another facet, Ezema and Igbo(2016) discussed the impacts of digital revolution on the libraries and reading culture in Africa(Ezema & Igbo, 2016). He outlined that African countries stand in a highly disadvantaged position both in terms of globalization and digitalization. Although librarians and information professionals have tried to bridge the gap between their traditional means of storing information and the modern digital ways, there is still a lot that needs to be done in the field of digitalization of local contents, re-tooling, re-training, promoting African languages, and indexing local contents(Ezema, 2016).

Ridge and Birchall (2015) delved into the matter of cultural heritage in Middle East and Africa, and proposed that even though the technology-hungry young generation of these countries never miss out on their cultural heritages as they have all been stored online, they may not have high degrees of appreciation for them. In other words, since youngsters in MENA countries are deeply engaged with social media and other types of online entertainment such as gaming, they fall short of staging any deep-seated interest or keen enthusiasm about their own traditions, getting to know them, practice them, and enjoy them. Cultural heritages of MENA are widely accessible to a generation that does not care to experience them(Ridge & Birchall, 2015).

A vivid example of this is the highly ambitious Aderet project launched by the Israel government in April 2016, whereby they digitized all of their holdings (potentially 400 million pages of material) and it is now available online (Correa, 2017). Another example of such cultural heritage preservation program in this region is a massive project called(Correa-Baena et al., 2017). The Endangered Archaeology (Sunkar et al., 2022) in the Middle East and North Africa (EAMENA), where remote sensing was utilized to record archaeological and cultural heritage landscapes across twenty countries, from Morocco to Iran and from Syria to Yemen(Zerbini, 2018).

In another note, social sustainability, as one of the key elements of sustainable development, is always in the center of attention by chief executives and policy makers. Social sustainability and business ethics in any enterprise are inevitably affected by social and behavioral interactions of individuals. In the context of the Middle East, Ronaghi and Mosakhani (2022) discovered that the use of block chain technology has a direct impact on business ethics, corporate governance, and social sustainability. The reasons, they suggested, were the creation of a decentralized system as well as information transparency and traceability(Ronaghi & Mosakhani, 2022). Hence, digitalization, and one of the soldiers which it serves (blockchain technology and digital currencies) have promoted culture and ethics in business in the MENA nations.

*Table 3. The impact of digitalization in Middle East-North-Africa-Pakistan Afghanistan*

| Authors/Years | Conclusion |
|---|---|
| Olkhovikov et al., (2021) | Conferring tolerance of diversity in terms of religion, race, and faith, and the like. Bringing comfort, convenience, and security. |
| Ronaghi and Mosakhani (2022) | Direct impact on business ethics, corporate governance, and social sustainability. |
| Ridge and Birchall (2015) | Being deeply engaged with social media and other types of online entertainment , youngsters in MENA countries fall short of staging any deep-seated interest or keen enthusiasm about their own traditions |

## SUMMARY OF THE FINDINGS AND CONCLUSION

Digital transformation, which has always been important as a basic and strategic measure in countries, has become more important in recent years following the spread of the Corona virus, and the pressures caused by the Corona virus pandemic have accelerated the efforts of organizations to create digital transformation. Considering the current situation and being in the Corona situation, some experts believe that not only the increase in productivity, but also the survival of organizations and governments depends on being entrusted with digital transformation. The effect of digital increase during the covid-19 epidemic is evident, because the use of digital technologies has increased due to the emergence of social distancing norms around the world. People all over the world have been forced to adapt to new ways of work and life and have been forced to work from home. In the digital era, due to the emergence of new technologies, the traditional beliefs of business have fundamentally changed (Tolboom, 2016). Organizations have only one way forward and that is to keep pace with existing changes, otherwise they will be removed from the competition. Transformational technologies have marked the digital transformation of business, and digital transformation has entered business literature as a concept. Due to the fact that the corona situation has brought an unprecedented crisis to the world, which is undergoing a digital transformation, millions of people started working remotely to prevent the spread of the disease and maintain business continuity, and the development of virtual human resources and alternative work strategies helped organizations. to adapt themselves to the current challenges and prepare to solve the disruption in the future. Therefore, one should seek to analyze the role of human resources development in the crisis and transition to a new era, so that in case of disruption and change, one can always help their organizations not only to survive this crisis, but also in a new era of work that is created by Technology changes, advances and increases performance (Bennett & McWhorter, 2021).

Digitalization is not only a matter of technology, but affects all employees and organizations (Aldieri et al.,). Therefore, every digital action needs coordination and alignment between technology, process and employees. Digital transformation has put a lot of pressure on organizations. What is certain is that digital transformation is a fundamental change and like any other organizational change, it must be managed very carefully (Nadeem et al., 2018). Digital culture can be considered as a tool through which an organization can plan for digital strategies in an environment to Start changing speed. Therefore, the existing organizational culture should encourage the employees of the organizations to challenge the accepted values and norms, as the first step of digitalization (Buvat et al., 2018). A huge amount of digital data available to companies can be a new source for creating value in organizations. As a result, this is a mechanism through which companies can use digital technologies to increase performance (Martinez-Caro et al., 2020). Having a digital culture that leads employees and teams in companies (Tunio et al., 2021) to share and create knowledge. It is necessary (Namaki & Aghasi, 2022). The willingness of employees to use and share knowledge to generate new and valuable ideas or to do work in an innovative and appropriate way enables the organization to use digital technologies (Dubey et al., 2019). A digital culture can cause behavioral stimulation. among the members of the organization to lead them to accept digital technologies as a source of value for the organization and strengthen the commitment towards them (Namaki & Aghasi, 2022). So, digitalization has had extensive impacts on all three classes of nations (Erum et al., 2022). In developed nations, where the Internet and its services enjoyed the highest internalization rate and have managed to improve swiftly owing to a liberal socio-political atmosphere, they transformed cultural values and created a whole new category of norms and values. They established digital culture from scratch. Communication and interactions were enhanced both in terms of quality and quantity thanks to social media. Digitalization altered the quality of relationships in different levels of families, circles of friends, communities, nations, peoples, and estates with diverse socioeconomic statuses. It also boosted social progress and cultural diplomacy. And last but not least, they triggered social innovation and contributed to the preservation of the culture.

In case of developing nations, the application of smart technologies in government was not as common and extensive as in developed nations. Digitalization has made education available to students in rural and remote areas at good quality. Tourism has managed to boom thanks to earning top recognition digital media brought about it. Indigenous knowledge now could be preserved and delivered to a broader array of individuals. However, the erosion of value systems in cultural communities, threats to self–determination, and lack of people's trust in online businesses (Tunio et al., 2021) are the challenges with digitalization in developed nations.

In the case of Middle-East-North-Africa-Pakistan-Afghanistan nations, the closed and limited sociopolitical environment has not allowed ample room for the improvement of digitalization and online services provision; nevertheless, digital transformation has conferred tolerance of diversity in terms of religion, race, faith, and the like in this region. Libraries and reading culture have been improved in Africa whereas a lot is yet to be done. Cultural heritages of MENA are widely accessible to their young generation while they tend not care to experience them. And social sustainability and business ethics have been fostered by the decentralization, information transparency and traceability that blockchain technology has brought about.

## PRACTICAL IMPLICATIONS

The findings of the present study could prove themselves useful to a wide array of researchers and practitioners in the realm of sociocultural research and practice. Hartl(2019) asserted that managing cultural change is crucial for the success of digital transformation, and Osmundsen and Iden(2018) added that research in the field of digital transformation lacks focus on change management. Given that the results of this study paint a picture of social and cultural changes in the new digital age, they could provide cultural decision makers with some perspective and assist them greatly in making management-related decisions(Hartl, 2019; Osmundsen et al., 2018).

The results of this study also confer implication to sociology researchers and anthropologists, whose main area of research and expertise lies in understanding human behaviors, what affects them, and how they are subject to change and transformation. Taking digitalization as a major change factor, the present study delineated alterations in the field of culture in various nation states.

Artists and men of pen and vision – such as journalists and movie critics – could also find the findings of the present study helpful, since it drops a number of hints as to how art and culture are presented, delivered, perceived and expected differently in the new digital age. IT men account for another group of stake holders of this study as the findings presented here could broaden their understanding as to how the products they produce and the systems they design could affect the new generation culture-wise.

## SUGGESTIONS FOR FURTHER RESEARCH

The present study managed to supply responses to various research questions investigating how the advent of digital transformation revolutionized cultural and sociocultural components in developed, developing, and MENAPA societies. However, in the light of the delimitations that the researcher had set as well as the limitations that the study suffered from, there remain several key points that could be placed in the spotlight and provide food for further academic pursuits. The classification of the nations in this study was set to be rather broad: Developed, developing, and MENAPA. Yet, further academic studies can break down each of these categories into more isolated classifications of nations, and delve into the sociocultural impacts of digital transformation on their zeitgeist. As a case in point, developed nations could be split into North America (i.e. The United States and Canada), European Union countries, the United Kingdom, Japan, and Australia. Developing countries could also be subcategorized into South East Asian nations (e.g. South Korea, Taiwan, and Malaysia), Eastern Europe nations (e.g. Romania, Bulgaria, and Belarus), and African ones (e.g. South Africa, Tunisia, and Morocco). Additionally, the current study merely placed the sociocultural impacts of digitalization on sociocultural elements of nations. Nevertheless, there is plenty of room left for probing other diverse societal elements and how they were influenced by the IT revolution. Economy, politics, business (Arabeche et al., 2022), education, transportation, entertainment, recreation, security, and media could be instances of such elements.

In current study the researcher deemed digitalization as a single unit, and analyzed its impacts on culture in the general sense. In further research, digitalization could be broken down into more isolated components, and the impact of each component could be scrutinized independently. Examples of such components could be smartphones, tablets, the Internet, social media, instant messengers, various Android and IOS applications, Windows- and MAC-based software packages, mobile and Internet banking, data processors, and the like. Further, this study delineated the impacts that digitalization has exerted on society and culture. It focused, hence, on the past and present, and it does not make any reference to the future. Further studies could target making estimations and prognostications as to what the future may hold in this field, and work out to what extent and in what ways could upcoming digital developments contribute to and revolutionize sociocultural components of societies.

## REFERENCES

Ali, M. S. B. (2022). *Digitalization and Economic Development: Insights from Developing Countries.* Taylor & Francis.

Aldieri, L., Brahmi, M., Bruno, B., & Vinci, C. P. (2021). Circular Economy Business Models: The Complementarities with Sharing Economy and Eco-Innovations Investments. *Sustainability, 13*(22), 12438. doi:10.3390u132212438

Andal-Ancion, A., Cartwright, P. A., & Yip, G. S. (2003). The digital transformation of traditional business. *MIT Sloan Management Review, 44*(4), 34.

Arabeche, Z., Soudani, A., Brahmi, M., Aldieri, L., Vinci, C. P., & Abdelli, M. E. A. (2022). Entrepreneurial Orientation, Organizational Culture and Business Performance in SMEs: Evidence from Emerging Economy. *Sustainability, 14*(9), 5160. doi:10.3390u14095160

Bennett, E. E., & McWhorter, R. R. (2021). Virtual HRD's role in crisis and the post Covid-19 professional lifeworld: Accelerating skills for digital transformation. *Advances in Developing Human Resources, 23*(1), 5–25. doi:10.1177/1523422320973288

Berman, S. J. (2012). Digital transformation: Opportunities to create new business models. *Strategy and Leadership, 40*(2), 16–24. doi:10.1108/10878571211209314

Bloomberg, J. (2018). Digitization, digitalization, and digital transformation: confuse them at your peril. *Forbes.*

Buvat, J., Solis, B., Crummenerl, C., Aboud, C., Kar, K., El Aoufi, H., & Sengupta, A. (2017). The Digital Culture Challenge: Closing the Employee-Leadership Gap. *Capgemini.* https://www. capgemini. com/consulting/wpcontent/uploads/sites/30/2017/07/dti_digitalculture_report. pdf

Correa-Baena, J.-P., Saliba, M., Buonassisi, T., Grätzel, M., Abate, A., Tress, W., & Hagfeldt, A. (2017). Promises and challenges of perovskite solar cells. *Science*, *358*(6364), 739–744. doi:10.1126cience. aam6323 PMID:29123060

Demlehner, Q., & Laumer, S. (2019). *Setting the hook–The digital transformation from a manufacturing point of view and what it really means.* Research Gate.

Dubey, R., Gunasekaran, A., Childe, S. J., Papadopoulos, T., Hazen, B., Giannakis, M., & Roubaud, D. (2017). Examining the effect of external pressures and organizational culture on shaping performance measurement systems (PMS) for sustainability benchmarking: Some empirical findings. *International Journal of Production Economics*, *193*, 63–76. doi:10.1016/j.ijpe.2017.06.029

Effah, J., & Nuhu, H. (2017). Institutional barriers to digitalization of government budgeting in developing countries: A case study of Ghana. *The Electronic Journal on Information Systems in Developing Countries*, *82*(1), 1–17. doi:10.1002/j.1681-4835.2017.tb00605.x

Erum, S.; Muhammad, N T.; Wali Muhammad, K.; Mohsen, B.; & Shahid, R., Chapter 16: The COVID-19 Pandemic Overlaps Entrepreneurial Activities and Triggered New Challenges: A Review Study, Book chapter: Managing Human Resources in SMEs and Start-ups, August 2022, 388 p. https://doi.org/ doi:10.1142/9789811239212_0008

Ezema, I. J. (2016). Globalistation, information revolution and cultural imperialism in africa: Implications for nigerian library and information professionals. *Middle East*, *439*(90), 4.

Ezema, I. J., & Igbo, H. U. (2016). Electronic theses and dissertations and the promotion of scholarship in African universities: Prospects and challenges. *The International Information & Library Review*, *48*(1), 21–30. doi:10.1080/10572317.2016.1146038

FEIGE, D. M. (2019). The Culture of Digitalization and the Digitalization of Culture. *Contemporary Research Topics In Arts Education*, *53*.

Feola, G. (2015). Societal transformation in response to global environmental change: A review of emerging concepts. *Ambio*, *44*(5), 376–390. doi:10.100713280-014-0582-z PMID:25431335

Fleischmann, A., Oppl, S., Schmidt, W., & Stary, C. (2020). *Contextual process digitalization: changing perspectives–design thinking–value-led design.* Springer Nature. doi:10.1007/978-3-030-38300-8

Gasmi, G., & Prlja, D. (2020). Perspectives of digitization of cultural heritage in european countries. *Fiat Iustitia,* (1).

Gasmi, G., Korać, V., & Prlja, S. (2019). Evropski propisi i digitalizacija kulturne i naučne baštine.

Gegenhuber, B., & Tollkuhn, J. (2020). Signatures of sex: Sex differences in gene expression in the vertebrate brain. *Wiley Interdisciplinary Reviews. Developmental Biology, 9*(1), e348. doi:10.1002/wdev.348 PMID:31106965

Gerards, R., van Wetten, S., & van Sambeek, C. (2021). New ways of working and intrapreneurial behaviour: The mediating role of transformational leadership and social interaction. *Review of Managerial Science, 15*(7), 2075–2110. doi:10.100711846-020-00412-1

Ghali-Zinoubi, Z. (2022). Examining Drivers of Environmentally Conscious Consumer Behavior: Theory of Planned Behavior Extended with Cultural Factors. *Sustainability, 14*(13), 8072. doi:10.3390u14138072

Goran, J., LaBerge, L., & Srinivasan, R. (2017). Culture for a digital age. *The McKinsey Quarterly, 3*(1), 56–67.

Gumenyuk, L. (2021). Cyber insurance: Modern requirements. *Economics & Education, 6*(4), 33–36. doi:10.30525/2500-946X/2021-4-5

Gumenyuk, T., Frotveit, M., Bondar, I., Horban, Y., & Karakoz, O. (2021). Cultural diplomacy in modern international relations: The influence of digitalization. *Journal of Theoretical and Applied Information Technology, 99*(7), 1549–1560.

Gurbaxani, V., & Dunkle, D. (2019). Gearing up for successful digital transformation. *MIS Quarterly Executive, 18*(3), 209–220. doi:10.17705/2msqe.00017

Hadžić, F. (2020). The influence of social media on threats to identity, stability and national security; institutional inefficiency and vulnerability of B&H. *Scholarly Journal for Protection, Security, Defense, Education and Training Issues, 24*(45-46), 67.

Hamrouni, B., Bourouis, A., Korichi, A., & Brahmi, M. (2021). Explainable Ontology-Based Intelligent Decision Support System for Business Model Design and Sustainability. *Sustainability, 13*(17), 9819. doi:10.3390u13179819

Hartl, E. (2019). A Characterization of Culture Change in the Context of Digital Transformation. AMCIS.

Hausberg, J. P., Liere-Netheler, K., Packmohr, S., Pakura, S., & Vogelsang, K. (2019). Research streams on digital transformation from a holistic business perspective: A systematic literature review and citation network analysis. *Journal of Business Economics, 89*(8), 931–963.

Hegmon, M., & Peeples, M. A. (2018). The human experience of social transformation: Insights from comparative archaeology. *PLoS One, 13*(11), e0208060. doi:10.1371/journal.pone.0208060 PMID:30496250

Henriette, E., Feki, M., & Boughzala, I. (2015). The shape of digital transformation: A systematic literature review. *AISEL.*

Kassim, H., Connolly, S., Dehousse, R., Rozenberg, O., & Bendjaballah, S. (2017). Managing the house: The presidency, agenda control and policy activism in the European Commission. *Journal of European Public Policy, 24*(5), 653–674. doi:10.1080/13501763.2016.1154590

Kondakov, V. L., Kopeikina, E. N., Voloshina, I. G., & Usatov, A. N. (2019). *Main directions digitalization in the higher education in the world and Russia (based on the example of physical culture and sports).* HR Pub.

Korhonen, J. J., & Halén, M. (2017). Enterprise architecture for digital transformation. *2017 IEEE 19th Conference on Business Informatics (CBI).* IEEE.

Legner, C., Eymann, T., Hess, T., Matt, C., Böhmann, T., Drews, P., Mädche, A., Urbach, N., & Ahlemann, F. (2017). Digitalization: Opportunity and challenge for the business and information systems engineering community. *Business & Information Systems Engineering, 59*(4), 301–308. doi:10.100712599-017-0484-2

Lodhi, S., & Mikulecky, P. (2010). Management of indigenous knowledge for developing countries. *Communication and management in technological innovation and academic globalization, 5.*

Lypak, H., Kunanets, N., Pasichnyk, V., & Veretennikova, N. (2020). Digitized Historical and Cultural Heritage Consolidation Technologies: From a Territorial Resource to a National Portal. *2020 10th International Conference on Advanced Computer Information Technologies.* IEEE.

Mahmoudi, A., Sadeghi, M., & Deng, X. (2022). Performance measurement of construction suppliers under localization, agility, and digitalization criteria: Fuzzy Ordinal Priority Approach. *Environment, Development and Sustainability*, 1–26. doi:10.100710668-022-02301-x PMID:35431618

Mahraz, M.-I., Benabbou, L., & Berrado, A. (2019). A Systematic literature review of Digital Transformation. *International Conference on Industrial Engineering and Operations Management. Anais.* IEOM Society International

Mamychev, A., Kazachanskaya, E., & Garashko, A. (2021). Value and Regulatory Foundations for Digital Transformation of Modern Social Relations: Theological and Conservative Legal Aspects. *Wisdom, 1*(1).

Martínez-Caro, E., Cegarra-Navarro, J. G., & Alfonso-Ruiz, F. J. (2020). Digital technologies and firm performance: The role of digital organisational culture. *Technological Forecasting and Social Change, 154*, 119962. doi:10.1016/j.techfore.2020.119962

Maseno, M., & Wanyoike, C. (2022). Social entrepreneurship as mechanisms for social transformation and social impact in East Africa an exploratory case study perspective. *Journal of Social Entrepreneurship, 13*(1), 92–117. doi:10.1080/19420676.2020.1755348

Mergel, I., Bretschneider, S. I., Louis, C., & Smith, J. (2014). *The challenges of Challenge. gov: Adopting private sector business innovations in the Federal Government.* 2014 47th Hawaii International Conference on System Sciences, Hawaii.

Mina, A. X. (2014). Batman, pandaman and the blind man: A case study in social change memes and Internet censorship in China. *Journal of Visual Culture, 13*(3), 359–375. doi:10.1177/1470412914546576

Nadeem, A., Abedin, B., Cerpa, N., & Chew, E. (2018). Digital transformation & digital business strategy in electronic commerce-the role of organizational capabilities. *Journal of Theoretical and Applied Electronic Commerce Research, 13*(2), 1–8. doi:10.4067/S0718-18762018000200101

Nadkarni, S., & Prügl, R. (2021). Digital transformation: A review, synthesis and opportunities for future research. *Management Review Quarterly, 71*(2), 233–341. doi:10.100711301-020-00185-7

Namaki, Z., & Aghasi, S. (2022)... *Presenting and Explaining the Organizational Performance Model Based on the Digital Status of the Organization in the Corona Eera with the Foundation Data Approach in the Ministry of Samt.*, *102*(30), 147–175.

Nikolaevich, L. S. (2020). Analysis of the development of the main directions of digitalization of the Russian economy. *Политематический сетевой электронный научный журнал Кубанского государственного аграрного университета [Polythematic network electronic scientific journal of the Kuban State Agrarian University],* (161), 309-324.

O'Brien, K. (2012). Global environmental change II: From adaptation to deliberate transformation. *Progress in Human Geography*, *36*(5), 667–676. doi:10.1177/0309132511425767

Oguamanam, C. (2009). Documentation and digitization of traditional knowledge and intangible cultural knowledge: Challenges and prospects. Intangible Cultural Heritage and Intellectual Property: Cultural Diversity and Sustainable Development. Intersentia.

Olkhovikov, K., Korobeynikov, A., Zarubina, E., Zhuravleva, L., & Ruchkin, A. (2021). Digitalizating rural areas: a traditional context. *IOP Conference Series: Earth and Environmental Science*

Osmundsen, K., Iden, J., & Bygstad, B. (2018). Digital Transformation: Drivers, Success Factors, and Implications. MCIS, Perez, C. (2010). Technological revolutions and techno-economic paradigms. *Cambridge Journal of Economics*, *34*(1), 185–202.

Porter, M. E., & Heppelmann, J. E. (2015). How smart, connected products are transforming companies. *Harvard Business Review*, *93*(10), 96–114.

Rabie, M. (2013). *Global economic and cultural transformation: The making of history*. Springer. doi:10.1057/9781137365330

Ridge, M., & Birchall, D. (2015). How digital tech can bridge gaps between museums and audiences. *Cultural Professional Network Article, the Guardian Online, Published on, 23.*

Roedder, N., Dauer, D., Laubis, K., Karaenke, P., & Weinhardt, C. (2016). The digital transformation and smart data analytics: An overview of enabling developments and application areas. *2016 IEEE International Conference on Big Data (Big Data).* IEEE.

Rogers, D. L. (2016). *The digital transformation playbook: Rethink your business for the digital age.* Columbia University Press. doi:10.7312/roge17544

Ronaghi, M. H., & Mosakhani, M. (2022). The effects of blockchain technology adoption on business ethics and social sustainability: Evidence from the Middle East. *Environment, Development and Sustainability*, *24*(5), 6834–6859. doi:10.100710668-021-01729-x PMID:34393620

Roper, S. D., & Chaudhari, N. (2017). Taste buds: Cells, signals and synapses. *Nature Reviews. Neuroscience*, *18*(8), 485–497. doi:10.1038/nrn.2017.68 PMID:28655883

Sadowski, B. (2022). Book review: A Modern Guide to the Digitalization of Infrastructure. *Digital Policy, Regulation and Governance.*

Saiko, D., Medvedkova, I., Kovaleva, E., Lemeshkin, A., Chernyaeva, S., & Matytsina, I. (2020). Educational and Cultural Aspects of Digitalization of Economy. *Russian Conference on Digital Economy and Knowledge Management (RuDEcK 2020).* Atlantic Press. 10.2991/aebmr.k.200730.061

Schuerkens, U. (2004). Global forces and local life-worlds: Social transformations. *Sage (Atlanta, Ga.).* doi:10.4135/9781446211328

Shaikh, E., Brahmi, M., Thang, P. C., Watto, W. A., Trang, T. T. N., & Loan, N. T. (2022). Should I Stay or Should I Go? Explaining the Turnover Intentions with Corporate Social Responsibility (CSR), Organizational Identification and Organizational Commitment. *Sustainability, 14*(10), 6030. doi:10.3390u14106030

Sokolova, O. (2021). Legal Regulation Of Toponyms In Cultural Landscape Of A Belarusian City. *Весці БДПУ. Серыя, 2*(4), 96–100.

Sokolovskaya, I. (2020). Socio-psychological factors of students' satisfaction in the context of digitalization of education during the COVID-19 pandemic and self-isolation. *Digital sociology, 3*(2), 46-54.

Sunkar, A., Lakspriyanti, A. P., Haryono, E., Brahmi, M., Setiawan, P., & Jaya, A. F. (2022). Geotourism Hazards and Carrying Capacity in Geosites of Sangkulirang-Mangkalihat Karst, Indonesia. *Sustainability, 14*(3), 1704. doi:10.3390u14031704

Teece, D. J. (2018). Profiting from innovation in the digital economy: Enabling technologies, standards, and licensing models in the wireless world. *Research Policy, 47*(8), 1367–1387. doi:10.1016/j.respol.2017.01.015

Todd, J. (2005). Social transformation, collective categories, and identity change. *Theory and Society, 34*(4), 429–463. doi:10.100711186-005-7963-z

Tolboom, I. H. (2016). The impact of digital transformation, Forcasting and social Journal, 101 (4), 875-895.

Tunio, M. N., Jariko, M. A., Børsen, T., Shaikh, S., Mushtaque, T., & Brahmi, M. (2021). How Entrepreneurship Sustains Barriers in the Entrepreneurial Process—A Lesson from a Developing Nation. *Sustainability, 13*(20), 11419. https://doi.org/10.3390/su132011419

Tunio, M. N., Chaudhry, I. S., Shaikh, S., Jariko, M. A., & Brahmi, M. (2021). Determinants of the Sustainable Entrepreneurial Engagement of Youth in Developing Country—An Empirical Evidence from Pakistan. *Sustainability, 13*(14), 7764. doi:10.3390u13147764

Viktorovna, K. O., Flyurovna, A., Anasovna, F., & Yuryevna, E. (2021). Priority directions for the development of the agrarian economy in the context of the digitalization of the agro-industrial complex. *BIO Web of Conferences.*

Vlasov, M., Buchinskaia, O., & Sukhikh, V. (2022). Intercountry differences in apprehension of the digitalization. *SHS Web of Conferences.* SHS. 10.1051hsconf/202214101006

Vujadinović, N., & Jaksic-Stojanovic, A. (2022). Digitalization and Implementation of Modern ICT in Tourism and Creative Industries on the Example of the Cultural Routes. *International Conference "New Technologies, Development and Applications."* Springer. 10.1007/978-3-031-05230-9_67

Wismar, M. (2021). 2. K. Round table: Everything you always wanted to know about (COVID-19 and) EU-health policy. *European Journal of Public Health*, 31.

Yatsenko, O. Y., & Starovoytova, I. E. (2020). *Digitization and problems of national culture. 13th International Scientific and Practical Conference-Artificial Intelligence Anthropogenic nature Vs.* Social Origin.

Yuryevna, K. T. (2022). The model of labor potential economic assessment at the regional level: Reproduction-factor approach. *AIP Conference Proceedings*, 070017. doi:10.1063/5.0074674

Zerbini, A. (2018). Developing a heritage database for the Middle East and North Africa. *Journal of Field Archaeology, 43*(sup1), S9-S18.

# Chapter 7
# Business Model Data Tools and Artificial intelligence (AI): Current State and Future Challenges

**Basma Hamrouni**
*Kasdi Merbah Ouargla University, Algeria*

**Abdelhabib Bourouis**
*University of Oum El Bouaghi, Algeria*

**Ahmed Korichi**
*Kasdi Merbah Ouargla University, Algeria*

**Brahmi Mohsen**
https://orcid.org/0000-0002-0995-0761
*University of Sfax, Tunisia*

## ABSTRACT

*An important axis of the contribution of business models is building a base for computer-assisted management tools. Management scholars are important actors that generate models and concepts. Nevertheless, these concepts are rarely translated into software-based tools, which could deliver huge value to management. However, the highly creative task of business model innovation is not effectively supported by these studied tools. Also, trust is not offered by these AI-based DSS systems to allow extremely accurate decisional guidance. To address these issues, the authors combine findings with studying 18 software tools from research and practice from scholars on software tools for business model design to address these problems. First, the authors provide a comprehensive taxonomy that identifies five novel categories of software-based business model development tools. Second, they provide a new generation of tools using the AI for Business Model that can give explanations in order to increase trust in suggested solutions. The performance results provided demonstrate the advantages of the suggested method.*

DOI: 10.4018/978-1-6684-6766-4.ch007

## INTRODUCTION

The business model framework is the basis for the decision-making process (Hamrouni et al., 2021). It is considered by entrepreneurship as a cognitive device. The integration and organization of strategic objectives are done by this cognitive device to remain profitable in the long run and benefit from the business opportunities (Baden-Fuller &Morgan, 2010; Chesbrough &Rosenbloom, 2002; Hacklin & Wallnöfer, 2012). Due to the fast transformation in the business environment, companies are required to assess their Business Model (BM) in order to stay competitive (Henry Chesbrough, 2006), since the BM is essential to the success of any organization (Magretta, 2002). It offers a solid framework for comprehending, analyzing, communicating, and managing strategic decisions (Al-Debei &Avison, 2010; Osterwalder et al., 2005; Shafer et al., 2004). Business model research is a rapidly developing field that is still in itsearly stages and in need of a conceptual underpinning. The literature on BM originates in awide variety of study areas, including information systems (Gordijn & Akkermans, 2001), technology and innovation management (Chesbrough, 2007) and strategic management (Amit & Zott, 2001). The business model construct has the ability to add useful tools and theoretical insights to the strategy literature. Contrary to what adherents of the business model construct claim, we contend that the current business model literature has not yet completely tapped into the potential for theoretical contributions (Lanzolla et al., 2021).

However, several scholars have made contributions to the field of business model design (Bouwman et al., 2008; Gordijn & Akkermans, 2003), and innovation (Sinkovics et al., 2021; López-Nicolás et al., 2021). In the literature, there are many calls for additional tools to assist in the development and assessment of BM. As a result, computer-based tools were developed. Research in the Information Systems (IS) discipline and adjunct disciplines concluded the necessity of developing business model development tools (BMDT) (Spieth & Schneider, 2016), that contribute to the development of strategies and products. During the process of ideating, software-based tools allow the integration and documentation of information from various sources easily (Szopinskiet et al., 2017). According to academics, a software-based business model data tool (BMDT) is useful for designing and innovating business models, particularly when using AI techniques and machine learning (Ebel et al., 2016; Veit et al., 2014; Athanasopoulou & De Reuver, 2020). However, these AI-based DSS systems do not offer enough trust to allow extremely accurate decisional guidance. The majority of the business model innovation (BMI) tools documented in the academic literature are used to support design processes rather than for testing or implementation. The most of BMI tools are designed for and are most effective when used to experiment with the creation or redesign of a business model and integrate it into a value. chain and value network ecosystem, which has implications for managers according to (Munir et al., 2022). Athanasopoulou et al. (2020) has argued that the existent business model tools enable the building of a business model, but they typically do not support evaluating several business models and selecting the best one. He proposed that future business model tools should include functions that facilitate choosing amongst different business model options.

The potential of an intelligent system to produce an explanation that is meaningful for its decisions is a critical aspect in determining the system's acceptability (Dellermann et al., 2019). For that reason, systems must provide explanations to encourage end-users to trust, understand, and manage these systems effectively. Moreover, existing BM design tools (BMDTs) must place emphasis on assisting the users to be creative, which has been ignored from subsequent research. Incorporate functions for exploring business model patterns were argued by (Szopinskiet et al., 2017). In addition, the challenge inherent in designing innovative business models and the limits to creativity in the practices of BM related education are stated in (Snihuret al., 2018). The author argued that the idea is to create a virtuous learning loop that combines explanation and experience-based learning methodologies.

There is currently no demonstration for the usefulness of the different methods used in designing and implementing BMDTs. This study's objective is to make such research possible and to lay the foundation for evaluating the importance of various methods and techniques used in designing and implementing BMDTs in specific use contexts.

The purpose of this chapter is to classify these tools according to the method used in their design, and also we have exposed their responses to the requirements of user needs in the field of design and innovation of BM. Thus the purpose of this research is to prepare a solid foundation for further research to develop and implement future BMDTs. In addition, a new generation of advanced business model decision support systems is proposed in this chapter. They are capable of providing explanations for suggested solutions, hence increasing trust in them.

## BACKGROUND

### 1. Business Model Data Tool

An important axis of the contribution of business models is building a base for computerassisted management tools. Management scholars are important actors that generate models and concepts.

However, rarely are these concepts translated into software-based tools, which could deliver huge value to management. Several functions of the business model can be understood if digitized. In addition, software-based tools accomplish some operations much more quickly than manual methods like visualization, comparison, and design. These ontologies appear as efficient tools for describing, integrating, comparing, and classifying business models (Shaikh et al., 2022). However, these researched results do not adequately assist the extremely creative task of business model design tools that do not support the ideation phase. They admit that most of these approaches are fill-in-the-blank tools where information is added manually. In most cases, users need knowledge and information about how to fill in the different elements of the BM. Furthermore, current methods must focus on assisting users in being creative, which has been ignored in recent studies. The authors of (Szopinskiet et al., 2017) argued that functions for exploring business model patterns should be included. In addition, difficulties in prototyping new business models (Erum et al., 2022) and limits to creativity in the practices of BM-related education are stated in (Snihur et al., 2018). The author argued that the solution is to merge explanation and experience-based learning approaches into a virtuous learning cycle. Therefore, methods of creative task and ideation should also be included, and this is precisely one of the dissertation's goals. Research has handled the development of software tools that support BM, which is still interesting, especially by facilitating the visualization of a BM during the design phase (Veit et al., 2014). Nowadays, there is a call for more sophisticated tools that evolve into high-level decision support tools (Çınar, 2009).

BM tooling are defined as "the use of methods, frameworks or templates (here referred to as tools) to facilitate communication and collaboration regarding Business Model analysis, (re-)design, adop tion, implementation and exploitation" (Bouwman et al., 2020).

In addition, trust is not offered by these AI-based DSS systems to allow extremely accurate decisional guidance. Meanwhile, the capability of an intelligent system to provide a meaningful explanation of its actions is a crucial factor affecting the acceptance of the system (Majchrzak et al., 1991). For that reason, systems must provide explanations to allow end users to trust, understand, and effectively manage these systems. What we suggest that software based Business Model Data Tool BMDTs could provide important assistance for designing and innovating Business Models, specifically with employing Artificial Intelligence techniques to provide more guidance in the ideation, design and validation phase. Also to provide explanation allowing end users to trust the proposed solution.

For building a taxonomy of methods and techniques used for BMDTs, we draw on literature that is concerned with software support for business model development and literature from adjacent disciplines in which experience has been gained in designing software for BMDTs. Thereby, this study seeks to systemize and build upon existing research and promote more cumulative research for BMDTs that still new line of inquiry.

## 2. Case-Based Reasoning

Humans commonly solve problems using case-based reasoning. As a result, this approach is widely used in business, even when people are unaware that they are doing so. Researchers asserted that the approach of case-based reasoning, as incorporated in information systems, may be efficiently used in business (Bergmann, 2003). It is an appropriate experience management methodology for assisting those who must accomplish hard and knowledge-intensive activities. Case-based reasoning CBR mimics the way humans think, comprehend, and predict. It is based on the human cognitive model. The main goal of CBR systems is to save user experiences as cases in the knowledge base. When a new problem, we must search the knowledge base to find previous instances of comparable problems and their solutions. Hence, we can have an acceptable case as a reference. The case can be adjusted to match the problem at hand if the user is not satisfied with it. Finally, the user stores the revised case in the case base (Gordijn & Akkermans, 2003). The current problem and all cases that has been saved into the system are described with the Case representation.

*Figure 1. The CBR process (Aamodt & Plaza, 1994)*

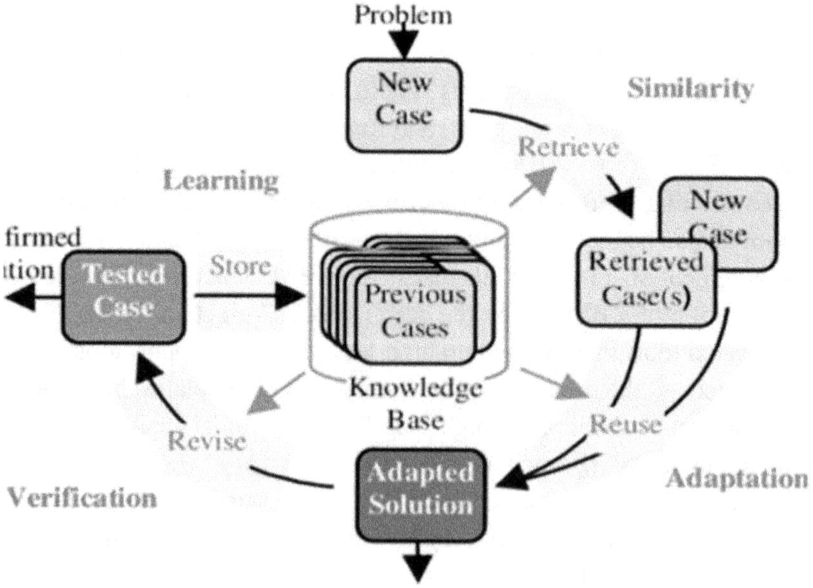

CBR problem-solving process is composed of a four-step, Case Retrieval, Case Adaptation, Case Revisingand Case Retainingas illustrated in Figure 1:

## 3. Explanation of System Decisions

Additionally, it is well-known that in everyday human-to-human interactions, transmitting information to understand one another is well done by explanations. Explanations increase the communication partners' understanding so that they may accept specific statements and allow people to make good choices. It's been known for a long time that to increase user trust about the decision of the intelligence system, he should comprehend system reasoning (Williamet al., 1984). CBR systems provide natural explanations. Unlike other techniques as neural networks, the outputs of CBR systems outputs are intuitively explained by describing the cases on which decisions are based and then comparing the solution to the prior cases to evaluate their applicability. Some CBR research saw the example as an adequate explanation; more current research is advancing a richer view (Sørmoet al., 2005). Elements affecting conclusions are examined, such as the contribution of similarity calculations fulfilling explanation (Massie et al., 2004).

# CLASSIFICATION OF BUSINESS MODEL DATA TOOLS

We propose a new classification of Business Model Data tools to five main new categories namely, Modeling languages, Digital Tools that represent and change business models, Business model patterns that stimulate analogical reasoning, Analytical Methods and DSS Based AI.

## 1. Modeling Languages

A number of scholars have proposed modeling languages, visual notation, and vocabulary as provided by these tools for capturing and presenting information on business models (e3value (Gordijn & Akkermans, 2003); the strategic business model ontology (Samavi & Topaloglou, 2009); The Business Model Canvas (Çınar, 2009). The visualization of all components of the business model is allowed with these modeling languages, and business model ideas are explicit and more appreciable. A business model simplifies activities such as communicating and understanding business logic (Samavi & Topaloglou, 2009). These languages are defined as a favored domain for the IS branch (Veit et al., 2014; Osterwalder & Pigneur, 2012), and have presented a frequent topic in recent IS business model research (Zott et al., 2011).

*The Business Model Canvas:* The Business Model Canvas has had the most impact on academic studies and practice and is regarded as the quasi-standard representation (Strategyzer, 2015, Spieth et al., 2014; Szopinski et al., 2020). The related book (Osterwalder & Pigneur, 2010), has sold about one million copies (Strategyzer, 2015; John et al., 2017).

The most complete framework, having the highest number of components, is the Business Model Canvas proposed by (Osterwalder et al., 2010).It is composed of nine components: key activities (KA), key resources (KR), key partnerships (KP), cost structure (C$), value propositions (VP), channels (CH), customer relationships (CR), customer segments (CS), revenue streams (R$).BMC is a schematic representation that presents how a company will deliver, capture, and create value. The BMC is the basis of many frameworks and IT tools because it offers the ontology of the business model domain and provides the domain's ontology for business models that allow using computer assistance.

*Figure 2. Selected business model modeling languages (Hamrouni et al., 2022)*

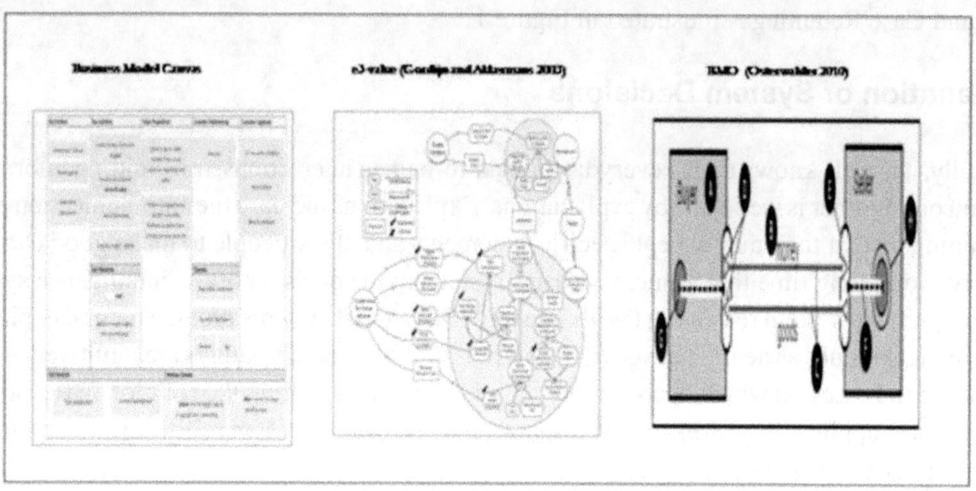

E3 value: The "e3-value" language was proposed by (Gordijn et al., 2003). It allows evaluating and capturing BMs from a financial point of view. The e3-value allows evaluating and clarifying an idea. This approach begins with an e-commerce idea to build a value model. The e3-value methodology has been used in different domains such as banking, energy, entertainment, and telecommunications (Gordijn et al., 2005). The main concepts of e3-value are actors, value ports, value exchanges, and value objects. Identifying involved actors is the first step to designing an e3-value model and the value exchanges that appear with these actors. After that, the value exchanges are valued financially to determine which economic performance each actor in the network is expected to have. The E3 value provides an initial idea of the economic attractiveness of the business model by automatically generating profitability sheets, which include the number of incoming and outgoing value objects and their value. Calculating the sum of an actor's inflows and outflows to calculate cash flow for a given period (Lindgren et al.2013). These main concepts and their relations are part of an ontology that has been formalized in the Unified Modeling Language (UML) (Gordijn et al., 2003).

Strategic business model ontology (SBMO): The decision-making process is completely expressed by the SBMO ontology by capturing the communication and cooperation with several stakeholders outside and inside a company. In the operational view, actors are represented by their tasks, relationships, and (operational) goals. The strategic view visualizes how these operational goals are linked to strategic goals (Samavi et al., 2009).

## 2. Digital Tools That Represent and Change Business Models

A variety of software solutions have been suggested to enhance the use of the current modeling languages (Szopinski et al., 2017; Gordijn et al., 2000; Peinel et al., 2010; Ebel et al., 2016; Athanasopoulo et al., 2020) in research and practice (Strategyzer, BM Designer1, Canvanizer 2.02).

Online repositories and online platforms are accessible, as BusinessMakeover.eu and BMToolBox.net and, which present different business model tools, supporting users in satisfying their demands (Bocken et al., 2019).

These tools enable making changes to business models and represent and allow collaborative development that is not even possible with "pen & paper" tools (Ebel et al., 2016). In addition, these tools can support their users more efficiently in performing some actions such as versioning and annotating business models than with the modeling languages' "pen & paper" versions. Some of these tools have already become rather popular in real life, as seen by the fact that the web application Canvanizer has more than 1,000,000 business model projects, while the app Business Model Canvas & SWOT has more than 100,000 downloads (Szopinski et al., 2020).

*Figure 3. Selected business model modeling languages from practice (Hamrouni et al., 2022)*
*BM Designer: https://bmdesigner.com/Canvanizer 2.0: https://canvanizer.com/*

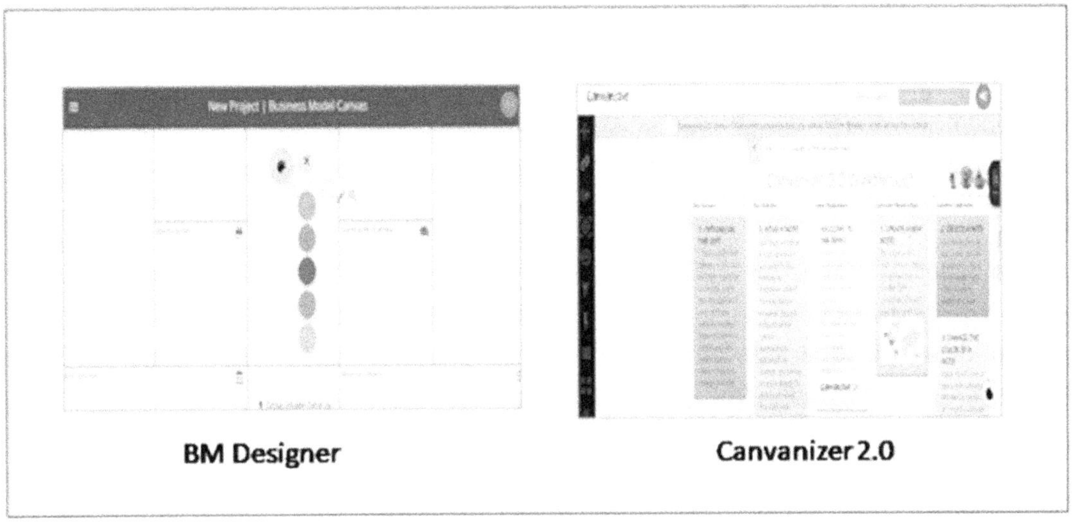


*Figure 4. The developed prototype (Athanasopoulou et al., 2018)*

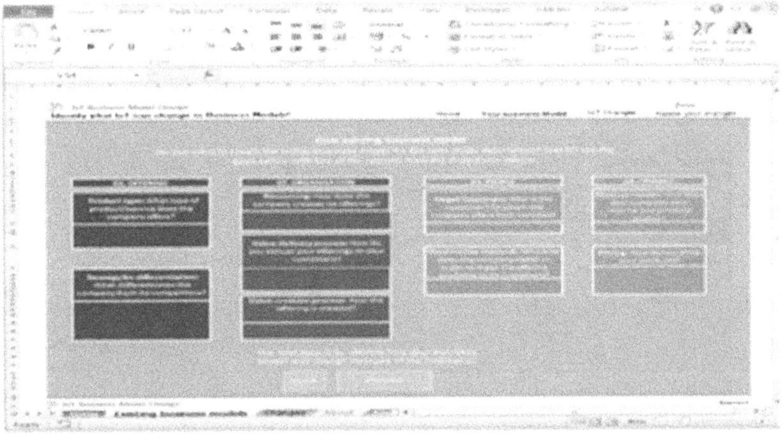

Finally, these tools use a fill-in-the-blank method, so information is entered manually by the user; they are click-and-fill-out tools. Nonetheless, users asked for clarifications on what the components (or building blocks) signify and examples of how to fill them up (William et al., 1984). This is because some prefilled software tools were developed.

## 3. Business Model Patterns that Stimulate Analogical Reasoning

The description of successful BMIs supports the ideation of novel business models. Recent research has shown that generating ideas for new business models is possible with two cognitive processes: conceptual combination and analogical reasoning (Martinset al., 2015). Patterns of BM are identified to stimulate analogical reasoning, which has gotten more and more interest in business model ideation techniques (Gassmann et al., 2014; Abdelkafi et al., 2013; Täuscher et al., 2017; Remane et al., 2017).

The Gassmann's 55 patterns (Gassmann et al., 2014) this catalog of BM inspired managers and entrepreneurs of all sorts to creatively develop or imitate solutions by recombining existing patterns, authors use a "who-what-how-why" framework to describe these patterns. However, this classification lacks a meta-structure that brings order to the 55 patterns [130]. To support business model innovation, this approach is widely recommended. It refers to the process of "generative cognition," which is envisioning future business models in the sense of seeing with one's mind. (Remane et al., 2017): utilizing the Business Model Canvas to develop a database of 182 patterns and describe pattern characteristics. The author proposed a strong approach to define patterns among these scholars. The author explains that different problems can be solved with the generalization and combination of these patterns in different domains. The elements that describe a problem-solution combination are: problem statement, solution statement, pattern name, context description, examples, and explanations.

(Abdelkafi et al., 2013): the author introduced a new framework in which a business model denotes a value-focused concept with five value dimensions: value proposition, value communication, value creation, value delivery, and value capture. The framework enables the classification of business model patterns, identified in the literature, into five categories.

*Figure 5. 50_business_model_examples (Gassmann, 2014; Hamrouni et al., 2022)*

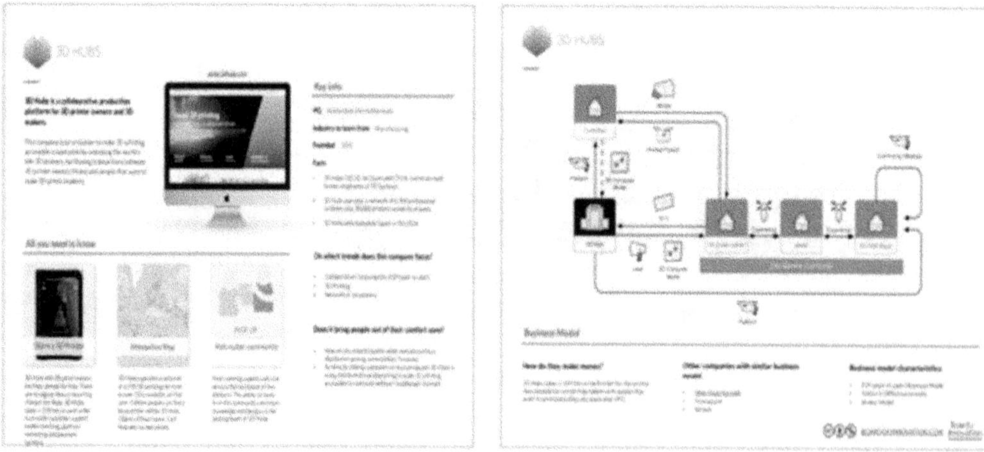

Business Model Gallery: The largest business model database that is a publicly available database on business models, as a resource for learning about different BM designs. In this database, BMs from all kinds of industries are explained, allowing learning about various patterns. This project aspires to capture the power of analogies by being a place for inspiration. https://www.businessmodelideas.com/

## 4. Analytical Methods

### Modeling, Simulation Tools and Stochastic analysis

An additional study area concentrated on validating the BM using analytical techniques like modeling and simulation. (Haakeret al., 2017; Daas et al., 2013). Business model adaptations can be done with simulations to comprehend the results without exposing the organization to risk (Bocken et al. 2019). To predict the viability of the business model decisions, quantitative and qualitative scenario analysis were adopted(Bouwman et al., 2008;Zoric et al., 2011; Pagani et al., 2008; Euchner & Ganguly, 2014; Latora et al., 2018).

*Figure 6. Service pricing dashboard (Daas et al., 2013)*

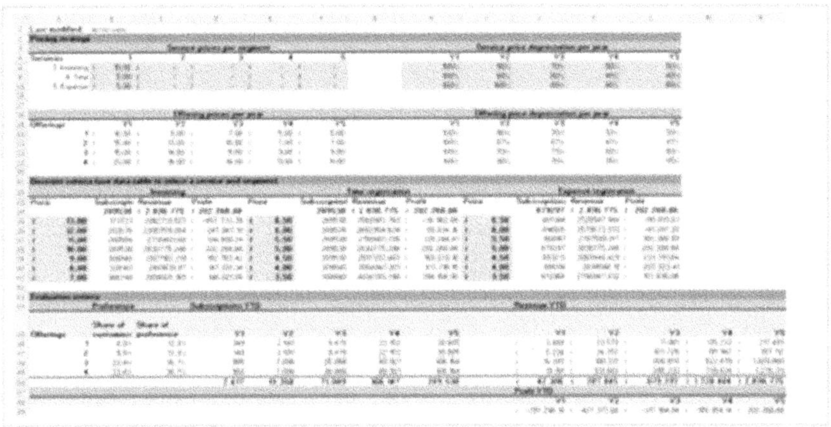

Daas et al. (2013) presented a tool that supports the evaluation of alternative business models by incorporating market analysis data. The tool helps analyze alternative BM solutions. The DSS uses flexible spreadsheet-based technology. The DSS is composed of three parts: (1) the business model design, (2) market analysis, and (3) decision analysis.

Figure 6 shows the conceptual design of the DSS. Each worksheet provided a dashboard, including design parameters and evaluation indicators tailored to a particular decision-maker within the business units of the SaaS providers or within a structural partner's organization.

Bouwman et al. 2008: used scenario analysis to test the robustness of the BM choices. The scenarios represent the different probable future changes in the environment, consumer attitudes, and towards IPTV service and industry structure. Telecom operators can realize economic benefits and deliver customer value with the selection of the optimal business model.

Zoric et al 2011: A techno-business modeling approach was discussed in this work for quantitative analysis of services and platforms (Tunio et al., 2021). The roles, responsibilities, and incentives of collaborating business actors in service delivery and provision were used in business analyses and valuations.

Pagani et al.2008: developed an operative planning tool with scenario evaluation and analysis through Repeated Cross-impact Handling. This tool generates quantitative and qualitative scenarios.

In other studies, the principal drivers of the financial performance of financial models were identified by using stochastic analysis.

Euchner et al. 2014: used stochastic methods to quantify the probability of business success and identify the variables that are likely to have the most effect on the success (or failure) of the business model. They used a tornado diagram.

Latora et al. 2018: proposed a (BM-DST) Business Model Decision Support Tool. He used a Multiple Criteria Decision Analysis (MCDA) called the Analytic Hierarchy Process (AHP) to estimate the business solutions.A software application was implemented by using a common spreadsheet in order to prove the "lean" characteristic of the Business Model Decision Support Tool (BMDST), which is easy to implement in any business context.

In other studies, the principal drivers of the financial performance of financial models were identified by using stochastic analysis.

## SIMULATION TOOLS

The alternatives and changes of an actual BM to a future one are defined in the tool BM Road Mapping, proposed by (De Reuver et al., 2013). The viability of a BM in front of the BM, value network, and regulations and standards is achieved using the Viability Radar BM tool (Bouwman et al., 2018). The robustness of a BM under several scenarios is experimented with using the BM stress-testing tool proposed by (Haakeret al., 2017; Gudiksen, 2015).

*Figure 7. Haaker et al., 2017*

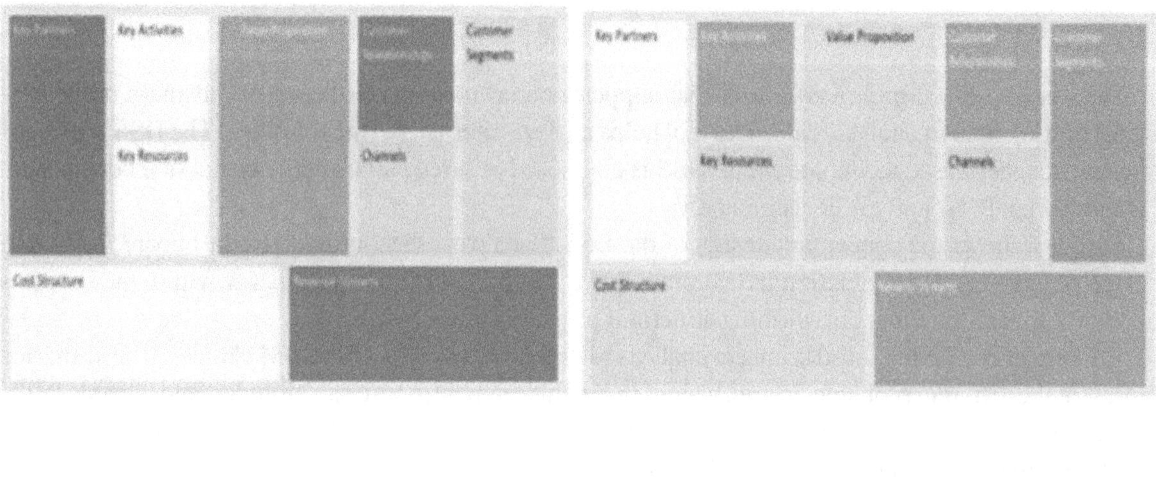

## 5. DSSBasedAI

Dellermann et al. designed a hybrid system that enables combining human input into an artificial intelligence system throughout the systems' process in order to build, add to, and assess the systems' capabilities (Dellermann et al., 2019). According to the authors, using the advantages of artificial intelligence and human intelligence will result in a more intelligent system than either one alone (Kamar, 2016).

*Figure 8. Complementary strengths of humans and machines (Dellermann, 2021)*

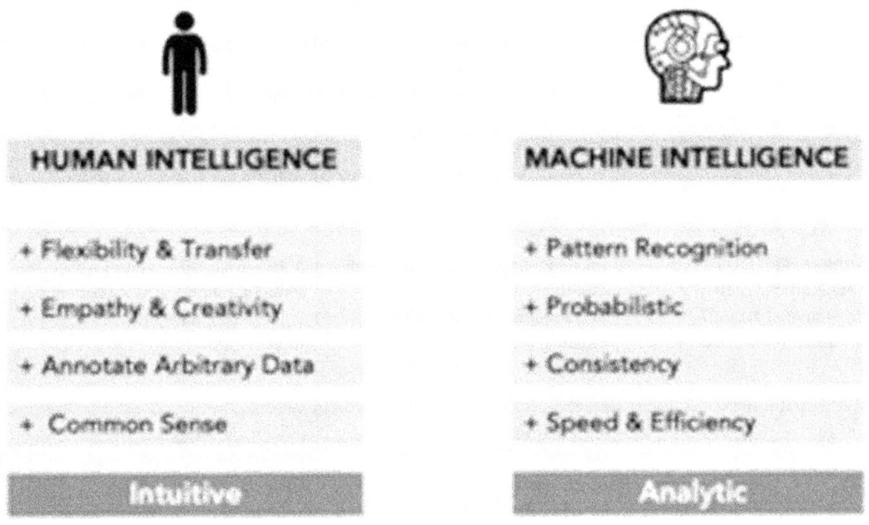


The HI-DSS artifact was offered as a cloud-based online service by Dellerman. A graphic user interface (GUI) that enables input and display of the entrepreneur's business model makes up the prototype of the artifact. He used Angular 3 to create a web application. The business model was represented in a standardized manner using a dynamically changeable structure. Each component of the company Business Model is chosen by the entrepreneur: value proposition, value delivery, value creation, and value capture dimensions of the business model. Information about startup business models that is publicly available was used to train the machine learning algorithm. The open-source machine learning framework TensorFlow4 was used to develop the machine learning part of the prototype.

In the following, we present our classification of BMDTs, which comprises advantages and disadvantages of each category with requirements to the decisional guidance for BM design and innovation.

The state of the art of decision support systems for Business Model is reviewed, assessed, and criticized. The limitations and shortcomings of the suggested models result in a wide range of issues and challenges. Software tools have demonstrated considerable promise for assisting business models innovation and development. They appear to be useful tools for defining, integrating, comparing, and categorizing business models as well. However, the software under consideration does not appear to be particularly helpful during the ideation phase, making it difficult to support the highly creative task of business model innovation.

*Table 1. Advantages and disadvantages for each category of BMDT's*

| Categories | BMDT | Advantageous | Disadvantageous | Needs |
|---|---|---|---|---|
| Modeling languages | E3 value (Gordijn et al., 2003)<br>Strategic business model ontology(SBMO) (Samavi et al., 2009)<br>The Business Model Canvas (Osterwalder et al., 2010)<br>The creative business model canvas(Carter et al 2020) | These tools are useful for defining, analyzing, integrating, and comparing business models. | These tools does not appear to be particularly helpful during the ideation phase, making it difficult to support the hard creative task of business model innovation. | The researchers suggested moving to a new type of ontology that contains more knowledge and information, from the well-known BM canvas. |
| Digital Tools that represent and change business models | Canvaniseur 2.02, 2014.<br>BM Designer1<br>Ebel et al., 2016<br>Athanasopoulo et al. 2020 | More efficient in performing versioning and annotation of BMs than with "pen and paper" modeling language versions. | The most common approach used in these business model tools is fill-inthe-blank, where information is added manually. Alternative of business model was enabled by current systems, but decision-making was not sufficiently facilitated. | In most cases, users need knowledge and information about how to fill the various BM components. |
| Business model patterns that stimulate analogical reasoning | Remane et al. 2017<br>Abdelkafi et al., 2013<br>Gassmann et al.,2014<br>Business Model Gallery | These BM catalogs and tools stimulated managers because many of them develop creatively BM by imitating and recombining solutions of existing patterns enabling BM idea generation, through the use of analogy. | These are catalogs and static tools that do not allow proper exploitation and retrieve of information . | Users need interactive tools that allow searching for BMs. |
| Analytical Methods and simulation | Daas et al. (2013)<br>Bouwman et al. (2008)<br>Latora et al.<br>Gudiksen et al. (2015) | Simulations provide efficient time and help decision makers understand the consequences of BM adaptations without exposing the organization to risk, to predict theviability of the business model decisions. | These tools focused on the financial aspect and the validation of the BM, and did not help in the design of the BM. | Users need tools that enable both the ideation, design and validation of the BM. |
| DSS Based AI | Dellermann et al. (2019) | In order to validate the BM, this tool uses artificial intelligence techniques, namely machine learning to learn from collective intelligence. | Little focus has been placed on providing decision support by building trust in these tools. | Provide intelligent systems that has the capacity of explaining the result in order to boost the trust in the suggested solutions. |

We concluded that the most common approach used in business model tools is fill-inthe-blank, where information is added manually. In most cases, users need knowledge andinformation about how to fill in the different elements of the BM. In other side, existing tools supportedthe financial validation of the BM by developing alternative of business models, however they did not help the decision-making process enough.

What we realized from Table 1, is that scholars have stated that software based Business Model Data Tool BMDTs provide important assistance for designing and innovating Business Models, specifically with employing machine learning and other AI techniques. However, trust is not offered by these AI-based DSS systems to allow extremely accurate decisional guidance. Meanwhile, An important element influencing the acceptance of a system is its capacity to explain its results (Osterwalder, 2004) .For that reason, systems must provide explanations to allow end users to trust, understand, and effectively manage these systems.

## PROPOSED CBR BASED ONTOLOGY SYSTEM FOR BUSINESS MODEL DESIGN

In an increasingly competitive and global market, most businesses agree that knowledge is a critical asset for success and survival. This awareness has been one of the main factors in the exponential expansion of knowledge management over the last few years. Our approach to BM design is founded on ontologies, and it intelligently makes knowledge assets available to individuals in organizations, where information previously resided exclusively in people's minds.

Motivated by the need of more knowledge to assist managers in the step of ideation and design of the BM, we developed a system that assist decision maker in the design of the BM and contain more knowledge while ensuring both the ideation and design of BM and sustainable development.

In its sophisticated decision-making process, business model creation frequently necessitates the knowledge and expertise of people's ability to handle enormous amounts of data. The availability of skilled decision-makers, on the other hand, is frequently constrained (Roth-Berghofer et al., 2012). The typical working style of the expert (which is based on his/her knowledge of past records) in dealing with BM design could be reproduced using the CBR technique. CBR is an artificial intelligence technique, as explained in the precedent section. There are numerous definitions of "CBR technique" in the literature:

- Making a decision based on previous cases
- To solve, analyze, or understand a new situation by referring to prior, similar cases.
- Using historical events as a model.
- Using appropriate solutions to recent problems to solve new ones, the CBR approach differs from other techniques (such as rule-based/black box methods) in that it uses a concrete knowledge base or experimental facts to infer knowledge.

Combining Case-based Reasoning system with ontologies allow using the power of ontologies. In this way Ontology-based CBR "[...] can take advantage of this domain knowledge and generate more accurate findings," according to (Recio-García et al., 2008). Integrating domain knowledge to the case-based reasoning system is advantageous, to minimize the knowledge acquisition bottleneck and to minimize the time it takes to acquire knowledge. "The more knowledge is embedded into the system, the more effective [it] is expected to be" (Recio-García et al., 2008).

The system enables decision-makers to evaluate, comprehend, measure, change, discuss, or even simulate their business models (Arabeche et al., 2022), as well as introduce modifications and experiment with them to learn about emerging opportunities.

On the one hand, the system provides a visualization tool for a firm's actual business model, but on the other hand, it also allows for the representation of almost all imaginable business models. This would assist managers in understanding competitors' business models (Aldieri et al., 2021), which would help them innovate. The previous cases of BM are carefully cataloged and arranged, making it easier for decision makers to create the BM. Then, based on the CBR system's adaption phase, a new business model could be recommended. Managers can conduct risk-free experiments without risking their organization by employing a number of iterations for learning.

## CBR APPLICATION

The presented system is a novel way for SBM design. The advantages of this approach are based on the opportunity to reuse existing domain knowledge on BM, management and sustainability during the execution of the CBR cycle. The application of this paradigm by DSS for SBM design holds great promise for supporting design and innovation.

The outcome of this approach is a CBR BASED ONTOLOGY system that provides knowledge to help decision-makers on the environment, production processes, and products by focusing on ideas of sustainable development to create new market opportunities for new processes and products, and innovations on how companies save natural resources and make better use of them.

### 1. Case Representation

In general, a case is described by a pair (problem, solution) that includes both problem and solution aspects. As a result, the problem part of our model corresponds to the enterprise description section, whereas the BM component belongs to the solution part. As a result, there are two primary parts: a description part that describes the setting and the enterprise, and a BM part that describes the various possible values of the BM components. In order to improve communication between the case base and the domain model, the case model is represented within an ontology that integrates the domain model, as suggested by (Rese et al., 2013).

BM experiences are taken into account as cases in this study in the sense of case-based paradigm. CBR may be used to retrieve BM experiences from the Case base, an ontology-based knowledge base.

Ontology serves as the case basis and the domain ontology in the CBR-based ontology system. Ontologies for the domain and the case base combined will provide the Knowledge-Intensive CBR (KICBR) (Bouwman et al., 2008). This model represents the knowledge about the business in general, the business model and the sustainability domain, in an ontological structure. The domain model is represented by ontologies which contain the vocabularies, concepts, and relations for defining knowledge related Business Models following the suggested classification by (Baader et al., 2003).

we have designed two different kinds of ontologies: one is generic, containing concepts like "the value delivered to the client," which can be a product, a service, or a mix of the two (Magretta, 2002), and the sectors of the economy. A domain ontology describing the business model domain, including the components of the business model. Its items, which are specializations of other base ontology concepts, include: key activities, cost structure, value propositions, channels, customer relationships, key partnerships, customer segments, revenue streams, key resources.

Based on BMO, this ontology includes information on the four major BM pillars, which are the firm's offerings of goods and services, infrastructure and partner network, human resources, and financial aspects (Osterwalder et al., 2002).

Accordingly, there are two primary parts: a description part that gives information about the firm and a BM part that gives information about the potential values of the BM components. The case model is expressed in an ontology that incorporates the domain model to enhance communication in between case base and the domain model, as suggested by CBR ONTO (Rese et al., 2013).

CBR-CASE, which includes all possible case, types in the system;

CBR-DESCRIPTION, which includes Business company description (Number of Employees, Name,Country) and BM Components of the Case (Customer Segment, Value Proposition, Customer Relationships, Key Activities, Cost Structure, Key Resources, Flows revenue from key partners).

CBR-INDEX, makes it possible to combine the concepts of the domain model necessary for the definition of the cases.

*Figure 9. EIDSS BM Process*

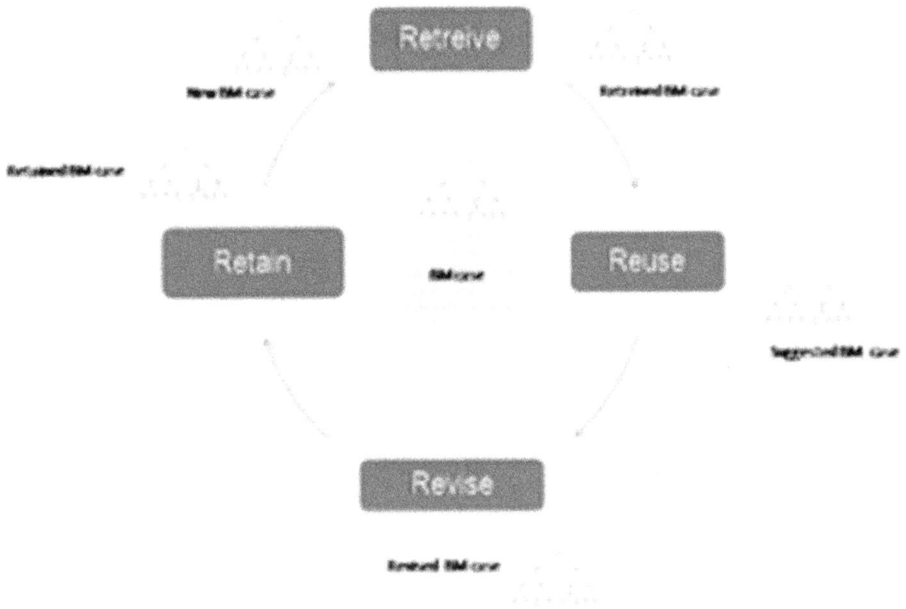


## 2. Business Model Retrieval

The primary concerns in developing the case retrieval method included in Business Models should be considered, we are based on the BMC of osterwalder with its nine components.

The user describes the problem by providing data about the sector, the country, and the establishment year. The query is submitted to the retrieve module, generates then checks the case base for the instances that are the most similar. The system searches in the database of previous (similar) cases useful in solving the current problem. The alternatives of BM possibilities for the present project make up the solution space.

## 3. Case Matching

Cases might be matched using semantic criteria rather than only syntactic ones based on this concept of generic domain knowledge. By adjusting the solutions of the best matched instances, the goal is to provide an appropriate solution for the new input case. The similarity value was calculated using the nearest neighbor technique (Xu et al., 2018).

## 4. Case Updating

When case matching is completed successfully, the actual business model results can be saved into the case base.

## 5. Explanation

The system will be able to produce targeted explanations for the user as well as for its internal reasoning process due to the general domain model and CBR. The generating explanation sub process seeks to explain the degree of similarity or relevancy among knowledge base concepts. The system includes the three goals of explanation which are the Conceptual, Transparency and the Justification Goal

- Implementation of the Conceptual Explanations, when the user hovers the mouse over conceptual explanations appear. The system describes all ontology concepts. The explanation includes a brief listing of URLs with a description to additional documents. For example, Wikipedia or Google define what it means to "start up."
- Implementation of Transparency Goal, In response to a query, the system ranks the case base. However, the retrieval result could be unexpected and require some explanation. To reply to this query: "How did the system come to the similarity evaluation of a given case?" The technology delivers a thorough the retrieval process's recording. As a result, it is possible to track each step of the similarity computation.
- Implementation of Justification Goal, the answer to the question: "Which arethe most similar aspects of a case? Which are the least?". An aspect is a single attribute, and myCBR may display the local similarity value of an aspect's similarity.

## IMPLEMENTATION AND EVALUATION

Various programming tools, both free and commercially available, can be used to construct a CBR system. The most extensively utilized and well-known frameworks for academic research and teaching are myCBR and jCOLIBRI. MyCBR contains a lot of capabilities and makes developing case-based reasoning apps very simple. It enables rapid prototyping and the integration of reduced CBR capabilities. It can be used as a standalone application or as a Protégé plugin. The developed system uses the CBR. A Case-Base database with cases has been created, containing parameters (attributes) of the different Business Models. The main functions include retrieve, adapt and explain the result to design and innovate BMs.

Testing of retrieval functionality: Figure 10 gives a schematic overview of the Retrieval GUI. The names of the classes' attributes are presented with the rows of the table. The area is divided into several columns. The left most column is used for query specification. The others are used to show the retrieval results. The rightmost column lists all cases of the case base, ordered by their similarity to the query.

The retrieval function is enhanced with using ontology, a domain-specific ontology or user-defined ontology represents specific domain knowledge or relation between words using class and subclass (Staab et al., 2010). Terms of a case can be compared with other cases by exact matching. However, some slots like the "industries" of the company can have a relationship with other synonyms or industries. The weight of such terms can be increased automatically using a domain specific ontology defined by experts.

For example, the term "education" is related to "learning" and "training", and it is more similar to some industries, so that enhance the result of the user query.

*Figure 10. Retrieval of a case query (Hamrouni et al., 2022)*

The performance of the proposed EIDSS-BM has been assessed following implementation (Hamrouni et al., 2021; Hamrouni et al., 2022).The evaluation process's objective is to determine the end user's views of the system's importance and value.

As a resource for learning about various BM designs, the "Business Modcl Gallery" dataset, which is a publicly accessible database on business models, and the largest business model database that is considered as a resource for learning about different BM designs. In this database, BMs from all kinds of industries are explained, allowing learning about various patterns. This project aspires to capture the power of analogies by being a place for inspiration. The "Business Model Gallery" dataset served as the basis for the primary data utilized in this study. This database contains descriptions of BMs from a variety of businesses, making it possible to discover distinct patterns. By serving as a source of inspiration, this research seeks to harness the potency of analogies. However, the system does not employ intelligent techniques. It offers a simple retrieval for wide range of information, such as the company's industry, employees, country of foundation, business type, yearly income, and many BM component values.

The evaluation was done in the second phase to evaluate the system's success in locating pertinent cases (*Hamrouni* et al., 2022; *Hamrouni* et al., 2021). By comparing the Business Model Gallery with our knowledge-enhanced retrieval approach, the accuracy and recall are determined. Figure 11shows the results of comparing the precision and recall of the two systems, with 0.6 as the threshold value. The results show that the Business Model Gallery's average precision of four test cases is 81.5%, whereas our upgraded system has a precision of 95%. Similarly, EIDSS-BM has a 95.5% average recall, whereas the

Business Model Gallery has a lower score of 46%. Overall, the results imply that the enhanced system performs better in this CBR system in terms of precision and recall. The results showed that CBR is an excellent method for solving and recommending BM. More advanced features will be investigated in this area as the study progresses (*Hamrouni* et al., 2022; *Hamrouni* et al., 2021).

*Figure 11. Comparison recall and precision of EIDSS-BM against the Business Model Gallery (Hamrouni et al., 2022)*

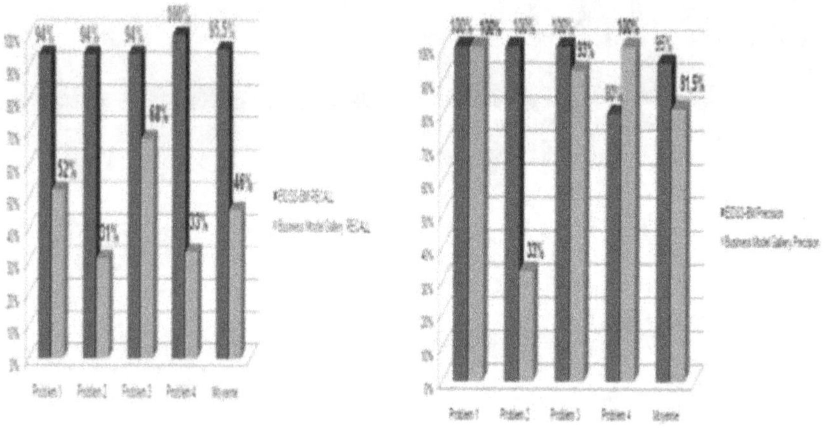

## FUTURE RESEARCH DIRECTIONS

As a potential future research area, we suggest extending the development of taxonomies for Business Model Data tools to facilitate, the implementation of software tools to automate the design, innovation and validation of the business models. Especially, with using intelligent and artificial intelligence techniques. There are still the need for more sophisticated and intelligent software tools to help managers in designing and validating their BM (Bouwman et al., 2020).

In this vein we suggest extending EIDSS-BM system with a Rule-Based Reasoning module to predict the success of early-stage BMs. The SWRL language may be used to convey the factors that affect how well organizational rules work based on the examination of classes and characteristics in the BM ontology model. Moreover, the development of the ontology is a long task, and the initial work is done. To add more management knowledge to the ontology, significant further work is needed.

Additionally, we want to add a balanced scorecard module to the intelligent system, enabling the decision-maker to track and visualize the effectiveness of his business model.

## CONCLUSION

This chapter brings together different important papers on BM. BM tooling is a growing field of IS research stream. However, there are still many questions to be answered in terms of research, not only the ones presented in this study. However, we sincerely believe that tools are necessary to make scholarly BM work useful for managers. Thereby, this study seeks to systemize and build upon existing research and promote more cumulative research for methods and techniques used for designing and implementing BMDTs that still a new line of inquiry. What we suggest that software based Business Model Data Tool BMDTs could provide important assistance for designing and innovating Business Models, specifically with employing Artificial Intelligence techniques to provide more guidance in the ideation, design and validation phase for the BM.

The AI contributions to an explainable intelligent system for BM design and exposed the usefulness of different methods and techniques used in designing the existant BMDTs. As a result, digital technologies and AI can aid in the development of BMs.

Our technique leads to an explainable decision support system for BM design based on ontologies, and it intelligently tends to make knowledge assets available to people in companies where knowledge previously resided only in people's minds. In addition, the valuable knowledge of specialists in previous business models is captured, allowing for the reuse of existing domain knowledge as well as the transmission and sharing of knowledge.

As a result, trying to apply this paradigm to business model development software tools holds great promise for improving business model design and innovation.

## REFERENCES

Aamodt, A., & Plaza, E. (1994). Case-based reasoning: Foundational issues, methodological variations, and system approaches. *AI Communications*, *7*(1), 39–59. doi:10.3233/AIC-1994-7104

Abdelkafi, N., Makhotin, S., & Posselt, T. (2013). Business model innovations for electric mobility—What can be learned from existing business model patterns? *International Journal of Innovation Management*, *17*(01), 1340003. doi:10.1142/S1363919613400033

Al-Debei, M. M., & Avison, D. (2010). Developing a unified framework of the business model concept. *European Journal of Information Systems*, *19*(3), 359–376. doi:10.1057/ejis.2010.21

Aldieri, L., Brahmi, M., Bruno, B., & Vinci, C. P. (2021). Circular Economy Business Models: The Complementarities with Sharing Economy and Eco-Innovations Investments. *Sustainability*, *13*(22), 12438. doi:10.3390u132212438

Amit, R., & Zott, C. (2001). Value creation in e-business. *Strategic Management Journal*, *22*(6-7), 493–520. doi:10.1002mj.187

Arrieta, A. B., Díaz-Rodríguez, N., Del Ser, J., Bennetot, A., Tabik, S., Barbado, A., & Herrera, F. (2020). Explainable Artificial Intelligence (XAI): Concepts, taxonomies, opportunities and challenges toward responsible AI. *Information Fusion*, *58*, 82–115. doi:10.1016/j.inffus.2019.12.012

Arabeche, Z., Soudani, A., Brahmi, M., Aldieri, L., Vinci, C. P., & Abdelli, M. E. A. (2022). Entrepreneurial Orientation, Organizational Culture and Business Performance in SMEs: Evidence from Emerging Economy. *Sustainability*, *14*(9), 5160. doi:10.3390u14095160

Athanasopoulou, A., & De Reuver, M. (2020). How do business model tools facilitate business model exploration? Evidence from action research. *Electronic Markets*, *30*(3), 495–508. doi:10.100712525-020-00418-3

Athanasopoulou, A., Haaker, T., & de Reuver, M. (2018). Designing digital tooling for business model exploration for the Internet-of-Things. In *DESRIST 2018-13th International Conference on Design Science Research in Information Systems and Technology*.

Baader, F., Calvanese, D., McGuinness, D., Patel-Schneider, P., & Nardi, D. (Eds.). (2003). *The description logic handbook: Theory, implementation and applications*. Cambridge university press.

Baden-Fuller, C., & Morgan, M. S. (2010). Business models as models. *Long Range Planning*, *43*(2-3), 156–171. doi:10.1016/j.lrp.2010.02.005

Bergmann, R. (Ed.). (2002). *Experience management: foundations, development methodology, and internet-based applications*. Springer Berlin Heidelberg. doi:10.1007/3-540-45759-3

Bocken, N., Boons, F., & Baldassarre, B. (2019). Sustainable business model experimentation by understanding ecologies of business models. *Journal of Cleaner Production*, *208*, 1498–1512. doi:10.1016/j.jclepro.2018.10.159

Bouwman, H., De Reuver, M., Heikkilä, M., & Fielt, E. (2020). Business model tooling: Where research and practice meet. *Electronic Markets*, *30*(3), 413–419. doi:10.100712525-020-00424-5

Bouwman, H., de Vos, H., & Haaker, T. (Eds.). (2008). *Mobile service innovation and business models*. Springer Science & Business Media. doi:10.1007/978-3-540-79238-3

Bouwman, H., Heikkilä, J., Heikkilä, M., Leopold, C., & Haaker, T. (2018). Achieving agility using business model stress testing. *Electronic Markets*, *28*(2), 149–162. doi:10.100712525-016-0243-0

Bouwman, H., Zhengjia, M., Van der Duin, P., & Limonard, S. (2008). A business model for IPTV service: a dynamic framework. *info*.

Buur, J., & Gudiksen, S. (2012, October). Interactive pinball business. In *Proceedings of the 7th Nordic Conference on Human-Computer Interaction: Making Sense Through Design* (pp. 129-138).

Carter, M., & Carter, C. (2020). The creative business model canvas. *Social Enterprise Journal*, *16*(2), 141–158. doi:10.1108/SEJ-03-2019-0018

Chesbrough, H. (2006). *Open business models: How to thrive in the new innovation landscape*. Harvard Business Press.

Chesbrough, H. (2007). Business model innovation: It's not just about technology anymore. *Strategy and Leadership*, *35*(6), 12–17. doi:10.1108/10878570710833714

Chesbrough, H., & Rosenbloom, R. S. (2002). The role of the business model in capturing value from innovation: Evidence from Xerox Corporation's technology spin-off companies. *Industrial and Corporate Change*, *11*(3), 529–555. doi:10.1093/icc/11.3.529

Çınar, A. K. (2009). *Integrating Case Based Reasoning and Geographic Information Systems in a Planing Support System: Çeşme Peninsula Study* [Doctoral dissertation, Izmir Institute of Technology, Turkey].

Crunchbase. (2021). Business model gallery. *Crunchbase company profile and funding*. https://www.crunchbase.com/organization/business-model-gallery

Daas, D., Hurkmans, T., Overbeek, S., & Bouwman, H. (2013). Developing a decision support system for business model design. *Electronic Markets*, *23*(3), 251–265. doi:10.100712525-012-0115-1

De Reuver, M., Bouwman, H., & Haaker, T. (2013). Business model roadmapping: A practical approach to come from an existing to a desired business model. *International Journal of Innovation Management*, *17*(01), 1340006. doi:10.1142/S1363919613400069

Dellermann, D. (2021). Accelerating Entrepreneurial Decision-Making Through Hybrid Intelligence. *arXiv preprint arXiv:2105.03365.*

Dellermann, D., Lipusch, N., Ebel, P., & Leimeister, J. M. (2019). Design principles for a hybrid intelligence decision support system for business model validation. *Electronic Markets*, *29*(3), 423–441. doi:10.100712525-018-0309-2

Ebel, P., Bretschneider, U., & Leimeister, J. M. (2016). Leveraging virtual business model innovation: A framework for designing business model development tools. *Information Systems Journal*, *26*(5), 519–550. doi:10.1111/isj.12103

Erum, S.; Muhammad, N T.; Wali Muhammad, K.; Mohsen, B.; & Shahid, R., Chapter 16: The COVID-19 Pandemic Overlaps Entrepreneurial Activities and Triggered New Challenges: A Review Study, Book chapter: Managing Human Resources in SMEs and Start-ups, August 2022, 388 p. https://doi.org/doi:10.1142/9789811239212_0008

Euchner, J., & Ganguly, A. (2014). Business model innovation in practice. *Research Technology Management*, *57*(6), 33–39.

Gassmann, O., Frankenberger, K., & Csik, M. (2014). *The business model navigator: 55 models that will revolutionise your business.* Pearson UK.

Gordijn, J. (2005). A design methodology for modeling trustworthy value webs. *International Journal of Electronic Commerce*, *9*(3), 31–48. doi:10.1080/10864415.2005.11044333

Gordijn, J., & Akkermans, H. (2001). Designing and evaluating e-business models. *IEEE Intelligent Systems*, *16*(04), 11–17. doi:10.1109/5254.941353

Gordijn, J., Akkermans, H., & Vliet, H. V. (2000, October). Business modelling is not process modelling. In *International Conference on Conceptual Modeling* (pp. 40-51). Springer, Berlin, Heidelberg.

Gordijn, J., & Akkermans, J. M. (2003). Value-based requirements engineering: Exploring innovative e-commerce ideas. *Requirements Engineering*, *8*(2), 114–134. doi:10.100700766-003-0169-x

Gudiksen, S. (2015). Business model design games: Rules and procedures to challenge assumptions and elicit surprises. *Creativity and Innovation Management*, *24*(2), 307–322. doi:10.1111/caim.12114

Haaker, T., Bouwman, H., Janssen, W., & de Reuver, M. (2017). Business model stress testing: A practical approach to test the robustness of a business model. *Futures*, *89*, 14–25. doi:10.1016/j.futures.2017.04.003

Hacklin, F., & Wallnöfer, M. (2012). The business model in the practice of strategic decision making: Insights from a case study. *Management Decision*, *50*(2), 166–188. doi:10.1108/00251741211203515

Hamrouni, A., & Korichi, B. Bourouis, (2022). *Explainable Ontology-Based Intelligent Decision Support System For Business Model Design And Sustainability*. [Thesis, Kasdi Merbah Ouargla University, Algeria].

Hamrouni, B., Bourouis, A., Korichi, A., & Brahmi, M. (2021). Explainable Ontology-Based Intelligent Decision Support System for Business Model Design and Sustainability. *Sustainability*, *13*(17), 9819. doi:10.3390u13179819

John, T., Kundisch, D., & Szopinski, D. (2017). Visual Languages for Modeling Business Models: A Critical Review and Future Research Directions. In ICIS.

Kamar, E. (2016, July). Directions in Hybrid Intelligence: Complementing AI Systems with Human Intelligence. In IJCAI (pp. 4070-4073).

Lanzolla, G., & Markides, C. (2021). A business model view of strategy. *Journal of Management Studies*, *58*(2), 540–553. doi:10.1111/joms.12580

Latora, A. G., Compagno, L., & Trapani, N. (2018). A decision support tool for business models analysis. *International Journal of the Analytic Hierarchy Process*, *10*(2), 219–242. doi:10.13033/ijahp.v10i2.516

Lindgren, P., & Rasmussen, O. H. (2013). The business model cube. *Journal of Multi Business Model Innovation and Technology*, *1*(3), 135–182.

López-Nicolás, C., Ruiz-Nicolás, J., & Mateo-Ortuño, E. (2021). Towards Sustainable Innovative Business Models. *Sustainability*, *13*(11), 5804. doi:10.3390u13115804

Lüdeke-Freund, F., Carroux, S., Joyce, A., Massa, L., & Breuer, H. (2018). The sustainable business model pattern taxonomy—45 patterns to support sustainability-oriented business model innovation. *Sustainable Production and Consumption*, *15*, 145–162. doi:10.1016/j.spc.2018.06.004

Magretta, J. (2002). Why business models matter.

Majchrzak, A., & Gasser, L. (1991). On using artificial intelligence to integrate the design of organizational and process change in US manufacturing. *AI & Society*, *5*(4), 321–338. doi:10.1007/BF02077438

Martins, L. L., Rindova, V. P., & Greenbaum, B. E. (2015). Unlocking the hidden value of concepts: A cognitive approach to business model innovation. *Strategic Entrepreneurship Journal*, *9*(1), 99–117. doi:10.1002ej.1191

Massie, S., Craw, S., & Wiratunga, N. (2004, December). A visualisation tool to explain case-base reasoning solutions for tablet formulation. In *International Conference on Innovative Techniques and Applications of Artificial Intelligence* (pp. 222-234). Springer, London.

Munir, H., Bengtsson, L., & Åkesson, E. (2022). Management tools for business model innovation–a review. *Innovation*, 141–158. doi:10.4324/9780429346033-11

Osterwalder, A. (2002). An e-business model ontology for the creation of new management software tools and IS requirement engineering.*Semantic Scholar.*

Osterwalder, A. (2004). *The business model ontology a proposition in a design science approach* [Doctoral dissertation, Université de Lausanne, Faculté des hautes études commerciales].

Osterwalder, A., & Pigneur, Y. (2010). *Business model generation: a handbook for visionaries, game changers, and challengers* (Vol. 1). John Wiley & Sons.

Osterwalder, A., & Pigneur, Y. (2012). Designing business models and similar strategic objects: The contribution of IS. *Journal of the Association for Information Systems*, *14*(5), 3.

Osterwalder, A., Pigneur, Y., & Tucci, C. L. (2005). Clarifying business models: Origins, present, and future of the concept. *Communications of the Association for Information Systems*, *16*(1), 1. doi:10.17705/1CAIS.01601

Pagani, M. (2009). Roadmapping 3G mobile TV: Strategic thinking and scenario planning through repeated cross-impact handling. *Technological Forecasting and Social Change*, *76*(3), 382–395. doi:10.1016/j.techfore.2008.07.003

Peinel, G., Jarke, M., & Rose, T. (2009). *Business Models For E-government the BMeG Method*. Semantic Scholar.

Recio-García, J. A., Díaz-Agudo, B., & González-Calero, P. (2008). jcolibri2 tutorial. Department of Software Engineering and Artificial Intelligence, University Complutense of Madrid, Madrid.

Remané, G., Hanelt, A., Tesch, J. F., & Kolbe, L. M. (2019). The business model pattern database: a tool for systematic BMI. In *Business model innovation in the era of the Internet of Things* (pp. 89–144). Springer. doi:10.1007/978-3-319-98723-1_5

Rese, M., Meier, H., Gesing, J., & Boßlau, M. (2013). An ontology of business models for industrial product-service systems. In *The Philosopher's Stone for Sustainability* (pp. 191–196). Springer. doi:10.1007/978-3-642-32847-3_32

Roth-Berghofer, T., Recio Garcia, J. A., Sauer, C., Bach, K., Althoff, K. D., Diaz-Agudo, B., & Gonzales Calero, P. A. (2012). Building case-based reasoning applications with myCBR and COLIBRI studio.

Samavi, R., Yu, E., & Topaloglou, T. (2009). Strategic reasoning about business models: A conceptual modeling approach. *Information Systems and e-Business Management*, *7*(2), 171–198. doi:10.100710257-008-0079-z

Shaikh, E., Brahmi, M., Thang, P. C., Watto, W. A., Trang, T. T. N., & Loan, N. T. (2022). Should I Stay or Should I Go? Explaining the Turnover Intentions with Corporate Social Responsibility (CSR), Organizational Identification and Organizational Commitment. *Sustainability*, *14*(10), 6030. doi:10.3390u14106030

Shafer, S. M., Smith, H. J., & Linder, J. C. (2005). The power of business models. *Business Horizons*, *48*(3), 199–207. doi:10.1016/j.bushor.2004.10.014

Sinkovics, N., Gunaratne, D., Sinkovics, R. R., & Molina-Castillo, F. J. (2021). Sustainable business model innovation: An umbrella review. *Sustainability*, *13*(13), 7266. doi:10.3390u13137266

Snihur, Y., Lamine, W., & Wright, M. (2021). Educating engineers to develop new business models: Exploiting entrepreneurial opportunities in technology-based firms. *Technological Forecasting and Social Change*, *164*, 119518. doi:10.1016/j.techfore.2018.11.011

Sørmo, F., Cassens, J., & Aamodt, A. (2005). Explanation in case-based reasoning–perspectives and goals. *Artificial Intelligence Review, 24*(2), 109–143. doi:10.100710462-005-4607-7

Spieth, P., Schneckenberg, D., & Ricart, J. E. (2014). Business model innovation–state of the art and future challenges for the field. *Research Management, 44*(3), 237–247.

Spieth, P., & Schneider, S. (2016). Business model innovativeness: designing a formative measure for business model innovation. *Journal of business Economics, 86*(6), 671-696.

Staab, S., & Studer, R. (Eds.). (2010). *Handbook on ontologies.* Springer Science & Business Media.

(2015). Strategyzer. The business model canvas: Why and how organizations around the world adopt it. Technical report. *Strategyzer Field Report, 13*, 27.

Szopinski, D., Schoormann, T., John, T., Knackstedt, R., & Kundisch, D. (2017). *How software can support innovating business models: A taxonomy of functions of business model development tools.* Semantic Scholars.

Szopinski, D., Schoormann, T., John, T., Knackstedt, R., & Kundisch, D. (2020). Software tools for business model innovation: Current state and future challenges. *Electronic Markets, 30*(3), 469–494. doi:10.100712525-018-0326-1

Täuscher, K., & Abdelkafi, N. (2017). Visual tools for business model innovation: Recommendations from a cognitive perspective. *Creativity and Innovation Management, 26*(2), 160–174. doi:10.1111/caim.12208

Tunio, M. N., Jariko, M. A., Børsen, T., Shaikh, S., Mushtaque, T., & Brahmi, M. (2021). How Entrepreneurship Sustains Barriers in the Entrepreneurial Process—A Lesson from a Developing Nation. *Sustainability, 13*(20), 11419. doi:10.3390u132011419

Van Melle, W., Shortliffe, E. H., & Buchanan, B. G. (1984). EMYCIN: A knowledge engineer's tool for constructing rule-based expert systems. *Rule-based expert systems: The MYCIN experiments of the Stanford Heuristic Programming Project*, 302-313.

Veit, D., Clemons, E., Benlian, A., Buxmann, P., Hess, T., Kundisch, D., Leimeister, J. M., Loos, P., & Spann, M. (2014). Business models: An information systems research agenda. *Business & Information Systems Engineering, 6*(1), 45–53. doi:10.100712599-013-0308-y

Xu, F., Liu, X., Chen, W., Zhou, C., & Cao, B. (2018). Ontology-based method for fault diagnosis of loaders. *Sensors (Basel), 18*(3), 729. doi:10.339018030729 PMID:29495646

Zoric, J. (2011). Connecting business models with service platform designs: Exploiting potential of scenario modeling. *Telematics and Informatics, 28*(1), 40–54. doi:10.1016/j.tele.2010.05.008

Zott, C., Amit, R., & Massa, L. (2011). The business model: Recent developments and future research. *Journal of Management, 37*(4), 1019–1042. doi:10.1177/0149206311406265

# Chapter 8
# Identifying and Analysing Entrepreneurship Barriers in Afghanistan

**Alireza Rajabipoor Meybodi**
*Yazd University, Iran*

**Elahe Hosseini**
https://orcid.org/0000-0003-3478-5320
*Yazd University, Iran*

**Joma Khan Kazimi**
*Yazd University, Iran*

**Ahsanullah Sazawar**
*Yazd University, Iran*

## ABSTRACT

*Despite of a vast amount of research about the significance effects of entrepreneurship on different economic and social aspects in developed and developing countries, there are limited studies about entrepreneurship barriers in developing countries; but in Afghanistan, due to unfavourable situations, this shortcoming is more serious. To the best of the authors' knowledge, still this important topic is not addressed in Afghanistan. This study aims to identify entrepreneurship barriers in Afghanistan. In this exploratory study, in a targeted sampling approach using chain-referral method, data collected through semi structured interviews and 11 participants, including defacto- entrepreneurs, potential entrepreneurs and one academic professional, were interviewed. Sample size depend on data saturation that happened in 8th and 9th. For data analysis, the authors use thematic analysis to investigate the research question.*

DOI: 10.4018/978-1-6684-6766-4.ch008

## INTRODUCTION

Beside other adversities, eradicating poverty and unemployment in all its forms remains one of the greatest challenges facing Afghanistan. More than one in four of work force was unemployed in 2019, poverty rate from 36% in 2012 increased to 55% in 2019 (United Nations Development Programme, 2020) and the World Bank estimation reported that poverty rate may project up to 72% in Afghanistan due to Covid-19 pandemic and y the end of 2020, Afghanistan's unemployment rate was projected to rise to 37.9%, while in 2019 unemployment rate was 23.9% (Social Inspector General for Afghanistan Reconstruction (SIGAR), 2021). According ILO estimation, around 400000 labour force enter into Afghanistan labour market each year, but job creation rate is manifold lower than new labour force. Economic crisis and unemployment are the main reason why Afghanistan have the highest migration rate. Survey by 'The Asia Foundation' shows that 72% of informants declared unemployment as their serious problems and 52% of informants claimed the economic situations as the main reason of migrating.

Despite of war, insecurity, instability; people have to earn their livelihood in any possible way. Knowing how to get rid of poverty and improve living standard of poor communities, are not beyond the human understanding as well as it is not easy too. Previous research shows that there is a close relationship between quality of life and socio-economic development with the existence of investment and manufacturing companies or entrepreneurship (Erdin & Ozkaya, 2020). To have a healthy, prosperous, harmonious, happy and life satisfied people; there should be a responsive, trustworthy and qualified state to provide an adequate Economic growth and social development (Liu et al., 2020), unfortunately often poor countries' policy maker just focus on foreign aid and policy interventions to change the situation, in Afghanistan it's a conspicuous issue that depending on foreign aid and concentrating on intervention policy could not alleviate the unemployment and poverty rate, there is just one way to eradicate poverty and unemployment, that is Economic growth and social development through creating job.

Entrepreneurial growth and activities are very slug and slow in non-developed and developing countries (Nikraftar et al.,2021). This is due to the presence of several factors such as economic and political factors, societal and cultural barriers, technical and educational barriers and so on. Lack of hard infrastructures, such as roads, bridges, transportation networks are evident in Afghanistan. Hard infrastructures are crucial to entrepreneurship, but lacking of it, is not that much serious obstacle, Entrepreneurship can work without a perfect system of hard infrastructure or, at least, can begin to work and often with minimal other resources (Desai, 2011). In Afghanistan despite of abundance resources and raw materials, but still entrepreneurship has not grew. It seems raw material, market availability, good opportunities are not enough to flourish entrepreneurship, in addition to raw material, resources and market; there should political and cultural ease and innate attitude (Hosseini et al., 2022). As Gunnar Myrdal said that Asian societies lack entrepreneurship, not because they lack money or raw materials, but because of their attitude. Here we reviewed some literatures about entrepereneurship and entrepreneurial barriers in other countries, then we will dicuss the findings and limitations.

## LITERATURE REVIEW

Entrepreneurship function is probably as old as the exchange and trade between individual in society back to 8000 years before(Edwards et al., 2020). But, the one who give it more precise economic meaning or proposed as an economic term, was Richard Cantillon (1680-1734) (Mazzarol & Reboud, 2020) and he defined the entrepreneur as those individuals, who bear the risk of buying at certain prices and selling at uncertain prices.

Entrepreneurship is a controversial topic, there is not unity between scholar about the definition of entrepreneurs and entrepreneurship (Tajpour et al.,2022). Some researchers argue it is a temporal experiences that consist of several stages or cumulative series of interdependent events from pre-venture experiences to emergence of venture or entrepreneurship that rooted in affect and emotions (Morris et al., 2012). In other words, Entrepreneurship is a journey consist of obstacles, failure and victories. The ability of entrepreneurs' in dealing with hindrances and barriers determine the ultimate outcome of entrepreneurship (Kollmann, Stöckmann & Kensbock, 2017). Some other define entrepreneurship as process consist of all activities and functions of perceiving opportunities and pursuing it through creating organization (Moroz & Hindle, 2012). Schumpeter define entrepreneurship as a creative destructions. It mean, the demise of previous model is essential entrepreneurship (Kraehe, 2019).

GEM define the Entrepreneurship as '*Any attempt at new business or new venture creation, such as self-employment, a new business organization, or the expansion of an existing business, by an individual, a team of individuals, or an established business*'. In this research we adopt the GEM definition of entrepreneurship.

Despite of a vast amount of research about the significance effects of Entrepreneurship on different economic and social aspects in developed and developing countries, like GDP/capita, unemployment, exports/GDP, patents per population (Doran et al, 2018), poverty reduction (Morris et al, 2020) economic growth (Pradhan et al., 2020) well-being and health (Wiklund et al., 2019) Sustainable Development (Dhahri et al., 2021) around the globe and specially in developed countries. Altogether, there are limited studies about entrepreneurship barriers in developing countries, but in Afghanistan, due to unfavourable situations, this shortcoming is more serious. To the best of our knowledge still this important topic is not addressed in Afghanistan, just a few report presented by foreign institutions and some other researches (Mohsen et al., 2020) that did not address exactly the barriers. In spite of higher entrepreneurial intentions among developing countries than developed, still there are not a significant progress in developing countries.

Barriers faced by budding entrepreneurs from developing countries (Tunio et al., 2021) may differ from those in developed countries (Meybodi et al., 2021). For, developed countries have more institutional support, high quality and suitable education system, good economic conditions, political and economic stability that reduce potential barriers (Sandhu et al., 2011). In this research, we try to answer the following questions:

1. What are Entrepreneurship Barriers in Afghanistan?
2. Under what categories can classify entrepreneurship Barriers in Afghanistan?

## Objectives of This Research

The main purpose of this research is to determine Entrepreneurship Barriers in Afghanistan, and answer to the question what factors influence entrepreneurship in Afghanistan and under what categories entrepreneurship barriers can be classified in Afghanistan.

*Table 1. Represent a summary of research and findings in other countries*

| Region | Author (Reference) | Statistical Population | Variables | Findings |
|---|---|---|---|---|
| **Australia** | (Kouriloff, 2000) | West Of N.S.W., Australia (Potential, Intending, Actual entrepreneurs, and no wish to start) | Age, Gender, Education, Range Of Barriers, Intensity Of Barriers, Domain Of Specific Barriers, Hidden Barriers, Combination of Barriers and Barriers sequences | The importance and sequentiality, combination and intensity of barriers are different according each groups. But, more important barriers are largely non-economic and intractable to government policy. |
| **South Africa** | (Cupido, 2002) | SMMEs (within the teclmical maintenance, chemical cleaners and specialised lubricant products suppliers to the petro-chemical, marine, industrial and power- generating industry in the Western Cape) | Gender, Age, Motivation, Business Plan and Managerial skills, Financial Aids and sources, Red Tap | Lack of Required Education and Management Skills, start business without any plan, Complexity of Finance Acquisition |
| **Albania** | (Bitzenis and Nito, 2005) | Companies in eleven Developed Cities of Albania (Tirana, Durres, Fieri, Vlora, Korca, Lushnje, Elbasan, Erseka, Saranda, Berati, Gjirokastra) | Enterprise Size and Life Span | Unfair competition, Changes in Taxation Procedures, Lack of Financial resources and problems related to Public Order |
| **USA (Illinois State University)** | (Elango, Hunter and Winchell, 2007) | Two Hospital Administrator, A Nurse Entrepreneur, An Ophthalmology Entrepreneur, A Dean of the nursing school familiar with nurse Entrepreneurship and 20 students in a nurse practitioner Program. . | Opportunity Recognition, Overcoming Entry Barriers, Operational Competencies | Legal Barriers, Personal and Ethical conflict, Knowledge Barriers (Lack of Management skills) |
| **Iran (Zanjan)** | (Yaghoubi, 2010) | Agricultural graduated students in higher education institutions of Zanjan province | Marital status, Education Level, Field of Study | Inappropriate teaching methods, Inappropriate educational content and syllabus, Poor educational and laboratory equipment and Inappropriate evaluation system |
| **Malaysia** | (Sandhu, Sidique and Riaz, 2011) | Postgraduate students studying at universities offering postgraduate education in Malaysia | Independent Variables: Risk Aversion, Stress and work Difficulty, Failure, Social Network, Financial resources, Demographic Factors.<br>Dependents Variables: Entrepreneurial Inclinations | Lack of Social Networking, Lack of Resources and Risk Aversion |
| **Iran (Persian Gulf University)** | (Raeesi et al., 2013) | Reviewing the most relevant available literature to elicit the major general barriers by utilizing Interpretive Structural Modelling (ISM) | | Among eleven Identified Entrepreneurship Barriers, Corrupted and Unsupportive business environment are the most serious. |
| **Albania, Georgia, Morocco, Nigeria and Pakistan** | (El Alaoui et al., 2016) | Data collected from officials of 149 Companies (mostly SMEs) through questionnaire disseminated from October to December 2015. | Type of Operation, Company size, Perception of the Environment, Activities' Expansion Plan | State Policy toward SMEs, Corruption and Political Instability, Tax Policy |

*continues on following page*

*Table 1. Continued*

| Region | Author (Reference) | Statistical Population | Variables | Findings |
|---|---|---|---|---|
| **India (Uttarakhand)** | (Sharma, 2018) | Students of professional courses | Gender and Regional Culture | Social Custom and Traditions (Gender Discriminations) |
| **Iraq** | (Kanabi and Tasie, 2020) | | | Political Instabilities, Lack of capital funding, lack of infrastructure, Barriers to entry and the Red tap |
| **sub-Saharan Africa** | (Osunmuyiwa, & Ahlborg,2022) | Rural district of Njombe, Tanzania | Gender and energy<br>Gender and entrepreneurship<br>Electricity access<br>Women's empowerment | Most women remained in low-growth enterprises due to existing socio-economic and power imbalances. |
| **Kazakhstan** | (Khanin et al.,2022) | Seven- teen interviews with the local entrepreneurs | Barriers to entrepreneurship, opportunity recognition, opportunity pursuit | Social-institutional factors may create access and legitimacy barriers; and economic-operational factors may erect location and magnitude barriers. |
| **India** | (Chaturvedi & Karri,2022) | Forty-four tech firms and ten non-tech firms | Entrepreneurship, Times of Pandemic, Barriers and Strategies | The prime barriers which affected the firms were organizational readiness, infrastructural support by government, technological inadequacy and financial crises. |
| **Iran** | (Tajpour et al.,2022) | Global Entrepreneurship Monitor (GEM) and its report during 2017 | International entrepreneurship, entrepreneurial opportunity perception, innovative, performance | International entrepreneurs balance the market by introducing a new product-market-to-market mix |
| **Pakistan** | (Tunio et al.,2021) | young entrepreneurs in the region of Hyderabad | entrepreneurship; entrepreneurial process; challenges; developing countries; sustainability; sustainable entrepreneurship | The findings of the study in the form of final themes suggest that trust issues, family barriers, financial issues, gender issues, educational barriers, corruption, and legal barriers are among the challenges which trigger changes in the entrepreneurial process and its sustainability. |
| **Poland** | (Wach & Bilan,2021) | students of seven different universities from Krakow | public support, administration barriers, institutional barriers, entrepreneurship education, entrepreneurship, entrepreneurial intentions | The results confirmed that positively perceived public support in favor of entrepreneurship strengthens the young generation's entrepreneurial intentions to start their own business, while negatively perceived administration barriers against entrepreneurship blunt the young generation's entrepreneurial intentions to start their own business. |

## RESULTS AND DISCUSSION

The article has sought to identify entrepreneurship barriers in Afghanistan. In the iterative analysis process, five themes were identified. The first theme being the economic and financial obstacles, administrative and institutional barriers is the second most predominant theme in this study. Lack of infrastructure, social-cultural barriers, and educational barriers are third, fourth and fifth predominant themes respectively. We will discuss each theme and sub-themes as follow.

*Figure 1. Themes and subthemes*

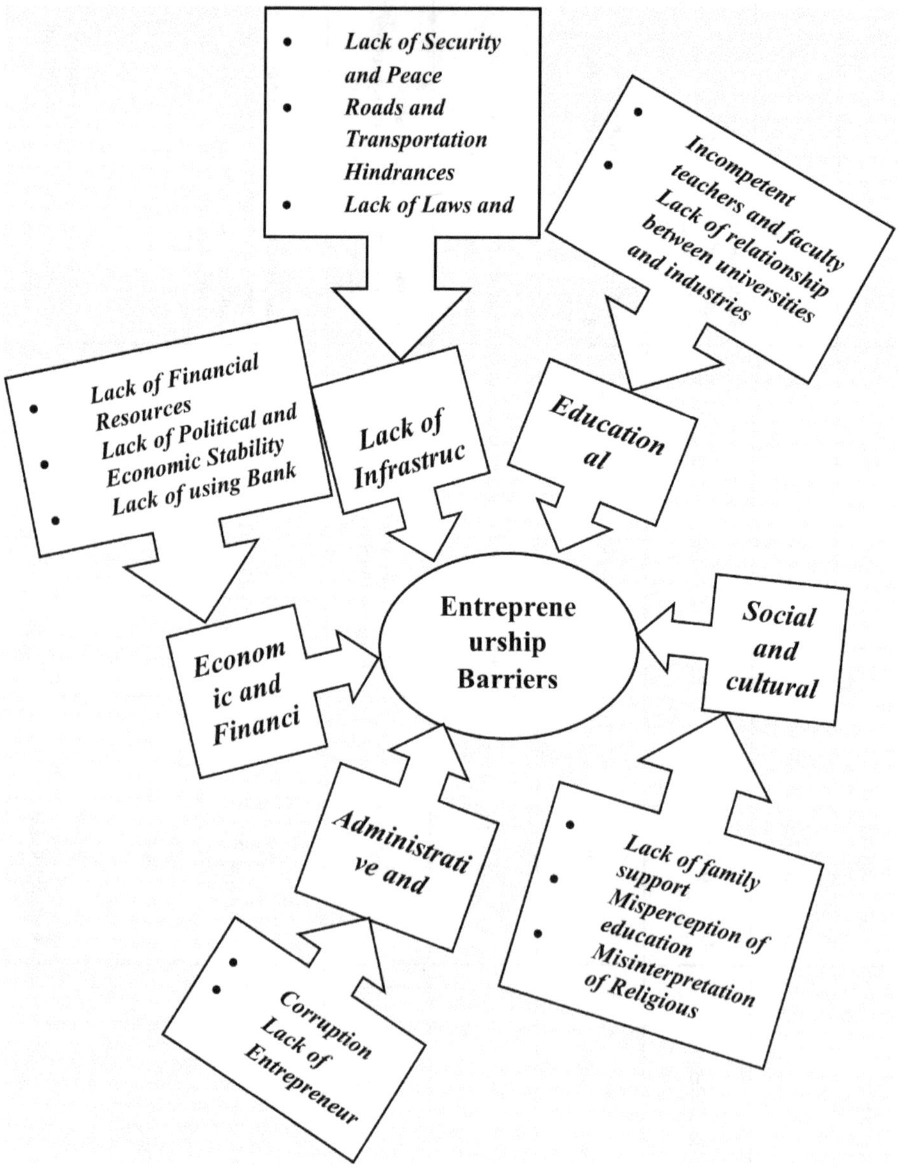

## Lack of Infrastructures

The entrepreneurship emersion and development is not an accidental phenomena rather than it depend on some economic, social, cultural and political factors which commonly can be listed as entrepreneurial activities friendly environment or simply as infrastructures.

The reason why in some region or countries entrepreneurial activities are more and in another is less or even none, is due to existence or non-existence of appropriate infrastructures. The infrastructures quality represent the quality of economic development and the growth of entrepreneurship and entrepreneurial activities directly depends on infrastructures. Infrastructures like transport, electricity, water, sanitation, information, communication technology, broadband (Ajide, 2020) institutional infrastructures and human capital (Nguyen et al., 2020) have a positive impact on entrepreneurial activities, many scholars believes that providing enough facilities and infrastructures like roads and energy sources are likely to reduce the poverty and unemployment. Lack of essential infrastructures such as road, electricity, institutions (law and entities) are a big challenge for entrepreneurs in Afghanistan that will explained as follow:

## Lack of Security

Security and peace are the panacea of everything. Security refers to the absence of threats to peace, stability, national cohesion and solidarity, absences of threats to socio-economic objective and Political achievement of a country. In other word, security refers to relative ability of a state to counter threats to its core values and interests.

Although some scholars like Olson and Higg's viewpoints are difference to war. Olson claim that major disruptions and crisis such as war by removing entrenched interest groups clean the way for productive reforms. Higgs believe that the U.S. government's growth in the 20th century was caused by a 'ratchet effect' stemming from crises (O'Reilly & Powell, 2015). But still War and Insecurity by increasing uncertainty, inflation, tax increment effects both potential and active businesses negatively, specially Civil war and proxy war have more negative effects on economy.

For more than four decades Afghanistan has engaged in a deadly Civil and Proxy war that caused infrastructures demolition, disappointment, frustration, suppression of entrepreneurial and critical thinking. Our finding shows that one of the serious obstacles to entrepreneurs are insecurity in Afghanistan. As per the informants of this study insecurity in Afghanistan stems either from corruption and legal malpractices or lack of government control in some region. As participants says:

*'…for ages Afghanistan is involved in wars – (P3, 6)'*

Or

*'In Afghanistan those who have a cake to eat, their liberty deprived, their family and their children are in risk of abduction and there is no authority to save them. You know security issues are more serious than financial problems. We have many entrepreneurs who left the country due to insecurity and invest in some other countries – (P7, 7)'*

## Roads and Transportation Hindrances

The transportation infrastructures essentiality and effectiveness on economic development is an importance topic in economic development research that many researchers, policy makers and scholars interested on(Saidi et al., 2018). Studies shows that between productivity and transport infrastructures are direct relationship, in long run it accelerate the economic development especially in developing countries and investing on roads in rural areas enhance social welfare through reducing the transport cost, improving the market and escalating the schools and university enrolment(Khandker & Koolwal, 2011).

Unfortunately in Afghanistan especially in rural area due to insecurity and more than decades civil wars transport infrastructures are not developed and mostly districts, villages and cities are connected through dirt and rough roads. Lack of transport infrastructures and asphalted roads are an obstacles to running business. As one the informant say complain about:

*'There are many opportunities in Afghanistan, especially in rural areas, but due to lack of good and asphalted roads we cannot utilize these opportunities - (P2, 27)'*

Another problem is that government do not supervise and control the roads effectively, heavy vehicle damage the roads.

## Lack of Laws and Order

The existence of Law and regulations; defining individual's relationship and responsibilities and clarifying its consequences are crucial for societies, the absence or malfunctioning of it create a distrust and mistrust environment that cripple the countries' economic and social development. As Hobbes says, absences of law and order and entrepreneurs distrust on law sanction discourage entrepreneurs from entry. Or as per Weber economic development is the result of a formal and rational legal system(Ogus, 2004).

In last two decades economic has changed in two dimension; Globalization and emersion of e-commerce along with internet expansion around the countries that both requires suitable legislation as per new problems(Hadfield, 2012). Beside, as economic development requires hard infrastructures as well as it need soft infrastructures and an integrated and developed legal system, especially free market economy depends more on rule and regulation and code of conducts. Overall, in addition to Accounting system and Cultural Attitudes, in a market economy legal system is the third essential institution. Weak rule of law, lack of good governance and absence of regulations pose a major threat to social and economic development over the world, and they have hindered progress in attaining the Millennium Development Goals (United Nations, 2013).

The lack of rule of law and absence of rules of regulation in some cases in Afghanistan pose barriers against entrepreneurs and cause confusion and uncertainty. The current research finding indicates that the lack of rules and regulation are a major obstacles for entrepreneurs. One of participant says:

*'Rules and regulations in Afghanistan are not as per new market and business requirements, it's for past, the nature of business has changed, and they have not enacted new law for new business- (P10, 21)'*

Lack of tax exemption law is another challenges as per entrepreneurs in Afghanistan.

## Absence of Entities to Support Entrepreneurial Ideas and Activities

It's believed that the way small business is managed determines its success. Often the absence of an effective institutional support system, lack of a systematic human resource development plan and skills in nascent entrepreneurship leads to mismanagement (Jegede & Irewole, 2020). One of the main role of Entrepreneurship Support Agencies (Entities) are providing Business Development Services to fill the gaps. Regulative (government policy toward financial support of entrepreneurs), Cognitive (developing managerial skills through general and practical knowledge) and Normative (developing entrepreneurial culture) are the triplet essential environment for entrepreneurship development. Governments enhance these three elements through establishing Entrepreneurship Support Agencies (Sayyedi & Taqi-Khani, 2011).

Unfortunately in Afghanistan still there is not established any specific entities to support entrepreneurs either financially or administratively. As one of the participant says;

*'Right now there is not any investment company...government should establish a specific agency or ministry to support entrepreneurs... at least there should be a specific address for entrepreneurs to recourse for solving the problems – (P11, 14)'*

## Lack of Energy (Electricity)

Electricity is an essential part of modern life and important to economic development that without electricity technological and industrial development, informational and security advancement will lag behind. Electricity through creating entrepreneurial opportunities, improving production process and wealth creation; effects individuals' perceptions of their social position and increase the households' income and there is a significant relationship between electrification and economic development.

Even though access to electricity increased from five per cent of Afghanistan population in 2001 to 30% in 2016, but still 70% of population has no access to electricity, including 90% of people living in rural areas. Lack of electricity is a big challenges for entrepreneurs and households. Often power pylons are blown up by extortionists and terrorist groups that cause power outage for days.

*'Another problem is the shortage of electricity. For example often due to power pylons destruction, power cut happens and we have to provide from other sources that it effects on final price of goods –(P8,9)'*

In addition to lack of access, the country's electric power sector is also plagued by reliance on imports, high consumer costs, and unreliability and Afghanistan pays at least $280 million annually to import 670 megawatts of power from neighbouring countries (Mian, 2021).

# ECONOMIC AND FINANCIAL BARRIERS

## Lack of Financial Resources

Access to capital plays an important role in entrepreneurship, both in direct and indirect ways. In many developing countries where Financial and Legal system are not developed, access to financial resources are a critical issues for entrepreneurs. Some study shows that access to financial resources and Entrepreneurial Propensities are different in different countries (Dvorský *et al.*, 2019).

In Afghanistan lack of financial resources and financial exclusion are a serious barriers for entrepreneurs. As all participant in this study with unanimously claimed lack of financial as their major barriers. One says;

*'The first problem that I had, was lack of finance. We with our team estimated the costs, we had to bear a huge expense, and we were students and financially were not independent. So, for me the financial problem were the only barrier – (P9, 3'*

## Lack of Entrepreneurial Loans

Lack of Entrepreneurial Loans and the ***High rate of interest*** are other barriers that entrepreneurs face in Afghanistan. Many nascent entrepreneurs and young enterprises in Afghanistan lack enough equity. As a result, the way to self-employment is often blocked from the very beginning. Hardly a bank is willing to grant a loan to a borrower who does not or cannot provide a strong collateral in Afghanistan. As participant say:

*'Public Bank do not provide any entrepreneurial Loan, Private sector either do not have any program in this regard. Private Banks just provide loans for those who have a high pay jobs, not for nascent entrepreneurs – (P11, 18)'* **or** *'Banks do not trust on us, for that they set difficult conditions and require collateral that have higher value than the amount of loans that we can't provide them – (P6, 27)'*

New business founders and young enterprises need small loan and more relaxed collateral requirements for their bank loan. Often Governments take action through Microfinance Loans programs to develop entrepreneurship(Chan, 2018). Nowadays Microfinance recognize as a primary engine of economic growth, note that success and efficiency of Microfinance also depend on institutional quality, poor institutional quality lead to unproductive or even destructive entrepreneurial activities(Nair & Njolomole, 2020).

In Afghanistan some bank grant Microfinance loans, but hardly provide nascent entrepreneurs, they mostly provide loans for business expansion not for new businesses. Also Afghanistan institutional and legal system act poorly.

## Lack of using Bank Account and Online services

Certainly, banking system through gathering and attracting deposit from savers and providing loans and resources for investment projects and business expansion, play an important role in economic growth. Greater banking sector openness and more access to banking services facilitate access to more sources and significantly increases new business formations (Ghosh, 2021). In addition, using bank account and banking services, especially e-banking provide a save transaction environment, decrease customer costs, save time and facilitated swift movement of funds domestically and across borders.

Unfortunately, in Afghanistan a vast majority of population are unbanked and not using any kind of banking services, have no saving account and do not deposit. Lack of internet coverage in most part of the country and lack of online banking and online transaction caused hindrance for businesses, especially e-business in Afghanistan.

*'The business that I am going to involve, need some infrastructures such as e-banking, online transaction, e-market and internet coverage. In Afghanistan we have not yet all of these – (P8, 13)'*

## Lack of Political and Economic Stability

Political instability refers to events or situation that government face a serious extra-parliamentary or extra-institutional threat and propensity to collapse the government. Political instability cause due to social conflict or fierce competition of political parties (Fraj et al., 2020). Studies shows a converse relationship between political instability and growth. political instability reduce investment activities and adversely affects growth by lowering the rates of productivity (Aisen & Veiga, 2013). Political instability and economic instability have a reciprocal relationships. Income inequality by fueling social dissatisfaction cause socio-political instability, political instability decrease investment and it leads to decrease economic growth.

Although some study (Yakubu *et al.*, 2021) found that political stability does not gave evidence of causing growth, but in Afghanistan entrepreneurs sees political and economic instability as a big challenge for their businesses. In last four decades due to civil war and proxy war Afghanistan lost the hard and soft infrastructures; uncertainty and inflation rate is high (in past 20 years Afghanistan experienced an average 8.1 inflation rate that is manifold higher than universal average rate 3.7); future is unpredictable and all together made an unfavourable environment for investors and entrepreneurs. As participants says;

*'There is no political and economic stability, people can't trust to financial system; when people do not believe on economic system, it is clear they won't enter to market – (P10, 6)'*

## ADMINISTRATIVE AND INSTITUTIONAL BARRIERS

Entrepreneurial success of any nation is largely dependent on the policy behaviour of the government. Government as the lead entity in entrepreneurship development, are responsible in providing resources for entrepreneurs. The government policy in support of entrepreneurs includes codifying and defining the rules and regulations (Aldieri et al., 2021), law enforcement, establishment of a transparent legal system, providing financial resources, pursue a supportive policies and training the entrepreneurs (Obaji, 2014). Management barriers such as the lack of proper analysis of the current status of social issues and planning to eliminate them, lack of specific operational programs for responding to social problems, lack of proper participatory management in solving community's social problems, management based on relationships rather than criteria (relationships instead of rules), failure to address real entrepreneurial activities due to community managers' lack of understanding of entrepreneurship (many costs are allocated to useless tasks), and lack of necessary managerial competencies in the field of entrepreneurship among managers and members firms(Naderi et al.,2022). Managerial skills also affect the performance of entrepreneurship(Khan & Burki, 2020). The main problems related to management are financing issues, personal issues, leadership, technical and lack of experience, which have been considered the principal obstacles to the success of businesses, particularly entrepreneurship(Hosseini et al.,2022). Managers in entrepreneurial entrepreneurship do not possess enough knowledge of how to manage financial matters, which results in the underutilisation of resources and even failure. entrepreneurship business is risky, but efficient managerial knowledge and skills can bring success(Khan,2022). As per this study's informants, in Afghanistan due to mismanagement and corruption, Government could not provide a suitable and supportive institutional environment. The major institutional and administrative barrier in Afghanistan includes Corruption, Lack of Funding, Lack of Entrepreneurial Insurance, and Lack of Financial Institution Support.

## Corruption

Corruption is a big challenge for all countries and have negative effects on economic growth and development. In developing countries corruption is one of the main reason behind economic crisis and conflicts. According Economist, Corruption refers to the misuse of power for private gain. Corruption exist everywhere, in different levels of a system, emerges in different forms; but mostly take root in countries with a weak incentives and poor monitoring, transparency and accountability of public agents(Bahoo et al., 2020).

Due to war; poor performance of executive, legislative, and judicial system; Aid dependency and lack of supervision on foreign organization corruption become an impossible puzzle that hinder the developmental and entrepreneurial activities. Corruption erupt in different forms in Afghanistan, like extortion, bribe, graft and peculation of developmental projects, nepotism in recruitments and government contracts, legal corruptions and bureaucratic obstacles.

*'You know there is corruption in law execution, this corruption discourage entrepreneurs to engage in business. I have seen how they hinders in registration process, even they asked us bribe … we have to obey, because there is no way – (P11, 16)'*

## Lack of Entrepreneurial Subsidies and Entrepreneurial Insurances

Subsidies are an important economic intervention tools to budgeting nascent entrepreneurs and target groups. Usually, entrepreneurs and companies relies on subsidies to decrease the expenses and prevent the likely risks in a new market. Governments invest on R&D through granting Soft Loans and subsidies to develop entrepreneurship and innovation, especially for Tech-Related Business to facilitate turning research results into marketable products(Hottenrott & Richstein, 2020). Subsidies can be grant in the form of cash payment, soft loans, tax exemption, In-kind subsidies, Procurement subsidies and Regulation subsidies.

According participant in this study, Lack of entrepreneurial subsidies are a barriers for nascent entrepreneurs who are mostly students and youths with no income.

*'… like other countries, there is not any supportive programs such as subsidies and tax exemptions in Afghanistan. Government should support domestic products against dumping policy of other countries by granting subsidies and incentives – (P10, 23)'*

It is a well-known fact that one key feature of entrepreneurship is business risk. Bearing this in mind, the decision to become self-employed always entails a far-reaching willingness to accept risk to a lesser or greater extent, to decrease failure costs and encourage entrepreneurs, countries establish entrepreneurial Insurance. Lack of entrepreneurial Insurance in Afghanistan discourage the entrepreneurs from entry to marke.

## SOCIAL AND CULTURAL BARRIERS

Culture can be defined as a collective programming of the mind which distinguish the behaviour of one group members from another. In other words Culture is defined as a set of shared values, beliefs, and expected behaviours (Hofstede & Hofstede, 1984). Cultural values are able to lead or even manipulate the societies' ways of thinking and mind-set, it refers the degrees to which a society considers entrepreneurial behaviors, such as risk taking and independent thinking, to be worthwhile and favourable. Cultures that value such behaviour, obviously help to promote a propensity to develop entrepreneurial activities, while culture that enforce group interests and conformity are not likely to shows entrepreneurial behaviour.

We found that, in Afghanistan not only the cultural and social context are helpful for entrepreneurial activities, but also it discourage and even hinders entrepreneurs in their efforts to pursue entrepreneurial activities. People sees the entrepreneurship or self-employment as an in-genuine work. In other words, they think those who are not much educated and are not enough genius, and those who cannot find genuine job; will start their own business (entrepreneurship out of necessity).

*'People mock him, humiliate and look him as inferior. They think those who are self-employed, absolutely they are lazy and educated in a low level that could not find any honoured job – (P3, 16)*

### Lack Of Family Support

Entrepreneurship is an acquired process rather than inherent, family play an important role in forming entrepreneurial behaviours. Cultural values influence the social networks' propensity toward entrepreneurial activities which is an important primary resources for entrepreneurs and social network that consist of family and friends, influence on entrepreneurs decision making (Klyver &Foley, 2012). In Afghanistan most of family and friends are not interested in entrepreneurial activities. One reason, especially for family can be risk aversion, but the main factor is the negative view of family to self-employment. Family and friends looks at entrepreneurship, especially those jobs that are less education oriented (like animal husbandry, aviculture, greenhouse and etc.).

*'Family do not support us, especially if we want to run some business which already exist in its customary manners, like livestock job and greenhouse. Personally I faced this barriers, I am an educated person, when I shared my Idea with my family and friends, somehow they mocked me and said 'this kind of job is not fit for an educated person' – (P9, 5)'*

### Misperception of Education

Another problem in Afghanistan is the misperception of people from education. Most of people perceive that education entails having government or office jobs. One of participant said about;

*'One who studies for 16-18 years, if s/he run a self-owned business, what people may say about? They will what is difference between s/he and some uneducated one – (P3, 15)'*

*Illiteracy* is another obstacle that it seems the most of cultural barriers rooted in illiteracy of society. An-alphabet have a negative effect on people views about self-owned business and investment, especially financial illiteracy.

## Misinterpretation of Religious Decrees and Instructions

In some cases, the misinterpretation of some religious tenets and instructions create barrier. Before starting any job or making decision, people refers to social values and norms that usually rooted in their believe system's principles. Sometime these norms or at least misinterpretation of it prevent them from taking action(Block et al., 2020).

If entrepreneurs have not personal or household financial resource, nowadays borrowing money from Bank or others in a specific rate of interest are the most common way of financing. But as discussed above, interest earned on money (Riba) is foremost among the unacceptable business practices and strongly condemned in Islam. Riba by definition is the extra sum the money- lender charges from the borrower for deferred payment. Afghanistan as an Islamic country and predominantly governed by a conservative Islamic law, in some cases face barriers in this way. As one of participant says;

*'... either I should say fortunately or unfortunately the religious values in some case do not allow us to use facilities provided. One clear example is borrowing money from banks, because Riba (usury) is prohibited in Islam – (P9, 18)'*

## Lack of Social Trust and Social Capital

Social trust can be defined as a generalized trust between people in their routine, as much as the level of social trust be high in a society, they deal more confidently. Social trust is often said to be the essence of social capital or Social Trust is a dimension of social capital (Newton, 2004). Trust is the cornerstone of relationships that help to create a transparent, confident, and save interaction environment that leads to stabilize the behaviour of economic actors. Successful business activity and entrepreneurial activity are significantly influenced by the stable behaviour of economic actors as well as by the transparency of the macro and micro business environment.

One of the critical resources for entrepreneurship development is social capital which consist of a wide social network between entrepreneurs, friends and shareholder; norms and trust that leads people to cooperation(Mickiewicz & Rebmann, 2020). Social capital through providing and issuing information, financial and human resources, motivating and encouraging help in developing entrepreneurship.

Due to war, poor performance of legal system and corruptions, illiteracy and uncertainty damaged trust between Entrepreneurs-investors, entrepreneurs-customers, entrepreneurs-society that in result entrepreneurs access to a narrow network of social capital. As one said;

*'It's difficult to finance, no one interested to support us and loan us, it is because of distrusts between entrepreneurs and investors – (P7, 21)'*

## Risk Aversion and Fear of Failure

Risk taking propensity is a prerequisite for entrepreneurship development. Generally entrepreneurship rewards are more uncertain than salary or wage, for that individual with low risk taking propensity or high risk aversion rarely take the risk of starting a business. Financial risk is the most predominate risk that entrepreneurs face to (Tunio et al., 2021). Family and social risk, occupational risks, and psychological risks are other risk that can be considered.

In a situation like Afghanistan, where there is no security, financial resources are scarce, and more importantly due to political and economic instability, uncertainty rate is high; it is hard that one risks to start new business.

*'... There is no security, political and economic instability is high, no one knows what will happen..., future is not predictable, so, it is hard to risk in this situation (P10, 10)'*

## EDUCATIONAL BARRIERS

Nowadays universities increasingly try to foster Entrepreneurial Mind-set and spirit on their Students(Mackie & Leuthardt, 2018) as long as entrepreneurial mind-set improve one's performance and enhance the social inclusion (Bacigalupo *et al.*, 2016), boost the success in a digital world and globalization(Balocco *et al.*, 2019) and also improve the key decision making skills such as financing the projects (Schückes & Gutmann, 2020).

Many studies shows that a hopeful activities to foster entrepreneurial mind-set, is entrepreneurial education. Entrepreneurship Education refers to a Pedagogical Programme to develop entrepreneurial intentions and foster entrepreneurial skills and Entrepreneurial Competences (Riepe et al., 2020; Secundo *et al.*, 2020). The core objectives of entrepreneurial education is to alter students' mind-set and views on risk taking and innovation on business, to improve critical thinking, changes the attitudes, to develop technological knowledge and skills which crucial in current digital era (Ratten & Usmanij, 2021).

**Lack of Entrepreneurial Education** is a big challenges in Afghanistan. Due to importance of entrepreneurship in economic development and job creation, nowadays countries have specific policies to develop entrepreneurship, like establishing entrepreneurship centre in Universities and entrepreneurship supportive agency in government body(Tajpour et al.,2022). In Afghanistan government still did not constitute any specific address for that. This shortcoming is noticeable in different part of education system. Such as lack of specific subject about entrepreneurship in school, late major specification, teachers and faculty incompetency, lack of relationship between universities and industries, out of date and low quality materials, lack of specialist and Consulting Services.

**Incompetent Teachers and Faculty**; competent faculty and teacher significantly effects on developing critical thinking, improve problem solving skills, innovation and Ideation. This days, industries and start-ups rely on universities' number one product; Ideas. Idea generation factors includes excellent facilities, funding and excellent faculty, trainees and staff (Mackie & Leuthardt, 2018). As the report of participant in this research, most of faculty are not familiar with entrepreneurial issues, especially about online business.

*'Faculty are not know much about entrepreneurship, only about 20% may know about, 80% do not know and even they are not familiar with 'entrepreneurship concepts' – (P11, 13)'*

**Lack of Relationship Between Universities and Industries;** the impact of field visit or industrial visit on knowledge gaining, promoting active learning, deepen the understanding, improving cognitive complexity and practical competence among students has been well acknowledged (Rajasulochana & Senthil Ganesh, 2019). In field visit each student observes the phenomenon under study in a realistic setting, attaches personally relevant meaning to the experience, which in turn allows the student to play with concepts or activities often not possible in the classroom. Thus, the course content becomes relevant as students assimilate and accommodate new understanding and cognition.

Most universities have field visit in their curricular to improve learning quality and develop critical thinking and problem solving skills on their students. But in Afghanistan, either higher education do not defined any specific program for this importance or the university staff do not follow. As reported by informants, they did not formally participated any field visit during their educational careers.

*'In my point of view, during education period, students should visit some entrepreneurship centre and business or some production company. It helps students to develop a perspective about future. Universities should facilitate field visit, ask some business man or business owner to give seminar for student about their success and failure – (P5, 29)'*

Lack of competent human capital, especially in tech-related business, is another obstacle to entrepreneurship in Afghanistan. As reported;

*'We have not specialist human resources, specifically if one going to start a technological related business. Beside, outsourcing is costly and unaffordable for nascent entrepreneurship – (P3, 8)'*

## METHODOLOGY

Research is a systematic process of collecting, analysing, and interpreting information and data to increase our understanding of a phenomenon we are interested in or concerned about(Leedy & Ormrod, 2016). In other words, research is the process of collecting and analysing data to increase our understanding of a subject. In a nutshell; Research is a systematic method of finding the answer or solving a research problem (Creswell *et al.*, 2007).

### Data Collection

This qualitative study with an exploratory approach, sought to examine and interpret the Entrepreneurship Barriers in Afghanistan. It was performed between August 2020 and Jun 2021.Through a semi-structured interview and theoretical sampling in a chin referral (snowball approach), eleven participant, including one Faculty, one Business manager, five active entrepreneurs and four potential entrepreneurs were interviewed.

Initially, the researchers interviewed two potential entrepreneur introduced by a co-worker. After each interview, they were asked if they know anybody who are interested in this subject. As in most qualitative studies, the sample size in this study depended on data saturation. It means we discontinued the interviews at the point that additional data or further interview do not led to any new emergent themes. The saturation happened in 8th -9th interviews, to make sure, we interviewed few more participants.

There are many studies (Sitaridis & Kitsios, 2017; Hoogendoorn et al, 2019; Kwapisz, 2019) that investigate both perceived and actual barriers that some cases there are different what entrepreneur perceives as barriers before launching their business and what they face actually after entry. To cover all suppositions, we selected three group of participants; defacto- entrepeneurs, potential entrepreneurs and academic professional. All participant were male, with at least graduate education and aged between 25 and 35.

The purpose, application of the study and their desired time and place of the interview were determined through phone calls and direct messages. The interviews were performed either F2F or CMC, in both conditions the interviews were recorded for transcription and better understanding. For better organizing and avoiding disorder, we followed seven stage of interview introduced by Steinar Kvale (Kvale, 1996). Each interview lasted between 30 to 60 min. The major question asked was, 'What are the barriers to run and develop a business in Afghanistan?' To deepen the interviews, some exploratory questions such as 'What do you mean by entrepreneurship? Name some entrepreneurial opportunity you know and explain more about' were also asked.

After the interview transcription, by using 'MAXQDA', we applied thematic analysis to interpret the data. Thematic analysis is a combination of structured approach with the researcher's subjective interpretation for systematically describing and interpreting the meaning of qualitative data (Wæraas, 2022).

In a six steps that normally followed in each thematic analysis; Familiarize with data, Assigning preliminary codes, Search for themes, Reviews the themes, Define and name the themes and finally produced the report with an iterative process based on thematic analysis, the initial concepts related to the subject outlined. Eventually, 271 codes and 52 subtheme formed 17 main themes. One of the main themes (Lack of Infrastructure) which is the result of 4th stage, represented on (Table 1).

To Maintain Privacy and Confidentiality, we used 'Pmn' as descriptive code for each participant and theme numbers. 'P' represent the participant, 'm' show participant's number and 'n' signify code number which extracted from interviews. For instance, 'P2,27', represent the interviewee 2 and 27th Code extracted from this interview.

To assess validity, researchers recommend a series of techniques that contribute to valid research findings.Researchers should make sure that the findings reflect the experience of participants or the context in a believable way. Qualitative research cannot be assessed through a single test or step in the research process, but should rather follow the rules of a processual validity that depend on decisions made in every steps of the research process (Steils, 2021). To examine the reliability and Validity of codes, we applied triangulation (validity checking through contribution of three or more co-researchers in coding and theme extraction) and Member checking with Holsti's Method. Holsti's Formula is;

$$PA = \frac{2}{(nA + nB)}$$

Where PAo represents percentage of agreement between two coders, $\overline{A}$ is the number of two coders' consensus decisions, and $nA$ and $nB$ are numbers of decisions coders have made respectively. The statistic ranges from '0.00' (no agreement) to '1.00' (perfect agreement). (Table 3) Show the calculation.

*Table 2. Themes and subthemes*

| Sr. No | Themes | subthemes | Descriptive code | Ref | Freqs. |
|---|---|---|---|---|---|
| 1 | Lack of appropriate Infrastructure | Lack of Security | lack of Financial and self-security | {P1,13} {P2,8} {P3,6} {P4,4} {P5,4} {P6,9} {P7,7} {P8,10} {P9,4} {P11,7} | 38 |
| | | | security threats, Kidnaping | | |
| | | | Lack of security for businessmen and entrepreneurs | | |
| | | | worry about security, existence of terrorist groups | | |
| | | | security challenges, investors do not have self and financial safety | | |
| | | | Entrepreneurs are not save | | |
| | | | Terrorise of capitalist and investors | | |
| | | | disinclination to invest due to security situations | | |
| | | | theft, a dire security situation | | |
| | | | Lack of investment because of security problems | | |
| | | | Self and financial threats | | |
| | | Absence of Law | rules and regulation are limit to the past, it does not give clarification for new business | {P11,15} {P7,14} {P6,30} {P10,21} | |
| | | | lack of law transparency and lack of law on online businesses | | |
| | | | lack of law for online businesses | | |
| | | | Lack of Law for New businesses | | |
| | | Lack of Tax exemption | Lack of Tax exemption for nascent entrepreneurs | {P1,19} {P2,25} {P3,23} {P4,21} {P5,27} {P6,28} {P9,19} | |
| | | | Statutory they should exempt the tax | | |
| | | | They should not collect tax from nascent entrepreneurs | | |
| | | | The concerned entity should provide incentives | | |
| | | | Lack of financial aids and tax exemption | | |
| | | | Tax law should not be applicable on new entrepreneurs, instead they should be provide with a sum of money | | |
| | | | either do not collect the tax or decrease it | | |
| | | Lack of Financial Backing of Entrepreneurial Ideas | The government should establish a system to grant us loan | {P3,24} {P4,22} {P2,24} {P11,10} {P5,26} {P8,24} | |
| | | | They should give interest free loan to entrepreneurs | | |
| | | | There is not any specific entity and address to support entrepreneurial Ideas | | |
| | | | There is not any financial organization to support entrepreneurial Ideas | | |
| | | | Central Bank should ease and simplify the process and condition of lending | | |
| | | | Government should work on lending management systems | | |
| | | Lack of road infrastructure | Lack of suitable route in some areas | {P4,5} {P10,16} {P3,26} {P2,27} {P9,9} {P5,7} | |
| | | | Bad roads cause hindrance on Entrepreneurship | | |
| | | | Lack of Road and water supply system | | |
| | | | Dirt and bad roads | | |
| | | | Lack of communication path between rural and urban areas | | |
| | | | Defective communication channel between rural and urban areas | | |
| | | Lack of Energy | Lack of energy sources | {P5,12} {P2,13} {P7,8} {P8,9} | |
| | | | Lack of Electricity | | |
| | | | Power shortage | | |
| | | | electricity shortage | | |

*Table 3. Holsti's coefficient calculation*

| Coder | Sr. | Interviewee | Total Codes | Number of agreement | Number of disagreement | Inter-coder reliability |
|---|---|---|---|---|---|---|
| A | 1 | P2 | 66 | 28 | 10 | 0.84848485 |
| | 2 | P3 | 70 | 32 | 6 | 0.91428571 |
| | 3 | P8 | 65 | 28 | 9 | 0.86153846 |
| | **Total** | | **201** | **88** | **25** | **0.87562189** |
| B | 1 | P2 | 74 | 34 | 6 | 0.91891892 |
| | 2 | P3 | 65 | 28 | 9 | 0.86153846 |
| | 3 | P8 | 58 | 24 | 10 | 0.82758621 |
| | **Total** | | **197** | **86** | **25** | **0.87309645** |
| **Grand Total** | | | 398 | 174 | 50 | **0.87437186** |

The statistical calculation of Holsti's coefficient (0.874) show a high agreement between Coders.

In Member checking approach, researchers share the codes and themes extracted from interviews with related participant to check if the researcher could extract what the participant means. In this study, after transcription, we sent the extracted codes and theme to selected participants and asked them to share freely there opinion about the codes and themes extracted from their recorded interviews. They were strongly agree what we extracted.

## CONCLUSION

The article has sought to identify entrepreneurship barriers in Afghanistan. The data collected through both field and desk study. We used qualitative method with an exploratory approach and the primary data collected through semi-structured interview. The target group are included active and potential entrepreneurs, faculty members of economic and management fields, elites and managers of small enterprises. Using thematic analysis, eleven participant interviewed in a Chain-referral targeted sampling approach. Then with recursive process approach based on thematic analysis, the related key concept to our subject were Identified. Finally, 271 codes, 52 subthemes Identified and in four part including entrepreneurship concept as per interviewees, motive behind entrepreneurial activities by interviewees, entrepreneurial opportunities according participant and Barriers to Entrepreneurship. Barriers classified under five categories which consist; Lack of Infrastructures, Financial Barriers, Administrative barriers, Social-Cultural Barriers and Educational barriers.

The Government of Afghanistan should continue its anticorruption operations to reduce the level of corruption and bribery in the system. The study also confirms that the infrastructure is not very developed in Afghanistan. Therefore, steps should be taken to improve the road system in the country. The communication system should be improved to increase interactions between customers and producers.

The management skills of owners and managers also play a key role in entrepreneurship performance. Management should be trained in the business. Workshops and seminars should be arranged by different organisations to give knowledge of management skills, such as record-keeping, marketing and accounting, to help them manage their business on a daily basis. These skills will enhance the overall performance of entrepreneurship (Shaikh et al., 2022). Entrepreneurship owners can also receive suggestions from more established firms about how to conduct their business (Arabeche et al., 2022), and management should hire skillful, trustworthy and educated people to run their businesses.

Findings shows that even though most barriers such as financial, legal, infrastructural and educational barriers are the same as in other developing and specially neighbouring countries (Hamrouni et al., 2021), but still there are a significant differences in some points and special in Afghanistan. For example, cultural and educational barriers are a good cross section of this type. Mostly, cultural and educational barriers are a common phenomenon in developing countries, but the nature is different with Afghanistan. In other developing countries, usually female face cultural and gender discrimination barriers; but in Afghanistan cultural barriers are a pervasive matter regardless the gender diversity. Along with other educational shortage such as facilities and material qualities; students' and people's perception of education are disappointing. People perceive education as a path to bureaucrat or official jobs rather than to become a self-employed or entrepreneurs, society degrade the self-employed and entrepreneurs.

## LIMITATIONS AND DIRECTIONS FOR FUTURE RESEARCH

We note key limitations of this study that provide opportunities for further research. First, this study is the first step in entrepreneurship fields, it means we lacked a rich literature review in Afghanistan, so we posed the question that drafted as per other developing countries, probably this effect on our finding. For that, we highly recommend the future researcher to address each barriers identified in this study as separate topic. Second, there are many factors influence each barriers, like political factors, financial factors, cultural factors, educational factors and etc. but all factors do not have equal impact, there is need to assess the extent each factors influence entrepreneurship in Afghanistan. Third, in this study due to having tight schedule and other limitation, we interviewed just the male informants, obviously the finding shows barriers as per male perspectives and not say anything about barriers may face female entrepreneurs in Afghanistan, so there is need a research to assess barriers faced by female entrepreneurs.

## REFERENCES

Aisen, A., & Veiga, F. J. (2013). How does political instability affect economic growth? *European Journal of Political Economy*, *29*, 151–167. doi:10.1016/j.ejpoleco.2012.11.001

Ajide, F. M. (2020). Infrastructure and Entrepreneurship: Evidence from Africa. *Journal of Developmental Entrepreneurship*, *25*(3), 2050015. doi:10.1142/S1084946720500156

Aldieri, L., Brahmi, M., Bruno, B., & Vinci, C. P. (2021). Circular Economy Business Models: The Complementarities with Sharing Economy and Eco-Innovations Investments. *Sustainability*, *13*(22), 12438. https://doi.org/10.3390/su132212438

Arabeche, Z., Soudani, A., Brahmi, M., Aldieri, L., Vinci, C. P., & Abdelli, M. E. A. (2022). Entrepreneurial Orientation, Organizational Culture and Business Performance in SMEs: Evidence from Emerging Economy. *Sustainability*, *14*(9), 5160. doi:10.3390u14095160

Bacigalupo, M. (2016). EntreComp: The entrepreneurship competence framework. *Luxembourg. Publication Office of the European Union, 10*, 593884.

Bahoo, S., Alon, I., & Floreani, J. (2020). Corruption in economics: A bibliometric analysis and research agenda. *Applied Economics Letters, 28*(7), 1–14. doi:10.1080/13504851.2020.1764476

Balocco, R., Cavallo, A., Ghezzi, A., & Berbegal-Mirabent, J. (2019). Lean business models change process in digital entrepreneurship. *Business Process Management Journal, 25*(7), 1520–1542. doi:10.1108/BPMJ-07-2018-0194

Block, J., Fisch, C., & Rehan, F. (2020). *Religion and entrepreneurship: a map of the field and a bibliometric analysis, Management Review Quarterly*. Springer International Publishing. doi:10.100711301-019-00177-2

Chan, S. K. L. (2018). Hierarchical microcredit networks: Lending and borrowing cliques in self-help groups in Phnom Penh. *The International Journal of Sociology and Social Policy, 38*(11–12), 1008–1023. doi:10.1108/IJSSP-06-2017-0078

Chaturvedi, R., & Karri, A. (2022). Entrepreneurship in the times of pandemic: Barriers and strategies. *FIIB Business Review, 11*(1), 52–66. doi:10.1177/23197145211043799

Creswell, J. W., Hanson, W. E., Clark Plano, V. L., & Morales, A. (2007). Qualitative research designs: Selection and implementation. *The Counseling Psychologist, 35*(2), 236–264. doi:10.1177/0011000006287390

Desai, S. (2011). Measuring entrepreneurship in developing countries. In *Entrepreneurship and economic development* (pp. 94–107). Springer. doi:10.1057/9780230295155_4

Dhahri, S., Slimani, S. & Omri, A. (2021) 'Behavioral entrepreneurship for achieving the sustainable development goals', *Technological Forecasting and Social Change, 165*(June 2017), 120561. doi:. doi:10.1016/j.techfore.2020.120561

Doran, J., McCarthy, N., & O'Connor, M. (2018). The role of entrepreneurship in stimulating economic growth in developed and developing countries. *Cogent Economics and Finance, 6*(1), 1–14. doi:10.1080/23322039.2018.1442093

Dvorský, J., Petráková, Z., Çera, G., & Folvarčna, A. (2019). Important factors for the entrepreneurship in Central Europe. *Innovative Marketing, 15*(2), 71–83. doi:10.21511/im.15(2).2019.06

Edwards, C. J. (2020). Entrepreneurship within the history of marketing. *Journal of Business Research, 108*(April 2019), 259–267. doi:. doi:10.1016/j.jbusres.2019.10.040

Erdin, C., & Ozkaya, G. (2020). Contribution of small and medium enterprises to economic development and quality of life in Turkey. *Heliyon, 6*(2), e03215. doi:10.1016/j.heliyon.2020.e03215 PMID:32055722

Fraj, S. H., Bouchoucha, N. and Maktouf, S. (2020). Political stability and economic growth: the role of exchange rate regime. *Munich Personal RePEc Archive Political (MPRA)*, (104586).

Ghosh, A. (2021). Banking sector openness and entrepreneurship. *Journal of Financial Economic Policy*. doi: . doi:10.1108/JFEP-03-2020-0042

Hadfield, G. K. (2012). Legal infrastructure and the new economy. *ISJLP, 8*, 1.

Hamrouni, B., Bourouis, A., Korichi, A., & Brahmi, M. (2021). Explainable Ontology-Based Intelligent Decision Support System for Business Model Design and Sustainability. *Sustainability, 13*(17), 9819. doi:10.3390u13179819

Hofstede, G. & Hofstede, G. H. (1984) *Culture's consequences: International differences in work-related values*. sage.

Hoogendoorn, B., Van der Zwan, P., & Thurik, R. (2019). Sustainable entrepreneurship: The role of perceived barriers and risk. *Journal of Business Ethics, 157*(4), 1133–1154. doi:10.100710551-017-3646-8

Hosseini, E., Ardekani, S. S., Sabokro, M., & Almodarresi, S. M. (2021). Developing a model for knowledge employee voice: The case study of information technology enterprises. *Organizational Culture Management, 19*(4), 655–682. doi:10.22059/jomc.2021.305993.1008085

Hosseini, E., Tajpour, M., Salamzadeh, A., & Ahmadi, A. (2022). Team Performance and the Development of Iranian Digital Start-ups: The Mediating Role of Employee Voice. In Managing Human Resources in SMEs and Start-ups: International Challenges and Solutions (pp. 109-140).

Hottenrott, H., & Richstein, R. (2020). Start-up subsidies: Does the policy instrument matter? *Research Policy, 49*(1), 103888. doi:10.1016/j.respol.2019.103888

Jegede, C. T., & Irewole, O. E. (2020). 'Agencies for Entrepreneurship Development and SMEs' Promotion in Nigeria'. *Revista Cimexus, 15*(2), 165–193. doi:10.33110/cimexus150208

Khan, M. A. (2022). Barriers constraining the growth of and potential solutions for emerging entrepreneurial SMEs. *Asia Pacific Journal of Innovation and Entrepreneurship, 16*(1), 38–50. doi:10.1108/APJIE-01-2022-0002

Khan, M. A., & Burki, M. (2020). Determinants of small and medium enterprises with the interaction effect of managerial activities. *International Journal of Research in Business and Social Science (2147-4478), 9*(4), 153-160. doi:10.20525/ijrbs.v9i4.750

Khandker, S. R., & Koolwal, B. G. (2011). *Estimating the long-term impacts of rural roads: a dynamic panel approach.* The World Bank. doi:10.1596/1813-9450-5867

Khanin, D., Rosenfield, R., Mahto, R. V., & Singhal, C. (2022). Barriers to entrepreneurship: Opportunity recognition vs. opportunity pursuit. *Review of Managerial Science, 16*(4), 1147–1167. doi:10.100711846-021-00477-6

Klyver, K., & Foley, D. (2012). Networking and culture in entrepreneurship. *Entrepreneurship and Regional Development, 24*(7–8), 561–588. doi:10.1080/08985626.2012.710257

Kollmann, T., Stöckmann, C., & Kensbock, J. M. (2017). Fear of failure as a mediator of the relationship between obstacles and nascent entrepreneurial activity—An experimental approach. *Journal of Business Venturing, 32*(3), 280–301. doi:10.1016/j.jbusvent.2017.02.002

Kraehe, A. M. (2019). Entrepreneurship as Creative Destruction. *Art Education, 72*(5), 4–7. doi:10.1080/00043125.2019.1640037

Kvale, S. (1996). *InterViews: an introduction to qualitive research interviewing.* Sage.

Kwapisz, A. (2019). Do government and legal barriers impede entrepreneurship in the US? An exploratory study of perceived vs. actual barriers. *Journal of Business Venturing Insights*, *11*, e00114. doi:10.1016/j.jbvi.2019.e00114

Leedy, P. D., & Ormrod, J. E. (2016). *Practical Research: Planning and Design* (11th ed.). Pearson Education, Inc.

Liu, H., Gao, H., & Huang, Q. (2020). Better Government, Happier Residents? Quality of Government and Life Satisfaction in China. *Social Indicators Research*, *147*(3), 971–990. doi:10.100711205-019-02172-2

Mackie, T. R., & Leuthardt, E. (2018). Managing Institutional Barriers to Entrepreneurship. In K. E. Behrns, B. Gingles, & M. G. B. T.-M. I. Sarr (Eds.), *Academic Press* (pp. 129–138). doi:10.1016/B978-0-12-814926-3.00013-9

Mazzarol, T., & Reboud, S. (2020). Entrepreneurship and Innovation Theory, Practice and Context. In *Gateway East, Singapore 189721* (pp. 1–34). Springer Nature Singapore Pte Ltd., doi:10.1007/978-981-13-9412-6

Mian, F. M. (2021) Exporting electricity to Afghanistan. *Dawn:The Business and Finance Weekly*.

Mickiewicz, T., & Rebmann, A. (2020). Entrepreneurship as trust. *Foundations and Trends in Entrepreneurship*, *16*(3), 44–309. doi:10.1561/0300000088

Mohsen, A., Ramadani, V., & Dana, L.-P. (2020). Green entrepreneurship prospects and challenges: the context of Afghanistan. In *Research Handbook on Entrepreneurship in Emerging Economies*. Edward Elgar Publishing. doi:10.4337/9781788973717.00008

Moroz, P. W., & Hindle, K. (2012). Entrepreneurship as a Process: Toward Harmonizing Multiple Perspectives. *Entrepreneurship Theory and Practice*, *36*(4), 781–818. doi:10.1111/j.1540-6520.2011.00452.x

Morris, M. H., Kuratko, D. F., Schindehutte, M., & Spivack, A. J. (2012). Framing the entrepreneurial experience. *Entrepreneurship Theory and Practice*, *36*(1), 11–40. doi:10.1111/j.1540-6520.2011.00471.x

Morris, M. H., Santos, S. C., & Neumeyer, X. (2020). Entrepreneurship as a solution to poverty in developed economies. *Business Horizons*, *63*(3), 377–390. doi:10.1016/j.bushor.2020.01.010

Naderi, N., Khosravi, E., Azadi, H., Karamian, F., Viira, A. H., & Nadiri, H. (2022). Barriers to developing social entrepreneurship in NGOs: Application of grounded theory in Western Iran. *Journal of Social Entrepreneurship*, *13*(2), 221–243. doi:10.1080/19420676.2020.1765409

Nair, M., & Njolomole, M. (2020). Microfinance, entrepreneurship and institutional quality. *Journal of Entrepreneurship and Public Policy*, *9*(1), 137–148. doi:10.1108/JEPP-07-2019-0061

Newton, K. (2004). Social trust: Individual and cross-national approaches. *Portuguese Journal of Social Science*, *3*(1), 15–35. doi:10.1386/pjss.3.1.15/0

Nguyen, B., Canh, N. P., & Thanh, S. D. (2020). Institutions, Human Capital and Entrepreneurship Density. *Journal of the Knowledge Economy*. Advance online publication. doi:10.100713132-020-00666-w

Nikraftar, T., Hosseini, E., & Mohammadi, E. (2021). The factors influencing technological entrepreneurship in nanotechnology businesses. *Revista de Gestão*, *29*(1), 76–99. doi:10.1108/REGE-02-2021-0029

O'Reilly, C., & Powell, B. (2015). War and the growth of government. *European Journal of Political Economy, 40*, 31–41. doi:10.1016/j.ejpoleco.2015.10.001

Obaji, N. O. (2014). The Role of Government Policy in Entrepreneurship Development. *Science Journal of Business and Management, 2*(4), 109. doi:10.11648/j.sjbm.20140204.12

Ogus, A. (2004) *The importance of legal infrastructure for regulation (and deregulation) in developing countries.*

Osunmuyiwa, O. O., & Ahlborg, H. (2022). Stimulating competition, diversification, or re-enforcing entrepreneurial barriers? Exploring small-scale electricity systems and gender-inclusive entrepreneurship. *Energy Research & Social Science, 89*, 102566. doi:10.1016/j.erss.2022.102566

Pradhan, R. P., Arvin, M. B., Nair, M., & Bennett, S. E. (2020). The dynamics among entrepreneurship, innovation, and economic growth in the Eurozone countries. *Journal of Policy Modeling, 42*(5), 1106–1122. doi:10.1016/j.jpolmod.2020.01.004

Rajabipoor Meybodi, A., Abasaltian, A., & Sabokro, M. (2021). Identifying and prioritizing the components of staff training in higher education institutions Based on Thematic analysis. *Journal of New Approaches in Educational Administration, 11*(46), 171–202.

Rajasulochana, S. R., & Senthil Ganesh, S. (2019). Is assessing learning outcomes a trade-off in experiential learning? Integrating field visit with managerial economics course. *International Review of Economics Education, 32*(May), 100169. doi:10.1016/j.iree.2019.100169

Ratten, V., & Usmanij, P. (2021). Entrepreneurship education: Time for a change in research direction? *International Journal of Management Education, 19*(1), 100367. doi:10.1016/j.ijme.2020.100367

Riepe, J., Rudeloff, M., & Veer, T. (2020). Financial literacy and entrepreneurial risk aversion. *Journal of Small Business Management, 00*(00), 1–20. doi:10.1080/00472778.2019.1709380

Saidi, S., Shahbaz, M., & Akhtar, P. (2018). The long-run relationships between transport energy consumption, transport infrastructure, and economic growth in MENA countries. *Transportation Research Part A, Policy and Practice, 111*(January), 78–95. doi:10.1016/j.tra.2018.03.013

Sandhu, M. S., Sidique, S. F., & Riaz, S. (2011). Entrepreneurship barriers and entrepreneurial inclination among Malaysian postgraduate students. *International Journal of Entrepreneurial Behaviour & Research, 17*(4), 428–449. doi:10.1108/13552551111139656

Sayyedi & Taqi-Khani, A. (2011) Entrepreneurship Development Barriers and The Role of Government in Facilitating Entrepreneurship Development. *Work and Sociaty*, 35.

Shaikh, E., Brahmi, M., Thang, P. C., Watto, W. A., Trang, T. T. N., & Loan, N. T. (2022). Should I Stay or Should I Go? Explaining the Turnover Intentions with Corporate Social Responsibility (CSR), Organizational Identification and Organizational Commitment. *Sustainability, 14*(10), 6030. doi:10.3390u14106030

Schückes, M., & Gutmann, T. (2020). Why do startups pursue initial coin offerings (ICOs)? The role of economic drivers and social identity on funding choice. *Small Business Economics*. doi:10.100711187-020-00337-9

Secundo, G., Mele, G., Sansone, G., & Paolucci, E. (2020). Entrepreneurship Education Centres in universities: Evidence and insights from Italian "Contamination Lab" cases. *International Journal of Entrepreneurial Behaviour & Research*, *26*(6), 1311–1333. doi:10.1108/IJEBR-12-2019-0687

Sitaridis, I. K. & Kitsios, F. (2017). Students' perceptions of barriers to entrepreneurship. *Ekpaídeush, Dia Bíou Máqhsh, Ereuna kai Tecnologikή Anáptuxh, Kainotomía kai Oikonomía, 1*, 524–535.

Social Inspector General for Afghanistan Reconstruction (SIGAR). (2021) *Quaterly Report to the United States Congress: Economic and Social Development*. SIGAR. https://www.sigar.mil/pdf/quarterlyreports/2021-01-30qr.pdf

Steils, N. (2021). Qualitative Experiments for Social Sciences. *New Trends in Qualitative Research*, *6*, 24–31. doi:10.36367/ntqr.6.2021.24-31

Tajpour, M., Hosseini, E., & Brahmi, M. (2022). Effect of international entrepreneurship indicators on innovative performance: The mediating role of motivation. *International Journal of Technology Transfer and Commercialisation*, *19*(1), 142–162. doi:10.1504/IJTTC.2022.123090

Tajpour, M., Salamzadeh, A., Ramadani, V., Palalić, R., & Hosseini, E. (2022). Knowledge sharing and achieving competitive advantage in international environments: The case of Iranian digital start-ups. In *International Entrepreneurship in Emerging Markets* (pp. 206–224). Routledge. doi:10.4324/9781003218357-13

Tunio, M. N., Jariko, M. A., Børsen, T., Shaikh, S., Mushtaque, T., & Brahmi, M. (2021). How entrepreneurship sustains barriers in the entrepreneurial process—A lesson from a developing nation. *Sustainability*, *13*(20), 11419. doi:10.3390u132011419

Tunio, M. N., Chaudhry, I. S., Shaikh, S., Jariko, M. A., & Brahmi, M. (2021). Determinants of the Sustainable Entrepreneurial Engagement of Youth in Developing Country—An Empirical Evidence from Pakistan. *Sustainability*, *13*(14), 7764. doi:10.3390u13147764

United Nations. (2013). *United Nations Office on Drugs and Crime: Weak rule of law and lack of good governance a major threat to development*. United Nations Population Fund. (News)

United Nations Development Programme. (2020) *About Afghanistan: Livelihoods, UNDP*. UN. https://www.af.undp.org/content/afghanistan/en/home/countryinfo.html#

Wach, K., & Bilan, S. (2021). Public support and administration barriers towards entrepreneurial intentions of students in Poland. *Administratie si Management Public*, (36), 67-80. doi:10.24818/amp/2021.36-04

Wæraas, A. (2022) 'Thematic Analysis: Making Values Emerge from Texts', *Researching Values: Methodological Approaches for Understanding Values Work in Organisations and Leadership*, 153.

Wiklund, J., Nikolaev, B., Shir, N., Foo, M.-D., & Bradley, S. (2019). Entrepreneurship and well-being: Past, present, and future. *Journal of Business Venturing*, *34*(4), 579–588. doi:10.1016/j.jbusvent.2019.01.002

Yakubu, Z. (2021). 'Do Financial Development, Trade Openness and Political Stability Complement for Egypt's Economic Growth?', Journal of International Commerce, *Economic Policy*, *12*(01), 2150001.

## ABBREVIATIONS

**ILO:** International Labour Organization
**GEM:** Global Entrepreneurship Monitor
**F2F:** Face-to face
**CMC:** Computer mediated communication

# Chapter 9
# Impact of Knowledge Diffusion on the Performance of Indian Pharmaceutical Companies

**Amit Banerji**
*Maulana Azad National Institute of Technology, India*

**Nirbhay Mahor**
*Maulana Azad National Institute of Technology, India*

## ABSTRACT

*The study aims to improve understanding of knowledge dissemination on performance determinants in the Indian pharmaceutical industry. Panel data analyses have been used to describe R&D spillover mediated through fixed assets act as a knowledge diffusion pathway, along with five other factors that affect profitability. R&D spillover mediated through physical capital points to knowledge diffusion, albeit in a small way, indicating that such things can take a permanent shape all across the industry. Fixed assets' negative relationship with profitability results from a directional shift in the last two decades.*

## INTRODUCTION

The Indian pharmaceutical industry (IPI) had reached around INR 1.40 lakh crore (US$ 20 billion) to US$ 50 billion by 2025. IPI supplies more than half of the global requirements for various drugs and vaccines, 40% of the generic market in the United States (US) and 25% of all drugs in the United Kingdom (UK). In 2020, US$ 16 billion more pharmaceuticals were exported than imported, and these exports comply with the strict regulatory standards of many countries around the world (IBEF 2020). Between 2018 and 2021, finished drug approvals granted by the USA were 3021, much more than that of China (Bureau, 2022) Its contribution to the commodity export structure had already doubled to 7% from 2.6% from FY 2011-12 to FY 2020-21 (Economic Survey of India, 202)

Growth opportunities exist in generics as approximately 120 drugs are expected to be denied patents by 2030 (IBEF 2019).

DOI: 10.4018/978-1-6684-6766-4.ch009

IPI is known for its technological strength, generic drugs, self-reliance, low production expenditure, relatively low investment in research and development (R&D), and skilled and innovative scientific human resources. Presently Indian pharma ranks third in pharmaceutical production and has become an emerging sector of the Indian economy. The government is actively supporting the expansion and Mergers & Acquisitions in IPI to attract additional R&D investments (Singh & Singh, 2014). Some of the prominent acquisitions include Matrix Lab acquired by Mylan Inc., Shantha Biotech acquired by Sanofi Aventis, the generic drug arm of Piramal Healthcare by US-based Abbott Laboratories, Dabur Pharma acquired by Fresenius Kabi, and Orchid Chemicals by Hospira. Between 2003 and 2010, these acquisitions lead to a significant increase (about ten percentage points) in the market share of MNCs (Goldar, 2013)

## Significance of R&D in Indian Pharmaceutical's Export

Being a Hi-Tech Manufactured product, based on science, the pharmaceutical industry has consistently invested heavily in R&D. Post accession to TRIPS (in 1995), IPI increased R&D investments and increased it further from 2005, upon introduction of the product patent regime Due to the large investments, companies have developed strong product pipelines for the generics exports, but a New Chemical Entity (NCE) is still elusive (Suri & Banerji 2016). Steadily from 1994 onwards R&D intensity (RDI= R&D expenditure/Sales) increased from a little over 1.6% to over 6.0%, which is much lower than global standards, wherein pharma MNCs have an RDI of 17% (Pharma Intelligence 2019).

*Figure 1. R&D Intensity between 1993-94 and 2018-19*

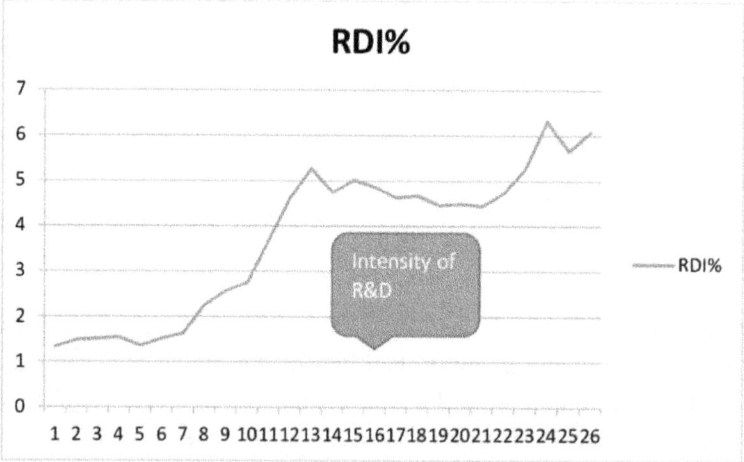


By FY 21, R&D investments by IPI reached 7.2% of sales, (IBEF 2021). The pharmaceutical industry is a high-value, knowledge-intensive sector where competition is focused on continuous product innovation and best-selling drugs for market order (Salazar & Hackney, 2003).

According to the OECD's Frascati Manual (1993), R&D is defined as: "Research and experimental development (R&D) comprises of creative work undertaken on a systematic basis to increase the stock of knowledge including knowledge of man, culture and society, and the use of this stock of knowledge to devise new applications". Rogers., (1998) defined it as "systematic investigation or experimentation involving innovation or technical risk, the outcome of which is new knowledge, with or without a specific practical application of new or improved products, processes, materials, devices or services."

On the other hand. knowledge can be defined as "a fluid mix of framed experience, values contextual information, and expert insight that provides a framework for evaluating and incorporating new experiences and information" (Baskerville & Dulipovici, 2006).

Although both explicit and tacit knowledge had a substantial impact on IPI innovation potential, tacit information transfer had a more prominent role than its explicit counterpart. The exchange of knowledge is more than just effective communication; it is an integrated process of encoding and dissemination. Knowledge exchange is a significant technique to properly operate lengthy and costly innovation processes. In this aspect, IPI must compete with global giants, which have institutionalized formal knowledge transfer mechanisms across organizations. Finally, managers may consider implementing enhanced knowledge managerial techniques or tools to assure the accessibility of high-quality knowledge production (Ganguly et al., 2020).

IPI focuses less on innovation and provides less finance in R&D as compared to developed countries. MNCs do not offer new drugs in the Indian market, inhibiting innovation and drug development as chances of knowledge diffusion decrease (Carboni & Medda, 2018).

In 1984, Hatch-Waxman Amendments (Drug Price Competition and Patent Term Restoration Act) passed in the United States paved the way for worldwide competition in the generic (off-patent) drug market of the USA. Indian firms used the provisions of this act to enter the US market. American industry was profitable but highly regulated, and corporations needed to increase R&D spending to remain competitive. These two legislative reforms made R&D and innovation spending vital to the survival and growth of firms (Chaudhuri, 2005).

Product patents on pharmaceuticals in India were recognized under the Indian Patent (Amendment) Act 2005 (IPA 2005). Before 2005, domestic firms derived a substantial portion of their earnings by reverse engineering drugs offered in global markets. After reverse engineering was declared illegal in 2005, IPI was forced to develop new drugs and remain competitive. The Post-TRIPS regime transformed IPI to acquire knowledge and develop intellectual strategies. Indian firms with limited prior experience in the development of new drugs increased R&D investments. Cooperative partnerships between Indian and pharmaceutical MNCs have been rising with a focus on innovation. Apart from indigenous R&D, Indian firms have been proactive in technology transfer and outsourcing knowledge involving MNCs. (Srivastava, 2020).

Ashwin et al (2016) observed that R&D increases as the board size and proportion of independent directors rise, indicating that more financial slack is allocated to R&D in such circumstances. This allows a firm to extract more resources from the environment, allowing more resources to be diverted into R&D also supports the assumption of independent directors as resource suppliers.

R&D and innovation activities have been identified as the growth engines. Technology investment is essential for productivity growth. Spillover has been an important source of industrial expansion and productivity, so industrial and innovation policies that encourage knowledge and technology spillover need to be encouraged. Fungibility characteristic of technology allows its development through internal R&D. Dissemination of knowledge is possible in several ways, including international trade, foreign direct investment (FDI), and technology transfer (Sharma, 2016).

Absorptive capacity has become an essential quality in the process of designing products and developing a new strategic position of the firm in response to a particular market situation. The absorption capacity of innovation and R&D management of a firm is described as: "the existence of prior related knowledge which confers an ability to recognize the value of new information, assimilate it, and apply it to commercial ends" (Cohen and Levinthal, 1990).

Zahra, S. A., & George, G. (2002) defined absorptive capacity as "a set of organizational routines and processes by which firms acquire, assimilate, transform and exploit knowledge to produce a dynamic organizational capability."

Absorption capacity is a technique of acquiring and using knowledge acquired from an external source which can be subdivided into four main stages: acquisition, assimilation, modification, and finally the application of knowledge. Acquisitions are activities that focus on identifying, evaluating, and acquiring external knowledge important to the operation of the firm. Assimilation is the process of adapting external knowledge into an understandable form that allows external information to be further modified. Finally, the acquired, assimilated and modified knowledge becomes usable and applied for the creation of new products and services to satisfy the competitive environment of the firm (Ma, 2013).

Absorption capacity helps a firm to improve its innovation performance by acting as a method of absorbing new knowledge and transferring the required knowledge to various innovation activities within the firm. Absorption capacity and knowledge flow have been considered a direct precursor to innovation and financial performance (ROA and ROS). Absorption capacity empowers firms to identify more available knowledge flows and more innovatively exploit a certain amount of accumulated externally sourced knowledge. Absorption as an attribute improves innovation and financial performance. It also increases efficiency, as well as converts external information flows into associated firm performance (Kostopoulos et al., 2011).

R&D is influential in increasing the absorption capacity of external technology and developing new and better products. In particular, assessing the effective contribution and absorption capacity of spillovers from others also includes the firm's ability to exploit more intermediate types of external knowledge, such as the core that provides subsequent applied R&D (Poldahl, 2012).

Firms with higher absorbing potential benefited more from net knowledge spillovers than from rental spillovers in areas (or economic environments) where the former is more relevant than the latter. Innovation not only benefits the innovator, but it also "spreads" to other firms - pure knowledge spillover occurs in the form of imperfect idea appropriation. Rent spillover occurs when the prices of raw materials purchased from other firms or nations are not fully adjusted for quality improvement due to a lack of R&D investment. Firms in economic sectors that are closer to the global technological frontier areas have benefited from net (knowledge) spillovers compared to rental spillovers with the same level of absorption capacity. Firms located in non-technological frontier areas appeared to benefit the most from rent spillovers (Aldieri et al., 2018).

There is no research that deals with the impact on TFP (profitability) due to spillover of R&D and its interaction with physical assets on market leaders in IPI. This study will analyze the behavior of market leaders of IPI in the context of R&D spillover (technology& knowledge), investments in physical capital, interaction with R&D spillover, and other firm-specific variables and their association with the firm's profitability which in turn can create a firm's capability in innovation transfer, knowledge acquisition, and adaptive capacities.

## LITERATURE REVIEW

R&D stock is a substitute for knowledge stock, giving R&D a role similar to physical investment in output production (Nadiri, 1993). This is an assumption made in these studies.

Stock R&D as input is assumed under Constant Returns to Scale (CRS), Cobb-Douglas production function to be generated through the concept of perpetual inventory, with an arbitrary depreciation rate, more so for process R&D, which is what Indian pharmaceutical firms do more (Suri & Banerji 2019a).

Growing demand for a firm/industry plays a significant role in productivity improvements along with the growth and magnitude of the contribution of R&D stock. Pathways of R&D knowledge transfer from outside the firm, leading to performance enhancement have been proven to exist in inter-industry frameworks, especially in technologically embodied products (Griliches, Z., & Lichtenberg, F. R. 1984).

An aspect of R&D that sets it apart from other forms of investments, is that firms that invest, can never prevent others from freely reaping the benefits of R&D initiatives (Bernstein, J. and Nadiri, I M. 1989) Benefits include cost reduction as knowledge increases. Inventions may be regulated by general conditions in financial, factor, and product markets. If favorable, they might lead to a bandwagon effect, an extension of the Long Cycle hypothesis. The theory is that if many unrelated innovations had main phases of life cycles modulated by macroeconomic conditions, contemporaneous diffusion of such innovations might be regulated (Rosenberg, N. & Frischtak, RC., 1984).

Own process R&D has been observed to impact total factor productivity more than own product R&D. This is valid in IPI where process R&D is given more importance (Suri & Banerji 2019b). R&D conducted in one firm/sector/country may favor other firms/sectors/countries. Since the supplier and recipient are associated, such spillovers are more prevalent and significant. Non-pecuniary spillovers are also useful, apart from financial spillovers, since they transfer knowledge created by R&D to other firms (Hall et al., 2009).

Bernstein, J. and Nadiri, I M. (1988) observed that in the case of Canadian firms, industries such as aircraft parts, electrical products, and chemical products, had the most inter-industry spillovers. In these (knowledge-based industries for the period 1958 and 1981) industries, an increase in R&D or knowledge spillover benefitted rival firms (Hamrouni et al., 2022) in the same industry with better ability to spend on R&D. In these specific examples, complementary relationships exist between firms' demand for R&D capital and intra-industry spillover. The requirement of physical capital (fixed assets and cash & cash equivalents) depends upon the relative propensity to spend on R&D capital. R&D spillovers reduce variable costs in technology-based industries. The return on invested R&D was consistently significantly more extensive than physical capital, which justified continued investment in R&D.

Frantzen D. (2000) carried out an international technology spillover of OECD countries taking human capital interaction as an additional variable from 1961-1991. It was observed that countries with lower levels of TFP growth tended to grow faster with international technology spillover (taking only the R&D factor into account). OLS indicated a significant contribution to foreign technology spillover. However, human capital development seemed to have a significant impact on TFP through foreign R&D spillover, suggesting a higher impact of process R&D through imported technologically embodied products. Dynamic OLS results with error correction modeling posited comparatively higher elasticity of TFP concerning foreign R&D. About larger economies (G-7), contradictory but reasonably logical evidence was obtained. Co-integration was observed with ECM. One lagged value of R&D was observed to be significant for growth in TFP. Indian technology-based industries (pharmaceuticals and software) have had significant spillovers of technology and knowledge in recent years (Haakonsson et al., 2013; Lorenzen, M., & Mudambi, R. 2013).

Sharma (2016) investigated the impact of R&D capital and technology transfer in IPI for the period 1994-2010. It was observed that the productivity of R&D investing firms was superior to non-R&D investing firms. In the production function approach (linearized Cobb-Douglas function), R&D capital was observed to be insignificant in explaining the firm's output. Technology transfer was also a contributory factor. TFP was affected negatively by R&D and positively by technology transfer. Suri and Banerji (2019b) reported a negative impact of patents on exports, with the reasoning that a more significant part of IPI on R&D is spent on product clearances from regulated markets and optimizing production processes for global generic competition (Aldieri et al., 2021). Technology transfer in the Indian context can be understood from the pre-2005 Patent Act (1970), which disallowed product patents in pharmaceuticals for almost twenty-five years (Banerji 2012).

Cincera (2005) studied the productivity of 625 firms for the period 1988-1994. The impact of fixed capital, firm size, labor employed, R&D industry, and firm stocks was observed to impact slightly but positively. Local R&D spillover (local stock refers to externalities) from firms operating in rigidly defined technological domains of specialty was notable. It was observed to be highly significant compared to external R&D spillover (Jaffe 1986). The rate of disembodied technological progress was 2%, emphasizing a rapid decline in the impact of pre-existing physical and R&D capital investments.

Plunket, A. (2009) studied spillover in French manufacturing industries from1992-2002, focusing on local R&D spillover along vertical chain – upstream and downstream industries. A firm's innovation output increases if it's located in an area of pre-existing high innovation-oriented firms. Patenting activities increase when apart from urbanization; a firm is located in a cluster where it finds itself as a part of a value chain comprising of R&D intensive firms. For, Hi-Medium tech firms (e.g., tier -1 auto parts), firms benefit from spillover mostly from suppliers.

Firms implementing a dynamic allocation strategy of R&D were worse off regarding both quantity and quality of their outputs. Within the estimation variability, the unpredicted portion hurts output and the predicted part can have some positive impact. The importance of the lagged effect of R&D, albeit asymmetric, emphasizes the role of R&D stock in leading to quality innovations. Developing a quality invention takes time for R&D research, but the destruction of quality occurs immediately when the R&D budget allocation is reduced. IPI so far has avoided pioneering R&D in pharmaceuticals. This has led to avoidance of technological uncertainty associated, which is relatively high. Adaptation may even require a firm to create new pathways for reshaping organizational aspects like leadership behaviors and invention mindsets (Pennetier., et al 2019).

Gkypali et al (2018) found that export orientation and internal knowledge development capability are endogenously linked, implying that R&D-active firms self-select into foreign markets. The mechanism underlying this relationship is based on the development and expansion of firms' technical capacities (Arabeche et ala., 2022), as well as their absorptive capability. Firms' absorptive capacity, in particular, appeared to be the only variable that showed a direct and statistically significant impact on innovation efficiency, emphasizing its knowledge filtering and integrating function. Also, firms' exporting output and portfolio of types of partners, in combination with absorptive ability, create a self-feeding cycle in which incoming information flows from external partners complement firms' capacity, which boosts exporting performance. This indirect learning through exporting effect indicates that engaging in exporting activities helps the firms develop purposeful connections abroad, leading them to migrate and acquire valuable externally sourced knowledge and information within their boundaries. Only the absorptive potential of firms had a statistically significant impact on innovation efficiency. According to the research, absorptive capability acted as a filtering mechanism for export efficiency and innovation. This is in line with work reported by Banerji (2012) and Banerji & Suri (2019), which investigated the role of R&D stock and export intensity in IPI exports.

Other studies have also highlighted the importance of exporting success as a key determinant in the innovation phase of businesses, and it has been linked to both the input and output sides. In the relevant literature, two well-known hypotheses of 'learning by exporting' and 'self-selection' have been observed. While previous theories have been used separately, the presence of an endogenous, two-way association between export and innovation performance has been established (Gkypali et al., 2012; Harris & Li, 2009). Foreign market exposure expands a firm's reservoir of innovative concepts, know-how, and other critical resources of knowledge that can draw the elements required for its innovation process. Innovation success can impact export performance since it is the outcome of firms' endeavors to diversify, compete, and separate themselves from competitors and establish or preserve their competitive advantage (Love & Ganotakis, 2013).

Absorptive ability appears to mediate the association between firm efficiency and R&D spillovers. Firms that are not on the technical frontier benefit the most from rent spillover. Certain findings indicate that firms are more likely to change and adjust their learning practices to take advantage of the current form of expertise in the external world. External knowledge gained from firms (Tunio et al., 2021) operating in related technical areas had been shown to improve the output of the recipient firm in complementing its previous competencies and offset the potential adverse effects of external competition. This was especially true for large firms with different competencies that could benefit from outside expertise (Arora et al., 2001).

Gleadle & Haslam, (2010) examined the financial operating ratios of 500 Alternative Investment Market (AIM) listed firms from Medco's published annual reports between 2003 and 2007. Medco is a financial R&D-intensive firm. Although Medco incorporated other firms to increase its market reach, these strategic acquisitions were recognized at market value. This action contributed to greater balance sheet capitalization before cash income (cash ROCE) without reducing corporate earnings potential. Mark-to-Market accounting requires firms to consider the market value of capital market transactions on their financial statements. When asset markets increase a company's market value, cash often exceeds revenue. It was pointed out that when the parent firm takes over such a firm, the consolidated reported ROCE is reduced. R&D (in itself) may not be enough to generate significant financial success for the firm, and the relationship between R&D and financial performance is not as obvious. Akintola & Cole, (2020) examined the influence of combined leverage on the capital employed in Nigerian Stock Exchange-listed manufacturing firms from 2008 to 2014. Capital structure has a positive influence on ROCE. It assesses how efficiently assets can be managed to generate profits. A portfolio containing more ROCE firms (Erum et al., 2022) should outperform a portfolio containing firms with reduced ROCE. An organization needs the financial resources to continue operating and engage in its prime objective of revenue generation, and it demonstrates the management's ability to allocate funds effectively. A high ROCE indicates a well-managed and profitable firm.

Andersson et al., (2006) deconstructed S&P 500 ROCE and showed how gains from excess cash and earnings are offset by an inflated balance sheet capitalization. The shareholder value of Pfizer and P&G hasn't changed over a decade of shareholder value relative to prior periods, even after extensive corporate restructuring. The financial performance of S&P 500 companies, forms the "Survivor Index" of companies from 1980–2003. After the acquisition of Pharmacia by Pfizer, the combined business of Pfizer and Pharmacia was providing an average ROCE of over 40%. The ROCE decreased to 5% in 2003 based on the market value of the transaction. Management had already set up a "scale adaptation" initiative in anticipation. The financial statements of Pfizer and Procter & Gamble show how share buybacks boost capitalization before profits. This is because executives must reduce costs to raise cash, which can be used to reduce the cost of capital involved in financing such buybacks.

## HYPOTHESES DEVELOPMENT

Extant work (not covered here) and literature Review suggests that the profitability of industry leaders of IPI(ROA and ROCE) has a long-term (run) relationship with working capital management, sales, physical capital intensity, R&D, and R&D spillover mediated through physical capital intensity.

## DATA AND METHODOLOGY

Six pharmaceutical firms viz., Abbott India Ltd., Aurobindo Pharma Ltd., Cipla Ltd., Dr. Reddy'S Laboratories Ltd., Lupin Ltd., and Sun Pharmaceutical Inds. Ltd. has been short-listed for being consistently among the top 10 pharmaceutical firms in revenue terms since 2016. These firm also makes a major contribution to the overall industry R&D investment, profitability, and fixed assets.

Data has been taken from CMIE Prowess for the period from the financial year (FY) 1993- 94 to 2020 - 21. Further data has been median scaled (Chauhan, 2019). Eviews 10 has been used for econometric analyses. Data for FY 2021-22 is missing/incomplete and hence not considered.

ROCE and ROA are reliable measures of profitability. ROCE is determined by dividing operating profit (EBIT) by capital employed or shareholders' funds. ROCE provides facts about a firm's financial performance because it includes both operating and non-operating returns (for example, revenue from the sale of assets). Because the operating margin is evaluated by total funds used, it allows comparison of firms concerning financial criteria (eg, depreciation) and various capital raising and financing techniques. ROCE represents the rate of return on capital employed and reflects the efficiency of overall capital resource used Pomerleano, M. (1998). ROA refers to how efficient an organization is with the use of its assets. ROA represents the net profits generated by total assets. ROA represents the rate of return on total assets for a while and reflects the efficiency of overall resources used by a firm. Further ROA has been studied by using the interaction of NFA with R&D to judge the spillover effect between the two.

### EQUATION ESTIMATION

$$\begin{aligned} ROA = {} & \beta_1 + \beta_2 ROA_{t-1} + \beta_3 NWCR_{ti} + \beta_4 FAT_{ti} + \beta_5 NFAT_{ti} \\ & + \beta_6 LEV_{ti} + \beta_7 RDI_{ti} + \beta_8 INNFATSORD_{ti} + \mu_{ti} \end{aligned} \tag{1}$$

$$ROCE = \beta_1 + \beta_2 NWCR_{ti} + \beta_3 FAT_{ti} + \beta_4 NFAT_{ti} + \beta_5 LEV_{ti} + \beta_6 RDI_{ti} + \mu_{ti} \left( error\ term \right) \tag{2}$$

Variables will be tested for stationary. In the event of variables (series) being I(0) and I(1) then the ARDL cointegration technique will be used to check for short-run and long cointegration. ARDL approach generates the error correction mechanism (ECM). Inclusion of the ECM reflects long-term interaction between the variables (series). A brief description of these approaches is available in Shrestha & Bhatta, (2018). Granger Causality (GC) will check for homogenous causation (Banerjee and Suri 2019).

## Empirical Analysis

Table 1 shows descriptive data about all the variables. The range of ROA is between 3.746 and -1.181, with a standard deviation (SD) of 0.621. ROCE ranges between 3.417 and -0.901 with an SD of 0.682. Both the profitability ratios are positively skewed. The variables- NWCR, FAT, NFAT, LEV, SORD, and RDI are more positively skewed than the profitability ratios. The Jarque- Beara test shows that all variables are normally distributed.

*Table 1. Descriptive data*

| | ROA | ROCE | NWCR |
|---|---|---|---|
| FAT | NFAT | LEV | SORD |
| RDI | | Mean | 1.013 |
| 1.022 | 1.199 | 1.651 | 1.559 |
| 2.207 | 2.726 | 1.044 | |
| Median | 0.972 | 0.972 | 0.964 |
| 0.994 | 0.987 | 0.986 | 0.966 |
| 0.963 | | Maximum | 3.746 |

ROCE and ROA are reliable measures of profitability. ROCE is determined by dividing operating profit (EBIT) by capital employed or shareholders' funds. ROCE provides facts about a firm's financial performance because it includes both operating and non-operating returns (for example, revenue from the sale of assets). Because the operating margin is evaluated by total funds used, it allows comparison of firms concerning financial criteria (eg, depreciation) and various capital raising and financing techniques. ROCE represents the rate of return on capital employed and reflects the efficiency of overall capital resource used Pomerleano, M. (1998). ROA refers to how efficient an organization is with the use of its assets. ROA represents the net profits generated by total assets. ROA represents the rate of return on total assets for a while and reflects the efficiency of overall resources used by a firm. Further ROA has been studied by using the interaction of NFA with R&D to judge the spillover effect between the two.

Table 2 Karl Pearson coefficient presents the results of the correlation coefficient. The correlation coefficient represents the intensity of the association relationship between two or more variables. A significant positive correlation between ROA and ROCE indicates a strong association with assets creation with Capital Employed (including shareholder's fund). Furthermore, RDI has a significantly negative correlation with both ROA and ROCE. This shows that a reduction in R&D increases profitability, a possible reason for this being innovation is a more costly and time-consuming process. NWCR has a moderate and positive relationship with ROA and ROCE. It shows that firms use suppliers' credit as a captive source of funds. NFAT has a moderate and negative correlation with ROA and ROCE indicating incurring capital expenditure reduces profitability. LEV has a negative relationship with ROA and ROCE. Borrowings require servicing, directly affecting profits. ROA and ROCE have a moderate positive relationship with FAT. A possible reason could be the realization of the economics of scale (variable return to scale). The spillover interaction term INNFATSORD has a negative relationship with ROA and ROCE, along expected lines.

*Table 2. Correlation matrix*

| | ROA | ROCE | RDI | NWCR | NFAT | LEV | FAT | INNFATSORD |
|---|---|---|---|---|---|---|---|---|
| ROA | 1 | | | | | | | |
| ROCE | 0.796*** | 1 | | | | | | |
| RDI | -0.242** | -0.421** | 1 | | | | | |
| NWCR | 0.200* | 0.123** | 0.161** | 1 | | | | |
| NFAT | -0.176*** | -0.257*** | -0.189* | -0.232** | 1 | | | |
| LEV | -0.405*** | -0.261*** | 0.490** | 0.072** | 0.082** | 1 | | |
| FAT | 0.307** | 0.177* | -0.444* | 0.398* | -0.268*** | -0.223** | 1 | |
| INNFATSORD | -0.287* | -0.323** | 0.771*** | 0.277** | -0.189** | 0.322*** | -0.401** | 1 |
| Note. ***, **, and * represent 1%, 5%, and 10% significance level respectively. | | | | | | | | |

Homogeneous panel GC test results presented in Table 3, show the directional causal relationship between the variables.

Bi-directional GC is observed between ROA and RDI at two lags. GC was observed from ROA to NWCR ($p < .05$) and from LEV to ROA at ($p < .05$). Similarly, GC at two lags from INNFATSORD to ROA was observed ($p < .05$) and vice versa ($p < .05$). GC observed from RDI to NWCR ($p < .05$) and from FAT to RDI ($p < .05$) level. Bi-directional causality was observed between FAT to NWCR ($p < .05$).

The interaction term, INNFATSORD showed GC toward NWCR along with FAT showing GC towards INNFATSORD ($p<0.05$)

Investment in R&D & NWCR seems to increase profitability among the sample firms. Investment in fixed assets and its interaction with spillover R&D, GC reduction in profitability. It is to be noted that fixed assets show a negative effect on profitability measures. Except for Aurobindo, all the sample firms show a marked decrease in NFA in nominal terms in the study period. Total factor productivity growth was shown to account for technological change rather than productivity change (Singh & Singh, 2014). The decline in NFA can be attributed to the diminishing production of Active Pharmaceutical Ingredients (API) in India since the 1990s, which requires large investments in plants and machinery. (Cherian et al., 2021).

## Panel Autoregressive Distributed Lag (ARDL)

Results of the overall sample estimation with linear panel ARDL (2, 2, 2, 2, 2, 2, 2) model using the Aikake Information Criterion (AIC) are shown in Table 4. Error correction is significant and negative. An error correction of 37.50% indicates that any deviation from the long-run equilibrium path is corrected in 32 months.

*Table 3. Pairwise Dumitrescu Hurlin Panel Causality Tests (Lags:2)*

| Null Hypothesis: | W-Stat. | Zbar-Stat. | Prob. |
|---|---|---|---|
| RDI does not homogeneously cause ROA | 4.26845 | 2.05175 | 0.0402 |
| ROA does not homogeneously cause RDI | 4.36917 | 2.15216 | 0.0314 |
| INNFATSORD does not homogeneously cause ROA | 5.63201 | 3.41121 | 0.0006 |
| ROA does not homogeneously cause INNFATSORD | 4.53380 | 2.31630 | 0.0205 |
| NWCR does not homogeneously cause ROA | 3.61192 | 1.39719 | 0.1624 |
| ROA does not homogeneously cause NWCR | 5.12235 | 2.90309 | 0.0037 |
| LEV does not homogeneously cause ROA | 4.36242 | 2.14543 | 0.0319 |
| ROA does not homogeneously cause LEV | 1.42117 | -0.78698 | 0.4313 |
| NWCR does not homogeneously cause RDI | 3.06955 | 0.85644 | 0.3918 |
| RDI does not homogeneously cause NWCR | 5.83552 | 3.61412 | 0.0003 |
| FAT does not homogeneously cause RDI | 7.28004 | 5.05430 | 0.0007 |
| RDI does not homogeneously cause FAT | 1.87546 | -0.33406 | 0.7383 |
| FAT does not homogeneously cause NWCR | 7.10428 | 4.87907 | 0.0000 |
| NWCR does not homogeneously cause FAT | 7.04249 | 4.81746 | 0.0000 |
| INNFATSORD does not homogeneously cause NWCR | 6.70632 | 4.48231 | 0.0010 |
| NWCR does not homogeneously cause INNFATSORD | 2.91820 | 0.70555 | 0.4805 |
| INNFATSORD does not homogeneously cause FAT | 1.72378 | -0.48528 | 0.6275 |
| FAT does not homogeneously cause INNFATSORD | 7.56791 | 5.34131 | 0.0006 |

LEV with one lag is significant. A 10% change in lagged LEV change produces a change of 9.8% of ROA in opposite direction. A 10 percent increase in FAT leads to a 4.7 percent increase in ROA. 10 percent change in NFAT produces approximately 5.2 percent change in ROA. The overall firm variables INNFATSORD and INNFATSORD at one lag are insignificant in the short run.

At the individual firm level, Abbot, Aurobindo, Cipla, Lupin, and Sun Pharma show error correction of 56.2%, 7.3%, 77.8%, 1.6%, and 84.5%, respectively. All error corrections are highly significant. Only in Dr. Reddy's Lab (DRL), the error correction is positive thereby showing over-correction. DRL is not discussed any further in the ARDL cointegration model. Reversion to equilibrium, in Abbot, Aurobindo, Cipla, Lupin, and Sun Pharma takes place in 21 months (approx.), 164 months (approx.), 15 months (approx.), 750 months (approx.) and 14 months (approx.), respectively.

A 10 percent change in NWCR of Abbott, Cipla, and Sun Pharma produces a change in ROA in the opposite direction by -1.2, -0.3, and -2.7 percent, respectively. 10 percent change in NWCR of Aurobindo and Lupin results in 4.8 and 0.3 percent change in ROA, respectively, in the same direction. This shows that the short-run, efficient management of WC has a positive and concurrent effect on the profitability of Sun Pharma and Abbott.

On the contrary, expanded WC has a positive and concurrent impact on the profitability of Aurobindo's ROA. The most likely reason is Aurobindo sacrificed profit to generate sales through increased receivables. The direction of the impact of NWCR at one lag remains the same on ROA, however, the magnitude differs individually.

A 10% decrease in LEV results in -0.6, -0.1, -1.02, and -7.9 percent changes in ROA for Aurobindo, Cipla, Lupin, and Sun Pharma, respectively. Debt reduction significantly increases profits in Sun Pharma. The direction of the influence of LEV on ROA at one lag remains constant, but the amount varies.

The coefficients of FAT, of all the five firms, are highly significant and positive. However, lagged values of FAT for Aurobindo and Lupin are negative at 1 percent significance. Lupin incurred debt to finance receivables, whereas, Aurobindo incurred debt to finance payables.

In the case of Aurobindo, Cipla, Lupin, and Sun Pharma, a 10 percent change in NFAT caused to change by 5.1, 4.3, 0.4, and 18.2 percent in the same direction as ROA respectively. In the case of Sun Pharma contemporaneous investments in fixed assets showed a disproportionately large impact in the same direction on ROA. The coefficient of lag NFAT is negative in the case of Aurobindo and Sun Pharma. Debt repayments incurred in building physical capital affect net profit, thereby impacting ROA negatively.

Cipla, Lupin, and Sun Pharma show a significant positive impact of R&D investment on profitability. A 10 percent change at one lagged RDI causes changes in the same direction of ROA by 7.71, 2.03, and 8.7 percent, respectively. The direction (positive) of the association depends on the R&D phase, knowledge acquisition & assimilation, and the time taken for innovative activities to result in gains.

Mediation of R&D spillover through physical capital (INNFATSORD), has been observed to be positive and significant at 1 percent, for Cipla, Lupin, and Sun Pharma. A 10 percent increase in the interaction, increases the ROA of Cipla, Lupin, and Sun Pharma by approx. 7, 10, and 2 percent, respectively.

INNFATSORD produces interesting results. Cipla, Lupin, and Sun Pharma have shown to be leaders in acquiring and assimilating R&D-generated knowledge from within the sample firms and transferring/translating (Shaikh et ala., 2022) the same in the usage of their respective fixed assets. It is quite likely that these three firms had the first mover advantage in R&D investments and fixed assets.

Table 5 exhibits the variables' long-run coefficients. All the variables are statistically significant ($p<0.05$). A 10% increase in NWCR results in a 1.65% increase in ROA. Increased supplier credit and shorter receivables boost NP. LEV, FAT, NFAT, and RDI all had a negative impact on profitability, with a 10% change in LEV, FAT, NFAT, and RDI causing -1.22, -0.09, -4.70, and -11.35 percent changes in ROA, respectively. Fixed asset accretion has reduced the long-term profitability of these companies because these firms were invested heavily (in terms of NFA) in manufacturing active pharmaceutical ingredient (API) manufacturing, which has been adversely affected by Chinese exports in recent years. (Cherian et al., 2021). As a result, the effects of FAT, NFAT, and the interaction term are all negative. It has been proposed that most multinational enterprises from developing nations (India) will only show partial support for the "S" curve theory, because their level of internationalization and performance association is only represented by a U-shaped curve (Kumar & Singh, 2008). A 10% change in INNFATSORD results in a -2.45% change in ROA at the 5% level of significance. Companies that invest extensively in knowledge transfer and technological capabilities accrue greater levels of expenditure and investment, which diminishes profitability.

## Panel Data Least Square (Fixed Effect)

A fixed effects regression is a panel data estimation technique that allows one to control for time-invariant unobserved individual characteristics that can be correlated with the observed independent variables (Stock & Watson 2015).

The dependent variable is ROCE. INNFATSORD, NWCR, LEV, FAT, and NFAT are all independent variables.

*Table 4. Short run coefficient Dependent Variable: ROA*

| Variable | Overall (Firms) | Abbot | Aurobindo | Cipla | Dr. Reddy Lab | Lupin | Sun Pharma |
|---|---|---|---|---|---|---|---|
| | Coefficient (T-value) | Coefficient (T-value) | Coefficient (T-value) | Coefficient (T-value) | Coefficient (T-value) | Coefficient (T-value) | Coefficient (T-value) |
| COINTEQ01 | -0.375*** (-2.307) | -0.562*** (-16.948) | -0.073*** (-4.613) | -0.778*** (-95.986) | 0.021*** (4.531) | -0.016*** (-181.868) | -0.845*** (-10.435) |
| ROA(-1) | -0.236* (-1.890) | -0.072** (-2.630) | -0.381*** (-18.991) | 0.279*** (26.568) | -0.501*** (-24.431) | -0.216*** (-11.502) | -0.528*** (-15.466) |
| NWCR | 0.031 (0.294) | -0.121*** (-18.282) | 0.485*** (19.880) | -0.039*** (-38.177) | 0.102*** (37.630) | 0.036*** (9.805) | -0.276*** (-77.373) |
| NWCR(-1) | 0.015 (0.157) | -0.190*** (-37.999) | 0.160*** (24.935) | -0.024*** (-23.861) | 0.226*** (51.766) | 0.272*** (43.655) | -0.349*** (-26.176) |
| LEV | -0.1604 (-1.251) | 0.018 (0.289) | -0.066*** (-23.398) | -0.013*** (-14.478) | -0.003*** (-3.892) | -0.102*** (-82.998) | -0.794*** (-30.755) |
| LEV(-1) | -0.098** (-2.409) | 0.066 (0.834) | -0.178*** (-58.647) | -0.035*** (-47.772) | -0.117*** (-92.468) | -0.118*** (-98.362) | -0.205*** (-17.636) |
| FAT | 0.047*** (3.156) | 0.002*** (347.619) | 0.018*** (70.270) | 0.041*** (866.937) | 0.066*** (1002.031) | 0.105*** (351.678) | 0.048*** (96.044) |
| FAT(-1) | 0.0054 (0.375) | 0.004*** (807.392) | -0.012*** (-206.442) | 0.011*** (130.665) | 0.008*** (132.449) | -0.043*** (-95.825) | 0.064*** (211.459) |
| NFAT | 0.5199* (1.924) | 0.1334 (0.724) | 0.510*** (7.889) | 0.434*** (49.626) | 0.178*** (8.660) | 0.042*** (707.316) | 1.819*** (3.739) |
| NFAT(-1) | 0.1895 (0.763) | 1.317*** (8.095) | -0.166*** (-4.539) | 0.365*** (10.037) | 0.027*** (3.603) | 0.003*** (70.686) | -0.408** (-2.932) |
| RDI | 3.0378 (1.052) | 17.4140 (0.135) | 0.2641 (0.137) | 0.074 (1.700) | -0.344*** (-6.397) | -0.528*** (-3.195) | 1.3470 (2.103) |
| RDI(-1) | -0.3080 (-0.700) | -0.7242 (-.008) | -1.6302 (-1.096) | 0.771*** (15.380) | -1.340*** (-17.343) | 0.203* (1.870) | 0.8708** (2.754) |
| INNFATSORD | -3.7591 (-1.082) | -20.692 (-0.103) | -4.1333 (-0.852) | 0.682*** (9.129) | 0.502*** (13.085) | 0.911*** (10.325) | 0.174*** (4.478) |
| INNFATSORD(-1) | -8.4550 (-1.014) | -50.055 (-0.099) | -2.6161 (-0.745) | 0.328*** (61.663) | 0.631*** (7.803) | 0.996*** (12.182) | -0.014 (-1.584) |
| C | 0.125** (2.425) | 0.195*** (32.191) | 0.035*** (27.625) | 0.266*** (159.681) | -0.002*** (-4.260) | 0.004*** (78.041) | 0.255*** (41.982) |

Note. ***, **, and * represent 1%, 5%, and 10% significance level respectively

*Table 5. Long run coefficient variable*

| Dependent Variable: ROA | | | | |
|---|---|---|---|---|
| **Variable** | **Coefficient** | **Std. Error** | **t-Statistic** | **Prob.*** |
| NWCR | 0.161861 | 0.033160 | 4.881253 | 0.0000 |
| LEV | -0.122348 | 0.016635 | -7.354817 | 0.0000 |
| FAT | -0.009186 | 0.003345 | -2.746524 | 0.0076 |
| NFAT | -0.470122 | 0.128337 | -3.663179 | 0.0005 |
| RDI | -1.113558 | 0.245423 | -4.537297 | 0.0000 |
| INNFATSORD | -0.245178 | 0.121586 | -2.016509 | 0.0475 |

The Hausmann test on a random effect model confirms the presence or absence of (cross-section) fixed effects. The Hausman test confirms the existence of a cross-section fixed effect (table 6)

*Table 6. Correlated random effects - Hausman Test*

| Test cross-section random effects | | | |
|---|---|---|---|
| **Test Summary** | **Chi-Sq. Statistic** | **Chi-Sq. d.f.** | **Prob.** |
| Cross-section random | 23.797534 | 5 | 0.0002 |
| ** WARNING: estimated cross-section random effects variance is zero | | | |

*Table 7. Fixed effect*

| Dependent Variable: ROCE | | | | |
|---|---|---|---|---|
| Cross-sections included: 6 | | | | |
| Total panel (balanced) observations: 168 | | | | |
| **Variable** | **Coefficient** | **Std. Error** | **t-Statistic** | **Prob.** |
| INNFATSORD | 0.009887 | 0.005111 | 1.934482 | 0.0549 |
| NWCR | 0.189485 | 0.034504 | 5.491628 | 0.0000 |
| FAT | 0.047851 | 0.027928 | 1.713361 | 0.0886 |
| NFAT | -0.018852 | 0.024298 | -0.775868 | 0.4390 |
| LEV | -0.020822 | 0.012166 | -1.711397 | 0.0890 |
| C | 0.763922 | 0.073023 | 10.46134 | 0.0000 |
| | **Effects Specification** | | | |
| Cross-section fixed (dummy variables) | | | | |
| R-squared | 0.471361 | Mean dependent var | | 1.021655 |
| Adjusted R-squared | 0.437690 | S.D. dependent var | | 0.682438 |
| S.E. of regression | 0.511742 | Akaike info criterion | | 1.561242 |
| Sum squared resid | 41.11516 | Schwarz criterion | | 1.765788 |
| Log-likelihood | -120.1444 | Hannan-Quinn criteria. | | 1.644257 |
| F-statistic | 13.99892 | Durbin-Watson stat | | 1.369134 |
| Prob(F-statistic) | 0.000000 | | | |

The linear equation with cross-section fixed effect:-

ROCE = 0.00988738067873*SOR_D + 0.189484502258*NWCR - 0.0188518253577*NFAT + 0.0478505470378*FAT - 0.0208216307549*LEV + 0.763921562565 + [CX=F]

The model fit is good as it is able to explain 47.13% of variation ($R^2 = 0.4713$) with F-statistic value of 13.99 ($p<0.05$). Autocorrelation is absent as Durbin–Watson statistic value is 1.369. Residual cross-section correction was found to be absent in estimation (table 8).

*Table 8. Residual cross-section Dependence Test*

| Null hypothesis: No cross-section dependence (correlation) in residuals | | | |
|---|---|---|---|
| Total panel observations: 168 | | | |
| Cross-section effects were removed during estimation | | | |
| **Test** | **Statistic** | **d.f.** | **Prob.** |
| Breusch-Pagan LM | 23.01267 | 15 | 0.0839 |
| Pesaran scaled LM | 1.462906 | | 0.1435 |
| Bias-corrected scaled LM | 1.351795 | | 0.1764 |
| Pesaran CD | 0.074752 | | 0.9404 |

INNFATSORD, NWCR, FAT, and LEV are all between 5% and 10% significant. A 10% increase in NWCR leads to a 1.89% increase in Profitability in the same direction, implying that a longer AR improves profitability. A 10% increase in FAT translates to a 0.5% increment in ROCE in the same direction. Increased sales increase ROCE when capital is fixed.

The cross-section fixed effect is also highly significant, with a 5% significance level. Table 9 exhibits the individual cross-section fixed effects.

*Table 9. Cross-section fixed effects*

| S. No. | Company Name | Effect |
|---|---|---|
| 1 | Abbott India Ltd. | 0.530081 |
| 2 | Aurobindo Pharma Ltd. | -0.158249 |
| 3 | Cipla Ltd. | 0.005153 |
| 4 | Dr. Reddy'S Laboratories Ltd. | -0.220824 |
| 5 | Lupin Ltd. | 0.109621 |
| 6 | Sun Pharmaceutical Inds. Ltd. | -0.265783 |

Controlling for individual firm fixed effects, a 10% increase in R&D spillover mediated by fixed assets raises ROCE by 0.10 percent. R&D and knowledge transfer can be more inventive and efficient as a result of knowledge inflow and outflow from cross-firm activities involving each other's manufacturing capabilities (NFA).

## CONCLUSION

This study adds to the empirical literature by expanding our understanding of knowledge diffusion on performance determinants in Indian pharmaceutical companies. The factors explaining the interaction terms R&D spillover, RDI, NWCR, LEV, NFAT, and FAT of the top six firms in the IPI are studied using ARDL and cross-section fixed-effects panel models. NWCR, NFAT, FAT, LEV, RDI, and interaction factors are key variables influencing profitability, according to empirical findings. They differ, however, in terms of strength and direction of influence. The interaction between NFAT and spillover R&D (knowledge diffusion) in these six firms has had a direct impact on their performance predicated on the inflow and outflow of knowledge transfer and fixed asset utilization. The accumulated knowledge can be mediated through the efficient utilization of fixed assets.

The IPI's R&D contribution appears to be significantly influenced by knowledge transfer and new technology orientation, as both are important determinants of in-house R&D. IPI's previous reserve engineering capabilities were also advantageous. Profit from the previous year appeared to function as an enabling fund to invest in R&D as well as an incentive to improve R&D, but higher LEV appeared to limit managers' ability to spend on R&D. Different approaches to working capital funding (aggressive vs. moderate) result in an efficient trade-off between NWCR and profitability. Profitability is also dependent on internal financing from WC and external financing at a competitive interest rate from financial institutions.

The low coefficient of interaction between NFAT and R&D diffusion within firms is due to low NFAT. The ARDL short-run coefficient of the interaction term is significant and positive in the cases of Cipla, Lupin, and Sun Pharma. In the short run, these three firms have benefited from knowledge diffusion mediated by fixed assets. The long-run coefficient, on the other hand, is significantly negative. Scaled net fixed assets (NFAT) began to decline in all of these firms beginning in the fiscal year 2000The precipitous drop was caused by an increase in Chinese API imports into India. Indian firms began to shift away from developing APIs and toward developing formulations, which require far fewer fixed assets.

## REFERENCES


Akintola, A. F., & Cole, A. A. (2020)... *Impact of Combined Leverage on Capital Employed Of Selected Listed Manufacturing Firms in Nigeria.*, *11*(3), 51–56. doi:10.9790/5933-1103055156

Aldieri, L., Sena, V., & Vinci, C. P. (2018). Domestic R&D spillovers and absorptive capacity: Some evidence for US, Europe, and Japan. *International Journal of Production Economics, 198*(April 2017), 38–49. doi:10.1016/j.ijpe.2018.01.015

Aldieri, L., Brahmi, M., Bruno, B., & Vinci, C. P. (2021). Circular Economy Business Models: The Complementarities with Sharing Economy and Eco-Innovations Investments. *Sustainability*, *13*(22), 12438. doi:10.3390u132212438

Andersson, T., Haslam, C., & Lee, E. (2006). Financialized accounts: Restructuring and return on capital employed in the S&P 500. *Accounting Forum*, *30*(1), 21–41. doi:10.1016/j.accfor.2006.01.001

Arabeche, Z., Soudani, A., Brahmi, M., Aldieri, L., Vinci, C. P., & Abdelli, M. E. A. (2022). Entrepreneurial Orientation, Organizational Culture and Business Performance in SMEs: Evidence from Emerging Economy. *Sustainability*, *14*(9), 5160. doi:10.3390u14095160

Arora, A., Fosfuri, A., & Gambardella, A. (2001). Technology markets and their implications for corporate strategy. *Industrial and Corporate Change*, *10*(2), 419–452. doi:10.1093/icc/10.2.419

Ashwin, A. S., Krishnan, R. T., & George, R. (2016). Board Characteristics, Financial Slack and R&D Investments: An Empirical Analysis of the Indian Pharmaceutical Industry. *International Studies of Management & Organization*, *46*(1), 8–23. doi:10.1080/00208825.2015.1007007

Banerji, A. (2012). A selective study of exports of manufactured goods from India: Auto parts and pharmaceuticals. *Journal of International Business Research, 11*(2), 89.

Banerji, A., & Suri, F. (2019). Does R&D Intensity and Innovative Activities drive Indian Pharmaceutical Exports? *Journal of Scientific and Industrial Research, 78*, 664–666.

Baskerville, R. L., & Dulipovici, A. (2006). The theoretical foundations of knowledge management. *Knowledge Management and Research, 4*, 83-105.

Bernstein, J., & Nadiri, I. M. (1988). Inter-industry R&D spillovers, rates of return and Production in High Tech Industries. *The American Economic Review, 78*, 429–434.

Bernstein, J., & Nadiri, I. M. (1989). Research and Development and Intra-industry Spillovers: An Empirical Application of Dynamic Duality. *The Review of Economic Studies, 56*(2), 249–269. doi:10.2307/2297460

Bureau, E. P. N. (2022, February 9). Slowing trend of ANDA approvals in 2021: Pandemic effect or selective filings? *Express Pharma*. https://www.expresspharma.in/slowing-trend-of-anda-approvals-in-2021-pandemic-effect-or-selective-filings/

Carboni, O. A., & Medda, G. (2018). R&D, export and investment decision: Evidence from European firms. *Applied Economics, 50*(2), 187–201. doi:10.1080/00036846.2017.1332747

Chaudhuri, S. (2005). *The WTO and India's pharmaceuticals industry: Patent protection, TRIPS, and developing countries*. Oxford University Press.

Chauhan, G. S. (2019). Are working capital decisions truly short-term in nature? *Journal of Business Research, 99*(August 2018), 238–253. doi:10.1016/j.jbusres.2019.02.032

Cherian, J. J., Rahi, M., Rinwa, N., Singh, S., Reddy, S. E., Gupta, Y. K., Katoch, V. M., Kumar, V., Selvaraj, S., Das, P., Gangakhedkar, R. R., Dinda, A. K., Sarkar, S., Vaghela, P. D., & Bhargava, B. (2021). India's road to independence in manufacturing active pharmaceutical ingredients: Focus on essential medicines. *Economies, 9*(2), 1–18. doi:10.3390/economies9020071

Cohen, W. M., & Levinthal, D. A. (1989). Innovation and learning: The two faces of R & D. *Economic Journal (London), 99*(397), 569–596. doi:10.2307/2233763

Dawar, G., Singh, S., Joshi, M., & Kumar, P. (2020). Effective Corporate Social Responsibilty in Small Medium Entreprises. In *Organizing entrepreneurship and MSME across India*. World Scientific Publishers.

Erum, S.; Muhammad, N T.; Wali Muhammad, K.; Mohsen, B.; & Shahid, R., Chapter 16: The COVID-19 Pandemic Overlaps Entrepreneurial Activities and Triggered New Challenges: A Review Study, Book chapter: Managing Human Resources in SMEs and Start-ups, August 2022, 388 p. https://doi.org/doi:10.1142/9789811239212_0008

Frantzen, D. (2000). R&D, Human Capital and International Technology Spillovers: A Cross Country Analysis. *The Scandinavian Journal of Economics, 102*(1), 55–75. doi:10.1111/1467-9442.00184

Ganguly, A., Talukdar, A., & Chatterjee, D. (2020). Social capital, knowledge quality, knowledge sharing, and innovation capability: An empirical study of the Indian pharmaceutical sector. *Knowledge and Process Management, 27*(1), 25–42. doi:10.1002/kpm.1614

Gkypali, A., Arvanitis, S., & Tsekouras, K. (2018). Absorptive capacity, exporting activities, innovation openness and innovation performance: A SEM approach towards a unifying framework. *Technological Forecasting and Social Change*, *132*, 143–155. doi:10.1016/j.techfore.2018.01.025

Gkypali, A., Tsekouras, K., & von Tunzelmann, N. (2012). Endogeneity between internationalization and knowledge creation of global R&D leader firms: An econometric approach using scoreboard data. *Industrial and Corporate Change*, *21*(3), 731–762. doi:10.1093/icc/dtr057

Gleadle, P., & Haslam, C. (2010). *An exploratory study of an early stage R & D-intensive firm under.* *34*, 54–65. doi:10.1016/j.accfor.2009.10.002

Goldar, B. (2013). R&D intensity and exports: A study of Indian pharmaceutical firms. *Innovation and Development*, *3*(2), 151–167. doi:10.1080/2157930X.2013.828878

Griliches, Z., & Lichtenberg, F. R. (1984). R&D and productivity growth at the industry level: is there still a relationship? In *R&D, patents, and productivity* (pp. 465–502). University of Chicago Press. doi:10.7208/chicago/9780226308920.001.0001

Haakonsson, S. J., Jensen, P. D. Ø., & Mudambi, S. M. (2013). A co-evolutionary perspective on the drivers of international sourcing of pharmaceutical R&D to India. *Journal of Economic Geography*, *13*(4), 677–700. doi:10.1093/jeg/lbs018

Hall, B. H., Mairesse, J., & Mohnen, P. (2010). Measuring the Returns to R&D. In *Handbook of the Economics of Innovation* (Vol. 2, pp. 1033–1082). North-Holland.

Hamrouni, B., Bourouis, A., Korichi, A., & Brahmi, M. (2021). Explainable Ontology-Based Intelligent Decision Support System for Business Model Design and Sustainability. *Sustainability*, *13*(17), 9819. doi:10.3390u13179819

Harris, R., & Li, Q. C. (2009). Exporting, R&D, and absorptive capacity in UK establishments. *Oxford Economic Papers*, *61*(1), 74–103. doi:10.1093/oep/gpn011

IBEF. (2019). Pharmaceutical Companies in India, Indian Pharma Industry- IBEF. *India Brand Equity Foundation.* https://www.ibef.org/industry/pharmaceutical-india.

IBEF. (2020). Pharmaceutical Companies in India, Indian Pharma Industry- IBEF. *India Brand Equity Foundation*. https://www.ibef.org/industry/pharmaceutical-india.

Jaffe, A. B. (1986). Technological Opportunity and Spillovers of R&D: Evidence from Firms' Patents, Profits, and Market Value. *The American Economic Review*, *76*(5), 984–1001.

Joshi, M. (2018). Workforce Trends and Challenges: A Peek Into the Future. *Management Techniques for a Diverse and Cross-Cultural Workforce*, 39-53.

Joshi, M. (2018). Burnout and Stressors as influencers on Work engagement among law enforcement agents in selected cities. In Chaudhary, N., Sharma, M., Singh: Vol. K. Management Techniques for Employee Engagement in Contemporary Organizations. IGI Global USA.

Joshi, M. (2022 Forthcoming). *A mediation based analysis of Emotional Intelligence effect on Cognition and Consumer Decision Making*. IJPSPM.

Joshi, M., Joshi, G., & Pathak, S. (2020). Awareness, entrepreneurial event theory and theory of planned behaviour as antecedents of student entrepreneurial intentions: An Indian perspective. *International Journal of Business and Globalisation*, *25*(2), 170–184. doi:10.1504/IJBG.2020.107885

Joshi, M., & Singh, V. K. (2017). Electronic Word of Mouth and Influence on Consumer Purchase Intention. *Dynamics of Public Administration*, *34*(2), 149–159. doi:10.5958/0976-0733.2017.00012.8

Joshi, M., Tyagi, S., Ansari, N., & Singh, V. K. (2019) Impact of IoT to accomplish a vision of digital transformation of the cities. In A handbook of IOT and Big Data, USA: CRC Press, Taylor and Francis.

Kostopoulos, K., Papalexandris, A., Papachroni, M., & Ioannou, G. (2011). Absorptive capacity, innovation, and fi nancial performance. *Journal of Business Research*, *64*(12), 1335–1343. doi:10.1016/j.jbusres.2010.12.005

Kumar, Vikas & Singh, N. (2008). Comments on "The parting gift.". *Thunderbird International Business Review*, *50*(5), 321–330. doi:10.1002/tie.20217

Lorenzen, M., & Mudambi, R. (2013). Clusters, connectivity and catch-up: Bollywood and Bangalore in the global economy. *Journal of Economic Geography*, *13*(3), 501–534. doi:10.1093/jeg/lbs017

Love, J. H., & Ganotakis, P. (2013). Learning by exporting: Lessons from high-technology SMEs. *International Business Review*, *22*(1), 1–17. doi:10.1016/j.ibusrev.2012.01.006

Ma, S. J. (2013). *Journal of Engineering and Product portfolio decision-making and absorptive capacity : A simulation study*. doi:10.1016/j.jengtecman.2013.09.004

Manual, F. Paris, OECD, (1993). The Oslo Manual: Proposed Guidelines for Collecting and Interpreting Technological Innovation Data. Paris, OECD.

Nadiri. (1993). *Nadiri-Innovation-and-Spillovers-1993-W4423*.

Pennetier, C., Girotra, K., & Mihm, J. (2019). R&D Spending: Dynamic or Persistent? *Manufacturing & Service Operations Management*, *21*(3), 636–657. doi:10.1287/msom.2018.0715

Plunket, A. (2009). Firms' inventiveness and localized vertical r&d spillovers. *Journal of Innovation Economics Management*, *4*(2), 147–170.

Poldahl, A. (2012). The Two Faces of R&D: Does Firm Absorptive Capacity Matter? *Journal of Industry, Competition and Trade*, *12*(2), 221–237. doi:10.100710842-010-0094-x

Pomerleano, M., & Shaw, W. (2005). *Corporate restructuring: lessons from experience*. World Bank Publications. doi:10.1596/0-8213-5928-2

Rogers, M., & Rogers, M. (1998). *The definition and measurement of innovation* (Vol. 98). Melbourne Institute of Applied Economic and Social Research.

Rosenberg, N., & Frischtak, R. C. (1984). Technological innovation and long waves. *Cambridge Journal of Economics*, *8*, 7–24.

Salazar, A., Hackney, R. A. Y., & Howells, J. (2003). The Strategic Impact of Internet Technology in Biotechnology and Pharmaceutical Firms. *Information Technology and Managment*, *4*(2/3), 289–301. doi:10.1023/A:1022910614411

Sharma, C. (2016). R&D, technology transfer and productivity in the Indian pharmaceutical industry. *International Journal of Innovation Management*, *20*(1), 1–24. doi:10.1142/S1363919616500109

Shaikh, E., Brahmi, M., Thang, P. C., Watto, W. A., Trang, T. T. N., & Loan, N. T. (2022). Should I Stay or Should I Go? Explaining the Turnover Intentions with Corporate Social Responsibility (CSR), Organizational Identification and Organizational Commitment. *Sustainability*, *14*(10), 6030. doi:10.3390u14106030

Shrestha, M. B., & Bhatta, G. R. (2018). Selecting appropriate methodological framework for time series data analysis. *Journal of Finance and Data Science*, *4*(2), 71–89. doi:10.1016/j.jfds.2017.11.001

Singh, J., & Singh, P. (2014). Decomposition of Technical Efficiency and Productivity Growth in Indian Pharmaceutical Industry:A Non-Parametric Analysis. *Artha Vijnana: Journal of The Gokhale Institute of Politics and Economics*, *56*(4), 456. doi:10.21648/arthavij/2014/v56/i4/111174

Srivastava, R. K. (2020). Managing mergers and acquisitions in health care: A case study in the pharmaceutical sector. *International Journal of Healthcare Management*, *13*(sup1, S1), 61–73. doi:10.1080/20479700.2017.1422337

Stock, J. H., & Watson, M. W. (2015). Introduction to econometrics (3rd ed). Pearson.

Suri, F. K., & Banerji, A. (2016). A study of disaggregated R&D expenditure on Indian pharmaceutical exports. *Journal of Developing Areas*, *50*(3), 167–190. doi:10.1353/jda.2016.0108

Suri, F. K., & Banerji, A. (2019a). Does R&D Intensity and Innovative Activities drive Indian Pharmaceutical Exports? *Journal of Scientific and Industrial Research*, *78*(10), 664–666.

Suri, F. K., & Banerji, A. (2019b). Impact of R&D Intensity, Patents and Regulatory filings on Export Intensity of Indian Pharmaceutical Industry. *Indian Journal of Pharmaceutical Education and Research*, *53*(4), 638–648. doi:10.5530/ijper.53.4.125

Tunio, M. N., Chaudhry, I. S., Shaikh, S., Jariko, M. A., & Brahmi, M. (2021). Determinants of the Sustainable Entrepreneurial Engagement of Youth in Developing Country—An Empirical Evidence from Pakistan. *Sustainability*, *13*(14), 7764. doi:10.3390u13147764

Zahra, S. A., & George, G. (2002). Absorptive capacity: A review, reconceptualization, and extension. *Academy of Management Review*, *27*(2), 185–203. doi:10.2307/4134351

# Chapter 10

# It Takes Two to Tango:
## The Ecosystem Engagement and Coopetition Paradoxes

**Sabrina Schneider**
https://orcid.org/0000-0001-6027-5282
*Management Center Innsbruck, Austria*

## ABSTRACT

*Business ecosystems have emerged as an increasingly popular and powerful mode of inter-firm collaborations. As such, business ecosystems are highly complex forms of joint value creation and capture activities between actors who, while partly loosely connected, depend on one another. Building on a combination of stakeholder and paradox theories, this chapter provides insights into two emerging paradox tensions: (1) The ecosystem engagement paradox (balancing the diverging interests of the focal firm and the overall ecosystem); and (2) the ecosystem coopetition paradox (balancing competition and cooperation with other ecosystem actors). This view allows displaying the complementary nature of both theoretical perspectives and their joint contribution to the ecosystem context. Further, by identifying two paradox tensions inherent to the business ecosystem context, this chapter offers insights for managers on how to engage in business ecosystem and how to deal with ecosystem competitiveness.*

## INTRODUCTION

Ecosystem actors join forces to create a cooperative value offering for customers by building on complementary resource inputs and multiple actors' competencies (Dattée et al., 2018; Hannah & Eisenhardt, 2018; Roundy et al., 2018). Since none of the actors possesses the capacity in terms of capabilities and resources to create the ecosystem's value offering on its own, all actors depend strongly on one another (Gueler & Schneider, 2021; Iansiti & Levien, 2004; Ihrig & MacMillan, 2017; Thomas & Ritala, 2022). At the same time, in contrast to other forms of inter-firm collaborations, ecosystem actors tend to be more loosely connected, specifically due to an ecosystem's reliance on many indirect ties between actors. These relationships go beyond transparent dyadic and multilateral formal collaborations. Owing to

DOI: 10.4018/978-1-6684-6766-4.ch010

ecosystem members' dependence on one another to create the joint value offering, each member shares an interest in the others' survival and success. Further, competition is likely to move from the level of a firm's business model to the ecosystem level, where one ecosystem is competing against another ecosystem. Consequently, being part of a strong ecosystem becomes fundamentally important to enable the success of a firm's business model as even the most promising business model – when it is stuck in a weak ecosystem – may become subject to failure. Scholars widely agree that the ecosystem concept has become key to innovation in the digital environment (e.g., Cohendet et al., 2021).

Despite rising interest in the ecosystem concept (e.g., Daymond et al., 2022), scholars acknowledge that the ecosystem environment requires actors to diverge from traditional thought patterns (Krome & Pidun, 2022; Stonig et al., 2022; Thomas & Ritala, 2022). The emergence of ecosystems requires a shift in mind-set among managers. Whereas managers have experience in maximising the benefits for their focal firm's business model, the ecosystem context requires them to balance the interests of the overall business ecosystem and their firm's business model. This implies that ecosystem members need to simultaneously act in the best interest of the ecosystem and their focal firm's business model – two objectives that are likely to be contradictory, however interdependent and potentially synergetic. We frame this persistent tension as the "ecosystem engagement paradox". In addition, we argue that ecosystem members face a second paradoxical tension, the "ecosystem coopetition paradox". This paradox is about balancing competition and cooperation behaviours with other ecosystem actors. Paradox tensions are "elements that seem logical individually but inconsistent and even absurd when juxtaposed" (Smith & Lewis, 2011, p. 382). Recent management literature has illustrated that while it is an innate human reaction to focus on one demand at the other demand's expense (Lewis, 2000), seemingly distinct and opposing demands can potentially be synergetic (Andriopoulos et al., 2018; Miron-Spektor et al., 2018; Schad et al., 2016). However, to leverage this potential, the actors involved need to encode the paradoxical situations, which is a challenging endeavour (Clegg et al., 2002; Smith & Lewis, 2011; Smith & Tushman, 2005).

So far, our explicit knowledge of business ecosystems as a new mode of the inter-firm organisation of value co-creation (Shaikh et al., 2022), capture and appropriation is limited. The objective of this chapter is to use a paradoxical lens to explore two of the major challenges in business ecosystems, the ecosystem engagement and coopetition paradoxes. Building on paradox and stakeholder theories, we explain how managers in business ecosystem contexts need to engage in increasingly paradox journeys. Further, this view allows us to explain the synergetic potential of these tensions as a source of competitive advantage in the inter-ecosystem context. This enables us to display the complementary character of both perspectives and their joint contribution to the ecosystem context. In addition, we thereby contribute to the emerging ecosystem theory by disentangling some of the fuzziness of the business ecosystem concept. Further, through raising the relevance of considering the inter-ecosystem perspective, we demonstrate the relevance of managerial coping mechanisms to deal with paradox tensions in the business ecosystem context. We show how balancing the focal firm's and the ecosystem's interests as well as the collaboration and competition with other ecosystem actors has become an essential capability for firms to master the internal ecosystem challenge and to be prepared for the emerging inter-ecosystem competition.

## BACKGROUND

### Business Ecosystems

Business ecosystems are an increasingly popular mode of inter-firm value creation and capture. In the context of a business ecosystem, we define stakeholders as any group or individual who creates and/or captures any type of value in interaction with the other firms involved in the ecosystem. An ecosystem offers its customers a value proposition that merges the multiple value offerings of the ecosystem's individual stakeholders into one joint value offering (Adner, 2017). We see an increasingly popular example of business ecosystems in the delivery of mobility services with the emergence of "Mobility-as-a-Service (MaaS)" offerings. Here, providers of different transportation options – ranging from public transportation to individual on-demand transportation services – bundle their offerings to offer a joint mobility valuer offering to their customers. Examples include whim, skedgo, transit, or skipr.[1] These stakeholders thus join forces to create the ecosystem's value offering by providing resources and capabilities and, in exchange, they participate in the appropriation of the ecosystem's output. A key feature of an ecosystem is that, individually, none of its members could achieve the ecosystem's value offering, because the ecosystem output relies on their inputs' complementarity (Hannah & Eisenhardt, 2018; Jacobides et al., 2018; Roundy et al., 2018). Further, if the ecosystem's members' were to engage in bilateral and multilateral relations only, they could not achieve the same value offering that their joint effort enables (Adner, 2017).

The high level of interdependence implies that an ecosystem's joint value creation is a highly complex endeavour that requires the collaboration of manifold actors (Adner, 2006; Dattée et al., 2018; Pagani, 2013). Even though these actors tend to be only loosely connected within the ecosystem and to act autonomously, such actors are highly dependent on one another (Dattée et al., 2018; Iansiti & Levien, 2004; Ihrig & MacMillan, 2017; Jacobides et al., 2018). This leads to ecosystem members being interested in their ecosystem partners' success (Adner, 2013), which in return requires firms to find the right balance between their cooperation and competition efforts (Hannah & Eisenhardt, 2018). In comparison to other forms of inter-firm value creation, such as strategic alliances (Hamrouni et al., 2021) and joint ventures, ecosystems tend to comprise a higher degree of complexity (Roundy et al., 2018). The loose form of collaboration between ecosystem members is one cause of this complexity. While there are formal, bilateral agreements between some ecosystem actors – particularly those that interact directly – not all ecosystem actors have concluded such agreements. This lack in existing bilateral agreements distinguishes ecosystems from other modes of joint value creation. Ecosystem actors might benefit from other ecosystem stakeholders' complementary resources, even if they do not have direct ties or interactions with the owners of these resources. Further, depending on an actor's positioning within an ecosystem, the actor might not have full transparency and influence on who joins and leaves the ecosystem. The reliability of the ecosystem's mechanisms is therefore a potential risk for any actor. Further, ecosystem complexity emerges through the ecosystem connecting and aligning its members' manifold business models. Each business model follows a distinct logic that explains how value is generated and captured; that is, how the firm makes money (Baden-Fuller & Morgan, 2010). Ecosystem actors provide the value offering of their business models, or a part of this value offering, or any other resources and capabilities they possess as their input into the ecosystem. Their strategic intentions can vary – the actors might expect access to new customer segments or markets, they might feel the ecosystem threatens their business model (Arabeche et ala., 2022), or they might just want to leverage their resource base. Furthermore, firms might hide their strategic intentions from other ecosystem members.

In ecosystem contexts, understanding individual ecosystem members' utility functions is a key challenge. A utility function captures the attractiveness of the inputs and outcomes of certain firm activities (Harrison et al., 2010). Each ecosystem member joins an ecosystem with distinct expectations built on this member's individual utility function. Based on the individual business models that underpin their utility functions, the ecosystem members evaluate their own input and output components. This evaluation determines their willingness to provide a certain input in exchange for an expected output. While some of these utility functions' components are likely to be transparent to all the ecosystem members, others might be less evident elements. Additionally, individual stakeholders might hesitate to share sensitive information about their individual utility functions, because this information could be used to their disadvantage. The perception of an individual ecosystem member's utility function might therefore be distinct to different ecosystem members, depending on their knowledge of the other actor's business model.

The value that an individual ecosystem member's input contributes to the ecosystem and what this member receives in return can vary in terms of its objective value to the ecosystem (Sunkar et al., 2022) and its subjective value to the individual ecosystem members. A particular input might, for example, be a secondary resource of little value within its owner's current business model, but make a beneficial or even crucial contribution to some of the ecosystem's members or to the system as a whole (Gueler & Schneider, 2021). In such constellations, ecosystem members are likely to hesitate to reveal the resource's limited value for themselves to avoid receiving a relatively low return for their input. Also, the benefits that the resource offers, might only emerge in combination with other ecosystem members' complementary resources. Such complements have a huge potential for disruption without new entrants entering the field (Adner & Lieberman, 2021). Ecosystems build on complementarities, which implies that the bundling of resources and/or capabilities makes them more valuable than their stand-alone merit (Adner, 2006; Hannah & Eisenhardt, 2018; Pagani, 2013). While all ecosystem actors must add value to the overall ecosystem's output to legitimise their inclusion and continuation in the ecosystem, some are likely to possess more relevant resources and capabilities than others (Aldieri et al., 2021). These actors have strategic resources and capabilities that are difficult or impossible for others to obtain and without which bottlenecks could potentially occur in the overall ecosystem's development (Adner & Kapoor, 2016; Baldwin, 2015; Hannah & Eisenhardt, 2018). In the MaaS-context, valuable resources often include the offer of public transportation providers, as they are difficult to copy or substitute (Gueler & Schneider, 2021).

## Stakeholder Theory

The stakeholder perspective has always emphasised the need to understand firms as elements of a network of ties and relationships with manifold stakeholders (Barringer & Harrison, 2000; Freeman, 1984; Freeman et al., 2007; Jones et al., 2018; Rowley, 1997). Freeman and Reed (1983, p. 89) emphasise that stakeholders are "those groups without whose support the organization would cease to exist". A firm's stakeholders may include primary stakeholders, such as owners, employees, customers and suppliers (Harrison et al., 2010), as well as less transparent, secondary stakeholders, such as community activists or non-governmental organisations (Clarkson, 1995). Particularly salient stakeholders of a firm distinguish themselves by their power, legitimacy and urgency (Mitchell et al., 1997). Their power refers to the "relative access to resources for the stakeholder group with respect to the firm being targeted"

(Eesley & Lenox, 2006, p. 766). In line with the resource dependence theory (Pfeffer & Salancik, 1978), which argues that firms depend on resources in their environment for survival, stakeholder theory claims that those stakeholders in a firm's environment that possess critical resources deserve particular attention (Agle et al., 1999; Frooman, 1999; Kreiner & Bhambri, 1991; Pfeffer, 1982). Their legitimacy is grounded in the perception that a stakeholder's actions are aligned with the prevailing social norms, values and beliefs (Mitchell et al., 1997). Their urgency describes the importance of and need for managerial attention to a stakeholder's demands (Eesley & Lenox, 2006; Mitchell et al., 1997). Within the body of stakeholder theories, three traditions have evolved: the normative tradition based on ethical frameworks, that emphasizes the behavioural implications for stakeholders; the descriptive tradition that focuses on stakeholders' actions during their interactions; and the instrumental tradition that attempts to explain stakeholder behaviour's performance implications in response to other stakeholders' interests and needs (Donaldson & Preston, 1995; Eesley & Lenox, 2006; Jones, 1995; Wood, 1991). In essence, the instrumental stakeholder view claims that firms that engage with stakeholders on a basis of mutual trust and cooperation and that pay attention to their interests are likely to enjoy a competitive advantage over those that do not (Donaldson & Preston, 1995; Jones, 1995). Freeman (1994, p. 174) summarizes this in the "stakeholder enabling principle", stating that "corporations shall be managed in the interests of its stakeholders".

Stakeholder management is widely acknowledged as a "bewilderingly complex" task (Mitchell et al., 1997, p. 857). It requires firms to understand and match multiple parties' interests and demands with their strategic goals (Ackermann & Eden, 2011). In contrast to an arms-length approach, which regards stakeholders as interchangeable actors and where power is the primary criterion in negotiations with stakeholders (Tunio et al., 2021) who concentrate solely on their own interests, the managing-for-stakeholders approach pays attention to understanding the implications of actions for all the stakeholder network's members (Harrison et al., 2010; Sisodia et al., 2007). Trust is therefore a vital ingredient for successful relationships between stakeholders. It refers to the "mutual confidence that no party to an exchange will exploit another's vulnerabilities" (Barney & Hansen, 1994, p. 176). Mutual trust increases the likelihood that stakeholders would be willing to reveal sensitive information to their partners (Harrison ct al., 2010). Each stakeholder enters a collaboration based on an individual utility function, which describes the subjective value of the stakeholders' invested input and received output (Harrison et al., 2010). Only when they trust their partners will stakeholders be likely to share the essential ingredients of their individual utility functions (Harrison et al., 2010).

In the current business environment, we perceive a shift from physical goods and resources to digital resources, knowledge and intellectual property (Asher et al., 2005; Powell & Snellman, 2004) and we face a wider distribution of these resources among multiple stakeholders (Amin & Cohendet, 2000; Grant, 1996). Consequently, joint value creation endeavours, defined as "mutually supportive contributions to value creation from multiple stakeholders whose tasks and outcomes are highly interdependent", have gained prominence (Bridoux & Stoelhorst, 2016, p. 229). Given the increasing levels of interdependency between a firm and its stakeholders, the success, or just the possible survival, of both are often jointly determined (Bundy et al., 2018), which emphasises the need for managing-for-stakeholders approaches.

Furthermore, appropriating the collective outcome becomes a challenging task. It is often impossible to appropriate value between the contributors to the joint value creation's highly interdependent outcomes in proportion to individual contributions' value (Alchian & Demsetz, 1972; Bridoux et al., 2001; Lindenberg & Foss, 2011), which results in a lack of value creation-appropriation correspondence (Brandenburger & Stuart, 1996; Lieberman et al., 2017; MacDonald & Ryall, 2004). Building on the latter, stakeholders might – in a situation where contribution is costly – be inclined to refuse to contribute to the value creation. This could result in a socially and economically detrimental or unfavourable outcome known as the public good or the team production dilemma (Donaldson & Preston, 1995; Jones, 1995), which entails that while the stakeholders' contribution could lead to better results from a collective perspective, they resist making a contribution for reasons of self-interest (Kollock, 1998; Olson, 1965). Achieving transparency about individual firms' utility functions is therefore even more important in the context of highly interdependent stakeholders engaged in complex forms of joint value creation. Whereas most research in this field has examined formal modes of collaboration such as alliances and joint ventures (e.g., Dyer and Nobeoka, 2000; Ingram and Roberts, 2000; Sonnenshein et al., 2017; Zollo et al., 2002), little is known about relational models in less formal modes of collaboration, such as in business ecosystems.

## Paradox Theory

There has been a rapidly growing interest in the study of paradoxes in organization and strategy studies (Pina e Cunha & Putnam, 2019; Waldman et al., 2019). Competing tensions and demands are omnipresent in today's ambiguous and complex business environment (Keller et al., 2017; Schad et al., 2019) – and the transformational potential of digital technologies is likely to further increase tensions' magnitude. Paradox tensions refer to "elements that seem logical individually but inconsistent and even absurd when juxtaposed" (Smith & Lewis, 2011, p. 382) that are persistent over time (Schad et al., 2016). It is these three characteristics that differentiate paradoxes from other forms of tensions: persistence, contradiction, and interdependence (Putnam et al., 2016; Schad et al., 2019). While paradox tensions can occur in various occasions, we focus in this paper on one particular type of paradoxes, the strategic paradox. Strategic paradoxes refer to organizational-level tensions that are persistent, contradicting and interdependent demands within an organization's goals (Smith, 2014; Smith & Lewis, 2011). In the context of the business ecosystem engagement paradox, these continuously competing and interwoven demands reflect the firm's desire to maximize the profits stemming from its business model, and the firm's intention to be a member of a strong business ecosystem. In the context of the ecosystem coopetition paradox, the competing demands stem again from the firm's profit maximization desire (competition) meanwhile striving to achieve a joint value offering that exceeds the firm's capabilities and capacities (collaboration). In the MaaS context, all actors are interested in maximizing the profitability of their distinct business models, while contributing to the long-term success of the ecosystem development, potentially also to ensure the ecosystem's competitiveness against emerging rivalling ecosystems. These objectives (maximizing their own business model's successes vs. supporting the ecosystem's growth and prosperity) are likely to demand trade-off decisions from all actors, as both objectives will not always be perfectly aligned.

In any paradox situation, the innate human reaction would be to focus on one alternative of the tension at the other alternative's expense (Lewis 2000). However, contradicting demands provide a rich potential: Seemingly distinct and opposing elements can be of synergetic nature by being tied through informing, enabling and reinforcing mechanisms (Andriopoulos et al. 2018; Lewis 2000; Schad et al. 2016). To activate the synergetic potential of tensions, individuals need to recognize the complex interrelationships between the opposing elements (Clegg et al. 2002; Lewis 2000; Smith and Lewis 2011). The encoding of such situations is a highly challenging and subjective experience (Smith & Lewis, 2011; Smith & Tushman, 2005). There is no clarity about whether paradoxical thinking can be learned (Audebrand et al., 2017; Schad et al., 2016). However, being aware of the inherent nature of paradox tensions will help us to prepare for the situation (Dubé & Robey, 2008). Further, to effectively cope with paradoxes, we have to learn to gain comfort in the discomfort provided by the tensions (Miron-Spektor et al., 2018).

To deal with the complexity and ambiguity of paradox tensions, managers apply cognitive frames that build on prior experiences and help them to organize and interpret what they perceive to be the most relevant elements in the information provided (Hahn et al., 2014; Mervis & Rosch, 1981; Nadkarni & Barr, 2008). Such cognitive frames or mental templates help managers to recognize and accept the simultaneous existence of contradictory demands and to engage in paradoxical thinking – the effective embracement, rather than avoidance, of these contradictions (Lewis, 2000; Lüscher and Lewis, 2008; Smith and Tushman, 2005). Indeed, paradoxical frames support "both/and" thinking instead of "either/or" thinking, which enables individuals in determining ties between the conflicting elements and the development of new ideas (Lewis 2000; Luscher and Lewis 2008). The adoption of paradox frames can help individuals to build a paradox mindset. A paradox mindset, "the extent to which one is accepting of and energized by tensions", has been acknowledged as critical to unravel the synergetic potential of tensions (Miron-Spektor et al., 2018, p. 26). Individuals with a paradox mindset understand the contradicting character of the tensions, however they also recognize that combining elements from both poles can lead to an overall more beneficial solution (Gebert et al., 2010; Miron-Spektor et al., 2018). The paradox mindset thereby activates a constructive coping response to the tension that allows the individual to develop creative strategies to meet the competing demands (Zheng et al., 2018).

## THE ECOSYSTEM PARADOXES

Strategic paradoxes, such as the ecosystem paradoxes introduced above, are constructs at the intersection of paradox and stakeholder theories (Pinto, 2019). The stakeholder perspective helps us to identify the relevant stakeholders in the ecosystem context. The theory argues that those stakeholders that own critical resources deserve particular attention (Eesley & Lenox, 2006; Frooman, 1999; Mitchell et al., 1997). In the ecosystem context, this can be either some of the other ecosystem actors that possess bottleneck resources (Hannah & Eisenhardt, 2018), or it can also be the ecosystem itself that may offer some valuable market access to a focal firm. The stakeholder theory further provides us with the rationale for managers to act in the interest of all stakeholders (Freeman, 1994; Freeman et al., 2007). However, these interests – at least in the short-run – can be conflicting as the maximization of an ecosystem actor's value appropriation might interfere with the ecosystem's wellbeing. The stakeholder theory does not deny that acting in the interest of all stakeholders can easily become a complex task, given the low transparency of each other's utility functions and of the value creation-appropriation relations (Lieberman et al., 2017; Mitchell et al., 1997). The theory emphasizes the mutual reliance on trust (Barney & Hansen, 1994; Harrison et al., 2010) and stresses that in the case of disappointment, individual stakeholders might resist to contribute to the joint endeavour in favour of self-interested motivations (Kollock, 1998; Olson, 1965). This team production dilemma could easily emerge in the ecosystem context, when one actor observes that other actors display self-interested behaviour.

The paradox perspective sensitizes us for the persistency, contradiction and interdependence of the competing demands inherent to the strategic paradox (Putnam et al., 2016; Schad et al., 2019). We need to be aware, accept and gain comfort with the fact that there is no one-time solution to the diverging interests (Dubé & Robey, 2008; Miron-Spektor et al., 2018). In the ecosystem context, this means that we will always have to balance interests of the ecosystem with our own interests, as well as the interests of other ecosystem actors with our own interests. The persistency of this tension requires us to continuously balance the diverging interests with a "both/and", rather than an "either/or" mindset (Lewis, 2000; Luscher and Lewis, 2008). This effort is done in return for hoping to leverage the synergetic potential inherent to the paradox tension (Andriopoulos et al. 2018; Lewis 2000; Schad et al. 2016). Paradox tensions are particularly likely to occur under the conditions of complexity, scarcity and plurality (Smith & Lewis, 2011), which describes most ecosystem contexts (Roundy et al., 2018). Paradox theory furthers shows that an individual's low paradox mindset might be a limiting factor to successfully cope with a paradox tension (Miron-Spektor et al., 2018).

Figure 1 provides an overview of the two ecosystem paradoxes discussed in more detail below, the ecosystem engagement and the ecosystem coopetition paradox. Following Whetten's (1989) core building blocks of a theory, we illustrate how stakeholder and paradox theory in combination serve to explain each of the paradox tension.

*Figure 1. Ecosystem paradoxes overview (own illustration)*

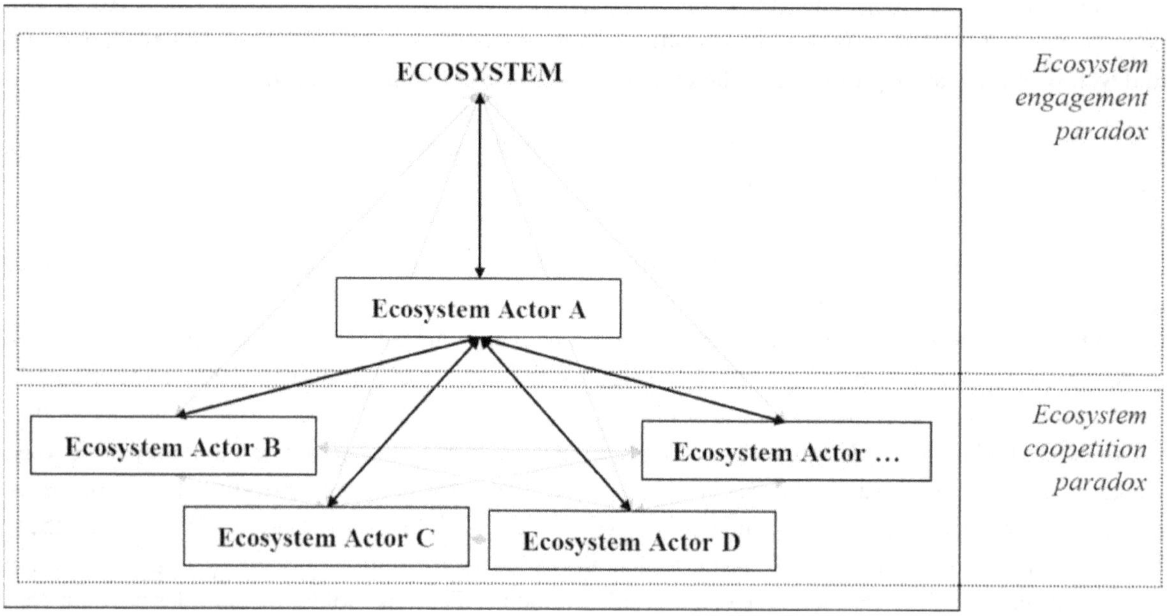


## The Ecosystem Engagement Paradox

In comparison to other forms of inter-firm value creation, such as strategic alliances and joint ventures, ecosystems tend to comprise a higher degree of complexity (Roundy et al., 2018). The loose form of collaboration between ecosystem members, while being interdependent, is one cause of this complexity. Most ecosystems require a potentially large and diverse set of actors to collaborate in order to achieve an attractive joint value offering (Adner, 2017; Dattée et al., 2018). While from a traditional, non-collaborative single firm business model perspective, the optimization of the firm's value capture is obviously the most salient firm objective, firms operating in a business ecosystem context need to balance the ecosystem's well-being and their own value capture. The contradiction of ecosystem members' self-interest in their individual value maximization and the acknowledgement of the ecosystem's overall well-being intensifies the complexity of the relationships between ecosystem actors (Adner, 2013; Hannah & Eisenhardt, 2018). We frame this tension around the relationship between one ecosystem actor and the overall ecosystem as the "ecosystem engagement paradox".

The ecosystem engagement paradox centres on the diverging interests of the overall ecosystem and a focal firm. Whereas the stakeholder perspective helps us to identify the relevant stakeholders (the ecosystem and the focal firm), the paradox perspective focuses on the persistent, contradictory and interrelated tension that exists between those stakeholders (optimization of the outcomes for the focal firm's business model vs. strengthening the overall ecosystem competitiveness). The stakeholder perspective further argues that in order to create mutual trust among the stakeholders (the overall ecosystem and the focal firm as an individual ecosystem actor), a managing-for-stakeholders approach that offers valuable outcomes to all stakeholders is suitable. Whereas the stakeholder perspective does not explain in detail how to achieve this, the paradox perspective offers some relevant insights. The paradox perspective also acknowledges the necessity to balance the stakeholders' diverging demands, rather than to focus on one side only. However, the paradox perspective further emphasizes the necessity to understand this balancing act as a continuous endeavour that requires the actors involved to accept its persistency and to engage in paradoxical thinking. This means that the focal firm's managers need to understand and become aware of the persistency of the competing demands of their business model (Tunio et al., 2021) and the overall ecosystem. Further, instead of always acting in favour of their own business model only, they need to balance the interests of ecosystem and their business model. The rationale for the suggested actions from both perspectives differs slightly. The stakeholder perspective suggests engaging in building mutual trust among all stakeholders in order to achieve their strong commitment towards the ecosystem. The theory assumes that this will help to avoid the situations in which individual participants refrain from contributing to the ecosystem because they privilege self-interested motivations. On the other hand, the paradox perspective explains the rationale for the acceptance and coping with persistent tensions by focusing on the synergetic potential of the contradictory demands. The focal firm would benefit from a strong ecosystem while at the same time the ecosystem would profit from the focal firm's commitment and contribution to the ecosystem. This contribution, however, depends on the focal firm's perception of the appropriated value from the ecosystem. Firms can create a synergy if they manage to contribute value to the ecosystem in a way that allows them to appropriate value through their business model from the increased ecosystem strength. Table 1 illustrates how both views – the stakeholder and the paradox perspectives – inform us about the ecosystem engagement paradox.

*Table 1. The ecosystem engagement paradox informed by stakeholder and paradox theories*

| *Building block* | *Stakeholder perspective* | *Paradox perspective* |
|---|---|---|
| Subject *(what)* | *Relevant stakeholders*: The ecosystem and the focal firm | *Persistent, contradictory and interrelated demands*: The interests of the focal firm's business model and the ecosystem's competitiveness |
| Subject *(how)* | *Create mutual trust through managing-for-stakeholders*: Making valuable contributions to the ecosystem and appropriating valuable contributions from the ecosystem | *Accepting and coping with the persistent tension*: Balancing the divergent demands of the ecosystem and the focal firm's business model using paradoxical thinking |
| Explanation *(why)* | *Avoidance of team production problem*: Achieve strong commitment of the stakeholders to the ecosystem | *Leveraging the synergetic potential*: The focal firm benefits from the strength of the ecosystem and its attraction of other ecosystem members and customers, whereas the ecosystem benefits from the firm's commitment, which in return depends on the firm's perceptions of the appropriated value |

## The Ecosystem Coopetition Paradox

An additional cause of business ecosystems' complexity arises as business ecosystems often bring unconventional actors from previously unrelated industries or even competitors together. Furthermore, ecosystem members usually have a limited transparency of the other member's utility functions and motivations to engage in the business ecosystem and thus their minimum requirements in order to enter the joint endeavour. Ecosystem actors join forces to create a cooperative value offering for customers by building on complementary resources' inputs and multiple actors' competencies (Dattée et al., 2018; Hannah & Eisenhardt, 2018; Roundy et al., 2018). Since none of these actors possess the capacity in terms of capabilities and resources to achieve this value offering on their own, they depend strongly on one another (Iansiti & Levien, 2004; Ihrig & MacMillan, 2017). Owing to ecosystem members that depend on one another to create the joint value offering, each shares an interest in the other's survival and success. Consequently, they are motivated to find a balance between cooperation and competition (Adner, 2013; Hannah & Eisenhardt, 2018). We frame this tension around the relationship between one ecosystem actor and individual members of the ecosystem as the "ecosystem coopetition paradox".

The ecosystem coopetition paradox centres on the diverging interests of two or more ecosystem actors. Whereas the stakeholder perspective again helps us to identify the relevant stakeholders, it is the paradox perspective that highlights the persistent, contradictory, and interrelated coopetition conflict that exists between those stakeholders. The coopetition paradox captures the simultaneous cooperation and competing of various actors (Bengtsson et al., 2016; Raza-Ullah et al., 2014). The ecosystem actors might include rivals that collaborate within the ecosystem context, but compete outside of this context or actors that collaborate only for some aspects within the ecosystem context. The contradictions that arise may stem from the joint value creation vs. individual value appropriation, knowledge-sharing vs. unintended diffusion of information or short-term vs. long-term orientations (Brandenburger & Nalebuff, 1997; Das & Teng, 2000; Raza-Ullah et al., 2014). The stakeholder theory suggests that ecosystem actors should pay attention to the implications of their actions to all ecosystem stakeholders in order to build mutual trust. In comparison, the paradox perspective stresses the ecosystem actor's awareness of and willingness-to-engage in coping with this coopetition context as a persistent tension. The rational for the suggested engagement in trust building from the stakeholder perspective builds upon the idea that in a context where all ecosystem actors trust each other, their behaviour will reflect their commitment to the ecosystem and encourage other ecosystem actors to follow them. The paradox perspective, in contrast, stresses the potential synergies that firms may leverage if they manage to balance the coopetition challenge. Table 2 provides a summary of the stakeholder and the paradox perspectives' contribution to the ecosystem coopetition paradox.

*Table 2. The ecosystem coopetition paradox informed by stakeholder and paradox theories*

| *Building block* | *Stakeholder perspective* | *Paradox perspective* |
|---|---|---|
| Subject *(what)* | *Relevant stakeholders*: The individual ecosystem actors | *Persistent, contradictory and interrelated demands*: The interests of the focal firm's business model and the other ecosystem actors |
| Subject *(how)* | *Create mutual trust through managing-for-stakeholders*: Making valuable contributions for the other ecosystem actors and receiving valuable contributions from the ecosystem and/or other ecosystem actors | *Accepting and coping with the persistent tension*: Balancing the divergent demands of the focal firm's business model and of other ecosystem actors using paradoxical thinking |
| Explanation *(why)* | *Avoidance of team production problem*: Achieve strong commitment of all ecosystem actors to the ecosystem | *Leveraging the synergetic potential*: The focal firm benefits from the contributions of other ecosystem actors whereas the other ecosystem actors benefit from the focal firm's input |

## DISCUSSION AND CONCLUSION

### Implications for Theory

In this study, we focus on the business ecosystem phenomena, a highly complex form of inter-organisational collaboration; in which multiple stakeholder engage in a joint value creation endeavour. This form of collaboration is often rich in tensions as we are facing a wide variety of stakeholders with diverging interests and objectives as well as with different understandings, perceptions and expectations concerning the ecosystem's role and development. Applying a combined stakeholder and paradox theory perspective, we identify and explore two strategic, paradox tensions in this context, the ecosystem engagement paradox and the ecosystem coopetition paradox. This allows us to make two distinct contributions to theory. The first one addresses the complementary nature of both theoretical perspectives. We show that in the ecosystem context, stakeholder and paradox theories provide two complementary lenses. The second one allows us to contribute to ecosystem theory. By identifying two paradox tensions inherent to the business ecosystem context, we contribute to the understanding of how to engage in business ecosystem successfully and how to manoeuvre the overall ecosystem competitiveness.

Our first contribution addresses the complementary character of stakeholder and paradox theories in the business ecosystem context. In line with Pinto (2019), we argue that both theoretical perspectives contribute to explaining some of the perceived complexity of strategic paradoxes. Using the business ecosystem phenomena (Erum et al. 2022), a particularly complex form of inter-organisational collaboration (Roundy et al., 2018) that is home to two strategic paradoxes, we show how both theoretical perspectives help us in understanding the persistent, contradictory and interrelated nature of these paradox tensions. Stakeholder theory emphasizes the identification of relevant stakeholders that deserve particular attention: Those stakeholders that own critical resources (Eesley & Lenox, 2006; Frooman, 1999; Mitchell et al., 1997). Further, the stakeholder perspective provides us with the rationale that to ensure those stakeholders' commitment, we need to build mutual trust though actions that consider the interests of all stakeholders rather than pursuing self-interested motivations (Freeman, 1994; Freeman et al., 2007; Harrison et al., 2010). Complementarily, the paradox perspective emphasizes the persistent, diverging, however interrelated demands of different stakeholders (Putnam et al., 2016; Schad et al., 2019). The rationale to engage continuously in these tensions offered by paradox theory concentrates on the synergetic potential of these tensions (Andriopoulos et al. 2018; Lewis 2000; Schad et al. 2016). Both theoretical perspectives suggest different, however complementary approaches to deal with the situation. The stakeholder perspective emphasizes the relevance of building mutual trust and commitment to the joint endeavour to avoid a relevant ecosystem actor's disappointment and consequent refusal to complement to the ecosystem (Kollock, 1998; Olson, 1965). The paradox perspective stresses the persistent nature of the tensions and in consequence, the necessity to apply a paradoxical thinking to become aware, to accept and to gain comfort with the fact that there is no one-time solution to the diverging interests (Dubé & Robey, 2008; Miron-Spektor et al., 2018).

Our second contribution adds to the still infant field of ecosystem theory. By identifying two paradox tensions inherent to the business ecosystem contest, we shed light on some of the underlying mechanisms of business ecosystems. Engaging in business ecosystems is a complex, stressful, risky and potentially costly step for any ecosystem actor. However, taking advantage of the complementary inputs of other ecosystem actors (Adner, 2017; Hannah & Eisenhardt, 2018; Jacobides et al., 2018) might be worth the effort and motivate firms to engage in business ecosystems. So far, we have very limited insights into how firms should engage and behave in ecosystem contexts. We enhance this understanding by identifying the paradox nature of a firm's ecosystem engagement. Ecosystems work as long as the ecosystem actors are committed to the ecosystem and enhance it with valuable contribution. An ecosystem's competitiveness stems from these contributions. While the contribution to the ecosystem might sometimes contradict a focal firm's interests, they are also likely to benefit from the overall ecosystem's strength – reflecting the synergetic potential inherent to the ecosystem engagement paradox. As the ecosystem will compete not only with the offerings of other individual firms, but also with other ecosystems, ecosystem actors need to show interest in their ecosystem's competitiveness. This reflects upon a new level of competition, the inter-ecosystem level.

### Implications for Managerial Practice

Engaging in business ecosystems remains to be highly complex and demanding endeavour. The conclusions of this study allow us to describe two particular tensions in the ecosystem context, which managers are likely to experience as challenges throughout their ecosystem journey. Thereby, we manage to disentangle some of the prevalent ecosystem complexity and to derive practical guidance on how to deal with the situations.

The first tension identified, the ecosystem engagement paradox, refers to the way a company engages with an ecosystem. We highlight that there will be situations that require managers to make a choice between decisions that directly favour the profits obtained by their firm's business model and decisions that favour the overall ecosystem development. For example, in the Maas context, each individual actor is likely to face competing demands for marketing budget – to finance campaigns for their particular business model offering vs. the ecosystem offering. While this situation might appear obvious at a first glance, our discussion of this tension reveals the synergetic potential of simultaneously considering both demands. This implies that ecosystem actors cannot make an either/or choice, but rather, they need to constantly balance both choices to achieve the best possible outcome. The second tension identified, the ecosystem coopetition paradox, shows how a partly familiar challenge for many experienced managers – the necessity to balance cooperation and competition with rival companies – is also inherent to the ecosystem context.

Both paradox tensions underline the increasing necessity for managers to enhance their paradoxical thinking. This starts with the need to raise awareness for the existence and an understanding of the mechanisms of these contradictory and interrelated tensions. Further, due to the tensions' inherent persistency, managers need to understand the management of these tensions as an ongoing, rather than a one-time effort, which requires them constantly to re-evaluate the options. In addition, the discussion of the ecosystem engagement paradox reveals a new level of competition, the inter-ecosystem competition. This also requires a shift in mindset as more and more firms need to see themselves as part of a team that jointly competes against other ecosystem-teams. This further implies that even a very competitive business model – once it becomes part of an ecosystem that loses in strength – may become subject to failure.

## LIMITATIONS AND FUTURE RESEARCH

In this study, we accomplish to identify two paradox tensions embedded in the business ecosystem context. While, informed by the complementary contributions of stakeholder and paradox theories, we provide a rich description of both paradoxes; we cannot provide any guidance on how to establish the prerequisites for successful engagement in the ecosystem commitment and coopetition paradoxes. The understanding and acknowledgement of the relevance of ecosystem engagement requires a fundamental mindshift from managers used to the pre-ecosystem era. In particular individuals in managerial positions in incumbent firms are likely to struggle with their heritage and traditional understanding of how power is distributed (Gueler & Schneider, 2019). This might hinder them to develop an ecosystem mindset that reflects the awareness and willingness-to-engage in establishing a balanced ecosystem engagement and coopetition environment. Future research should take this up by reflecting upon the key ingredients and training opportunities for developing an ecosystem mindset. Furthermore, in this study we assume that the relevance of individual ecosystem actors to the overall ecosystem is transparent. This is a crucial piece of information for managers to be capable of finding the right balances in both paradoxical situations. While this might hold true for the providers of obvious bottleneck resources (Hannah & Eisenhardt, 2018), it is likely to be less transparent in most other situations. The value a resource has for a focal firm's business model differs from the value the same resource has for other ecosystem actors as well as for the overall ecosystem (Gueler & Schneider, 2021). Additionally, tied to the resource contribution, the question of governance, roles and power distribution within business ecosystem remains challenging. While this topic has recently received rising attention (see Altman et al., 2022 for a review), this field requires further investigation.

## REFERENCES


Ackermann, F., & Eden, C. (2011). Strategic management and stakeholders: Theory and practice. *Long Range Planning*, *44*(3), 179–196. doi:10.1016/j.lrp.2010.08.001

Adner, R. (2006). Match your innovation strategy to your innovation ecosystem. *Harvard Business Review*, *84*(4), 98–107. PMID:16579417

Adner, R. (2013). *The wide lens: What successful innovators see that others miss*. Portfolio/Penguin.

Adner, R. (2017). Ecosystem as structure: An actionable construct for strategy. *Journal of Management*, *43*(1), 39–58. doi:10.1177/0149206316678451

Adner, R., & Kapoor, R. (2016). Innovation ecosystems and the pace of substitution: Re-examining technology S-curves. *Strategic Management Journal*, *37*(4), 625–648. doi:10.1002mj.2363

Adner, R., & Lieberman, M. (2021). Disruption Through Complements. *Strategy Science*, *6*(1), 91–109. doi:10.1287tsc.2021.0125

Agle, B. R., Mitchell, R. K., & Sonnenfeld, J. A. (1999). Who matters to CEOs? An investigation of stakeholder attributes and salience, corporate performance, and CEO values. *Academy of Management Journal*, *42*(5), 507–525. doi:10.2307/256973

Alchian, A., & Demsetz, H. (1972). Production, information costs, and economic organization. *The American Economic Review*, *62*, 777–795.

Aldieri, L., Brahmi, M., Bruno, B., & Vinci, C. P. (2021). Circular Economy Business Models: The Complementarities with Sharing Economy and Eco-Innovations Investments. *Sustainability, 13*(22), 12438. doi:10.3390u132212438

Altman, E. J., Nagle, F., & Tushman, M. L. (2022). The Translucent Hand of Managed Ecosystems: Engaging Communities for Value Creation and Capture. *The Academy of Management Annals, 16*(1), 70–101. doi:10.5465/annals.2020.0244

Amin, A., & Cohendet, P. (2000). Organisational learning and governance through embedded practices. *The Journal of Management and Governance, 4*(1/2), 93–116. doi:10.1023/A:1009913429932

Andriopoulos, C., Gotsi, M., Lewis, M. W., & Ingram, A. E. (2018). Turning the sword: How NPD teams cope with front-end tensions. *Journal of Product Innovation Management, 35*(3), 427–445. doi:10.1111/jpim.12423

Arabeche, Z., Soudani, A., Brahmi, M., Aldieri, L., Vinci, C. P., & Abdelli, M. E. A. (2022). Entrepreneurial Orientation, Organizational Culture and Business Performance in SMEs: Evidence from Emerging Economy. *Sustainability, 14*(9), 5160. doi:10.3390u14095160

Asher, C. C., Mahoney, J. M., & Mahoney, J. T. (2005). Towards a property rights foundation for a stakeholder theory of the firm. *The Journal of Management and Governance, 9*(1), 5–32. doi:10.100710997-005-1570-2

Audebrand, L. K., Camus, A., & Michaud, V. (2017). A mosquito in the classroom: Using the cooperative business model to foster paradoxical thinking in management education. *Journal of Management Education, 41*(2), 216–248. doi:10.1177/1052562916682552

Baden-Fuller, C., & Morgan, M. S. (2010). Business models as models. *Long Range Planning, 43*(2/3), 156–171. doi:10.1016/j.lrp.2010.02.005

Baldwin, C. (2015). *Bottlenecks, modules, and dynamic architectural capabilities*. HBS Working Paper 15-028.

Barney, J. B., & Hansen, M. H. (1994). Trustworthiness as a source of competitive advantage. *Strategic Management Journal, 15*(S1), 175–190. doi:10.1002mj.4250150912

Barringer, B. R., & Harrison, J. S. (2000). Walking a tightrope: Creating value through interorganizational relationships. *Journal of Management, 26*(3), 367–404. doi:10.1177/014920630002600302

Bengtsson, M., Raza-Ullah, T., & Vanyushyn, V. (2016). The coopetition paradox and tension: The moderating role of coopetition capability. *Industrial Marketing Management, 53*, 19–30. doi:10.1016/j.indmarman.2015.11.008

Brandenburger, A., & Nalebuff, B. J. (1997). *Co-opetition*. Currency Doubleday.

Brandenburger, A. M., & Stuart, H. Jr. (1996). Value-based business strategy. *Journal of Economics & Management Strategy, 5*(1), 5–25. doi:10.1111/j.1430-9134.1996.00005.x

Bridoux, F., Coeurderoy, R., & Durand, R. (2001). Heterogeneous motives and collective value creation. *Academy of Management Review, 36*, 711–730.

Bridoux, F., & Stoelhorst, J. W. (2016). Stakeholder relationships and social welfare: A behavioral theory of contributions of joint value creation. *Academy of Management Review*, *41*(2), 229–251. doi:10.5465/amr.2013.0475

Bundy, J., Vogel, R. M., & Zachary, M. A. (2018). Organization–stakeholder fit: A dynamic theory of cooperation, compromise, and conflict between an organization and its stakeholders. *Strategic Management Journal*, *39*(2), 476–501. doi:10.1002mj.2736

Clarkson, M. B. E. (1995). A stakeholder framework for analyzing and evaluating corporate social performance. *Academy of Management Review*, *20*(1), 92–117. doi:10.2307/258888

Clegg, S. R., Da Cunha, J. V., & Cunha, M. P. (2002). Management paradoxes: A relational view. *Human Relations*, *55*(5), 483–503. doi:10.1177/0018726702555001

Cohendet, P., Simon, L., & Mehouachi, C. (2021). From business ecosystems to ecosystems of innovation: The case of the video game industry in Montréal. *Industry and Innovation*, *28*(8), 1046–1076. doi:10.1080/13662716.2020.1793737

Das, T. K., & Teng, B.-S. (2000). A resource-based theory of strategic alliances. *Journal of Management*, *26*(1), 31–61. doi:10.1177/014920630002600105

Dattée, B., Alexy, O., & Autio, E. (2018). Maneuvering in Poor Visibility: How Firms Play the Ecosystem Game when Uncertainty is High. [buh.]. *Academy of Management Journal*, *61*(2), 466–498. doi:10.5465/amj.2015.0869

Daymond, J., Knight, E., Rumyantseva, M., & Maguire, S. (2022). Managing ecosystem emergence and evolution: Strategies for ecosystem architects. *Strategic Management Journal*. doi:10.1002/smj.3449

Donaldson, T., & Preston, L. E. (1995). The stakeholder theory of the corporation: Concepts, evidence, and implications. *Academy of Management Review*, *20*(1), 65–91. doi:10.2307/258887

Dubé, L., & Robey, D. (2008). Surviving the paradoxes of virtual teamwork. *Information Systems Journal*, *19*(1), 3–30. doi:10.1111/j.1365-2575.2008.00313.x

Dyer, J. H., & Nobeoka, K. (2000). Creating and managing a high-performance knowledge-sharing network: The Toyota case. *Strategic Management Journal*, *21*(3), 345–367. doi:10.1002/(SICI)1097-0266(200003)21:3<345::AID-SMJ96>3.0.CO;2-N

Eesley, C., & Lenox, M. J. (2006). Firm responses to secondary stakeholder action. *Strategic Management Journal*, *27*(8), 765–781. doi:10.1002mj.536

Erum, S.; Muhammad, N T.; Wali Muhammad, K.; Mohsen, B.; & Shahid, R., Chapter 16: The COVID-19 Pandemic Overlaps Entrepreneurial Activities and Triggered New Challenges: A Review Study, Book chapter: Managing Human Resources in SMEs and Start-ups, August 2022, 388 p. https://doi.org/doi:10.1142/9789811239212_0008

Freeman, R. E. (1984). *Strategic management: A stakeholder approach*. Pitman Publishing.

Freeman, R. E. (1994). The politics of stakeholder theory: Some future direction. *Business Ethics Quarterly*, *4*(4), 409–421. doi:10.2307/3857340

Freeman, R. E., Harrison, J. S., & Wicks, A. C. (2007). *Managing for stakeholders: Survival, reputation, and success*. Yale University Press.

Freeman, R. E., & Reed, D. L. (1983). Stockholders and shareholders: A new perspective on corporate governance. *California Management Review*, *25*(3), 88–106. doi:10.2307/41165018

Frooman, J. (1999). Stakeholder influence strategies. *Academy of Management Review*, *24*(2), 191–205. doi:10.2307/259074

Gebert, D., Boerner, S., & Kearney, E. (2010). Fostering team innovation: Why is it important to combine opposing action strategies? *Organization Science*, *21*(3), 593–608. doi:10.1287/orsc.1090.0485

Grant, R. M. (1996). Prospering in dynamically-competitive environments: Organizational capability as knowledge integration. *Organization Science*, *7*(4), 375–387. doi:10.1287/orsc.7.4.375

Gueler, M. S., & Schneider, S. (2019). Transformation from industries towards ecosystems: How behemoths approach ecosystem thinking. *Academy of Management Proceedings*. Academy of Management Annual Conference. doi:10.5465/AMBPP.2019.14272abstract

Gueler, M. S., & Schneider, S. (2021). The resource-based view in business ecosystems: A perspective on the determinants of a valuable resource and capability. *Journal of Business Research*, *133*, 158–169. doi:10.1016/j.jbusres.2021.04.061

Hahn, T., Preuss, L., Pinske, J., & Figge, F. (2014). Cognitive frames in corporate sustainability: Managerial sensemaking with paradoxical and business case frames. *Academy of Management Review*, *39*(4), 463–487. doi:10.5465/amr.2012.0341

Hannah, D. P., & Eisenhardt, K. M. (2018). How firms navigate cooperation and competition in nascent ecosystems. *Strategic Management Journal*, *39*(12), 3163–3192. doi:10.1002mj.2750

Harrison, J. S., Bosse, D. A., & Phillips, R. A. (2010). Managing for stakeholders, stakeholder utility functions, and competitive advantage. *Strategic Management Journal*, *31*(1), 58–74. doi:10.1002mj.801

Iansiti, M., & Levien, R. (2004). *The keystone advantage: What the new dynamics of business ecosystems mean for strategy, innovation, and sustainability*. Harvard Business School Press.

Ihrig, M., & MacMillan, I. C. (2017). How to get ecosystem buy-in. *Harvard Business Review*, *95*(2), 102–107.

Ingram, P., & Roberts, P. W. (2000). Friendships among competitors in the Sydney hotel industry. *American Journal of Sociology*, *106*(2), 387–423. doi:10.1086/316965

Jacobides, M. G., Cennamo, C., & Gawer, A. (2018). Towards a theory of ecosystems. *Strategic Management Journal*, *39*(8), 2255–2276. doi:10.1002mj.2904

Jones, T. M. (1995). Instrumental stakeholder theory: A synthesis of ethic and economics. *Academy of Management Review*, *20*(2), 404–437. doi:10.2307/258852

Jones, T. M., Harrison, J. S., & Felps, W. (2018). How Applying Instrumental Stakeholder Theory Can Provide Sustainable Competitive Advantage. *Academy of Management Review*, *43*(3), 371–391. doi:10.5465/amr.2016.0111

Keller, J., Loewenstein, J., & Yan, J. (2017). Culture, conditions and paradoxical frames. *Organization Studies*, *38*(3–4), 539–560. doi:10.1177/0170840616685590

Kollock, P. (1998). Social dilemmas: The anatomy of cooperation. *Annual Review of Sociology*, *22*(1), 183–205. doi:10.1146/annurev.soc.24.1.183

Kreiner, P., & Bhambri, A. (1991). Influence and information or organization-stakeholder relationships. In L. E. Preston (Ed.), *Research in corporate social performance and policy* (Vol. 12, pp. 3–36). JAI Press.

Krome, M. J., & Pidun, U. (2022). *Conceptualization of research themes and directions in business ecosystem strategies: A systematic literature review*. Management Review Quarterly. doi:10.100711301-022-00306-4

Lewis, M. W. (2000). Exploring Paradox: Toward a More Comprehensive Guide. *Academy of Management Review*, *25*(4), 760–776. doi:10.2307/259204

Lieberman, M. B., Balasubramanian, N., & Garcia-Castro, R. (2017). Toward a dynamic notion of value creation and appropriation in firms: The concept and measurement of economic gain. *Strategic Management Journal*, *39*(6), 1546–1572. doi:10.1002mj.2708

Lindenberg, S., & Foss, N. (2011). Managing joint production motivation: The role of goal framing and governance mechanisms. *Academy of Management Review*, *36*, 500–525.

Lüscher, L. S., & Lewis, M. W. (2008). Organizational change and managerial sensemaking: Working through paradox. *Academy of Management Journal*, *51*(2), 221–240. doi:10.5465/amj.2008.31767217

MacDonald, G., & Ryall, R. D. (2004). How do value creation and competition determine whether a firm appropriates value? *Management Science*, *50*(10), 1319–1333. doi:10.1287/mnsc.1030.0152

Mervis, C. B., & Rosch, E. (1981). Categorization of natural objects. *Annual Review of Psychology*, *32*(1), 89–115. doi:10.1146/annurev.ps.32.020181.000513

Miron-Spektor, E., Ingram, A., Keller, J., Smith, W. K., & Lewis, M. W. (2018). Microfoundations of organizational paradox: The problem is how we think about the problem. *Academy of Management Journal*, *61*(1), 26–45. doi:10.5465/amj.2016.0594

Mitchell, R. K., Agle, B. R., & Wood, D. J. (1997). Toward a theory of stakeholder identification and salience: Defining the principle of who and what really counts. *Academy of Management Review*, *22*(4), 853–886. doi:10.2307/259247

Nadkarni, S., & Barr, P. S. (2008). Environmental context, managerial cognition, and strategic action: An integrated view. *Strategic Management Journal*, *29*(13), 1395–1427. doi:10.1002mj.717

Olson, M. (1965). *The logic of collective action*. Harvard University Press.

Pagani, M. (2013). Digital business strategy and value creation: Framing the dynamic cycle of control points. *Management Information Systems Quarterly*, *37*(2), 617–632. doi:10.25300/MISQ/2013/37.2.13

Pfeffer, J. (1982). *Organizations and organization theory*. Pitman Publishing.

Pfeffer, J., & Salancik, G. R. (1978). *The external control of organizations: A resource dependence perspective*. Harper and Row.

Pina e Cunha, M., & Putnam, L. L. (2019). Paradox theory and the paradox of success. *Strategic Organization, 17*(1), 95–106. doi:10.1177/1476127017739536

Pinto, J. (2019). Key to effective organizational performance management lies at the intersection of paradox theory and stakeholder theory. *International Journal of Management Reviews, 21*(2), 185–208. doi:10.1111/ijmr.12199

Powell, W. W., & Snellman, K. (2004). The knowledge economy. *Annual Review of Sociology, 30*(1), 199–220. doi:10.1146/annurev.soc.29.010202.100037

Putnam, L. L., Fairhurst, G. T., & Banhart, S. G. (2016). Contradictions, dialectics, and paradoxes in organizations: A constitutive approach. *The Academy of Management Annals, 10*(1), 65–171. doi:10.5465/19416520.2016.1162421

Raza-Ullah, T., Bengtsson, M., & Kock, S. (2014). The coopetition paradox and tension in coopetition at multiple levels. *Industrial Marketing Management, 43*(2), 189–198. doi:10.1016/j.indmarman.2013.11.001

Roundy, P. T., Bradshaw, M., & Brockman, B. K. (2018). The emergence of entrepreneurial ecosystems: A complex adaptive systems approach. *Journal of Business Research, 86*, 1–10. doi:10.1016/j.jbusres.2018.01.032

Rowley, T. J. (1997). Moving beyond dyadic ties: A network theory of stakeholder influences. *Academy of Management Review, 22*(4), 887–910. doi:10.2307/259248

Schad, J., Lewis, M. W., Raisch, S., & Smith, W. K. (2016). Paradox Research in Management Science: Looking back to move forward. *The Academy of Management Annals, 10*(1), 5–64. doi:10.5465/19416520.2016.1162422

Schad, J., Lewis, M. W., & Smith, W. K. (2019). Quo vadis, paradox? Centripetal and centrifugal forces in theory development. *Strategic Organization, 17*(1), 107–119. doi:10.1177/1476127018786218

Shaikh, E., Brahmi, M., Thang, P. C., Watto, W. A., Trang, T. T. N., & Loan, N. T. (2022). Should I Stay or Should I Go? Explaining the Turnover Intentions with Corporate Social Responsibility (CSR), Organizational Identification and Organizational Commitment. *Sustainability, 14*(10), 6030. doi:10.3390u14106030

Sisodia, R., Wolfe, D. B., & Sheth, J. (2007). *Firms of endearment: How world-class companies profit from passion and purpose*. Wharton School Publishing.

Smith, W. K. (2014). Dynamic decision making: A model of senior leaders managing strategic paradoxes. *Academy of Management Journal, 57*(6), 1592–1623. doi:10.5465/amj.2011.0932

Smith, W. K., & Lewis, M. W. (2011). Toward a theory of paradox: A dynamic equilibrium model of organizing. *Academy of Management Review, 36*(2), 381–403.

Smith, W. K., & Tushman, M. L. (2005). Managing strategic contradictions: A top management model for managing innovation streams. *Organization Science, 16*(5), 522–536. doi:10.1287/orsc.1050.0134

Sonnenshein, S., Nault, K., & Obodaru, O. (2017). Competition of a different flavor: How a strategic group identity shapes competition and cooperation. *Administrative Science Quarterly*, *62*(4), 626–656. doi:10.1177/0001839217704849

Stonig, J., Schmid, T., & Müller-Stewens, G. (2022). From product system to ecosystem: How firms adapt to provide an integrated value proposition. *Strategic Management Journal*, *43*(9), 1927–1957. doi:10.1002mj.3390

Sunkar, A., Lakspriyanti, A. P., Haryono, E., Brahmi, M., Setiawan, P., & Jaya, A. F. (2022). Geotourism Hazards and Carrying Capacity in Geosites of Sangkulirang-Mangkalihat Karst, Indonesia. *Sustainability*, *14*(3), 1704. doi:10.3390u14031704

Thomas, L. D. W., & Ritala, P. (2022). Ecosystem Legitimacy Emergence: A Collective Action View. *Journal of Management*, *48*(3), 515–541. doi:10.1177/0149206320986617

Tunio, M. N., Jariko, M. A., Børsen, T., Shaikh, S., Mushtaque, T., & Brahmi, M. (2021). How Entrepreneurship Sustains Barriers in the Entrepreneurial Process—A Lesson from a Developing Nation. *Sustainability*, *13*(20), 11419. doi:10.3390u132011419

Tunio, M. N., Chaudhry, I. S., Shaikh, S., Jariko, M. A., & Brahmi, M. (2021). Determinants of the Sustainable Entrepreneurial Engagement of Youth in Developing Country—An Empirical Evidence from Pakistan. *Sustainability*, *13*(14), 7764. doi:10.3390u13147764

Waldman, D. A., Putnam, L. L., Miron-Spektor, E., & Siegel, D. (2019). The role of paradox theory in decision making and management research. *Organizational Behavior and Human Decision Processes*, *155*, 1–6. Advance online publication. doi:10.1016/j.obhdp.2019.04.006

Whetten, D. A. (1989). What Constitutes a Theoretical Contribution? *Academy of Management Review*, *14*(4), 490–495. doi:10.2307/258554

Wood, D. J. (1991). Corporate social performance revisited. *Academy of Management Review*, *16*(4), 691–719. doi:10.2307/258977

Zheng, W., Kark, R., & Meister, A. L. (2018). Paradox versus dilemma mindset: A theory of how women leaders navigate the tensions between agency and communion. *The Leadership Quarterly*, *29*(5), 584–596. doi:10.1016/j.leaqua.2018.04.001

Zollo, M., Reuer, J. J., & Singh, H. (2002). Interorganizational routines and performance in strategic alliances. *Organization Science*, *13*(6), 701–713. doi:10.1287/orsc.13.6.701.503

## ENDNOTE

1 Whim: https://whimapp.com; skedgo: https://skedgo.com; skipr: https://skipr.co; transit: https://transitapp.com

# Chapter 11
# It's Too Friendly!!
## Acceptance of Social Media Platforms in the Virtual World

**Kirti Sharma**
*Chandigarh University, India*

**Tania Mittal**
*Gurukula Kangri Vishwavidyalaya, India*

**Pankaj Madan**
https://orcid.org/0000-0002-4648-9863
*Gurukula Kangri Vishwavidyalaya, India*

## ABSTRACT

*With the widespread use of the Internet, social networks have become an important tool for online marketing. The authors designed and tested various social media platforms to enrich the literature on the effectiveness of multiple types of posts with web links. In this article, researchers investigated the impact of social media marketing campaigns on continued intentions and purchase intentions. For data analysis, this study performed an online survey of 100 social media users, which was examined using SEM analysis. It was concluded that continuance intention has more influence on social media marketing as comparison to purchase intention.*

## INTRODUCTION

### Social Media Marketing

Since its inception, the internet has evolved into a more social environment. The internet generates value-added content webs. Using web 3.0 social media is a premium and appealing method of connecting individuals worldwide. The primary aim of social media in the past was to allow individuals with similar interests to exchange information and voice their views. However, social media as a communica-

DOI: 10.4018/978-1-6684-6766-4.ch011

tion medium is no longer restricted to individuals who have similar interests (Barreto, 2013). Marketers are starting to recognise the impact of social communities in terms of interaction, including customised sections, purchasing experiences, increased convenience, and broad information search (Duffett, 2015). Social media marketing is a subcategory of digital marking where communication and promotion tools are employed to support organisational marketing strategy.

In short, SMM (Social media marketing) is the use of social networking sites to promote their brands, and products. SMM is under the umbrella of online marketing activities. Social networking sites offer customers a speech and enable individuals to engage and share their experiences with people anywhere globally (Kozinets et al., 2010). Although businesses use social media marketing to increase sales and acquire more customers, how to purchase intention through social marketing affects continuous choice to use social media. Social media marketing could be used as both active and passive approaches to target their audience by listening to what social media users are sharing with each other or by customising user experience by direct marketing and publication relation (Constantinides, 2014). Social media marketing techniques provide customers with complete information without human intervention and create loyal customers by providing good customer service (Nadaraja & Yazdanifard, 2013). Social media marketing, ties between businesses and customers are direct and engaging. These connections make it possible to launch new goods and services to many people. If social media marketing actions (Shaikh et al., 2022) align with the company's vision and objective, they are crucial components for the success of the business. The main goal of this study is to provide a thorough understanding of the myriad aspects that determine how social media marketing affects buy intention and continuous intention(Kim & Ko, 2012). As customers move from one device to another, continuous interaction on digital and social media leads to seamless interaction between user and brand, customised social media marketing is required to target customers.(Dwivedi et al., 2021). Social media characteristics of entertainment, interaction, trendiness, personalisation, and word-of-mouth are included in social media marketing for small and large businesses (Kim & Ko, 2012). Content that generates two-way communication on social media is done through chatbots, direct messages and live sessions on Facebook, WhatsApp, and Instagram handles. Being emotionally intelligent along with cognitively intelligent is essential aspect to consider when defining factors of purchase intention (Joshi, 2018)

Regardless of the approval of social media, experts believe that the ongoing viability of an information source depends on its continuous use of social media (Bhattacherjee, 2011). With widespread 5G and the Internet, it is easy for users to switch social network types. It is essential to understand the motivations of consumers for indefinite use of social networks (Sunkar et al., 2022), also known as "continuous use of social networks. social media intention "or simply referred to as" continue to use. " Intention'. Additionally, this research attempts to discover how social media marketing and purchase intentions affect ongoing purchase intentions. Social media marketing is booming due to the omnipresence of social media for continuous usage. Continuous usage of social media is affected by the emotional and social presence of users on social networking sites (Park, Ji Yeon, Shin, 2019).

## LITERATURE REVIEW

### Social Media Marketing

Web 3.0 results from technological advances that let companies react quickly according to customers' needs by reading and understanding various touchpoints on the Internet. With this information, firms can contact their customers to personalise their brand experience using social media. Social networks have become an indispensable source of entertainment for their users. Researchers have examined various aspects of usage time and the impact of user-generated content on brand value(Bolton et al., 2013). Researchers have recognised the importance of social interaction on social networks as it affects the purchase intention of their users. (Yin et al., 2019). Researchers have identified entertainment, electronic word of mouth, trendiness, perceived risk, events, advertisements for luxurious brands (Kim & Ko, 2012), and insurance service companies (Drucker & Oster, 2015). Many researchers have found the media society's acceptance of the health service and identified characteristics and early acceptance as important (Zilber et al., 2019). e-Wom on social media now turned as a stage for advocacy for loyalist and satisfied consumer(Mihir Joshi, 2017)

### Purchase Intention

Purchase intent is the customer trust stage, which determines the process by which customers trust the brand and are willing to buy. Customer purchase intention for a brand is strongly affected by their friends and family's recommendation and ratings of different products on websites and e-application(Chu & Kim, 2018). Escobar-Rodríguez et al. (2017) researched Spanish customers and reported that online purchase intention is influenced by perceived value and trust in online transactions. Social media has made it possible for users to purchase directly and influences offline purchase intention(Dabbous & Barakat, 2020). Consumers in Italy were confirmed to be affected by continuous and intensive use of social media to purchase wine, given the basic knowledge of the same(Pucci et al., 2019). Social media strengthens the relationship between Generation Y and the brand through continuous interaction, ultimately creating sales for the company (Prasad et al., 2017). When the study's findings were implemented, it was established that social media marketing efforts have a beneficial impact on purchasing behaviours, as suggested by the theory of reasoned action (TRA) and the theory of planned behaviour (TPB)(Joshi et al., 2020).

### Continuance Intention

The factors of the TAM model, such as perceived usefulness and perceived ease of use, are determined to influence college students' continuous use of social networks (Wang et al., 2015). Usage and Gratifications theory is considered important in understanding your continued use of social media based on social media needs or usage satisfaction (Coursaris et al., 2013). Perceived trust and perceived enjoyment are essential factors for the continuous intention of social networking sites (Bataineh et al., 2015). Other researchers (Tunio et al., 2021) have identified information quality on social media, concern for security and privacy affects attitude towards social media and their continuous involvement through social networks(Safwa Farook & Abeysekera, 2016). For those with greater levels of education and money, entertainment is a significant motivator for ongoing use of social media.(Hsu et al., 2015). Social media operators providing necessary functions to the users positively affect their continuous intention

(Ruangkanjanases et al., 2020). Continued usage of social media is influenced by social factors like information support from social media and virtual community whom the individual is a part of and trust community members and brands that appear on social media (Prasad et al., 2017). continuous intention to use social media is impacted by playfulness on social media networks which also positively affects attitude towards social media(Chiang, 2013).

## METHODOLOGY

This research examines and evaluates the engagement of social media marketing on customers' intentions to buy for commercial purposes/currency transactions and social media continuity intentions. To collect the requisite data, a quantitative technique was used. In this study, researchers took **Social Media Marketing** as an Independent Variable and **Purchase Intention** and **Continuance Intention** as the dependent variable. The conceptual framework was constructed.

## CONCEPTUAL FRAMEWORK

This is the study's conceptual framework, which shows that we are determining whether social media marketing is influenced by purchase intention and continuance intention of social media, demonstrated in figure 1.

## HYPOTHESES

After the conceptual framework was developed, the hypotheses were generated, and these were as follows:

(i) The use of social media platforms positively correlates with purchase intentions.
(ii) Usage of social networking sites/ media positively related to continuance intention.

### Sampling Technique

A stratified random sampling technique was used for the data collection. It was used so that Social Media users using different social media are covered in our sample i.e. Facebook users, Instagram users, YouTube users and combination of them were taken. For each social media user, strata were made (Aldieri et al., 2021), which was shown as below with number of respondents in Table 1.

## RELIABILITY STATISTICS

Cronbach's alpha is used for calculating dependability estimates in Table 2. It specifies the relationship between the objects to be examined and whether they belong to the same domain. If the Cronbach's alpha value of the created questionnaire is greater than 0.70, the project is consistent with the project. (Gliem, J. A., & Gliem, 2003). In our study, the value is .876, which is considered to be very good.

*Figure 1. Conceptual framework*

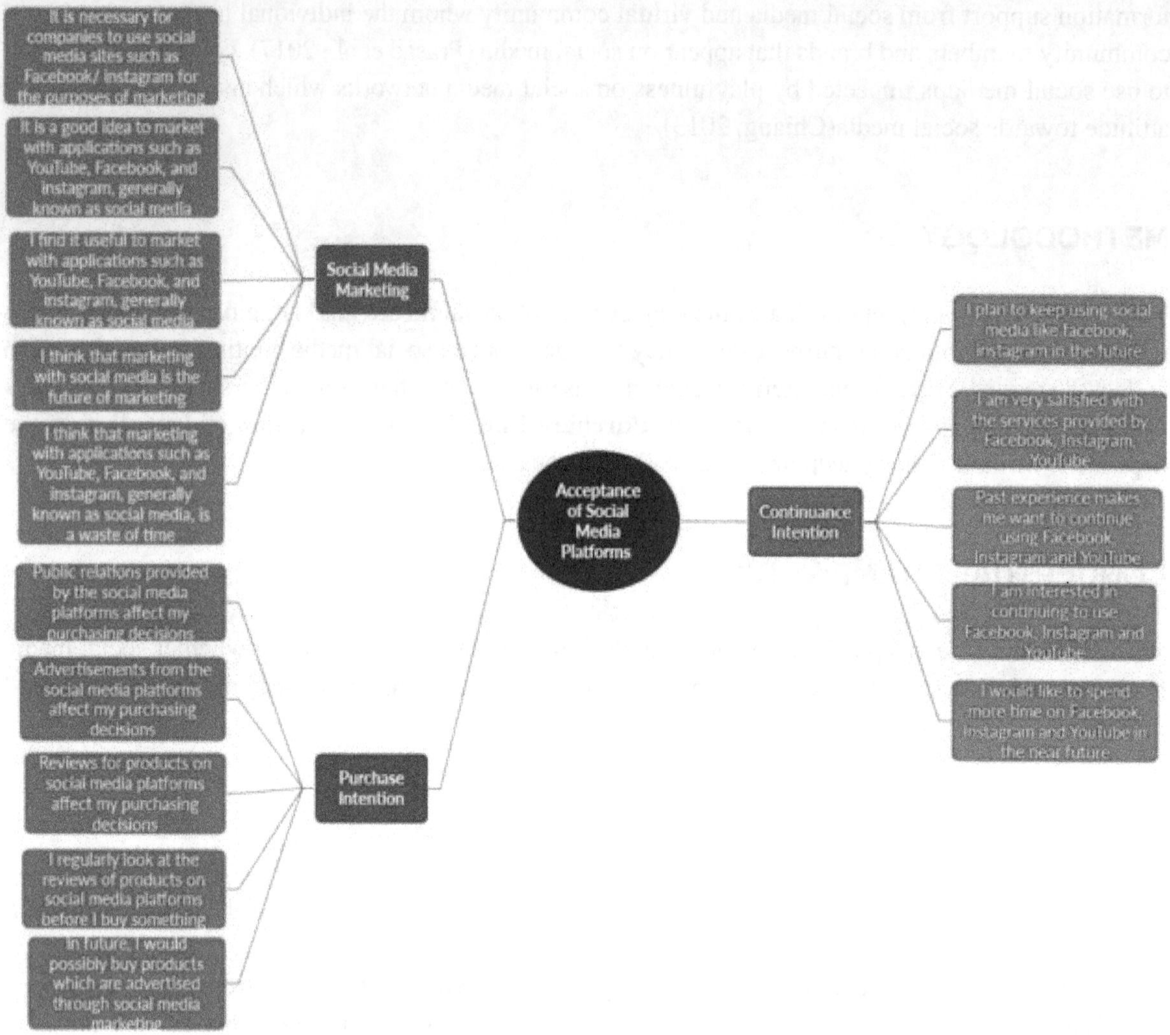


## DATA ANALYSIS AND INTERPRETATIONS

Structural Equation Modeling technique was used in this survey with the help of AMOS Graphics Software. It is a method for examining several dependency relationships altogether. It is beneficial for evaluating hypotheses containing dependency relationships that many equations can describe (Arabeche et al., 2022). These equations represent the relationship between various structures (Hair et al., 2019). After designing the model, its validity was tested by applying second-order confirmatory factor analysis. The CFA model of this study shown below shows that all the factor loadings are good, and all variables are closely correlated with their latent variable shown in figure 2.

*Table 1. Social media users*

| Social Media | Number of Users |
|---|---|
| Facebook | 22 |
| Instagram | 31 |
| YouTube | 24 |
| Combination of any above | 23 |
| **Total** | **100** |

*Table 2. Reliability statistics*

| Cronbach's Alpha | N of Items |
|---|---|
| .876 | 15 |

## Model Fitness of CFA Model

In table 3: The model is fit if the CMIN/DF value is less than 3, and it is good if the value is between 3 and 5. The CMIN/DF value in our study is 2.806, which is considered to be good for model fitness(Hair, 1998) shown in Table 3. A residual value is the result of a prediction error for each term of covariance. It is regarded as favorable for the model fitness if it is less than 0.08. GFI stands for Goodness of Fit Index, and AGFI stands for Adjusted Goodness of Fit Index. Both range from 0 to 1. If their values are close to 1, they are considered good. In our study, the GFI value is .768 and AGFI value is .701; both are considered to be good (Byrne, 2016).

*Figure 2. CFA model*

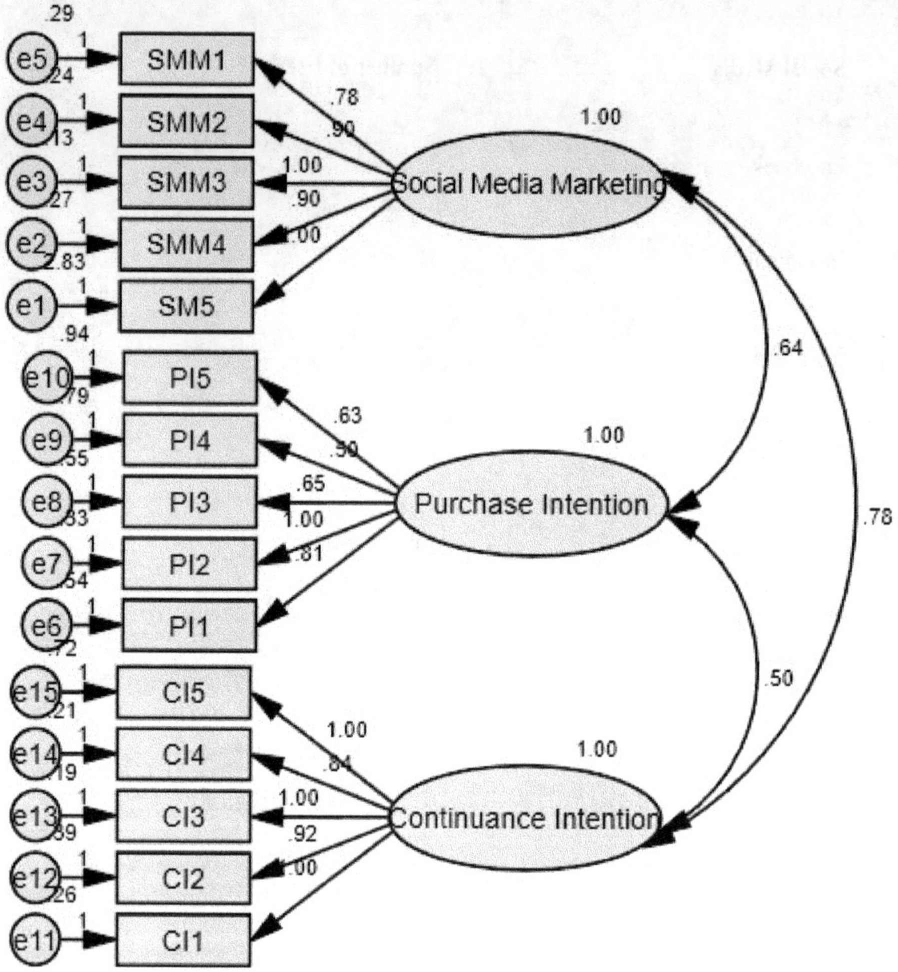


NFI stands for normed fit index, and CFI stands for comparative fit index. NFI and CFI range from 0 to 1; higher the value indicates a good fit. If the value is close to 1, our model is fit. Our study's NFI value is .740, and the CFI value is .814, which indicates an excellent fit. RMSEA **Execution time summary** stands for root mean square error of approximation. Its value is between 0.05 to 0.08, which shows the model's goodness of fit. In our study, the RMSEA value is .134, which is relatively high for the model fitness. So, we have to consider other values to determine the model fitness's accuracy (Hair et al., 1998).

## SEM Model

This is the hypothesised SEM model (figure 3) of the study, which indicates that if we compare which dependent variable (Purchase Intention and Continuance Intention) has more impact on social media marketing, so it shows that continuance intention has more impact on social media marketing as compared to purchase choice as it has more factor loading

*Table 3. Model fitness of CFA model*

| Model | CMIN/DF | Acceptable Limit |
|---|---|---|
| **CMIN/DF** | 2.806 | <3 good; <5 acceptable |
| **RMR** | .380 | Less than .08 |
| **GFI** | .768 | Value near to 1 |
| **AGFI** | .701 | Value near to 1 |
| **NFI** | .740 | Value near to 1 |
| **CFI** | .814 | Value near to 1 |
| **RMSEA** | .134 | 05-.08 good |

**Source:** (Byrne et al., 2016a ; Hair et al., 1998)

*Figure 3. SEM Model*

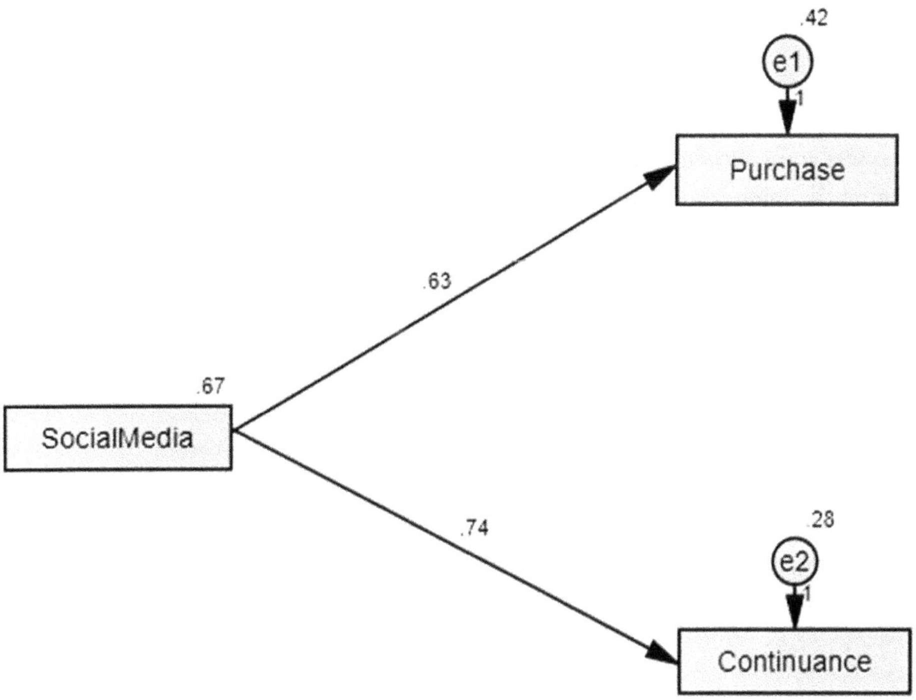

## Model Fitness Values of SEM Model

Table 4 shows the fitness value of the SEM model that interprets all values as being below the acceptable range of model fitness. The results show that the use of social network platforms is positively allied along the willingness to buy, and the usage of social media platforms is simply linked with willingness to continue. Therefore, H1 and H2 are accepted, which means that the original hypothesis has been rejected and the alternative hypothesis has been accepted.

*Table 4. Model Fitness Values of SEM Model*

| Model | Values Obtained | Acceptable Limit |
|---|---|---|
| CMIN/DF | 2.140 | <3 good; <5 acceptable |
| RMR | .007 | Less than .08 |
| GFI | .999 | Value near to 1 |
| AGFI | .991 | Value near to 1 |
| NFI | .998 | Value near to 1 |
| CFI | 1.000 | Value near to 1 |
| RMSEA | .000 | 05-.08 good |

**Source:** (Byrne et al., 2016a ; Hair et al., 1998)

Figure 4 depicts some crucial aspects that play the most critical role in adopting social media marketing concerning the intention to buy and continuance intention. Most people said media is the most critical aspect of SMM. Here perceived usefulness, and intention to purchase are significant factors for adoption. As supported by previous studies, satisfaction being a key factor for continuous usage of social networking (Ruangkanjanases et al., 2020). satisfaction

*Figure 4. Adoption of SMM*

## CONCLUSION AND IMPLICATION

This study has investigated the influence of SMM on future purchase intent and continued use of social networking sites. The study's results found that the willingness to continue using social media has a more excellent bearing on the social media marketing activities of different brands. Social media is used to promote, sell and buy items and services using social commerce. It acts as a new communication tool for companies and sure does impact the purchase intention of its users. This research has made important notional contributions first, brands have understood that social media has become a dominant and culturally important means of communication. Due to constant changes in customer behavior, brands need to develop profitable social media marketing strategies (Tunio et al., 2021) by first attracting the attention of potential customers. Then let them spend time exploring their products, and finally, allow them to spend money to create experiences with these products. This research broadens the approach towards social media marketing. With the emergence of 5G technology and the widespread use of social media, this research gives away practical implacability for small and large brands. Customers' desire to utilise social media is more aggressive than their intention to make purchases through social media as an impact of social media marketing. So to improve sales through social media, one has to increase the scale of social commerce, which can be done by enhancing the social media interface (Hamrouni et al., 2021), making shopping on social media more reliable and secure. It is necessary to establish social media advertising protocols so that customers can avoid bogus websites and enjoy better customer service.

## REFERENCES

Aldieri, L., Brahmi, M., Bruno, B., & Vinci, C. P. (2021). Circular Economy Business Models: The Complementarities with Sharing Economy and Eco-Innovations Investments. *Sustainability*, *13*(22), 12438. https://doi.org/10.3390/su132212438

Arabeche, Z., Soudani, A., Brahmi, M., Aldieri, L., Vinci, C. P., & Abdelli, M. E. A. (2022). Entrepreneurial Orientation, Organizational Culture and Business Performance in SMEs: Evidence from Emerging Economy. *Sustainability*, *14*(9), 5160. doi:10.3390u14095160

Bataineh, A. Q., Al-Abdallah, G. M., & Alkharabsheh, A. M. (2015). Determinants of Continuance Intention to Use Social Networking Sites SNS's: Studying the Case of Facebook. *International Journal of Marketing Studies*, *7*(4), 121–135. doi:10.5539/ijms.v7n4p121

Bolton, R. N., Parasuraman, A., Hoefnagels, A., Migchels, N., Kabadayi, S., Gruber, T., Loureiro, Y. K., & Solnet, D. (2013). Understanding Generation Y and their use of social media: A review and research agenda. *Journal of Service Management*, *24*(3), 245–267. doi:10.1108/09564231311326987

Byrne, B. M. (2016). *Structural Equation Modeling with Mplus : Basic Concepts, Applications, and Programming*. Structural Equation Modeling with Mplus. doi:10.4324/9781315757421

Chu, S. C., & Kim, J. (2018). The current state of knowledge on electronic word-of-mouth in advertising research. *International Journal of Advertising*, *37*(1), 1–13. doi:10.1080/02650487.2017.1407061

Constantinides, E. (2014). Foundations of Social Media Marketing. *Procedia: Social and Behavioral Sciences*, *148*, 40–57. doi:10.1016/j.sbspro.2014.07.016

Coursaris, C., Van Osch, W., Sung, J., & Yun, Y. (2013). Disentangling Twitter's Adoption and Use (Dis)Continuance: A Theoretical and Empirical Amalgamation of Uses and Gratifications and Diffusion of Innovations. *AIS Transactions on Human-Computer Interaction*, *5*(1), 57–83. https://aisel.aisnet.org/thci/vol5/iss1/5. doi:10.17705/1thci.00054

Dabbous, A., & Barakat, K. A. (2020). Bridging the online offline gap: Assessing the impact of brands' social network content quality on brand awareness and purchase intention. *Journal of Retailing and Consumer Services, 53*(November 2018), 101966. doi:10.1016/j.jretconser.2019.101966

Drucker, J., & Oster, H. (2015). *An empirical study of the effect of social media marketing activities upon customer satisfaction, positive word-of-mouth and commitment in indemnity insurance service*. March.

Dwivedi, Y. K., Ismagilova, E., Hughes, D. L., Carlson, J., Filieri, R., Jacobson, J., Jain, V., Karjaluoto, H., Kefi, H., Krishen, A. S., Kumar, V., Rahman, M. M., Raman, R., Rauschnabel, P. A., Rowley, J., Salo, J., Tran, G. A., & Wang, Y. (2021). Setting the future of digital and social media marketing research: Perspectives and research propositions. *International Journal of Information Management*, *59*(May), 102168. doi:10.1016/j.ijinfomgt.2020.102168

Gliem, J. A., & Gliem, R. R. (2003). *Calculating, Interpreting, And Reporting Cronbach's Alpha Reliability Coefficient For Likert-Type Scales*. Scholar Works. https://scholarworks.iupui.edu/handle/1805/344

Hair, J. F., Black, W. C., Babin, B. J., & Anderson, R. E. (2019). *Multivariate Data Analysis*. Cengage Learning.

Hair. (1998). *Multivariate data analysis: Its approach, evolution, and impact*. Springer. https://link.springer.com/chapter/10.1007/978-3-030-06031-2_16

Hamrouni, B., Bourouis, A., Korichi, A., & Brahmi, M. (2021). Explainable Ontology-Based Intelligent Decision Support System for Business Model Design and Sustainability. *Sustainability*, *13*(17), 9819. doi:10.3390u13179819

Hsu, M. H., Tien, S. W., Lin, H. C., & Chang, C. M. (2015). Understanding the roles of cultural differences and socio-economic status in social media continuance intention. *Information Technology & People*, *28*(1), 224–241. doi:10.1108/ITP-01-2014-0007

Joshi, M. (2018). Workforce Trends and Challenges: A Peek Into the Future. In Management Techniques for a Diverse and Cross-Cultural Workforce. doi:10.4018/978-1-5225-4933-8.ch003

Joshi, M., Joshi, G., & Pathak, S. (2020). Awareness, entrepreneurial event theory and theory of planned behaviour as antecedents of student entrepreneurial intentions: An indian perspective. *International Journal of Business and Globalisation*, *25*(2), 170–184. doi:10.1504/IJBG.2020.107885

Kim, A. J., & Ko, E. (2012). Do social media marketing activities enhance customer equity? An empirical study of luxury fashion brand. *Journal of Business Research*, *65*(10), 1480–1486. doi:10.1016/j.jbusres.2011.10.014

Mihir Joshi, V. K. S. (2017). Electronic Word of Mouth and Influence on Consumer Purchase Intention. *Dynamics of Public Administration*, 149–159. https://www.ajol.info/index.php/jfas/article/view/171488

Nadaraja, R., & Yazdanifard, R. (2013). Social Media Marketing Advantages And Disadvantages. *Center of Southern New Hempshire University*, 1–10.

Park, J. Y. Shin, J. K. (2019). *Predicting Continuous Usage Behavior in Social Network Service: Focusing on Affective Commitment and Users' Characteristics*. DBPIA. https://www.dbpia.co.kr/Journal/articleDetail?nodeId=NODE09233668

Prasad, S., Gupta, I. C., & Totala, N. K. (2017). Social media usage, electronic word of mouth and purchase-decision involvement. *Asia-Pacific Journal of Business Administration*, *9*(2), 134–145. doi:10.1108/APJBA-06-2016-0063

Pucci, T., Casprini, E., Nosi, C., & Zanni, L. (2019). Does social media usage affect online purchasing intention for wine? The moderating role of subjective and objective knowledge. *British Food Journal*, *121*(2), 275–288. doi:10.1108/BFJ-06-2018-0400

Ruangkanjanases, A., Hsu, S. L., Wu, Y. J., Chen, S. C., & Chang, J. Y. (2020). What drives continuance intention towards social media? Social influence and identity perspectives. *Sustainability (Switzerland)*, *12*(17), 1–15. doi:10.3390u12177081

Safwa Farook, F., & Abeysekera, N. (2016). Influence of Social Media Marketing on Customer Engagement. *International Journal of Business and Management Invention*, *5*(12), 115–125. www.ijbmi.org

Sen Chiang, H. (2013). Continuous usage of social networking sites: The effect of innovation and gratification attributes. *Online Information Review*, *37*(6), 851–871. doi:10.1108/OIR-08-2012-0133

Shaikh, E., Brahmi, M., Thang, P. C., Watto, W. A., Trang, T. T. N., & Loan, N. T. (2022). Should I Stay or Should I Go? Explaining the Turnover Intentions with Corporate Social Responsibility (CSR), Organizational Identification and Organizational Commitment. *Sustainability*, *14*(10), 6030. https://doi.org/10.3390/su14106030

Sunkar, A., Lakspriyanti, A. P., Haryono, E., Brahmi, M., Setiawan, P., & Jaya, A. F. (2022). Geotourism Hazards and Carrying Capacity in Geosites of Sangkulirang-Mangkalihat Karst, Indonesia. *Sustainability*, *14*(3), 1704. https://doi.org/10.3390/su14031704

Tunio, M. N., Jariko, M. A., Børsen, T., Shaikh, S., Mushtaque, T., & Brahmi, M. (2021). How Entrepreneurship Sustains Barriers in the Entrepreneurial Process—A Lesson from a Developing Nation. *Sustainability*, *13*(20), 11419. https://doi.org/10.3390/su132011419

Tunio, M. N., Chaudhry, I. S., Shaikh, S., Jariko, M. A., & Brahmi, M. (2021). Determinants of the Sustainable Entrepreneurial Engagement of Youth in Developing Country—An Empirical Evidence from Pakistan. *Sustainability*, *13*(14), 7764. doi:10.3390u13147764

Wang, D., Xu, L., & Chan, H. C. (2015). Understanding the continuance use of social network sites: a computer self-efficacy perspective, *34*(2), 204–216. doi:10.1080/0144929X.2014.952778

Yin, X., Wang, H., Xia, Q., & Gu, Q. (2019). How Social Interaction Affects Purchase Intention in Social Commerce: A Cultural Perspective. *Sustainability, 11*(8), 2423. doi:10.3390/SU11082423

Zilber, S., Monken, S., & Quevedo-Silva, F. (2019). Adoption of Social Media by Small- and Medium-Sized Healthcare Enterprises. *BBR. Brazilian Business Review*, *16*(5), 453–469. doi:10.15728/bbr.2019.16.5.3

# Chapter 12

# Ride-Hailing Apps' Continuance Intention Among Millennials in the Indian Emerging Market:

## A Mediation and Moderation Analysis

**Rambabu Lavuri**
https://orcid.org/0000-0002-0976-8126
*Indian Institute of Management, Jammu, India*

## ABSTRACT

*The study aims to explore the continuous usage intention of ride-hailing apps by millennials utilizing the TAM model with the mediation role of service quality. Purposive sampling was employed to collect primary data from 277 Indian millennials, and structural equation modeling was utilized to analyze the data. The findings showed that perceived ease of use boosted perceived usefulness, attitude, and hedonic value, while perceived usefulness substantially affected utilitarian value and perspective. It was shown that utilitarian and hedonic values strongly impacted millennials' opinions and continued the desire to use ride-hailing applications. Service quality seems to significantly moderate impact attitudes, utilitarian and hedonic values, and ride-hailing applications' continuous intention.*

## 1. INTRODUCTION

The rising sharing economy, technological innovation, and travel demand have encouraged the introduction and marketing of new travel choices, aided by the widespread use of ride-hailing applications (Fauzi & Sheng, 2020). Ride-hailing applications are used to book a car, a taxi, or another method of transportation using a mobile device (Carlson & O'Cass, 2010; Jain et al., 2014). Most ride-hailing services do not own or operate cars; instead, they serve as intermediaries, connecting providers and passengers while earning fees for each voyage (Anderson, 2014). Ride-hailing applications are becoming a more common mode of transportation (Cheah et al., 2020). Many governments on the continent have actively promoted this service (Kang et al., 2021). Technology advancements have enabled smartphone users

DOI: 10.4018/978-1-6684-6766-4.ch012

to instantly access ride-hailing applications while creating a market for transportation services based on sharing private automobiles (Anderson, 2014). UBER, OLA DiDi, Lyft, and Grab cab are popular ride-hailing companies that provide various distinct services and have quickly been interwoven into people's lives in India.

An estimated 175 to 225 billion dollars in global ride-hailing app bookings were made last year, with that figure set for an increase of more than 100% by 2021 (Gawer & Srnicek, 2021). India's shared mobility (including ride-hailing services) is expected to account for 35 per cent of all global miles travelled by 2023 (Statista report 2022).

Ride-hailing services are viable in India because of the growing population and the increasing number of mobile phone owners (Fauzi & Sheng, 2020). It is no surprise, therefore, that India is rapidly evolving into an enticing ride-hailing industry, attracting domestic and international players. There is little doubt that competition in India will heat up in the coming years as more players join the ride-hailing sector there, given India's immense potential. Ride-hailing service providers are urged to concentrate on either recruiting new customers or maintaining existing customers due to an extreme business competitiveness situation. Providers of ride-hailing services may have difficulty attracting and maintaining customers. In the ride-hailing business, the alternative appeal is the critical element determining users' switching behaviours, making it more challenging to keep current customers than it is to bring in new ones (Kang et al., 2021). In this regard, only some app providers can easily maintain the sustainability of their customers' usage of their applications because of the danger of other comparable apps. Customers may also switch to comparable services if they want, as they can do so through their cell phones, which they can access from any location and at any time. Consumers can no longer be locked into a single ride-hailing app provider when there are no obstacles in terms of changeover fees at this time (Cheah et al., 2020). As a result, the desire of current customers to continue using ride-hailing applications becomes an important consideration. Ride-hailing apps include the hailing of taxis and bikes through smartphone apps, and there are two facets in the case of ride-hailing digital platforms, i.e. the drivers and the riders. Some of India's most common ride-hailing apps are Uber, Ola, Taxi, Rapido, etc. With the increased usage of smartphones and Smartphone apps post-COVID, the markets are expanding with a potential for a vast customer base, especially for capturing the millennial market. The study is specific to the riders and investigates the reasons and changes in millennial travel behaviour induced by ride-hailing apps and the continuance of the intention to use them.

The present research focuses on the Indian millennial generation between the ages of 22 and 37 (Lavuri, 2020; Indian Census, 2011). One-third of India's population comprises millennials with enormous financial power (Morgan Stanley, 2017). Moreover, they were technology-savvy, and affluent group members used their mobile phones extensively to make phone calls, send emails, book travel reservations, and use web services to their fullest potential (Devaraj *et al.*, 2020). However, with the outbreak of the COVID-19 epidemic (Erum et al. 2022), users' opinions and attitudes toward ride-sharing applications have evolved substantially (Fauzi & Sheng, 2020). The epidemic has also prompted companies (Tunio et al. 2021) and industries to adapt to shifting customer preferences, particularly among millennials (imarcgroup.com report, 2022). Ride-hailing applications are expected to see an increase in use as a result of this shift.

However, there is still a paucity of continuous usage of ride-hailing apps literature and market research, particularly for Indian millennials. Thus, an empirical study has been conducted to address a research gap by operationalizing and verifying triggers driving ride-hailing apps' continuous usage. This study followed the trend and used the TAM theoretical framework to better understand of usage intention of ride-hailing apps. Thus, the present study intends to address these research gaps by examining the factors that influence the continuous usage of ride-hailing apps and adding two variables (Uteliterian value and hedonic value) to the TAM model to understand continuous millennial usage of ride-hailing apps better. Therefore, we address three research questions (**RQs**):

**RQ1.** Do TAM constructs (perceived ease of use and usefulness) positively influence millennials' attitudes towards continuous usage intention of ride-hailing apps?
**RQ2.** Do perceived values (utilitarian and hedonic values) and attitudes positively influence millennials' continuous usage intention of ride-hailing apps?
**RQ3.** Will service quality positively mediate between perceived value and continuous usage intention of ride-hailing apps?

Non-probability sampling (purposive sampling method) was used to collect data from 277 Indian millennials, which was then empirically evaluated using the structural equation modelling (SEM) method. This research contributes to the sharing economy literature, particularly studies on ride-hailing applications' ongoing intention behaviour. This study report covered the following sections: theoretical foundation, literature review assessment, and hypotheses formulation. In this manner, the research methodology examines future research results, implications, and limitations on potential study pathways.

## 2. THEORETICAL BACKGROUND

### 2.1 Technology Acceptance Model (TAM)

The theory of reasoned action model was used to build the technology acceptance model (TAM) to understand better user adoption of technology and computer-based information systems (Venkatesh & Davis, 2000). In order to address the challenges of technology adoption and use, the TAM is a widely acknowledged paradigm based on an individual's psychological interactions with technology. An essential factor to consider is whether or not the user expects a new system to be simple to use and beneficial to their current situation (Lee et al., 2011).

According to the TAM model, PU and PEOU are critical components and foretell a big part in deciding the willingness to embrace and use any technology and enhance its utility (Venkatesh & Davis, 2000). Many researchers independently validated this model and evaluated whether or not consumers want to use the Internet to their advantage as a platform by looking at how well it can predict model adoption in a variety of IT-enabled applications, such as mobile learning (Liu & Wayne Xu, 2018).

TAM's predictive power is enhanced by including perceived values (utility and hedonic values). These three variables strongly predicted ride-hailing app use among millennials. The research paradigm shown in Figure 1 will be examined experimentally in this research.

## 3. REVIEW OF LITERATURE AND HYPOTHESES DEVELOPMENT

### 3.1 Perceived Ease of Use (PEOU)

PEOU is the user's ability to freely utilize the system or technology to find mobile applications they require (Davis & Venkatesh, 1996). Making things easy to use increases user usefulness (Davis, 1993). Perceived ease of use, perceived usefulness, increased hedonic value, and improved individual attitudes about using new technology are linked (Fauzi & Sheng, 2020). PEOU describes the simplicity and comfort of a ride-hailing app's trip reservation procedure (Arora et al., 2021). Users are more inclined to use programs with big rewards (Kumar et al., 2017).

PEOU affects an app's perceived usefulness, allowing users to utilize it (Fauzi & Sheng, 2020) freely. Hedonic value is customers' joy, pleasure, and satisfaction from using a service. It reflects the service's uniqueness and emotional connection to its users (Fauzi & Sheng, 2020). In a sharing economy, it is a better predictor of customer happiness (Arora *et al.*, 2021). PEOU helps adopt new technology. This study examined millennials' views, hedonic values, PEOU, PU, and attitude factors concerning ride-hailing applications. Therefore, the proposed hypothesize were

H1a: PEOU has a positive influence on PU.
H1b: PEOU has a positive influence on millennial attitudes
H1c: PEOU has a positive impact on the millennial's HV

### 3.2 Perceived Usefulness

"Perceived usefulness" refers to users' expectations of technology's benefits (Davis, 1993). This way of thinking will change how people feel about new technology and how much they want to use it (Bhattacherjee, 2001). Before using PU, a user may think about it, compare prices, and look up information. It is a crucial part of using any new technology for every user (Weinberg & Gottwald, 1982). PU is a strong predictor of satisfaction and intention. It changes customers' attitudes and increases their hedonic and utilitarian values when they make online purchases (Kumar et al., 2017). Davis (1993) says that this is one of the most important reasons why people use new technologies.

Perceived usefulness in ride-hailing relates to how fast end-users achieve utilitarian duties with ease, price comparison, and information availability. Fauzi and Sheng (2020) say that the service will seem more useful to end users if they can use their phones to book rides. Customers believe essential technologies provide more benefits than advantages (Ryu et al., 2010). The mobile technology in ride-hailing apps is likely helpful, and users are happy with them and want to keep using them. The number of users grows annually (Kumar et al., 2017). Therefore, the proposed hypothesize were

H2a: PU has a positive influence on millennial' HV
H2b: PU has a positive influence on millennial' attitudes

## 3.3 Utilitarian Value

Utilitarian value is the customer-perceived operational and functional advantages (Overby & Lee, 2006; Lavuri et al., 2022b). It has been assessed based on the cost and advantages of fair, effective, and inexpensive peer-to-peer internet connections. It is also one of the attributes users look for when assessing mobile applications and a ranking element (Fauzi & Sheng, 2020; Kim & Hwang, 2011). Past research has demonstrated that a customer's opinion of a product's usefulness is a significant determinant of purchase intent (Lavuri, 2021). This may be one of the main reasons consumers love ride-hailing apps (Voss *et al.*, 2018; Lavuri et al., 2022b). When goods and services are problem-solving and goal-directed, the client has gained utility from them; hence, utilitarian value is crucial in establishing product or service worth (Lavuri, 2021). The positive utilitarian value increases positivity and reduces the desire for alternatives. The interaction between utilitarian value and attitude boosts internet usage and online shopping (Vieira et al., 2018).

Individual ingenuity of ride-hailing app users leads to a proper perception of the utilitarian value, sustaining continued usage. According to research, the perceived utilitarian value affects app users' retention intentions (Aw et al., 2019; Fauzi & Sheng, 2020; Lavuri et al., 2022b). In ride-hailing apps, utilitarian value mediates user innovation and retention (Hartman et al., 2006). In the case of ride-hailing applications, the claimed utilitarian value should affect users' views, changing their motivation to continue using the program. Therefore, the proposed hypothesize were

H3a: UV has a positive influence on millennial' attitudes
H3b: UV positively influences millennial ride-hailing app's continuous usage intention?

## 3.4 Hedonic Value (HV)

*Hedonic value* is "those parts of consumer behaviour that relate to the multisensory, imaginative, and emotional aspects of one's interaction with things." Hedonic value (Hirschman and Holbrook, 1982). "HV" is derived from the user's assessment of the system's quality, whereas "perceived informativeness" and "credibility" emphasize the "utilitarian features of the system," which are more critical to the user. How a user views a system's quality determines how much fun they have with it, how engaged they are, and how arousing they are (Li & Mao, 2015; Lavuri et al., 2022b). It is typical for a product or service user to have nostalgic memories of previous hedonistic experiences related to the event, leading to the user's perceived satisfaction with the product or service (Lavuri, 2021). When people participate in tourist activities, for example, they get a higher hedonic value, increasing their levels of enjoyment and, thus, their expenditure (Ponsignon et al., 2021). Hedonic value and user attitudes have positively correlated in previous studies, which impacts users' motivation to continue using new technology (Lavuri, 2021). End-of-trip experiences, whether favourable or unfavourable, influence the value of a ride-hailing program's hedonic value to the user (Lavuri et al., 2022b). Ride-hailing applications may be seen more favourably by users if they have a positive hedonic value from their previous experience. Therefore, the proposed hypothesize were

H4a: HV has a positive influence on millennial' attitude?
H4b: HV has a positive influence on millennial' ride hailing apps continuous usage intention?

## 3.5 Attitude

A person's attitude toward a subject may be either favourable or unfavourable, and it can be expressed in their remarks about other people, things, or events (Ajzen & Fishbein, 1980). Positive or bad past experiences and readily available emotional and cognitive information contribute to the construction of attitudes by influencing a user's behaviour in reaction to a particular activity (Lavuri, 2021). TAM and UTAUT agree that attitudes play a significant role in determining whether or not a person intends to use new technologies. That is because the UTAUT and TAM theories of technology adoption and usage have a lot in common (Davis, 1993; Dwivedi et al., 2019). Thus, it is impossible to overstate this component's importance (Chang et al., 2020; Lavuri, 2021). As a result, users who have a favourable view of the mobile app intend to use it repeatedly. When customers have an unfavourable opinion of a mobile app, they are more likely to stop using it altogether if they have a terrible experience with it (Lavuri et al., 2022b). Therefore, the proposed hypothesize was

H5: Millennia's attitudes have a positive influence on continuous usage intention of ride-hailing apps?

## 3.6 Moderation Role: Service Quality

Service quality is complicated; from one perspective, it should be evaluated in terms of the technical and operational components of the service provided (van Tonder and Petzer, 2021). Second, reliability, attention, compassion, tangibility, and certainty contribute to service excellence (Parasuraman et al., 1988). Third, it is influenced by customer views of service conditions, (Hamrouni et al., 2021) behavior, and satisfaction (Gong and Yi, 2018). The current research-validated the third point of view by evaluating the service quality of mobile ride-hailing applications (van Tonder and Petzer, 2021). Positive user emotions, satisfaction, trustworthiness, perceived values, a strong reputation, and behavioural intent may benefit service providers (Arguello et al., 2020). Service quality may lead to engagement, user pleasure, and customer loyalty (Kasiri et al., 2017). Service quality heavily influences personal views (Carlson and O'Cass, 2010). Similarly, providing outstanding ride-hailing services increases people's perceived worth. The quality of service has affected ride-hailing clients' ongoing usage of the service (Nguyen-Phuoc et al., 2021). Therefore, proposed hypothesize was

H6: Service quality has a positive moderation association between UV (H6a), HV (H6b), attitude (H6c), and continuance usage intention of ride-hailing apps.

# 4. METHODOLOGY

## 4.1 Research Design and Procedure

To evaluate the suggested model, we employed a quantitative technique to investigate the continuation intention of ride-hailing apps among millennial in India. To gather respondents, we used a purposive sampling strategy. Purposive sampling, also known as judgmental, subjective, or selective sampling, is a method in which researchers pick groups to sample based on their judgement. It is a well-known method that is suited for the present research (Lavuri et al., 2022a). In order to acquire primary data

*Figure 1. Current study model*

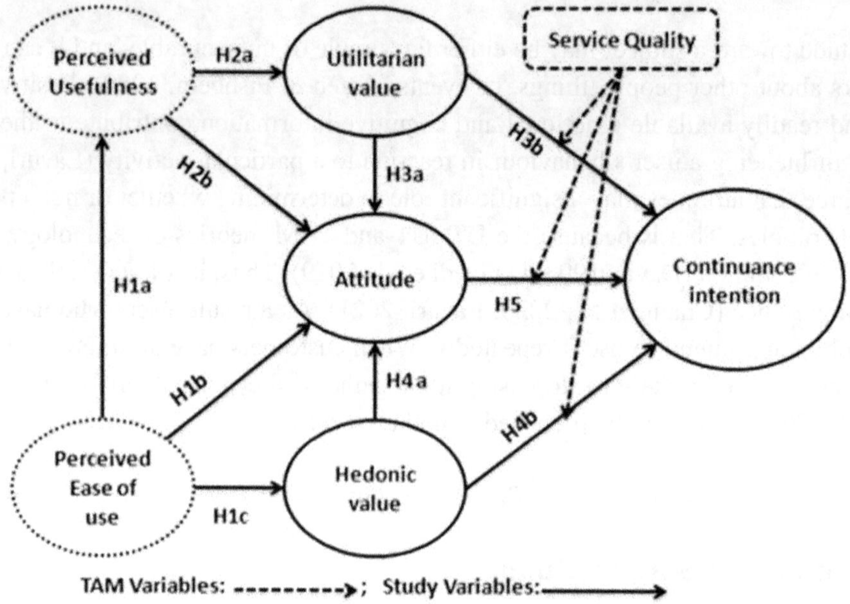


from millennial who had previously used ride-hailing applications, we used a structured questionnaire to gather information.

Ride-hailing app users were asked to answer screening questions on their intent to continue using the service to identify authentic replies. Afterwards, they were free to provide whatever further information they wished. Only those who met the participation requirements were allowed to participate, and the restrictions were quite strict in this regard. 389 questionnaires were sent, with 277 (71.2 per cent) deemed suitable for the final research. This percentage is higher than the 20% minimum response rate permitted (Hair et al., 2015). Table 1 depicts the characteristics of millennials.

## 4.2 Measures

For this study, a structured questionnaire was designed using pre-validated scale items. As part of the research, the researcher conducted a pilot study with 67 participants to determine the validity and reliability of our survey instrument. A few minor changes were made to the questionnaire after the pre-test to address any issues raised by the participants. One part of the questionnaire reveals the sample's demographic features and general questions about ride-hailing apps, and the second section consists of seven variables with 25 items. We used the 3-item scales Malik & Rao (2019) developed to measure PU and PEOU. Similarly, the 5-item scales for measuring UV were adopted from the research of Fauzi and Sheng (2021), and the 3-item scale for assessing HV was derived from the study of (Wu et al., 2018). A 3-item scale for assessing ATT was adopted from a study by Weng et al. (2017), a 3-item scale for measuring SQ was adapted from a research by van Tonder and Petzer (2021), and a 3-item scale for measuring CI of ride-hailing apps was adapted from a study by Hong et al. (2017). We used a 1 to 5 Likert scale (1-strongly agree and 5-strongly disagree). The data was evaluated using structural equation modelling (SEM), and the model was tested using AMOS 23v (Hair et al., 2015).

*Table 1. Millennials characteristics (**n=277**)*

| Characteristics | *F* | % |
|---|---|---|
| **Sex** | | |
| **Male** | 144 | 52.0 |
| **Female** | 133 | 48.0 |
| **Age (in years)** | | |
| **22 years to 29 years** | 159 | 57.4 |
| **30 years to 37 years** | 118 | 42.6 |
| **Education** | | |
| **Intermediate** | 72 | 26.0 |
| **Degree** | 77 | 27.8 |
| **Post graduation** | 58 | 20.9 |
| **Above Post graduation** | 70 | 25.3 |
| **Occupation** | | |
| **Students** | 29 | 10.5 |
| **private employee** | 91 | 32.9 |
| **Govt employee** | 51 | 18.4 |
| **Business** | 70 | 25.3 |
| **Home maker** | 36 | 13.0 |
| **Monthly income in rupees** | | |
| **below 35,000** | 21 | 7.6 |
| **35,001- 40,000** | 45 | 16.2 |
| **40,001 -45,000** | 107 | 38.6 |
| **45,001-50,000** | 70 | 25.3 |
| **50,001 and Above** | 34 | 12.3 |

# 5. RESULTS

## 5.1 Common Method Bias (CMB)

Common method bias was assessed using the Harman single factor test (CMB). The test indicated that a single factor accounted for 39.24% of the entire variation (Lavuri et al., 2022). The Kurtosis and skewness tests confirmed data normality. The study findings were within the suggested limit of 1. Predictor factor VIF values were below 3. The data set is not multicollinear; hence there's no common method bias.

## 5.2 Reliability and Validity

We employed a two-stage structural equation modelling (SEM) technique using AMOS 23.0v, first evaluating the measurement model and then assessing the structural one. The results of confirmatory factor analysis (CFA) first indicated excellent fit: with reasonably high fit indices- X2/df = 2.541, NFI

*Table 2. General awareness of ride hailing apps in India*

| Characteristics | F | % |
|---|---|---|
| *Which ride-hailing applications do you use the most while travelling?* | | |
| **Uber** | 27 | 9.7 |
| **Ola** | 40 | 14.4 |
| **Savari** | 63 | 22.7 |
| **Zoom car** | 83 | 30.0 |
| **Rapido** | 64 | 23.1 |
| *Use of ride-hailing applications* | | |
| **Regular** | 149 | 53.8 |
| **Sometimes** | 96 | 34.7 |
| **Rarely** | 32 | 11.5 |
| *Reasons to use app-based ride-hailing services* | | |
| **Saves time** | 45 | 16.2 |
| **Scarcity of public transit** | 27 | 9.7 |
| **Reasonable Cost** | 38 | 13.7 |
| **Limitations on using private car** | 101 | 36.5 |
| **Problems with parking** | 66 | 23.8 |

= .942, RMSA= .041, CFI= .958, TLI = .961, RFI= .921 and IFI= .934 and the indices' results align with recognized norms (Hair *et al.*, 2015). The convergent and discriminant validity of the constructs was determined using the construct reliabilities, as presented in Table 2.

Convergent validity was used to examine the constructs' homogeneity through average variance extracted (AVE). The findings reveal that Factor loading values ranged between .709 to 0.894, which were more than threshold value (>.70). Likewise, Cronbach Alpha values ranged between .798 to .894 which is more than threshold value (>.70), Composite Reliability values ranged between .813 to .905 (>.6), and average variance extracted values ranged between .611 to .762 (>.5). All values were over the threshold value which was suggested by Hair *et al.*, (2015) (Table 3), therefore, the convergent validity is excellent.

The findings of discriminant validity indicated that the square root of the squared root of AVE of each construct is larger than the absolute value of inter-construct correlation; consequently, discriminant validity is confirmed (Table 4). The inter-construct coefficient result show that PEOU has a strong positive correlation with UV ($r = .401, p < .01$) and ATT ($r = .354, p < .01$), at the 2-tailed significance level.

Similarly, PU has a significant association with ATT ($r = .406, p < .01$) and UV ($r = .351, p < .01$); UV has a strong association with ATT ($r = .255, p < .01$) and CI ($r = .205, p < .01$); ATT has a positive correlation with CI ($r = .198, p < .01$) and HV has a strong correlation with CI ($r = .209, p <.01$) at the 2 tailed significance level.

*Table 3. Results of reliability and validity*

| Constructs/Measurement items | Factor loading | Composite reliability | Avg. Variance Extraction | Cronbach Alpha |
|---|---|---|---|---|
| Perceived ease of use *(PEOU)* | | | | |
| It is easy for me to learn how to use a ride hailing app for booking a vehicle | 0.822 | .813 | .592 | .804 |
| It is easy for me to smartly use the ride hailing app for booking a vehicle | 0.709 | | | |
| Overall using the ride hailing service app process was easy to use | 0.775 | | | |
| *Perceived Usefulness (PU)* | | | | |
| It is easy for me to book a vehicle and travel anywhere and improves my lifestyle | 0.889 | .885 | .72 | .855 |
| My travelling and lifestyle is enhanced by using rise hailing app | 0.847 | | | |
| Ride hailing apps are very useful and I was missing using it in the past years | 0.808 | | | |
| *Utilitarian value (UV)* | | | | |
| I can book a vehicle easily and effortlessly using a ride hailing app | 0.894 | .905 | .707 | .821 |
| I can book a vehicle easily and efficiently using ride hailing app and travel anywhere relentlessly | 0.808 | | | |
| I save a lot of time by booking a vehicle using ride hailing app for transportation | 0.875 | | | |
| My mobility has improved a lot since I have stated using ride hailing app for transportation | 0.782 | | | |
| *Hedonic value (HV)* | | | | |
| I enjoy the service of the cab by using online ride hailing app | 0.855 | .884 | .717 | .798 |
| It is exciting to book a cab using ride hailing app for transportation as I always used traditional ways to book a cab. | 0.817 | | | |
| It is thrilling to book a cab through ride hailing app and look for discounts and offers | 0.869 | | | |
| *Attitude (ATT)* | | | | |
| I think ride hailing app is a very good option for booking a ride | 0.812 | .823 | .737 | .894 |
| I todays world booking a ride through rise hailing app is the correct approach | 0.849 | | | |
| It will be a good habit in today's world to book a ride through rise hailing app | 0.807 | | | |
| Continuance intention of ride hailing apps *(CI)* | | | | |
| I will keep using ride hailing apps for booking a vehicle in future also | 0.726 | .862 | .639 | .805 |
| I have started to use ride hailing app frequently for booking a cab for transportation easily | 0.786 | | | |
| I will recommend my friends and relatives also to use the ride hailing apps for booking a vehicle | 0.825 | | | |

*Table 4. Discriminant Validity of Measurement Model*

| Constructs | *Mean* | *Std. D* | *PEOU* | *PU* | *UV* | *ATT* | *HV* | *CI* |
|---|---|---|---|---|---|---|---|---|
| ***PEOU*** | 3.94 | .987 | *(.77)* | | | | | |
| ***PU*** | 4.04 | 1.022 | .354* | ***(.848)*** | | | | |
| ***UV*** | 4.62 | 1.546 | .401** | .351** | ***(.841)*** | | | |
| ***ATT*** | 3.75 | 1.992 | .354** | .406** | .255* | ***(.847)*** | | |
| ***HV*** | 3.22 | 1.452 | .104* | .112* | .136** | .115* | *(.78)* | |
| ***CI*** | 3.82 | 1.544 | .217** | .282** | .204** | .198** | .209** | ***(0.822)*** |

*: $p < .05$ and **: $p < .01$

## 5.3 Hypotheses Testing

The hypothesis findings showed that H1a to H5 were supported. The findings of the hypotheses showed that PEOU had a favourable effect on the PU (H1a: β= .344, p< .05); ATT (H1b: β= .094, p< .001); and HV (H1b: β= .411, p< .001). Likewise, PU had a beneficial impact on the UV (H2a: β=.522, p < .001) and ATT (H1a: β= .292, p< .001); UV had a strong impact on the millennials attitude (H3a: β= .453, p< .001) and CI (H3b: β= .099, p< .001); HV had a favourable impact on the ATT (H4a: β= .108, p< .05) and and (H4b: β= .092, p< .001) millennials attitude had a significant impact on the continuous usage intention of ride hailing apps (H5: β= .268, p< .001) (Table 5); hence, the millennial' utilitarian and hedonistic values were bolstered by the ride-hailing apps' ease of use and utility. These values encouraged and strengthened their attitude toward the continued use of the applications.

*Table 5. Hypotheses results*

| Hypotheses | Path | β | C.R. | Sig. | Supported |
|---|---|---|---|---|---|
| *H1a* | PEOU -----> PU | .344 | 1.051 | *p < .05* | Yes |
| *H1b* | PEOU ----->ATT | .094 | 1.322 | *p < .001* | Yes |
| *H1c* | PEOU ----->HV | .411 | 1.361 | *p< .001* | Yes |
| *H2a* | PU -----> UV | .522 | 2.668 | *p< .001* | Yes |
| *H2b* | PU -----> ATT | .292 | .987 | *p< .001* | Yes |
| *H3a* | UV -----> ATT | .453 | 1.658 | *p < .001* | Yes |
| *H3b* | UV -----> CI | .099 | .954 | *p< .001* | Yes |
| *H4a* | HV -----> ATT | .108 | 1.548 | *p< .05* | Yes |
| *H4b* | HV -----> CI | .092 | 1.954 | *p< .001* | Yes |
| *H5* | ATT -----> CI | .268 | 3.254 | *p< .001* | Yes |

## 5.4 Moderation Effect of SQ

We used moderation analysis to determine whether the association between UV, ATT, HV and CI were moderated by SQ. We used the PROCESS macro with a bootstrapping effect of five thousand times to examine the moderating impact on five proposed associations. The model includes interaction variables to assess the moderating effects of SQ association among UV, ATT, and HV. First, the fix factors of UV, ATT, HV, CI, SE and SE were assigned standardized values. Additionally, we calculated the values for the interaction variable. The effect of the interaction variable was determined, and the structural model was validated using AMOS v23. Numerous studies have already employed this strategy and obtained factual findings (Butcher *et al.*, 2017). In moderation results, SQ has a noteworthy moderation relationship between UV and CI (H7a: β = .102, p < .001); ATT and CI (H7b: β = .249, p < .001) and HV and CI (H7c: β = .345, p < .05) (see Table 6). Therefore, Reusability of the ride-hailing applications was dependent on the service quality.

*Table 6. Moderation results*

| Hypotheses | Path | β | C.R. | Sig. | Supported |
|---|---|---|---|---|---|
| *H6a* | UV----> SQ ---->CI | .102 | .988 | *p< .001* | Yes |
| *H6b* | ATT----> SQ ---->CI | .249 | 1.328 | *p < .001* | Yes |
| *H6c* | HV----> SQ---->C1 | .345 | 1.249 | *p < .05* | Yes |

## 6. DISCUSSIONS AND CONCLUSION

This study empirically explored the continuance intention of ride-hailing apps among millennials in India. It is also one of the few efforts that examine the long-term objective of financial service sharing. The study explores the ride-hailing app's ongoing use intention using the TAM model and service quality as moderating variables. These results are remarkable regarding millennials' willingness to continue utilising ride-hailing services.

Results have shown that PEOU strongly affects PU (H1a), ATT (H1b), and HV (H1c), and these findings are corroborated by Arora et al. (2021). Perceives usefulness is established by the user's assessment of the model's ease of use and acceptance (Ofori et al., 2021), and PEOU is a crucial factor in building a good attitude about using and embracing new technologies like ride-hailing services(van Tonder and Petzer, 2021). Due to the ease and flexibility with which users may schedule trips, ride-hailing apps enjoy great popularity among millennials. This positive experience and subsequent enjoyment have led to the development of significant hedonic value for millennials. It indicates that users would get hedonistic value from ride-hailing services if they discovered them to be as user-friendly as other online utility apps.

User PU was shown to have positive effects on UV (H2a) and ATT (H2c), as demonstrated by the results of this study (Fauzi and Sheng, 2020). Ride-hailing apps provide several advantages, including service information, precise mapping, pricing information, and a simple payment option. This means that ride-hailing apps like Uber and Lyft will keep millennials using them for future journeys because of their ease and versatility.

The millennial attitude (H3a) and continuous intention of ride-hailing (H3b) were significantly influenced by the perceived utilitarian value, and these results were validated by research by Fauzi and Sheng (2020); Voss et al. (2018). Customers who use ride-hailing services are more likely to continue using them if they have had a positive experience. The link between utilitarian value and attitude increases ride-hailing app bookings because good utilitarian value fosters a favourable attitude among millennials and minimises risk (Vieira et al., 2018). Realistic perception of the perceived utilitarian value is fostered by ride-hailing app users' technical preparedness (Tunio et al., 2021), which motivates them to keep using the apps in question.

Millennials' attitudes (H4a) and long-term intentions (H4b) to use ride-hailing services were shown to be strongly influenced by their perceptions of hedonic value (Voss et al., 2016). (2018). People use ride-hailing apps because they make it simple to receive various rides and make it possible for them to have more fun while doing so (Huang, 2018). Zhu et al. (2017) found that positive sentiments and excitement among users may increase their hedonic value and long-term desire to continue with the service (H5), and this finding was validated by previous research on ride-hailing applications (Devaraj et al., 2020). Finally, in the developing industry, users' utility, hedonic value, and attitude all play significant roles in their continued intention to use ride-hailing applications. Utilitarian value influenced intention more than hedonic value, while the latter had more of an overall effect on continuous intention (Ryu et al., 2010; Lavuri et al., 2022b). Despite this, users are more inclined to use ride-hailing applications frequently because of their hedonic value (Zhang et al., 2019).

Concerning SQ as a moderation effect, the findings showed that SQ had a substantial moderating link between the UV (H7a), ATT (H7b), HV (H7c), and CI of ride-hailing apps. SQ is one of the factors that enhance the continuous use of ride-hailing apps. If the service provider provides high-quality services and protects users' sensitive information (such as financial and private data), they are more inclined to continue using the service; high levels of consumer satisfaction and brand loyalty go hand in hand. For corporations and academics, this research will help them better comprehend why millennial continue to use ride-hailing apps and the most important factors that influence their use of ride-hailing apps.

## 7. IMPLICATION

### 7.1 Theoretical Implications

This study extends the technology acceptance model for ride-hailing applications by looking at the long-term use intention of these apps. When it comes to developing market ride-hailing, this research goes further than the standard TAM to examine the role that hedonic and utilitarian value perceptions have in the TAM for millennials. Findings from this research show that millennial Indian users' opinions are affected by the model's fundamental elements, such as PU and PEOU. Ride-hailing marketing is a unique area of study, and the suggested model provides new insights into the effect of attitudes and values on millennials' behavioural intentions. Research on the influence of ride-hailing applications on millennials, in particular, has only looked at these components. They've all been studied in their own right, but they've also formed the basis of several conceptual models (Fauzi and Sheng, 2021). This survey was conducted in an Asian nation where no such research has been done. As a result, the study contributes dynamically to the body of knowledge. After COVID-19 (Erum et al, 2022), millennials began utilising ride-hailing applications extensively to participate in mobility, leading to the continued use of ride-hailing apps and the study of these structures. As a result of this study, we can better understand how and service quality affect the frequency with which people use ride-hailing applications. Millennials' continued use of ride-hailing applications may be influenced by their poor while utilising these services. The quality of the ride-hailing app's service was a significant predictor of how often people will use it.

### 7.2 Practical Implication

The 2020 pandemic has affected the features, psychographic behaviour, perspective, and connectivity of millennials, leading to accelerated growth in online applications like taxi-hailing apps (Zwanka & Buff, 2020). This current technology revolution was made feasible by the epidemic, and consumer acceptance relies on technical handiness, convenience, necessity, and safety (Zwanka & Buff, 2020). These criteria connect to our study's premise. This research suggests long-term alterations in millennials' behaviour toward marketers, resulting in consumer movements toward ride-hailing applications. It also helps digital firms design ride-hailing applications based on how users perceive their utility, simplicity of use, and utilitarian and hedonic value, which changes their attitude towards the app's continuation and results in improvements. The simplicity of use significantly influences continued intention; thus, ride app designers should create user-friendly applications. To achieve customer expectations, service providers should prioritize quality. Service providers' quality affects their continuous use. It may also be a favourable or unfavourable system attitude. When a ride-hailing platform becomes multisided, adoption studies or other market research will be exciting. These studies will include the platform's social and economic impact (van Tonder & Petzer, 2021).

Ride-hailing app developers could employ practical value-based service techniques in the form of more user-friendly, affordable, and easy-to-navigate apps with lower wait times (Fauzi & Sheng, 2020a). It should also concentrate on hedonistic value-based service techniques, such as offering more pleasant services that engage customers. Companies may achieve this by pushing customization elements that enable consumers to optimize their preferences, such as allowing the clients to pick their desired car, payment methods, and driver alternatives. The app supplier could also consider developing loyalty programmes to establish long-term consumer relationships that will lead to continuing app use. Managers should focus on marketing strategies that promote applications' economic benefits while advertising its hedonistic components to increase user happiness.

## 7.3 Social Implication

Given the inefficiency of public transportation, residents in these places are more likely to rely on personal automobiles for their travel needs. The findings, however, suggest that inhabitants of these farther-flung neighbourhoods may have been drawn to these services with the introduction of these new, more flexible, and economically viable operators. In addition to improving people's health, cutting down on traffic, and making mobility more accommodating to the requirements of the community, the door-to-door service they provide eliminates the need for users to locate a parking place at the destination, saving both time and energy. Therefore, these services will have helped increase accessibility in underserved regions, hence increasing people's access to the labour market and stimulating economic development. Additionally, these services have the ability to enhance the integrated transport system without adding additional costs, since they cater to the mobility requirements of modes of travel with a greater propensity to produce congestion (private automobiles) and extend the reach of the integrated transport network (last mile) (AFI, 2017).

People choose not to own vehicles since alternative forms of transportation are handier, versatile, and cheaper (Ride-Hailing Global Market Report, 2021). Monthly car rental is more affordable than buying and maintaining a new vehicle for a year. 55% of Generation Z feels that mobility is vital but having a car is superfluous, according to a 2019 Cox Automotive poll. 45% of millennials, 34% of Gen Xers, and 28% of boomers agree. On-demand transportation services and a decline in car ownership are driving the expansion of the ride-hailing industry. This study informs ride-hailing platform management on the importance of hedonic and economic value in driving app usage. The research examines hedonic and financial matters. This underscores the importance of service quality and user while utilizing apps. Post-covid, ride-hailing service companies in India might leverage this market segment.

Mitra et al. (2019) found that smartphone ownership and internet availability impact older people's usage of on-demand ride-hailing services. Despite restrictions, many older folks remain separated from the digital revolution. Physical and technical constraints exist. Companies should teach elderly individuals to use new technologies. "Lyft Concierge" may help millennials without telephones utilize ride-hailing services, enhancing their hedonic and utilitarian value.

Previous user intention studies on online apps focused on e-banking, e-marketing, and online shopping. Millennials' attitudes regarding ride-hailing applications in India aren't studied. In conclusion, our empirical research helps management guidance on ride-hailing app use.

## 8. LIMITATIONS AND SCOPE FOR FURTHER RESEARCH

This research is based on ride-hailing applications and the continual intention of millennials' cross-sectional data and changes in user behaviour over time; longitudinal data might be employed in future studies to examine how the correlations observed shift over time. Data acquired from millennials in India cannot be applied to other nations because of their cultural differences. The usage of a ride-hailing app in a particular country should be weighed against other aspects, including the industry, law, competition, and public awareness. Additional research should be carried out as a representative poll.

## ACKNOWLEDGMENT

I acknowledge the prior reports as sources for their essential advice to improve the research framework for this study.

**RESEARCH FUNDING:** Nobody supported this study.

## REFERENCES

Aldieri, L., Brahmi, M., Bruno, B., & Vinci, C. P. (2021). Circular Economy Business Models: The Complementarities with Sharing Economy and Eco-Innovations Investments. *Sustainability, 13*(22), 12438. doi:10.3390u132212438

Ajzen, I., & Fishbein, M. (1980). *Understanding Attitudes and Predicting Social Behavior*. Prentice-Hall.

Anderson, D. N. (2014). Not just a taxi'? For-profit ridesharing, driver strategies, and VMT. *Transportation, 41*(5), 1099–1117. doi:10.100711116-014-9531-8

Arabeche, Z., Soudani, A., Brahmi, M., Aldieri, L., Vinci, C. P., & Abdelli, M. E. A. (2022). Entrepreneurial Orientation, Organizational Culture and Business Performance in SMEs: Evidence from Emerging Economy. *Sustainability, 14*(9), 5160. doi:10.3390u14095160

Arguello, M. I., Monferrer Tirado, D., & Estrada Guillén, M. (2020). Service quality in a post-crisis context: Emotional effects and behaviours. *International Journal of Bank Marketing, 38*(1), 175–198. doi:10.1108/IJBM-02-2019-0045

Arora, M., Singh, H., & Gupta, S. (2021). What drives e-hailing apps adoption? An analysis of behavioral factors through fuzzy AHP. *Journal of Science and Technology Policy Management, 13*(2), 382–404. doi:10.1108/JSTPM-12-2020-0177

Aw, E. C. X., Basha, N. K., Ng, S. I., & Sambasivan, M. (2019). To grab or not to grab? The role of trust and perceived value in on-demand ridesharing services. *Asia Pacific Journal of Marketing and Logistics*, *31*(5), 1442–1465. doi:10.1108/APJML-09-2018-0368

Bandura, A. (1977). Self-efficacy: Toward a unifying theory of behavioral change. *Psychological Review*, *84*(2), 191–215. doi:10.1037/0033-295X.84.2.191 PMID:847061

Bhattacherjee, A. (2001). Understanding Information Systems Continuance: An Expectation-Confirmation Model. *Psychology Computer Science*, *25*(3), 351–370.

Bhattacherjee, A., Perols, J., & Sanford, C. (2015). Information Technology Continuance: A Theoretic Extension and Empirical Test. *Journal of Computer Information Systems*, *49*(1), 17–26. doi:10.1080/08874417.2008.11645302

Branscombe, M. (2020). The network impact of the global COVID-19 pandemic. *The New Stack*, *14*. https://thenewstack.io/the-network-impact-of-the-global-covid-19-pandemic/

Butcher, L., Phau, I., & Shimul, A. S. (2017). Uniqueness and status consumption in Generation Y consumers: Does moderation exist? *Marketing Intelligence & Planning*, *35*(5), 673–687. doi:10.1108/MIP-12-2016-0216

Cao, J., Li, J., Wang, Y., & Ai, M. (2022). The Impact of Self-Efficacy and Perceived Value on Customer Engagement under Live Streaming Commerce Environment. *Security and Communication Networks*, *2022*, 1–13. Doi.org/10.1155/2022/2904447. doi:10.1155/2022/2904447

Carlson, J., & O'Cass, A. (2010). Exploring the relationships between e-service quality, satisfaction, attitudes and behaviours in content-driven e-service web sites. *Journal of Services Marketing*, *24*(2), 112–127. doi:10.1108/08876041011031091

Census 2011 India. (n.d.). Population Census. https://www.census2011.co.in/

Chang, W.-C., Ardiyanto, A. N., Wu, C.-W., & Lin, C.-N. (2020). The Application of SERVQUAL Model to Construct Indicators for Improvement of Agricultural Products. *Exhibitions Service Quality*, *7*(6), 1–9.

Cheah, I., Shimul, A. S., Liang, J., & Phau, I. (2022). Consumer attitude and intention toward ridesharing. *Journal of Strategic Marketing*, *30*(2), 115–136. doi:10.1080/0965254X.2020.1733050

*COVID-19 Digital Transformation & Technology*. (n.d.). McKinsey. https://www.mckinsey.com/business-functions/strategy-and-corporate-finance/our-insights/how-covid-19-has-pushed-companies-over-the-technology-tipping-point-and-transformed-business-forever

Davis, F. D. (1993). User acceptance of information technology: System characteristics, user perceptions and behavioral impacts. *International Journal of Man-Machine Studies*, *38*(3), 475–487. doi:10.1006/imms.1993.1022

De', R., Pandey, N., & Pal, A. (2020). Impact of digital surge during Covid-19 pandemic: A viewpoint on research and practice. *International Journal of Information Management*, *55*, 102171. doi:10.1016/j.ijinfomgt.2020.102171 PMID:32836633

Devaraj, A., Ambi Ramakrishnan, G., Nair, G. S., Srinivasan, K. K., Bhat, C. R., Pinjari, A. R., Ramadurai, G., & Pendyala, R. M. (2020). Joint Model of Application-Based Ride Hailing Adoption, Intensity of Use, and Intermediate Public Transport Consideration among Workers in Chennai City. *Transportation Research Record: Journal of the Transportation Research Board*, *2674*(4), 152–164. doi:10.1177/0361198120912237

Dwivedi, Y. K., Rana, N. P., Jeyaraj, A., Clement, M., & Williams, M. D. (2019). Re-examining the Unified Theory of Acceptance and Use of Technology (UTAUT): Towards a Revised Theoretical Model. *Information Systems Frontiers*, *21*(3), 719–734. doi:10.100710796-017-9774-y

Erum, S.; Muhammad, N T.; Wali Muhammad, K.; Mohsen, B.; & Shahid, R., Chapter 16: The COVID-19 Pandemic Overlaps Entrepreneurial Activities and Triggered New Challenges: A Review Study, Book chapter: Managing Human Resources in SMEs and Start-ups, August 2022, 388 p. https://doi.org/doi:10.1142/9789811239212_0008

Fauzi, A. A., & Sheng, M. L. (2020). Ride-hailing apps' continuance intention among different consumer groups in Indonesia: The role of personal innovativeness and perceived utilitarian and hedonic value. *Asia Pacific Journal of Marketing and Logistics*, *33*(5), 1195–1219. doi:10.1108/APJML-05-2019-0332

Ferguson, R., & Brohaugh, B. (2010). The aging of Aquarius. *Journal of Consumer Marketing*, *27*(1), 76–81. doi:10.1108/07363761011012976

Gong, T., & Yi, Y. (2018). The effect of service quality on customer satisfaction, loyalty, and happiness in five Asian countries. *Psychology and Marketing*, *35*(6), 427–442. doi:10.1002/mar.21096

Hair, J. F., Celsi, M., Money, A., Samouel, P., & Page, M. (2015). The essentials of business research methods: Third Edition. The Essentials of Business Research Methods (3rd ed.), 1–494 doi:10.4324/9781315704562

Hartman, J. B., Shim, S., Barber, B., & O'Brien, M. (2006). Adolescents' utilitarian and hedonic Web consumption behavior: Hierarchical influence of personal values and innovativeness. *Psychology and Marketing*, *23*(10), 813–839. doi:10.1002/mar.20135

Hamrouni, B., Bourouis, A., Korichi, A., & Brahmi, M. (2021). Explainable Ontology-Based Intelligent Decision Support System for Business Model Design and Sustainability. *Sustainability*, *13*(17), 9819. doi:10.3390u13179819

Hirschman, E. C., & Holbrook, M. B. (1982). Hedonic Consumption: Emerging Concepts, Methods and Propositions. *Journal of Marketing*, *46*(3), 92–101. doi:10.1177/002224298204600314

Hong, J. C., Lin, P. H., & Hsieh, P. C. (2017). The effect of consumer innovativeness on perceived value and continuance intention to use smartwatch. *Computers in Human Behavior*, *67*, 264–272. doi:10.1016/j.chb.2016.11.001

Kang, Q., Li, H., Cheng, Y., & Kraus, S. (2021). Entrepreneurial ecosystems: Analysing the status quo. *Knowledge Management Research and Practice*, *19*(1), 8–20. doi:10.1080/14778238.2019.1701964

Kasiri, L. A., Guan Cheng, K. T., Sambasivan, M., & Sidin, S. M. (2017). Integration of standardization and customization: Impact on service quality, customer satisfaction, and loyalty. *Journal of Retailing and Consumer Services*, *35*, 91–97. doi:10.1016/j.jretconser.2016.11.007

Kim, D. J., & Hwang, Y. (2010). A study of mobile internet user's service quality perceptions from a user's utilitarian and hedonic value tendency perspectives. *Information Systems Frontiers*, *14*(2), 409–421. doi:10.100710796-010-9267-8

Kim, S., & Eastin, M. S. (2011). Hedonic tendencies and the online consumer: An investigation of the online shopping process. *Journal of Internet Commerce*, *10*(1), 68–90. doi:10.1080/15332861.2011.558458

Kumar, V. V. R., Lall, A., & Mane, T. (2017). Extending the TAM Model: Intention of Management Students to Use Mobile Banking: Evidence from India. *Global Business Review*, *18*(1), 238–249. doi:10.1177/0972150916666991

Lavuri, R. (2021). Intrinsic factors affecting online impulsive shopping during the COVID-19 in emerging markets. *International Journal of Emerging Markets*, Emerald Group Holdings Ltd. doi:10.1108/IJOEM-12-2020-1530/FULL/XML

Lavuri, R. (2022). Extending the theory of planned behavior: Factors fostering millennials' intention to purchase eco-sustainable products in an emerging market. *Journal of Environmental Planning and Management*, *65*(8), 1507–1529. doi:10.1080/09640568.2021.1933925

Lavuri, R., Jabbour, C.J.C., Grebinevych, O. & Roubaud, D., (2022a). Green factors stimulating the purchase intention of innovative luxury organic beauty products: Implications for sustainable development", *Journal of Environmental Management*, *.301*, 113899.

Lavuri, R., Jindal, A., & Umair, A. (2022b). How Perceived Utilitarian and Hedonic value influence online impulse shopping in India? Moderating role of Perceived Trust and Perceived Risk. *International Journal of Quality and Service Sciences*.

Li, M., & Mao, J. (2015). Hedonic or utilitarian? Exploring the impact of communication style alignment on user's perception of virtual health advisory services. *International Journal of Information Management*, *35*(2), 229–243. doi:10.1016/j.ijinfomgt.2014.12.004

Liu, X. & Wayne Xu, W. (2018). Adoption of ride-sharing apps by Chinese taxi drivers and its implication for the equality and wellbeing in the sharing economy. *JITSM.12* (1), 7–24.

Malik, G., & Rao, A. S. (2019). Extended expectation-confirmation model to predict continued usage of ODR/ride hailing apps: Role of perceived value and self-efficacy. *Information Technology & Tourism*, *21*(4), 461–482. doi:10.100740558-019-00152-3

Mitra, S. K., Bae, Y., & Ritchie, S. G. (2019). Use of Ride-Hailing Services among Older Adults in the United States. *Transportation Research Record: Journal of the Transportation Research Board*, *2673*(3), 700–710. doi:10.1177/0361198119835511

Nguyen-Phuoc, D. Q., Vo, N. S., Su, D. N., Nguyen, V. H., & Oviedo-Trespalacios, O. (2021). What makes passengers continue using and talking positively about ride-hailing services? The role of the booking app and post-booking service quality. *Transportation Research Part A, Policy and Practice*, *150*, 367–384. doi:10.1016/j.tra.2021.06.013

Ofori, K. S., Anyigba, H., Adeola, O., Junwu, C., Osakwe, C. N., & David-West, O. (2021). Understanding post-adoption behaviour in the context of ride-hailing apps: The role of customer perceived value. *Information Technology & People*, *35*(5), 1540–1562. doi:10.1108/ITP-06-2019-0285

Overby, J. W., & Lee, E. J. (2006). The effects of utilitarian and hedonic online shopping value on consumer preference and intentions. *Journal of Business Research*, *59*(10–11), 1160–1166. doi:10.1016/j.jbusres.2006.03.008

Owusu Kwateng, K., Yobanta, A. L., & Amanor, K. (2021). Hedonic and utilitarian perspective of mobile phones purchase intention. *Journal of Contemporary Marketing Science*, *4*(1), 44–68. doi:10.1108/JCMARS-08-2020-0035

Ponsignon, F., Lunardo, R., & Michrafy, M. (2021). Why Are International Visitors More Satisfied with the Tourism Experience? The Role of Hedonic Value, Escapism, and Psychic Distance. *Journal of Travel Research*, *60*(8), 1771–1786. doi:10.1177/0047287520961175

Rasheed Gaber, H., & Elsamadicy, A. M. (2021). What drives customers to continue using ride-sharing apps during the COVID-19 pandemic? The case of Uber in Egypt. *Cogent Business & Management. Cogent*, *8*(1), 1–21.

Robbins, S. P., Judge, T., & Vohra, N. (n.d.). *Organizational behavior.*

Ryu, K., Han, H., & Jang, S. S. (2010). Relationships among hedonic and utilitarian values, satisfaction and behavioral intentions in the fast-casual restaurant industry. *International Journal of Contemporary Hospitality Management*, *22*(3), 416–432. doi:10.1108/09596111011035981

Shankar, A., & Datta, B. (2018). Factors affecting mobile payment adoption intention: An Indian perspective. *Global Business Review, 19*(3_suppl), S72-S89.

Sharma, T. G., Hamari, J., Kesharwani, A., & Tak, P. (2020). Understanding continuance intention to play online games: Roles of self-expressiveness, self-congruity, self-efficacy, and perceived risk. *Behaviour & Information Technology*, *41*(2), 348–364. doi:10.1080/0144929X.2020.1811770

Sunkar, A., Lakspriyanti, A. P., Haryono, E., Brahmi, M., Setiawan, P., & Jaya, A. F. (2022). Geotourism Hazards and Carrying Capacity in Geosites of Sangkulirang-Mangkalihat Karst, Indonesia. *Sustainability, 14*(3), 1704. doi:10.3390u14031704

Tunio, M. N., Chaudhry, I. S., Shaikh, S., Jariko, M. A., & Brahmi, M. (2021). Determinants of the Sustainable Entrepreneurial Engagement of Youth in Developing Country—An Empirical Evidence from Pakistan. *Sustainability*, *13*(14), 7764. doi:10.3390u13147764

Tunio, M. N., Jariko, M. A., Børsen, T., Shaikh, S., Mushtaque, T., & Brahmi, M. (2021). How Entrepreneurship Sustains Barriers in the Entrepreneurial Process—A Lesson from a Developing Nation. *Sustainability*, *13*(20), 11419. doi:10.3390u132011419

Van Tonder, E., & Petzer, D. J. (2018). The interrelationships between relationship marketing constructs and customer engagement dimensions. *Service Industries Journal*, *38*(13–14), 948–973. doi:10.1080/02642069.2018.1425398

Venkatesh, V., & Davis, F. D. (2000). Theoretical Extension of the Technology Acceptance Model: Four longitudinal field studies. *Management Science*, *46*(2), 186–204. doi:10.1287/mnsc.46.2.186.11926

Vieira, V., Santini, F. O., & Araujo, C. F. (2018). A meta-analytic review of hedonic and utilitarian shopping values. *Journal of Consumer Marketing*, *35*(4), 426–437. doi:10.1108/JCM-08-2016-1914

Voss, K. E., Spangenberg, E. R., & Grohmann, B. (2018). Measuring the Hedonic and Utilitarian Dimensions of Consumer Attitude. *JMR, Journal of Marketing Research*, *40*(3), 310–320. doi:10.1509/jmkr.40.3.310.19238

Weinberg, P., & Gottwald, W. (1982). Impulsive consumer buying as a result of emotions. *Journal of Business Research*, *10*(1), 43–57. doi:10.1016/0148-2963(82)90016-9

Weng, G. S., Zailani, S., Iranmanesh, M., & Hyun, S. S. (2017). Mobile taxi booking application service's continuance usage intention by users. *Transportation Research Part D, Transport and Environment*, *57*, 207–216. doi:10.1016/j.trd.2017.07.023

Wu, W., Huang, V., Chen, X., Davison, R. M., & Hua, Z. (2018). Social value and online social shopping intention: The moderating role of experience. *Information Technology & People*, *31*(3), 688–711. doi:10.1108/ITP-10-2016-0236

Yan, R., Zhang, K. Z. K., & Yu, Y. (2019). Switching from hotels to peer-to-peer accommodation: An empirical study. *Information Technology & People*, *32*(6), 1657–1678. doi:10.1108/ITP-12-2017-0444

Zhang, T. C., Gu, H., & Jahromi, M. F. (2019). What makes the sharing economy successful? An empirical examination of competitive customer value propositions. *Computers in Human Behavior*, *95*, 275–283. doi:10.1016/j.chb.2018.03.019

Zhu, G., So, K. K. F., & Hudson, S. (2017). Inside the sharing economy: Understanding consumer motivations behind the adoption of mobile applications. *International Journal of Contemporary Hospitality Management*, *29*(9), 2218–2239. doi:10.1108/IJCHM-09-2016-0496

Zwanka, R. J., & Buff, C. (2020). COVID-19 Generation: A Conceptual Framework of the Consumer Behavioral Shifts to Be Caused by the COVID-19 Pandemic. *International Consumer Marketing*, *33*(1), 58–67. doi:10.1080/08961530.2020.1771646

# Chapter 13
# The Circular Business Model:
## A Solution for a Sustainable Business Ecosystem

**Priti Saxena**
*Welingkar Institute of Management, India*

**Abhineet Saxena**
https://orcid.org/0000-0003-0467-7900
*Amity University, Jaipur, India*

**Garima Sharma**
*Welingkar Institute of Management, India*

## ABSTRACT

*Technological disruptions, hyper innovation, and a more globalized world has changed the way businesses were done. Competitive pressure in today's world is ever increasing; one of the most effective ways of staying competitive in these challenging times is through building efficient business ecosystems. This economic community leverages the services of its members to offer value to customers. Over time, they co-evolve their capabilities and roles and tend to align themselves with the directions set by one or more central companies. With growing concern towards environment safety more and more companies are putting effort to include element of sustainability in their business ecosystem. This chapter will be structured around how to build sustainable business ecosystem through circular business model.*

## INTRODUCTION

The term "ecosystem" was coined by British botanist Arthur Tansley to indicate the interaction of living organisms with each other and their natural habitat of air, water, soil etc., drawing the analogy between James Moore imported the concept to the business ecosystem. He wrote in a Harvard Business article in 1993 that "Successful businesses are those that evolve rapidly and effectively." Yet innovative businesses can't evolve in a vacuum. They must attract resources of all sorts, drawing in capital, partners,

DOI: 10.4018/978-1-6684-6766-4.ch013

suppliers, and customers to create cooperative networks. It is advisable that company be viewed not as a member of a single industry but as part of a business ecosystem that crosses a variety of industries. In a business ecosystem, companies co-evolve capabilities around a new innovation. They work cooperatively and competitively to support new products, satisfy customer needs, and eventually incorporate the next round of innovations. Moore's concept of business ecosystem has garnered immense attention in the present times where we see organisations like Apple, Facebook, Maruti Suzuki, Tata Motors, Reliance Industries etc. increasingly conceiving their products and services as part of an ecosystem and not just confined to the narrow concept of self-contained organizations. Incremental value creation has become an ongoing activity for most of the new age firms, and this can be achieved only by way of inter-connection, collaboration, and integration with various members of the ecosystem, viz., suppliers, channel partners, financers, technology support providers, government bodies, and even competitors. A strong business ecosystem is quickly emerging as an effective competitive edge for organizations, as evidenced by the CXOs of SoftBank and Nokia, who have emphasized the importance of creating a strong ecosystem that competitors will not be able to easily replicate (Canning & Eamonn, 2015).

*Figure 1. Cultural economy benefits*
*Source- https://unctad.org/*

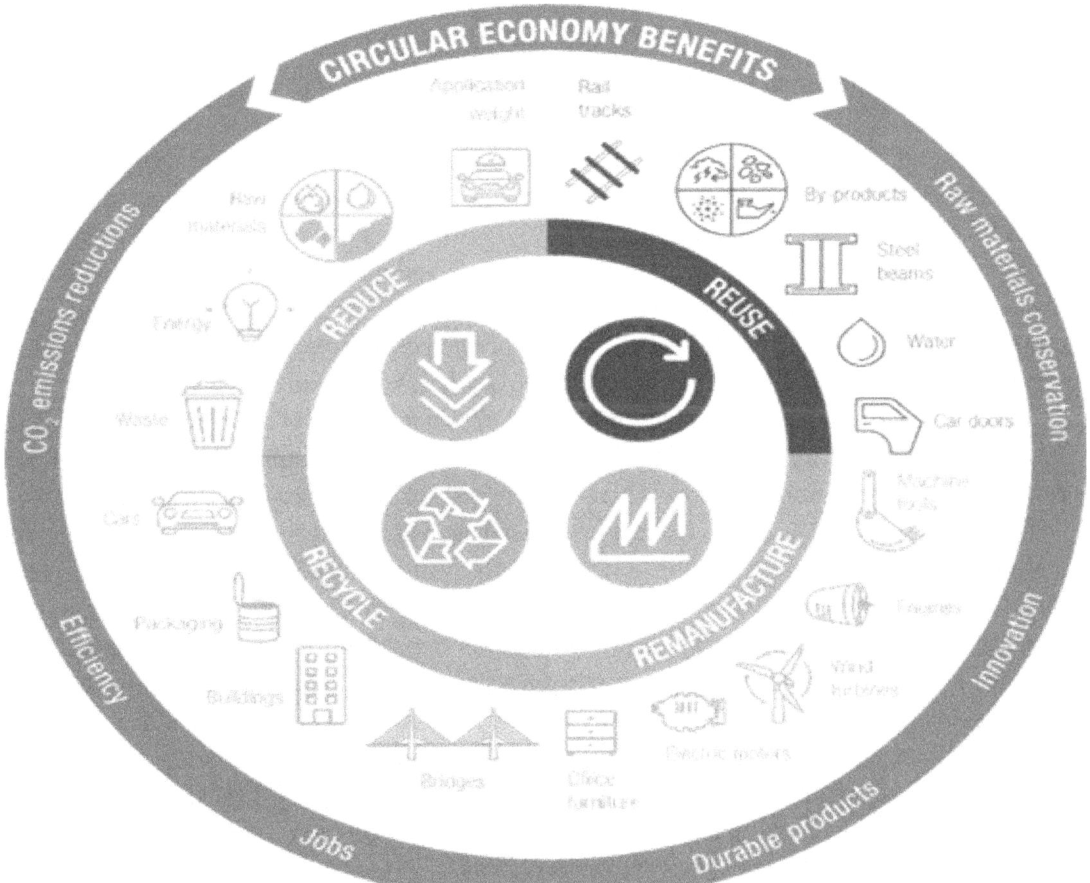

Recently, Delhi and Kolkata featured as the two most polluted cities in the world by PM2.5 level according to a research conducted by US based Health Effects Institute (Mohan, 2022). Such developments have led to the increased concern towards environment and social safety, the element of sustainability is progressively being embedded in the eco systems of agile businesses. Concept of Circular economy, that reward consumers for reusing things rather than throwing them away and requiring fresh resources has emerged as an effective tool to embrace sustainability. In a circular economy, all kinds of garbage are recycled or repurposed, including textiles, scrap metal, and outdated gadgets. As a result, the environment may be protected while new industries, jobs, and capabilities can be created, and old products get regenerated or repurposed. The mantra for Circular Economy is "at today's resource costs, we have today's goods and tomorrow's resources."

## BACKGROUND

In the words of Moore Business Ecosystem may be defined as network of suppliers, manufacturers, channel partners, competitors, customers, and other stakeholders. This economic community leverages the services of its members to offer value to customers. Over time, they co-evolve their capabilities and roles and tend to align themselves with the directions set by one or more central companies. The vitality of such business ecosystem can be understood from the anthropological analogy of co evolution cited by Gregory Bateson in the book Mind and Nature, He has defined Co evolution as a process in which interdependent species evolve in an endless reciprocal cycle.

There are several benefits of an efficient business ecosystem, to cite a few, strong entry barriers for new competitors as it's not very easy to replicate such strong network of stakeholders, it enables organizations to excel in research and competency, accomplish better collaboration, lowering cost of production, novel ways to address human needs etc.

With growing concern towards environment safety more and more companies are putting effort to include element of sustainability in their business ecosystem, many organizations have started thinking and acting beyond the boundaries of business to incorporate sustainable practices, however, to have a real impact on environment collective action is imperative whereby a group of dynamic businesses work together to build a coherent sustainable solution. Often the crucial concern of environment safety remains unaddressed as companies follow the conventional approach to tackle competition and ever-changing business environment and focus primarily on gaining larger share of the market in usual traditional ways. However, developments and events in the last few years have adequately highlighted the limitations of such traditional approach towards staying competitive and valuable. There is a definite growing shift towards adoption of circular economy model of business eco system as the age old linear economic models are archaic, this transition further deepens the much-needed emphasis on sustainable economic growth which eventually leads to global competitiveness and enable jobs creation. If done in the right way, this model has the potential to significantly reduce the pressure on environment due to economic activities which in turn drives the transition towards a resource efficient way. In India, where a sizeable contribution to economy is made by Micro, Small and Medium Enterprises (MSMEs), it is noteworthy that such small organizations are increasingly trying to develop an ecosystem of stakeholders to sustain and grow their present and future business prospects (Dana, Sharma, & Acharya, 2020)

Circular economy model framework is generated gradually over a period in peace meal and is heavily dependent on innovations.

Unlike traditional economic system which was based on a linear process that begins with the extraction of raw materials from the Earth, continues with their transformation into products, and concludes with their disposal as waste. Circular Economy on the other hand prevents the very generation of trash of any kind. The three pillars of the circular economy:

- Remove all waste and contamination from the environment.
- Distribute goods and materials to those who need them (at their highest value)
- Nature's rebirth or regeneration

In order to support this shift, sustainable energy and materials must be used in an Economy. The use of finite resources is separated from economic activity in a circular economy. As a result, it is a robust system that benefits companies, employees, and the environment as well.

## REVIEW OF LITERATURE

With non-renewable resources depleting and becoming more expensive (EMF, 2015), customers becoming more environmentally conscious, and technological advancements across sectors, geographies, and functions reaching unprecedented heights, an increasing number of organizations are embracing sustainability as an integral part of their business model (Antikainen & Valkokari, 2016).

Sustainability is not a new concept for Indian policy makers and corporates. It was enshrined in the 1950's when the first constitution of independent India came alive by way of social policies. In the subsequent decades, the environment and forest ministries consistently upheld the environment focus in their policies and frameworks. However, post liberalization, when foreign companies and the private sector emerged, GDP growth garnered the major attention of Indian policymakers. These efforts led to reduction in poverty but at the cost of a debilitating impact on the environment. Seven of the 10 most polluted cities in the world are in India. Protected forest lands have been opened up for mining, road and rail construction, oil drilling, pipeline and canal construction. Despite progress on poverty parameter, it still remains a major challenge. According to the United Nations Development Programme's 2018 Multidimensional Poverty Index, a staggering 364 million Indians continue to experience acute deprivations in health, nutrition, schooling, and sanitation. "And inequality has worsened dramatically over time" (Krishna, 2019).

Such grim situations led the Indian Companies Act, 2013 to make corporate social responsibility mandatory for companies operating in India, subject to certain conditions. After all these efforts, the concept of sustainability is not fully realized in India as corporates mostly engage in sustainable practices as a matter of compliance, ignoring the true spirit of such engagements. This is due to a lack of any pressure from the customer side to move the focus towards sustainability.

There is abundant research globally proving the positive impact of firms' sustainable practises on profitability (Naseem, Shahzad, Asim, Rehman, & Nawaz (2020); Tashman, Marano, & Kostova, 2017; Newman, Carol; Rand, John; Tarp, Finn; Trifkovic, Neda, 2020; Hou Liu, Fan, & Wei, 2016; Vázquez & Licandro, 2013 ; Shen & Chang, 2009; Waddock, & Graves, 1997). Though such research is scant in the Indian context, nevertheless the findings of some of the studies on the topic provide evidence of a positive impact of sustainable practices on the profitability of Indian firms as well (Rani & Mann, 2018; Arpita Ghosh, 2013; Mishra & Suar, 2010, Kaur & Singh,2020). Even after such evidence at both global and national level, the importance of sustainable practices as a strong social and economic risk management tool hasn't been well recognized in the Indian setting. There are enough examples of economic risk accruing due to non-sustainable practices—firms like Grasim Pulp and Fiber plant and Reliance Plastic had to close operations because of depleted water table. There are enough instances of social risk as well, emanating due to unfriendly environmental practices, like public demonstrations against Vedanta Sterlite copper plant and Unilever's Mercury plant in 2018 and 2015 respectively.

## Circular Economy: A Solution to Environment, Social and Economic Risks

To mitigate the occurrence and possibility of such debilitating environment, social and in turn economic loss, circular economy is a go to strategy, it eliminates waste, regenerates ecosystems, and reuses products. Decoupling the economy from material flows—improving resource productivity faster than economic growth—is another guide. By integrating tactics across thematic areas, Circle Economy's Key Features Framework (KE) makes circular economy elements salient and serves as a framework for contextual strategies and interventions.

**Core Elements** are Activities directly handling product or material flows; **Enabling Elements** reduce barriers for actors. Prioritize regeneration - Use renewable, reusable, non-toxic materials and energy efficiently. Lifespan -Maintain, repair, and improve in-use resources to maximise their lifetime and provide them a second life through take-back measures when applicable. (Circle Economy, n.d)

Recycle trash-Recover waste streams for reuse and recycling. Business model redesign- Consider ways to create value and align incentives based on product-service interactions. Future-proofing- Use the suitable materials, consider the system's lifespan, and plan for future use. Digitize-Use digital platforms and technology to track and optimise resource use, increase supply chain relationships, and apply circular models. Co-create value-Increase transparency throughout the supply chain, within organisations, and with the public sector and communities. Improve knowledge -Develop research, organise knowledge, encourage innovation networks, and responsibly communicate discoveries.

The definite advantage of circular economy as compared to linear economy is extension of the duration that resources remain in the system. The materials are reused, hence decreasing the extraction of fresh raw materials and minimizing waste. Using the same zinc, copper, etc., it is possible to create a second phone or even many more. The wood from the wooden dining table can be recycled into four side tables and other pieces of furniture. The t-shirt can be used into a tote bag.

Due to the finite nature of Earth's resources, an economy predicated on production, use, and disposal is untenable. In addition, the effects of pollution and waste on climate change make the transition to a circular economy vital. However as not everything can be reused and it might not be resource-efficient, there will be some leakage from the circular economy as well. Therefore, it cannot be either/or, but rather a gradual progression. Joshi and Singh (2017) found that electronic word of mouth has a positive influence as a predictor of purchase intention in the Indian context. Hence, creating awareness and spreading positive word-of-mouth regarding circular economy and sustainable business models deploying the Internet and social media will have far-reaching effects on the top and bottom lines of green enterprises.

Arruda, Melatto, Levy, and Conti (2021) opine that Economic dynamics and development processes have led to global environmental and ecological degradation. They recommend Circular Economy is an excellent tool for sustainable development. Authors explain circular economy from several perspectives by undertaking a thorough qualitative study and systematic literature review. The inclusion criteria for choosing literary texts were scientific papers indexed in Scielo, Science Direct, or Google Scholar;

published in the duration 2015 – 2020; in lingua-franca-English; with at least 100 citations and theme-relevant. The paper presented excerpts of the investigated articles and a comparison of the scientific literature on the topic demonstrating the growth of some components of the Circular Economy, such as the creation of new goods (eco-friendly), emergence of new regulations to stem the rise in environmental degradation and the industry's adoption of the practice. The study urges future research to utilise case studies as a model for evaluating the evolution of Circular Economy particularly considering emergent law and evolving commercial interest.

## OBJECTIVES/ RQ

a) Is the current Business ecosystem sustainable?
b) What are the barriers in creating a sustainable business ecosystem?
c) What are the practices followed by new age business and established players to achieve sustainability?
d) Can circular economy help in making a business system sustainable?

## RESEARCH DESIGN

Qualitative Research design was adopted for collecting data/information by way of tapping secondary data sources such as company websites, periodicals, newspaper articles, journal research papers and interviews of corporate experts from varied fields like Fintech, Pharmaceuticals, using qualitative content analysis the information gleaned from multiple resources was examined. (Hsieh, H.-F., & Shannon, S.E. (2005). The focus was on examining the occurrence of the two chosen terms - Sustainable Business Ecosystem and Circular Economy -within a text or texts, whether or not the terms were explicit.

In the next stage relational analysis was conducted with the aim to go beyond studying existence and investigating the connections between the selected ideas or notions of Sustainable Business Ecosystem and Circular economy. This was more of a semantic analysis (Palmquist, Carley, & Dale, 1997). In other words, relational analysis focus was on identifying semantic or meaningful linkages between the two concepts of Sustainable Business Ecosystem and Circular Economy. Qualitative Researchers believe that individual notions have no intrinsic value. Rather, the meaning of a concept/idea/notion is derived by the interactions between them. Relational analysis is a technique that investigates the connections between identified concepts in a text. This sort of research deploys non-statistical techniques to investigate the links between concepts contained in text collections. Text collections/secondary data for this study included Case studies gleaned from company websites and databases as also Journal Research papers and articles. An analysis and discussion on the secondary data including Case studies pertaining to Start-ups and established players across Industries is being presented in the ensuing section.

## CASES AND DISCUSSION

- **Innovative Practices Followed by Established as Well As Start-Up Organizations To Imbibe Sustainable Business Ecosystems:**

Joshi, Joshi & Pathak(2020) inform Start-up India project has provided Indians with a forum that promotes aspiring entrepreneurs in a variety of fields Unsurprisingly, like many other product categories and business spaces, most of the innovative and transformational ideas for sustainability also emanate from new age sustainability driven eco- entrepreneurs and startups. They are supported by multiple sustainability-driven business ecosystems.

A few such start-ups are Kisan Hub, committed towards the reduction of food waste; Freightfox, which with the help of technology and analytics is trying to integrate a cost-effective, efficient, and future-ready logistics system; Plastic for Change is working towards the reduction of plastic waste; Erthos is into designing and developing alternate packaging materials to reduce plastic consumption. These start-ups are aided by the 100+ Accelerator programme supported by veteran organisations like AB InBev, The Coca-Cola Company, Colgate-Palmolive, and Unilever. The incubator programme supports the funding and pilot launch, hence ensuring access to funds and scalability to organisations that are working towards sustainable supply chain management.

Several other start-ups, like Waste Ventures, Invest in Clean Technology Firms. JITO Angel Network has funded Nexus Power, which manufactures batteries from crop residue. ZunRoof, a Gurgaon-based home start-up, provides solar energy, and Phool. Co is a flower recycling technology start-up that uses flower waste to make luxury fragrance products. All these innovations and the support by established conglomerates are providing a much-needed boost to the creation of a sustainable business ecosystem for the startups.

Similarly, Circular economics is being adopted by some of the world's greatest corporations in order to capture new values, improve resilience and meet social and environmental goals. A few businesses have made a firm commitment to moving toward a circular economy and have begun providing products and services to aid in that process. Few case studies of organizations following sustainable practices through circular economy are listed below;

## CASE STUDIES OF ESTABLISHED ORGANIZATIONS

### Royal Philips (Healthcare Equipment's)

Philips' size and scope make it well-suited to drive a circular healthcare business. The company uses product-as-a-service, take-back programmes, and upgrading and refurbishment to implement circular economy ideas. Philips' goal appears to be to remove the link between expansion and finite resource consumption. The company embeds circularity in its DNA, empowers all employees to contribute, and incorporates it into its products and solutions. Philips also works with various environmental groups on sustainability agenda. The firm is expanding its circularity through product design, business model innovation, and deployment of digital and new tech. Philips' circular transition includes closing equipment loopholes by taking up repair of customers' used medical equipment.

Digital devices and services are used owing to their potential for minimizing emissions and material consumption by enabling remote patient-caregiver communication or extending equipment life through upgrades and predictive maintenance. Resource-intensive and wasteful healthcare delivery components are common in Healthcare Segment. Each hospital bed creates 13 kg of garbage daily, of which 15 to 25% is toxic.

Circular innovation can help the global healthcare industry develop solutions that improve patient outcomes and access to care while saving the environment. Philips believes a circular economy benefits customer, but a more efficient supply chain may boost quality and performance. Hence adoption of Circular Economy is helping Philips to build a sustainable business Ecosystem.

Circular economy can benefit Philips in three ways.

- Gaining a competitive advantage and long-term value as more customers consider the environment.
- Product-as-a-service, take-back, and upgrade programs build client relationships and encourage recurring business.
- Less raw material utilization reduces business costs.

## Case Study: H&M (Clothing and Fashion)

H&M Group -Clothes & Fashion major from Sweden- says a linear economic system's inefficient and polluting fashion paradigm must be altered. H&M Group plans to become climate-positive and circular by 2040. Several H&M stores collect clothes and materials. Any brand and condition are accepted. 50-60% of discarded textiles are reused. Most remnants become insulation or cleaning cloths.

H&M Group's circular economy and climate-positive aims inspired a 'circular environment' approach. This strategy promotes climate and biodiversity and tackles water insecurity. H&M's 'circular environment' idea has three pillars: Circular items are made with recyclable, non-hazardous, eco-friendly materials that can be reused. Circular supply networks recycle products, processes, and materials. Circular consumer travels allow participants to experience circular fashion, in which products are used more often, repaired, reused, and recycled. H&M's initiatives to incorporate industry stakeholders widen its supply chain reform. H&M's external supply chain programme. Treadler (B2B Supply chain partner) allows non-H&M Group enterprises to use H&M's circular supply chain, accelerating their own circular transformation. H&M wants to improve its supply chain and fashion industry. H&M Group is investigating strategies to suit shifting consumer demands (e.g., environmentally conscious purchasing) while reducing climate, water, and waste. H&M wants 100% recycled or sustainably sourced goods by 2030. The corporation plans to recycle 30% by 2025. Thus H& M is taking enormous strides for sustainable business ecosystem.

## HUL has Clearly Articulated its Commitment to a "Waste-Free Future"

"The plastics problem is too big for us to solve alone. A movement to a circular economy approach for plastics requires system-level change, beyond our industry. That is why we are working with governments to support development of waste infrastructure. We want to make sure the systems our products flow into are robust, and ideally, circular." FMCG major has successfully partnered with the United Nations Development Programme (UNDP), and Xynteo (business consulting firm helping clients grapple with environment and social challenges) for end-to-end waste management projects in India's financial capital-Mumbai, "right from collection, to segregation and recycling" HUL is invested in recycling and reusing of packaging as well as "waste free manufacturing" (Hindustan Unilever Limited, n.d)

### Mahindra Group Website (2022) Proclaims Concerted Effort to Achieve Zero Trash to Landfill

Indian Automobile major, Mahindra writes Mahindra.com (2022) "The Circular economy will be key for the economic development of India, especially in light of the fact that the world faces resource constraints." It adds that "Virgin material mining" is bad for the environment, and soon we will have plenty of resources without having to mine for them. The matter of reverse logistics can be dealt with by enlisting the assistance of the informal economy, which is already a part of the ecosystem. This would be highly beneficial for the country and the industry. Mahindra encourages employees, vendors and suppliers to incorporate sustainability and reduce waste and energy consumption and focus on enhancing biodiversity. (Mahindra Rise, 2020)

The cornerstone of **Birla Carbon's (Aaditya Birla Group, 2022) success strategy is its commitment to sustainability.** As the industry leader in carbon black production, the company strives to disconnect economic activity from the consumption of natural resources and eliminate excess waste from the system. 75% of the company's plants are net energy positive, 100% of its sites use recycled process water or rainfall in their operations, and 60% of the company's material waste is repurposed. (Aditya Birla Group, n.d)

## CASE STUDIES OF INDIAN STARTUP ORGANIZATIONS

A 2016 World Bank report estimates that India would be one of the countries with the biggest garbage output by the year 2050, with yearly trash production of 543.3 million tons, up from 387.8 million tons in 2030. If businesses in India adopt circular economy practices, they may be able to avoid contributing to the country's waste problem, which would have significant positive consequences for the environment. By adopting circular strategies for products like electronics, plastics, textiles, and food, India may be able to reduce its contribution to global warming.

## WASTE VENTURES INDIA

By altering solid waste management paradigms, Waste Ventures India, a for-profit social enterprise based in Telangana, is increasing the value for all stakeholders along the value chain. The startup asserts that it may reduce trash in a given gated community or business by up to 90 percent while leaving a green impact. Its R&D group has devised a scientific, fly-free, and odourless method for consolidating organic waste. Local community members are gaining a better understanding of recycling, composting, and other eco-friendly practices as a result of the waste management education being disseminated during the collection of ground debris. It is one of the first startups in Hyderabad to offer a digital doorstep recycling pickup service. Since late 2013, the firm has prevented approximately 3000 tonnes of garbage from entering Indian dumpsites.

## Nexus Power

Utilizing nanotechnology, Nexus Power develops biodegradable electric vehicle batteries from crop residue. The company manufactures rechargeable energy-storage cells from one of the most significant causes of air pollution, unburned crops, by employing a unique extraction and filtration technology. These cells are afterwards installed in electric vehicles since they are employed to create the sensor-enabled IoT and AI-based battery pack.

## ZunRoof

A residential solar startup- founded in 2016 at Gurugram, develops next-generation solar and IoT energy technology. In India, it boasts 10,000 rooftop solar installations and 30,000 system designs. The five-year-old firm claims to have saved INR 50 crore in electricity costs. Godrej family office, Intellicap Investment Network, and IIT Kharagpur alumni fund the startup.

## Phool.Co

By recycling floral waste into luxury fragrance products with charcoal, Phool.Co promotes the circular economy. They gather waste flowers from Uttar Pradesh temples and mosques, keeping 7600 kilogrammes of flowers and 97 kg of chemicals from entering the river daily. Rural women's self-help groups recycle flowers into organic fertiliser and fragrance sticks.

## Binbag Recycling

Established in 2014 by Achitra Borgohain, Bangalore Headquartered, Binbag utilizes technical know-how "to collect and recycle" electronic garbage. Their two plants are situated in Andhra Pradesh and Assam to recycle air conditioners, computer-hardware, and mobile devices among other items.

## Namo e-Waste Management

Namo e-waste is a company that was founded in 2014 by the entrepreneur Akshay Jain and has its headquarters in Faridabad, in the state of Haryana. The company is in the business of pulling out metals from electronic-waste and separating hazardous chemicals from garbage. The foundries that specialise in casting the metals and polymers receive the "recovered metals and plastics." For instance, the aluminum that is salvaged from old refrigerators is repurposed into secondary aluminum, which is then used in the manufacturing of automobiles. (Change Started,2021)

## Attero Recycling Services

Recognized as the first player in the e-waste circular economy segment in India, Attero - founded by Rajat Vishnoi -was started all the way back in 2008 in the Noida, UP area and specialises in full-cycle e-waste recycling as well as metal extraction. With its network presence Pan India, the company's value chain connects garbage pickers, aggregators, customers, and manufacturers. (Change started,2021)

## Recykal

Founded in 2017 by 3 partners namely, Abhay Deshpande, Vikram Prabakar, and Nitin Padawar Recykal operates out of the state capital of Telangana- Hyderabad. "Recykal is an end-to-end waste management company that use technology to link garbage providers, processors, recyclers, and brand owners." (Change started,2021)

## Saahas

Wilma Rodrigues founded Saahas in 2001 to encourage trash management principles. "Saahas manages two distinct organisations: Saahas and Saahas Zero Waste".(Saahaszerowaste.com, n.d) Saahas Zero Garbage works with enterprises, residential complexes, educational institutions, hotels, and other bulk waste generators. The abandoned debris is then transformed into roofing sheets, clipboards, stationery, repurposed textile goods, and so on.

## Twirl.Store

Established in 2017 by Sujata Chatterjee, Twirl.store in Kolkata enables individuals to sell their old clothing, which is repaired and given a new look by the Twirl crew. The repurposed garments might be sold back to the consumer, donated, or sold separately.

## The Clothes Box Foundation (CBF)

It is a not-for profit(NPO) organization that provides clothing to those in need. The clothes that are in decent shape are sorted, separated, and dry-cleaned prior to distribution by the Clothes Box Foundation. (Invest India,2021)

The cases enumerated above highlight the attempts made by firms -across formats, sectors and consumer segments served- to embed circular economy in their operations and product and service offerings as also their efforts to contribute in the direction of Sustainable Business Ecosystem.

## Role of Leadership for Sustainable Business Ecosystem

The Global Compact Network India, one of the leading corporate sustainability efforts in India, conducted a study of Indian executives and found that "Indian business leaders are focused mostly on regulatory compliance, not fundamental sustainability." It should not come as a surprise that this is the case given that ninety percent of CEOs polled stated that they are under no pressure whatsoever from investors to move the needle on sustainability. For India to achieve quick development, pressure would need to be increased, and it will need to come from all directions.

The biggest challenge for most organisations in today's rapidly changing business scenario is to remain relevant. They need to continuously change, adapt, unlearn, re-learn, and self-disrupt to keep up with the ever-evolving business environment. This requires an immense amount of agility, but the irony of the situation is that organisations are hard wired and designed for stability. To serve this purpose, people, policies, processes, and functions are organised in a zero-deviance way.

Mostly, leaders in various organisations are trained and expected to ensure consistency and stability in operations and processes. So the big question is, how do leaders ensure adaptability of the organisation so that it remains relevant to the requirements of the changing business world? The answer is being provided by Bien & Arena, 2018. They say, the answer is not to abandon stability but to manage stability and disruption simultaneously, this may be termed as Stablerupting. Leaders, in a rapidly changing business world, need to pursue both short-term stability and long-term innovation (disruption). This would require creativity, energy, and tenacity. "Becoming a leader who adeptly drives both stability and disruption is the key to ensuring performance for today (Aldieri et al., 2021) while at the same time unleashing innovation for tomorrow" (Winn, Brad 2020). Another major challenge to embrace sustainable business eco system is lack of talent management which is specially true for MSME sector. Since the firms are smaller in size with stakeholder viz. partners, suppliers and customers spread far and wide, managing human resource to plan and execute such sustainable ecosystem is quite a challenge. (Dana, Sharma, & Singh, 2022)

## MAJOR FINDINGS

After in depth analysis of available literature it was deduced that the popularity and acceptance of Moore's concept of business ecosystem with both established and new age firms like Apple, Facebook, Maruti Suzuki, Tata Motors, and Reliance Industries, phool.co, Zunroof, Twirl stores, etc. is increasing, the organizations are increasingly conceiving their products and services as part of an ecosystem and not just confined to the narrow concept of self-contained organizations,

Some of the major barriers to creating sustainable business ecosystem as explained by BCG Henderson Institute are Fragmented Supply, Fragmented demand, Lack of Trust, Lack of co-innovation and lack of coordination among player. Fragmented supply, as 33.4% of India's manufacturing output and 45% of overall exports from India come from MSMEs (CII, 2022) and these MSMEs are highly fragmented hence adopting sustainable practices across different stakeholders of these MSMEs is a challenge (Arabeche et al., 2022; Shaikh et al., 2022); Fragmented demand, as India's per capita real private final consumption reached its 3 years low to Rs.55,783/ in 1920-21 (Swamy, 2021); Lack of trust among various inter connected organizations in the business ecosystem; Difficulty to co-innovate with and co-ordinate across different players, since suppliers are fragmented.

The extant survey enshrined that more and more startups and established organizations while working on the principles of Reduce, Reuse and Recycle are coming up with innovative practices to attain sustainable business eco system (Erum et al.2022). In our study we have given several examples of established conglomerates like Amazon, Visa, H&M etc. and shared case studies of various organizations including new age startups like clothes box foundation (CBF), Saahas, Recykal that are using powerful ecosystems of omnichannel players, payment platforms, suppliers, supply chain Partners, various eco-friendly techniques of recycling the finished goods, reusing raw material to attain a competitive edge over their counterparts, more and more companies are exploring ways to imbibe sustainability and planet protection elements while designing and developing robust business ecosystems (Tunio et al., 2021), the literature survey also highlighted the indispensability of agile leadership for embracing sustainability.

Review of related literature also revealed the lack of clear understanding about How to incorporate sustainable (Hamrouni et al. 2021) business ecosystem in their existing business model?

Young and Gerard (2021) through their study attempted to answer this burgeoning question, they proposed four steps to attain competitive advantage through a sustainable business model. The steps are as below:

### Wider and More Inclusive Outlook Towards the Business Canvas

The first step to developing a sustainable business model is to identify the stakeholders, environmental and social issues, and other factors that might affect the business ecosystem. This step will throw light on the impact of several micro and macroeconomic factors on the business ecosystem. The analysis will help in understanding the pool of business opportunities and threats related to environmental and societal issues.

### Innovation is Key to Resilient Business Model

The first step would be to highlight the opportunity spaces for both financial and societal values. At the second stage, the prevailing business model should be reimagined to incorporate changes so as to seize the opportunities. The business model should either be transformed or a new business model would be required so as to innovate and develop new facets of the business model that would be financially, socially, and environmentally advantageous.

### Testing and Refinement of Business Model Developed at Second Stage

At the third stage, it is advised by Young & Gerard that the business model developed at the second stage needs to be tested, repeated, and refined further. This is required to ensure that social, environmental, and financial benefits are duly embedded in the business model. Financial benefit, along with social and environmental benefits, is paramount as an organisation with low profits won't be able to support research and development required for social and environmental causes.

### Scale the Initiative

The real advantage of such sustainable business model is attained only when it is not limited to an individual or few members of the business ecosystem but scales to engage people in the company, across supply chain, in the company's wider network and overall ecosystem. This scaling can be achieved through partnership with other organizations either in or across industries enabling partnering organizations to pool resources, fill capability gaps and explore new markets.

## CONCLUSION

*"The circular economy, which promotes the elimination of waste and the continued safe use of natural resources, offers an alternative that can yield up to $4.5 trillion in economic benefits by 2030".* – World Economic Forum

Due to the increased traction that sustainability has garnered, increasingly organizations are trying to imbibe the concept of sustainability in their business eco system. Businesses have evolved from focusing primarily on shareholder wealth maximization to now when focus is on more intangible assets like ESG and GRI (Global Reporting Initiative), Ministry of corporate affairs has made BRSR (Business Responsibility and Sustainability Report) mandatory. Development from regulatory perspective is assuring however there is need to move from regulatory compliance to core sustainability, beyond continued government push via incentives and punitive actions there is need for involvement of private sector, researchers and academia to develop new technologies related to green, renewable and sustainable energy, it is important to create awareness at general population level through the involvement & support of media, civil society, NGOs academic institutes in shaping the public support. Kalaari Capital predicts India's circular economy could reach $45 billion by 2030. Adopting circular economy practices might save India $624 billion by 2050 in food, agriculture, infrastructure, and mobility (livemint.com, 22 April 2022).

The move towards sustainability through circular economy is indispensable for India, where a large population stresses resources, impact of climate change is being felt across the nation (Tunio et al., 2021) with temperature soaring over 50 degrees Celsius, making many regions uninhabitable and conditions are set to worsen. This directly impacts not just individuals but also business operations and increases their risk profile unfavorably

## MANAGERIAL IMPLICATIONS

The study is a guide to business organizations to expand their horizon of strategic planning and imbibe sustainability as a core principle through the practice of sustainable business ecosystem. Advocacy and adoption of concept of circular economy has immense benefits for corporates. It is an established fact that a sustainable business ecosystem is not just a strong competitive strategy, it also serves as an efficient mode to mitigate economic, social and environmental risk. Such ecosystems are highly conducive to drive sustainable goals as sustainability can be achieved only through collective participation of interrelated organizations. Such results have higher implications for the business organizations from developing countries, as in such economies there is a major transition towards sustainability from the traditional approach where profit maximization was paramount objective.

## REFERENCES

Aditya Birla Group. (n.d) *Designed for circularity – Stories*. Aditya Birla Group. https://www.adityabirla.com/media/stories/designed-for-circularity

Aldieri, L., Brahmi, M., Bruno, B., & Vinci, C. P. (2021). Circular Economy Business Models: The Complementarities with Sharing Economy and Eco-Innovations Investments. *Sustainability*, *13*(22), 12438. doi:10.3390u132212438

Antikainen, M., & Valkokari, K. (2016). A framework for sustainable circular business model innovation. *Technology Innovation Management Review*, *6*(7).

Arabeche, Z., Soudani, A., Brahmi, M., Aldieri, L., Vinci, C. P., & Abdelli, M. E. A. (2022). Entrepreneurial Orientation, Organizational Culture and Business Performance in SMEs: Evidence from Emerging Economy. *Sustainability*, *14*(9), 5160. doi:10.3390u14095160

Arruda, E. H. Melatto, R., Levy, W., & de Melo. C. D. (2021) Circular economy: A brief literature review (2015–2020). *Science Direct.* https://www.sciencedirect.com/science/article/pii/S2666412721000167)

Change started. (2021). Year in Review – 11 Indian Green Startups Working for the Climate. *Change Started.* https://changestarted.com/year-end-round-up-10-indian-green-startups-working-for-the-climate/

Circle Economy. (n.d.). The Key Elements Of The Circular Economy Framework A Comprehensive Landscape Of Circular Economy. *Circle Economy.* https://www.circle-economy.com/resources/the-key-elements-of-the-circular-economy- framework#:~:text=The%20principles%20of%20a%20circular,guide%20%5B8%5D%5B9%5D

Circle Economy. (n.d.). Trade and Environment. *Circle Economy.* https://unctad.org/topic/trade-and-environment/circular-economy#:~:text=A%20circular%20economy%20entails%20markets,economy%20or%20used%20more%20efficiently

Circular economy. (2022). A $45 billion opportunity by 2030 in India: report *Live Mint.* https://www.livemint.com/news/india/circular-economy-a-45-billion-opportunity-by-2030-in-india-report-11650628743418.html

Dana, L. P., Sharma, N., & Acharya, S. R. (Eds.). (2020). *Organizing entrepreneurship and MSMEs across India* (Vol. 11). World Scientific.

Dana, L. P., Sharma, N., & Singh, V. K. (Eds.). (2022). *Managing Human Resources in SMEs and Start-ups: International Challenges and Solutions* (Vol. 5). World Scientific. doi:10.1142/12341

Ellen MacArthur Foundation. (2015). *Circularity Indicators Project.* Ellen MacArthur Foundation. https://www.ellenmacarthurfoundation.org/programmes/insight/circularity-indicators

Erum, S.; Muhammad, N T.; Wali Muhammad, K.; Mohsen, B.; & Shahid, R., Chapter 16: The COVID-19 Pandemic Overlaps Entrepreneurial Activities and Triggered New Challenges: A Review Study, Book chapter: Managing Human Resources in SMEs and Start-ups, August 2022, 388 p. https://doi.org/doi:10.1142/9789811239212_0008

Fiksel, J., Sanjay, P., & Raman, K. (2021). Steps toward a resilient circular economy in India. *Clean Technologies and Environmental Policy*, *23*(1), 203–218. doi:10.100710098-020-01982-0 PMID:33199980

Ghosh, A. (2013). Corporate sustainability and corporate financial performance: the Indian context.2013 Hindustan Unilever Limited. *Waste free world.* https://www.hul.co.in/

Hamrouni, B., Bourouis, A., Korichi, A., & Brahmi, M. (2021). Explainable Ontology-Based Intelligent Decision Support System for Business Model Design and Sustainability. *Sustainability*, *13*(17), 9819. doi:10.3390u13179819

Hou, M., Liu, H., Fan, P., & Wei, Z. (2016, March). Does CSR practice pay off in East Asian firms? A meta-analytic investigation. *Asia Pacific Journal of Management*, *33*(1), 195–228. doi:10.100710490-015-9431-2

Hsieh, H.-F., & Shannon, S. E. (2005). Three Approaches to Qualitative Content Analysis. *Qualitative Health Research, 15*(9), 1277–1288. doi:10.1177/1049732305276687 PMID:16204405

Invest India. (2021). India's Sustainable Start-ups. Invest India, National Investment Promotion and Facilitation Agency. https://www.investindia.gov.in/siru/indias-sustainable-start-ups

Joshi, M., Joshi, G., & Pathak, S. (2020). Awareness, entrepreneurial event theory and theory of planned behaviour as antecedents of student entrepreneurial intentions: An Indian perspective. *International Journal of Business and Globalisation, 25*(2), 170–184. doi:10.1504/IJBG.2020.107885

Joshi, M., & Singh, V. K. (2017, July-December).. . *Electronic Word of Mouth and Influence on Consumer Purchase Intention Dynamics of Public Administration, 34*(2), 149–159. doi:10.5958/0976-0733.2017.00012.8

Kaur, N., & Singh, V. (2020). Empirically examining the impact of corporate social responsibility on financial performance: Evidence from Indian steel industry. *Asian Journal of Accounting Research., 2020*(Dec), 15.

Krishnan, D. (2019, September 11) *Making Indian businesses sustainable*. Strategy Business. https://www.strategy-business.com/article/Making-Indian-businesses-sustainable

Mishra, S., & Suar, D. (2010, September). Does corporate social responsibility influence firm performance of Indian companies? *Journal of Business Ethics, 95*(4), 571–601. doi:10.100710551-010-0441-1

Mohan, V. (2022). Delhi, Kol most polluted cities globally by PM2.5, Says Study. *Times of India.*

Naseem, T., Shahzad, F., Asim, G. A., Rehman, I. U., & Nawaz, F. (2020, March). Corporate social responsibility engagement and firm performance in Asia Pacific: The role of enterprise risk management. *Corporate Social Responsibility and Environmental Management, 27*(2), 501–513. doi:10.1002/csr.1815

Newman, C., Rand, J., Tarp, F., & Trifkovic, N. (2020, August 2). Corporate social responsibility in a competitive business environment. *The Journal of Development Studies, 56*(8), 1455–1472. doi:10.1080/00220388.2019.1694144

Palmquist, M. E., Carley, K. M., & Dale, T. A. (1997). Two applications of automated text analysis: Analyzing literary and non-literary texts. In C. Roberts (Ed.), *Text Analysis for the Social Sciences: Methods for Drawing Statistical Inferences from Texts and Transcripts*. Lawrence Erlbaum Associates.

Rani P, Mann VK. (2018) The Impact of Ethical and Philanthropic Component of CSR on Financial Performance: A Panel Data Study of BSE 500 Companies. *IUP Journal of Corporate Governance, 1;17*(4).

Rise, M. (2020, May 28) The Time For Sustainability Has Come. *Mahindra.* https://www.mahindra.com/news-room/knowledge-centre/impact-stories/the-time-for-sustainability-has-come

Saahas Zero Waste (n.d). About us. *Saahas Zero Waste.* https://saahaszerowaste.com/ /about-us/

Shen, C. H., & Chang, Y. (2009, April). Ambition versus conscience, does corporate social responsibility pay off? The application of matching methods. *Journal of Business Ethics, 88*(1), 133–153. doi:10.100710551-008-9826-9

Swamy, M. (2021). Per capita consumption expenditure regresses by 3 years. *CMIE*. https://cmie.com/kommon/bin/sr.php?kall=warticle&dt=20210605142154&msec=730#:~:text=India's%20private%20final%20consumption%20expenditure,123.1%20trillion%20in%202019%2D20

Sunkar, A., Lakspriyanti, A. P., Haryono, E., Brahmi, M., Setiawan, P., & Jaya, A. F. (2022). Geotourism Hazards and Carrying Capacity in Geosites of Sangkulirang-Mangkalihat Karst, Indonesia. *Sustainability*, *14*(3), 1704. doi:10.3390u14031704

Tashman, P., Marano, V., & Kostova, T. (2017) Talking the talk and walking the walk: CSR reporting and CSP of emerging market multinationals. In Academy of Management Proceedings 2017 (Vol. 2017, No. 1, p. 11183). Briarcliff Manor, Academy of Management.

Tunio, M. N., Jariko, M. A., Børsen, T., Shaikh, S., Mushtaque, T., & Brahmi, M. (2021). How Entrepreneurship Sustains Barriers in the Entrepreneurial Process—A Lesson from a Developing Nation. *Sustainability*, *13*(20), 11419. doi:10.3390u132011419

Tunio, M. N., Chaudhry, I. S., Shaikh, S., Jariko, M. A., & Brahmi, M. (2021). Determinants of the Sustainable Entrepreneurial Engagement of Youth in Developing Country—An Empirical Evidence from Pakistan. *Sustainability*, *13*(14), 7764. doi:10.3390u13147764

Uhl-Bien, M., & Arena, M. (2018). Leadership for organizational adaptability: A theoretical synthesis and integrative framework. *The Leadership Quarterly*, *29*(1), 89–104. doi:10.1016/j.leaqua.2017.12.009

Vázquez, J. L., Lanero, A., & Licandro, O. (2013, October). The added value of corporate social responsibility. Some insights from a research in Uruguay. *International Review on Public and Nonprofit Marketing*, *10*(3), 187–200. doi:10.100712208-013-0099-3

Waddock, S. A., & Graves, S. B. (1997, April). The corporate social performance–financial performance link. *Strategic Management Journal*, *18*(4), 303–319. doi:10.1002/(SICI)1097-0266(199704)18:4<303::AID-SMJ869>3.0.CO;2-G

*What is Circular Economy and Linear Economy?* (2021) Changestarted.com. https://changestarted.com/circular-economy-why-is-it-better-than-linear-economy/

Winn, B. (2020,March 26) Driving Stability & Disruption: How Stablerupting Leaders Unleash Innovation. *Huntsman.* https://huntsman.usu.edu/mba/management-minute/articles/leaders-status-quo

Young, D., Reeves, M., & Gerard, M. (2021) *The Secrets of Sustainability Front-Runners.* BCG. https://www.bcg.com/publications/2021/keys-to-being-a-leader-in-sustainable-business-model-innovation

# Chapter 14
# The Impact of Financial Technology on Profitability for Banks

**Abdel Rahman Mohamed Rashwan**
*University College of Science and Technology, Palestine*

**Zeinab Abd-Elhafiz Ahmed Kassem**
https://orcid.org/0000-0002-9311-2794
*Faculty of Business, Ain Shams University, Egypt*

## ABSTRACT

*The study aims to investigate the impact of the use of financial technology (FINTECH) on the profitability of banks; indicate the impact of using FINTECH to increase the quality of bank's services to provided customers; and clarify the impact of use on raising the operational efficiency of banks. The results of the study found that the use of financial technology in banks facilitates the procedures for securing the necessary financing for customers, and activating electronic services such as credit card payments, mobile phone technology, and other electronic services. FINTECH increases competition in banks by reducing barriers to entry for new products to the market. Banks use FINTECH to achieve efficient results in terms of reducing costs, increasing revenue growth, reducing risks, raising operational efficiency, and increasing profitability.*

## INTRODUCTION

Digital development is one of the most important pillars of the future of the financial and banking sector, as customers are increasingly moving towards carrying out their banking transactions through electronic applications and smart solutions. FINTECH has a real ability to change the structure of traditional financial services, as financial technology can make financial services faster, cheaper, safer, transparent, and available, as the speed of development in FINTECH services and emerging companies that provide innovative financial solutions that mimic what they offer. Banking sectors and simplify banking op-

DOI: 10.4018/978-1-6684-6766-4.ch014

erations, constitutes a threat that must be hedged and take all precautionary measures that achieve the safety, integrity and stability of the banking and financial sector and its various applications represent opportunities and challenges at the same time for banks and financial institutions.

Where FINTECH is considered one of the most important inventions and modern technological innovations in the field of the financial sector, these inventions include a set of digital programs that are used in the financial operations of banks, including transactions with customers' financial services. Such as, money transfer, currency exchange, calculations of interest rates and profits, knowing the expected profits for investments, and so on. Of banking operations.

FINTECH also constituted a great opportunity for the banking system through the advanced electronic systems and programs that helped banks develop and improve their performance and increased their efficiency in services and transactions. It also became the key to success and distinction for these banks. It constitutes a new way for this banking system to help it become more familiar with its products and services, and therefore it is an urgent necessity and a strategic policy for these banks that must give their right to further progress and successes to the banking system.

Although the uses of FINTECH included a limited number of services such as: Internet payment, phone banking services and others, these banks were able to introduce their products and improve their services through their work with financial technology. This technology has also contributed to increasing the efficiency and profitability of these banks.

Fin-tech is a technological innovation used in the financial services sector. Regarding the application of financial technology, fin-tech products are a system designed to carry out certain financial transaction procedures. Payment systems, market support, investment and risk management, loans, financing and capital provision, and financial services are the categories into which the regulator subdivides fin-tech. Fintech uses the Internet and cards to make transactions simpler. Finch affects the effectiveness of banks in payment, clearing, and settlement systems.

## PROBLEM OF THE STUDY

Over the past few years, the FINTECH sector has revolutionized the global financial systems, as companies in the field FINTECH. It has succeeded in providing a variety of banking financial services to banks, including payments services, digital currencies, money transfer, as well as lending, financing and wealth management, which casts a shadow on the future of traditional financial services. Therefore, banks are seeking to introduce some changes in their business models by expanding the adoption in their infrastructure, to improve their competitiveness and increase reliance on modern FINTECH in providing financial services with high efficiency.

The main motive for writing this modest study was to accurately understand the importance of the emergence of FINTECH in the field of banking services, as banks face intense competition in light of rapid technological progress striving to seize opportunities in the financial services market, and based on the above, the study questions can be formulated as follows:

The main question:

- Is there an impact of the use of FINTECH on the profitability of banks?

The following sub-questions are derived from the main question:

- Is there any effect of using FINTECH on increasing the quality of the bank's services provided to customers?
- Is there an impact of the use of financial technology FINTECH on raising the operational efficiency of banks?

## OBJECTIVES OF THE STUDY

The primary objective of the research is to determine how the implementation of FINTECH affects the profitability of banks. To accomplish this goal, the study can develop a set of the following sub-objectives: Clarify the impact of using FINTECH on improving the quality of the services the Bank provides to customers.

## IMPORTANCE OF THE STUDY

The importance of the study is based on the role of the banking system and its impact on the state's economy, it is important and effective role in society, and interest in the issue of the use of financial technology in general. Given the role of financial technology in accelerating the system and working mechanisms in order to increase the quality of services provided to customers, and raise operational efficiency as conscious banks operate efficiently as part of their primary work to increase profitability, researchers and professionals understand the importance of banks and thus the importance of FINTECH.

## LITERATURE REVIEW

### Study (Njogu, 2014)

The study aimed to measure the impact of electronic banking services on the profitability of Kenyan commercial banks. Data were collected from the Central Bank of Kenya and commercial banks. A regression analysis was conducted to determine the effects of electronic banking services on the profitability of commercial banks in Kenya by measuring the relationship between the application of modern electronic services and the cost of services. Modern electronics and the speed of completion of tasks and between the rate of return on assets and the rate of return on the owner's property rights during the period from 2008 to 2013. The study found a positive relationship between the application of electronic banking services and profitability indicators represented in the rate of return. the rate of return on assets and the rate of return on rights to Al-Asid property, and that there is a significant relationship between the cost of providing services, and the profitability of banks, and that there is a significant relationship between the speed of completion of electronic banking services and profitability rates.

## Study (Sheikh & Muhammad, 2015)

This study aimed to identify the extent of the availability of controls over the application of electronic accounting information systems with its three axes, and its impact on the quality of profits in Palestinian banks. In addition, that the Palestinian banks under study have high quality profits, and the study recommended the necessity of activating the role of the Palestinian Monetary Authority in supervising banks and obligating them to control systems for accounting information systems applications and their application to obtain high-quality profits.

## Study (Wu & Wang, 2020)

This study aimed to examine the relationship between the profitability of commercial banks and business cycles in China using a panel data analysis method that dealt with the rate of return on assets, loan growth rate, non-performing loans ratio, and net interest margin for 34 commercial banks listed from (2001) to (2018) as variables. As well as, the GDP growth rate, unemployment rate, and industry value added growth rate in China from (2001 to 2018). As indicators of business cycles, and the results of the study concluded that business cycles have a negative impact on the profitability of commercial banks in China based on the result of the conclusions. The study also showed a positive impact of business cycles on the profitability of commercial banks from the perspective of the loan, the net interest spread. The results of the study recommended the need to conduct further research on the factors that affect the profitability of banks in addition to the factors those Affect business cycles that have a bearing on the profitability of commercial banks.

## Study (Amariah, Bakhti. Ghania, & Majan, 2020)

The study aimed to shed light on the basic concepts about financial technology, as an introduction to the subject. then the study will analyze the role of financial technology companies in developing and supporting the banking sector, and the results of the study concluded that financial technology contributes to the development of financial services, and that the development of electronic financial services includes money transfer, payments and borrowing and insurance, and the study recommends the need for financial technology companies to participate with banks in order to maintain customers' confidence in banks on the one hand and on the other hand reduce the risks resulting from the lack of controls over FINTECH companies and thus there is an integration to support the growth of the banking sector in addition to ensuring its stability.

## Study (Broby, 2021)

This study aimed to create an analytical framework to describe the banking business model. It is based on the classical theory of banking and the literature on financial technology. The study also reviews the options that existing banks must consider in order mitigating the threat to their profitability. Where deposit and lending are taken into account in the context of the challenge posed by digital banks. This study also contributes to understanding the future of banking, and then the study discussed four possible strategies for market participants, (1) customer retention, (2) customer acquisition, (3) banking as a service, and (4) social media payment. The results showed that the use of financial technology would maintain confidence in banking services. However, transfer of liquidity will continue to play an important role, and banks face several challenges, including balance sheet risk.

### Study (Dur & Aljughaiman, 2021)

The study aimed to find out the impact of FINTECH services provided by banks on their financial performance, and to analyze the verification of the differences between conventional banks (CBs) and Islamic banks (IBs) in this relationship. The study used a sample of 40 listed banks from the Gulf Co-operation Council countries, where the use of FINTECH was impressive. In the period 2014-2019. The results of the study showed a negative relationship between FINTECH services and the performance of banks for both types of banks. Moreover, we show that the growth of FINTECH companies in a country negatively affects the financial performance of central banks.

### Study (Piotrowski., 2022)

The study aimed to determine the bank's activities that customers consider ethical and to what extent they affect the ethics perceived by the consumer, using electronic services and artificial intelligence technology. The results showed that FINTECH improves the quality of banking services and has a significant positive impact on consumers' moral perception of banks in Poland. It also negatively affects the use of financial advisory services and banks' manipulation of information about financial products on the perceived ethics of consumers, as well as having a positive impact on consumer confidence, satisfaction and loyalty.

### Study (Wang, Yini, & Nor, (2022))

The purpose of this research is to examine how finch innovation and profits affect traditional banks. Design/methodology/approach: To determine how finch in China is influencing traditional banks' revenue, a quantitative analysis methodology is used. Findings: According to the study, the finch index significantly increases the net assets of conventional banks. By expanding the use of finch, conventional banks' profitability may essentially be refined. Constraints and implications of the research this essay uses primarily quantitative analytical approaches. The main source of the data is the financial statements of this study demonstrates how traditional banks can increase their profits through Internet finance. Therefore, banks can boost operating earnings by using financial technology. The major purpose of this essay is to serve as a guide for banks as they change Internet finance. The number of technology workers, the growth rate of automated machines, and the rate at which electronic banking is substituting for traditional banking are all factors in the financial technology model built in this article.

## COMMENTING ON PREVIOUS STUDIES

The differences between the current chapter and previous studies:

Previous studies dealt with discussing the topic of "the role of using FINTECH on the profitability of banks", but they focused on studying the reality of financial technology in companies and its impact on the profitability of banks.

What distinguishes the current study from previous studies: the current study is distinguished in several points; the most important ones:

- The current study is a cognitive and cumulative building for previous studies on the subject, and it comes as a continuation of what the researchers started; it is based on their findings and recommendations.
- The current study focuses on studying the role of the use of financial technology (FINTECH) on the profitability of banks, which is thus considered more specialized than previous studies, as it dealt with the study of the impact between two variables in its subject, namely, financial technology and the profitability of the bank.

## THE INTELLECTUAL FRAMEWORK OF FINANCIAL TECHNOLOGY

FINTECH is a term used in the financial services industry to combine the latest innovations in technology and finance. Besides the development of FINTECH, today's financial services are not only required to facilitate transactions alone. Rather, the need for financial services has become a way of life and entertainment for some people in the world today - these people are generally known as "Millennials". They need financial services that can indulge their lives, self-esteem and social status, as some of the activities that fall into the FINTECH category are lending and borrowing money using financial technology systems, remittances, buying and selling of shares, and other transactions. One of the reasons why FINTECH is so important to the lifestyles and financial conditions of the global community is that it helps develop new start-ups. Many new start-ups are trying to create innovation in the field of FINTECH. (Dede Suryanto., 2018)

## THE IMPACT OF FINANCIAL TECHNOLOGY ON TRANSACTION COSTS

The use of FINTECH is helped in the process of financing, providing services and lending (Subanidja, Legowo, Sorongan, Wahyudi, 2020), and the use of FINTECH contributed to reducing transaction costs by reducing the fixed and marginal costs of producing financial services. Technological advances are not new to finance. FINTECH has brought about significant improvements in systems connectivity, computing power and cost. These improvements have reduced transaction costs and led to the emergence of new business models. As technology has increased information exchange and lowered transaction costs. (Feyen, Frost, Gambacorta, Natarajan, & Saal., 2021).

## THE INFLUENCE COVID-19 ON FINANCIAL TECHNOLOGY

The COVID-19 virus has severely affected the financial system and the way the financial industry operates. Front-end or face-to-face operations are hampered, and the payment system is increasingly reserved as the financial service. The nature of the COVID-19 shock is different from many of the shocks we have known in the world; the world has never seen such a pandemic, precisely because the virus emerged in an era of hyperactive globalization and interconnectedness of systems. This interdependence linked to the systemic nature of the financial sectors increases global financial vulnerability and creates cracks in the financial fabric of economies. The current vulnerability is much higher among asset managers, in the corporate sector, reflecting a prolonged period of stagnation and the high cost of financing would lead to business bankruptcy; in the sovereign sector and in the insurance sector. Then the insurance sector showed a significant loss of portfolios, and this has serious consequences for international capital flows and leads to disruption of global financial stability. Contrary to the case of the global financial crisis. (Pinshi, 2021)

The impact COVID-19 pandemic of FINTECH in the is on transportation as digital technology collaborates with the online transportation that many large companies are using to meet the needs of consumers. Millennials will be in terms of accessibility, speed and value of the financial services that are in high demand. It is used to not complete a problem submission for Digital Technology 4.0 using digital applications in Jakarta, Depok and Tangerang surrounding quantitative data analysis methods. Technological advances have accelerated the development of the digital payments industry, providing more efficient and faster access to financial services during this pandemic of financial literacy, and the adoption of financial technology. (Candy, Robin, Estina Sativa, Sephia Septiana, Hansen Can, Alice, 2022)

In the opinion of the researchers, the Banks and customers have realized that they are able to operate remotely in a safe and efficient manner. Banks may face renewed competition from shadow banks and new digital participants who were already challenging the traditional banking business model before the pandemic. FINTECH companies have had significant successes in the emerging markets, large digital platforms, such as Alipay in China; have become dominant in some market segments such as payment systems.

When lockdown measures to combat COVID-19 that the pace of change in the banking sector may surprise everyone. This acceleration, in turn, may precipitate the adoption of various forms of digital currencies, including by central banks. The financial services market, FINTECH will intensify competitive pressures and constrain the profitability of banks in the short term. However, its long-term effect will be more ambiguous, and will depend on the market structure that will eventually prevail. Because it can control the ability to reach a fragmented customer base that lives in different financial ecosystems. In this case, clients register their orders on a platform, and financial service providers compete to provide it to them.

COVID-19 has been a catalyst for FINTECH, because this is particularly true of financial services and FINTECH, and it is worth noting that as governments continue to implement positive incentives and regulatory initiatives, opportunities will continue to evolve, giving the region's FINTECH industry the ability to raise the level of general welfare of the participating countries. We are also witnessing government actions and investments in this area (such as Saudi Arabia, Bahrain, Egypt and the UAE) with the aim of creating job opportunities, as well as greater financial independence. The investment varies greatly.

## THE ROLE OF USING FINANCIAL TECHNOLOGY IN BANKS

Mobile phones have become the primary tool used by FINTECH providers to reach existing and potential customers. Two out of three adults who do not have access to financial services have access to mobile phones, a phenomenon that has enabled companies specialized in providing FINTECH services to successfully enter emerging markets and expand their activities. (Innes & Andrieu, 2022), and access to Services have become much easier and an example of this is taking financial loans where there is no need at present to submit credit applications, as one of the advantages of using FINTECH is the speed of obtaining loans that can take only two days. (Guliyev., 2018)

## FINANCIAL TECHNOLOGY FACTORS AFFECTING THE PROFITABILITY OF BANKS

There are many factors affecting the profitability of banks, and among those factors, we mention four of the groups that contain these factors. (Akhtar, Khizar, & Shama, 2011)

**First**: the technical factors: they are represented in the size of the bank and the techniques used by it, and the size of the bank is only a reflection of the volume of its available resources, meaning that there is often a direct relationship between the size of the bank and its profitability.

**Second**: The nature of management: Experience has shown that the banks on which the owners are based have outperformed the banks that are managed by departments separate from ownership, and similarly it was found that these banks achieve a higher return on investment, and this positively affects the allocation of resources in those banks. Which banks are more efficient, this is due to the reason that the managers are less willing to take risks than the owners are, and this can be attributed to the administrative corruption that infects the Islamic banking business.

**Third**: Administrative success: lies in the relationship between individuals within the bank, as the bank is made up of several departments, each department specializes in performing a specific work, and therefore it is natural for the members of each department to have a close relationship, and this relationship is necessary to affect the profitability of The Bank. (Achi, Adel, 2001).

**Fourth**: Environmental factors: There are environmental factors that the bank can control and control that affect its profitability, and among these factors, liquidity, which means the amount of funding sufficient to meet deposit withdrawals and other financial obligations realized by the bank on time or on demand (Al-Jamil, 2002). Alternatively, it represents the bank's ability to meet its immediate and expected obligations immediately. The other factor is paid-up capital is represented in the total funds actually provided by the bank's shareholders. When it was established, their participation in the formation of its capital, but it is necessary to pay attention to it. Because it helps to increase Confidence in the hearts of dealers with the bank, especially the owners of current deposits among them. (Hamad & Adour, 2005, p. 60) and at the same time enhances the position of the bank in various circles.

## FINANCIAL TECHNOLOGY AND IMPROVING THE PROFITABILITY OF BANKS

Banks measure the possibilities of implementing FINTECH in light of its ability to change the traditional financial services sector. One of the common advantages of adopting. FINTECH has developed its ability to provide efficient services in order to meet the needs of customers at a lower cost, thus winning market share at the expense of traditional banks, financial institutions and other established companies. Despite the tendency to view FINTECH as an agent of change, the bank's market positions are stable in the national economy. Looking at the various banking revenue streams, the ability of banks to win market share in deposits and lending is minimal, as this business is capital intensive. In addition, in order to overcome the possibilities of withdrawing deposits and directing them to FINTECH companies, the banks themselves can improve and utilize their technological capabilities to overcome any potential competition. One possible scenario is to increase profitability.

It is necessary to plan the local FINTECH environment to enable the banks' strategy to achieve its goal of achieving the highest possible profitability. Bank's authority assists in launching and quickly shifting to the use of FINTECH in the scope of their work. As, the introduction of automated teller machines had a positive impact on the banks' performance, adding the expanded use of communication technology, which helped speed up the performance of operations and reduce costs through the use of advanced digital devices and computer and service improvements Increasing profitability in addition to many benefits such as ease of dealing, external contracting with banks around the world and improving the service provided.

## THE IMPACT OF THE USE OF FINANCIAL TECHNOLOGY ON RAISING THE EFFICIENCY OF THE OPERATIONAL PERFORMANCE OF BANKS

The use of FINTECH helps mitigate transaction costs and enables a wide range of new financial services business models. Adoption intersects with both traditional and new providers. FINTECH can help reduce the costs of collecting, storing, processing and exchanging information including study costs, transcription costs, tracking costs and verification costs in finance, and can help borrowers more quickly find a suitable loan offer, or help savers find an investment product. Suits their specific needs. FINTECH can also help parties automate event verification, enabling the creation of a wide range of state-driven products (Jon et al., 2021).

The emergence of innovative FINTECH has also affected the financial world - including the banking, online payments, and cryptocurrency and e-commerce sectors -, which is growing rapidly. Thus, the use of FINTECH will form an important part of the development of new digital technology. Digital banking and the digital society can also be considered as constituting those parts of the banking and community work that are linked to digital systems to provide banking services to the digital community.

## THE IMPACT OF THE USE OF FINANCIAL TECHNOLOGY ON PROVIDING BANKING SERVICES TO CUSTOMERS

There are a number of banking services including prepaid credit cards, lending and leasing. Where the emergence of banking services that depend on the use of FINTECH must be understood as directly competing with traditional banks. The use of FINTECH facilitates the online lending process, and services.

## RESULTS AND RECOMMENDATIONS OF THE STUDY

Based on the results of data analysis and hypothesis testing, the study reached a set of results and made a set of recommendations as follows:

## THE RESULTS OF THE STUDY

1. FINTECH in banks facilitates the procedures for securing the necessary financing for customers, and activating electronic services such as credit card payments, mobile phone technology and other electronic services.
2. The Corona epidemic is causing an increase in the development of FINTECH, through the following: The number of startups in the field of FINTECH has increased, The "Payment and Remittance" sector, "Lending and Crowdfunding" and "Wealth and Financial Management"
3. Banks using FINTECH achieve more efficient results in terms of reducing costs, increasing revenue growth, reducing risks, raising operational efficiency, and increasing profitability.

## RECOMMENDATIONS OF THE STUDY

Based on the results, the researchers recommend the following recommendations:

1. The necessity for banks to develop legal frameworks for the use of FINTECH, which contribute significantly to the development of its products.
2. The necessity of investing in FINTECH techniques in the context of developing electronic financial services to reduce the traditional methods used by banks.
3. The need for the various components of the banking sector to pay attention to training their employees on the mechanisms and techniques of FINTECH, given its role in diversifying economic activity and developing banking work to become more responsive to the changing and multiple needs of customers and dealers with this pioneering and vital sector.
4. The importance of encouraging banks, in keeping pace with FINTECH, and the process of transforming banks from the stage of the traditional economy to the stage of the digital economy, coinciding with containing the risks of this transformation and its repercussions.
5. Increasing spending on FINTECH applications to improve banking services provided to customers, especially through electronic applications and technologies.
6. Working on developing a legislative framework for FINTECH related to electronic transactions, electronic identification, and electronic signature in order to unleash electronic financial and banking transactions to keep pace with technological developments and protect private and public interests.

## FUTURE RESEARCH DIRECTIONS

Financial technology (FINTECH) has a real ability to change the structure of traditional financial services. As FINTECH can make financial services faster, cheaper, safer, transparent and available. In addition, its various applications represent opportunities and challenges at the same time for banks and financial institutions.

Where FINTECH is modern technological innovations it includes a set of digital programs that are used in the financial operations of banks, including transactions with customers and financial services such as money transfer, currency exchange, calculations of interest rates and profits, knowing the expected profits for investments, and so on. Of banking operations.

FINTECH constituted a great opportunity for the banking system through the advanced electronic systems and programs that helped banks develop and improve their performance and increased their efficiency in services and transactions. It also became the key to success and distinction for these banks.

Although the uses of FINTECH included a limited number of services such as: Internet payment, phone banking services and others, these banks were able to introduce their products and improve their services through their work with financial technology. This technology has also contributed to increasing the efficiency and profitability of these banks.

## CONCLUSION

Over the past few years, the FINTECH sector has revolutionized the global financial systems. The main motive for writing this modest study was to accurately understand the importance of the emergence of FINTECH in the field of banking services, as banks face intense competition in light of rapid technological progress striving to seize opportunities in the financial services market, and based on the above, The main question: Is there an impact of the use of FINTECH on the profitability of banks?.

The study aims to investigate the impact of the use of FINTECH on the profitability of banks, indicate the impact of using financial technology to increase the quality of bank's services to provide customers, and clarify the impact of using financial technology on raising the operational efficiency of banks. The results of the study found that the use of financial technology in banks facilitates the procedures for securing the necessary financing for customers, and activating electronic services such as credit card payments, mobile phone technology and other electronic services.

The Corona epidemic is causing an increase in the development of financial technology, through the following: The number of startups in the field of financial technology has increased, The "Payment and Remittance" sector, "Lending and Crowdfunding" and "Wealth and Financial Management". Banks that use FINTECH achieve more efficient results in terms of reducing costs to increase revenue growth, reducing risks, raising operational efficiency, and increasing profitability. Based on the results, the researchers recommend the following recommendations: The necessity for banks to develop legal frameworks for the use of financial technology, which contribute significantly to the development of financial technology products. The necessity of investing financial technology techniques in the context of developing electronic financial services to reduce the traditional methods used by banks. Increasing spending on financial technology applications to improve banking services provided to customers, especially electronic applications, and technologies.

## REFERENCES

Achi, A. (2001). *The financial performance of the economic institution, measuring and evaluating - a case study of the institution of the cable industry in Biskra.* [Unpublished master's thesis, University of Mohamed Khider, Biskra, Algeria.]

Akhtar, M. F., Ali, K., & Sadaqat, S. (2011). Factors Influencing the Profitability of Islamic Banks of Pakistan. *International Research Journal of Finance and Economics, 66.*

Al-Jamil, S. K. (2002). *International Finance: Introduction to Structures, Processes and Tools.* Dar Al-Jamieh for Printing and Publishing.

Ali, S. & Muhammad, M. (2015). The availability of controls on the applications of electronic accounting information systems and their impact on the quality of profits - An applied study on the Palestinian banks whose shares are listed on the stock exchange Al-Quds. Open University Journal for Research and Administrative and Economic Studies, 1(2), 337-375.

Amariah, B. & Ghania, M. (2020). The Role of Financial Technology in Supporting the Banking Sector. *Al-Mudabber journal, 70*(72), pp. 99-111.

Broby, D. (2021). Financial technology and the future of banking. *Broby Finance Innov, VOL, 7*(1), 47. doi:10.118640854-021-00264-y

Dur, A. & Aljughaiman, A. (2021). Does financial technology matter? Evidence from an alternative banking system. *Cogent Economics & Finance*. doi:. doi:10.1080/23322039.2021.1934978

Feyen, E., Frost, J., Gambacorta, L., Natarajan, H., & Saal, M. (2021). FINTECH and the digital transformation of financial services: implications for market structure and public policy. BIS Papers, No 117, The Bank for International Set.

Guliyev, A. (2018). *The Impact of FINTECH on Banking Industry in Portugal Master's Degree in Innovation and Technological Entrepreneurship 2016-2018.* FEUP - Faculdade de Engenharia da Universidade do Porto.

Innes, C. & Andrieu, J. (2022). *Banking on FINTECH in Emerging Markets.* IFC, a member of the World Bank Group. www.ifc.org/thoughtleadership

Njogu, N. J. (2014). (Manuscript submitted for publication). The Effect of Electronic Banking on Profitability of Commercial Banks in Kenya. [In Partial Fulfillment of the Requirements for the Award of the Degree Of Master of Science In Finance, School Of Business, and University Of Nairobi.]. *Research Project.*

Piotrowski, D.(2022). Consumer perceived ethicality of banks in the era of digitalization: The case of Poland. *Economics and Business Review, 8* (22). doi:10.18559/ebr.2022.1.690-114

Subanidja, S., Legowo, M., Sorongan, F., & Wahyudi, E. (2020). The Choice of Collaborating with FINTECH Entities for Competitive Advantage through Leadership Styles Scientific. *Papers of the University of Pardubice, Series D: Faculty.*

Suryanto, D. (2018). Bank Strategy when Facing Financial Technology *Competition. 3rd International Conference on Vocational Higher Education (ICVHE 2018),* (pp. 149-154). IEEE.

Wang, Y.s & Nor, E. (2022). The Impact of FinTech on the Profitability of Traditional banks. *Global Business and Management Research*, 14.

Wu, B. & Wang, M, (2020). *The Impact of Business Cycles on the Profitability of Chinese Commercial Banks.* [Master Thesis Within: Business Administration, Jonkoping University, China].

## ADDITIONAL READING

Carbó-Valverde, S., Cuadros-Solas, P. J., & Rodríguez-Fernández, F. (2022). Entrepreneurial, institutional and financial strategies for FINTECH profitability. *Financial Innovation*, *8*(1), 1–36. doi:10.118640854-021-00325-2

Chhaidar, A., Abdelhedi, M., & Abdelkafi, I. (2022). The Effect of Financial Technology Investment Level on European Banks' Profitability. *Journal of the Knowledge Economy*, 1–23. doi:10.100713132-022-00992-1

Najaf, K., Mostafiz, M. I., & Najaf, R. (2021). FINTECH firms and banks sustainability: Why cybersecurity risk matters? *International Journal of Financial Engineering*, *8*(02), 2150019. doi:10.1142/S2424786321500195

Phan, D. H. B., Narayan, P. K., Rahman, R. E., & Hutabarat, A. R. (2020). Do financial technology firms influence bank performance? *Pacific-Basin Finance Journal*, *62*, 101210. doi:10.1016/j.pacfin.2019.101210

Wang, Y., Xiuping, S., & Zhang, Q. (2021). Can FINTECH improve the efficiency of commercial banks?—An analysis based on big data. *Research in International Business and Finance*, *55*, 101338. doi:10.1016/j.ribaf.2020.101338

Zhao, J., Li, X., Yu, C. H., Chen, S., & Lee, C. C. (2022). Riding the FINTECH innovation wave: FINTECH, patents and bank performance. *Journal of International Money and Finance*, *122*, 102552. doi:10.1016/j.jimonfin.2021.102552

## KEY TERMS AND DEFINITIONS

**Bank Operating Efficiency:** This is a key performance metric used to assess a bank's profitability. It is calculated by dividing a bank's operating expenses by its total income and is therefore referred to as a bank's "Cost to Income Ratio.

**Bank Performance:** This means the value calculated using the financial metrics, determined by the Board, in most cases annually on the last day of each fiscal year or such more frequent intervals as may be determined in the discretion of the Board Such as factors has been assigned a weighting indicating the proportion of that metric to be used in the overall calculation of Bank Performance.

**Digital Banking:** This is banking done through the digital platform, doing away with all the paperwork like pay-in slips, Demand Drafts, and so on. It means availability of all banking activities online.

**Digital Currency:** This is a form of currency that is available only in digital or electronic form. It is also called digital money, electronic money, electronic currency, or cyber-cash.

**FINTECH:** This is utilized to help companies, business owners, and consumers had better manage their financial operations, processes, and lives by utilizing specialized software and algorithms that are used on computers and, increasingly, smartphones. Fintech, the word, is a combination of "financial technology.

**Quality of Customer Service:** it This means Quality customer service involves providing efficient, quick, and friendly service to customers as well as building strong relationships with them. It also entails responding to customers' issues in time and handling any complaints swiftly.

**Technological Innovation:** This is a new or improved product or process whose technological characteristics are significantly different from before. Implemented technological product innovations are new products (product innovations) or processes in application (process innovations) that have been brought to market. The product or process is considered an innovation if it achieves specified advantages for the enterprise concerned; these need not be new from the point of view of other companies or the market.

**Traditional Financial Services:** These are typically offered by regulated financial institutions, such as banks and credit unions, and include checking and savings accounts and home mortgage and auto loans. "Fringe" financial service providers offer check cashing and payday and title loans.

# Chapter 15
# The Importance of Innovation Diffusion in the Renewable Energy Sector

**Luca Esposito**
*University of Salerno, Italy & University of Eastern, Finland*

**Mohsen Brahmi**
https://orcid.org/0000-0002-0995-0761
*University of Sfax, Tunisia*

**Mihir Joshi**
https://orcid.org/0000-0001-6922-3489
*Banasthali Vidyapith University, India*

## ABSTRACT

*In the last decade, one of the most discussed topics globally concerns the difficult management of climate change and the need for an energy and cultural transition that pays attention so as not to increase territorial inequalities. This chapter aims to provide a clear and comprehensive picture of the importance of innovation in the renewable energy sector and the role of their deployment to ensure climate change mitigation and sustainable growth. The authors will start from the environmental Kuznets curve (EKC) and then examine the metabolism of current societies, focusing on the trend of the diffusion of technological innovation and its contribution to the energy transition.*

## INTRODUCTION

Natural balances have been put in serious difficulty, due to a metabolism of a society that is too hectic. In fact, with the development of the economy, degradation and environmental problems become increasingly important. (Zhang et al., 2020). The increase in temperatures and the exploitation of natural resources have caused irreversible transformations, with on average profound consequences also on people's health.

DOI: 10.4018/978-1-6684-6766-4.ch015

(Zhao et al., 2020). Currently it is on the political agendas of all states, the need for the construction of a sustainable economic system that allows an efficient allocation of resources and reduces negative externalities. To achieve the 2°C climate targets, the share of renewable energy must increase from 19% in 2017 to 65% by the end of 2050. Negotiation between stakeholders is needed to set emission and quality standards. Some studies believe that "eco-economic decoupling" should be put into practice. Since the existing scientific literature documents that an increase in GDP exerts a strong environmental pressure, a new economic paradigm should be generated that allows growth in this respect and at the same time aims to reduce environmental impacts. Currently renewable energy is classified as the energy of the future, as it does not generate pollution (Sadorsky, 2014) and allows to improve energy security (Irandoust, 2016) and redesign a new low-carbon society. Technological progress plays a key role; however, care must be taken not to generate what in economics, is called paradox or Jevons effect. This paradox arises because of a series of research and studies conducted by William Stanley Jevons, an English economist, of international renown. In 1865, it observed that technological improvements, instead of reducing consumption, increased them. In fact, the analysis took place by looking at coal mines and how a technological improvement implied an excessive increase in coal consumption. Subsequently, Daniel Khazzoom and Leonard Brookes, revisited and restudied the Jevons model and came to the conclusion that the reduction of energy consumption through an increase in energy efficiency, implies an increase in energy demand. Later Saunders said that greater energy efficiency normally tends to increase energy consumption. This is due to two reasons, from an economic point of view, the increase in efficiency, as a rule, makes the use of energy cheaper, generating what in economics is called the rebound effect. This effect, in line with what is specified, occurs when we have a greater efficiency (in terms of production or in terms of efficiency), it generates a reduction in costs, and a chain increase in demand.

Saunders examined the problem from two profiles, both microeconomic and macroeconomic, and concluded that technological progress certainly improves efficiency, but will generate an increase in overall consumption, causing an increase in demand. Reducing emissions into the atmosphere, in a "frenetic" society and prone to consumerism is not a simple factor, however it is estimated that the reduction of CO2 emissions can take place through four channels, they are:

- From an economic point of view, one could think of a reduction in economic growth, in fact as a result of the serious economic crisis, emissions into the atmosphere have suffered a 7% drop. However, economic decline causes serious negative impacts in terms of employment.
- From an energy point of view, one could think of reducing the use of coal and replacing these substances with natural gas and renewables.
- From a behavioral point of view, one could think of a change in the behavior of individuals to reduce waste and emissions.
- From a technological point of view, innovation plays a key role in removing emissions. However, it could give rise to some opportunistic behaviour.

## BACKGROUND

Climate change can trigger another equally worrying aspect that takes the name of "climate sensitivity", or the problems that would cause an alteration of the amounts of dioxide in the atmosphere, with consequences not only environmental but also economic and social. Although global warming is characterized by a strong margin of uncertainty and discontinuity, the certain element is that technology and its diffusion, in particular specific sectors for example (renewable energy), can offer solutions that allow to overcome this type of adversity, to combat climate change, a reorganization of the energy sector is needed. (Abufotuh, 2007; Apergis et al., 2012; Balsalobre-Lorente et al., 2018). The spread of patents allows the production of household appliances with better energy classes, with consequences on the reduction of energy consumption. It can promote and disseminate innovation, reducing what can be classified as transaction costs (Sag et al.; 2007; Thomas, 2002).

Innovation and modernization funds play a key role in promoting investment in this respect. The introduction of innovative design methodologies that can guarantee effectiveness, efficiency and cost-effectiveness, are particularly important, especially in sectors in constant updating and improvement, they are a strategic tool and can promote the energy independence of the various States. Before examining the diffusion, the focus will be on both innovative input indicators, i.e., R&D, and innovative output indicators, i.e., patents. Both are fundamental tools, as well as necessary to allow a homogeneous diffusion on the territory. This branch of study is extremely broad, multidisciplinary, and variable, and the results depend very much on the geographical area of reference and the regulation put into practice by policy makers and individual lines of government. With this in mind, it was considered appropriate to examine the speed of diffusion and how closely it is interconnected with the type and the historical, political and cultural context. Rogers Everett, in his famous book "Diffusion of Innovation" believes that diffusion is identifiable as the process by which an innovation enters the market and is disseminated among the participants. This definition has been shared by sociologists, politicians, and marketing scholars. At the base of the diffusion, it is possible to observe that a fundamental role is played by the behavior not only of companies but also of the end user, that is, the consumer. To adopt a new technology, it must have a perception of the innovativeness of the product and the benefits that could derive from it and derive from it. The diffusion of an innovation, in fact, depends on countless factors, including for example the target audience and the categories of users to whom it is intended. You can divide user categories into five sections: "innovators, adopters, early majority, late majority, and finally retarded." Each of these subjects has a different degree of interest in the modern technology and drives its diffusion with a different intensity. Over the years, various models have been structured to study the consequences of innovation, which can be divided into three macro categories, desirable and undesirable, direct and indirect and anticipated against the unexpected. It is not always true that efficient technological innovation, appreciated and in the process of diffusion, is adopted by all economic operators. Often the trend of the "diffusion paths" takes on a sigmoidal form, where innovation follows an initial phase of growth and diffusion and then in the short-term decreases, as it is replaced by new "more modern" innovations. The existing scientific literature and the studies conducted document two distinct types of diffusion path (symmetrical and asymmetrical), which will be explained in detail in this chapter. Through the correct dissemination of innovations and the application of information and communication technologies (ICT) it is possible to achieve significant energy savings and build a sustainable society in line with the objectives set by Europe 2030. In fact, increasing the diffusion of technologies matured in the renewable energy sector is a fundamental element to reduce climate change mitigations on a global scale.

The energy sector has received a lot of attention, thanks to the long life of complex energy infrastructure. (Ebinger et al.; 2011). The increase in technological maturity in the field of renewables, especially in some geographical areas (Japan, China, Korea, Germany, and the United States), has allowed a widespread diffusion, with improvements in terms of emissions. The recent geopolitical flows testify to the importance and commitment in the various countries of the world to allow the energy transition and the reduction of emissions into the atmosphere. The diffusion of innovation and all the tools used to ensure the mitigation of climate change, will be examined both through basic models of product and process innovation, and through the selection and imitation that takes place between innovative companies. In addition, particular attention will be paid to the difference between business size models and models with strategic interaction. However, it is believed that a key role is played by the degree and level of innovation, in fact a lack of useful information, implies a decrease in the expected number of diffusions. It is estimated, especially in the field of renewable energy, that crucial information, coming not from suppliers, but from other agents who have already used this technology, can produce positive externalities in terms of the spread of patents. Although in this chapter it was considered appropriate to examine only and exclusively the energy sector, it is appropriate to specify how it is not the only one that allows the mitigation of climate change, currently the principle of benign by design is very developed. In fact, the goal is to design products, which have the same characteristics, but with a lower degree of toxicity and which are generators of positive externalities. Briefly, the aim is to provide a general vision, aimed at explaining how a correct diffusion of innovations and patents combined with a strong regulation, can contribute to reducing negative externalities towards the environment and guarantee the healthiness of the air. It should be pointed out that the degree of wealth of a country is not measurable, only and through GDP per capita and the presence of a structured industrial fabric. One of the fundamental conditions that allows a country to label itself as "rich" is dictated by the low percentage of pollution it generates and the positive externalities. Have high rates of pollution and produce negative externalities (desertification, soil erosion, loss of biodiversity, environmental irreversibility), implies self-destruction as well as early population death and habitat destruction. For this reason, it is important that each state reaches equilibrium, not going beyond the optimal pollution threshold. A correct diffusion of innovations would guarantee a co-creation and dissemination of patents among companies, as well as ensuring the protection of ecosystems. Even the energy mix (photovoltaic, biomass, wind, hydroelectric, geothermal) if effectively managed can allow the development of energy independence and guarantee a low-carbon future. Technological innovation arises from the evolution of knowledge, with the consequent creation of new services and new tools that can be inserted within society. Back on February 20, 1999, in "Economist", a definition of innovation was published, which is still extremely current today. In one section it is explained, in a pointed way, how innovation has become: "the industrial religion of the late twentieth century. Businesses see it as the key tool to increase profits and market share. Governments rely on it when trying to improve the economy. In the world, the rhetoric of innovation has recently replaced that of the economy of well-being, present since the Second World War. It is the innovative technology that unites left and right at the political level (...). But what exactly innovation is difficult to say, even more so to measure it". About twenty years after this extremely precise and precise definition, it is possible to confirm how innovation is a difficult element to measure and how it does not develop in a homogeneous way, creating profound territorial inequalities between the various countries. The relationship between companies and innovation is also very variable and difficult in its understanding to outline its boundaries. Within the following chapter, attention will be focused on the role of technological innovation in the renewable energy sector and how systemic innovation can contribute to the mitigation of climate change and generate positive externalities. To achieve the objectives set by the European Green Deal, radical changes of course are indispensable, possible through a greater diffusion and promotion of energy technologies. Many environmental innovations, especially in the energy sector, were born from the need to remedy and reduce emissions with new tools. Most of the technologies patented in 2002 entered the market about 10 years later, due to the difficulty of installation and the changes made to allow better yields. The existing scientific literature documents how a correct development of renewable energy sources contributes to reducing pollution, but not to reducing energy consumption and lends itself as a valid tool to combat the climate crisis. Although measuring innovation is a complicated process to study, many times patents are the tool used to evaluate and quantify how much innovation is happening in each country. The biggest challenge of the 21st century can and must be addressed through innovation, to achieve net emissions by 2050 and contribute to the achievement of climate goals.

*Figure 1. Patent Renewable Energy Sector - Source: Economics and Statistics Division, WIPO*

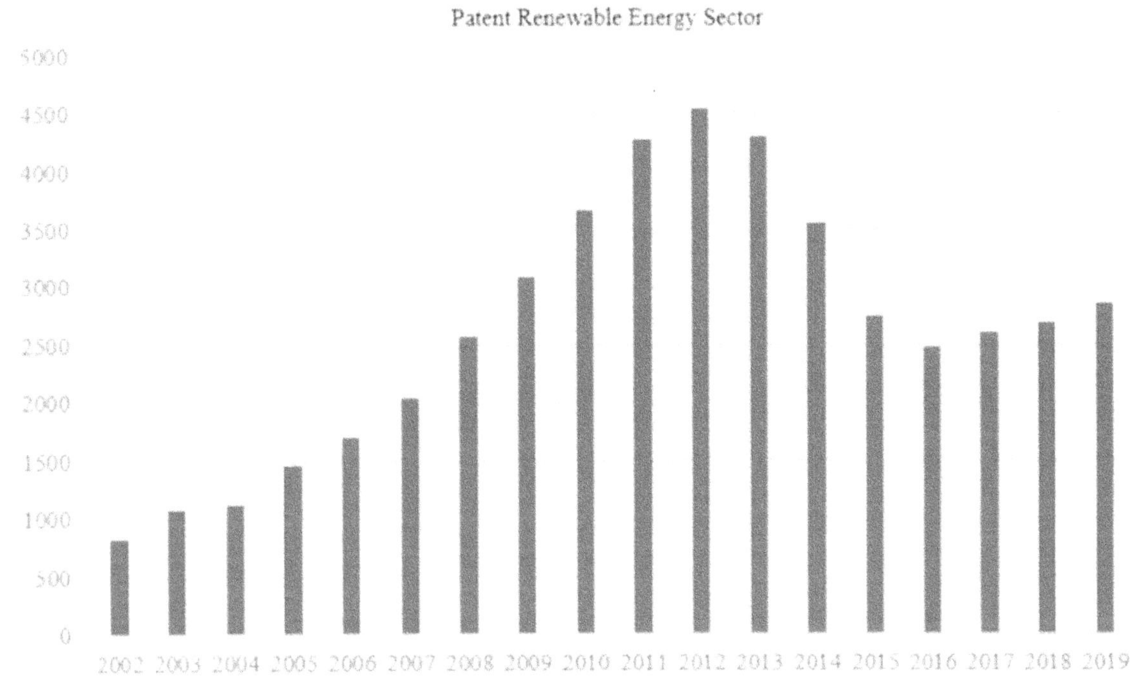


From the image it is possible to observe a gradual increase from 2002 to 2012 and subsequently a reduction from 2013 to 2018 of patents in the renewable sector. However, it is appropriate to clarify how patents are classifiable as long-term investments and therefore, many technologies designed about a decade earlier come into full operation a decade later. Technological innovation and renewables, turn out to be the winning combination and one of the strategic tools to allow the correct energy transition. Through a simple mathematical formula, it is possible to calculate the environmental pressure that is generated to produce one euro of output. In the field of fossil fuels, it is extremely high. A simple decomposition will be proposed below to explain what has been previously described.

$$E_t = \sum_{ffi} E_{tffi} = \sum_{ffi} \left( \frac{E_{tffi}}{Y_{tffi}} * \frac{Y_{tffi}}{Y_t} * Y_t \right)$$

It is possible to observe three different effects, starting by defining $\left(\frac{E_{tffi}}{Y_{tffi}}\right)$ it represents the technical effect, or how much environmental pressure is generated to produce a euro of output in the sector of the fossil fuel industry **(ffi)**. In the second section, on the other hand, $\left(\frac{Y_{tffi}}{Y_t}\right)$ it represents the composition effect, aimed at measuring how environmental pressures change, as a result of the various shifts in production. An additional effect that has been considered is the scale effect ($Y_t$).

The diffusion of innovation, in the sphere of renewables, plays a significant role, in two respects. In fact, they go primarily to change the global energy market, thanks to constantly evolving technologies and offer a particularly important contribution in terms of climate change mitigation. In fact, most of the decarbonisation we wish to achieve can be ensured simply by stimulating renewables more and with-it technological progress. The current situation of emissions in the world is truly tragic, but there are tools, already tested, such as renewables that allow a slow and gradual reduction. Currently it has been estimated that energy production, which takes place mainly through fossil fuels, represents about three-fourths of global emissions. To it, profound consequences are associated such as prohibitive costs on human health, with a high number of vit e losses, attributed to air pollution. Renewable systems and technologies are entering the market faster and faster, both due to energy inflation and environmental and geopolitical issues. And their diffusion can contribute to the creation of a sustainable economic system. Great attention must be paid to the concept of waste absorption and allow resources the normal rate of natural regeneration. In fact, in today's society the socio-economic metabolism is characterized by the extraction of resources with the consequent generation of negative externalities. To conduct such a study you can use, the response state pressure model that we will propose below:

*Figure 2. Reworking of the author on OECD Source 1994 p.11*

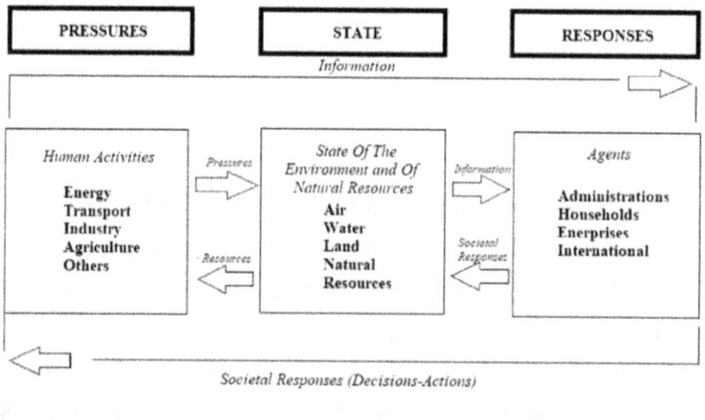


The externalities produced by the production and consumption of fossil fuels can be assessed through three indicators:

- Pressure indicators
- Status indicators
- Response indicators

Pressure indicators describe the pressure exerted by human activity on the environment, they are often used to assess socio-economic scenarios and to be subsequently used as indicators for environmental policies. Status indicators aim to describe the qualitative and quantitative transformations taking place on the environment, while response indicators aim to describe the activities carried out by society to reduce negative externalities and react to environmental problems. Through the Kuznets curve it is possible to represent environmental damage in relation to the level of per capita income of the population. In the explanation of the curve, it is appropriate to explain first of all its role, it is a function that explains the environmental damage and the distributive effects of pollution. Starting from the assumptions made by the economist Kuznets, a distinction will be made between poor societies and rich societies. In poor societies the level of environmental degradation is minimal, due to the absence of a structured industrial fabric. In many countries, under-developed, the economic-productive activity is based on food consumption that comes from the agricultural world. However, within the curve, we can distinguish three separate phases. We have a first phase in which there is a strong economic development, dictated by the presence of companies in the area. In it, we can observe the spread of industries, which inevitably have an impact in terms of growth, but also in environmental terms. Kuznets believes that the relationship between economic growth and pollution is interrupted at some point (Y*) and the relationship is reversed.

*Figure 3. Environmental Kuznets curve*

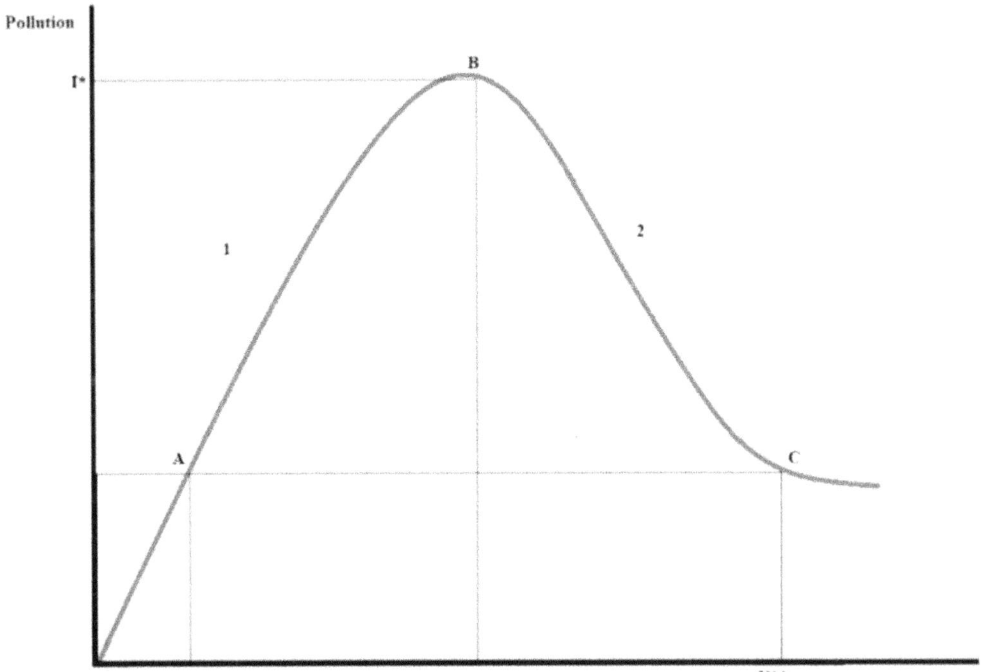

In recent years it has been possible to observe many response indicators as potential tools for climate change mitigation. In the renewable sector, the adoption and consequent diffusion of different technologies in the fields of energy production, transport, buildings, and agriculture. In the energy sector, we have witnessed the application of recent technologies, capable of being easily installed even in urban contexts. Having mentioned the various indicators, we believe it is appropriate to analyze the externalities produced by conventional energy production.

Energy production, through a system that can be defined as "conventional", has strong repercussions on the environment. Moreover, it is characterized by a margin of uncertainty, scientifically proven that documents how within the next 104 years it will run out. Being strongly dependent makes fossil fuels, generates negative externalities not only of an environmental nature, but also of an economic nature[1].

*Figures 4. Effects of conventional electricity production*

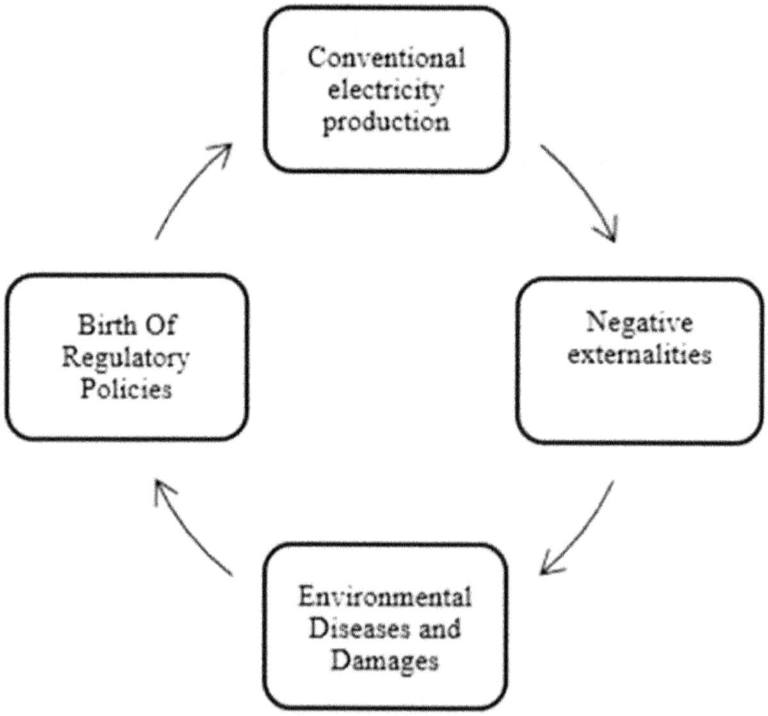


Dependence on fossil fuels translates into a threat to national energy security and a brake on economic development, triggering geopolitical problems. Thanks to the use of technology development and new energy infrastructure paradigms, global emissions over the period (2014-2015) remained unchanged. The consequences in environmental, economic and health terms have pushed since 1999, political leaders to adopt new political practices that are rare to defuse climate change. However, the existing scientific literature testifies to how the political apparatus has provided incorrectly adequate answers (Eskander et al 2020). In the last decade, in the same way as the spread of innovation, there has been a diffusion of the political proposals of the various states that aim to remove the principle: "the polluter pays"

and promote a carbon taxation system that allows to guarantee reductions of environmental pollution. (Carattini et al., 2019). All States have a "common concern" linked to climate change and the continuous rise in global energy demand. (Liu et al., 2021; Umar et al., 2022) and engage collectively to ensure sustainable economic development by promoting energy production through renewable energy sources to limit environmental impoverishment (Hao et al., 2021).

## MAIN FOCUS OF THE CHAPTER

### Issues, Controversies, Problems

The study and analysis of the concept of diffusion of innovation, was originally studied for the first time by the sociologist [2]*Gabriel Trade, sociologist French (1843-1904) in the late 1900s. However, most of the studies related to the field of diffusion of innovation have been carried out in the field of rural sociology and in the context of agricultural technology, to examine the application in the soil of hybrid seeds. Subsequently, Rogers provided a fundamental contribution on the study of the diffusion of innovation, thanks to a wide range of methodologies and lines of thought offered. In the energy sector, the diffusion of innovation and innovative technologies is characterized as a cumulative process, through which the innovative technology turns out to be the result of a recombination and modernization of existing technology (Arthur, 2007). Moreover, being a highly diversified sector that requires the combination of different technical-practical knowledge, it does not depend on a single factor but on a plurality of mechanisms and conditions, closely related and interconnected. (Nemet, 2012; Garrone et al., 2014; Noailly and Smeets, 2015; Popp, 2017). The speed with which an innovation spreads, depends on countless factors and the type of technology, however, recent studies, testify to how the technologies of the green branch go to exert a greater impact on the diffusion and future inventions (Barbieri et al; 2020) and how overall the most cited technologies and patents are inherent in wind and solar technologies (Noailly et al; 2017). The diffusion of innovation is closely interconnected and linked to two processes that can be classified as dissemination and implementation processes. The studies conducted by [3]*E. M Rogers – Diffusion of innovation (1962), have allowed the predisposition of the Rogers curve, which is considered by most scholars as one of the best models to be used to explain how different individuals decide to adopt the innovation. Subsequently, the five types of users will be analyzed in detail. However, there are also other models, such as Bass' model which instead believes that the diffusion of innovation follows an "S" shaped curve which depends on three parameters. These three parameters are respectively: [4]

- The maximum market demand, i.e., the potential demand
- Coefficient of innovation
- Imitation coefficient

### The Model

This model has long been used in forecasts, particularly in sales forecasts. It is based on an apparently quite simple model that is modeled on a simple equation, where there are two dissimilar categories of adopters, who can be classified as innovators and imitators and the time of adoption strongly depends on how users interact. It was considered appropriate to explain the specified model, starting by defining the two coefficients of innovation (p) and imitation (q), while F(t) and f(t), represent respectively the installed base fraction and the variation of the installed fraction.

$$\frac{'(t)}{1-F(t)} = p + qF(t)$$

Subsequently, it was considered appropriate to express what was explained above through an ordinary differential equation.

$$\frac{dF}{dt} = p(1-F) + q(1-F)F$$

$$s(t) = mf(t)$$

$$s(t) = m\frac{(p+q)^2}{P} \frac{e^{-(p+q)t}}{(1+\frac{q}{p}e^{-(p+q)t})^2}$$

In the end, you get the moment of peak sales that will be indicated with (t*)

$$t^* = \frac{\ln q - \ln p}{p+q}$$

Through the reading of the [4*]F. Bass – Bass Model or Bass diffusion model (1969), it is possible to intercept how potential and current users interact with each other on the management of a new product. However, those who decide to adopt an innovative technology can be classified as innovators or imitators and the degree of diffusion of the technology is closely interconnected with the degree of imitation among the adopters. Most renewable technologies designed for emerging countries tend to be exported to mature markets and continue in their diffusion process. In fact, the emerging country is seen as a place to elaborate and generate innovative ideas that are then transferred to the markets. In the renewable energy sector, there is a circular relationship that is present between the spread of innovation and profitability, in fact, companies operating in the same economic sector, are often in competition with each other and innovation turns out to be an efficient alternative to increase profits. However, the results of diffusion are often by their nature uneven. In any sector, technologies before entering the market follow a well-defined linear cycle, which is usually classified into four parts: invention, innovation, commercialization and finally the diffusion of technology, which depends very much on how strong innovation and commercialization are on the market. Several studies have been conducted over the years with the aim of studying and evaluating the trend of the diffusion of innovation. In chronological order, the first studies are attributed to Tarde, a sociologist French of international fame and who matured and perfected the idea that the diffusion of innovations and ideas had an “S” shape, and how on this curve it was possible to observe three points (innovation, growth and maturity). In line with the studies conducted by Rayan and Gross, we specify that the diffusion of innovation is closely interconnected with entrepreneurs and their willingness to adopt it or not; in fact, we can distinguish five types of entrepreneurs, we have the innovators, or those who innovate and circulate a new innovation, the anticipators, or those who decide to adopt the new technology first and who in turn fit into the group of the anticipatory majority. This is the first group of entrepreneurs, then it is possible to observe the majority of latecomers, or those who decide not to innovate immediately because of the initial investments too excessive and the group of latecomers. In this respect, the leading role of the entrepreneur takes on a key meaning and of fundamental importance and the decision-making activities themselves take on a significant role. However, especially in the renewable sector it is not easy given the conditions of extreme uncertainty. And examination the diffusion of innovations, we must consider some particularly key factors that will be divided into three macro-categories, which will be described below:

- Major features of innovation
- Characteristics of innovators
- Context and environmental characteristics

The characteristics of innovation are fundamental, as a well-structured innovation and the result of updates due to learning by doing and using activities, will attract more investors who will be able to observe the trends of previous years and make simple projections on the advantage that the new technology can have in terms of profit maximization and in terms of environmental maximization, with the aim of producing positive externalities on the market. However, from the point of view of diffusion, the characteristics of those who must innovate are fundamental, but this aspect is extremely variable and depends on some crucial factors that are for example the familiarity and the degree of knowledge of innovation. The environmental context also plays a key role, just think of the large projects of onshore wind farms, which are often hindered by the environmental context and morphological characteristics, but it does not turn out to be the only problem as there are many geographical features and diverse cultural ideologies. In line with the existing scientific literature, the innovative technologies that develop in the world of renewables, spread very slowly, they can attract investors and consequently dominate the market, only after several years and their use allows benefits in economic and environmental terms. In recent years there has been an increase in energy patents, particularly in renewable energy. (Hötte et al., 2021; Perrons et al., 2021). In fact, most of the technologies belonging to the energy context and specifically of renewables, take on a sigmoidal form, implementing the creation of two different paths of diffusion, symmetrical and asymmetrical. In the first years of the development of photovoltaics, we witnessed the formation of asymmetric diffusion paths, they are characterized by a strong diffusion and success of innovation, right from the start. The world of renewables is complex, and the diffusion of a given technology spreads at different speeds, based on the geographical, morphological context and the type of sources available in each area.

The link between innovation and diffusion is certainly also interconnected to the type of innovation that is observed. Currently it is customary to distinguish two distinct types of innovation: product innovation and process innovation.

- Product innovation consists in the introduction of a new service on the market. In this case the service corresponds to the production of energy from renewable energy sources. This phase began

in the nineteenth century, a period of inventions, in which, Auguste Mouchot, built the first solar engine, through which it was possible to produce thermal energy by solar energy.
- Process innovation, on the other hand, is closely interconnected with production processes and the consequent introduction of new methods of production and distribution of a service that was currently already on the market, but of which improvements are presented, an example could be the production of agrivoltaic, or other technologies that develop and become an important support for the energy context.

The selection of the market in the choice of mature technologies is one of the elements that is taken into greater consideration because the mature technology acts as a guarantee towards investors, who are aware that they are buying a product that has already been tested and is currently being improved.

In studying the spread of innovations, not only in the context of renewables, but in any sector, it is important to delineate and determine boundaries. However, it is not always easy to observe precisely where an innovation stops, as the diffusion of innovations depends on multiple factors, which will be described below:

- It is possible to intercept the advantages that those who adopt the innovation expect to receive, in the context of renewables. These advantages can be classified into three different subcategories, economic aspect, environmental aspect, and social aspect.
- Adaptability and compatibility, for potential adopters of an innovative technology and adaptability and compatibility of the old technology with the new one that takes over. Adopting a renewable innovation, incompatible, would imply an unnecessary expenditure of money and resources, with the risk that the absorption of the innovative technology in the context in which it falls does not happen.
- The complexity of innovation is another closely interconnected element to diffusion. More complex technologies, with substantial investments on the infrastructure side, are not easily "understandable" and "manageable" and this generates delays because they require a study and understanding to allow their durability and at the same time to be effective, efficient and economical. In the varied world of renewables, offshore wind power is characterized by its high complexity, both in terms of installations and in terms of maintenance. In fact, it has only spread in recent years, thanks to modern installation and maintenance techniques. These wind farms enjoy countless advantages, including speed and the stability of the winds in the open sea, which is greater than on land. Moreover, since there are no morphological problems, it is possible to allow the installation of several turbines, without space limits. The slow diffusion of this technology is due both to the maintenance costs that are quite high and the difficulty in management and installation, which today thanks to modern technologies, takes place in a much faster time.

Previously we have indicated that innovation spreads not constantly and that their diffusion depends on economic, social and environmental factors. In this respect, climate change is the driving force behind the spread of innovations. Many studies refer to Kaya's identity to explain the trend in carbon emissions.

$$GHGE = P\frac{Y}{E}\frac{E}{Y}\frac{M}{E}$$

According to Kaya's identity, emissions (GHGE) are respectively equal to the number of people, i.e., population (P), gross domestic product (Y) and (E) represents primary energy use and (M) represents global anthropogenic carbon dioxide emissions. Therefore (Y/E), it represents the gross domestic product, while (E/Y) it represents the energy intensity of the gross domestic product and finally (M/E), it turns out to be the carbon footprint in this case, of the energy.

However, in line with the studies conducted by Richard J. Tol (2014), we agree that despite being an identity it would be more appropriate if it were expressed in proportional growth, as we report below:[5]

$$\frac{\partial lnM}{\partial t} = \frac{\partial lnP}{\partial t} + \frac{\partial ln^{y} \setminus P}{\partial t} + \frac{\partial ln^{E} \setminus Y}{\partial t} + \frac{\partial ln^{M} \setminus E}{\partial t}$$

$$\frac{\partial lnX}{\partial t} = \frac{1}{X} + \frac{\partial X}{\partial t} = \frac{\Delta}{X}$$

With the aim of fighting the current crisis, the innovators themselves aim to build more resilient business models that can better adapt to the society in which we live.

In the complex just transition scenario, a significant role in the dissemination of innovations is played by banking institutions and the funding they grant.

## THE ROLE OF INNOVATION FOR PROMOTING RENEWABLE ENERGY

Innovation plays a fundamental role in promoting the development of modern technologies capable of producing energy from renewable energy sources and in addressing the ongoing energy and global crisis. Thanks to it has been possible to develop modern technologies that allow to overcome the problems present. In the following section, the main five most well-known and widespread types of renewable energy sources will be explained and then the new emerging renewable energy sources that have been the result of the diffusion and innovation of the previous ones will be listed. Renewable energy sources (Mohsen, Karim & Sonia, 2013 ; Mohsen & Sonia, 2013) have been extraordinarily successful since the 70s, in fact, following the oil crisis of that period, the awareness is maturing that we must find an alternative and change course.

We will start by indicating the traditional renewable energy sources, which will be divided into six categories:

- Solar
- Wind
- Biomass
- Bioenergy
- Geothermal
- Hydropower

Solar energy, it turns out to be, inevitably one of the most widespread in the world both for the speed in the installation and for the initial investment not always excessively high. Some studies, testify how solar parks installed on roofs, turn out to be a convenient tool to increase energy production and reduce climate-changing emissions. (Arnette, 2013) Currently China enjoys the advantage of being the world's leading producer of energy from renewable sources, followed by Japan, the USA, the European Union, and India. The origin of the sun as a source of renewable energy dates to 1800, by many scholars, identified as the century of scientific research. Edmond Becquerel, in 1839, discovered the photoelectric effect, this project was the starting point for the spread of this type of innovation. In 1869, Smith Willoughby discovered the advantages of selenium in the composition of photovoltaic panels, but the first photovoltaic panel was built about ten years later and its commercialization starting in the sixties. However, the production of energy through these systems takes place only at the turn of the eighties and nineties. Conversely, wind energy discovered its first application with windmills, they were used to grind the grain that came from crops and to pump water. Subsequently, many studies have been carried out observing the ability of mills to transform wind energy into mechanical energy, which have allowed the creation and diffusion of more sophisticated structures. In 1887, following the creation of the dynamo, the first turbines began to be built and in 1900 the first models were developed, to allow the construction of a new paradigm of wind energy, with the consequent construction of real wind farms in Denmark and the United States. While in the hydroelectric energy sector, initially, there were only plants that were able to exploit the power of the water that came out of the basins. Subsequently, technological innovation and technological progress have made it possible to exploit the energy of the tides and waves. Another potential to produce energy from renewable sources is geothermal energy, some rocks present below the earth's mantle can be hot and through the establishment of geothermal power plants, it is possible to exploit this heat to transform water into steam. In the last decade, biogas plants have also found an excellent margin of success, through which it is possible to produce thermal energy, electricity and organic fertilizers that can be used for agriculture. The analysis will aim to examine the economic and environmental impact of these renewable sources (Akhdar & Mohsen 2019), highlighting their progress and changes in recent years. The analysis will start from the photovoltaic sector, the companies, are promoting innovative technologies that aim to reduce land use. Technological innovation has allowed the development of agrivoltaic, thanks to this technology it is possible to guarantee the production of energy within farms. The construction of a modular and mobile structure allows both to produce energy and to proceed with agricultural processing. The spread of this technology has generated countless advantages especially among farms that can aim to achieve energy independence and allow the conduct of agricultural activities. Moreover, according to recent studies (Marrou et al., 2013), it has been possible to observe how through the agrivoltaic it is possible to produce a particular microclimate that allows the production of certain crops, producing benefits and advantages also from an economic point of view. In fact, thanks to the diffusion of this technology it is possible to guarantee a better and greater production of food, a considerable water saving and a greater production of renewable energy. The diffusion of this technology could prove to be extremely advantageous because thanks to the use of agrivoltaic, a synergy is created between agricultural production and the production of energy from renewable sources, which allows crops a reduced exposure to the sun and extreme weather conditions. Moreover, thanks to the spread of modern technologies for the preparation of foundations, it was possible to guarantee the installation of these systems, without the use of concrete. The innovative technology c.d. Spinachor, takes its cue from the roots of a tree to build an anchor structure, resistant, which does not make any changes to the soil. The rapid spread of this type of plant is generating the birth of new incentives that go to support farms and ensure the birth of new plants. In the last decade, the rapid spread of innovation has allowed the development of models aimed at ensuring the possibility of energy storage, this process plays a key role, as renewable energy sources (Douah & Mohsen, 2019), especially solar and wind, are characterized by their discontinuity that makes it difficult to ensure a balance of supply and demand. Agrivoltaic allows both agricultural entrepreneurs and agro-industrial enterprises to generate countless benefits. In addition, in the photovoltaic sector, the CSP (Concentrating Solar Power) technology offers the opportunity to store energy, which can be used later, especially on cloudy days. However, the installation of such parks, requires large sums for initial investments, the availability of the land to be used will fluctuate according to the technology that will be decided to be used, as a rule, the existing scientific literature, testifies to how for such plants about ten acres of land per megawatt (MW) are needed. Even the spread of marine energy has found countless successes in the last decade, thanks to countless technologies that have allowed the creation of energy parks located on the seabed that manage to combine the preservation of biodiversity and the energy transition. However, in all cases, the degree of diffusion of renewable technologies is closely interconnected with the degree and level of technological maturity. In addition, substantial public funding has expanded markets, allowing energy financing that has redesigned the energy scenario of renewables. The exploitation of resources, the incessant growth of the population, have made it possible to develop innovative technologies to exploit renewable resources. As population growth has increased and living standards have improved, we have seen an increase in the amount of energy required in most places in the world, and this has prompted several industrialized economies of the world, including for example the "BRICS" to change direction. Since the two thousand years, important technologies have been introduced with renewable sources that are characterized by their low environmental impact. Currently fossil fuels provide about 80% of energy needs and only a small part is covered through renewable energy sources, which are characterized by high rates of inconsistency and ungovernability. However, the banks themselves play a key role in terms of spreading innovation through financing. However, if on the one hand financing and incentives from banking institutions increase in the renewable sector, those in the oil sector do not stop and continue to be substantial. In the dispute of wind energy, the technology has been widely spread among the various companies operating in the area, up to making significant changes that have allowed improvements in terms of energy production and in terms of installation. To overcome the problems related to noise pollution and visual impact, which could be an obstacle to the landscape, offshore wind farms were designed. The offshore wind farms being in the open sea, allow a greater constancy of the winds, however the installation costs are quite high due to the materials that must be used, and it is possible to reduce the forms of noise pollution, which especially near the inhabited centers can be particularly annoying. To describe the life cycle of renewable technologies, we will refer to Kondratiev's life cycles. We can divide this cycle into four phases, which will be described in detail below:

- The first phase is research and development, it is a phase of experimentation, where the fusion between research and innovation occurs to evaluate the economic and environmental advantages in a cost-benefit perspective. In this phase the risk of failure of the innovative technology that aims to enter the market is extremely high, but the co-creation between companies and universities that occurs at this stage, allows the possibility of reorganizing and reshaping the technology and making corrective measures.
- The second phase is of ascent, where technologies begin to take shape and begin to enter the market, we are at point (A). The technologies belonging to the context of renewables, have an average slow development and many processes are subjected to remodulation.

- The third phase is the stage of maturity that we have indicated with the point (M), in this phase the gain and expansion of the technology has taken place successfully.
- The fourth point concerns the phase of decline of technology that is being replaced by a new, younger technology. This process occurs frequently especially in this industrial sector.

*Figure 5. Technology distribution*

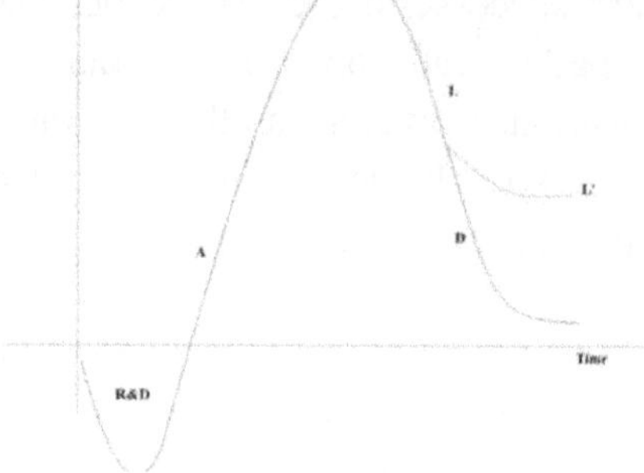


The four phases of technology distribution can also be described as the phase of innovation, commercialization, diffusion, and substitution and follow different cycles, depending on the type of technology and the type of renewable source used. The greater the spread of innovation, the faster consumers will adopt a new product or service. An interesting aspect to examine is the achievement of critical mass, it occurs when a fairly substantial number of individuals adopt the new technology. It has been repeatedly pointed out that the adoption rate is extremely variable. The existing scientific literature highlights two main trends. In the first case, the aim is to observe the diffusion process in an overall perspective, with the aim of not linking the diffusion process only and exclusively to an adoption discourse but also to problems that may arise in this process, an example of selection and entry. In accordance with the studies conducted by Francesco Lissoni, it is considered appropriate to specify that in this respect, both the life cycles of the product (Klepper, 1996) and the industrial dynamics of an evolutionary type play a key role. In the second case it is important to affirm the key role of information externalities, that is, how information is disseminated. Moreover, the adoption of various mechanisms that differ from each other, can generate new political implications that could facilitate the spread of innovation (Alcalde, 2013). Information externalities play a fundamental role, as at the center of the topic for climate change mitigation, there is the reorganization of energy infrastructure (Abufotuh, 2007; Apergis et al., 2012; Balsalobre-Lorente et al., 2018). There is an increase in energy patents integrated into the sciences (Hötte et al., 2021; Perrons et al., 2021). An interesting aspect is to be intercepted not only in the consequence of the diffusion of innovations, but also the impact of current patents on new innovations to be patented (Chen et al; 2010). Examining the problem, under the macroeconomic aspect, the dissemination of knowledge through spillovers, plays a fundamental role in endogenous economic growth (Grossman et al., 1991; Griliches, 1992; Aghion et al., 1992; Acemoglu et al., 2012). Conversely, from a microeconomic point of view, the spread of innovation plays a key role in the productivity of individual states. (Baumol, 1991). However, the spread of renewables generates positive effects on the rate of future growth (Islam et al., 2022).

## SOLUTIONS AND RECOMMENDATIONS

It is necessary to translate knowledge into awareness to change the metabolism of today's society and to guarantee these models are necessary policies to support the development of renewables, these must be not only desirable but also dutiful on the part of governments.

## FUTURE RESEARCH DIRECTIONS

The internal package of renewable energies and their diffusion on the territory, are undoubtedly an invaluable resource that in a long-term perspective can only translate into a growth compatible with the external environment and, through the implementation and subsequent development of modern technologies, to ensure effective coordination between the various actors, aimed at promoting greater environmental justice.

## CONCLUSION

The study of the diffusion of innovation is extremely vast and at times heterogeneous, due to the various methodological perspectives that have been adopted by various scholars over the years. Understanding the way in which an innovation is adopted in the world of renewables and how it is spread among the various companies is a question that has a key role to accelerate the dissemination processes and ensure greater information externalities between the various agents. The diffusion of promising technologies has allowed us to develop a new paradigm in energy production and it is thanks to their diffusion that today it is possible to build offshore wind farms that allow to produce energy in an alternative way and favor transition cycles. Despite the incompleteness and non-exhaustive treatment of a topic with multiple implications and facets and despite the topicality of the theme, constantly evolving, it is still possible to draw some final considerations in the light of future evolutions and innovations. In the energy sector, support from the state and financial institutions is more than necessary, and the promotion of incentive mechanisms could encourage agents to make green investments. Ensuring its correct diffusion would generate important implications, both in terms of energy independence from foreign countries, and as an important energy resource from an economic point of view thanks to the lower costs associated with domestic production and above all for the positive contribution it could make to our public debt. Renewable energies, in fact, could be a strong point for the creation of new jobs in the various sectors of the production chain, generating sustainable and environmentally friendly economic growth, which aims to reduce negative externalities and social costs.

## REFERENCES

Abufotuh, F. (2007). Energy efficiency and renewable technologies: the way to sustainable energy future. *Desalination Journal, 209* (1–3), 275-282.

Acemoglu, D., Akcigit, U. (2012). Intellectual property rights policy, competition, and innovation. *Journal of the European economic association, 10*(1), 1-42.

Aghion, P., & Howitt, P. (1992). *A model of growth through creative destruction* (Vol. 60). Econometrica.

Akhdar, B., & Mohsen, B. (2019). Transition économique vs. Résistances sociopolitiques et de la gouvernance institutionnelle: évidence de la politique économique algerienne. Revue Européenne du Droit Social, Vol.44 (03): 80-98.doi https://www.ceeol.com/search/article-detail?id=768418

Alcalde, P. (2013). *A behavioral model of non-linear peer effects in cognitive achievement.* [PhD thesis: University of Pennsylvania].

Apergis, N., Payne, J.E. (2012). Renewable and non-renewable energy consumption-growth nexus: evidence from a panel error correction model. *Energy Economics, 34* (3), 733-738.

Arnette, A. N. (2013). *Integrating rooftop solar into a multi-source energy planning optimization model* (Vol. 111). Applied Energy.

Arthur, W.B. (2007). The structure of invention. *Resource Policy, 36* (2), 274-287.

Balsalobre-Lorente, D., Shahbaz, M., Roubaud, D., & Farhani, S. (2018). *How economic growth, renewable electricity and natural resources contribute to CO2 emissions?* (Vol. 113). Energy Policy.

Barbieri, N., Marzucchi, A., & Rizzo, U. (2020). Knowledge sources and impacts on subsequent inventions: Do green technologies differ from non-green ones? *Resources Policy*, *49*(2), 103901. doi:10.1016/j.respol.2019.103901

Baumol, W. J. (1991). Technological imperatives, productivity, and insurance costs. Geneva documents on risk and insurance. The Geneva Papers on Risk and Insurance. Issues and Practice, (pp. 154–165). Springer.

Brahmi, M., Zouari, S., & Rossi, M. (2014). L'industrie minière et ses effets écologiques. État socio-économique et environnemental dans le bassin minier tunisien. In E. D. Y. T. E. M. Collection (Ed.), *Cahiers de géographie, numéro 17, Exploitations minières passées et présentes. Impacts environnementaux et sociétaux* (pp. 109–120)., doi:10.3406/edyte.2014.1279

Carattini, S., Kallbekken, S., & Orlov, A. (2019). *How to win public support for a global carbon tax.* Nature Journal. doi:10.1038/d41586-019-00124-x

Chen, Y.S., Chang, K.C. (2010). The relationship between the quality of a company's patent and its market value: the case of the US pharmaceutical industry. *Technological forecasting and social change, 77* (1), 20 – 33. .

Douah, B., & Mohsen, B. (2019). *Issue 3* (Vol. 44). Renewable energies and their contribution in development in the context of competitiveness: evidence of specific oil Territory, European Review of Social L. DOI., https://www.ceeol.com/search/article-detail?id=768416

Ebinger, J., & Vergara, W. (2011). *Climate Impacts on Energy Systems: key issues for energy sector adaptation.* The World Bank. doi:10.1596/978-0-8213-8697

Eskander, S. M. S. U., & Fankhauser, S. (2020). Reduction in greenhouse gas emissions from national climate legislation. Natural Climate change, 10, 750–756. . doi:10.103841558-020-0831-z

Garrone, P., Piscitello, L., Wang, Y. (2014). Innovation performance and international knowledge spillovers: evidence from the renewable energy sector in OECD countries. *Industry and Innovation Journal, 21* (7–8), 574-598. .

Griliches, Z. (1992). The Search for R&D Spillovers Scandinavian. Journal of economics, 94, 29-47.

Grossman, G. M., & Helpman, E. (1991). *Innovation and growth in the global economy*. MIT Press.

Hao, L.N., Umar, M., Khan, Z., and Ali, W. (2021). Green Growth and Low Carbon Emission in G7 Countries: How Critical the Network of Environmental Taxes, Renewable Energy and Human Capital Is? *Sci. Total Environ. Science of total environment.*

Hötte, K., Pichler, A., & Lafond, F. (2021). The rise of science in low-carbon energy technologies. Renewable and sustainable energy reviews, 139. doi:10.1016/j.rser.2020.110654

Irandoust, M. (2016). *The renewable energy-growth nexus with carbon emissions and technological innovation: evidence from the Nordic countries.* Ecological Indicators.

Islam, M., Irfan, M., Shahbaz, M., & Vo, X. V. (2022). [Renewable Energy.]. *Renewable and Non-renewable Energy Consumption in Bangladesh: The Relative Influencing Profiles of Economic Factors, Urbanization, Physical Infrastructure, and Institutional Quality., 184*, 1130–1149.

Klepper, S. (1996). Entry, Exit, Growth, and Innovation over the Product Life Cycle. *The American Economic Review.*

Liu, J., Zhang, D., Cai, J., & Davenport, J. (2021). Legal Systems. *National Governance and Renewable Energy Investment: Evidence from Around the World., 32*, 579–610.

Marrou, H., Guilioni, L., Dufour, L., Dupraz, C., & Wery, J. (2013). Microclimate under agrivoltaic systems: Is crop growth rate affected in the partial shade of solar panels? *Agricultural and Forest Meteorology, 177*, 117–132. doi:10.1016/j.agrformet.2013.04.012

Mohsen, B., Karim,B., & Sonia, Z.(2013). History vs. Reality, Mining industry diagnostic and environmental effects: Illustration case in real size of Tunisian mining basin. IOSR Journal of Environmental Science, Toxicology and Technology (IOSR-JESTFT) 3 (2), 56-64.

Mohsen, B., & Sonia, Z. (2013). Indicateurs statistiques de performance économique et du positionnement mondial de l'industrie minière en Tunisie (1990 - 2010): Regard avant la révolution 2011. Book of Acts of collective, Informal economy and development: employment, financing and regulation in a context of crisis, "the University Paris-Est-Créteil, 6, 7 and 8 June 2013 Paris, France

Nemet, G.F. (2012). Spillover of inter-technological knowledge for energy technologies. *Energy economics, 34* (5), 1259 – 1270.

Noailly, J., & Shestakova, V. (2017). Knowledge spillovers from renewable energy technologies: lessons from patent citations. Environmental innovation and societal transitions, 22, 1-14. .

Noailly, J., Smeets, R. (2015). Directing technical change from fossil-fuel to renewable energy innovation: an application using firm-level patent data. *Journal of Environmental Economics and Management, 72*, 15-37.

Perrons, R. K., Jaffe, A. B., & Le, T. (2021). Linking scientific research and energy innovation: A comparison of clean and dirty technologies. *Energy Research & Social Science, 78*, 102122. doi:10.1016/j.erss.2021.102122

Popp, D. (2017). From science to technology: the value of knowledge from different energy research institutions. *Resource Policy, 46* (9), 1580-1594. .

Sadorsky, P. (2014). The effect of urbanization on CO2, emissions in emerging economies. *Energy Economics, 41*(1) pp. 147-153. .

Sag, M., Rohde, K. (2007). Patent reform and differential impact. *Minnesota Journal of Law,* Science & Technology, 8 (1), 1-93. .

Thomas, J. R. (2002). *No. 2* (Vol. 17). The responsibility of the rule maker: comparative approaches to patent administration reform. Berkeley Technology Law Journal.

Tol, R. J. (2014). *Climate economics: economic analysis of climate, climate change and climate policy, Book*. Edward Elgar.

Umar, M., Farid, S., & Naeem, M. A. (2022). Time-frequency connection between clean energy stocks and fossil fuel markets: Comparison between the financial, oil and pandemic crises. *Energy, 240*, 122702. doi:10.1016/j.energy.2021.122702

Zhang, W., Zhang, X., Liu, F., Huang, Y., & Xie, Y. (2020). Evaluation of the urban low-carbon sustainable development capability based on the TOPSIS-BP neural network and grey relational analysis. *Complexity, 2020*, 1–16. doi:10.1155/2020/6616988

Zhao, R., Zhan, L., Yao, M., Yang, L. (2020). A geographically weighted regression model augmented by Geodetector analysis and principal component analysis for the spatial distribution of PM2. *Sustainable Cities and Society, 5.*

## ENDNOTES

1. B. Petroleum, "BP Statistical Review of World Energy."
2. Gabriel Trade, sociologist French (1843-1904)
3. E. M Rogers – Diffusion of innovation (1962)
4. F. Bass – Bass Model or Bass diffusion model (1969)
5. Richard J. Tol – Full Professor University of Sussex – Climate economics: economic analysis of climate, climate change and climate policy, Edward Elgar Pub Oct. 26 - 2014

# Chapter 16
# The Relationship Between Total Quality Management Practices and Their Impacts on Product Innovation:
## An Empirical Study

**Oumayma Tajouri**
*High Institute of Management of Sousse, Tunisia*

## ABSTRACT

*The relationship between Total Quality Management (TQM) practices and product innovation is conflictual. Although some scholars have confirmed that TQM promotes product innovation, many others have reported that TQM and product innovation are negatively associated. Furthermore, most of these studies have not studied the direct and indirect impact of TQM practices on product innovation and they have neglected the interrelation between quality practices. The purpose of this paper is to analyze the causal relation between TQM practices and product innovation in the Tunisian ISO 9001-certified industries. Using a self-administered survey to sample ISO9001-certified industries, the present investigation tests ten hypotheses linked TQM practices and product innovation. The present study supports the significant and positive relations among TQM practices. Then, only the impact of data and analysis on both incremental and radical product innovation was supported.*

## INTRODUCTION

Introducing the appropriate methods which enable product innovation is an increasingly important challenge for the industries (Yusr et al., 2022). Total quality management (TQM) is widely recognized as a useful managerial tool that can lead organization to develop product innovation (Honarpour et al., 2017), (Prajogo & Sohal, 2003). In the literature, several empirical studies have been proposed to explain the impact of TQM practices on product innovation (Yusr et al., 2022) (Honarpour et al., 2017).

DOI: 10.4018/978-1-6684-6766-4.ch016

The existing literature showed conflictual results about the extent of TQM and its impact on product innovation (Manzani et al. 2019) (Khan & Naeem, 2016). Although many studies (Honarpour et al., 2017) (Prajogo & Sohal, 2003) (Khan & Naeem, 2016) (Khalfallah et al., 2022) have affirmed the positive effect of TQM on product innovation, other have showed that both these variables are negatively associated (Yusr et al., 2022).

Furthermore, the most drawback of these studies is the ignorance of the causal relation among TQM practices and their impact on product innovation. The most of previous empirical studies have considered TQM as one dimensional construct or they have carried on only the direct impact of TQM on innovation and they are neglected the impact of interaction between TQM practices (Manzani et al. 2019) (Kim et al., 2012). Although some previous investigations have tested the direct impact TQM practices on product innovation (Arshad & Su, 2015) (Àbu Salim et al., 2019), only few studies have focused on the interrelation among TQM practices and their impacts on product innovation (Kim et al., 2012).

The literature lacks of systematic empirical evidence regarding the interrelation of TQM practices and its effects on product innovation in Tunisian context. This paper fills these gaps. The objective of this paper is to explore the relation between TQM practices and their impacts on product innovation in Tunisian certified industries. The structure of this study is organized as follows. The next section describes the extant literature, develop hypothesis and establish a research model. The third section presents methodology, results. Finally, this study concludes with a discussion.

## LITERATURE REVIEW AND HYPOTHESIS DEVELOPEMENT

### A. TQM Practices

TQM is a holistic management philosophy that fosters all functions of an organization through continuing improvement and organizational change (Kayna, 2003). According to Lakhal and al. (Lakhal et al., 2006), TQM is defined as an action plan aimed at produce or deliver products and \ or services which are compatible with customer needs at best, by requirements, faster, safer, cheaper than processing easier with competitors through the participation of all employees under the senior management direction. A review of extent literature shows that TQM is a multidimensional construct. Table 1 presents the most influential practices selected in innovation field.

*Table 1. TQM Practices in the present study*

| **PRACTICES SUPPORTING REFERENCE IN INNOVATION FIELD**Employee relations (ER) (Kim et al., 2012) (Hung et al., 2011) (Zeng et al., 2015)(et al., 2018) Continuous improvement (CI)(Khan & Naeem, 2016)(Abu Salim et al., 2019) Customer focus (CF) (Honarpour et al., 2017)(et al., 2018)(Khan & Naeem, 2016)(Kim et al., 2012)(Arshad & Su, 2015)(Abu Salim et al., 2019)(Hung et al., 2011)(Prajogo & Sohal, 2004)(Zhang et al., 2016) Process management (PM) (Honarpour et al., 2017)(et al., 2018)(Kim et al., 2012) (Zeng et al., 2015)(Zhang et al., 2016)(Ershadi et al., 2019) Data and analysis (DA) (Honarpour et al., 2017)(Prajogo & Sohal, 2003) (Khan & Naeem, 2016)(Kim et al., 2012) |
|---|

## B. Product Innovation

Product innovation split into incremental product innovation and radical product innovation (Manzani et al., 2019) (Kim et al., 2012). This classification can be made when considering the degree of innovation (Kim et al., 2012). While Incremental product innovation (IPI) refers to innovation related to the introduction of products that provide improvements or new advantage to existing technology in the market, radical product innovation (RPI) is defined as innovation associated with the introduction of products that incorporate ultimatly different technology from that already used for existing products (Kim et al., 2012), (Chandy & Tellis, 1998).

## C. Hypotheses Development

### 1) The Interrelation Between TQM Practices

#### *a) Employees Relations*

Many researchers have asserted that employees' relations are an elementary component in TQM. In fact, TQM could be viewed as involvement all the employees at all the level. Involving employees in quality activities and supporting this responsibility play a crucial role in successful TQM implementation in the industries (Kayna, 2003) (Lakhal et al., 2006). According Fuentes-Fuentes and al. (2004) have argued that employee's awareness about quality and employee's participation in quality decisions lead to better understand continuous improvement principles. They have supported that continuous improvement is consistent with teamwork.Furthermore, according previous empirical studies (Kim et al., 2012) (Fuentes-Fuentes et al., 2004), the involvement of the employees at all level in quality improvement allows organization to success customer oriented employees. Then, they have argued that supporting quality responsibility and the participation in quality improvement quality are required to make the contact with the customers more flexible. Similarly, Kim and al. (2012) have stressed that employee's relations may facilitate quality tools learning such as check sheets, flow charts, and statistical process control. Then, supporting quality responsibilities and collaboration among employees can help organization to reduce process variation and interruption production, also, guarantee regular preventive equipment maintenance (Kim et al., 2012).

As such, we suggest the following hypotheses:

**H1a.** Employees relations are positively associated to customer focus.
**H1b.** Employees relations are positively associated to continuous improvement.
**H1c.** Employees relations are positively associated to process management.

#### *b) Customer Focus*

Customer focus is considered as elementary practice of TQM (Honarpour et al., 2017) (Manzani et al. 2019) (Khan & Naeem, 2016) (Kim et al., 2012) (Arshad & Su, 2015) (Abu Salim et al., 2019). Customer focus refers to the extent to which a firm is following, understanding customer expectations (Manzani and al. 2019) (Kim et al., 2012). In fact, TQM is a highly customer oriented strategies. Kim and al. (2012) have suggested that identifying and understanding customers' exceptions can help the organizations to use quality data and analysis it. Then following customer needs allows organization to get at update their product quality information dealing with a changing demand. Prior empirical investigations (Kim et al., 2012) have showed that customer focus is positively associated with data and analysis. Hence, the following hypothesis is proposed:

**H2a.** Customer focus is positively associated with data and analysis

## 2) TQM Practices and Product Innovation

### *a) Continuous Improvement*

Continuous improvement is one of the most influential practices of TQM (Khan & Naeem, 2016)(Arshad & Su, 2015) (Abu Salim et al., 2019). In fact, continuous improvement allows to reduce failure rate (Arshad & Su, 2015) and allows firm to align their product with customer needs. Abu Salim and al. (2019) have asserted the elementary role of continuous improvement to produce innovation. Many scholars (Honarpour et al., 2017)(Khan & Naeem, 2016) have affirmed the positive effect of TQM on product innovation including continuous improvement practice. Arshad and al. (2015) have emphasized on continuous improvement role on product innovation. As such, we can propose the following hypotheses:

**H3a.** Continuous improvement is positively associated with incremental product innovation
**H3b.** Continuous improvement is positively associated with radical product innovation

### *b) Data and Analysis*

Data and analysis play crucial role to introduce product innovation (Honarpour et al., 2017)(Prajogo & Sohal, 2003)(Khan & Naeem, 2016)(Kim et al., 2012). An empirical study was conducted by Khan and al. (2016) have affirmed that TQM practices including data and analysis linked significantly and positively with product innovation. Arshad and al. (2015) have supported that the use of data and analysis it can influence product innovation. Hence, the following hypotheses are proposed:

**H4a.**Quality and analysis is positively associated with incremental product innovation
**H4b.**Quality and analysis is positively associated with radical product innovation

### *c) Process Management*

Process management is considered a key part of TQM practices (Honarpour et al., 2017) (Manzani and al. 2019) (Kim et al., 2012) (Zeng et al., 2015). Khan and al. (Khan & Naeem, 2016) found that TQM including process management affect positively product innovation. Kim and al. (2012) have supported the positive link between process management and both incremental and radical product innovation. They have argued the positive effect of process management by encouraging routines and by developing new ideas through improvement these routines. As such, we can formulate the following hypotheses:

**H5a.** Process management is positively associated with incremental product innovation
**H5b.**Process management is positively associated with radical product innovation

# METHODOLOGY

## A. Sample and Data Collection

This study concerns quality certified Tunisians industries. They were selected using the agency for the promotion of industry and innovation (APII) database. The data collection method used was quantitative method based on questionnaire. It has been used in many empirical studies of quality management (Kim et al., 2012) (Zeng et al., 2015). Of 836 Tunisian quality certified, the questionnaire was posted to 594 certified quality industries. A total of 99 questionnaires were returned. The Table 2 presents the characteristics of firm and respondent.

*Table 2. Characteristics of Firms and Respondents*

| FIRM CHARC. FREQ. % RESPONDEN T CHAR. FREQ. %Num. of employees<50 <200 >20018 51 30 18.2 51.6 30.3Gendre Female Male23 76 23.2 76.8Industry sector Agro-foods indus Mat., cer. and glass const.Mechanical and metall. Electric, electronic Chemistry Textils Other12 7 28 13 25 12 2 12.1 7.1 28.3 13.1 25.3 12.1 2Position Manager Head of departement Engineer CEO Other16 19 53 5 6 16.2 19.2 53.5 5.1 6.1 |
|---|

## B. Measures

### 1) TQM Practices

In order to measure TQM practices in quality certified Tunisian industries, this study includes (1) employee relations, (2) customer focus, (3) continuous improvement, (4) data and analysis and (5) process management as total quality practices.

This study assessed TQM using 25 measurement items developed from previous studies (Ahire et al., 1996) (Coyle-Shapiro, 2002) (Gradzol & Gershon, 1998) (Hunt, 1992) (Saraph et al., 1989) (Zeitz et al., 1997). TQM measurements were adapted from those employed by (Kim et al., 2012) (Kayna, 2003) (Lakhal et al., 2006) (Hung et al., 2011) (Zeng et al., 2015) (Jaca & Psomas, 2015) (Singh & Smith, 2004).

### 2) Product Innovation

The construct of product innovation has two dimensions. Multi-item scales were adopted to measure those dimensions. Four items for each of the dimensions were used. Incremental product innovation measurement scales (Muhammad et al., 2022; Geetika, Archana & Mohsen 2021) were developed based on the studies of (Chandy & Tellis, 1998) (Baker & Sinkula, 1999), (Prajogo & Sohal, 2004) used by (Kim et al., 2012) (Hung et al., 2011).

Radical product innovation measurement scales were adopted from (Chandy & Tellis, 1998) (Baker & Sinkula, 1999) (Prajogo & Sohal, 2004) used (Kim et al., 2012) (Hung et al., 2011).

## RESULTS

In order to test the research model for this study, a structural equation model was run using Partial Least Square (PLS-SEM). The data analysis with PLS model is conducted at two steps:

The first step is to assess the measurement model (outer model) through evaluating validity and reliability of the measures. The second step is to examine structural model (inner model) using bootstrapping method for testing hypothesis.

### A. Measurement Model

#### 1) Exploratory Factor Analysis (EFA)

In order to purify the measurement instruments, an exploratory factor analysis was executed. A factor analysis with principal component analysis (PCA) for each measurement scale was performed. PCA aims to determine the uni-dimensionality and reliability of dimensions underlying each construct in the proposed research model. The results of principles component analysis (PCA) reveal that several items should be eliminated from the analysis. We deleted the item that hasn't the corresponding the threshold level suggested. These are the following items EI4, DA1, IPI1. After iteration, the Principal Component Analysis and Varimax were adopted and reach the following results. TQM practices represents the five following factors; Employees relations (factor 1), Customer focus (factor2), Continuous improvement (factor3), Data and analysis (factor4) Process management (factor5). The total variance explained and the eigen value were calculated separately for each TQM practices. The results show that all the eigen value of each practices are superior than 1 and the total variance ranged from 59.981 to 73.852 per cent. The KMO for all dimensions were exceeded 0.50, vary between 0.659 and 0.883. In order to examine the reliability, the Cronbach's alpha for the factors vary between 0.743 and 0.928, which are exceeded the traditionally acceptable level of 0.70. The results show two factors of product innovation, Incremental product innovation (factor1), Radical product innovation (factor 2). The total variance explained and the eigen value were calculated separately for each dimension of product innovation. The result demonstrates that all the eigen value of each dimension is superior than 1 and the total variance and the KMO for all dimensions were exceeded 05. In order to examine the reliability, the Cronbach's alpha for the factors vary between 0.711 and 0.814, which are exceeded the traditionally acceptable level of 0.70.

#### 2) Confirmatory Factor Analysis CFA

As indicated by Hair and al. (2011) (2014), the convergent validity is assessed through the factor loading average variance extracted (AVE) and composite reliability (CR). As shown in Table 3, all the indicators loadings surpass 0.7, the average variance extracted (AVE) of each construct have to be about 0.50 or higher, and composite reliability for each construct take a value equal to or above 0.70. These results verify the convergent validity of the measurement model.

The discriminant validity is assessed through the means of the Fornell and Larcker (1981) criterion in which the AVE of each construct should be higher than the highest squared correlation with any other construct. Also, the discriminant validity is assessed through the cross loading. The loadings of each indicator on its construct have to be higher than the cross-loadings on other constructs. The estimation

*Table 3. Converent Validity*

| Construct | Number of items | Second order construct loading | Loading | CR | AVE |
|---|---|---|---|---|---|
| Employees relations | 3 | | 0.803-0.829 | 0.855 | 0.663 |
| Customer focus | 6 | | 0.818-0.894 | 0.944 | 0.738 |
| Data and analysis | 4 | | 0.739-0.800 | 0.857 | 0.599 |
| Process management | 5 | | 0.719-0.856 | 0.894 | 0.624 |
| Continuous improvement | 4 | | 0.764-0.924 | 0.904 | 0.702 |
| Incremental product and service innovation | 3 | 0.926 | 0.889-0.928 | 0.930 | 0.816 |
| Radical product and service innovation | 4 | 0.947 | 0.789 -0.934 | 0.927 | 0.762 |

results verify that the measurement model meets all common requirements and confirm the discriminant validity.

## B. Structural Model

After confirming construct validity and reliability, the next step is to assess the structural model. It consists to examine the proposed hypotheses and to validate the research model. A bootstrapping was executed to examine the significance of the path coefficients and the loadings. The assessment of the structural model is established by examination the coefficient of determination $R^2$ of dependant latent variable and the cross-validated redundancy ($Q^2$) (Hair et al., 2014) (Henseler et al., 2009). The current study considers the rule of thumb proposed by Cohen (1998) to evaluate and accept coefficient of determination $R^2$. Accordingly, to Cohen (1998), $R^2$ values of 0.26, 0.13 and 0.02 are respectively interpreted as substantial, medium, weak levels of predictive accuracy.

The $R^2$ for customer focus is medium and the $R^2$ for all other dependent latent variables (CI, PM, DA, IPI, RPI) are substantial with value superior than 0.260.

To evaluate the cross-validated redundancy ($Q^2$), the blindfolding procedure cross-validated redundancy ($Q^2$) was pursued. The evaluation of Stone–Geisser's $Q^2$ value is done accordingly to Henseler et al. (2009). For a dependent latent variable, a Stone–Geisser's $Q^2$ value superior to zero states that the proposed path model has a satisfactory predictive relevance. The $Q^2$ of endogenous constructs are acceptable with values superior than 0.

The results indicate a positive significant relationship between employees' relations and customer focus. Moreover, beta coefficient and T values are significant ($\beta$=0.436, T=5.396, $p<0.001$) showing that there is strong relationship between level of employees relations and customer focus, hence, H1a is supported. The results ($\beta$=0.615, T=11.430, $p<0.001$) indicate a positive significant relationship between

*Table 4. Coefficient of determination $R^2$*

| | CI | CF | PM | DA | IPI | RIP |
|---|---|---|---|---|---|---|
| $R^2$ | 0.379 | 0.190 | 0.434 | 0.286 | 0.431 | 0.349 |

ER: Employees relations, CF: Customer focus , DA: Data and analysis, PM: Process management , CI : Continuous improvement , IPSI : Incremental product ans service innovation , RPSI : Radical product and service innovation

*Table 5. $Q^2$ coefficient*

| | CI | CF | PM | DA | IPI | RPI |
|---|---|---|---|---|---|---|
| $Q^2$ | 0.258 | 0.130 | 0.260 | 0.168 | 0.319 | 0.212 |

ER : Employees relations, CF : Customer focus , DA : Data and analysis, PM :Process management , CI : Continuous improvement , IPSI : Incremental product ans service innovation , RPSI : Radical product and service innovation

employees' relations and continuous improvement, H1b is supported. The results ($\beta$=0.659, T=10.021, p<0.001) indicate a positive significant relationship between employees' relations and process management, H1c is supported. Hypothesis H2 states that customer focus has an effect on data and analysis. The results ($\beta$=0.535, T=8.163, p<0.001) indicate a positive significant relationship between customer focus and data and analysis, H2a is supported.

The findings between continuous improvement and incremental product innovation ($\beta$=-0.059, T=0.572, p>0.05) indicate not significant, H3 is rejected. Hypothesis H3b states that continuous improvement has an effect on radical product innovation. The findings ($\beta$=0.014, T=0.088, p<0.05) indicate not significant relationship between continuous improvement and radical product innovation, H3b is rejected.

The findings ($\beta$=0.527, T=4.567, p<0.001) indicate a significant relationship between data and analysis and incremental product innovation, H4a is supported. Hypothesis H4b states that data and analysis have an effect on radical product innovation. The findings ($\beta$=0.463, T=4.452, p<0.001) indicate a significant relationship between data and analysis and product innovation, H4b is supported. The findings ($\beta$=0.214, T=1.542, p<0.05) show an insignificant relationship between process management and incremental product innovation, H5a is rejected. The results manifest ($\beta$=0.164, T=1.275, p>0.05) indicate an insignificant relationship between process management and product innovation, H5 is supported.

## DISCUSSIONS AND CONCLUSION

The present study investigates the relationship between TQM practices and their effects on product innovation. This study has identified the following practices i.e.: employees' relations, continuous improvement, process management, customer focus, data and analysis. A proposed model comprises five TQM practices and both incremental and radical product innovation. In order to examine the proposed model, data were collected from 99 Tunisian ISO 9001 certified industries. The findings of this study show significantly and positive link between TQM practices. This study supports that employees' relations influence positively customer focus, continuous improvement and process management. These results are consistent with those obtained by (2004). In their study, Fuentes-Fuentes and al. (2004) have confirmed that the employees' involvement and supporting quality responsibility influence positively customer focus and continuous improvement. Similarly, the results of the present investigation support that customer focus is positively associated with quality data. This result is consistent with those obtained by (Kim et al., 2012).

The findings of this study support only the direct effect of data and analysis on both incremental and radical product innovation. This study supports that using quality information and analysis it may lead to introduce both incremental and radical product innovation in Tunisian certified industries. These results are consistent with those obtained by Abu Salim and al. (2019). Contrary of the results obtained by (Kim

*Table 6. Hypotheses test results*

| | Hypothesis | Path coefficient | Tstat | Pvalue | Decision |
|---|---|---|---|---|---|
| H1a | ER→CF | 0.436 | 5.396 | 0.000 | **Supported** |
| H1b | ER→ CI | 0.615 | 11.430 | 0.000 | **Supported** |
| H1c | ER →PM | 0.659 | 10.021 | 0.000 | **Supported** |
| H2 | CF →DA | 0.535 | 8.163 | 0.000 | **Supported** |
| H3a | CI →IPI | -0.059 | 0.572 | 0.567 | **Rejected** |
| H3b | CI →RPI | 0.014 | 0.088 | 0.930 | **Rejected** |
| H4a | DA →IPI | 0.527 | 4.567 | 0.000 | **Supported** |
| H4b | DA →RPI | 0.463 | 4.452 | 0.000 | **Supported** |
| H5a | PM →IPI | 0.214 | 1.542 | 0.123 | **Rejected** |
| H5b | PM →RPI | 0.164 | 1.275 | 0.203 | **Rejected** |

et al., 2012), their study has not supported the positive and significant impact of data and analysis on incremental and radical product innovation.

Contrary of theoretical suggestions, the findings show that there is no significant relationship between both process management and continuous improvement on incremental and radical product innovation. The findings are consistent partially with the results obtained by Manzani et al. (2019) and Abu Salim and al. (2019). But the results of the present study desalign with the study of Kim and al. (2012). The results of their study have affirmed that process management is an enabler of both incremental and radical product innovation.

The results indicate that only data and analysis can introduce incremental and radical product innovation. An explanation for this results is that Tunisian certified industries didn't focus enough on process management and continuous improvement and allow the most importance to the other practices (Employees relations, customer focus and data and information). This focus on the three other practices was be explained by their ease to be implemented (El Manzani and al. 2019). Also, the motivation to be certified may drive to superficial implementation Manzani and al. (2019).

Theoretically, the present study is the first research that focuses on the relationship between TQM practices and their impacts on both incremental and radical product innovation in Tunisian certified industries. This empirical study fills the gap in TQM research field in the emerging countries. That bring us to invite practioners to review the implementation of TQM especially process management and continuous improvement and remedy its anomalies. The present study includes many limitations. The size of our sample is relatively small that it does not generalize the results. Another limitation, the respondents are the managers of Tunisian certified industries. It is recommended to replicate this study with a large sample with multiple informants from each company including other position.

## REFERENCES

Abu Salim, T., Sundarakani, B., & Lasrado, F. (2019). The relationship between TQM practices and organisational innovation outcomes Moderating and mediating the role of slack. *The TQM Journal*, *31*(6), 874–907. doi:10.1108/TQM-11-2018-0160

Ahire, S. L., Golhar, D. Y., & Waller, M. A. (1996). Development and validation of TQM implementation constructs. *Decision Sciences*, *27*(1), 23–56. doi:10.1111/j.1540-5915.1996.tb00842.x

Arshad, A. M., & Su, Q. (2015). Role of Total Quality Management in service innovations: An empirical study of Pakistans financial services firms. *Journal of Applied Business Research*, *31*(3), 891–910. doi:10.19030/jabr.v31i3.9225

Baker, W. E., & Sinkula, J. M. (1999). Learning orientation, market orientation and innovation: Integrating and extending models of organizational performance. *Journal of Market Focused Management*, *4*(4), 295–308. doi:10.1023/A:1009830402395

Chandy, R. K., & Tellis, G. J. (1998). Organizing for radical product innovation: The overlooked role of willingness to cannibalize. *JMR, Journal of Marketing Research*, *35*(4), 474–487. doi:10.1177/002224379803500406

Cohen, J. (1998). *Statistical power analysis for the behavioral sciences* (2nd ed.). Erlbaum.

Coyle-Shapiro, J. (2002). 'Changing employee attitudes: The independent effects of TQM & profit sharing on continuous improvement orientation'. *The Journal of Applied Behavioral Science*, *38*(1), 55–77. doi:10.1177/0021886302381004

Manzani, Sidmou & Cegarra. (2019). Does ISO 9001quality management system support product innovation? An analysis from the sociotechnical systems theory. *International Journal of Quality*.

Ershadi, M. J., Najafi, N., & Soleimani, P. (2019). Measuring the impact of soft and hard total quality management factors on customer behavior based on the role of innovation and continuous improvement. *The TQM Journal*, *31*(6), 1093–1115. doi:10.1108/TQM-11-2018-0182

Fornell, C., & Larcker, D. (1981). Evaluating Structural Equation Models with Unobservable Variables and Measurement Error. *JMR, Journal of Marketing Research*, *18*(1), 39–50. doi:10.1177/002224378101800104

Fuentes-Fuentes, M. M., & Albacete, C. ALlor Ãens-Montes, F. J. (2004). The impact of environmental characteristics on TQM principles and organizational performance. *Omega*, *32*(6), 425–442. doi:10.1016/j.omega.2004.02.005

Geetika, J., Archana, S., & Mohsen, B. (2021). *Consumer acceptance toward Blockchain Technology for Anti-counterfeiting: Hype, Credence or Future*. International Journal of Business Innovation and Research., doi:10.1504/IJBIR.2021.10042862

Gradzol, J. R., & Gershon, M. (1998). A survey instrument for standardizing TQM modelling research. *International Journal of Quality Science*, *3*(1, N1pp), 80–81. doi:10.1108/13598539810203887

Hair, J. F., Ringle, C. M., & Sarstedt, M. (2011). 'PLS-SEM: Indeed a Silver Bullet'. *Journal of Marketing Theory and Practice*, *19*(2), 139–151. doi:10.2753/MTP1069-6679190202

Henseler, J., Ringle, C. M., & Sinkovics, R. R. (2009). The use of partial least squares path modeling in international marketing. In *New challenges to international marketing*. Emerald Group Publishing Limited. doi:10.1108/S1474-7979(2009)0000020014

Honarpour, A., Jusoh, A., & Nor, K. M. (2017). *Total quality management, knowledge management, and innovation.* Business Excellence.

Hung, R. Y. Y., Lien, B. Y. H., Yang, B., Wu, C. M., & Kuo, Y. M. (2011). Impact of TQM and organizational learning on innovation performance in the high-tech industry. *International Business Review*, *20*(2), 213–225. doi:10.1016/j.ibusrev.2010.07.001

Hunt, V. D. (1992). *Quality in America: How to implement a competitive quality program.* Irwin.

Jaca, C. & Psomas, E. (2015). Total quality management practices and performance outcomes in Spanish service companies. *Total Quality Management & Business Excellence, 26*(9-10).

Hair, JSarstedt, MHopkins, LKippelwieser, G. (2014). Partial least squares structural equation modeling (PLS-SEM). *European Business Review*, *26*(2), 106–121. doi:10.1108/EBR-10-2013-0128

Kafetzopoulos, D., Gotzamani, K., & Gkana, V. (2015). Relationship between quality management, innovation and competitiveness. Evidence from Greek companies. *Journal of Manufacturing Technology Management*, *26*(No. 8), 1177–1200. doi:10.1108/JMTM-02-2015-0007

Kayna, H. (2003). The relationship between total quality management practices and their effects on firm performance. *Journal of Operations Management*, *21*(4), 405–435. doi:10.1016/S0272-6963(03)00004-4

Khalfallah, M.,, Ben Salem, A.,, & Zorgati, HLakhal, L. (2022). Innovation mediating relationship between TQM and performance: cases of industrial certified companies. *The TQM Journal*, *34*(3), 552-575 ().

Khan, B. A., & Naeem, H. (2016). *Measuring the impact of soft and hard quality practices on service innovation and organisational performance.* Total Quality Management & Business Excellence.

Kim, D. Y., Kumar, V., & Kumar, U. (2012). Relationship between quality management practices and innovation. *Journal of Operations Management*, *30*(4), 295–315. doi:10.1016/j.jom.2012.02.003

Lakhal, L., Pasin, F., & Liman, M. (2006). Quality management practices and their impact on performance. *International Journal of Quality & Reliability Management*, *23*(6), 625–646. doi:10.1108/02656710610672461

Muhammad, T., Erum, S., Naveeda, K., Brahmi,M. (2022). Nascent entrepreneurs and challenges in the digital market in developing countries, International Journal of Public Sector Performance Management, 2022, Vol.9, in-press. doi doi:10.1504/IJPSPM.2022.10138750

Prajogo, D. I., & Sohal, A. S. (2003). The relationship between TQM practices, quality performance, and innovation performance An empirical examination. International Journal of Quality & *Reliability Management*, *20*(8), 901–918.

Prajogo, D. I., & Sohal, A. S. (2004). The multidimensionality of TQM practices in determining quality and innovation performance an empirical examination. *Technovation*, *24*(6), 443–453. doi:10.1016/S0166-4972(02)00122-0

Saraph, J. V., Benson, G. P., & Schroeder, R. G. (1989). An instrument for measuring the critical factors of quality management. *Decision Sciences*, *20*(4), 810–829. doi:10.1111/j.1540-5915.1989.tb01421.x

Singh, P. J., & Smith, A. (2004). 'Relationship between TQM and innovation: An empirical Study'. *Journal of Manufacturing Technology Management*, *15*(5), 394–401. doi:10.1108/17410380410540381

Yusr, M. M., Mokhtar, S. S. M., Perumal, S., & Salimon, M. G. (2022). The impact of customer knowledge management, TQM and marketing capabilities on product innovation performance of Malaysian SMEs: An empirical study. *International Journal of Innovation Science*, *14*(No. 2), 316–338. doi:10.1108/IJIS-03-2021-0053

Zeitz, G., Johannesson, R., & Jr, J. E. (1997). Employee survey measuring total quality management practices and culture. *Group & Organization Management*, *22*(4), 414–444. doi:10.1177/1059601197224002

Zeng, J., Phan, C. A., & Matsui, Y. (2015). The impact of hard and soft quality management on quality and innovation performance: An Empirical study. *International Journal of Production Economics*, *162*, 162. doi:10.1016/j.ijpe.2014.07.006

Zhang, Q., Feng, X., & Xiang, X. (2016). The Impact of Quality Management Practices on Innovation in China: The Moderating Effects of Market Turbulence. *American Journal of Industrial and Business Management*, *6*(03), 291–304. doi:10.4236/ajibm.2016.63027

# Chapter 17
# Value Creation Through Innovation:
## Renewable Energy Community

**Luca Esposito**
*Department of Economics and Statistics, University of Salerno, Italy*

**Mohsen Brahmi**
*University of Sfax, Tunisia*

## ABSTRACT

*Innovation has become in recent years a tool to promote and allow the creation of value, that is, the ability of a company or a company to generate utility, wealth, and growth. In this chapter, the contribution of innovation in decarbonization and in combating the climate crisis is illustrated, paying particular attention to the role of renewable energy communities. They are classified as a means capable of guaranteeing environmentally friendly wealth that aims not only at maximizing profit but also at creating economically sustainable models. Currently, digitalization allows a connection to nodes, peer to peer, while initially, the model was based on one-to-many transmissions, which did not allow the decentralization that are the basis of renewable energy communities; they also have a strong social impact, aiming to increase the production and consumption of energy by renewable sources, with the aim of achieving high levels of energy efficiency within society.*

## INTRODUCTION

Interest in environmental issues and commitment to reducing emissions has grown exponentially in recent years (Jin, 2020). Technological innovation and innovation processes make an extremely important contribution in terms of decarbonization and combating the climate crisis. (Aldieri et al., 2019). The present link between energy and climate change, turns out to be increasingly worrying, complex and difficult to manage and in the last decade much scientific work has been done to analyze climate change policies, internationally (Helm et al., 2009; Giddens, 2011), national (Lisowski, 2002; Harris

DOI: 10.4018/978-1-6684-6766-4.ch017

2011; Bailey et al., 2012) and local (Bulkeley et al., 2003; Rootes et al., 2012). Many technologies that belong to the sphere of energy transition are emerging technologies that have not yet been able to fully express their potential in terms of value creation. Increasing energy efficiency and enabling a transition from fossil fuels to green is the challenge of the future. In fact, only by changing the sources of energy supply and limiting emissions and consumption will it be possible to avoid a catastrophe on a global scale and in this respect, innovation has become a tool to face the challenges of the current era and promote sustainable development (Horgan et al., 2018). Following the industrial era, the human being has generated enormous amounts of greenhouse gases (anthropogenic greenhouse effect), which comes from the consumption of conventional fossil fuels (oil, coal, gas), from all sources of pollution from intensive agriculture, livestock (methane) and deforestation. Currently the green lungs are suffering from a serious pathology, in fact they cannot perform a function of vital importance, namely the regulation of the climate that took place by absorbing CO2. Malthus, Pigou, Boulding, all have a common denominator, the study of the impact of man on the environment, the incessant growth of the population and the now well-known Malthusian trap, all factors that have occurred centuries later.

Their ability to study the succession of events, despite the very few means available, have allowed them to conduct extraordinary research that is still the subject of careful studies.

Boulding himself states that: “Albeit in a picturesque way I will call the open economy ‘cowboy economy’; the cowboy is the symbol of the endless plains, of the tireless, romantic, violent and robbery behavior that is characteristic of open societies. The closed economy of the future will have to resemble the economy of the astronaut: the Earth must be considered a spaceship, in which the availability of anything has a limit, as regards both the possibility of use and the ability to accept waste, and in which therefore it is necessary to behave as in a closed ecological system capable of continuously regenerating materials, using only an external supply of energy”, with the aim of highlighting that the environment should not be seen as an open, infinite system, but a closed system, where resources are available in limited stocks. Later Herman Daly (1973) introduced the concept of steady state. It is considered the pioneer of ecological economics, it affirmed that economic and population growth must be limited and cannot grow indefinitely, as an ever-changing economic growth becomes unsustainable, dangerous and cause of wars. Throughout history, changing lifestyles and increasing well-being have driven the spread of innovation, which can be achieved through the placing on the market of new products and new organizational structures (Schumpeter 1934).

Climate change and the loss of biodiversity are just some of the signs that have forced the entire world economy to move from linear economy models to circular economy models, with the aim of having to not only maximize profit but allow a harmonious development of society.

## BACKGROUND

In this chapter, reference will be made to the concept of transition from linear to circular energy, i.e., that produced through energy communities. There has been a process of transition from classical models of economic growth to models of economic development. In fact, the model of economic growth is based on a positive increase in production, vice versa economic development implies an increase in production and together with technological progress, aimed at ensuring better and sustainable living standards. In this perspective it is possible to speak of sustainable economic development. Over the past decade, the transition process to a low-carbon economy has been the key element in enabling climate change mitigation and reducing the impact on the environment and human health, and aims to ensure environmentally friendly economic growth, with the potential to enable the job creation of the future. This chapter arises from the need to provide a broad treatment of value creation through innovation. Since the end of the 20th century, it has become one of the main tools to enable companies to increase profits, as well as being a tool that has allowed governments to make improvements to the economy. The first part aims to present an analysis on the aspects related to the relationship between innovation and value creation, i.e., the ability of companies to generate utility and wealth. In the second part, the key role of innovation in value creation in the renewable energy sector and their contribution to the energy transition and climate change mitigation will be examined. In addition, the term energy democracy will often be used to outline how citizens and businesses can decide where and how to invest in clean energy. Currently, all over the world, a change of course is underway, aimed at promoting sustainable and environmentally friendly economic growth, with the aim of ensuring the promotion of a new development model capable of combining innovation and sustainability. In the last decade, innovation has played a key role in terms of business competitiveness, becoming one of the main tools to acquire new customers and allow good export profits with foreign countries. However, due to climate change, it plays a key role not only in terms of "rationalization" of processes, but also in terms of sustainability. There are many studies that confirm that companies operating in heterogeneous sectors integrate the principles of environmental sustainability within their business strategy. The current historical context is very dynamic, the company must not only and exclusively observe the maximization of profit but must produce sustainable services with low environmental impact. This process allows the promotion of social sustainability, through which it is possible to build a synergy between internal and external stakeholders. Innovation, if managed correctly, can enable companies (Brahmi & Zouari 2014) to achieve positive effects on costs, in addition to environmental certifications that act as a guarantee for companies to differentiate themselves from the competition, improving relations with shareholders and enabling collaboration with international customers. The promotion of renewable energy communities is not only developed at the company level, a fundamental contribution, in fact, is offered by small local communities. It is possible to allow a change of direction aimed at fostering a sustainable mentality, based on self-consumption and the sharing of energy from renewable sources (Akhdar & Mohsen 2019; Douah & Mohsen 2019). The implementation of such sources of innovation will generate a twofold benefit, aimed at reducing the carbon footprint and enabling significant savings on energy bills. If everyone transformed their environment into a source of clean energy, a circle would be generated at the end of which everyone would have a contribution in economic terms. We should direct the production of renewable energy through a model that we could call "PAD", based respectively on the production, storage and finally distribution of clean energy. This process would make it possible to obtain economic resources and would contribute to the promotion of some services to be distributed free of charge both for citizens and for companies. Currently, countless populations do not have access to electricity and in this sense, innovation plays a significant role in terms of energy efficiency. In fact, through the implementation of renewable energy communities, installed in a widespread way throughout the territory, it will be possible to promote the electrification of remote areas and contribute to the reduction of emissions into the atmosphere. Through the scores of the Energy Transition Index (ETI), on a sample of about 115 countries, energy performance has recorded a clear improvement. However, to promote an acceleration of electrification, both more funding for research and more cross-sectoral collaboration are needed. In addition, innovation, as a value creator, must not only contribute to ensuring access to energy, preferably from renewable sources, but also an affordable supply, to ensure the eradication of poverty and inequalities between states. For example, in Germany, the number of energy communities is increasing from 889 (2013) to 1.024 (2017), (Debor, 2014) and the renewable energy community model, allows to obtain resources from wind farms and offers a contribution of about 4,000 euros to each citizen who connects to the grid and also thanks to an agreement it was possible to finance car sharing, through electric cars, which is provided free of charge, generating a sustainable service and creating added value for all citizens. Energy communities play a key role, as the real pillar of innovation and sustainability is people and their habits. To enable a transition to a low-carbon economy, we need a cultural change and the sacrifice of having to "give up" to allow future generations a quality of life no lower than the one we have inherited. The effectiveness and success of renewable energy communities and the very creation of value through innovation, is strongly influenced both by the institutional context and technological policies that each state promotes to create added value. Institutional aspects and the role of policy makers can generate significant impacts both on innovative performance and in ensuring technological cooperation. Briefly, the purpose of the next chapter is to illustrate the new paradigm of innovation economics in value creation and how innovation, through the creation of renewable energy communities, can contribute to climate change mitigation and energy poverty reduction and allow an increase in prosperity and a reduction in territorial inequalities. Briefly summarizing, the purpose of this chapter is to provide managers and researchers working in the energy sector with contextual information on the European energy system, highlighting the impact of policies and the effects of investments, as an incentive to promote sustainable economic growth and a fair energy transition leading to a reduction in territorial disparities. Climate change and energy inflation have an impact on the whole structure and economic system; in this respect, this chapter documents the feasibility of value creation through strategic management of renewable energy communities, describing their strengths and weaknesses and the economic and environmental benefits for the creation of added value.

## MAIN FOCUS OF THE CHAPTER

### Issues, Controversies, Problems

Technological innovation has proved over the years to be a fundamental tool to allow the creation of new values and to combat global warming and it is estimated that a 1% increase in renewable energy generates a 0.193% reduction in carbon emissions (Mohsin et al., 2021), and how its correct supply can subsequently be spent to obtain social results (Crisan 2020). Innovation, therefore, has become necessary not only to allow the creation of value, but also to ensure the birth of new products or services that can be introduced not only at the company level but also within companies. Through this process, the aim is to increase competitiveness and provide innovative solutions that, especially in the context of renewables, allow us to design future scenarios that leave us hopeful. Some studies document that by 2050 we could move towards a renewable system (Hansen et al., 2019) and already starting from 2040 renewable energies could provide 20-30% of energy. In the last decade, innovation is observed not only as a tool to launch a new innovation on the market, but also in the creation of a service (renewable energy communities) that bases its pillars on the collaboration and co-creation of citizens and companies to promote the development of a shared technology that allows to produce, consume and sell the energy produced by each small community. In fact, most of the revolutionary waves have all focused and focused on innovation to create future value and generate wealth. (Lee et al., 2012). We live in a society in which we must foster creativity, developing innovation at all its levels and in all its angles and aiming through innovation to organize and manage an energy community. Innovation has a complex task, it must be able to co-create visions and objectives shared between people, aiming to obtain a harmonious result. (Porter et al., 2011; Ramaswammy et al., 2014). Currently, we live in the era of the knowledge economy and the economy of collaboration, they are the basis of the current era, and fundamental to share resources and obtain advantages from an economic, social, and environmental point of view. The same energy sharing, will change the electricity system, redesigning the way of producing and consuming energy. This innovation generates wealth, as it produces benefits and effects not only of an economic but also of an environmental nature, which will be explained in detail, later. The advantages are not only in the increased use of clean energy, but also in terms of energy savings with the consequent reduction in costs. In addition, modern innovative techniques allow the accumulation of the energy produced, which is stored inside the batteries that allow you to conserve the energy and then make it available in times of need. This innovation generates value from two different perspectives, in fact, it aims to reduce both poverty and energy dependence. Although the scores of the Energy Transition Index (ETI), testify through an analysis conducted on a sample of about 115 countries of how energy performance has recorded a clear improvement, nevertheless there are many developing countries and third and fourth world countries that do not have access to energy, as well as recording high rates of unemployment due to illiteracy and the lack of a structured industrial fabric. In the European political scenario, this issue is present within the energy package and one of the tools to combat it are the local communities. Innovation can contribute to the creation of a resilient energy system and allow the creation of new "players" that are able to promote decarbonization and guarantee through renewable energy communities, not only the generation of energy, but also the possibility of monitoring storage and consumption. The possibility of managing the accumulation in peak periods is relevant since renewable sources are characterized by a high rate of fluctuation. It can take place through different systems. The classic system involves electrochemical storage, through batteries, while the hydroelectric system comes using pumping plants. The energy produced in excess by the prosumers is conveyed into an accumulator and made available in times of need, while the remaining part is fed into the national electricity grid.

## THE EUROPEAN ENERGY SYSTEM AND THE ROLE OF FINANCING

The European Union promotes the production and use of energy from renewable energy sources. In the last decade, there are several European directives that aim to ensure an energy transition and a low-carbon future. Relevant in this respect, are the European directives, they are legislative acts, through which the European Union sets objectives and standards that the various member states must achieve, using the tools they deem most appropriate. The EU Directive 2018/2001 (RED II) was created to promote the consumption of energy from renewable sources and to allow citizens to collaborate and create energy communities. It introduces two important concepts, the concept of Collective Self-Consumption (AUC) and the concept of renewable energy communities (REC). The rapid spread of renewables has allowed the development of an increasingly distributed electricity system thanks to the presence of small plants. Citizens, their behavior, and habits, play a central and dominant role in the transition process, transforming themselves from passive and external subjects to active subjects. The European Union in 2019, has relaunched and updated the energy strategy, through the Clean Energy for all European Package (CEP), it aims to find a balance to allow a correct transition using renewable energy, with the aim of improving efficiency and energy performance both in buildings and at company level. Renewable energy communities can offer a fundamental contribution, although it remains important to allow the energy mix, to avoid "black-out" phenomena. Their goal is to produce, exchange and store energy, promoting a model based on energy democracy, where everyone can become the protagonist of the transition and decide where and how to invest in clean energy. The current historical period is characterized by excessive consumerism that has strong repercussions from an environmental and social point of view. Energy demand is increasing and with it also price volatility. Therefore, it is necessary to ensure energy security, which is denoted (Sovacool et al., 2017): "as a global energy system that fairly distributes both the benefits and burdens of energy services, and one that contributes to more representative and inclusive energy decision-making", with the aim of providing reliability supplies and ensuring reasonable market prices. A strategy must be implemented, which considers not only security of supply, but also sustainability and competitiveness. Only by aiming in this direction and changing consumer behavior will it be possible to reduce greenhouse gases by 40% by 2030. Back in 1992, with the Maastricht Treaty, the Objectives were assigned to the European Union to try to promote sustainable economic growth and that should not be excessively dependent on fluctuations in energy prices, subsequently, about five years later, the Treaty of Amsterdam (1997) was introduced through which renewables played a central role and it was estimated that by 2010, should cover about 12% of renewable energy. Currently, the European Union, thanks to better energy efficiency, consumes less energy and, especially thanks to photovoltaics and wind, manages to gradually get rid of fossil fuels, although it remains the prevailing energy source. Thanks to policies to support substantial investments, renewable energy is growing rapidly, in fact, recent studies show that the role of banks is fundamental in two respects, meeting the needs and expectations of families and individuals and offering financial services to those working in the private sector (Beck et al., 2006; Wang, 2016). To enable the process of transition to a sustainable society, a radical change is needed, which requires huge investments in this sector. Renewable energy sources have proved to be a powerful engine both in terms of economic growth and employment, above all, for example for the BRICS and SAARC countries. Suffice it to say that it is estimated that in 2016 in developing countries a number of green loans were recorded with an amount of about 1.5 trillion dollars, which according to studies conducted by the International Finance Corporation, are equivalent to 7% of credit in emerging sectors. Unlocking private sector investment, aiming to create a bridge between supply and demand, carrying out assessments on environmental and economic risks, is the new role of banks in this respect. Today, where it is believed that banking services have their own margin of responsibility, it is not uncommon to come across studies conducted on green banking. There is no single definition and universally shared by all scholars on this term (Alexander, 2016), however we could define this concept, as a theory oriented towards sustainability, through which banks offer services by promoting green finance with the aim of generating a positive effect on people and the environment. (Weber et al., 2011). The change of course of the various banking institutions, especially in recent years, is dictated by the fact that different financial risks have been found, which are closely related to climate change, this has pushed a large number of banks to be less short-sighted and observe the problem in all its angles (Monnin, 2018). A substantial number of investors see banks as one of the key drivers to enable the transition to a green economy. Despite this, according to the latest studies conducted by the World Resource Institute, many banks continue to finance those fuel-related sectors. Recently, banking institutions around the world offer a range of services and products aimed at ensuring the transition. However, especially from a business point of view, the three key factors for the measurability of investments: "Environmental, Social and Governance", are still considered only a purely reputational factor. The attention of the global public to green issues has allowed the creation of ad hoc investments by the various credit institutions, in line with the objectives set by the 2030 agenda. A classic example in this perspective are green loans and green bonds. They are characterized as green loans, i.e., forms of financing to finance projects and offer a contribution to the achievement of environmental objectives. In the case of both Green Loans and Green Bond Principles, both must be used to finance 100% green investments. Obviously, they are subject to a process of project evaluation, project management, reporting and publication of results, or the Green Loans Principles. The existing scientific literature demonstrates how the use of sustainable and environmentally responsible practices improves shareholder activity, but also the value of non-financial stakeholders. Green loans are one of the main tools that the bank can provide to its consumers. Through green loans, a person can receive financing for his company to allow him to implement sustainable investments. According to recent studies (Wang et al., 2020), the green bond market has increased incrementally since 2013, recording consistent growth. Moreover, the same study shows that countries such as China, Sweden and Japan have recorded an increase in green bond emissions, confirming the energy transition processes underway within the BRICS countries. Within this section, the results proposed by a study conducted by the Institute for Sustainability Leadership Initiative (EIB) of the University of Cambridge will be used, in 2020, about 100 interviews were conducted, with the aim of building a survey, of which about 80% were submitted to senior bankers, with experience gained in the sector, operating in Europe, Asia and the Americas. The aim is to analyze how financial institutions can facilitate and contribute to the promotion of economic growth and a green economy. In fact, in recent years, the role of banks has profoundly changed, they deal with "Social Economy", that is the branch of the economy that aims to reduce social disparities, poverty rates and promote equality.

*Figure 1. Reworking the author*
*Bank 2030: Accelerating the transition to a low-carbon economy; Source: Cambridge Institute for Sustainability Leadership, University of Cambridge January 30, 2020*

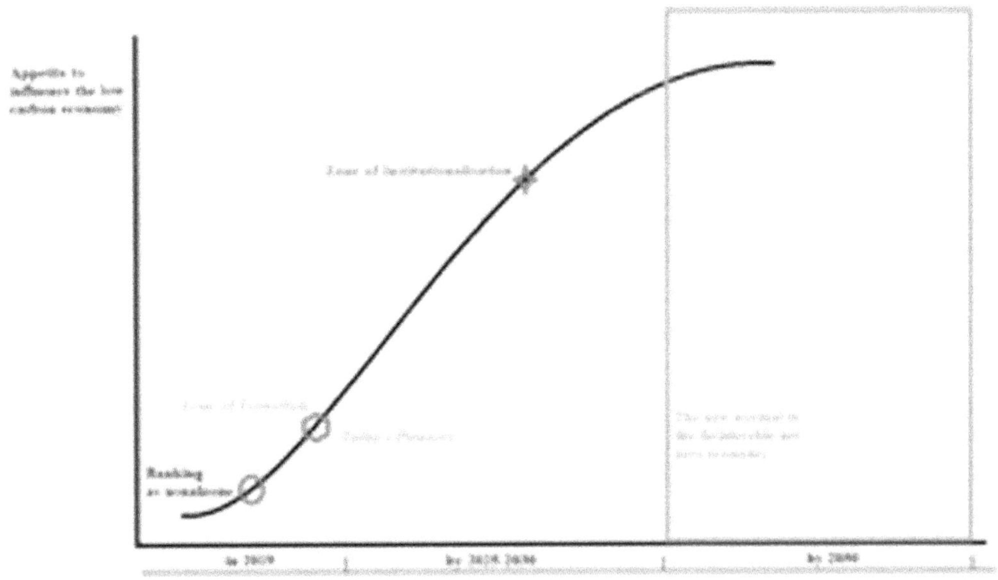

Within this graphic section, it is possible to observe a distribution, where on the axis of the abscissa time is placed, vice versa on the axis of the ordinates, "Appetite to influence the low carbon economy" is placed, to observe the three different perspectives:

- Banking as-usual zone, examining this point we note, how banks have a passive role towards sustainability, considering sustainability only from a reputational point of view.
- Zone of transition, create sustainable practices and have a forward-looking vision, promoting an activity and a commitment towards a low-carbon transition.
- Zone of institutionalization, through the alignment of business models, with zero emissions.

Banks do not yet have an "active mindset" towards issues such as sustainability and climate change and continue not to provide substantial financing to fossil fuel producers. This confirms how many banks have a (reactive) approach, with the ability to react to the event, but not to predict it before it happens and consequently produce negative externalities. This vision stems from the need of banks to respond to the needs of customers who in most cases are simply interested in maximizing profit. The study also confirms how in the event that banks decide to apply a series of business models, with the aim of promoting a low-carbon economy, they can offer facilitations on green leasing activities, to promote the rental of electric vehicles, make it easier and increase lending capacities to carry out sustainable activities, facilitate crowdfunding activities to also allow the dissemination of smaller projects. However, the study confirms that banking institutions can accelerate this transition process, creating a synergy between innovation and collaboration, moreover the analysis shows that in recent years, the non-commitment of a bank, could translate into bad reputation and loss of customers. From the analysis, conducted on a sample of about one hundred respondents, only 50% said they had an "active mentality", on the need for banks to accelerate the transition process. It should be clarified that each individual banking institution has a board of directors, which specializes in climate change risks, and which also plays a key role in speeding up this process. However, the percentage of people who see climate change as a real threat is an element that varies from country to country and depends on distinct factors, such as quality of life, education, and employment rates. Furthermore, legal liability and compensation should not be overlooked, which can become a problem when the parties to the dispute claim compensation for losses suffered as a result of climate risks. China plays a significant role in terms of green banking. In particular, the Industrial Bank in China (IBC), has offered different loans to both large and small and medium-sized enterprises, currently playing a leading role within green finance, it represents a classic example of the relationship between banks and customers to allow sustainable economic growth. In conclusion, the financial sector plays a fundamental role in promoting the green economy and reducing carbon emissions. However, collaboration between banks and companies is necessary to use appropriate tools on which to invest. In recent years it is possible to observe how the existing literature testifies that the interest of savers in environmental issues is substantial. However, following the results obtained, it is clear that policy measures focused on obtaining environmental results are fundamental to change the behavior of companies to prefer environmentally friendly environmental strategies. It is believed, however, that it is appropriate to draw up a Common Action Plan with the aim of giving companies greater incentives to access these new forms of financing, guaranteeing benefits both in terms of image, economic and environmental and allowing the possibility of accessing subsidized rates and guaranteeing the development of energy communities. Each bank should make known a strategic action plan, including a series of climate considerations and information, carefully examining the allocation of resources and observing the market, both with a view to exclusion, not financing those who could be potential producers of negative externalities from an environmental point of view and favoring positive inclusion, towards all those companies that are producers of positive externalities that can contribute to providing new technologies and solutions useful to climate change.

## DIFFUSION OF RENEWABLE ENERGY COMMUNITIES

Technological innovation plays a key role in improving energy efficiency and maximizing energy needs. Localized energy systems are important from two perspectives, self-sufficiency, and sustainability, and in recent years scientific research in this direction has significantly increased. (Rogers et al., 2008; Walker et al., 2010; Bradley et al., 2012; Wirth, 2014) Among the most widespread and mature technologies, there are photovoltaics and wind energy. It is produced in seven countries, which produce around 90% of the EU's wind energy. The main installations are present in Germany, Spain, and Denmark, but medium-large plants are also present in Portugal, France, the Netherlands, and Italy where the orographic characteristics allow a greater and better strength of the winds that can power the wind turbines. Currently in Europe, there are both on-shore and off-shore wind farms. It is estimated that by 2050, in Europe, a wind farm with a capacity of about 150 GW will be built in the North Sea. In the photovoltaic sector, too, the EU plays a winning role. In first place is Germany, while in second place in terms of production Italy, followed by Spain which enjoys the primacy of being the largest photovoltaic solar power plant in the world. Renewable energy communities have the objective of self-producing energy and offering it at advantageous prices on the market, they are based on a collaborative approach, which is from the bottom up and it is precisely through the collaboration of citizens and local companies that it is possible to generate value creation. In addition, the existing scientific literature shows that renewable energy communities can provide social benefits (Brauwer et al., 2020) and ensure a deployment and maximization of the network (Koirala et al., 2016) and ensure better social acceptance of renewables (Baxter et al., 2013). Local generation plants are based on the principle of decentralization and the correct location of these plants. Those who become part of this community are defined as "prosumers", i.e., citizens/users who become producers and consumers of a part of the energy they produce, injecting the remaining part into the national electricity grid, so that all the subjects that are connected to the "smart grid", can benefit from it. One of the ingredients that allows energy communities to spread is the active participation of participants, as well as a comprehensive legal framework. (Hicks et al., 2018) Before describing the economic and environmental benefits of prosumer community groups (Rathnayaka et al., 2015), it is considered appropriate to explain the previously mentioned concept of smart grid. Today, digitalization has influenced the energy transition, on several fronts, thanks to digitalization, not only improves productivity, but also the maintenance and safety of plants, this allows greater efficiency and greater economy that translate into revenue growth and cost savings. The term smart-grid is widely used in electrical engineering to indicate the management of the electricity grid. Currently, digitization allows a connection to nodes, peer to peer, while initially, the model was based on one-to-many transmissions, it did not allow the decentralization that is the basis of renewable energy communities. To date, the creation of energy communities is possible on three levels: "individual, collective and community". At the individual level, there is the individual citizen who produces the energy and consumes the energy produced. At the collective level, we observe the presence of more family groups and a greater number of subjects that produce energy. At the community level, aimed at sharing energy, based on local exchange in a spirit of collaboration. The creation of such plants brings benefits and advantages, not only from an economic point of view, but also from an environmental point of view and from the point of view of combating energy poverty. It is due to the increase in energy prices and every year affects the health of about fifty-four million people living in Europe. Through ambitious policies and a modernization of Europe's energy parks, the aim is to reduce this problem, which currently affects around 11% of the EU's population (equivalent to fifty-four million). The modern technology, thanks to the development of IT (Information Technology) tools, allows a better design and management of renewable communities. In fact, through Information Technology, it is possible to use an energy community simulator to evaluate the different scenarios and the most suitable technology and a management platform to evaluate their progress and operation.

## ECONOMIC BENEFITS

The first advantage that is obtained through an energy community is the economic advantage. In the UK, an estimated £2.9 million has been saved through renewable communities and a saving of 65,000 tons of CO2 in 2020 alone. In fact, those who decide to build an energy community, access three different economic advantages:

- Savings in the bill, as a car consuming the energy produced, there are considerable savings on what are called costs of the variable components of the bill and the taxes provided for by current legislation on the subject.
- Gain on the energy produced, it occurs from the moment in which the excess energy is fed into the national electricity grid.
- Tax breaks and support from the State of origin aimed at encouraging the construction of these plants through special facilities, providing economic support on the entire value of the investment.

The second advantage that is obtained through an energy community is the environmental advantage. In fact, since these communities are managed through renewable parks, they allow the reduction of CO2 emissions into the atmosphere and other types of climate-changing gases (Douah & Mohsen 2019). The term energy poverty usually indicates the impossibility for a family not to be able to buy a minimum energy basket and this has repercussions in terms of well-being. This topic has taken on a vital importance in recent years, until it has been included in the Energy 2030 package. Currently there are several energy communities present both on EU territory and on non-EU territory, they offer a fundamental contribution, especially for developing countries to combat energy poverty and ensure greater access to electricity. Currently, the construction of renewable energy communities takes place exclusively through hydroelectric, photovoltaic and biomass plants. The preparation of energy communities powered by wind energy is complex and difficult to manage (Brahmi et al. 2018). In recent years, technological innovation has made it possible to develop a very wide range of innovations, including the birth of integrated Community energy systems (ICES), they allow to face current challenges and redesign the energy landscape through micro community networks (Mendes et al., 2011) and peer-to-peer energy systems. Another interesting aspect concerns the overcoming of the visual impact and allowing its installation even in inhabited centers. In fact, as has been specified above, within renewable energy communities, the aim is to prefer photovoltaic and hydroelectric installations. However, there are several wind turbines that thanks to their small size could be installed in urban centers. For example, bradless vortex which develops in height and produces energy thanks to an aerodynamic effect called vortex detachment. A true engineering excellence and technological innovation, a small jewel of 2.75 meters, which allows you to produce energy and thanks to its minimal visual impact and ease of installation, can be installed in urban centers and close to city streets. To date, the models in production sleep two, a first model of four kilowatt hours and a second model of 1 kWh. The advantages of this technology allow a saving of 53% compared to a normal wind turbine, with an 80% reduction in maintenance costs compared to traditional turbines. In this context, it is considered appropriate to mention the tyer wind. It simulates the typical movement adopted by the wings of hummingbirds to produce energy from the force of the winds. Also, in this case the small size allows the installation of urban and inhabited centers, like his peer vortex bradless. Projects with an innovative design, which have also received positive feedback from the environmental wing, since a normal wind turbine can become a real threat to birds. Finally, it is considered necessary to mention an additional technology, which could be installed within renewable communities. This technology is called wind trees, the result of high technology French. It consists of a section of 3 stems and the leaves with a particular shell shape, can move thanks to the force of the wind, in any direction this blows, like a real tree. On each tree there are about thirty-six leaves, they can move both with slight gusts and with stronger gusts of wind. By observing the UN Sustainable Development Goals (SDGs), it is possible to intercept how they are in line with the following objectives: clean and accessible energy, decent work and economic growth, sustainable cities and communities and the fight against climate change. Energy communities can generate new jobs, in fact with the development of circular economy models and the importance of environmental issues at European and national level, new professional figures have developed (green jobs). The advantages deriving from these professional figures vary, in fact they produce benefits in traditional and new sectors (Esposito et al., 2014). Certainly, in the short term, employment will experience increasing rates in sectors where there are facilitations, aimed for example at generating new green jobs, aimed at the production of goods and services that are in line with the various European directives, but employment could decrease along the whole chain of goods and services that will be replaced on the market. All this will make it necessary to implement industrial reconversion processes, with the aim of ensuring the maintenance of jobs. In the medium term, however, employment will change according to the degree of impact of green policy in the various states, unlike the long term in which we should look at established technologies, which generate new investment opportunities (Missaoui, Mohsen & Jaleleddine 2018) and the impact of policies will always be present but gradually. In 2020 alone, the renewable energy sector generated around twelve million jobs. In the last decade it has been possible to witness exponential growth, particularly in the solar photovoltaic energy sector, in the bioenergy and wind industries that have ranked as the largest employers.

Returning to renewable communities, in Europe, there are several examples. One of the main European countries that adopts this technology is Denmark, where the origin of the first communities' dates to the dawn of the seventies. In this geographical area, the first groups of organized communities produced energy through wind farms, they initially had a power between 5-7 Kw, but the rapid spread of innovation, has allowed the preparation of turbines with capacities between 50 and 600 kW. In fact, this source is very developed, thanks to the orographic characteristics of the territory and the advanced technologies that have developed over the years. In the following years, the Danish model was the benchmark for other states interested in designing renewable communities. The trigger for the spread of CREs was the oil crisis of 1973. The United Kingdom also demonstrates its commitment to the energy communities' sector, followed by Germany. Most of the renewable energy communities are powered by photovoltaic systems, it has countless advantages, as it allows installation on the roofs of inhabited centers, thanks to the modularity and ease of installation, it is also silent and does not require any maintenance to the mechanical parts that are absent. In line with the concept of circular economy at the end of the product life cycle, all the parts that compose it (glass, aluminum, and silicon) are recyclable.

## SOLUTIONS AND RECOMMENDATIONS

A correct regulatory evolution, with targeted and structured investments would inevitably contribute to the spread of energy communities and to generate new opportunities especially for disadvantaged or rural areas, with the aim of promoting a more inclusive energy market to produce energy from renewable sources in a decentralized way and guarantee the production of local energy and at the same time aim to reduce energy poverty.

## FUTURE RESEARCH DIRECTIONS

We are witnessing a re-evaluation and redefinition of capitalism, where knowledge and innovation become the "guide" to explore sustainable innovative solutions and to spread a new strategy of responsible capitalism. This theory contributes both to generating value and to ensuring competition between companies. The decentralization of production through renewable communities turns out to be a fundamental tool not only at the condominium level, but also at the corporate level for the creation of value, with the aim of generating wealth and contributing to decarbonization and the achievement of the sustainable development objectives, promoted by the European Union.

## CONCLUSION

This chapter aims to provide a clear and comprehensive explanation of electricity generation through renewable energy communities. The first part focuses on the role of innovation in the creation of value. Subsequently, a study is conducted on the complex European regulatory apparatus, through legislative analysis and its evolution. Subsequently, the various technological configurations were taken into account, making a classification between the most and least profitable. It is believed that the role of financial institutions plays a central role, as they can activate incentive or disincentive mechanisms. Despite this, these maneuvers often meet with the resistance of interests, not only of an economic but also of an industrial nature. For the achievement of the ambitious goals set by the European Union, the combination of renewable energy and consumer, is becoming increasingly important. A consumer who, from a passive subject, becomes the engine and protagonist of the transition, thanks to the distributed management of renewable energy communities. In fact, it is necessary to take responsibility, through the leading role of information and through integrated territorial development plans, it is possible to obtain benefits in economic, environmental and employment terms. Currently, we are witnessing a rapid expansion of renewable communities, in fact, in Europe alone there are more than 1000 small power plants that produce energy. They are mainly concentrated in the countries of Northern Germany and Denmark and the numbers are constantly growing. In fact, energy communities also have a social impact, in line with the seventh Sustainable Development Goal (Ensuring access to affordable, reliable, sustainable and modern energy systems for all). The intent of the SDGs objective is to increase the production and consequently the consumption of energy by renewable sources, with the aim of achieving high levels of energy efficiency within society and ensuring equitable access to energy, avoiding disparities and generating well-being. We need to promote and raise awareness among the consumer and political actors, in order to avoid the not infrequent phenomena of Not In My Backyard (NIMBY) and Not In My Terms Of Office (NIMTO - not during my mandate). Over the years, many engineering works, which would have allowed, inevitably, to offer an important contribution to the energy transition, have been hindered by local populations or by the environmental wing. However, an important element during the transition process is the non-creation of inequalities and energy communities also pay particular attention to the social impact. The legislator should aim to promote the inclusiveness of these micro-macro organizations, so as to allow a greater numberof individuals to be able to join and improve the performance of the territory. By adopting the energy communities you will have the opportunity to transform every small house and every condominium into a generation plant through which it is possible to produce clean energy and use the surplus to feed it into the national electricity grid. It is inevitably necessary to promote a more effective use of energy in buildings, through renovation works and to develop individual methodologies for territorial planning at local, provincial and regional level, through targeted and non-rain investments, which are able to respond to the technical-morphological needs of each geographical area concerned.

## REFERENCES

Aldieri, L., Kotsemir, M., & Concetto, P.V. (2020). The role of environmental innovation through the technological proximity in the implementation of the sustainable development. *Business Strategy and the Environment.*

Akhdar, B., & Mohsen, B. (2019). Transition économique vs. Résistances sociopolitiques et de la gouvernance institutionnelle: évidence dc la politique économique algerienne. Revue Européenne du Droit Social, Vol.44 (03):80-98. DOI https://www.ceeol.com/search/article-detail?id=768418

Alexander, K. (2016). Greening banking policy. In *Support of the G20 Green Finance*. Study Group.

Bailey, I., & Compston, H. (2012). *Feeling the heat: climate policy in rapidly industrializing countries.* Palgrave. doi:10.1057/9780230374973

Baxter, J., Morzaria, R., & Hirsch, R. (2013). A case-control study of support/opposition to wind turbines: Perceptions of health risk, economic benefits, and community conflict. *Energy Policy*, *61*, 931–943. doi:10.1016/j.enpol.2013.06.050

Beck, T., & Demirguc-Kunt, A. (2006). Small and medium-sized enterprises: Access to finance as a growth constraint. *Journal of Banking & Finance*, *30*(11), 2931–2943. doi:10.1016/j.jbankfin.2006.05.009

Bradley, F., & Rae, C. (2012). *Energy autonomy in sustainable communities: a review of key issues* (Vol. 16). Renewable and Sustainable. Energy Reviews.

Brahmi, M., Zouari, S., & Rossi, M. (2014). L'industrie minière et ses effets écologiques. État socio-économique et environnemental dans le bassin minier tunisien. In E. D. Y. T. E. M. Collection (Ed.), *Cahiers de géographie, numéro 17, Exploitations minières passées et présentes. Impacts environnementaux et sociétaux* (pp. 109–120)., doi:10.3406/edyte.2014.1279

Brauwer, C., & Cohen, J. J. (2020). Analysing the potential of citizen-financed community renewable energy to drive Europe's low-carbon energy transition. *Renewable & Sustainable Energy Reviews.*

Brahmi, M., & Zouari, S. (2014). TIC, innovation et impacts sur l'analyse concurrentielle: Leader Firme du Bassin Minier Tunisien. *International Journal of Innovation and Applied Studies*, *10*(1), 195–217.

Bulkeley, H., & Betsill, M. (2003). *Cities and climate change. Urban sustainability and global environmental governance*. Routledge.

Crisan, D. (2020). *Buying with intention: public procurement for innovation by provincial and municipal administrations*. The School of Public Policy Publications.

Debor, S. (2014). *The Socio-Economic Power of Renewable Energy Production Cooperatives in Germany. Results of an Empirical Assessment*. Wuppertal Papers.

Douah, B., & Mohsen, B. (2019). Renewable energies and their contribution in development in the context of competitiveness: evidence of specific oil Territory, European Review of Social L, Vol.44, Issue 3, pp: 44-61 (Co-Author.,) DOI https://www.ceeol.com/search/article-detail?id=768416

Energy England Community. (2021). *Community Energy State of the Sector 2021*. Community Energy England.

Esposito, M., Haider, A., Samaan, D., & Semmler, W. (2014). Improving job creation through green transformation. In K. Schlegelmilch, H. Eichel, & A. Pegels (Eds.), Green Industrial Policy: Concept, Policies, Country Experiences (Vol. 30, pp. 469-491). Academic Press.

Giddens, A. (2011). *The policy of climate change*. Polity Press.

Hansen, K., Breyer, C. & Lund, H. J. E. (2019). Status and perspectives on 100% renewable energy systems. *Energy*.

Harris, P. (2011). *China's responsibility for climate change: ethics, fairness, and environmental policy*. Political Press.

Helm, D., & Hepburn, C. (Eds.). (2009). *Economics and politics of climate change*. Oxford University Press. doi:10.1093/acprof:osobl/9780199573288.001.0001

Hicks, J., & Ison, N. (2018). *An exploration of the boundaries of 'community' in community renewable energy projects: Navigating between motivations and context* (Vol. 113). Energy Policy.

Horgan, D., & Dimitrijević, B. (2018). *Social innovation systems to build resilient communities*. Urban Science.

Jin, S. (2020). COVID-19, Climate Change, and Renewable Energy Research: We Are All in This Together, and the Time to Act Is Now. *ACS Energy Letter*.

Joshi, M. (2018). Burnout and Stressors as influencers on Work engagement among law enforcement agents in selected cities. In *Management Techniques for Employee Engagement in Contemporary Organizations*. IGI Global.

Joshi, M (2018). Workforce trends and challenges: a peek into future. In N. Sharma (Ed.), *Management Techniques for a Diverse and Cross-Cultural Workforce*. IGI Global.

Joshi, M., Joshi, G., & Pathak, S. (2020). *Awareness, entrepreneurial event theory and theory of planned behavior as antecedents of student entrepreneurial intentions: an Indian perspective. International Journal of Business and Globalisation*. Inderscience Publishers.

Joshi, M., Tyagi, S., Ansari, N., & Singh, V. K. (2019). Impact of IoT to accomplish a vision of digital transformation of the cities. In *A handbook of IOT and Big Data*. CRC Press, Taylor and Francis.

Koirala, B. P., Koliou, E., Friege, J., Hakvoort, R. A., & Herder, P. M. (2016). Energetic communities for community energy: A review of key issues and trends shaping integrated community energy systems. *Renewable & Sustainable Energy Reviews*, *56*, 722–744. doi:10.1016/j.rser.2015.11.080

Lee, S. M., Olson, D. L., & Trimi, S. (2012). Co-innovation: Convergence, collaboration, and co-creation for organizational values. *Management Decision*, *50*(5), 817–831. doi:10.1108/00251741211227528

Lisowski, M. (2002). *The two-tier game: US President Bush's decision to repudiate the Kyoto Protocol*. Environmental Policy.

Mendes, G., Loakimidis, C., & Ferraro, P. (2011). *On the planning and analysis of integrated community energy systems: A review and survey of available tools* (Vol. 15). Renewable and Sustainable Energy Review.

Missaoui, I., Mohsen, B., & Jaleleddine, B. (2018). Quantitative relationship between corruption ad development of the Tunisian stock market. *Public and Municipal Finance Journal*, *7*(2), 39–47. doi:10.21511/pmf.07(2).2018.04

Mohsin, M., Kamran, H. W., Nawaz, M. A., Hussain, M. S., & Dahri, A. S. (2021). Assessing the impact of transition from nonrenewable to renewable energy consumption on economic growth-environmental nexus from developing Asian economies. *Journal of Environmental Management*, *284*, 111999. doi:10.1016/j.jenvman.2021.111999 PMID:33556829

Monnin, P. (2018). *Central banks and the transition to a low-carbon economy. Technical report, discussion note*. Council on Economic Policies.

Porter, M. E., & Kramer, M. R. (2011). *Creating shared value* (Vol. 89). Harvard Business Review.

Ramaswammy, V., & Ozcan, K. (2014). *The paradigm of co-creation*. Stanford University Press. doi:10.1515/9780804790758

Rathnayaka, A. J. D., Potdar, V. M., Dillon, T., & Kuruppu, S. (2015). *Framework to manage multiple objectives in the community-based energy sharing network in smart grid* (Vol. 73). International Journal Electric Power Energy Systems.

Rogers, J. C., Simmons, E. A., & Convery, A. (2008). *Weatherall Public perceptions of opportunities for community-based renewable energy projects* (Vol. 36). Energy Policy.

Rootes, C., Zito, A., & Barry, J. (2012). *Climate change, national policy, and grassroots action: an introduction*. Environmental Policy.

Schumpeter, J. (1934). *The Theory of Economic Development* (1st ed.). Harvard University Press.

Sovacool, B. K., Burke, M., Baker, L., Kotikalapudi, C. K., & Wlokas, H. (2017). New frontiers and conceptual frameworks for energy justice. *Energy Policy*, *105*, 677–691. doi:10.1016/j.enpol.2017.03.005

Walker, G., Devine-Wright, P., Hunter, S., High, H., & Evans, B. (2010). *Trust and community: exploring the meanings, contexts, and dynamics of community renewable energy* (Vol. 38). Energy Policy.

Walker, G., & Simcock, N. (2012). *Community energy systems* (Vol. 1). International Encyclopedia of Housing and Home.

Wang, Y. (2016). *What are the biggest obstacles to growth of SMEs in developing countries? An Empirical evidence from an enterprise survey*. Instanbul Stock Exchange Review. doi:10.1016/j.bir.2016.06.001

Weber, O., & Remer, S. (2011). *Social banking and the future of sustainable finance*. Routledge. doi:10.4324/9780203827871

Wirth, S. (2014). Communities matter: Institutional preconditions for community renewable energy. *Energy Policy*, *70*, 236–246. doi:10.1016/j.enpol.2014.03.021

# Compilation of References

Aamodt, A., & Plaza, E. (1994). Case-based reasoning: Foundational issues, methodological variations, and system approaches. *AI Communications*, *7*(1), 39–59. doi:10.3233/AIC-1994-7104

Abbas, A. F., Jusoh, A., Mas'od, A., Alsharif, A. H., & Ali, J. (2022). Effect of intrinsic and extrinsic motivations on cyber-market mavenism: Their role in information-sharing behavior. *Innovative Marketing*, *18*(2), 198–211. doi:10.21511/im.18(2).2022.17

Abdelkafi, N., Makhotin, S., & Posselt, T. (2013). Business model innovations for electric mobility—What can be learned from existing business model patterns? *International Journal of Innovation Management*, *17*(01), 1340003. doi:10.1142/S1363919613400033

Abu Salim, T., Sundarakani, B., & Lasrado, F. (2019). The relationship between TQM practices and organisational innovation outcomes Moderating and mediating the role of slack. *The TQM Journal*, *31*(6), 874–907. doi:10.1108/TQM-11-2018-0160

Abufotuh, F. (2007). Energy efficiency and renewable technologies: the way to sustainable energy future. *Desalination Journal, 209* (1–3), 275-282.

Acemoglu, D., Akcigit, U. (2012). Intellectual property rights policy, competition, and innovation. *Journal of the European economic association, 10*(1), 1-42.

Achi, A. (2001). *The financial performance of the economic institution, measuring and evaluating - a case study of the institution of the cable industry in Biskra.* [Unpublished master's thesis, University of Mohamed Khider, Biskra, Algeria.]

Ackermann, F., & Eden, C. (2011). Strategic management and stakeholders: Theory and practice. *Long Range Planning*, *44*(3), 179–196. doi:10.1016/j.lrp.2010.08.001

Adams, D., & Hess, M. (2010). Social innovation and why it has policy significance. London, UK. *Sage (Atlanta, Ga.)*. doi:10.1177/103530461002100209

Aditya Birla Group. (n.d) *Designed for circularity – Stories.* Aditya Birla Group. https://www.adityabirla.com/media/stories/designed-for-circularity

Adner, R. (2006). Match your innovation strategy to your innovation ecosystem. *Harvard Business Review*, *84*(4), 98–107. PMID:16579417

Adner, R. (2012). The wide lens: A new strategy for innovation. London, England: Penguin. Adner, R. (2017). Ecosystem as structure: An actionable construct for strategy. *Journal of Management*, *43*(1), 39–58. doi:10.1177/0149206316678451

Adner, R. (2013). *The wide lens: What successful innovators see that others miss.* Portfolio/Penguin.

Adner, R., & Kapoor, R. (2010). Value creation in innovation ecosystems: How the structure of technological interdependence affects firm performance in new technology generations. *Strategic Management Journal, 31*(3), 306–333. doi:10.1002mj.821

Adner, R., & Kapoor, R. (2016). Innovation ecosystems and the pace of substitution: Re-examining technology S-curves. *Strategic Management Journal, 37*(4), 625–648. doi:10.1002mj.2363

Adner, R., & Lieberman, M. (2021). Disruption Through Complements. *Strategy Science, 6*(1), 91–109. doi:10.1287tsc.2021.0125

*Advanced analysis of strategic environment (Uncertainty, complexity and intelligence).* (2020). University of Tehran Publications.

Agha, N., & Rascher, D. A. (2016). An explanation of economic impact: Why positive impacts can exist for smaller sports. *Sport, Business and Management, 6*(2), 182–204. doi:10.1108/SBM-07-2013-0020

Aghion, P., & Howitt, P. (1992). *A model of growth through creative destruction* (Vol. 60). Econometrica.

Agle, B. R., Mitchell, R. K., & Sonnenfeld, J. A. (1999). Who matters to CEOs? An investigation of stakeholder attributes and salience, corporate performance, and CEO values. *Academy of Management Journal, 42*(5), 507–525. doi:10.2307/256973

Aguilera, R. V., Rupp, D. E., Williams, C. A., & Ganapathi, J. (2007). Putting the S back in corporate social responsibility: A multilevel theory of social change in organizations. *Academy of Management Review, 32*(3), 836–863. doi:10.5465/amr.2007.25275678

Ahire, S. L., Golhar, D. Y., & Waller, M. A. (1996). Development and validation of TQM implementation constructs. *Decision Sciences, 27*(1), 23–56. doi:10.1111/j.1540-5915.1996.tb00842.x

Aisen, A., & Veiga, F. J. (2013). How does political instability affect economic growth? *European Journal of Political Economy, 29*, 151–167. doi:10.1016/j.ejpoleco.2012.11.001

Ajide, F. M. (2020). Infrastructure and Entrepreneurship: Evidence from Africa. *Journal of Developmental Entrepreneurship, 25*(3), 2050015. doi:10.1142/S1084946720500156

Ajzen, I., & Fishbein, M. (1980). *Understanding Attitudes and Predicting Social Behavior.* Prentice-Hall.

Akhdar, B., & Mohsen, B. (2019). Transition économique vs. Résistances sociopolitiques et de la gouvernance institutionnelle: évidence de la politique économique algerienne. Revue Européenne du Droit Social, Vol.44 (03): 80-98.doi https://www.ceeol.com/search/article-detail?id=768418

Akhdar, B., & Mohsen, B. (2019). Transition économique vs. Résistances sociopolitiques et de la gouvernance institutionnelle: évidence de la politique économique algerienne. Revue Européenne du Droit Social, Vol.44 (03):80-98. DOI https://www.ceeol.com/search/article-detail?id=768418

Akhtar, M. F., Ali, K., & Sadaqat, S. (2011). Factors Influencing the Profitability of Islamic Banks of Pakistan. *International Research Journal of Finance and Economics, 66.*

Akintola, A. F., & Cole, A. A. (2020).. . *Impact of Combined Leverage on Capital Employed Of Selected Listed Manufacturing Firms in Nigeria., 11*(3), 51–56. doi:10.9790/5933-1103055156

Al-Abdin, A., Roy, T., & Nicholson, J. D. (2018). Researching corporate social responsibility in the Middle East: The current state and future directions. *Corporate Social Responsibility and Environmental Management, 25*(1), 47–65. doi:10.1002/csr.1439

Albelbisi, N. A., Al-Adwan, A. S., Habibi, A., & Rasool, S. (2022). The relationship between students' attitudes toward online homework and mathematics anxiety. *International Journal of Mathematical Education in Science and Technology*, 1–19. doi:10.1080/0020739X.2021.2023769

Alcalde, P. (2013). *A behavioral model of non-linear peer effects in cognitive achievement.* [PhD thesis: University of Pennsylvania].

Alchian, A., & Demsetz, H. (1972). Production, information costs, and economic organization. *The American Economic Review, 62*, 777–795.

Al-Debei, M. M., & Avison, D. (2010). Developing a unified framework of the business model concept. *European Journal of Information Systems, 19*(3), 359–376. doi:10.1057/ejis.2010.21

Aldieri, L., Kotsemir, M., & Concetto, P.V. (2020). The role of environmental innovation through the technological proximity in the implementation of the sustainable development. *Business Strategy and the Environment.*

Aldieri, L., Sena, V., & Vinci, C. P. (2018). Domestic R&D spillovers and absorptive capacity: Some evidence for US, Europe, and Japan. *International Journal of Production Economics, 198*(April 2017), 38–49. doi:10.1016/j.ijpe.2018.01.015

Aldieri, L., Brahmi, M., Bruno, B., & Vinci, C. P. (2021). Circular Economy Business Models: The Complementarities with Sharing Economy and Eco-Innovations Investments. *Sustainability, 13*(22), 12438. doi:10.3390u132212438

Aldrich, H. E. (1979). Organizations and Environment. Englewood cliffs. NJ, NewJersey: Prentice Hall.

Alexander, K. (2016). Greening banking policy. In *Support of the G20 Green Finance*. Study Group.

Alhaddad, A. (2015). Perceived quality, brand image and brand trust as determinants of brand loyalty. *Journal of Research in Business and Management, 3*(4), 01-08.

Ali, S. & Muhammad, M. (2015). The availability of controls on the applications of electronic accounting information systems and their impact on the quality of profits - An applied study on the Palestinian banks whose shares are listed on the stock exchange Al-Quds. Open University Journal for Research and Administrative and Economic Studies, 1(2), 337-375.

Ali, M. S. B. (2022). *Digitalization and Economic Development: Insights from Developing Countries*. Taylor & Francis.

Al-Jamil, S. K. (2002). *International Finance: Introduction to Structures, Processes and Tools*. Dar Al-Jamieh for Printing and Publishing.

Allah Pitchay, A., Ganesan, Y., Zulkifli, N. S., & Khaliq, A. (2022). Determinants of customers' intention to use online food delivery application through smartphone in Malaysia. *British Food Journal, 124*(3), 732–753. doi:10.1108/BFJ-01-2021-0075

Allen, Donald M. (2020). "Don Allen: Grove's First Editor." Interview with SE Gontarski. *Writing Into the Future: New American Poetries from" the Dial" to the Digital, 10*(3), 297.

Alperen, M. J. (2017). *Foundations of homeland security: Law and policy*. John Wiley & Sons. doi:10.1002/9781119289142

Altman, E. J., Nagle, F., & Tushman, M. L. (2022). The Translucent Hand of Managed Ecosystems: Engaging Communities for Value Creation and Capture. *The Academy of Management Annals*, *16*(1), 70–101. doi:10.5465/annals.2020.0244

Alyahya, M., & McLean, G. (2022). Examining tourism consumers' attitudes and the role of sensory information in virtual reality experiences of a tourist destination. *Journal of Travel Research*, *61*(7), 1666–1681. doi:10.1177/00472875211037745

Amariah, B. & Ghania, M. (2020). The Role of Financial Technology in Supporting the Banking Sector. *Al-Mudabber journal, 70*(72), pp. 99-111.

Amin, A., & Cohendet, P. (2000). Organisational learning and governance through embedded practices. *The Journal of Management and Governance*, *4*(1/2), 93–116. doi:10.1023/A:1009913429932

Amit, R., & Zott, C. (2001). Value creation in e-business. *Strategic Management Journal*, *22*(6-7), 493–520. doi:10.1002mj.187

Andal-Ancion, A., Cartwright, P. A., & Yip, G. S. (2003). The digital transformation of traditional business. *MIT Sloan Management Review*, *44*(4), 34.

Anderson, D. N. (2014). Not just a taxi'? For-profit ridesharing, driver strategies, and VMT. *Transportation*, *41*(5), 1099–1117. doi:10.100711116-014-9531-8

Andersson, T., Haslam, C., & Lee, E. (2006). Financialized accounts: Restructuring and return on capital employed in the S&P 500. *Accounting Forum*, *30*(1), 21–41. doi:10.1016/j.accfor.2006.01.001

Andriopoulos, C., Gotsi, M., Lewis, M. W., & Ingram, A. E. (2018). Turning the sword: How NPD teams cope with front-end tensions. *Journal of Product Innovation Management*, *35*(3), 427–445. doi:10.1111/jpim.12423

Antikainen, M., & Valkokari, K. (2016). A framework for sustainable circular business model innovation. *Technology Innovation Management Review, 6*(7).

Apergis, N., Payne, J.E. (2012). Renewable and non-renewable energy consumption-growth nexus: evidence from a panel error correction model. *Energy Economics, 34* (3), 733-738.

Arabeche, Z., Soudani, A., Brahmi, M., Aldieri, L., Vinci, C. P., & Abdelli, M. E. A. (2022). Entrepreneurial Orientation, Organizational Culture and Business Performance in SMEs: Evidence from Emerging Economy. *Sustainability*, *14*(9), 5160. doi:10.3390u14095160

Aragon, S. R., & Johnson, E. S. (2008). Factors influencing completion and noncompletion of community college online courses. *American Journal of Distance Education*, *22*(3), 146–158. doi:10.1080/08923640802239962

Arevalo, Jorge A, & Aravind, Deepa. (2011). Corporate social responsibility practices in India: approach, drivers, and barriers. *Corporate Governance: The international journal of business in society, 11*(4), 399-414.

Arguello, M. I., Monferrer Tirado, D., & Estrada Guillén, M. (2020). Service quality in a post-crisis context: Emotional effects and behaviours. *International Journal of Bank Marketing*, *38*(1), 175–198. doi:10.1108/IJBM-02-2019-0045

Argyropoulou, A., Dionyssopoulou, P., & Miaoulis, G. (2011). Tourist Destination Marketing and Management Using Advanced ICTs Technologies. *Advances on Information Processing and Management*, *365*, 369.

Arnette, A. N. (2013). *Integrating rooftop solar into a multi-source energy planning optimization model* (Vol. 111). Applied Energy.

Arora, A., Fosfuri, A., & Gambardella, A. (2001). Technology markets and their implications for corporate strategy. *Industrial and Corporate Change*, *10*(2), 419–452. doi:10.1093/icc/10.2.419

Arora, M., Singh, H., & Gupta, S. (2021). What drives e-hailing apps adoption? An analysis of behavioral factors through fuzzy AHP. *Journal of Science and Technology Policy Management, 13*(2), 382–404. doi:10.1108/JSTPM-12-2020-0177

Arrieta, A. B., Díaz-Rodríguez, N., Del Ser, J., Bennetot, A., Tabik, S., Barbado, A., & Herrera, F. (2020). Explainable Artificial Intelligence (XAI): Concepts, taxonomies, opportunities and challenges toward responsible AI. *Information Fusion, 58*, 82–115. doi:10.1016/j.inffus.2019.12.012

Arruda, E. H. Melatto, R., Levy, W., & de Melo. C. D. (2021) Circular economy: A brief literature review (2015–2020). *Science Direct.* https://www.sciencedirect.com/science/article/pii/S2666412721000167)

Arshad, A. M., & Su, Q. (2015). Role of Total Quality Management in service innovations: An empirical study of Pakistans financial services firms. *Journal of Applied Business Research, 31*(3), 891–910. doi:10.19030/jabr.v31i3.9225

Arthur, W.B. (2007). The structure of invention. *Resource Policy, 36* (2), 274-287.

Asher, C. C., Mahoney, J. M., & Mahoney, J. T. (2005). Towards a property rights foundation for a stakeholder theory of the firm. *The Journal of Management and Governance, 9*(1), 5–32. doi:10.100710997-005-1570-2

Ashwin, A. S., Krishnan, R. T., & George, R. (2016). Board Characteristics, Financial Slack and R&D Investments: An Empirical Analysis of the Indian Pharmaceutical Industry. *International Studies of Management & Organization, 46*(1), 8–23. doi:10.1080/00208825.2015.1007007

Athanasopoulou, A., Haaker, T., & de Reuver, M. (2018). Designing digital tooling for business model exploration for the Internet-of-Things. In *DESRIST 2018-13th International Conference on Design Science Research in Information Systems and Technology.*

Athanasopoulou, A., & De Reuver, M. (2020). How do business model tools facilitate business model exploration? Evidence from action research. *Electronic Markets, 30*(3), 495–508. doi:10.100712525-020-00418-3

Attig, N., Boubakri, N., Ghoul, S. E., & Guedhami, O. (2016). Firm internationalization and corporate social responsibility. *Journal of Business Ethics, 134*(2), 171–197. doi:10.100710551-014-2410-6

Atzeni, M., Del Chiappa, G., & Mei Pung, J. (2022). Enhancing visit intention in heritage tourism: The role of object-based and existential authenticity in non-immersive virtual reality heritage experiences. *International Journal of Tourism Research, 24*(2), 240–255. doi:10.1002/jtr.2497

Audebrand, L. K., Camus, A., & Michaud, V. (2017). A mosquito in the classroom: Using the cooperative business model to foster paradoxical thinking in management education. *Journal of Management Education, 41*(2), 216–248. doi:10.1177/1052562916682552

Avram, E. & Avasilcai, S. (2014). Symbiosis Process in Business Ecosystem. *Advanced Materials Research (vol. 1036).* Trans Tech Publications. doi:10.4028/www.scientific.net/AMR.1036.1066

Aw, E. C. X., Basha, N. K., Ng, S. I., & Sambasivan, M. (2019). To grab or not to grab? The role of trust and perceived value in on-demand ridesharing services. *Asia Pacific Journal of Marketing and Logistics, 31*(5), 1442–1465. doi:10.1108/APJML-09-2018-0368

Baader, F., Calvanese, D., McGuinness, D., Patel-Schneider, P., & Nardi, D. (Eds.). (2003). *The description logic handbook: Theory, implementation and applications.* Cambridge university press.

Bacigalupo, M. (2016). EntreComp: The entrepreneurship competence framework. *Luxembourg. Publication Office of the European Union, 10*, 593884.

Baden-Fuller, C., & Morgan, M. S. (2010). Business models as models. *Long Range Planning, 43*(2-3), 156–171. doi:10.1016/j.lrp.2010.02.005

Bahoo, S., Alon, I., & Floreani, J. (2020). Corruption in economics: A bibliometric analysis and research agenda. *Applied Economics Letters, 28*(7), 1–14. doi:10.1080/13504851.2020.1764476

Bailey, I., & Compston, H. (2012). *Feeling the heat: climate policy in rapidly industrializing countries.* Palgrave. doi:10.1057/9780230374973

Baker, W. E., & Sinkula, J. M. (1999). Learning orientation, market orientation and innovation: Integrating and extending models of organizational performance. *Journal of Market Focused Management, 4*(4), 295–308. doi:10.1023/A:1009830402395

Baldwin, C. (2015). *Bottlenecks, modules, and dynamic architectural capabilities.* HBS Working Paper 15-028.

Balocco, R., Cavallo, A., Ghezzi, A., & Berbegal-Mirabent, J. (2019). Lean business models change process in digital entrepreneurship. *Business Process Management Journal, 25*(7), 1520–1542. doi:10.1108/BPMJ-07-2018-0194

Balsalobre-Lorente, D., Shahbaz, M., Roubaud, D., & Farhani, S. (2018). *How economic growth, renewable electricity and natural resources contribute to CO2 emissions?* (Vol. 113). Energy Policy.

Bamel, N., & Dhir, S. Sushil, (2019) "Inter-partner dynamics and joint venture competitiveness: A fuzzy TISM approach. *Benchmarking*. doi:10.1108/ BIJ-02-2018-0041

Bandura, A. (1977). Self-efficacy: Toward a unifying theory of behavioral change. *Psychological Review, 84*(2), 191–215. doi:10.1037/0033-295X.84.2.191 PMID:847061

Banerji, A. (2012). A selective study of exports of manufactured goods from India: Auto parts and pharmaceuticals. *Journal of International Business Research, 11*(2), 89.

Banerji, A., & Suri, F. (2019). Does R&D Intensity and Innovative Activities drive Indian Pharmaceutical Exports? *Journal of Scientific and Industrial Research, 78*, 664–666.

Bansal, P., & Song, H.-C. (2017). Similar but not the same: Differentiating corporate sustainability from corporate responsibility. *The Academy of Management Annals, 11*(1), 105–149. doi:10.5465/annals.2015.0095

Barbieri, N., Marzucchi, A., & Rizzo, U. (2020). Knowledge sources and impacts on subsequent inventions: Do green technologies differ from non-green ones? *Resources Policy, 49*(2), 103901. doi:10.1016/j.respol.2019.103901

Barnes, S. J. (2011). Understanding use continuance in virtual worlds: Empirical test of a research model. *Information & Management, 48*(8), 313–319. doi:10.1016/j.im.2011.08.004

Barney, J. B., & Hansen, M. H. (1994). Trustworthiness as a source of competitive advantage. *Strategic Management Journal, 15*(S1), 175–190. doi:10.1002mj.4250150912

Barringer, B. R., & Harrison, J. S. (2000). Walking a tightrope: Creating value through interorganizational relationships. *Journal of Management, 26*(3), 367–404. doi:10.1177/014920630002600302

Baskerville, R. L., & Dulipovici, A. (2006). The theoretical foundations of knowledge management. *Knowledge Management and Research, 4*, 83-105.

Basole, R. C., & Karla, J. (2011). On the evolution of mobile platform ecosystem structure and strategy. *Business & Information Systems Engineering, 3*(5), 313–322. doi:10.100712599-011-0174-4

Bataineh, A. Q., Al-Abdallah, G. M., & Alkharabsheh, A. M. (2015). Determinants of Continuance Intention to Use Social Networking Sites SNS's: Studying the Case of Facebook. *International Journal of Marketing Studies*, *7*(4), 121–135. doi:10.5539/ijms.v7n4p121

Baumol, W. J. (1991). Technological imperatives, productivity, and insurance costs. Geneva documents on risk and insurance. The Geneva Papers on Risk and Insurance. Issues and Practice, (pp. 154–165). Springer.

Baxter, J., Morzaria, R., & Hirsch, R. (2013). A case-control study of support/opposition to wind turbines: Perceptions of health risk, economic benefits, and community conflict. *Energy Policy*, *61*, 931–943. doi:10.1016/j.enpol.2013.06.050

Beamish, P. W. (1999). The role of alliances in international entrepreneurship, pp. 43-61. Research in Global Strategic Management, Emerald Group Publishing Limited. doi:10.1016/S1064-4857(99)07056-4

Beck, T., & Demirguc-Kunt, A. (2006). Small and medium-sized enterprises: Access to finance as a growth constraint. *Journal of Banking & Finance*, *30*(11), 2931–2943. doi:10.1016/j.jbankfin.2006.05.009

Bengtsson, M., & Kock, S. (2014). Coopetition - quo vadis? Past accomplishments and future challenges. *Industrial Marketing Management*, *43*(2), 180–188. doi:10.1016/j.indmarman.2014.02.015

Bengtsson, M., Raza-Ullah, T., & Vanyushyn, V. (2016). The coopetition paradox and tension: The moderating role of coopetition capability. *Industrial Marketing Management*, *53*, 19–30. doi:10.1016/j.indmarman.2015.11.008

Bennett, E. E., & McWhorter, R. R. (2021). Virtual HRD's role in crisis and the post Covid-19 professional life-world: Accelerating skills for digital transformation. *Advances in Developing Human Resources*, *23*(1), 5–25. doi:10.1177/1523422320973288

Bergenholtz, C., & Waldstrøm, C. (2011). Inter-organizational network studies—A literature review. *Industry and Innovation*, *18*(6), 539–562. doi:10.1080/13662716.2011.591966

Bergmann, R. (Ed.). (2002). *Experience management: foundations, development methodology, and internet-based applications*. Springer Berlin Heidelberg. doi:10.1007/3-540-45759-3

Berman, S. J. (2012). Digital transformation: Opportunities to create new business models. *Strategy and Leadership*, *40*(2), 16–24. doi:10.1108/10878571211209314

Bernstein, J., & Nadiri, I. M. (1988). Inter-industry R&D spillovers, rates of return and Production in High Tech Industries. *The American Economic Review*, *78*, 429–434.

Bernstein, J., & Nadiri, I. M. (1989). Research and Development and Intra-industry Spillovers: An Empirical Application of Dynamic Duality. *The Review of Economic Studies*, *56*(2), 249–269. doi:10.2307/2297460

Bharucha, J. (2019). Sustainability of kirana stores in India: Reengineering physical with some digital. *World Review of Entrepreneurship, Management and Sustainable Development*, *15*(6), 751–764. doi:10.1504/WREMSD.2019.104866

Bhattacherjee, A. (2001). Understanding Information Systems Continuance: An Expectation-Confirmation Model. *Psychology Computer Science*, *25*(3), 351–370.

Bhattacherjee, A. (2002). Individual trust in online firms: Scale development and initial test. *Journal of Management Information Systems*, *19*(1), 211–241. doi:10.1080/07421222.2002.11045715

Bhattacherjee, A., Perols, J., & Sanford, C. (2015). Information Technology Continuance: A Theoretic Extension and Empirical Test. *Journal of Computer Information Systems*, *49*(1), 17–26. doi:10.1080/08874417.2008.11645302

Bingöl, D., & Begeç, S. (2020). Managing International Alliances: Joint Ventures: A Case Study. *Open Journal of Social Sciences*, *8*(04), 538–552. doi:10.4236/jss.2020.84039

Block, J., Fisch, C., & Rehan, F. (2020). *Religion and entrepreneurship: a map of the field and a bibliometric analysis, Management Review Quarterly*. Springer International Publishing. doi:10.100711301-019-00177-2

Bloomberg, J. (2018). Digitization, digitalization, and digital transformation: confuse them at your peril. *Forbes.*

Bocken, N., Boons, F., & Baldassarre, B. (2019). Sustainable business model experimentation by understanding ecologies of business models. *Journal of Cleaner Production, 208*, 1498–1512. doi:10.1016/j.jclepro.2018.10.159

Bogicevic, V., Seo, S., Kandampully, J. A., Liu, S. Q., & Rudd, N. A. (2019). Virtual reality presence as a preamble of tourism experience: The role of mental imagery. *Tourism Management, 74*, 55–64. doi:10.1016/j.tourman.2019.02.009

Bolton, R. N., Gustafsson, A., Tarasi, C. O., & Witell, L. (2022). Designing satisfying service encounters: Website versus store touchpoints. *Journal of the Academy of Marketing Science, 50*(1), 1–23. doi:10.100711747-021-00808-9 PMID:34608342

Bolton, R. N., Parasuraman, A., Hoefnagels, A., Migchels, N., Kabadayi, S., Gruber, T., Loureiro, Y. K., & Solnet, D. (2013). Understanding Generation Y and their use of social media: A review and research agenda. *Journal of Service Management, 24*(3), 245–267. doi:10.1108/09564231311326987

Borokhovski, E., Bernard, R. M., Tamim, R. M., Schmid, R. F., & Sokolovskaya, A. (2016). Technology-supported student interaction in post-secondary education: A meta-analysis of designed versus contextual treatments. *Computers & Education, 96*, 15–28. doi:10.1016/j.compedu.2015.11.004

Bouwman, H., Zhengjia, M., Van der Duin, P., & Limonard, S. (2008). A business model for IPTV service: a dynamic framework. *info.*

Bouwman, H., De Reuver, M., Heikkilä, M., & Fielt, E. (2020). Business model tooling: Where research and practice meet. *Electronic Markets, 30*(3), 413–419. doi:10.100712525-020-00424-5

Bouwman, H., de Vos, H., & Haaker, T. (Eds.). (2008). *Mobile service innovation and business models*. Springer Science & Business Media. doi:10.1007/978-3-540-79238-3

Bouwman, H., Heikkilä, J., Heikkilä, M., Leopold, C., & Haaker, T. (2018). Achieving agility using business model stress testing. *Electronic Markets, 28*(2), 149–162. doi:10.100712525-016-0243-0

Bradley, F., & Rae, C. (2012). *Energy autonomy in sustainable communities: a review of key issues* (Vol. 16). Renewable and Sustainable. Energy Reviews.

Brahmi, M., & Zouari, S. (2014). TIC, innovation et impacts sur l'analyse concurrentielle: Leader Firme du Bassin Minier Tunisien. *International Journal of Innovation and Applied Studies, 10*(1), 195–217.

Brahmi, M., Zouari, S., & Rossi, M. (2014). L'industrie minière et ses effets écologiques. État socio-économique et environnemental dans le bassin minier tunisien. In E. D. Y. T. E. M. Collection (Ed.), *Cahiers de géographie, numéro 17, Exploitations minières passées et présentes. Impacts environnementaux et sociétaux* (pp. 109–120)., doi:10.3406/edyte.2014.1279

Braithwaite, J. (2022). Complexity science. In *Implementation Science* (pp. 7–12). Routledge. doi:10.4324/9781003109945-3

Brandenburger, A. M., & Stuart, H. Jr. (1996). Value-based business strategy. *Journal of Economics & Management Strategy, 5*(1), 5–25. doi:10.1111/j.1430-9134.1996.00005.x

Brandenburger, A., & Nalebuff, B. J. (1997). *Co-opetition*. Currency Doubleday.

Branscombe, M. (2020). The network impact of the global COVID-19 pandemic. *The New Stack, 14*. https://thenewstack.io/the-network-impact-of-the-global-covid-19-pandemic/

Brass, D. J., Galaskiewicz, J., Greve, H. R., & Tsai, W. (2004). Taking stock of networks and organizations: A multilevel perspective. *Academy of Management Journal*, *47*(6), 795–817. doi:10.2307/20159624

Brauwer, C., & Cohen, J. J. (2020). Analysing the potential of citizen-financed community renewable energy to drive Europe's low-carbon energy transition. *Renewable & Sustainable Energy Reviews.*

Bridoux, F., Coeurderoy, R., & Durand, R. (2001). Heterogeneous motives and collective value creation. *Academy of Management Review*, *36*, 711–730.

Bridoux, F., & Stoelhorst, J. W. (2016). Stakeholder relationships and social welfare: A behavioral theory of contributions of joint value creation. *Academy of Management Review*, *41*(2), 229–251. doi:10.5465/amr.2013.0475

Brix, J. (2019). Innovation capacity building: An approach to maintaining balance between exploration and exploitation in organizational learning. *The Learning Organization*, *26*(1), 12–26. doi:10.1108/TLO-08-2018-0143

Broby, D. (2021). Financial technology and the future of banking. *Broby Finance Innov, VOL*, *7*(1), 47. doi:10.118640854-021-00264-y

Bulkeley, H., & Betsill, M. (2003). *Cities and climate change. Urban sustainability and global environmental governance*. Routledge.

Bundy, J., Vogel, R. M., & Zachary, M. A. (2018). Organization–stakeholder fit: A dynamic theory of cooperation, compromise, and conflict between an organization and its stakeholders. *Strategic Management Journal*, *39*(2), 476–501. doi:10.1002mj.2736

Bureau, E. P. N. (2022, February 9). Slowing trend of ANDA approvals in 2021: Pandemic effect or selective filings? *Express Pharma*. https://www.expresspharma.in/slowing-trend-of-anda-approvals-in-2021-pandemic-effect-or-selective-filings/

Burt, R. (1992). *Structural Holes: The Social Structure of Competition*. Cambridge, MA: Carayannis, E.G., Campbell, D.F.J., 2009. 'mode 3' and 'quadruple helix': toward a 21st century fractal innovation ecosystem. *International Journal of Technology Management*, *46*(3–4), 201–234.

Butcher, L., Phau, I., & Shimul, A. S. (2017). Uniqueness and status consumption in Generation Y consumers: Does moderation exist? *Marketing Intelligence & Planning*, *35*(5), 673–687. doi:10.1108/MIP-12-2016-0216

Buur, J., & Gudiksen, S. (2012, October). Interactive pinball business. In *Proceedings of the 7th Nordic Conference on Human-Computer Interaction: Making Sense Through Design* (pp. 129-138).

Buvat, J., Solis, B., Crummenerl, C., Aboud, C., Kar, K., El Aoufi, H., & Sengupta, A. (2017). The Digital Culture Challenge: Closing the Employee-Leadership Gap. *Capgemini*. https://www. capgemini. com/consulting/wpcontent/uploads/sites/30/2017/07/dti_digitalculture_report. pdf

Byrne, B. M. (2016). *Structural Equation Modeling with Mplus : Basic Concepts, Applications, and Programming.* Structural Equation Modeling with Mplus. doi:10.4324/9781315757421

Cao, J., Li, J., Wang, Y., & Ai, M. (2022). The Impact of Self-Efficacy and Perceived Value on Customer Engagement under Live Streaming Commerce Environment. *Security and Communication Networks*, *2022*, 1–13. Doi.org/10.1155/2022/2904447. doi:10.1155/2022/2904447

Carattini, S., Kallbekken, S., & Orlov, A. (2019). *How to win public support for a global carbon tax.* Nature Journal. doi:10.1038/d41586-019-00124-x

Carboni, O. A., & Medda, G. (2018). R&D, export and investment decision: Evidence from European firms. *Applied Economics*, *50*(2), 187–201. doi:10.1080/00036846.2017.1332747

Carlson, J., & O'Cass, A. (2010). Exploring the relationships between e-service quality, satisfaction, attitudes and behaviours in content-driven e-service web sites. *Journal of Services Marketing*, *24*(2), 112–127. doi:10.1108/08876041011031091

Carroll, A. B. (1979). A three-dimensional conceptual model of corporate performance. *Academy of Management Review*, *4*(4), 497–505. doi:10.2307/257850

Carroll, A. B. (1991). Corporate social responsibility: Evolution of a definitional construct. *Business & Society*, *38*(3), 268–295. doi:10.1177/000765039903800303

Carter, M., & Carter, C. (2020). The creative business model canvas. *Social Enterprise Journal*, *16*(2), 141–158. doi:10.1108/SEJ-03-2019-0018

Census 2011 India. (n.d.). Population Census. https://www.census2011.co.in/

Chandra, Y., & Shang, L. (2017). An RQDA-based constructivist methodology for qualitative research. *Qualitative Market Research*, *20*(1), 90–112. doi:10.1108/QMR-02-2016-0014

Chandy, R. K., & Tellis, G. J. (1998). Organizing for radical product innovation: The overlooked role of willingness to cannibalize. *JMR, Journal of Marketing Research*, *35*(4), 474–487. doi:10.1177/002224379803500406

Change started. (2021). Year in Review – 11 Indian Green Startups Working for the Climate. *Change Started.* https://changestarted.com/year-end-round-up-10-indian-green-startups-working-for-the-climate/

Chang, W.-C., Ardiyanto, A. N., Wu, C.-W., & Lin, C.-N. (2020). The Application of SERVQUAL Model to Construct Indicators for Improvement of Agricultural Products. *Exhibitions Service Quality*, *7*(6), 1–9.

Chan, S. K. L. (2018). Hierarchical microcredit networks: Lending and borrowing cliques in self-help groups in Phnom Penh. *The International Journal of Sociology and Social Policy*, *38*(11–12), 1008–1023. doi:10.1108/IJSSP-06-2017-0078

Chaturvedi, R., & Karri, A. (2022). Entrepreneurship in the times of pandemic: Barriers and strategies. *FIIB Business Review*, *11*(1), 52–66. doi:10.1177/23197145211043799

Chaudhuri, S. (2005). *The WTO and India's pharmaceuticals industry: Patent protection, TRIPS, and developing countries*. Oxford University Press.

Chauhan, G. S. (2019). Are working capital decisions truly short-term in nature? *Journal of Business Research, 99*(August 2018), 238–253. doi:10.1016/j.jbusres.2019.02.032

Cheah, I., Shimul, A. S., Liang, J., & Phau, I. (2022). Consumer attitude and intention toward ridesharing. *Journal of Strategic Marketing*, *30*(2), 115–136. doi:10.1080/0965254X.2020.1733050

Chell, E., Spence, L. J., Perrini, F., & Harris, J. D. (2016). Social entrepreneurship and business ethics: Does social equal ethical? *Journal of Business Ethics*, *133*(4), 619–625. doi:10.100710551-014-2439-6

Chen, Roger CY, Hung, Shih-Wei, & Lee, Chen-Hsun. (2018). Corporate Social Responsibility and Firm Idiosyncratic Risk in Different Market States. *Corporate Social Responsibility and Environmental Management*.

Chen, Y.S., Chang, K.C. (2010). The relationship between the quality of a company's patent and its market value: the case of the US pharmaceutical industry. *Technological forecasting and social change, 77* (1), 20 – 33. .

Chen, Y., Ding, D., Meng, L., Li, X., & Zhang, S. (2021). Understanding consumers' purchase intention towards online paid courses. *Information Development*, 02666669211027206.

Chen, Y., Yang, S., & Wang, Z. (2016). Service cooperation and marketing strategies of infomediary and online retailer with eWOM effect. *Information Technology Management*, *17*(2), 109–118. doi:10.100710799-015-0237-1

Cherian, J. J., Rahi, M., Rinwa, N., Singh, S., Reddy, S. E., Gupta, Y. K., Katoch, V. M., Kumar, V., Selvaraj, S., Das, P., Gangakhedkar, R. R., Dinda, A. K., Sarkar, S., Vaghela, P. D., & Bhargava, B. (2021). India's road to independence in manufacturing active pharmaceutical ingredients: Focus on essential medicines. *Economies*, *9*(2), 1–18. doi:10.3390/economies9020071

Chesbrough, H. (2006). *Open business models: How to thrive in the new innovation landscape*. Harvard Business Press.

Chesbrough, H. (2007). Business model innovation: It's not just about technology anymore. *Strategy and Leadership*, *35*(6), 12–17. doi:10.1108/10878570710833714

Chesbrough, H., & Rosenbloom, R. S. (2002). The role of the business model in capturing value from innovation: Evidence from Xerox Corporation's technology spin-off companies. *Industrial and Corporate Change*, *11*(3), 529–555. doi:10.1093/icc/11.3.529

Chinazzi, M., Davis, J. T., Ajelli, M., Gioannini, C., Litvinova, M., Merler, S., Pastore y Piontti, A., Mu, K., Rossi, L., Sun, K., Viboud, C., Xiong, X., Yu, H., Halloran, M. E., Longini, I. M. Jr, & Vespignani, A. (2020). The effect of travel restrictions on the spread of the 2019 novel coronavirus (COVID-19) outbreak. *Science*, *368*(6489), 395–400. doi:10.1126cience.aba9757 PMID:32144116

Chinomona, R. (2016). Brand communication, brand image and brand trust as antecedents of brand loyalty in Gauteng Province of South Africa. *African Journal of Economic and Management Studies*, *7*(1), 124–139. doi:10.1108/AJEMS-03-2013-0031

Choi, T. H., & Pae, J. (2011). Business ethics and financial reporting quality: Evidence from Korea. *Journal of Business Ethics*, *109*(3), 403–427. doi:10.100710551-011-0871-4

Chomvilailuk, R., & Butcher, K. (2010). Enhancing brand preference through corporate social responsibility initiatives in the Thai banking sector. *Asia Pacific Journal of Marketing and Logistics*, *22*(3), 397–418. doi:10.1108/13555851011062296

Chu, S. C., & Kim, J. (2018). The current state of knowledge on electronic word-of-mouth in advertising research. *International Journal of Advertising*, *37*(1), 1–13. doi:10.1080/02650487.2017.1407061

Çınar, A. K. (2009). *Integrating Case Based Reasoning and Geographic Information Systems in a Planing Support System: Çeşme Peninsula Study* [Doctoral dissertation, Izmir Institute of Technology, Turkey].

Circle Economy. (n.d.). The Key Elements Of The Circular Economy Framework A Comprehensive Landscape Of Circular Economy. *Circle Economy*. https://www.circle-economy.com/resources/the-key-elements-of-the-circular-economy-framework#:~:text=The%20principles%20of%20a%20circular,guide%20%5B8%5D%5B9%5D

Circle Economy. (n.d.). Trade and Environment. *Circle Economy*. https://unctad.org/topic/trade-and-environment/circular-economy#:~:text=A%20circular%20economy%20entails%20markets,economy%20or%20used%20more%20efficiently

Circular economy. (2022). A $45 billion opportunity by 2030 in India: report *Live Mint*. https://www.livemint.com/news/india/circular-economy-a-45-billion-opportunity-by-2030-in-india-report-11650628743418.html

Clapper, J. R. (2014). *The national intelligence strategy of the United States of America*. Office of the Director of National Intelligence.

Clarkson, M. B. E. (1995). A stakeholder framework for analyzing and evaluating corporate social performance. *Academy of Management Review*, *20*(1), 92–117. doi:10.2307/258888

Clegg, S. R., Da Cunha, J. V., & Cunha, M. P. (2002). Management paradoxes: A relational view. *Human Relations*, *55*(5), 483–503. doi:10.1177/0018726702555001

Cohendet, P., Simon, L., & Mehouachi, C. (2021). From business ecosystems to ecosystems of innovation: The case of the video game industry in Montréal. *Industry and Innovation*, *28*(8), 1046–1076. doi:10.1080/13662716.2020.1793737

Cohen, J. (1998). *Statistical power analysis for the behavioral sciences* (2nd ed.). Erlbaum.

Cohen, W. M., & Levinthal, D. A. (1989). Innovation and learning: The two faces of R & D. *Economic Journal (London)*, *99*(397), 569–596. doi:10.2307/2233763

Connor, T. (2003). Managing for competitiveness: A proposed model for managerial focus. *Strategic Change*, *12*(4), 195–207. doi:10.1002/jsc.633

Constantinides, E. (2014). Foundations of Social Media Marketing. *Procedia: Social and Behavioral Sciences*, *148*, 40–57. doi:10.1016/j.sbspro.2014.07.016

Cooper, R. G. (2019). The drivers of success in new-product development. *Industrial Marketing Management*, *76*, 36–47. doi:10.1016/j.indmarman.2018.07.005

Correa-Baena, J.-P., Saliba, M., Buonassisi, T., Grätzel, M., Abate, A., Tress, W., & Hagfeldt, A. (2017). Promises and challenges of perovskite solar cells. *Science*, *358*(6364), 739–744. doi:10.1126cience.aam6323 PMID:29123060

Coursaris, C., Van Osch, W., Sung, J., & Yun, Y. (2013). Disentangling Twitter's Adoption and Use (Dis)Continuance: A Theoretical and Empirical Amalgamation of Uses and Gratifications and Diffusion of Innovations. *AIS Transactions on Human-Computer Interaction*, *5*(1), 57–83. https://aisel.aisnet.org/thci/vol5/iss1/5. doi:10.17705/1thci.00054

*COVID-19 Digital Transformation & Technology* . (n.d.). McKinsey. https://www.mckinsey.com/business-functions/strategy-and-corporate-finance/our-insights/how-covid-19-has-pushed-companies-over-the-technology-tipping-point-and-transformed-business-forever

Coyle-Shapiro, J. (2002). 'Changing employee attitudes: The independent effects of TQM & profit sharing on continuous improvement orientation'. *The Journal of Applied Behavioral Science*, *38*(1), 55–77. doi:10.1177/0021886302381004

Creswell, J. W., Hanson, W. E., Clark Plano, V. L., & Morales, A. (2007). Qualitative research designs: Selection and implementation. *The Counseling Psychologist*, *35*(2), 236–264. doi:10.1177/0011000006287390

Crick, J. M., & Crick, D. (2020). Coopetition and COVID-19: Collaborative business-to-business marketing strategies in a pandemic crisis. *Industrial Marketing Management.*

Crisan, D. (2020). *Buying with intention: public procurement for innovation by provincial and municipal administrations.* The School of Public Policy Publications.

Cruickshank, J. (2003). *Critical realism: The difference it makes* (Vol. 6). Routledge. doi:10.4324/9780203512302

Crunchbase. (2021). Business model gallery. *Crunchbase company profile and funding.* https://www.crunchbase.com/organization/business-model-gallery

Csikszentmihalyi, M. (1975). *Beyond Boredom and Anxiety*. Jossey-Bass San Francisco.

D'Amato, D., Korhonen, J., & Toppinen, A. (2019). Circular, Green, and Bio Economy: How Do Companies in Land-Use Intensive Sectors Align with Sustainability Concepts? *Ecological Economics*, *158*, 116–133. doi:10.1016/j.ecolecon.2018.12.026

Daas, D., Hurkmans, T., Overbeek, S., & Bouwman, H. (2013). Developing a decision support system for business model design. *Electronic Markets*, *23*(3), 251–265. doi:10.100712525-012-0115-1

Dabbous, A., & Barakat, K. A. (2020). Bridging the online offline gap: Assessing the impact of brands' social network content quality on brand awareness and purchase intention. *Journal of Retailing and Consumer Services, 53*(November 2018), 101966. doi:10.1016/j.jretconser.2019.101966

Dacin, M. T., Dacin, P. A., & Tracey, P. (2011). Social entrepreneurship: A critique and future directions. *Organization Science, 22*(5), 1203–1213. doi:.1100.0620 doi:10.1287/orsc

Daft, R. (2006). Cengage learning. *Organization theory and design.*

Dana, L. P., Sharma, N., & Acharya, S. R. (Eds.). (2020). *Organizing entrepreneurship and MSMEs across India* (Vol. 11). World Scientific.

Dana, L. P., Sharma, N., & Singh, V. K. (Eds.). (2022). *Managing Human Resources in SMEs and Start-ups: International Challenges and Solutions* (Vol. 5). World Scientific. doi:10.1142/12341

Das, T. K., & Teng, B.-S. (2000). A resource-based theory of strategic alliances. *Journal of Management*, *26*(1), 31–61. doi:10.1177/014920630002600105

Dattée, B., Alexy, O., & Autio, E. (2018). Maneuvering in Poor Visibility: How Firms Play the Ecosystem Game when Uncertainty is High. [buh.]. *Academy of Management Journal*, *61*(2), 466–498. doi:10.5465/amj.2015.0869

Daugherty, T., & Hoffman, E. (2014). eWOM and the importance of capturing consumer attention within social media. *Journal of Marketing Communications*, *20*(1-2), 82–102. doi:10.1080/13527266.2013.797764

Davis, F. D. (1993). User acceptance of information technology: System characteristics, user perceptions and behavioral impacts. *International Journal of Man-Machine Studies*, *38*(3), 475–487. doi:10.1006/imms.1993.1022

Davis, F. D., Bagozzi, R. P., & Warshaw, P. R. (2002). X: User Acceptance of Computer Technology: A Comparison of Two Theoretical Models. *Management Science*, *35*(8), 10–1287.

Dawar, G., Singh, S., Joshi, M., & Kumar, P. (2020). Effective Corporate Social Responsibilty in Small Medium Entreprises. In *Organizing entrepreneurship and MSME across India*. World Scientific Publishers.

Dawes, S. S. (1996). Interagency information sharing: Expected benefits, manageable risks. *Journal of Policy Analysis and Management*, *15*(3), 377–394. doi:10.1002/(SICI)1520-6688(199622)15:3<377::AID-PAM3>3.0.CO;2-F

Dawson, P., & Daniel, L. (2010). Understanding social innovation: A provisional framework. *International Journal of Technology Management*, *51*(1), 9–21. doi:10.1504/IJTM.2010.033125

Daymond, J., Knight, E., Rumyantseva, M., & Maguire, S. (2022). Managing ecosystem emergence and evolution: Strategies for ecosystem architects. *Strategic Management Journal.* doi:10.1002/smj.3449

De Reuver, M., Bouwman, H., & Haaker, T. (2013). Business model roadmapping: A practical approach to come from an existing to a desired business model. *International Journal of Innovation Management*, *17*(01), 1340006. doi:10.1142/S1363919613400069

de Vasconcelos Gomes, L. A., Facin, A. L. F., Salerno, M. S., & Ikenami, R. K. (2018). Unpacking the innovation ecosystem construct: Evolution, gaps and trends. *Technological Forecasting and Social Change*, *136*, 30–48. doi:10.1016/j.techfore.2016.11.009

De', R., Pandey, N., & Pal, A. (2020). Impact of digital surge during Covid-19 pandemic: A viewpoint on research and practice. *International Journal of Information Management*, *55*, 102171. doi:10.1016/j.ijinfomgt.2020.102171 PMID:32836633

Debor, S. (2014). *The Socio-Economic Power of Renewable Energy Production Cooperatives in Germany. Results of an Empirical Assessment.* Wuppertal Papers.

Dellermann, D. (2021). Accelerating Entrepreneurial Decision-Making Through Hybrid Intelligence. *arXiv preprint arXiv:2105.03365.*

Dellermann, D., Lipusch, N., Ebel, P., & Leimeister, J. M. (2019). Design principles for a hybrid intelligence decision support system for business model validation. *Electronic Markets, 29*(3), 423–441. doi:10.100712525-018-0309-2

Demlehner, Q., & Laumer, S. (2019). *Setting the hook–The digital transformation from a manufacturing point of view and what it really means.* Research Gate.

Dent, E. B. (1999). Complexity science. *A worldview shift. Emergence, 1*(4), 5–19. doi:10.120715327000em0104_2

Desai, S. (2011). Measuring entrepreneurship in developing countries. In *Entrepreneurship and economic development* (pp. 94–107). Springer. doi:10.1057/9780230295155_4

Desai, S., & Acs, Z. J. (2008). *Democratic capitalism and philanthropy in a global economy Public policy in an entrepreneurial economy.* Springer.

Destination, B. C. (2014). Destination BC creates the wild within VR experience. *Tratto il giorno agosto, 11*, 2015.

Devaraj, A., Ambi Ramakrishnan, G., Nair, G. S., Srinivasan, K. K., Bhat, C. R., Pinjari, A. R., Ramadurai, G., & Pendyala, R. M. (2020). Joint Model of Application-Based Ride Hailing Adoption, Intensity of Use, and Intermediate Public Transport Consideration among Workers in Chennai City. *Transportation Research Record: Journal of the Transportation Research Board, 2674*(4), 152–164. doi:10.1177/0361198120912237

Dhahri, S., Slimani, S. & Omri, A. (2021) 'Behavioral entrepreneurship for achieving the sustainable development goals', *Technological Forecasting and Social Change, 165*(June 2017), 120561. doi:. doi:10.1016/j.techfore.2020.120561

Diaz Lopez, F. J., Bastein, T., & Tukker, A. (2019). Business Model Innovation for Resource-efficiency, Circularity and Cleaner Production: What 143 Cases Tell Us. *Ecological Economics, 155*, 20–35. doi:10.1016/j.ecolecon.2018.03.009

DiMaggio, P. J., & Powell, W. W. (1983). The iron cage revisited: Institutional isomorphism and collective rationality in organizational fields. *American Sociological Review, 48*(2), 147–160. doi:10.2307/2095101

Domenech, T., & Bahn-Walkowiak, B. (2017). Transition Towards a Resource Efficient Circular Economy in Europe: Policy Lessons From the EU and the Member States. *Ecological Economics.* doi:10.1016/J.ECOLECON.2017.11.001

Domenech, T., Bleischwitz, R., Doranova, A., Panayotopoulos, D., & Roman, L. (2019). Mapping Industrial Symbiosis Development in Europe_ typologies of networks, characteristics, 728 performance and contribution to the Circular Economy. *Resources, Conservation and Recycling, 141*, 76–98. doi:10.1016/j.resconrec.2018.09.016

Donaldson, T., & Preston, L. E. (1995). The stakeholder theory of the corporation: Concepts, evidence, and implications. *Academy of Management Review, 20*(1), 65–91. doi:10.2307/258887

Doran, J., McCarthy, N., & O'Connor, M. (2018). The role of entrepreneurship in stimulating economic growth in developed and developing countries. *Cogent Economics and Finance, 6*(1), 1–14. doi:10.1080/23322039.2018.1442093

Douah, B., & Mohsen, B. (2019). Renewable energies and their contribution in development in the context of competitiveness: evidence of specific oil Territory, European Review of Social L, Vol.44, Issue 3, pp: 44-61 (Co-Author.,) DOI https://www.ceeol.com/search/article-detail?id=768416

Douah, B., & Mohsen, B. (2019). *Issue 3* (Vol. 44). Renewable energies and their contribution in development in the context of competitiveness: evidence of specific oil Territory, European Review of Social L. DOI., https://www.ceeol.com/search/article-detail?id=768416

Drucker, J., & Oster, H. (2015). *An empirical study of the effect of social media marketing activities upon customer satisfaction, positive word-of-mouth and commitment in indemnity insurance service.* March.

Dubé, L., & Robey, D. (2008). Surviving the paradoxes of virtual teamwork. *Information Systems Journal, 19*(1), 3–30. doi:10.1111/j.1365-2575.2008.00313.x

Dubey, R., Gunasekaran, A., Childe, S. J., Papadopoulos, T., Hazen, B., Giannakis, M., & Roubaud, D. (2017). Examining the effect of external pressures and organizational culture on shaping performance measurement systems (PMS) for sustainability benchmarking: Some empirical findings. *International Journal of Production Economics, 193*, 63–76. doi:10.1016/j.ijpe.2017.06.029

Duncan, R. B. (1971). *The effects of perceived environmental uncertainty on organizational decision unit structure: A cybernetic model.* Yale University.

Duncan, R. B. (1972). Characteristics of organizational environments and perceived environmental uncertainty. *Administrative Science Quarterly, 17*(3), 313–327. doi:10.2307/2392145

Dur, A. & Aljughaiman, A. (2021). Does financial technology matter? Evidence from an alternative banking system. *Cogent Economics & Finance*. doi:. doi:10.1080/23322039.2021.1934978

Du, S., Bhattacharya, C. B., & Sen, S. (2007). Reaping relational rewards from corporate social responsibility: The role of competitive positioning. *International Journal of Research in Marketing, 24*(3), 224–241. doi:10.1016/j.ijresmar.2007.01.001

Dvorský, J., Petráková, Z., Çera, G., & Folvarčna, A. (2019). Important factors for the entrepreneurship in Central Europe. *Innovative Marketing, 15*(2), 71–83. doi:10.21511/im.15(2).2019.06

Dwivedi, Y. K., Ismagilova, E., Hughes, D. L., Carlson, J., Filieri, R., Jacobson, J., Jain, V., Karjaluoto, H., Kefi, H., Krishen, A. S., Kumar, V., Rahman, M. M., Raman, R., Rauschnabel, P. A., Rowley, J., Salo, J., Tran, G. A., & Wang, Y. (2021). Setting the future of digital and social media marketing research: Perspectives and research propositions. *International Journal of Information Management, 59*(May), 102168. doi:10.1016/j.ijinfomgt.2020.102168

Dwivedi, Y. K., Rana, N. P., Jeyaraj, A., Clement, M., & Williams, M. D. (2019). Re-examining the Unified Theory of Acceptance and Use of Technology (UTAUT): Towards a Revised Theoretical Model. *Information Systems Frontiers, 21*(3), 719–734. doi:10.100710796-017-9774-y

Dyer, J. H., & Nobeoka, K. (2000). Creating and managing a high-performance knowledge-sharing network: The Toyota case. *Strategic Management Journal, 21*(3), 345–367. doi:10.1002/(SICI)1097-0266(200003)21:3<345::AID-SMJ96>3.0.CO;2-N

Ebel, P., Bretschneider, U., & Leimeister, J. M. (2016). Leveraging virtual business model innovation: A framework for designing business model development tools. *Information Systems Journal, 26*(5), 519–550. doi:10.1111/isj.12103

Ebinger, J., & Vergara, W. (2011). *Climate Impacts on Energy Systems: key issues for energy sector adaptation.* The World Bank. doi:10.1596/978-0-8213-8697

Edwards, C. J. (2020). Entrepreneurship within the history of marketing. *Journal of Business Research, 108*(April 2019), 259–267. doi:. doi:10.1016/j.jbusres.2019.10.040

Eesley, C., & Lenox, M. J. (2006). Firm responses to secondary stakeholder action. *Strategic Management Journal*, *27*(8), 765–781. doi:10.1002mj.536

Effah, J., & Nuhu, H. (2017). Institutional barriers to digitalization of government budgeting in developing countries: A case study of Ghana. *The Electronic Journal on Information Systems in Developing Countries*, *82*(1), 1–17. doi:10.1002/j.1681-4835.2017.tb00605.x

Eisingerich, A. B., & Bell, S. J. (2008). Perceived service quality and customer trust: Does enhancing customers' service knowledge matter? *Journal of Service Research*, *10*(3), 256–268. doi:10.1177/1094670507310769

Ellen MacArthur Foundation. (2015). *Circularity Indicators Project*. Ellen MacArthur Foundation. https://www.ellenmacarthurfoundation.org/programmes/insight/circularity-indicators

Employment, European Commission. Directorate-General for. (2001). *Promoting a European Framework for Corporate Social Responsibility: Green Paper*: Office for Official Publications of the European Communities.

Energy England Community. (2021). *Community Energy State of the Sector 2021*. Community Energy England.

Environments of organizations. (1976). *Annual review of sociology*, 79-105. EOO.

Erdem, T., & Swait, J. (2004). Brand credibility, brand consideration, and choice. *The Journal of Consumer Research*, *31*(1), 191–198. doi:10.1086/383434

Erdin, C., & Ozkaya, G. (2020). Contribution of small and medium enterprises to economic development and quality of life in Turkey. *Heliyon*, *6*(2), e03215. doi:10.1016/j.heliyon.2020.e03215 PMID:32055722

Ershadi, M. J., Najafi, N., & Soleimani, P. (2019). Measuring the impact of soft and hard total quality management factors on customer behavior based on the role of innovation and continuous improvement. *The TQM Journal*, *31*(6), 1093–1115. doi:10.1108/TQM-11-2018-0182

Erum, S.; Muhammad, N T.; Wali Muhammad, K.; Mohsen, B.; & Shahid, R., Chapter 16: The COVID-19 Pandemic Overlaps Entrepreneurial Activities and Triggered New Challenges: A Review Study, Book chapter: Managing Human Resources in SMEs and Start-ups, August 2022, 388 p. https://doi.org/ doi:10.1142/9789811239212_0008

Eskander, S. M. S. U., & Fankhauser, S. (2020). Reduction in greenhouse gas emissions from national climate legislation. Natural Climate change, 10, 750–756. . doi:10.103841558-020-0831-z

Esposito, M., Haider, A., Samaan, D., & Semmler, W. (2014). Improving job creation through green transformation. In K. Schlegelmilch, H. Eichel, & A. Pegels (Eds.), Green Industrial Policy: Concept, Policies, Country Experiences (Vol. 30, pp. 469-491). Academic Press.

Etemad, H., Wright, R. W., & Dana, L. P. (2001). Symbiotic international business networks: Collaboration between small and large firms. *Thunderbird International Business Review*, *43*(4), 481–499. doi:10.1002/tie.1009

Etikan, I., Musa, S. A., & Alkassim, R. S. (2016). Comparison of convenience sampling and purposive sampling. *American Journal of Theoretical and Applied Statistics*, *5*(1), 1–4. doi:10.11648/j.ajtas.20160501.11

Euchner, J., & Ganguly, A. (2014). Business model innovation in practice. *Research Technology Management*, *57*(6), 33–39.

European Commission. (2015). *Closing the loop - An EU action plan for the Circular Economy*. COM.

Ezema, I. J. (2016). Globalistation, information revolution and cultural imperialism in africa: Implications for nigerian library and information professionals. *Middle East*, *439*(90), 4.

Ezema, I. J., & Igbo, H. U. (2016). Electronic theses and dissertations and the promotion of scholarship in African universities: Prospects and challenges. *The International Information & Library Review*, *48*(1), 21–30. doi:10.1080/10572317.2016.1146038

Fan, X., Jiang, X., & Deng, N. (2022). Immersive technology: A meta-analysis of augmented/virtual reality applications and their impact on tourism experience. *Tourism Management*, *91*, 104534. doi:10.1016/j.tourman.2022.104534

Fatikah, B. H., & Albanna, H. (2022). The Influence of E-Servqual and E-Trust on E-Loyalty: The Role of E-Satisfaction as an Intervening on Islamic Mobile Banking Customer. *Journal of Business Management and Islamic Banking*, *1*(1), 119–130. doi:10.14421/jbmib.2022.011-08

Fauzi, A. A., & Sheng, M. L. (2020). Ride-hailing apps' continuance intention among different consumer groups in Indonesia: The role of personal innovativeness and perceived utilitarian and hedonic value. *Asia Pacific Journal of Marketing and Logistics*, *33*(5), 1195–1219. doi:10.1108/APJML-05-2019-0332

FEIGE, D. M. (2019). The Culture of Digitalization and the Digitalization of Culture. *Contemporary Research Topics In Arts Education*, *53*.

Feola, G. (2015). Societal transformation in response to global environmental change: A review of emerging concepts. *Ambio*, *44*(5), 376–390. doi:10.100713280-014-0582-z PMID:25431335

Ferguson, R., & Brohaugh, B. (2010). The aging of Aquarius. *Journal of Consumer Marketing*, *27*(1), 76–81. doi:10.1108/07363761011012976

Feyen, E., Frost, J., Gambacorta, L., Natarajan, H., & Saal, M. (2021). FINTECH and the digital transformation of financial services: implications for market structure and public policy. BIS Papers, No 117, The Bank for International Set.

Fianto, A. Y. A., Hadiwidjojo, D., & Aisjah, S. (2014). The influence of brand image on purchase behaviour through brand trust. *Business Management and Strategy*, *5*(2), 58. doi:10.5296/bms.v5i2.6003

Fiksel, J., Sanjay, P., & Raman, K. (2021). Steps toward a resilient circular economy in India. *Clean Technologies and Environmental Policy*, *23*(1), 203–218. doi:10.100710098-020-01982-0 PMID:33199980

Fleischmann, A., Oppl, S., Schmidt, W., & Stary, C. (2020). *Contextual process digitalization: changing perspectives–design thinking–value-led design*. Springer Nature. doi:10.1007/978-3-030-38300-8

Fornell, C., & Larcker, D. (1981). Evaluating Structural Equation Models with Unobservable Variables and Measurement Error. *JMR, Journal of Marketing Research*, *18*(1), 39–50. doi:10.1177/002224378101800104

Forte, A. (2013). Corporate Social Responsibility in The United States and Europe: How Important Is It? The Future of Corporate Social Responsibility, International Business &. *Economic Research Journal*, *12*(7), N-7. doi:10.19030/iber.v12i7.7970

Fraccascia, L. (2020). Quantifying the direct network effect for online platforms supporting industrial symbiosis: An agent-based simulation study. *Ecological Economics*, *170*, 106587. doi:10.1016/j.ecolecon.2019.106587

Fraj, S. H., Bouchoucha, N. and Maktouf, S. (2020). Political stability and economic growth: the role of exchange rate regime. *Munich Personal RePEc Archive Political (MPRA)*, (104586).

Frantzen, D. (2000). R&D, Human Capital and International Technology Spillovers: A Cross Country Analysis. *The Scandinavian Journal of Economics*, *102*(1), 55–75. doi:10.1111/1467-9442.00184

Freeman, R. & Velamuri, S. (2006). A new approach to CSR: Company stakeholder responsibility Corporate social responsibility (pp. 9-23): Springer.

Freeman, R. E. (1984). *Strategic management: A stakeholder approach.* Pitman Publishing.

Freeman, R. E. (1994). The politics of stakeholder theory: Some future direction. *Business Ethics Quarterly, 4*(4), 409–421. doi:10.2307/3857340

Freeman, R. E., Harrison, J. S., & Wicks, A. C. (2007). *Managing for stakeholders: Survival, reputation, and success.* Yale University Press.

Freeman, R. E., & Reed, D. L. (1983). Stockholders and shareholders: A new perspective on corporate governance. *California Management Review, 25*(3), 88–106. doi:10.2307/41165018

Friedman, A. L., & Miles, S. (2006). *Stakeholders: Theory and practice.* Oxford University Press on Demand.

Frooman, J. (1999). Stakeholder influence strategies. *Academy of Management Review, 24*(2), 191–205. doi:10.2307/259074

Fuentes-Fuentes, M. M., & Albacete, C. ALlor Ãens-Montes, F. J. (2004). The impact of environmental characteristics on TQM principles and organizational performance. *Omega, 32*(6), 425–442. doi:10.1016/j.omega.2004.02.005

Ganguly, A., Talukdar, A., & Chatterjee, D. (2020). Social capital, knowledge quality, knowledge sharing, and innovation capability: An empirical study of the Indian pharmaceutical sector. *Knowledge and Process Management, 27*(1), 25–42. doi:10.1002/kpm.1614

Garrone, P., Piscitello, L., Wang, Y. (2014). Innovation performance and international knowledge spillovers: evidence from the renewable energy sector in OECD countries. *Industry and Innovation Journal, 21* (7–8), 574-598. .

Gasmi, G., & Prlja, D. (2020). Perspectives of digitization of cultural heritage in european countries. *Fiat Iustitia,* (1).

Gasmi, G., Korać, V., & Prlja, S. (2019). Evropski propisi i digitalizacija kulturne i naučne baštine.

Gasparin, M., Green, W., Lilley, S., Quinn, M., Saren, M., & Schinckus, C. (2020). Business as unusual: A business model for social innovation. *Journal of Business Research.*

Gassmann, O., Frankenberger, K., & Csik, M. (2014). *The business model navigator: 55 models that will revolutionise your business.* Pearson UK.

Gawer, A., & Cusumano, M. A. (2014). Industry platforms and ecosystem innovation. *Journal of Product Innovation Management, 31*(3), 417–433. doi:10.1111/jpim.12105

Gebert, D., Boerner, S., & Kearney, E. (2010). Fostering team innovation: Why is it important to combine opposing action strategies? *Organization Science, 21*(3), 593–608. doi:10.1287/orsc.1090.0485

Geetika, J., Archana, S., & Mohsen, B. (2021). *Consumer acceptance toward Blockchain Technology for Anti-counterfeiting: Hype, Credence or Future.* International Journal of Business Innovation and Research., doi:10.1504/IJBIR.2021.10042862

Gefen, D., & Straub, D. (2003). Managing user trust in B2C e-services. *e-Service, 2*(2), 7-24.

Gefen, D., Karahanna, E., & Straub, D. W. (2003). Trust and TAM in online shopping: An integrated model. *Management Information Systems Quarterly, 27*(1), 51–90. doi:10.2307/30036519

Gegenhuber, B., & Tollkuhn, J. (2020). Signatures of sex: Sex differences in gene expression in the vertebrate brain. *Wiley Interdisciplinary Reviews. Developmental Biology, 9*(1), e348. doi:10.1002/wdev.348 PMID:31106965

Gentili, P. L. (2021). Why is Complexity Science valuable for reaching the goals of the UN 2030 Agenda? *Rendiconti Lincei. Scienze Fisiche e Naturali, 32*(1), 117–134. doi:10.100712210-020-00972-0 PMID:33527036

Gerards, R., van Wetten, S., & van Sambeek, C. (2021). New ways of working and intrapreneurial behaviour: The mediating role of transformational leadership and social interaction. *Review of Managerial Science*, *15*(7), 2075–2110. doi:10.100711846-020-00412-1

Geyer, R. (2003). Europeanisation, Complexity and the British Welfare State. In *Unspecified, Sheffield, UK*. Unspecified.

Ghali-Zinoubi, Z. (2022). Examining Drivers of Environmentally Conscious Consumer Behavior: Theory of Planned Behavior Extended with Cultural Factors. *Sustainability*, *14*(13), 8072. doi:10.3390u14138072

Ghosh, A. (2013). Corporate sustainability and corporate financial performance: the Indian context.2013 Hindustan Unilever Limited. *Waste free world*. https://www.hul.co.in/

Ghosh, A. (2021). Banking sector openness and entrepreneurship. *Journal of Financial Economic Policy*. doi: . doi:10.1108/JFEP-03-2020-0042

Giddens, A. (2011). *The policy of climate change*. Polity Press.

Giret, A., & Botti, V. (2004). Holons and agents. *Journal of Intelligent Manufacturing*, *15*(5), 645–659. doi:10.1023/B:JIMS.0000037714.56201.a3

Gkypali, A., Arvanitis, S., & Tsekouras, K. (2018). Absorptive capacity, exporting activities, innovation openness and innovation performance: A SEM approach towards a unifying framework. *Technological Forecasting and Social Change*, *132*, 143–155. doi:10.1016/j.techfore.2018.01.025

Gkypali, A., Tsekouras, K., & von Tunzelmann, N. (2012). Endogeneity between internationalization and knowledge creation of global R&D leader firms: An econometric approach using scoreboard data. *Industrial and Corporate Change*, *21*(3), 731–762. doi:10.1093/icc/dtr057

Gleadle, P., & Haslam, C. (2010). *An exploratory study of an early stage R & D-intensive firm under. 34*, 54–65. doi:10.1016/j.accfor.2009.10.002

Gliem, J. A., & Gliem, R. R. (2003). *Calculating, Interpreting, And Reporting Cronbach's Alpha Reliability Coefficient For Likert-Type Scales*. Scholar Works. https://scholarworks.iupui.edu/handle/1805/344

Gnambs, T., & Kaspar, K. (2015). Disclosure of sensitive behaviors across self-administered survey modes: A meta-analysis. *Behavior Research Methods*, *47*(4), 1237–1259. doi:10.375813428-014-0533-4 PMID:25410404

Godovykh, M., Baker, C., & Fyall, A. (2022). VR in Tourism: A New Call for Virtual Tourism Experience amid and after the COVID-19 Pandemic. *Tourism and Hospitality*, *3*(1), 265–275. doi:10.3390/tourhosp3010018

Goh, S., & Yoon, T. (2011, January). If you build it will they come? An empirical investigation of facilitators and inhibitors of hedonic virtual world acceptance. In *2011 44th Hawaii International Conference on System Sciences* (pp. 1-9). IEEE. 10.1109/HICSS.2011.233

Goldar, B. (2013). R&D intensity and exports: A study of Indian pharmaceutical firms. *Innovation and Development*, *3*(2), 151–167. doi:10.1080/2157930X.2013.828878

Gond, J.-P., El Akremi, A., Swaen, V., & Babu, N. (2017). The psychological microfoundations of corporate social responsibility: A person-centric systematic review. *Journal of Organizational Behavior*, *38*(2), 225–246. doi:10.1002/job.2170

Gong, T., & Yi, Y. (2018). The effect of service quality on customer satisfaction, loyalty, and happiness in five Asian countries. *Psychology and Marketing*, *35*(6), 427–442. doi:10.1002/mar.21096

González-Gómez, D., Jeong, J. S., Airado Rodríguez, D., & Cañada-Cañada, F. (2016). Performance and perception in the flipped learning model: An initial approach to evaluate the effectiveness of a new teaching methodology in a general science classroom. *Journal of Science Education and Technology*, *25*(3), 450–459. doi:10.100710956-016-9605-9

Goran, J., LaBerge, L., & Srinivasan, R. (2017). Culture for a digital age. *The McKinsey Quarterly*, *3*(1), 56–67.

Gordijn, J. (2005). A design methodology for modeling trustworthy value webs. *International Journal of Electronic Commerce*, *9*(3), 31–48. doi:10.1080/10864415.2005.11044333

Gordijn, J., & Akkermans, H. (2001). Designing and evaluating e-business models. *IEEE Intelligent Systems*, *16*(04), 11–17. doi:10.1109/5254.941353

Gordijn, J., Akkermans, H., & Vliet, H. V. (2000, October). Business modelling is not process modelling. In *International Conference on Conceptual Modeling* (pp. 40-51). Springer, Berlin, Heidelberg.

Gordijn, J., & Akkermans, J. M. (2003). Value-based requirements engineering: Exploring innovative e-commerce ideas. *Requirements Engineering*, *8*(2), 114–134. doi:10.100700766-003-0169-x

Gradzol, J. R., & Gershon, M. (1998). A survey instrument for standardizing TQM modelling research. *International Journal of Quality Science*, *3*(1, N1pp), 80–81. doi:10.1108/13598539810203887

Granovetter, M. (1985). Embeddedness. *American Journal of Sociology*, *91*, 481–510.

Granovetter, M. S. (1985). Economic action and social structure: The problem of Granstrand, O., & Holgersson, M. (2020). Innovation ecosystems: A conceptual review and a new definition. *Technovation*, *90*, 102098.

Grant, R. M. (1996). Prospering in dynamically-competitive environments: Organizational capability as knowledge integration. *Organization Science*, *7*(4), 375–387. doi:10.1287/orsc.7.4.375

Green, T., & Peloza, J. (2011). How does corporate social responsibility create value for consumers? *Journal of Consumer Marketing*, *28*(1), 48–56. doi:10.1108/07363761111101949

Greenway, J. M., & Weiland, J. P. (2000). *Building capacity for innovation as a source of individual and organizational fulfillment* [Doctoral dissertation, Massachusetts Institute of Technology].

Griliches, Z. (1992). The Search for R&D Spillovers Scandinavian. Journal of economics, 94, 29-47.

Griliches, Z., & Lichtenberg, F. R. (1984). R&D and productivity growth at the industry level: is there still a relationship? In *R&D, patents, and productivity* (pp. 465–502). University of Chicago Press. doi:10.7208/chicago/9780226308920.001.0001

Grossman, G. M., & Helpman, E. (1991). *Innovation and growth in the global economy*. MIT Press.

Gudiksen, S. (2015). Business model design games: Rules and procedures to challenge assumptions and elicit surprises. *Creativity and Innovation Management*, *24*(2), 307–322. doi:10.1111/caim.12114

Gueler, M. S., & Schneider, S. (2019). Transformation from industries towards ecosystems: How behemoths approach ecosystem thinking. *Academy of Management Proceedings*. Academy of Management Annual Conference. doi:10.5465/AMBPP.2019.14272abstract

Gueler, M. S., & Schneider, S. (2021). The resource-based view in business ecosystems: A perspective on the determinants of a valuable resource and capability. *Journal of Business Research*, *133*, 158–169. doi:10.1016/j.jbusres.2021.04.061

Gulati, R., & Gargiulo, M. (1999). Where do interorganizational networks come from? *American Journal of Sociology*, *104*(5), 1439–1493. doi:10.1086/210179

Gulati, R., & Singh, H. (1999). The architecture of cooperation: Managing coordination costs and appropriation concerns in strategic alliances. *Administrative Science Quarterly*, *43*(4), 781–814. doi:10.2307/2393616

Guliyev, A. (2018). *The Impact of FINTECH on Banking Industry in Portugal Master's Degree in Innovation and Technological Entrepreneurship 2016-2018*. FEUP - Faculdade de Engenharia da Universidade do Porto.

Gulson, K. N., Lewis, S., Lingard, B., Lubienski, C., Takayama, K., & Webb, P. T. (2017). Policy mobilities and methodology: A proposition for inventive methods in education policy studies. *Critical Studies in Education*, *58*(2), 224–241. doi:10.1080/17508487.2017.1288150

Gumenyuk, L. (2021). Cyber insurance: Modern requirements. *Economics & Education*, *6*(4), 33–36. doi:10.30525/2500-946X/2021-4-5

Gumenyuk, T., Frotveit, M., Bondar, I., Horban, Y., & Karakoz, O. (2021). Cultural diplomacy in modern international relations: The influence of digitalization. *Journal of Theoretical and Applied Information Technology*, *99*(7), 1549–1560.

Gurbaxani, V., & Dunkle, D. (2019). Gearing up for successful digital transformation. *MIS Quarterly Executive*, *18*(3), 209–220. doi:10.17705/2msqe.00017

Gutiérrez, M. A. A., Vexo, F., & Thalmann, D. (2008). *Stepping into Virtual Reality*. Springer London. doi:10.1007/978-1-84800-117-6

Guttentag, D. A. (2010). Virtual reality: Applications and implications for tourism. *Tourism Management*, *31*(5), 637–651. doi:10.1016/j.tourman.2009.07.003

Haaker, T., Bouwman, H., Janssen, W., & de Reuver, M. (2017). Business model stress testing: A practical approach to test the robustness of a business model. *Futures*, *89*, 14–25. doi:10.1016/j.futures.2017.04.003

Haakonsson, S. J., Jensen, P. D. Ø., & Mudambi, S. M. (2013). A co-evolutionary perspective on the drivers of international sourcing of pharmaceutical R&D to India. *Journal of Economic Geography*, *13*(4), 677–700. doi:10.1093/jeg/lbs018

Hacklin, F., & Wallnöfer, M. (2012). The business model in the practice of strategic decision making: Insights from a case study. *Management Decision*, *50*(2), 166–188. doi:10.1108/00251741211203515

Hadfield, G. K. (2012). Legal infrastructure and the new economy. *ISJLP*, *8*, 1.

Hadžić, F. (2020). The influence of social media on threats to identity, stability and national security; institutional inefficiency and vulnerability of B&H. *Scholarly Journal for Protection, Security, Defense, Education and Training Issues*, *24*(45-46), 67.

Haefner, N., Wincent, J., Parida, V., & Gassmann, O. (2021). Artificial intelligence and innovation management: A review, framework, and research agenda. *Technological Forecasting and Social Change*, *162*, 120392. doi:10.1016/j.techfore.2020.120392

Hahn, T., Preuss, L., Pinske, J., & Figge, F. (2014). Cognitive frames in corporate sustainability: Managerial sensemaking with paradoxical and business case frames. *Academy of Management Review*, *39*(4), 463–487. doi:10.5465/amr.2012.0341

Hair, J. F., Celsi, M., Money, A., Samouel, P., & Page, M. (2015). The essentials of business research methods: Third Edition. The Essentials of Business Research Methods (3rd ed.), 1–494 doi:10.4324/9781315704562

Hair. (1998). *Multivariate data analysis: Its approach, evolution, and impact*. Springer. https://link.springer.com/chapter/10.1007/978-3-030-06031-2_16

Hair, F. Jr, J., Sarstedt, M., Hopkins, L., & G. Kuppelwieser, V. (. (2014). Partial least squares structural equation modeling (PLS-SEM) An emerging tool in business research. *European Business Review*, *26*(2), 106–121. doi:10.1108/EBR-10-2013-0128

Hair, J. F., Black, W. C., Babin, B. J., & Anderson, R. E. (2019). *Multivariate Data Analysis*. Cengage Learning.

Hair, J. F., Ringle, C. M., & Sarstedt, M. (2011). 'PLS-SEM: Indeed a Silver Bullet'. *Journal of Marketing Theory and Practice*, *19*(2), 139–151. doi:10.2753/MTP1069-6679190202

Hall, B. H., Mairesse, J., & Mohnen, P. (2010). Measuring the Returns to R&D. In *Handbook of the Economics of Innovation* (Vol. 2, pp. 1033–1082). North-Holland.

Hallikainen, H., Luongo, M., Dhir, A., & Laukkanen, T. (2022). Consequences of personalized product recommendations and price promotions in online grocery shopping. *Journal of Retailing and Consumer Services*, *69*, 103088. doi:10.1016/j.jretconser.2022.103088

Hamrouni, A., & Korichi, B. Bourouis, (2022). *Explainable Ontology-Based Intelligent Decision Support System For Business Model Design And Sustainability*. [Thesis, Kasdi Merbah Ouargla University, Algeria].

Hamrouni, B., Bourouis, A., Korichi, A., & Brahmi, M. (2021). Explainable Ontology-Based Intelligent Decision Support System for Business Model Design and Sustainability. *Sustainability*, *13*(17), 9819. doi:10.3390u13179819

Hancock, L., Schellinck, T., & Schrans, T. (2008). Gambling and corporate social responsibility (CSR): Re-defining industry and state roles on duty of care, host responsibility and risk management. *Policy and Society*, *27*(1), 55–68. doi:10.1016/j.polsoc.2008.07.005

Hannah, D. P., & Eisenhardt, K. M. (2018). How firms navigate cooperation and competition in nascent ecosystems. *Strategic Management Journal*, *39*(12), 3163–3192. doi:10.1002mj.2750

Hansen, K., Breyer, C. & Lund, H. J. E. (2019). Status and perspectives on 100% renewable energy systems. *Energy*.

Hao, L.N., Umar, M., Khan, Z., and Ali, W. (2021). Green Growth and Low Carbon Emission in G7 Countries: How Critical the Network of Environmental Taxes, Renewable Energy and Human Capital Is? *Sci. Total Environ. Science of total environment.*

Harris, P. (2011). *China's responsibility for climate change: ethics, fairness, and environmental policy*. Political Press.

Harrison, J. S., Bosse, D. A., & Phillips, R. A. (2010). Managing for stakeholders, stakeholder utility functions, and competitive advantage. *Strategic Management Journal*, *31*(1), 58–74. doi:10.1002mj.801

Harris, R., & Li, Q. C. (2009). Exporting, R&D, and absorptive capacity in UK establishments. *Oxford Economic Papers*, *61*(1), 74–103. doi:10.1093/oep/gpn011

Hartl, E. (2019). A Characterization of Culture Change in the Context of Digital Transformation. AMCIS.

Hartman, J. B., Shim, S., Barber, B., & O'Brien, M. (2006). Adolescents' utilitarian and hedonic Web consumption behavior: Hierarchical influence of personal values and innovativeness. *Psychology and Marketing*, *23*(10), 813–839. doi:10.1002/mar.20135

Hassanein, K., & Head, M. (2007). Manipulating perceived social presence through the web interface and its impact on attitude towards online shopping. *International Journal of Human-Computer Studies*, *65*(8), 689–708. doi:10.1016/j.ijhcs.2006.11.018

Hausberg, J. P., Liere-Netheler, K., Packmohr, S., Pakura, S., & Vogelsang, K. (2019). Research streams on digital transformation from a holistic business perspective: A systematic literature review and citation network analysis. *Journal of Business Economics*, *89*(8), 931–963.

Hebebci, M. T., Bertiz, Y., & Alan, S. (2020). Investigation of views of students and teachers on distance education practices during the Coronavirus (COVID-19) Pandemic. *International Journal of Technology in Education and Science*, *4*(4), 267–282. doi:10.46328/ijtes.v4i4.113

Hegmon, M., & Peeples, M. A. (2018). The human experience of social transformation: Insights from comparative archaeology. *PLoS One*, *13*(11), e0208060. doi:10.1371/journal.pone.0208060 PMID:30496250

Helfrich, P. (2000). *The emerging new worldview: An introduction and overview.* [*Unpublished* manuscript, Helfrich]. http://www. paulhelfrich. com/library/Helfrich_P_The_Emerging_New_Worldview. pdf

Helm, D., & Hepburn, C. (Eds.). (2009). *Economics and politics of climate change*. Oxford University Press. doi:10.1093/acprof:osobl/9780199573288.001.0001

Henriette, E., Feki, M., & Boughzala, I. (2015). The shape of digital transformation: A systematic literature review. *AISEL.*

Henseler, J., Ringle, C. M., & Sinkovics, R. R. (2009). The use of partial least squares path modeling in international marketing. In *New challenges to international marketing*. Emerald Group Publishing Limited. doi:10.1108/S1474-7979(2009)0000020014

Hew, J. J., Leong, L. Y., Tan, G. W. H., Lee, V. H., & Ooi, K. B. (2018). Mobile social tourism shopping: A dual-stage analysis of a multi-mediation model. *Tourism Management*, *66*, 121–139. doi:10.1016/j.tourman.2017.10.005

Hicks, J., & Ison, N. (2018). *An exploration of the boundaries of 'community' in community renewable energy projects: Navigating between motivations and context* (Vol. 113). Energy Policy.

Hill, R. C., & Hellriegel, D. (1994). Critical contingencies in joint venture management: Some lessons from managers. *Organization Science*, *5*(4), 594–607. doi:10.1287/orsc.5.4.594

Hinson, E. (2011). Online CSR reportage of award-winning versus non award-winning banks in Ghana. *Journal of Information. Communication and Ethics in Society*, *9*(2), 102–115. doi:10.1108/14779961111148622

Hirschman, E. C., & Holbrook, M. B. (1982). Hedonic Consumption: Emerging Concepts, Methods and Propositions. *Journal of Marketing*, *46*(3), 92–101. doi:10.1177/002224298204600314

Ho, J. L., Chen, K. Y., Wang, L. H., Yeh, S. S., & Huan, T. C. (2022). Exploring the impact of social media platform image on hotel customers' visit intention. *International Journal of Contemporary Hospitality Management.*

Hofstede, G. & Hofstede, G. H. (1984) *Culture's consequences: International differences in work-related values*. sage.

Holman, P. (2015). *Complexity, self-organization, and emergence. Dialogic organization development*. Berrett-Koehler.

Holsapple, C. W., & Wu, J. (2007). User acceptance of virtual worlds: The hedonic framework. *ACM SIGMIS Database: The DATABASE for Advances in Information Systems*, *38*(4), 86–89. doi:10.1145/1314234.1314250

Honarpour, A., Jusoh, A., & Nor, K. M. (2017). *Total quality management, knowledge management, and innovation.* Business Excellence.

Hong, J. C., Lin, P. H., & Hsieh, P. C. (2017). The effect of consumer innovativeness on perceived value and continuance intention to use smartwatch. *Computers in Human Behavior*, *67*, 264–272. doi:10.1016/j.chb.2016.11.001

Hoogendoorn, B., Van der Zwan, P., & Thurik, R. (2019). Sustainable entrepreneurship: The role of perceived barriers and risk. *Journal of Business Ethics, 157*(4), 1133–1154. doi:10.100710551-017-3646-8

Hooker, R., Wasko, M., & Paradice, D. (2009). *Linking flow, brand attitudes and purchase intent in virtual worlds.* In Proceedings of The Thirtieth International Conference on Information Systems(ICIS 2009), Phoenix, Arizona.

Horgan, D., & Dimitrijević, B. (2018). *Social innovation systems to build resilient communities.* Urban Science.

Hosseini, E., Tajpour, M., Salamzadeh, A., & Ahmadi, A. (2022). Team Performance and the Development of Iranian Digital Start-ups: The Mediating Role of Employee Voice. In Managing Human Resources in SMEs and Start-ups: International Challenges and Solutions (pp. 109-140).

Hosseini, E., Ardekani, S. S., Sabokro, M., & Almodarresi, S. M. (2021). Developing a model for knowledge employee voice: The case study of information technology enterprises. *Organizational Culture Management, 19*(4), 655–682. doi:10.22059/jomc.2021.305993.1008085

Hosseini, E., Tajpour, M., Salamzadeh, A., Demiryurek, K., & Kawamorita, H. (2021). Resilience and Knowledge-Based Firms' Performance: The Mediating Role of Entrepreneurial Thinking. *Journal of Entrepreneurship and Business Resilience, 4*(2), 7–29.

Hötte, K., Pichler, A., & Lafond, F. (2021). The rise of science in low-carbon energy technologies. Renewable and sustainable energy reviews, 139. doi:10.1016/j.rser.2020.110654

Hottenrott, H., & Richstein, R. (2020). Start-up subsidies: Does the policy instrument matter? *Research Policy, 49*(1), 103888. doi:10.1016/j.respol.2019.103888

Hou, M., Liu, H., Fan, P., & Wei, Z. (2016, March). Does CSR practice pay off in East Asian firms? A meta-analytic investigation. *Asia Pacific Journal of Management, 33*(1), 195–228. doi:10.100710490-015-9431-2

Hsieh, H.-F., & Shannon, S. E. (2005). Three Approaches to Qualitative Content Analysis. *Qualitative Health Research, 15*(9), 1277–1288. doi:10.1177/1049732305276687 PMID:16204405

Hsu, M. H., Tien, S. W., Lin, H. C., & Chang, C. M. (2015). Understanding the roles of cultural differences and socio-economic status in social media continuance intention. *Information Technology & People, 28*(1), 224–241. doi:10.1108/ITP-01-2014-0007

Huang, H., Chau, K. Y., Iqbal, W., & Fatima, A. (2022). Assessing the role of financing in sustainable business environment. *Environmental Science and Pollution Research International, 29*(5), 7889–7906. doi:10.100711356-021-16118-0 PMID:34480700

Huang, T. K., Wang, Y. T., & Lin, K. Y. (2022). Enhancing brand loyalty through online brand communities: The role of community benefits. *Journal of Product and Brand Management, 31*(5), 823–838. doi:10.1108/JPBM-08-2020-3027

Huang, Y. C., Backman, S. J., Backman, K. F., & Moore, D. (2013). Exploring user acceptance of 3D virtual worlds in travel and tourism marketing. *Tourism Management, 36*, 490–501. doi:10.1016/j.tourman.2012.09.009

Hung, R. Y. Y., Lien, B. Y. H., Yang, B., Wu, C. M., & Kuo, Y. M. (2011). Impact of TQM and organizational learning on innovation performance in the high-tech industry. *International Business Review, 20*(2), 213–225. doi:10.1016/j.ibusrev.2010.07.001

Hunt, V. D. (1992). *Quality in America: How to implement a competitive quality program.* Irwin.

Hussain, S., Ahmed, W., Jafar, R. M. S., Rabnawaz, A., & Jianzhou, Y. (2017). eWOM source credibility, perceived risk and food product customer's information adoption. *Computers in Human Behavior, 66*, 96–102. doi:10.1016/j.chb.2016.09.034

Iansiti, M., & Levien, R. (2004). *The keystone advantage: What the new dynamics of business ecosystems mean for strategy, innovation, and sustainability*. Harvard Business School Press.

IBEF. (2019). Pharmaceutical Companies in India, Indian Pharma Industry- IBEF. *India Brand Equity Foundation.* Error! Hyperlink reference not valid.https://www.ibef.org/industry/pharmaceutical-india.

IBEF. (2020). Pharmaceutical Companies in India, Indian Pharma Industry- IBEF. *India Brand Equity Foundation.* Error! Hyperlink reference not valid.https://www.ibef.org/industry/pharmaceutical-india.

Ihrig, M., & MacMillan, I. C. (2017). How to get ecosystem buy-in. *Harvard Business Review, 95*(2), 102–107.

Improving decision making in complexity environment. (2014). *Procedia Economics and Finance, 16*, 402-409.

Ingram, P., & Roberts, P. W. (2000). Friendships among competitors in the Sydney hotel industry. *American Journal of Sociology, 106*(2), 387–423. doi:10.1086/316965

Innes, C. & Andrieu, J. (2022). *Banking on FINTECH in Emerging Markets.* IFC, a member of the World Bank Group. www.ifc.org/thoughtleadership

Introduction to Complex Systems and Agent Based Modeling, s.l. (2014). *Awarness: Self-Awarness in Autonomic systems.*

Invest India. (2021). India's Sustainable Start-ups. Invest India, National Investment Promotion and Facilitation Agency. https://www.investindia.gov.in/siru/indias-sustainable-start-ups

Irandoust, M. (2016). *The renewable energy-growth nexus with carbon emissions and technological innovation: evidence from the Nordic countries.* Ecological Indicators.

Islam, M., Irfan, M., Shahbaz, M., & Vo, X. V. (2022). [Renewable Energy.]. *Renewable and Non-renewable Energy Consumption in Bangladesh: The Relative Influencing Profiles of Economic Factors, Urbanization, Physical Infrastructure, and Institutional Quality., 184*, 1130–1149.

Jaca, C. & Psomas, E. (2015). Total quality management practices and performance outcomes in Spanish service companies. *Total Quality Management & Business Excellence, 26*(9-10).

Jacobides, M. G., Cennamo, C., & Gawer, A. (2018). Towards a theory of ecosystems. *Strategic Management Journal, 39*(8), 2255–2276. doi:10.1002mj.2904

Jaffe, A. B. (1986). Technological Opportunity and Spillovers of R&D: Evidence from Firms' Patents, Profits, and Market Value. *The American Economic Review, 76*(5), 984–1001.

Jamali, J., & Mirshak, R. (2007). Corporate social responsibility (CSR): Theory and practice in a developing country context. *Journal of Business Ethics, 72*(3), 243–262. doi:10.100710551-006-9168-4

Jang, Y., & Park, E. (2019). An adoption model for virtual reality games: The roles of presence and enjoyment. *Telematics and Informatics, 42*, 101239. doi:10.1016/j.tele.2019.101239

Jarvenpaa, S. L., Tractinsky, N., & Vitale, M. (2000). Consumer trust in an Internet store. *Information Technology and Management, 1*(1/2), 45–71. doi:10.1023/A:1019104520776

Jegede, C. T., & Irewole, O. E. (2020). 'Agencies for Entrepreneurship Development and SMEs' Promotion in Nigeria'. *Revista Cimexus, 15*(2), 165–193. doi:10.33110/cimexus150208

Jenkins, H. (2009). A 'business opportunity'model of corporate social responsibility for small-and medium-sized enterprises. *Business Ethics (Oxford, England), 18*(1), 21–36. doi:10.1111/j.1467-8608.2009.01546.x

Jin, S. (2020). COVID-19, Climate Change, and Renewable Energy Research: We Are All in This Together, and the Time to Act Is Now. *ACS Energy Letter.*

John, T., Kundisch, D., & Szopinski, D. (2017). Visual Languages for Modeling Business Models: A Critical Review and Future Research Directions. In ICIS.

Jones, T. M. (1995). Instrumental stakeholder theory: A synthesis of ethic and economics. *Academy of Management Review, 20*(2), 404–437. doi:10.2307/258852

Jones, T. M., Harrison, J. S., & Felps, W. (2018). How Applying Instrumental Stakeholder Theory Can Provide Sustainable Competitive Advantage. *Academy of Management Review, 43*(3), 371–391. doi:10.5465/amr.2016.0111

Jörg, T. (2011). *New thinking in complexity for the social sciences and humanities: . A generative, transdisciplinary approach.* Springer Science & Business Media. doi:10.1007/978-94-007-1303-1

Joshi, M (2018). Workforce trends and challenges: a peek into future. In N. Sharma (Ed.), *Management Techniques for a Diverse and Cross-Cultural Workforce.* IGI Global.

Joshi, M (February, 2018). Workforce trends and challenges: a peek into future In N. Sharma, *Management Techniques for a Diverse and Cross-Cultural Workforce*, IGI Global USA.

Joshi, M. (2018). "Burnout and Stressors as influencers on Work engagement among law enforcement agents in selected cities. In Chaudhary, N. Sharma, & M. Singh (eds.) Management Techniques for Employee Engagement in Contemporary Organizations. IGI Global USA.

Joshi, M. (2018). Burnout and Stressors as influencers on Work engagement among law enforcement agents in selected cities. In Chaudhary, N., Sharma, M., Singh: Vol. K. Management Techniques for Employee Engagement in Contemporary Organizations. IGI Global USA.

Joshi, M. (2018). Workforce Trends and Challenges: A Peek Into the Future. In Management Techniques for a Diverse and Cross-Cultural Workforce. doi:10.4018/978-1-5225-4933-8.ch003

Joshi, M. (2018). Workforce Trends and Challenges: A Peek Into the Future. *Management Techniques for a Diverse and Cross-Cultural Workforce*, 39-53.

Joshi, M., Tyagi, S., Ansari, N., & Singh, V. K. (2019) Impact of IoT to accomplish a vision of digital transformation of the cities. In A handbook of IOT and Big Data, USA: CRC Press, Taylor and Francis.

Joshi, M. (2018). Burnout and Stressors as influencers on Work engagement among law enforcement agents in selected cities. In *Management Techniques for Employee Engagement in Contemporary Organizations.* IGI Global.

Joshi, M. (2022 Forthcoming). *A mediation based analysis of Emotional Intelligence effect on Cognition and Consumer Decision Making.* IJPSPM.

Joshi, M., Joshi, G., & Pathak, S. (2020). *Awareness, entrepreneurial event theory and theory of planned behavior as antecedents of student entrepreneurial intentions: an Indian perspective. International Journal of Business and Globalisation.* Inderscience Publishers.

Joshi, M., Joshi, G., & Pathak, S. (2020). Awareness, entrepreneurial event theory and theory of planned behaviour as antecedents of student entrepreneurial intentions: An Indian perspective. *International Journal of Business and Globalisation, 25*(2), 170–184. doi:10.1504/IJBG.2020.107885

Joshi, M., & Singh, V. K. (2017). Electronic Word of Mouth and Influence on Consumer Purchase Intention. *Dynamics of Public Administration*, *34*(2), 149–159. doi:10.5958/0976-0733.2017.00012.8

Joshi, M., Tyagi, S., Ansari, N., & Singh, V. K. (2019). Impact of IoT to accomplish a vision of digital transformation of the cities. In *A handbook of IOT and Big Data*. CRC Press, Taylor and Francis.

Kafetzopoulos, D., Gotzamani, K., & Gkana, V. (2015). Relationship between quality management, innovation and competitiveness. Evidence from Greek companies. *Journal of Manufacturing Technology Management*, *26*(No. 8), 1177–1200. doi:10.1108/JMTM-02-2015-0007

Kakabadse, Nada K, Kakabadse, Andrew P, & Lee-Davies, Linda. (2009). CSR leaders road-map. *Corporate Governance: The international journal of business in society*, *9*(1), 50-57.

Kamar, E. (2016, July). Directions in Hybrid Intelligence: Complementing AI Systems with Human Intelligence. In IJCAI (pp. 4070-4073).

Kamien, M. I., & Schwartz, N. L. (1975). Market structure and innovation: A survey. *Journal of Economic Literature*, *13*(1), 1–37.

Kamoun-Chouk, S. (2022). How Digital Literacy, Could Impact Environmental Scanning, Business Intelligence and Knowledge Management? *International Conference on Knowledge Management in Organizations* 10.1007/978-3-031-07920-7_8

Kang, Q., Li, H., Cheng, Y., & Kraus, S. (2021). Entrepreneurial ecosystems: Analysing the status quo. *Knowledge Management Research and Practice*, *19*(1), 8–20. doi:10.1080/14778238.2019.1701964

Kapoor, R., & Lee, J. M. (2013). Coordinating and competing in ecosystems: How organizational forms shape new technology investments. *Strategic Management Journal*, *34*(3), 274–296. doi:10.1002mj.2010

Kasiri, L. A., Guan Cheng, K. T., Sambasivan, M., & Sidin, S. M. (2017). Integration of standardization and customization: Impact on service quality, customer satisfaction, and loyalty. *Journal of Retailing and Consumer Services*, *35*, 91–97. doi:10.1016/j.jretconser.2016.11.007

Kassim, H., Connolly, S., Dehousse, R., Rozenberg, O., & Bendjaballah, S. (2017). Managing the house: The presidency, agenda control and policy activism in the European Commission. *Journal of European Public Policy*, *24*(5), 653–674. doi:10.1080/13501763.2016.1154590

Kaur, N., & Singh, V. (2020). Empirically examining the impact of corporate social responsibility on financial performance: Evidence from Indian steel industry. *Asian Journal of Accounting Research.*, *2020*(Dec), 15.

Kayna, H. (2003). The relationship between total quality management practices and their effects on firm performance. *Journal of Operations Management*, *21*(4), 405–435. doi:10.1016/S0272-6963(03)00004-4

Keller, J., Loewenstein, J., & Yan, J. (2017). Culture, conditions and paradoxical frames. *Organization Studies*, *38*(3–4), 539–560. doi:10.1177/0170840616685590

Khalfallah, M.,, Ben Salem, A.,, & Zorgati, HLakhal, L. (2022). Innovation mediating relationship between TQM and performance: cases of industrial certified companies. *The TQM Journal*, *34*(3), 552-575 ().

Khan, M. A., & Burki, M. (2020). Determinants of small and medium enterprises with the interaction effect of managerial activities. *International Journal of Research in Business and Social Science (2147-4478)*, *9*(4), 153-160. doi:10.20525/ijrbs.v9i4.750

Khan, B. A., & Naeem, H. (2016). *Measuring the impact of soft and hard quality practices on service innovation and organisational performance.* Total Quality Management & Business Excellence.

Khandker, S. R., & Koolwal, B. G. (2011). *Estimating the long-term impacts of rural roads: a dynamic panel approach.* The World Bank. doi:10.1596/1813-9450-5867

Khanin, D., Rosenfield, R., Mahto, R. V., & Singhal, C. (2022). Barriers to entrepreneurship: Opportunity recognition vs. opportunity pursuit. *Review of Managerial Science, 16*(4), 1147–1167. doi:10.100711846-021-00477-6

Khan, M. A. (2022). Barriers constraining the growth of and potential solutions for emerging entrepreneurial SMEs. *Asia Pacific Journal of Innovation and Entrepreneurship, 16*(1), 38–50. doi:10.1108/APJIE-01-2022-0002

Kilduff, M., & Tsai, W. (2003). Social networks and organizations. *Sage (Atlanta, Ga.).*

Killing, J. P. (1983). *Strategies for joint venture success.* Praeger.

Kim, A. J., & Ko, E. (2012). Do social media marketing activities enhance customer equity? An empirical study of luxury fashion brand. *Journal of Business Research, 65*(10), 1480–1486. doi:10.1016/j.jbusres.2011.10.014

Kim, D. J., & Hwang, Y. (2010). A study of mobile internet user's service quality perceptions from a user's utilitarian and hedonic value tendency perspectives. *Information Systems Frontiers, 14*(2), 409–421. doi:10.100710796-010-9267-8

Kim, D. Y., Kumar, V., & Kumar, U. (2012). Relationship between quality management practices and innovation. *Journal of Operations Management, 30*(4), 295–315. doi:10.1016/j.jom.2012.02.003

Kim, D., & Ko, Y. J. (2019). The impact of virtual reality (VR) technology on sport spectators' flow experience and satisfaction. *Computers in Human Behavior, 93*, 346–356. doi:10.1016/j.chb.2018.12.040

Kimes, S. E., & Wirtz, J. (2003). Has revenue management become acceptable? Findings from an international study on the perceived fairness of rate fences. *Journal of Service Research, 6*(2), 125–135. doi:10.1177/1094670503257038

Kim, J. Y., & Hwang, J. (2022). Who is an evangelist? Food tourists' positive and negative eWOM behavior. *International Journal of Contemporary Hospitality Management, 34*(2), 555–577. doi:10.1108/IJCHM-06-2021-0707

Kim, S., & Eastin, M. S. (2011). Hedonic tendencies and the online consumer: An investigation of the online shopping process. *Journal of Internet Commerce, 10*(1), 68–90. doi:10.1080/15332861.2011.558458

Klepper, S. (1996). Entry, Exit, Growth, and Innovation over the Product Life Cycle. *The American Economic Review.*

Klyver, K., & Foley, D. (2012). Networking and culture in entrepreneurship. *Entrepreneurship and Regional Development, 24*(7–8), 561–588. doi:10.1080/08985626.2012.710257

Kogut, B. (1988a). A Study of the Life Cycle of Joint Ventures. In F. J. Contractor & P. Lorange (Eds.), *Cooperative strategies in international business.* D.C. Heath.

Koirala, B. P., Koliou, E., Friege, J., Hakvoort, R. A., & Herder, P. M. (2016). Energetic communities for community energy: A review of key issues and trends shaping integrated community energy systems. *Renewable & Sustainable Energy Reviews, 56*, 722–744. doi:10.1016/j.rser.2015.11.080

Kollmann, T., Stöckmann, C., & Kensbock, J. M. (2017). Fear of failure as a mediator of the relationship between obstacles and nascent entrepreneurial activity—An experimental approach. *Journal of Business Venturing, 32*(3), 280–301. doi:10.1016/j.jbusvent.2017.02.002

Kollock, P. (1998). Social dilemmas: The anatomy of cooperation. *Annual Review of Sociology, 22*(1), 183–205. doi:10.1146/annurev.soc.24.1.183

Kondakov, V. L., Kopeikina, E. N., Voloshina, I. G., & Usatov, A. N. (2019). *Main directions digitalization in the higher education in the world and Russia (based on the example of physical culture and sports).* HR Pub.

Korhonen, J. J., & Halén, M. (2017). Enterprise architecture for digital transformation. *2017 IEEE 19th Conference on Business Informatics (CBI).* IEEE.

Kostopoulos, K., Papalexandris, A., Papachroni, M., & Ioannou, G. (2011). Absorptive capacity, innovation, and fi nancial performance. *Journal of Business Research, 64*(12), 1335–1343. doi:10.1016/j.jbusres.2010.12.005

Kotler, P., & Armstrong, G. M. (2018). *Marketing Mix: Selected Chapters From: Principles of Marketing, Philip Kotler and Gary Armstrong.* Pearson.

Koul, S., & Mishra, H. G. (2013). Customer perceptions for store attributes: A study of traditional retail stores in India. *Journal of Business and Economics, 5*(1), 79–103.

Kraaijenbrink, J., Spender, J. C., & Groen, A. J. (2010). The resource-based view: A review and assessment of its critiques. *Journal of Management, 36*(1), 349–372. doi:10.1177/0149206309350775

Kraehe, A. M. (2019). Entrepreneurship as Creative Destruction. *Art Education, 72*(5), 4–7. doi:10.1080/00043125.2019.1640037

Kreiner, P., & Bhambri, A. (1991). Influence and information or organization-stakeholder relationships. In L. E. Preston (Ed.), *Research in corporate social performance and policy* (Vol. 12, pp. 3–36). JAI Press.

Krishnan, D. (2019, September 11) *Making Indian businesses sustainable.* Strategy Business. https://www.strategy-business.com/article/Making-Indian-businesses-sustainable

Krome, M. J., & Pidun, U. (2022). *Conceptualization of research themes and directions in business ecosystem strategies: A systematic literature review.* Management Review Quarterly. doi:10.100711301-022-00306-4

Kujala, S. I. (2008). Effective user involvement in product development by improving the analysis of user needs. *Behaviour & Information Technology, 27*(6), 457–473. doi:10.1080/01449290601111051

Kumar, V. V. R., Lall, A., & Mane, T. (2017). Extending the TAM Model: Intention of Management Students to Use Mobile Banking: Evidence from India. *Global Business Review, 18*(1), 238–249. doi:10.1177/0972150916666991

Kumar, V., Patwari, Y., & Ayush, H. (2008). Organised food retailing: A blessing or a curse? *Economic and Political Weekly, 43*(20), 67–75.

Kumar, Vikas & Singh, N. (2008). Comments on "The parting gift.". *Thunderbird International Business Review, 50*(5), 321–330. doi:10.1002/tie.20217

Kvale, S. (1996). *InterViews: an introduction to qualitive research interviewing.* Sage.

Kwapisz, A. (2019). Do government and legal barriers impede entrepreneurship in the US? An exploratory study of perceived vs. actual barriers. *Journal of Business Venturing Insights, 11*, e00114. doi:10.1016/j.jbvi.2019.e00114

Lakhal, L., Pasin, F., & Liman, M. (2006). Quality management practices and their impact on performance. *International Journal of Quality & Reliability Management, 23*(6), 625–646. doi:10.1108/02656710610672461

Lanzolla, G., & Markides, C. (2021). A business model view of strategy. *Journal of Management Studies, 58*(2), 540–553. doi:10.1111/joms.12580

Laroche, M., Kim, C., & Zhou, L. (1996). Brand familiarity and confidence as determinants of purchase intention: An empirical test in a multiple brand context. *Journal of Business Research, 37*(2), 115–120. doi:10.1016/0148-2963(96)00056-2

Latora, A. G., Compagno, L., & Trapani, N. (2018). A decision support tool for business models analysis. *International Journal of the Analytic Hierarchy Process*, *10*(2), 219–242. doi:10.13033/ijahp.v10i2.516

Lau, A., Lee, P., & Cheng, T. (2018). An empirical taxonomy of corporate social responsibility in china's manufacturing industries. *Journal of Cleaner Production*.

Lavuri, R. (2021). Intrinsic factors affecting online impulsive shopping during the COVID-19 in emerging markets. *International Journal of Emerging Markets*, Emerald Group Holdings Ltd. doi:10.1108/IJOEM-12-2020-1530/FULL/XML

Lavuri, R., Jabbour, C.J.C., Grebinevych, O. & Roubaud, D., (2022a). Green factors stimulating the purchase intention of innovative luxury organic beauty products: Implications for sustainable development", *Journal of Environmental Management*, *.301*, 113899.

Lavuri, R., Jindal, A., & Umair, A. (2022b). How Perceived Utilitarian and Hedonic value influence online impulse shopping in India? Moderating role of Perceived Trust and Perceived Risk. *International Journal of Quality and Service Sciences*.

Lavuri, R. (2022). Extending the theory of planned behavior: Factors fostering millennials' intention to purchase eco-sustainable products in an emerging market. *Journal of Environmental Planning and Management*, *65*(8), 1507–1529. doi:10.1080/09640568.2021.1933925

Lawrence, P., & Lorsch, J. (2015). Contingency Theory of Organizations—Differentiation and Integration. In *Organizational Behavior 2* (pp. 244–270). Routledge.

Leedy, P. D., & Ormrod, J. E. (2016). *Practical Research: Planning and Design* (11th ed.). Pearson Education, Inc.

Lee, H., Jung, T. H., tom Dieck, M. C., & Chung, N. (2020). Experiencing immersive virtual reality in museums. *Information & Management*, *57*(5), 103229. doi:10.1016/j.im.2019.103229

Lee, K. T., & Koo, D. M. (2012). Effects of attribute and valence of e-WOM on message adoption: Moderating roles of subjective knowledge and regulatory focus. *Computers in Human Behavior*, *28*(5), 1974–1984. doi:10.1016/j.chb.2012.05.018

Lee, M. K., Cheung, C. M., & Chen, Z. (2005). Acceptance of Internet-based learning medium: The role of extrinsic and intrinsic motivation. *Information & Management*, *42*(8), 1095–1104. doi:10.1016/j.im.2003.10.007

Lee, S. M., Olson, D. L., & Trimi, S. (2012). Co-innovation: Convergence, collaboration, and co-creation for organizational values. *Management Decision*, *50*(5), 817–831. doi:10.1108/00251741211227528

Lee, W. J., & Kim, Y. H. (2021). Does VR Tourism Enhance Users Experience? *Sustainability*, *13*(2), 806. doi:10.3390u13020806

Legner, C., Eymann, T., Hess, T., Matt, C., Böhmann, T., Drews, P., Mädche, A., Urbach, N., & Ahlemann, F. (2017). Digitalization: Opportunity and challenge for the business and information systems engineering community. *Business & Information Systems Engineering*, *59*(4), 301–308. doi:10.100712599-017-0484-2

Levi, R., Perakis, G., Shi, C., & Sun, W. (2020). Strategic Capacity Planning Problems in Revenue-Sharing Joint Ventures. *Production and Operations Management*, *29*(3), 664–687. doi:10.1111/poms.13128

Lewis, M. W. (2000a). Exploring paradox: Toward a more comprehensive guide. *Academy of Management Review*, *25*(4), 760–776. doi:10.2307/259204

Lieberman, M. B., Balasubramanian, N., & Garcia-Castro, R. (2017). Toward a dynamic notion of value creation and appropriation in firms: The concept and measurement of economic gain. *Strategic Management Journal, 39*(6), 1546–1572. doi:10.1002mj.2708

Li, F., & Miniard, P. W. (2006). On the potential for advertising to facilitate trust in the advertised brand. *Journal of Advertising, 35*(4), 101–112. doi:10.2753/JOA0091-3367350407

Lii, Y.-S., & Lee, M. (2012). Doing right leads to doing well: When the type of CSR and reputation interact to affect consumer evaluations of the firm. *Journal of Business Ethics, 105*(1), 69–81. doi:10.100710551-011-0948-0

Li, M., & Mao, J. (2015). Hedonic or utilitarian? Exploring the impact of communication style alignment on user's perception of virtual health advisory services. *International Journal of Information Management, 35*(2), 229–243. doi:10.1016/j.ijinfomgt.2014.12.004

Limbu, Y. B., Wolf, M., & Lunsford, D. (2012). Perceived ethics of online retailers and consumer behavioral intentions: The mediating roles of trust and attitude. *Journal of Research in Interactive Marketing, 6*(2), 133–154. doi:10.1108/17505931211265435

Lindenberg, S., & Foss, N. (2011). Managing joint production motivation: The role of goal framing and governance mechanisms. *Academy of Management Review, 36*, 500–525.

Lindgren, P., & Rasmussen, O. H. (2013). The business model cube. *Journal of Multi Business Model Innovation and Technology, 1*(3), 135–182.

Lin, Y. M., Lin, G. Y., & Laffey, J. M. (2008). Building a social and motivational framework for understanding satisfaction in online learning. *Journal of Educational Computing Research, 38*(1), 1–27. doi:10.2190/EC.38.1.a

Lisowski, M. (2002). *The two-tier game: US President Bush's decision to repudiate the Kyoto Protocol*. Environmental Policy.

Li, T., & Chen, Y. (2019). Will Virtual Reality Be a Double-Edged Sword? Exploring the Moderation Effects of the Expected Enjoyment of a Destination on Travel Intention. *Journal of Destination Marketing & Management, 12*, 15–26. doi:10.1016/j.jdmm.2019.02.003

Litschert, R. J., & Bonham, T. (1978). A conceptual model of strategy formation. *Academy of Management Review, 3*(2), 211–219. doi:10.2307/257662

Liu, X. & Wayne Xu, W. (2018). Adoption of ride-sharing apps by Chinese taxi drivers and its implication for the equality and wellbeing in the sharing economy. *JITSM.12* (1), 7–24.

Liu, H., Gao, H., & Huang, Q. (2020). Better Government, Happier Residents? Quality of Government and Life Satisfaction in China. *Social Indicators Research, 147*(3), 971–990. doi:10.100711205-019-02172-2

Liu, J., Zhang, D., Cai, J., & Davenport, J. (2021). Legal Systems. *National Governance and Renewable Energy Investment: Evidence from Around the World., 32*, 579–610.

Lodhi, S., & Mikulecky, P. (2010). Management of indigenous knowledge for developing countries. *Communication and management in technological innovation and academic globalization, 5*.

López-Nicolás, C., Ruiz-Nicolás, J., & Mateo-Ortuño, E. (2021). Towards Sustainable Innovative Business Models. *Sustainability, 13*(11), 5804. doi:10.3390u13115804

Lorenzen, M., & Mudambi, R. (2013). Clusters, connectivity and catch-up: Bollywood and Bangalore in the global economy. *Journal of Economic Geography, 13*(3), 501–534. doi:10.1093/jeg/lbs017

Love, J. H., & Ganotakis, P. (2013). Learning by exporting: Lessons from high-technology SMEs. *International Business Review, 22*(1), 1–17. doi:10.1016/j.ibusrev.2012.01.006

Lüdeke-Freund, F., Carroux, S., Joyce, A., Massa, L., & Breuer, H. (2018). The sustainable business model pattern taxonomy—45 patterns to support sustainability-oriented business model innovation. *Sustainable Production and Consumption, 15*, 145–162. doi:10.1016/j.spc.2018.06.004

Lu, J., Xiao, X., Xu, Z., Wang, C., Zhang, M., & Zhou, Y. (2022). The potential of virtual tourism in the recovery of tourism industry during the COVID-19 pandemic. *Current Issues in Tourism, 2021*(25), 441–457. doi:10.1080/13683500.2021.1959526

Lu, L. C., Chang, W. P., & Chang, H. H. (2014). Consumer attitudes toward blogger's sponsored recommendations and purchase intention: The effect of sponsorship type, product type, and brand awareness. *Computers in Human Behavior, 34*, 258–266. doi:10.1016/j.chb.2014.02.007

Lüscher, L. S., & Lewis, M. W. (2008). Organizational change and managerial sensemaking: Working through paradox. *Academy of Management Journal, 51*(2), 221–240. doi:10.5465/amj.2008.31767217

Lypak, H., Kunanets, N., Pasichnyk, V., & Veretennikova, N. (2020). Digitized Historical and Cultural Heritage Consolidation Technologies: From a Territorial Resource to a National Portal. *2020 10th International Conference on Advanced Computer Information Technologies*. IEEE.

Ma, S. J. (2013). *Journal of Engineering and Product portfolio decision-making and absorptive capacity : A simulation study*. doi:10.1016/j.jengtecman.2013.09.004

MacDonald, G., & Ryall, R. D. (2004). How do value creation and competition determine whether a firm appropriates value? *Management Science, 50*(10), 1319–1333. doi:10.1287/mnsc.1030.0152

Mackie, T. R., & Leuthardt, E. (2018). Managing Institutional Barriers to Entrepreneurship. In K. E. Behrns, B. Gingles, & M. G. B. T.-M. I. Sarr (Eds.), *Academic Press* (pp. 129–138). doi:10.1016/B978-0-12-814926-3.00013-9

Madjid, C. N. I. F., & Hermawan, A. (2022). The Influence of Viral Marketing and Brand Image on Purchase Decisions through E-Trust: Study on Avoskin Skincare Customers. *International journal of economics, management, business, and social science (ijembis), 2*(2), 315-321.

Magretta, J. (2002). Why business models matter.

Mahmoudi, A., Sadeghi, M., & Deng, X. (2022). Performance measurement of construction suppliers under localization, agility, and digitalization criteria: Fuzzy Ordinal Priority Approach. *Environment, Development and Sustainability*, 1–26. doi:10.100710668-022-02301-x PMID:35431618

Mahraz, M.-I., Benabbou, L., & Berrado, A. (2019). A Systematic literature review of Digital Transformation. *International Conference on Industrial Engineering and Operations Management. Anais.* IEOM Society International

Majchrzak, A., & Gasser, L. (1991). On using artificial intelligence to integrate the design of organizational and process change in US manufacturing. *AI & Society, 5*(4), 321–338. doi:10.1007/BF02077438

Malik, G., & Rao, A. S. (2019). Extended expectation-confirmation model to predict continued usage of ODR/ride hailing apps: Role of perceived value and self-efficacy. *Information Technology & Tourism, 21*(4), 461–482. doi:10.100740558-019-00152-3

Mamychev, A., Kazachanskaya, E., & Garashko, A. (2021). Value and Regulatory Foundations for Digital Transformation of Modern Social Relations: Theological and Conservative Legal Aspects. *Wisdom, 1*(1).

Manual, F. Paris, OECD, (1993). The Oslo Manual: Proposed Guidelines for Collecting and Interpreting Technological Innovation Data. Paris, OECD.

Manzani, Sidmou & Cegarra. (2019). Does ISO 9001quality management system support product innovation? An analysis from the sociotechnical systems theory. *International Journal of Quality.*

Marquis, C., & Qian, C. (2013). Corporate social responsibility reporting in China: Symbol or substance. *Organization Science, 25*(1), 127–148. doi:10.1287/orsc.2013.0837

Marrou, H., Guilioni, L., Dufour, L., Dupraz, C., & Wery, J. (2013). Microclimate under agrivoltaic systems: Is crop growth rate affected in the partial shade of solar panels? *Agricultural and Forest Meteorology, 177*, 117–132. doi:10.1016/j.agrformet.2013.04.012

Martínez-Caro, E., Cegarra-Navarro, J. G., & Alfonso-Ruiz, F. J. (2020). Digital technologies and firm performance: The role of digital organisational culture. *Technological Forecasting and Social Change, 154*, 119962. doi:10.1016/j.techfore.2020.119962

Martins, L. L., Rindova, V. P., & Greenbaum, B. E. (2015). Unlocking the hidden value of concepts: A cognitive approach to business model innovation. *Strategic Entrepreneurship Journal, 9*(1), 99–117. doi:10.1002ej.1191

Marzouk, Y. & Jin, J. (2022). Linking environmental scanning and organizational innovation with competitive advantage: evidence from Egyptian SMEs. *Management & Sustainability: An Arab Review.*

Maseno, M., & Wanyoike, C. (2022). Social entrepreneurship as mechanisms for social transformation and social impact in East Africa an exploratory case study perspective. *Journal of Social Entrepreneurship, 13*(1), 92–117. doi:10.1080/19420676.2020.1755348

Massie, S., Craw, S., & Wiratunga, N. (2004, December). A visualisation tool to explain case-base reasoning solutions for tablet formulation. In *International Conference on Innovative Techniques and Applications of Artificial Intelligence* (pp. 222-234). Springer, London.

Mazzarol, T., & Reboud, S. (2020). Entrepreneurship and Innovation Theory, Practice and Context. In *Gateway East, Singapore 189721* (pp. 1–34). Springer Nature Singapore Pte Ltd., doi:10.1007/978-981-13-9412-6

McKnight, D. H., & Chervany, N. L. (2001). What trust means in e-commerce customer relationships: An interdisciplinary conceptual typology. *International Journal of Electronic Commerce, 6*(2), 35–59. doi:10.1080/10864415.2001.11044235

McKnight, D. H., Choudhury, V., & Kacmar, C. (2002). Developing and validating trust measures for e-commerce: An integrative typology. *Information Systems Research, 13*(3), 334–359. doi:10.1287/isre.13.3.334.81

McWilliams, A., & Siegel, D. S. (2011). Creating and capturing value: Strategic corporate social responsibility, resource-based theory, and sustainable competitive advantage. *Journal of Management, 37*(5), 1480–1495. doi:10.1177/0149206310385696

Mendes, G., Loakimidis, C., & Ferraro, P. (2011). *On the planning and analysis of integrated community energy systems: A review and survey of available tools* (Vol. 15). Renewable and Sustainable Energy Review.

Mergel, I., Bretschneider, S. I., Louis, C., & Smith, J. (2014). *The challenges of Challenge. gov: Adopting private sector business innovations in the Federal Government.* 2014 47th Hawaii International Conference on System Sciences, Hawaii.

Merkx, C., & Nawijn, J. (2021). Virtual reality tourism experiences: Addiction and isolation. *Tourism Management, 87*, 104394. doi:10.1016/j.tourman.2021.104394

Mervis, C. B., & Rosch, E. (1981). Categorization of natural objects. *Annual Review of Psychology, 32*(1), 89–115. doi:10.1146/annurev.ps.32.020181.000513

Mian, F. M. (2021) Exporting electricity to Afghanistan. *Dawn:The Business and Finance Weekly.*

Miao, M., Jalees, T., Zaman, S. I., Khan, S., Hanif, N. U. A., & Javed, M. K. (2022). The influence of e-customer satisfaction, e-trust and perceived value on consumer's repurchase intention in B2C e-commerce segment. *Asia Pacific Journal of Marketing and Logistics, 34*(10), 2184–2206. doi:10.1108/APJML-03-2021-0221

Mickiewicz, T., & Rebmann, A. (2020). Entrepreneurship as trust. *Foundations and Trends in Entrepreneurship, 16*(3), 44–309. doi:10.1561/0300000088

Mihir Joshi, V. K. S. (2017). Electronic Word of Mouth and Influence on Consumer Purchase Intention. *Dynamics of Public Administration*, 149–159. https://www.ajol.info/index.php/jfas/article/view/171488

Mina, A. X. (2014). Batman, pandaman and the blind man: A case study in social change memes and Internet censorship in China. *Journal of Visual Culture, 13*(3), 359–375. doi:10.1177/1470412914546576

Miron-Spektor, E., Ingram, A., Keller, J., Smith, W. K., & Lewis, M. W. (2018). Microfoundations of organizational paradox: The problem is how we think about the problem. *Academy of Management Journal, 61*(1), 26–45. doi:10.5465/amj.2016.0594

Mishra, S., & Suar, D. (2010, September). Does corporate social responsibility influence firm performance of Indian companies? *Journal of Business Ethics, 95*(4), 571–601. doi:10.100710551-010-0441-1

Missaoui, I., Mohsen, B., & Jaleleddine, B. (2018). Quantitative relationship between corruption ad development of the Tunisian stock market. *Public and Municipal Finance Journal, 7*(2), 39–47. doi:10.21511/pmf.07(2).2018.04

Mitchell, R. K., Agle, B. R., & Wood, D. J. (1997). Toward a theory of stakeholder identification and salience: Defining the principle of who and what really counts. *Academy of Management Review, 22*(4), 853–886. doi:10.2307/259247

Mitra, S. K., Bae, Y., & Ritchie, S. G. (2019). Use of Ride-Hailing Services among Older Adults in the United States. *Transportation Research Record: Journal of the Transportation Research Board, 2673*(3), 700–710. doi:10.1177/0361198119835511

Mobarki, M., Ziyae, B., Rezvani, M., Tajpour, M. (2021). Conceptual Model of Internationalization of the Entrepreneurial University with an Interpretive Structural Modeling Approach. *Journal of Research on Management of Teaching in Marine Sciences.* doi:10.22034/rmt.2021.530319.1841

Mobini Dehkordi, A., & Heydari, H. (2014). *Fundamentals of Strategic Environmental Knowledge*. Concepts, Theories, Techniques and Applications.

Mobini-Dehkordi, A., Yadolai-Farsi, J., Arabiun, A., & Keshavarz-Turk, M. (2021). Identifying Applied Aspects, Medical Fields, and Technological Trends in Developing Future Entrepreneurial Opportunities in Telemedicine. *Health Information Management, 17*(6), 260–267.

Mohan, V. (2022). Delhi, Kol most polluted cities globally by PM2.5, Says Study. *Times of India.*

Mohr, L. A., & Webb, D. J. (2005). The effects of corporate social responsibility and price on consumer responses. *The Journal of Consumer Affairs, 39*(1), 121–147. doi:10.1111/j.1745-6606.2005.00006.x

Mohsen, B., & Sonia, Z. (2013). Indicateurs statistiques de performance économique et du positionnement mondial de l'industrie minière en Tunisie (1990 - 2010): Regard avant la révolution 2011. Book of Acts of collective, Informal economy and development: employment, financing and regulation in a context of crisis, "the University Paris-Est-Créteil, 6, 7 and 8 June 2013 Paris, France

Mohsen, B., Karim,B., & Sonia, Z.(2013). History vs. Reality, Mining industry diagnostic and environmental effects: Illustration case in real size of Tunisian mining basin. IOSR Journal of Environmental Science, Toxicology and Technology (IOSR-JESTFT) 3 (2), 56-64.

Mohsen, A., Ramadani, V., & Dana, L.-P. (2020). Green entrepreneurship prospects and challenges: the context of Afghanistan. In *Research Handbook on Entrepreneurship in Emerging Economies*. Edward Elgar Publishing. doi:10.4337/9781788973717.00008

Mohsin, M., Kamran, H. W., Nawaz, M. A., Hussain, M. S., & Dahri, A. S. (2021). Assessing the impact of transition from nonrenewable to renewable energy consumption on economic growth-environmental nexus from developing Asian economies. *Journal of Environmental Management*, *284*, 111999. doi:10.1016/j.jenvman.2021.111999 PMID:33556829

Monnin, P. (2018). *Central banks and the transition to a low-carbon economy. Technical report, discussion note*. Council on Economic Policies.

Moore, J. F. (1993). Predators and prey: A new ecology of competition. *Harvard Business Review*, *71*(3), 75–86. PMID:10126156

Moorman, C., Zaltman, G., & Deshpande, R. (1992). Relationships between providers and users of market research: The dynamics of trust within and between organizations. *JMR, Journal of Marketing Research*, *29*(3), 314–328. doi:10.1177/002224379202900303

Moroz, P. W., & Hindle, K. (2012). Entrepreneurship as a Process: Toward Harmonizing Multiple Perspectives. *Entrepreneurship Theory and Practice*, *36*(4), 781–818. doi:10.1111/j.1540-6520.2011.00452.x

Morris, M. H., Kuratko, D. F., Schindehutte, M., & Spivack, A. J. (2012). Framing the entrepreneurial experience. *Entrepreneurship Theory and Practice*, *36*(1), 11–40. doi:10.1111/j.1540-6520.2011.00471.x

Morris, M. H., Santos, S. C., & Neumeyer, X. (2020). Entrepreneurship as a solution to poverty in developed economies. *Business Horizons*, *63*(3), 377–390. doi:10.1016/j.bushor.2020.01.010

Muhammad, T., Erum, S., Naveeda, K., Brahmi,M. (2022). Nascent entrepreneurs and challenges in the digital market in developing countries, International Journal of Public Sector Performance Management, 2022, Vol.9, in-press. doi doi:10.1504/IJPSPM.2022.10138750

Muniapan, B., & Dass, M. (2008). Corporate social responsibility: A philosophical approach from an ancient Indian perspective. *International Journal of Indian Culture and Business Management*, *1*(4), 408–420. doi:10.1504/IJICBM.2008.018622

Munir, H., Bengtsson, L., & Åkesson, E. (2022). Management tools for business model innovation–a review. *Innovation*, 141–158. doi:10.4324/9780429346033-11

Murray, R., Caulier-Grice, J., & Mulgan, G. (2010). The open book of social innovation (p. 2). London: National endowment for science, technology and the art.

Nadaraja, R., & Yazdanifard, R. (2013). Social Media Marketing Advantages And Disadvantages. *Center of Southern New Hempshire University*, 1–10.

Nadeem, A., Abedin, B., Cerpa, N., & Chew, E. (2018). Digital transformation & digital business strategy in electronic commerce-the role of organizational capabilities. *Journal of Theoretical and Applied Electronic Commerce Research*, *13*(2), 1–8. doi:10.4067/S0718-18762018000200101

Naderi, N., Khosravi, E., Azadi, H., Karamian, F., Viira, A. H., & Nadiri, H. (2022). Barriers to developing social entrepreneurship in NGOs: Application of grounded theory in Western Iran. *Journal of Social Entrepreneurship*, *13*(2), 221–243. doi:10.1080/19420676.2020.1765409

Nadiri. (1993). *Nadiri-Innovation-and-Spillovers-1993-W4423.*

Nadkarni, S., & Barr, P. S. (2008). Environmental context, managerial cognition, and strategic action: An integrated view. *Strategic Management Journal, 29*(13), 1395–1427. doi:10.1002mj.717

Nadkarni, S., & Prügl, R. (2021). Digital transformation: A review, synthesis and opportunities for future research. *Management Review Quarterly, 71*(2), 233–341. doi:10.100711301-020-00185-7

Nah, F. F. H., Eschenbrenner, B., DeWester, D., & Park, S. R. (2012). Impact of flow and brand equity in 3D virtual worlds. In *Cross-disciplinary models and applications of database management: advancing approaches* (pp. 277–297). IGI Global. doi:10.4018/978-1-61350-471-0.ch011

Nair, M., & Njolomole, M. (2020). Microfinance, entrepreneurship and institutional quality. *Journal of Entrepreneurship and Public Policy, 9*(1), 137–148. doi:10.1108/JEPP-07-2019-0061

Namaki, Z., & Aghasi, S. (2022).. . *Presenting and Explaining the Organizational Performance Model Based on the Digital Status of the Organization in the Corona Eera with the Foundation Data Approach in the Ministry of Samt., 102*(30), 147–175.

Nambisan, S., & Baron, R. A. (2013). Entrepreneurship in innovation ecosystems: Entrepreneurs' self-regulatory processes and their implications for new venture success. *Entrepreneurship Theory and Practice, 37*(5), 1071–1097. doi:10.1111/j.1540-6520.2012.00519.x

Naseem, T., Shahzad, F., Asim, G. A., Rehman, I. U., & Nawaz, F. (2020, March). Corporate social responsibility engagement and firm performance in Asia Pacific: The role of enterprise risk management. *Corporate Social Responsibility and Environmental Management, 27*(2), 501–513. doi:10.1002/csr.1815

Nemet, G.F. (2012). Spillover of inter-technological knowledge for energy technologies. *Energy economics, 34* (5), 1259 – 1270.

Newman, C., Rand, J., Tarp, F., & Trifkovic, N. (2020, August 2). Corporate social responsibility in a competitive business environment. *The Journal of Development Studies, 56*(8), 1455–1472. doi:10.1080/00220388.2019.1694144

Newton, K. (2004). Social trust: Individual and cross-national approaches. *Portuguese Journal of Social Science, 3*(1), 15–35. doi:10.1386/pjss.3.1.15/0

Nguyen, B., Canh, N. P., & Thanh, S. D. (2020). Institutions, Human Capital and Entrepreneurship Density. *Journal of the Knowledge Economy.* Advance online publication. doi:10.100713132-020-00666-w

Nguyen-Phuoc, D. Q., Vo, N. S., Su, D. N., Nguyen, V. H., & Oviedo-Trespalacios, O. (2021). What makes passengers continue using and talking positively about ride-hailing services? The role of the booking app and post-booking service quality. *Transportation Research Part A, Policy and Practice, 150*, 367–384. doi:10.1016/j.tra.2021.06.013

Nikolaevich, L. S. (2020). Analysis of the development of the main directions of digitalization of the Russian economy. *Политематический сетевой электронный научный журнал Кубанского государственного аграрного университета [Polythematic network electronic scientific journal of the Kuban State Agrarian University],* (161), 309-324.

Nikraftar, T., Hosseini, E., & Mohammadi, E. (2021). The factors influencing technological entrepreneurship in nanotechnology businesses. *Revista de Gestão, 29*(1), 76–99. doi:10.1108/REGE-02-2021-0029

Njogu, N. J. (2014). (Manuscript submitted for publication). The Effect of Electronic Banking on Profitability of Commercial Banks in Kenya. [In Partial Fulfillment of the Requirements for the Award of the Degree Of Master of Science In Finance, School Of Business, and University Of Nairobi.]. *Research Project.*

Noailly, J., & Shestakova, V. (2017). Knowledge spillovers from renewable energy technologies: lessons from patent citations. Environmental innovation and societal transitions, 22, 1-14. .

Noailly, J., Smeets, R. (2015). Directing technical change from fossil-fuel to renewable energy innovation: an application using firm-level patent data. *Journal of Environmental Economics and Management, 72*, 15-37.

Nobari, N., Dehkordi, A. M., Akbari, M., & Padash, H. (2020). Innovation intelligence and its role in environmental uncertainty management: A conceptual framework. *VINE Journal of Information and Knowledge Management Systems.*

Nohria, N., & Eccles, R. (1992). *Networks and Organizations: Structure, Form and Action.* Harvard University Press.

O'Brien, K. (2012). Global environmental change II: From adaptation to deliberate transformation. *Progress in Human Geography*, *36*(5), 667–676. doi:10.1177/0309132511425767

O'regan, K. (2003). Emotion and e-learning. *Journal of Asynchronous Learning Networks*, *7*(3), 78–92.

O'Reilly, C., & Powell, B. (2015). War and the growth of government. *European Journal of Political Economy*, *40*, 31–41. doi:10.1016/j.ejpoleco.2015.10.001

Obaji, N. O. (2014). The Role of Government Policy in Entrepreneurship Development. *Science Journal of Business and Management*, *2*(4), 109. doi:10.11648/j.sjbm.20140204.12

Ofori, K. S., Anyigba, H., Adeola, O., Junwu, C., Osakwe, C. N., & David-West, O. (2021). Understanding post-adoption behaviour in the context of ride-hailing apps: The role of customer perceived value. *Information Technology & People*, *35*(5), 1540–1562. doi:10.1108/ITP-06-2019-0285

Oguamanam, C. (2009). Documentation and digitization of traditional knowledge and intangible cultural knowledge: Challenges and prospects. Intangible Cultural Heritage and Intellectual Property: Cultural Diversity and Sustainable Development. Intersentia.

Ogus, A. (2004) *The importance of legal infrastructure for regulation (and deregulation) in developing countries.*

Oh, J. C., Yoon, S. J., & Park, B. I. (2012). A structural approach to examine the quality attributes of e-shopping malls using the Kano model. *Asia Pacific Journal of Marketing and Logistics*, *24*(2), 305–327. doi:10.1108/13555851211218075

Olkhovikov, K., Korobeynikov, A., Zarubina, E., Zhuravleva, L., & Ruchkin, A. (2021). Digitalizating rural areas: a traditional context. *IOP Conference Series: Earth and Environmental Science*

Olmedo, E. (2016). Implications of complexity in strategic management. *International Journal of Complexity in Leadership and Management*, *3*(1-2), 101–114. doi:10.1504/IJCLM.2016.075047

Olson, M. (1965). *The logic of collective action.* Harvard University Press.

Ong, M., Mayer, D. M., Tost, L. P., & Wellman, N. (2018). When corporate social responsibility motivates employee citizenship behavior: The sensitizing role of task significance. *Organizational Behavior and Human Decision Processes*, *144*, 44–59. doi:10.1016/j.obhdp.2017.09.006

Osmundsen, K., Iden, J., & Bygstad, B. (2018). Digital Transformation: Drivers, Success Factors, and Implications. MCIS, Perez, C. (2010). Technological revolutions and techno-economic paradigms. *Cambridge Journal of Economics*, *34*(1), 185–202.

Osterwalder, A. (2002). An e-business model ontology for the creation of new management software tools and IS requirement engineering. *Semantic Scholar.*

Osterwalder, A. (2004). *The business model ontology a proposition in a design science approach* [Doctoral dissertation, Université de Lausanne, Faculté des hautes études commerciales].

Osterwalder, A., & Pigneur, Y. (2010). *Business model generation: a handbook for visionaries, game changers, and challengers* (Vol. 1). John Wiley & Sons.

Osterwalder, A., & Pigneur, Y. (2012). Designing business models and similar strategic objects: The contribution of IS. *Journal of the Association for Information Systems*, *14*(5), 3.

Osterwalder, A., Pigneur, Y., & Tucci, C. L. (2005). Clarifying business models: Origins, present, and future of the concept. *Communications of the Association for Information Systems*, *16*(1), 1. doi:10.17705/1CAIS.01601

Osunmuyiwa, O. O., & Ahlborg, H. (2022). Stimulating competition, diversification, or re-enforcing entrepreneurial barriers? Exploring small-scale electricity systems and gender-inclusive entrepreneurship. *Energy Research & Social Science*, *89*, 102566. doi:10.1016/j.erss.2022.102566

Overby, J. W., & Lee, E. J. (2006). The effects of utilitarian and hedonic online shopping value on consumer preference and intentions. *Journal of Business Research*, *59*(10–11), 1160–1166. doi:10.1016/j.jbusres.2006.03.008

Overholm, H. (2015). Collectively created opportunities in emerging ecosystems: The case of solar service ventures. *Technovation*, *39-40*, 14–25. doi:10.1016/j.technovation.2014.01.008

Owusu Kwateng, K., Yobanta, A. L., & Amanor, K. (2021). Hedonic and utilitarian perspective of mobile phones purchase intention. *Journal of Contemporary Marketing Science*, *4*(1), 44–68. doi:10.1108/JCMARS-08-2020-0035

Ozmel, U., Reuer, J. J., & Gulati, R. (2013). Signals across multiple networks: How venture capital and alliance networks affect interorganizational collaboration. *Academy of Management Journal*, *56*(3), 852–866. doi:10.5465/amj.2009.0549

Pagani, M. (2009). Roadmapping 3G mobile TV: Strategic thinking and scenario planning through repeated cross-impact handling. *Technological Forecasting and Social Change*, *76*(3), 382–395. doi:10.1016/j.techfore.2008.07.003

Pagani, M. (2013). Digital business strategy and value creation: Framing the dynamic cycle of control points. *Management Information Systems Quarterly*, *37*(2), 617–632. doi:10.25300/MISQ/2013/37.2.13

Page, S. E. (2009). Understanding Complexity. The Teching Company. chantilly, VA.

Palmquist, M. E., Carley, K. M., & Dale, T. A. (1997). Two applications of automated text analysis: Analyzing literary and non-literary texts. In C. Roberts (Ed.), *Text Analysis for the Social Sciences: Methods for Drawing Statistical Inferences from Texts and Transcripts*. Lawrence Erlbaum Associates.

Pardo, T. A., Cresswell, A. M., Dawes, S. S., & Burke, G. B. (2004). *Modeling the social & technical processes of interorganizational information integration.* Paper presented at the Hawaii International Conference on System Sciences (HICSS-37), Hawaii 10.1109/HICSS.2004.1265307

Park, J. Y. Shin, J. K. (2019). *Predicting Continuous Usage Behavior in Social Network Service: Focusing on Affective Commitment and Users' Characteristics*. DBPIA. https://www.dbpia.co.kr/Journal/articleDetail?nodeId=NODE09233668

Parker, J. (2015). *How Oculus and Cardboard Are Going to Rock the Travel Industry*. Bloomberg. https://www.bloomberg.com/news/articles/2015-06-19/how-oculus-and-cardboard-are-going-to-rock-the-travel-industry

Patrick, O. P. (2022). Assessment of the Impact of Environmental Scanning Intensity on Innovation among SMEs Owners in Oyo State Nigeria. *JSMR*.

Pavlou, P. A., & Dimoka, A. (2006). The nature and role of feedback text comments in online marketplaces: Implications for trust building, price premiums, and seller differentiation. *Information Systems Research*, *17*(4), 392–414. doi:10.1287/isre.1060.0106

Peinel, G., Jarke, M., & Rose, T. (2009). *Business Models For E-government the BMeG Method*. Semantic Scholar.

Pennetier, C., Girotra, K., & Mihm, J. (2019). R&D Spending: Dynamic or Persistent? *Manufacturing & Service Operations Management*, *21*(3), 636–657. doi:10.1287/msom.2018.0715

Perlusz, S. (2004, October). Emotions and technology acceptance: development and validation of a technology affect scale. In *2004 IEEE International Engineering Management Conference* (IEEE Cat. No. 04CH37574) (Vol. 2, pp. 845-847). IEEE. 10.1109/IEMC.2004.1407500

Perrons, R. K., Jaffe, A. B., & Le, T. (2021). Linking scientific research and energy innovation: A comparison of clean and dirty technologies. *Energy Research & Social Science*, *78*, 102122. doi:10.1016/j.erss.2021.102122

Peterson, R. T., & Jun, M. (2009). Perceptions on social responsibility: The entrepreneurial vision. *Business & Society*, *48*(3), 385–405. doi:10.1177/0007650307305758

Pfeffer, J. & Salancik, G. (1981). *Dependence Perspective*. New York: Harper and Row.

Pfeffer, J. (1982). *Organizations and organization theory*. Pitman Publishing.

Pfeffer, J., & G, R. Salancik. (1978). The External Control of Organizations. *Resource (Saint Joseph, Mich.)*.

Pfeffer, J., & Salancik, G. (1978). *The external con-trol of organizations. A Resource Dependence Approach*. Harp-er and Row Publishers.

Pfeffer, J., & Salancik, G. R. (1978). *The external control of organizations: A resource dependence perspective*. Harper and Row.

Phills, J. A., Deiglmeier, K., & Miller, D. T. (2008). Rediscovering social innovation. *Stanford Social Innovation Review*, *6*(4), 34–43.

Pina e Cunha, M., & Putnam, L. L. (2019). Paradox theory and the paradox of success. *Strategic Organization*, *17*(1), 95–106. doi:10.1177/1476127017739536

Pinto, J. (2019). Key to effective organizational performance management lies at the intersection of paradox theory and stakeholder theory. *International Journal of Management Reviews*, *21*(2), 185–208. doi:10.1111/ijmr.12199

Piotrowski, D.(2022). Consumer perceived ethicality of banks in the era of digitalization: The case of Poland. *Economics and Business Review, 8* (22). doi:10.18559/ebr.2022.1.690-114

Plunket, A. (2009). Firms' inventiveness and localized vertical r&d spillovers. *Journal of Innovation Economics Management*, *4*(2), 147–170.

Podolny, J. (2001). Networks as the pipes and prisms of the Market. *American Journal of Sociology*, *1*(1), 33–60. doi:10.1086/323038

Podolny, J. M., & Page, K. L. (1998). Network forms of organization. *Annual Review of Sociology*, *24*(1), 57–76. doi:10.1146/annurev.soc.24.1.57

Poldahl, A. (2012). The Two Faces of R&D: Does Firm Absorptive Capacity Matter? *Journal of Industry, Competition and Trade*, *12*(2), 221–237. doi:10.100710842-010-0094-x

Pomerleano, M., & Shaw, W. (2005). *Corporate restructuring: lessons from experience.* World Bank Publications. doi:10.1596/0-8213-5928-2

Ponsignon, F., Lunardo, R., & Michrafy, M. (2021). Why Are International Visitors More Satisfied with the Tourism Experience? The Role of Hedonic Value, Escapism, and Psychic Distance. *Journal of Travel Research, 60*(8), 1771–1786. doi:10.1177/0047287520961175

Popp, D. (2017). From science to technology: the value of knowledge from different energy research institutions. *Resource Policy, 46* (9), 1580-1594. .

Porter, M. E., & Heppelmann, J. E. (2015). How smart, connected products are transforming companies. *Harvard Business Review, 93*(10), 96–114.

Porter, M. E., & Kramer, M. R. (2011). *Creating shared value* (Vol. 89). Harvard Business Review.

Powell, W. W. (1990). Neither market nor hierarchy: Network forms of organizations. In B. Staw & L. L. Cummings (Eds.), *Research in Organizational Behavior*. JAI Press.

Powell, W. W., Koput, K. W., & Smith-Doerr, L. (1996). Interorganizational collaboration and the locus of innovation: Networks of learning in biotechnology. *Administrative Science Quarterly, 41*(1), 116–145. doi:10.2307/2393988

Powell, W. W., & Snellman, K. (2004). The knowledge economy. *Annual Review of Sociology, 30*(1), 199–220. doi:10.1146/annurev.soc.29.010202.100037

Pradhan, R. P., Arvin, M. B., Nair, M., & Bennett, S. E. (2020). The dynamics among entrepreneurship, innovation, and economic growth in the Eurozone countries. *Journal of Policy Modeling, 42*(5), 1106–1122. doi:10.1016/j.jpolmod.2020.01.004

Prajogo, D. I., & Sohal, A. S. (2003). The relationship between TQM practices, quality performance, and innovation performance An empirical examination. International Journal of Quality & *Reliability Management, 20*(8), 901–918.

Prajogo, D. I., & Sohal, A. S. (2004). The multidimensionality of TQM practices in determining quality and innovation performance an empirical examination. *Technovation, 24*(6), 443–453. doi:10.1016/S0166-4972(02)00122-0

Prasad, S., Gupta, I. C., & Totala, N. K. (2017). Social media usage, electronic word of mouth and purchase-decision involvement. *Asia-Pacific Journal of Business Administration, 9*(2), 134–145. doi:10.1108/APJBA-06-2016-0063

Pratiwi, L., Sunaryo, S., & Mugiono, M. (2021). The effect of e-service quality on e-loyalty mediated by e-trust and brand image variables: A study on OVO E-Wallet application users in Malang City. *International Journal of Research in Business and Social Science (2147-4478), 10*(6), 56-62.

Priem, R. L., Butler, J. E., & Li, S. (2013). Toward reimagining strategy research: Retrospection and prospection on the 2011 AMR decade award article. *Academy of Management Review, 38*(4), 471–489. doi:10.5465/amr.2013.0097

Pucci, T., Casprini, E., Nosi, C., & Zanni, L. (2019). Does social media usage affect online purchasing intention for wine? The moderating role of subjective and objective knowledge. *British Food Journal, 121*(2), 275–288. doi:10.1108/BFJ-06-2018-0400

Purtik, H., & Arenas, D. (2019). Embedding social innovation: Shaping societal norms and behaviors throughout the innovation process. *Business & Society, 58*(5), 963–1002. doi:10.1177/0007650317726523

Pustovrh, A., Rangus, K., & Drnovšek, M. (2020). The role of open innovation in developing an entrepreneurial support ecosystem. *Technological Forecasting and Social Change, 152*, 119892. doi:10.1016/j.techfore.2019.119892

Putnam, L. L., Fairhurst, G. T., & Banhart, S. G. (2016). Contradictions, dialectics, and paradoxes in organizations: A constitutive approach. *The Academy of Management Annals, 10*(1), 65–171. doi:10.5465/19416520.2016.1162421

Rabie, M. (2013). *Global economic and cultural transformation: The making of history*. Springer. doi:10.1057/9781137365330

Rahimizhian, S., Ozturen, A., & Ilkan, M. (2020). Emerging realm of 360-degree technology to promote tourism destination. *Technology in Society, 63*, 101411. doi:10.1016/j.techsoc.2020.101411

Rajabipoor Meybodi, A., Abasaltian, A., & Sabokro, M. (2021). Identifying and prioritizing the components of staff training in higher education institutions Based on Thematic analysis. *Journal of New Approaches in Educational Administration, 11*(46), 171–202.

Rajasulochana, S. R., & Senthil Ganesh, S. (2019). Is assessing learning outcomes a trade-off in experiential learning? Integrating field visit with managerial economics course. *International Review of Economics Education, 32*(May), 100169. doi:10.1016/j.iree.2019.100169

Ramadhan, A., Hidayanto, A. N., Evik, C. S., Rizkiandini, N., Rahimullah, N. A., Muthiah, R. H., Anggreainy, M. S., & Phusavat, K. (2022). Factors affecting the continuation to use and e-WOM intention of online library resources by university students: A study in Indonesia. *Journal of Academic Librarianship, 48*(6), 102592. doi:10.1016/j.acalib.2022.102592

Ramaswammy, V., & Ozcan, K. (2014). *The paradigm of co-creation*. Stanford University Press. doi:10.1515/9780804790758

Rana, S. (2012). Philanthropic innovation and creative capitalism: A historical and comparative perspective on social entrepreneurship and corporate social responsibility. *Alabama Law Review, 64*, 1121.

Rani P, Mann VK. (2018) The Impact of Ethical and Philanthropic Component of CSR on Financial Performance: A Panel Data Study of BSE 500 Companies. *IUP Journal of Corporate Governance, 1;17*(4).

Rasheed Gaber, H., & Elsamadicy, A. M. (2021). What drives customers to continue using ride-sharing apps during the COVID-19 pandemic? The case of Uber in Egypt. *Cogent Business & Management. Cogent, 8*(1), 1–21.

Rathnayaka, A. J. D., Potdar, V. M., Dillon, T., & Kuruppu, S. (2015). *Framework to manage multiple objectives in the community-based energy sharing network in smart grid* (Vol. 73). International Journal Electric Power Energy Systems.

Ratten, V., & Usmanij, P. (2021). Entrepreneurship education: Time for a change in research direction? *International Journal of Management Education, 19*(1), 100367. doi:10.1016/j.ijme.2020.100367

Ray, A., Bala, P. K., Chakraborty, S., & Dasgupta, S. A. (2021). Exploring the impact of different factors on brand equity and intention to take up online courses from e-Learning platforms. *Journal of Retailing and Consumer Services, 59*, 102351. doi:10.1016/j.jretconser.2020.102351

Ray, N., Clarke, G., & Waley, P. (2020). The rise of corporate retailing and the impacts on small-scale retailing: The survival strategies of Kirana stores and informal street vendors in Durgapur, India. *Singapore Journal of Tropical Geography, 41*(2), 269–283. doi:10.1111jtg.12312

Raza-Ullah, T., Bengtsson, M., & Kock, S. (2014). The coopetition paradox and tension in coopetition at multiple levels. *Industrial Marketing Management, 43*(2), 189–198. doi:10.1016/j.indmarman.2013.11.001

Recio-García, J. A., Díaz-Agudo, B., & González-Calero, P. (2008). jcolibri2 tutorial. Department of Software Engineering and Artificial Intelligence, University Complutense of Madrid, Madrid.

Remané, G., Hanelt, A., Tesch, J. F., & Kolbe, L. M. (2019). The business model pattern database: a tool for systematic BMI. In *Business model innovation in the era of the Internet of Things* (pp. 89–144). Springer. doi:10.1007/978-3-319-98723-1_5

Rese, M., Meier, H., Gesing, J., & Boßlau, M. (2013). An ontology of business models for industrial product-service systems. In *The Philosopher's Stone for Sustainability* (pp. 191–196). Springer. doi:10.1007/978-3-642-32847-3_32

Richter, N., Jackson, P., & Schildhauer, T. (2018). Outsourcing creativity: An abductive study of open innovation using corporate accelerators. *Creativity and Innovation Management*, *27*(1), 69–78. doi:10.1111/caim.12252

Ridge, M., & Birchall, D. (2015). How digital tech can bridge gaps between museums and audiences. *Cultural Professional Network Article, the Guardian Online, Published on, 23*.

Riepe, J., Rudeloff, M., & Veer, T. (2020). Financial literacy and entrepreneurial risk aversion. *Journal of Small Business Management*, *00*(00), 1–20. doi:10.1080/00472778.2019.1709380

Ring, P. S., & Van de Ven, A. H. (1994). Developmental processes of cooperative interorganizational relationships. *Academy of Management Review*, *19*(1), 90–118. doi:10.2307/258836

Rise, M. (2020, May 28) The Time For Sustainability Has Come. *Mahindra.* https://www.mahindra.com/news-room/knowledge-centre/impact-stories/the-time-for-sustainability-has-come

Robbins, S. P., Judge, T., & Vohra, N. (n.d.). *Organizational behavior.*

Roedder, N., Dauer, D., Laubis, K., Karaenke, P., & Weinhardt, C. (2016). The digital transformation and smart data analytics: An overview of enabling developments and application areas. *2016 IEEE International Conference on Big Data (Big Data).* IEEE.

Rogers, D. L. (2016). *The digital transformation playbook: Rethink your business for the digital age*. Columbia University Press. doi:10.7312/roge17544

Rogers, J. C., Simmons, E. A., & Convery, A. (2008). *Weatherall Public perceptions of opportunities for community-based renewable energy projects* (Vol. 36). Energy Policy.

Rogers, M., & Rogers, M. (1998). *The definition and measurement of innovation* (Vol. 98). Melbourne Institute of Applied Economic and Social Research.

Ronaghi, M. H., & Mosakhani, M. (2022). The effects of blockchain technology adoption on business ethics and social sustainability: Evidence from the Middle East. *Environment, Development and Sustainability*, *24*(5), 6834–6859. doi:10.100710668-021-01729-x PMID:34393620

Rootes, C., Zito, A., & Barry, J. (2012). *Climate change, national policy, and grassroots action: an introduction*. Environmental Policy.

Roper, S. D., & Chaudhari, N. (2017). Taste buds: Cells, signals and synapses. *Nature Reviews. Neuroscience*, *18*(8), 485–497. doi:10.1038/nrn.2017.68 PMID:28655883

Rosenberg, N., & Frischtak, R. C. (1984). Technological innovation and long waves. *Cambridge Journal of Economics*, *8*, 7–24.

Roth-Berghofer, T., Recio Garcia, J. A., Sauer, C., Bach, K., Althoff, K. D., Diaz-Agudo, B., & Gonzales Calero, P. A. (2012). Building case-based reasoning applications with myCBR and COLIBRI studio.

Roundy, P. T., Bradshaw, M., & Brockman, B. K. (2018). The emergence of entrepreneurial ecosystems: A complex adaptive systems approach. *Journal of Business Research*, *86*, 1–10. doi:10.1016/j.jbusres.2018.01.032

Rowley, T. J. (1997). Moving beyond dyadic ties: A network theory of stakeholder influences. *Academy of Management Review*, *22*(4), 887–910. doi:10.2307/259248

Ruangkanjanases, A., Hsu, S. L., Wu, Y. J., Chen, S. C., & Chang, J. Y. (2020). What drives continuance intention towards social media? Social influence and identity perspectives. *Sustainability (Switzerland)*, *12*(17), 1–15. doi:10.3390u12177081

Ryu, K., Han, H., & Jang, S. S. (2010). Relationships among hedonic and utilitarian values, satisfaction and behavioral intentions in the fast-casual restaurant industry. *International Journal of Contemporary Hospitality Management*, *22*(3), 416–432. doi:10.1108/09596111011035981

Saadé, R., & Bahli, B. (2005). The impact of cognitive absorption on perceived usefulness and perceived ease of use in on-line learning: An extension of the technology acceptance model. *Information & Management*, *42*(2), 317–327. doi:10.1016/j.im.2003.12.013

Saahas Zero Waste (n.d). About us. *Saahas Zero Waste.* https://saahaszerowaste.com/ /about-us/

Sadeghi, M. (2019). A shift from classroom to distance learning: Advantages and limitations. *International Journal of Research in English Education*, *4*(1), 80–88. doi:10.29252/ijree.4.1.80

Sadorsky, P. (2014). The effect of urbanization on CO2, emissions in emerging economies. *Energy Economics, 41*(1) pp. 147-153. .

Sadowski, B. (2022). Book review: A Modern Guide to the Digitalization of Infrastructure. *Digital Policy, Regulation and Governance.*

Saeed, N., Yang, Y., & Sinnappan, S. (2009). Emerging web technologies in higher education: A case of incorporating blogs, podcasts and social bookmarks in a web programming course based on students' learning styles and technology preferences. *Journal of Educational Technology & Society*, *12*(4), 98–109.

Safwa Farook, F., & Abeysekera, N. (2016). Influence of Social Media Marketing on Customer Engagement. *International Journal of Business and Management Invention*, *5*(12), 115–125. www.ijbmi.org

Sag, M., Rohde, K. (2007). Patent reform and differential impact. *Minnesota Journal of Law,* Science & Technology, 8 (1), 1-93. .

Sahebi, H., Nickel, S., & Ashayeri, J. (2015). Joint venture formation and partner selection in upstream crude oil section: Goal programming application. *International Journal of Production Research*, *53*(10), 3047–3061. doi:10.1080/00207543.2014.970708

Saidi, S., Shahbaz, M., & Akhtar, P. (2018). The long-run relationships between transport energy consumption, transport infrastructure, and economic growth in MENA countries. *Transportation Research Part A, Policy and Practice*, *111*(January), 78–95. doi:10.1016/j.tra.2018.03.013

Saiko, D., Medvedkova, I., Kovaleva, E., Lemeshkin, A., Chernyaeva, S., & Matytsina, I. (2020). Educational and Cultural Aspects of Digitalization of Economy. *Russian Conference on Digital Economy and Knowledge Management (RuDEcK 2020)*. Atlantic Press. 10.2991/aebmr.k.200730.061

Salamzadeh, A., Tajpour, M., Hosseini, E., & Salamzadeh, Y. (2022). Geotourism and Destination Brand Selection: Does Social Media Matter? In *Economics and Management of Geotourism* (pp. 105–124). Springer. doi:10.1007/978-3-030-89839-7_6

Salazar, A., Hackney, R. A. Y., & Howells, J. (2003). The Strategic Impact of Internet Technology in Biotechnology and Pharmaceutical Firms. *Information Technology and Managment*, *4*(2/3), 289–301. doi:10.1023/A:1022910614411

Samavi, R., Yu, E., & Topaloglou, T. (2009). Strategic reasoning about business models: A conceptual modeling approach. *Information Systems and e-Business Management*, *7*(2), 171–198. doi:10.100710257-008-0079-z

Sandhu, M. S., Sidique, S. F., & Riaz, S. (2011). Entrepreneurship barriers and entrepreneurial inclination among Malaysian postgraduate students. *International Journal of Entrepreneurial Behaviour & Research, 17*(4), 428–449. doi:10.1108/13552551111139656

Saraph, J. V., Benson, G. P., & Schroeder, R. G. (1989). An instrument for measuring the critical factors of quality management. *Decision Sciences, 20*(4), 810–829. doi:10.1111/j.1540-5915.1989.tb01421.x

Sarasvathy, S. D., & Dew, N. Velamuri, S Ramakrishna, & Venkataraman, Sankaran. (2010). Three views of entrepreneurial opportunity Handbook of entrepreneurship research (pp. 77-96): Springer.

Sawyerr, O. O., & Ebrahimi, B. P. (2022). Executive environmental scanning and strategic uncertainty: The impact of institutional context. *International Studies of Management & Organization, 52*(1), 7–24. doi:10.1080/00208825.2021.2023442

Sawyer, S. J., Eubanks, M. D., Beasley, J. C., Barton, B. T., Puckett, R. T., Tomeček, J. M., & Tomberlin, J. K. (2022). Vertebrate and invertebrate competition for carrion in human-impacted environments depends on abiotic factors. *Ecosphere, 13*(7), e4151. doi:10.1002/ecs2.4151

Sayyedi & Taqi-Khani, A. (2011) Entrepreneurship Development Barriers and The Role of Government in Facilitating Entrepreneurship Development. *Work and Sociaty*, 35.

Schad, J., Lewis, M. W., Raisch, S., & Smith, W. K. (2016). Paradox Research in Management Science: Looking back to move forward. *The Academy of Management Annals, 10*(1), 5–64. doi:10.5465/19416520.2016.1162422

Schad, J., Lewis, M. W., & Smith, W. K. (2019). Quo vadis, paradox? Centripetal and centrifugal forces in theory development. *Strategic Organization, 17*(1), 107–119. doi:10.1177/1476127018786218

Scherer, A. G., & Palazzo, G. (2011). The new political role of business in a globalized world: A review of a new perspective on CSR and its implications for the firm, governance, and democracy. *Journal of Management Studies, 48*(4), 899–931. doi:10.1111/j.1467-6486.2010.00950.x

Schiopu, A. F., Hornoiu, R. I., Padurean, M. A., & Nica, A. M. (2021). Virus tinged? Exploring the facets of virtual reality use in tourism as a result of the COVID-19 pandemic. *Telematics and Informatics, 60*, 101575. doi:10.1016/j.tele.2021.101575 PMID:36569994

Schückes, M., & Gutmann, T. (2020). Why do startups pursue initial coin offerings (ICOs)? The role of economic drivers and social identity on funding choice. *Small Business Economics.* doi:10.100711187-020-00337-9

Schuerkens, U. (2004). Global forces and local life-worlds: Social transformations. *Sage (Atlanta, Ga.).* doi:10.4135/9781446211328

Schumpeter, J. (1934). *The Theory of Economic Development* (1st ed.). Harvard University Press.

Secundo, G., Mele, G., Sansone, G., & Paolucci, E. (2020). Entrepreneurship Education Centres in universities: Evidence and insights from Italian "Contamination Lab" cases. *International Journal of Entrepreneurial Behaviour & Research, 26*(6), 1311–1333. doi:10.1108/IJEBR-12-2019-0687

Sen Chiang, H. (2013). Continuous usage of social networking sites: The effect of innovation and gratification attributes. *Online Information Review, 37*(6), 851–871. doi:10.1108/OIR-08-2012-0133

Sethi, S. (1975). Dimensions of corporate social performance: An analytical framework. *California Management Review, 17*(3), 58–64. doi:10.2307/41162149

Setiawan, R., & Achyar, A. (2012). *Effects of Perceived Trust and Perceived Price on Customers' Intention to Buy in Online Store in Indonesia.* Asean Marketing Journal.

Shafer, S. M., Smith, H. J., & Linder, J. C. (2005). The power of business models. *Business Horizons*, *48*(3), 199–207. doi:10.1016/j.bushor.2004.10.014

Shaikh, E., Brahmi, M., Thang, P. C., Watto, W. A., Trang, T. T. N., & Loan, N. T. (2022). Should I Stay or Should I Go? Explaining the Turnover Intentions with Corporate Social Responsibility (CSR), Organizational Identification and Organizational Commitment. *Sustainability*, *14*(10), 6030. https://doi.org/10.3390/su14106030

Shaikh, E, Brahmi, M, Thang, PC, Watto, WA, Trang, TTN, & Loan, NT. Should I Stay or Should I Go? Explaining the Turnover Intentions with Corporate Social Responsibility (CSR), Organizational Identification and Organizational Commitment.2022. *Sustainability*, *14*(10):6030. https://doi.org/ doi:10.3390u14106030

Shankar, A., & Datta, B. (2018). Factors affecting mobile payment adoption intention: An Indian perspective. *Global Business Review, 19*(3_suppl), S72-S89.

Sharma, C. (2016). R&D, technology transfer and productivity in the Indian pharmaceutical industry. *International Journal of Innovation Management*, *20*(1), 1–24. doi:10.1142/S1363919616500109

Sharma, S., Singh, S., Kujur, F., & Das, G. (2020). Social media activities and its influence on customer-brand relationship: An empirical study of apparel retailers' activity in India. *Journal of Theoretical and Applied Electronic Commerce Research*, *16*(4), 602–617. doi:10.3390/jtaer16040036

Sharma, T. G., Hamari, J., Kesharwani, A., & Tak, P. (2020). Understanding continuance intention to play online games: Roles of self-expressiveness, self-congruity, self-efficacy, and perceived risk. *Behaviour & Information Technology*, *41*(2), 348–364. doi:10.1080/0144929X.2020.1811770

Sharp, Z., & Zaidman, N. (2010). Strategization of CSR. *Journal of Business Ethics*, *93*(1), 51–71. doi:10.100710551-009-0181-2

Shaw, E., Gordon, J., Harvey, C., & Maclean, M. (2013). Exploring contemporary entrepreneurial philanthropy. *International Small Business Journal*, *31*(5), 580–599. doi:10.1177/0266242611429164

Shen, C. H., & Chang, Y. (2009, April). Ambition versus conscience, does corporate social responsibility pay off? The application of matching methods. *Journal of Business Ethics*, *88*(1), 133–153. doi:10.100710551-008-9826-9

Shipilov, A., & Gawer, A. (2020). Integrating Research on Interorganizational Networks and Ecosystems. *The Academy of Management Annals*, *14*(1), 92–121. doi:10.5465/annals.2018.0121

Shrestha, M. B., & Bhatta, G. R. (2018). Selecting appropriate methodological framework for time series data analysis. *Journal of Finance and Data Science*, *4*(2), 71–89. doi:10.1016/j.jfds.2017.11.001

Sihite, J., Harun, T. W., & Nugroho, A. (2016). The Low Cost Airline Consumer Price Sensitivity: An Investigation on the Mediating Role of Promotion and Trust in Brand. *International Research Journal of Business Studies, 7*(3).

Singh, A., Verma, P. (2014). A New Model of Corporate Social Responsibility in India. *International Journal of Academic Research in Business and Social Sciences,N-10.*

Singh, A., Majumdar, S., & Saini, G. K. (2017). Corporate Social Responsibility and Social Entrepreneurship: An Indian Context. *Journal of Entrepreneurship and Innovation in Emerging Economies*, *3*(1), 71–76. doi:10.1177/2393957516684451

Singh, H. (2009). *Retail Management – A Global Perspective: Text and Cases, S.* Chand Publishing.

Singh, J., & Singh, P. (2014). Decomposition of Technical Efficiency and Productivity Growth in Indian Pharmaceutical Industry:A Non-Parametric Analysis. *Artha Vijnana: Journal of The Gokhale Institute of Politics and Economics*, *56*(4), 456. doi:10.21648/arthavij/2014/v56/i4/111174

Singh, P. J., & Smith, A. (2004). 'Relationship between TQM and innovation: An empirical Study'. *Journal of Manufacturing Technology Management*, *15*(5), 394–401. doi:10.1108/17410380410540381

Sinha, P., Gokhale, S., & Rawal, S. (2015). Online retailing paired with kirana: A formidable combination for emerging markets. *Customer Needs and Solutions*, *2*(4), 317–324. doi:10.100740547-015-0057-9

Sinkovics, N., Gunaratne, D., Sinkovics, R. R., & Molina-Castillo, F. J. (2021). Sustainable business model innovation: An umbrella review. *Sustainability*, *13*(13), 7266. doi:10.3390u13137266

Sisodia, R., Wolfe, D. B., & Sheth, J. (2007). *Firms of endearment: How world-class companies profit from passion and purpose*. Wharton School Publishing.

Sitaraman, K. (2018). Traditional trade in India: The resilient retailer and implications for POS (point of sale) strategies. *Journal of Indian Business Research*, *10*(4), 337–344. doi:10.1108/JIBR-12-2017-0247

Sitaridis, I. K. & Kitsios, F. (2017). Students' perceptions of barriers to entrepreneurship. *Ekpaídeush, Dia Bíou Máqhsh, Έreuna kai Tecnologikή Anáptuxh, Kainotomía kai Oikonomía, 1,* 524–535.

Slaughter, R. A. (1999). A new framework for environmental scanning.. *Foresight-The journal of future studies, strategic thinking and policy, 1*(5), 441-451.

Smith, A. C. (2005). Complexity theory for organizational futures studies.. *Foresight.*

Smith, W. K. (2014). Dynamic decision making: A model of senior leaders managing strategic paradoxes. *Academy of Management Journal*, *57*(6), 1592–1623. doi:10.5465/amj.2011.0932

Smith, W. K., & Lewis, M. W. (2011). Toward a theory of paradox: A dynamic equilibrium model of organizing. *Academy of Management Review*, *36*(2), 381–403.

Smith, W. K., & Tushman, M. L. (2005). Managing strategic contradictions: A top management model for managing innovation streams. *Organization Science*, *16*(5), 522–536. doi:10.1287/orsc.1050.0134

Snihur, Y., Lamine, W., & Wright, M. (2021). Educating engineers to develop new business models: Exploiting entrepreneurial opportunities in technology-based firms. *Technological Forecasting and Social Change*, *164*, 119518. doi:10.1016/j.techfore.2018.11.011

Social Inspector General for Afghanistan Reconstruction (SIGAR). (2021) *Quaterly Report to the United States Congress: Economic and Social Development.* SIGAR. https://www.sigar.mil/pdf/quarterlyreports/2021-01-30qr.pdf

Sokolova, O. (2021). Legal Regulation Of Toponyms In Cultural Landscape Of A Belarusian City. *Весці БДПУ. Серыя*, *2*(4), 96–100.

Sokolovskaya, I. (2020). Socio-psychological factors of students' satisfaction in the context of digitalization of education during the COVID-19 pandemic and self-isolation. *Digital sociology, 3*(2), 46-54.

Solikhah, E. W. (2022). The Effect E-Wom Website Attractiveness E-Trust and Innovation on Purchase Decision Online Sales. *(JDS), 20*(11), 61-69.

Sonnenshein, S., Nault, K., & Obodaru, O. (2017). Competition of a different flavor: How a strategic group identity shapes competition and cooperation. *Administrative Science Quarterly*, *62*(4), 626–656. doi:10.1177/0001839217704849

Sørmo, F., Cassens, J., & Aamodt, A. (2005). Explanation in case-based reasoning–perspectives and goals. *Artificial Intelligence Review*, *24*(2), 109–143. doi:10.100710462-005-4607-7

Sovacool, B. K., Burke, M., Baker, L., Kotikalapudi, C. K., & Wlokas, H. (2017). New frontiers and conceptual frameworks for energy justice. *Energy Policy*, *105*, 677–691. doi:10.1016/j.enpol.2017.03.005

Spieth, P., & Schneider, S. (2016). Business model innovativeness: designing a formative measure for business model innovation. *Journal of business Economics, 86*(6), 671-696.

Spieth, P., Schneckenberg, D., & Ricart, J. E. (2014). Business model innovation–state of the art and future challenges for the field. *Research Management*, *44*(3), 237–247.

Srinivisan, S.R. (2015) Lessons from local self sustained retailers. *Free Press Journal, 12.*

Srivastava, R. K. (2020). Managing mergers and acquisitions in health care: A case study in the pharmaceutical sector. *International Journal of Healthcare Management*, *13*(sup1, S1), 61–73. doi:10.1080/20479700.2017.1422337

Staab, S., & Studer, R. (Eds.). (2010). *Handbook on ontologies*. Springer Science & Business Media.

Steils, N. (2021). Qualitative Experiments for Social Sciences. *New Trends in Qualitative Research*, *6*, 24–31. doi:10.36367/ntqr.6.2021.24-31

Stock, J. H., & Watson, M. W. (2015). Introduction to econometrics (3rd ed). Pearson.

Stonig, J., Schmid, T., & Müller-Stewens, G. (2022). From product system to ecosystem: How firms adapt to provide an integrated value proposition. *Strategic Management Journal*, *43*(9), 1927–1957. doi:10.1002mj.3390

Strogatz, S. H. (2012). *Sync: How order emerges from chaos in the universe, nature, and daily life.* . sustainable supply chains; a framework for environmental scanning practices. (2014). *International Journal of Operation & Production Managment.*

Subanidja, S., Legowo, M., Sorongan, F., & Wahyudi, E. (2020). The Choice of Collaborating with FINTECH Entities for Competitive Advantage through Leadership Styles Scientific. *Papers of the University of Pardubice, Series D: Faculty.*

Suhaily, L., & Darmoyo, S. (2017). Effect Of Product Quality, Perceived Priceand Brand Image On Purchase Decision Mediated By Customer Trust (Study On Japanese Brandelectronic Product). *Jurnal Manajemen*, *21*(2), 179–194. doi:10.24912/jm.v21i2.230

Sunkar, A., Lakspriyanti, A. P., Haryono, E., Brahmi, M., Setiawan, P., & Jaya, A. F. (2022). Geotourism Hazards and Carrying Capacity in Geosites of Sangkulirang-Mangkalihat Karst, Indonesia. *Sustainability*, *14*(3), 1704. doi:10.3390u14031704

Suri, F. K., & Banerji, A. (2016). A study of disaggregated R&D expenditure on Indian pharmaceutical exports. *Journal of Developing Areas*, *50*(3), 167–190. doi:10.1353/jda.2016.0108

Suri, F. K., & Banerji, A. (2019b). Impact of R&D Intensity, Patents and Regulatory filings on Export Intensity of Indian Pharmaceutical Industry. *Indian Journal of Pharmaceutical Education and Research*, *53*(4), 638–648. doi:10.5530/ijper.53.4.125

Suryanto, D. (2018). Bank Strategy when Facing Financial Technology *Competition. 3rd International Conference on Vocational Higher Education (ICVHE 2018)*, (pp. 149-154). IEEE.

Sussmann, S., & Vanhegan, H. (2000). Virtual Reality and the Tourism Product Substitution or Complement? *In Proceedings of the Eighth European Conference on Information Systems* (ECIS) (pp. 1077–1083). Vienna, Austria: Wirtschaftsuniversität Wien.

Su, W., Peng, M. W., Tan, W., & Cheung, Y.-L. (2016). The signaling effect of corporate social responsibility in emerging economies. *Journal of Business Ethics, 134*(3), 479–491. doi:10.100710551-014-2404-4

Swait, J., & Erdem, T. (2007). Brand effects on choice and choice set formation under uncertainty. *Marketing Science, 26*(5), 679–697. doi:10.1287/mksc.1060.0260

Swamy, M. (2021). Per capita consumption expenditure regresses by 3 years. *CMIE.* https://cmie.com/kommon/bin/sr.php?kall=warticle&dt=20210605142154&msec=730#:~:text=India's%20private%20final%20consumption%20expenditure,123.1%20trillion%20in%202019%2D20

Szopinski, D., Schoormann, T., John, T., Knackstedt, R., & Kundisch, D. (2017). *How software can support innovating business models: A taxonomy of functions of business model development tools.* Semantic Scholars.

Szopinski, D., Schoormann, T., John, T., Knackstedt, R., & Kundisch, D. (2020). Software tools for business model innovation: Current state and future challenges. *Electronic Markets, 30*(3), 469–494. doi:10.100712525-018-0326-1

Tai, F.-M., & Chuang, S.-H. (2014). Corporate social responsibility. *Ibusiness, 6*(03), 117–130. doi:10.4236/ib.2014.63013

Tajpour, M., Salamzadeh, A., Salamzadeh, Y., & Braga, V. (2021). Investigating social capital, trust, and commitment in family business: case of media firms. *Journal of Family Business Management.*

Tajpour, M. (2021). towards the entrepreneurial university. *Journal of Organizational Culture Communications and Conflict, 25*(3), 4–5.

Tajpour, M., Demiryurek, K., & Abaci, N. I. (2021). Design the pattern of increasing satisfaction for international students: A qualitative study with the grounded theory approach. *International Journal of Management Education, 15*(5), 458–476.

Tajpour, M., Hosseini, E., & Brahmi, M. (2022). Effect of international entrepreneurship indicators on innovative performance: The mediating role of motivation. *International Journal of Technology Transfer and Commercialisation, 19*(1), 142–162. doi:10.1504/IJTTC.2022.123090

Tajpour, M., Hosseini, E., Mohammadi, M., & Bahman-Zangi, B. (2022). The effect of knowledge management on the sustainability of technology-driven businesses in emerging markets: The mediating role of social media. *Sustainability, 14*(14), 8602. doi:10.3390u14148602

Tajpour, M., Salamzadeh, A., Ramadani, V., Palalić, R., & Hosseini, E. (2022). Knowledge sharing and achieving competitive advantage in international environments: The case of Iranian digital start-ups. In *International Entrepreneurship in Emerging Markets* (pp. 206–224). Routledge. doi:10.4324/9781003218357-13

Tajpour, M., Salamzadeh, A., Ramadani, Y., Palalić, R., & Hosseini, E. (2021). *Knowledge Sharing and Achieving Competitive Advantage in International Environments: Case of Iranian Digital Startups. International Entrepreneurship in Emerging Markets: Contexts, Behaviours, and Successful Entry.* Routledge.

Talwar, S., Kaur, P., Nunkoo, R., & Dhir, A. (2022). Digitalization and sustainability: Virtual reality tourism in a post pandemic world. *Journal of Sustainable Tourism*, 1–28. doi:10.1080/09669582.2022.2029870

Tan, Z., Sadiq, B., Bashir, T., Mahmood, H., & Rasool, Y. (2022). Investigating the Impact of Green Marketing Components on Purchase Intention: The Mediating Role of Brand Image and Brand Trust. *Sustainability, 14*(10), 5939. doi:10.3390u14105939

Tashman, P., Marano, V., & Kostova, T. (2017) Talking the talk and walking the walk: CSR reporting and CSP of emerging market multinationals. In Academy of Management Proceedings 2017 (Vol. 2017, No. 1, p. 11183). Briarcliff Manor, Academy of Management.

Täuscher, K., & Abdelkafi, N. (2017). Visual tools for business model innovation: Recommendations from a cognitive perspective. *Creativity and Innovation Management*, *26*(2), 160–174. doi:10.1111/caim.12208

Teece, D. J. (2007). Explicating dynamic capabilities: The nature and microfoundations of (sustainable) enterprise performance. *Strategic Management Journal*, *28*(13), 1319–1350. doi:10.1002mj.640

Teece, D. J. (2018). Profiting from innovation in the digital economy: Enabling technologies, standards, and licensing models in the wireless world. *Research Policy*, *47*(8), 1367–1387. doi:10.1016/j.respol.2017.01.015

Thatcher, J. B., Loughry, M. L., Lim, J., & McKnight, D. H. (2007). Internet anxiety: An empirical study of the effects of personality, beliefs, and social support. *Information & Management*, *44*(4), 353–363. doi:10.1016/j.im.2006.11.007

The new complex perspective in economic analysis and business management. . (2002). *Emergence, 4(1-2)*, 147-163.

The new dynamics of strategy: Sense-making in a complex and complicated world. (2003). *IBM systems journal, 42*(3), 462-483.

Thomas, J. R. (2002). *No. 2* (Vol. 17). The responsibility of the rule maker: comparative approaches to patent administration reform. Berkeley Technology Law Journal.

Thomas, L. D. W., & Ritala, P. (2022). Ecosystem Legitimacy Emergence: A Collective Action View. *Journal of Management*, *48*(3), 515–541. doi:10.1177/0149206320986617

Todd, J. (2005). Social transformation, collective categories, and identity change. *Theory and Society*, *34*(4), 429–463. doi:10.100711186-005-7963-z

Tolboom, I. H. (2016). The impact of digital transformation, Forcasting and social Journal, 101 (4), 875-895.

Tol, R. J. (2014). *Climate economics: economic analysis of climate, climate change and climate policy, Book.* Edward Elgar.

Tunio, M. N., Chaudhry, I. S., Shaikh, S., Jariko, M. A., & Brahmi, M. (2021). Determinants of the Sustainable Entrepreneurial Engagement of Youth in Developing Country—An Empirical Evidence from Pakistan. *Sustainability*, *13*(14), 7764. https://doi.org/10.3390/su13147764

Tunio, M. N., Jariko, M. A., Børsen, T., Shaikh, S., Mushtaque, T., & Brahmi, M. (2021). How Entrepreneurship Sustains Barriers in the Entrepreneurial Process—A Lesson from a Developing Nation. *Sustainability*, *13*(20), 11419. doi:10.3390u132011419

Tussyadiah, I. P., Wang, D., & Jia, C. (2017). Virtual reality and attitudes toward tourism destinations. In *Information and Communication Technologies in Tourism 2017: Proceedings of the International Conference in Rome*, (pp. 229-239). Springer International Publishing. 10.1007/978-3-319-51168-9_17

Uhl-Bien, M., & Arena, M. (2018). Leadership for organizational adaptability: A theoretical synthesis and integrative framework. *The Leadership Quarterly*, *29*(1), 89–104. doi:10.1016/j.leaqua.2017.12.009

Umar, M., Farid, S., & Naeem, M. A. (2022). Time-frequency connection between clean energy stocks and fossil fuel markets: Comparison between the financial, oil and pandemic crises. *Energy*, *240*, 122702. doi:10.1016/j.energy.2021.122702

United Nations Development Programme. (2020) *About Afghanistan: Livelihoods, UNDP*. UN. https://www.af.undp.org/content/afghanistan/en/home/countryinfo.html#

United Nations. (2013). *United Nations Office on Drugs and Crime: Weak rule of law and lack of good governance a major threat to development*. United Nations Population Fund. (News)

Valkokari, K. (2015). Business, innovation, and knowledge ecosystems: How they differ and how to survive and thrive within them. *Technol. Innov. Manage. Rev.*, *8*(5), 17–24. doi:10.22215/timreview/919

Valmohammadi, C. (2011). Investigating corporate social responsibility practices in Iranian organizations: An ISO 26000 perspective. *Business Strategy Series*, *12*(5), 257–263. doi:10.1108/17515631111166898

van der Wal, J. M., van Borkulo, C. D., Deserno, M. K., Breedvelt, J. J., Lees, M., Lokman, J. C., Borsboom, D., Denys, D., van Holst, R. J., Smidt, M. P., Stronks, K., Lucassen, P. J., van Weert, J. C. M., Sloot, P. M. A., Bockting, C. L., & Wiers, R. W. (2021). Advancing urban mental health research: From complexity science to actionable targets for intervention. *The Lancet. Psychiatry*, *8*(11), 991–1000. doi:10.1016/S2215-0366(21)00047-X PMID:34627532

Van Melle, W., Shortliffe, E. H., & Buchanan, B. G. (1984). EMYCIN: A knowledge engineer's tool for constructing rule-based expert systems. *Rule-based expert systems: The MYCIN experiments of the Stanford Heuristic Programming Project*, 302-313.

Van Oosterhout, J., & Heugens, P. (2008). Much ado about nothing: A conceptual critique of corporate social responsibility. In D. S. Siegel, D. Matten, A. McWilliams, & A. Crane (Eds.), *The Oxford handbook of corporate social responsibility* (pp. 197–223). Oxford University Press. doi:10.1093/oxfordhb/9780199211593.003.0009

Van Tonder, E., & Petzer, D. J. (2018). The interrelationships between relationship marketing constructs and customer engagement dimensions. *Service Industries Journal*, *38*(13–14), 948–973. doi:10.1080/02642069.2018.1425398

Vardomatski, S. (2021, September 14). Augmented and virtual reality after COVID-19. *Forbes*. https://www. forbes.com/sites/forbestechcouncil/2021/09/14/augmented-and-virtual-reality-after-covid-19/?sh=bc07d852d97c

Vázquez, J. L., Lanero, A., & Licandro, O. (2013, October). The added value of corporate social responsibility. Some insights from a research in Uruguay. *International Review on Public and Nonprofit Marketing*, *10*(3), 187–200. doi:10.100712208-013-0099-3

Veit, D., Clemons, E., Benlian, A., Buxmann, P., Hess, T., Kundisch, D., Leimeister, J. M., Loos, P., & Spann, M. (2014). Business models: An information systems research agenda. *Business & Information Systems Engineering*, *6*(1), 45–53. doi:10.100712599-013-0308-y

Venkatesh, V. (2000). Determinants of perceived ease of use: Integrating control, intrinsic motivation, and emotion into the technology acceptance model. *Information Systems Research*, *11*(4), 342–365. doi:10.1287/isre.11.4.342.11872

Venkatesh, V., & Davis, F. D. (2000). Theoretical Extension of the Technology Acceptance Model: Four longitudinal field studies. *Management Science*, *46*(2), 186–204. doi:10.1287/mnsc.46.2.186.11926

Vieira, V., Santini, F. O., & Araujo, C. F. (2018). A meta-analytic review of hedonic and utilitarian shopping values. *Journal of Consumer Marketing*, *35*(4), 426–437. doi:10.1108/JCM-08-2016-1914

Viktorovna, K. O., Flyurovna, A., Anasovna, F., & Yuryevna, E. (2021). Priority directions for the development of the agrarian economy in the context of the digitalization of the agro-industrial complex. *BIO Web of Conferences*.

Visser, W. (2011). *The age of responsibility: CSR 2.0 and the new DNA of business*. John Wiley & Sons.

Vlasov, M., Buchinskaia, O., & Sukhikh, V. (2022). Intercountry differences in apprehension of the digitalization. *SHS Web of Conferences*. SHS. 10.1051hsconf/202214101006

Voss, K. E., Spangenberg, E. R., & Grohmann, B. (2018). Measuring the Hedonic and Utilitarian Dimensions of Consumer Attitude. *JMR, Journal of Marketing Research*, *40*(3), 310–320. doi:10.1509/jmkr.40.3.310.19238

Vujadinović, N., & Jaksic-Stojanovic, A. (2022). Digitalization and Implementation of Modern ICT in Tourism and Creative Industries on the Example of the Cultural Routes. *International Conference "New Technologies, Development and Applications."* Springer. 10.1007/978-3-031-05230-9_67

Wach, K., & Bilan, S. (2021). Public support and administration barriers towards entrepreneurial intentions of students in Poland. *Administratie si Management Public*, (36), 67-80. doi:10.24818/amp/2021.36-04

Waddock, S. A., & Graves, S. B. (1997, April). The corporate social performance–financial performance link. *Strategic Management Journal*, *18*(4), 303–319. doi:10.1002/(SICI)1097-0266(199704)18:4<303::AID-SMJ869>3.0.CO;2-G

Wæraas, A. (2022) 'Thematic Analysis: Making Values Emerge from Texts', *Researching Values: Methodological Approaches for Understanding Values Work in Organisations and Leadership*, 153.

Waldman, D. A., Putnam, L. L., Miron-Spektor, E., & Siegel, D. (2019). The role of paradox theory in decision making and management research. *Organizational Behavior and Human Decision Processes*, *155*, 1–6. Advance online publication. doi:10.1016/j.obhdp.2019.04.006

Walker, G., Devine-Wright, P., Hunter, S., High, H., & Evans, B. (2010). *Trust and community: exploring the meanings, contexts, and dynamics of community renewable energy* (Vol. 38). Energy Policy.

Walker, G., & Simcock, N. (2012). *Community energy systems* (Vol. 1). International Encyclopedia of Housing and Home.

Walker, H., Seuring, S., Sarkis, J., & Klassen, R. (2014). Sustainable operations management: Recent trends and future directions. *International Journal of Operations & Production Management*, *34*(5). doi:10.1108/IJOPM-12-2013-0557

Walters, D., & Helman, D. (2020). *Strategic Capability Response Analysis*. Springer Books. doi:10.1007/978-3-030-22944-3

Wandoko, W., Panggati, I. E., & Sukmaningsih, D. W. (2020, August). Developing e-loyalty toward Online Retailer from e-WOM, Reputation, Information Quality and e-trust. In *2020 International Conference on Information Management and Technology (ICIMTech)* (pp. 238-243). IEEE. 10.1109/ICIMTech50083.2020.9211251

Wang, D., Xu, L., & Chan, H. C. (2015). Understanding the continuance use of social network sites: a computer self-efficacy perspective, *34*(2), 204–216. doi:10.1080/0144929X.2014.952778

Wang, Y. H., & Tsai, C. F. (2014). The relationship between brand image and purchase intention: Evidence from award winning mutual funds. *The international journal of business and finance research*, *8*(2), 27-40.

Wang, Y. H., and Tsai, C. F. (2014). The relationship between brand image and purchase intention: Evidence from award winning mutual funds. *The international journal of business and finance research*, *8*(2), 27-40.

Wang, Y. (2016). *What are the biggest obstacles to growth of SMEs in developing countries? An Empirical evidence from an enterprise survey*. Instanbul Stock Exchange Review. doi:10.1016/j.bir.2016.06.001

Wang, Y. D., & Emurian, H. H. (2005). An overview of online trust: Concepts, elements, and implications. *Computers in Human Behavior*, *21*(1), 105–125. doi:10.1016/j.chb.2003.11.008

Wang, Y.s & Nor, E. (2022). The Impact of FinTech on the Profitability of Traditional banks. *Global Business and Management Research*, 14.

Wasserman, S., & Faust, K. (1994). *Social network analysis: Methods and applications* (Vol. 8). Cambridge University Press. doi:10.1017/CBO9780511815478

Watts, D. (1999). Networks, dynamics and the small world phenomenon. *American Journal of Sociology*, *105*(2), 493–527. doi:10.1086/210318

Weber, O., & Remer, S. (2011). *Social banking and the future of sustainable finance*. Routledge. doi:10.4324/9780203827871

Weinberg, P., & Gottwald, W. (1982). Impulsive consumer buying as a result of emotions. *Journal of Business Research*, *10*(1), 43–57. doi:10.1016/0148-2963(82)90016-9

Weiss, A., Michels, C., Burgmer, P., Mussweiler, T., Ockenfels, A., & Hofmann, W. (2021). Trust in everyday life. *Journal of Personality and Social Psychology*, *121*(1), 95–114. doi:10.1037/pspi0000334 PMID:32816511

Wei, W., Qi, R., & Zhang, L. (2019). Effects of virtual reality on theme park visitors' experience and behaviors: A presence perspective. *Tourism Management*, *71*, 282–293. doi:10.1016/j.tourman.2018.10.024

Weng, G. S., Zailani, S., Iranmanesh, M., & Hyun, S. S. (2017). Mobile taxi booking application service's continuance usage intention by users. *Transportation Research Part D, Transport and Environment*, *57*, 207–216. doi:10.1016/j.trd.2017.07.023

*What is Circular Economy and Linear Economy ?* (2021) Changestarted.com. https://changestarted.com/circular-economy-why-is-it-better-than-linear-economy/

Whetten, D. A. (1989). What Constitutes a Theoretical Contribution? *Academy of Management Review*, *14*(4), 490–495. doi:10.2307/258554

Wiewel, W., & Hunter, A. (1985). The interorganizational network as a resource: A comparative case study on organizational genesis. *Administrative Science Quarterly*, *30*(4), 482–496. doi:10.2307/2392693

Wiklund, J., Nikolaev, B., Shir, N., Foo, M.-D., & Bradley, S. (2019). Entrepreneurship and well-being: Past, present, and future. *Journal of Business Venturing*, *34*(4), 579–588. doi:10.1016/j.jbusvent.2019.01.002

Wilber, K. (2000). Waves, streams, states and self. Further considerations for an integral theory of consciousness. *Journal of Consciousness Studies*, *7*(11-12), 145–176.

Wilis, R. A., & Nurwulandari, A. (2020). The effect of E-Service Quality, E-Trust, Price and Brand Image Towards E-Satisfaction and Its Impact on E-Loyalty of Traveloka's Customer. *Jurnal Ilmiah MEA (Manajemen, Ekonomi, & Akuntansi)*, *4*(3), 1061-1099.

Win, K. S. (2022). *Factors Influencing Patient Satisfaction and Loyatly Toward Aye Thitsar Specialist Clinic* (Doctoral dissertation, MERAL Portal).

Winn, B. (2020,March 26) Driving Stability & Disruption: How Stablerupting Leaders Unleash Innovation. *Huntsman.* https://huntsman.usu.edu/mba/management-minute/articles/leaders-status-quo

Winter, J., Zhai, J., & Cotton, D. (2022). Teaching environmental sustainability in China: Opportunities and challenges for business and economics faculty in higher education. *Environmental Education Research*, *28*(2), 318–332. doi:10.1080/13504622.2021.2012560

Wirth, S. (2014). Communities matter: Institutional preconditions for community renewable energy. *Energy Policy*, *70*, 236–246. doi:10.1016/j.enpol.2014.03.021

Wismar, M. (2021). 2. K. Round table: Everything you always wanted to know about (COVID-19 and) EU-health policy. *European Journal of Public Health*, 31.

Wood, D. J. (1991). Corporate social performance revisited. *Academy of Management Review*, *16*(4), 691–718. doi:10.2307/258977

Wu, B. & Wang, M, (2020). *The Impact of Business Cycles on the Profitability of Chinese Commercial Banks.* [Master Thesis Within: Business Administration, Jonkoping University, China].

Wu, C. H., Parker, S. K., & De Jong, J. P. (2014). Need for cognition as an antecedent of individual innovation behavior. *Journal of Management*, *40*(6), 1511–1534. doi:10.1177/0149206311429862

Wu, C. S., & Chen, T. T. (2019). Building brand's value: Research on brand image, personality and identification. *International Journal of Management* [IJMESS]. *Economics and Social Sciences*, *8*(4), 299–318.

Wu, W., Huang, V., Chen, X., Davison, R. M., & Hua, Z. (2018). Social value and online social shopping intention: The moderating role of experience. *Information Technology & People*, *31*(3), 688–711. doi:10.1108/ITP-10-2016-0236

Wu, X., & Lai, I. K. W. (2022). The use of 360-degree virtual tours to promote mountain walking tourism: Stimulus–organism–response model. *Information Technology & Tourism*, *24*(1), 85–107. doi:10.100740558-021-00218-1

Xu, F., Liu, X., Chen, W., Zhou, C., & Cao, B. (2018). Ontology-based method for fault diagnosis of loaders. *Sensors (Basel)*, *18*(3), 729. doi:10.339018030729 PMID:29495646

Yadav, P. L., Han, S. H., & Rho, J. J. (2016). Impact of environmental performance on firm value for sustainable investment: Evidence from large US firms. *Business Strategy and the Environment*, *25*(6), 402–420. doi:10.1002/bse.1883

Yadolahi Farsi, J., Arabiun, A., & Akbar Farjadian, A.(2021). Reconceptualizing opportunity construct: An answer to a theoretical dilemma through a systematic literature review.

Yakubu, Z. (2021). 'Do Financial Development, Trade Openness and Political Stability Complement for Egypt's Economic Growth?', Journal of International Commerce, *Economic Policy*, *12*(01), 2150001.

Yan, A., & Luo, Y. (2016). *International Joint Ventures: Theory and Practice: Theory and Practice*. Routledge. doi:10.4324/9781315501338

Yang, T. M., & Maxwell, T. A. (2011). Information-sharing in public organizations: A literature review of interpersonal, intra-organizational and inter-organizational success factors. *Government Information Quarterly*, *28*(2), 164–175. doi:10.1016/j.giq.2010.06.008

Yang, T., Lai, I. K. W., Fan, Z. B., & Mo, Q. M. (2021). The impact of a 360 virtual tour on the reduction of psychological stress caused by COVID-19. *Technology in Society*, *64*, 101514. doi:10.1016/j.techsoc.2020.101514 PMID:33424061

Yan, R., Zhang, K. Z. K., & Yu, Y. (2019). Switching from hotels to peer-to-peer accommodation: An empirical study. *Information Technology & People*, *32*(6), 1657–1678. doi:10.1108/ITP-12-2017-0444

Yatsenko, O. Y., & Starovoytova, I. E. (2020). *Digitization and problems of national culture. 13th International Scientific and Practical Conference-Artificial Intelligence Anthropogenic nature Vs.* Social Origin.

Yin, X., Wang, H., Xia, Q., & Gu, Q. (2019). How Social Interaction Affects Purchase Intention in Social Commerce: A Cultural Perspective. *Sustainability*, *11*(8), 2423. doi:10.3390/SU11082423

Young, D., Reeves, M., & Gerard, M. (2021) *The Secrets of Sustainability Front-Runners.* BCG. https://www.bcg.com/publications/2021/keys-to-being-a-leader-in-sustainable-business-model-innovation

Yuryevna, K. T. (2022). The model of labor potential economic assessment at the regional level: Reproduction-factor approach. *AIP Conference Proceedings*, 070017. doi:10.1063/5.0074674

Yusr, M. M., Mokhtar, S. S. M., Perumal, S., & Salimon, M. G. (2022). The impact of customer knowledge management, TQM and marketing capabilities on product innovation performance of Malaysian SMEs: An empirical study. *International Journal of Innovation Science*, *14*(No. 2), 316–338. doi:10.1108/IJIS-03-2021-0053

Zaheer, A., McEvily, B., & Perrone, V. (1998). Does trust matter? Exploring the effects of interorganizational and interpersonal trust on performance. *Organization Science*, *9*(2), 141–159. doi:10.1287/orsc.9.2.141

Zahra, S. A., & George, G. (2002). Absorptive capacity: A review, reconceptualization, and extension. *Academy of Management Review*, *27*(2), 185–203. doi:10.2307/4134351

Zahra, S. A., & Nambisan, S. (2012). Entrepreneurship and strategic thinking in business ecosystems. *Business Horizons*, *55*(3), 219–229. doi:10.1016/j.bushor.2011.12.004

Zeithaml, V. A., Parasuraman, A., & Malhotra, A. (2000). *A conceptual framework for understanding e-service quality: implications for future research and managerial practice* (Vol. 115). Marketing Science Institute.

Zeitz, G., Johannesson, R., & Jr, J. E. (1997). Employee survey measuring total quality management practices and culture. *Group & Organization Management*, *22*(4), 414–444. doi:10.1177/1059601197224002

Zeng, J., Phan, C. A., & Matsui, Y. (2015). The impact of hard and soft quality management on quality and innovation performance: An Empirical study. *International Journal of Production Economics*, *162*, 162. doi:10.1016/j.ijpe.2014.07.006

Zerbini, A. (2018). Developing a heritage database for the Middle East and North Africa. *Journal of Field Archaeology*, *43*(sup1), S9-S18.

Zhang, J., & Dawes, S. S. (2006). Expectations and perceptions of benefits, barriers, and success in public sector knowledge networks. *Public Performance & Management Review*, *29*(4), 433–466.

Zhang, Q., Feng, X., & Xiang, X. (2016). The Impact of Quality Management Practices on Innovation in China: The Moderating Effects of Market Turbulence. *American Journal of Industrial and Business Management*, *6*(03), 291–304. doi:10.4236/ajibm.2016.63027

Zhang, S. N., Li, Y. Q., Liu, C. H., & Ruan, W. Q. (2019). How does authenticity enhance flow experience through perceived value and involvement: The moderating roles of innovation and cultural identity. *Journal of Travel & Tourism Marketing*, *36*(6), 710–728. doi:10.1080/10548408.2019.1625846

Zhang, T. C., Gu, H., & Jahromi, M. F. (2019). What makes the sharing economy successful? An empirical examination of competitive customer value propositions. *Computers in Human Behavior*, *95*, 275–283. doi:10.1016/j.chb.2018.03.019

Zhang, W., Zhang, X., Liu, F., Huang, Y., & Xie, Y. (2020). Evaluation of the urban low-carbon sustainable development capability based on the TOPSIS-BP neural network and grey relational analysis. *Complexity*, *2020*, 1–16. doi:10.1155/2020/6616988

Zhao, R., Zhan, L., Yao, M., Yang, L. (2020). A geographically weighted regression model augmented by Geodetector analysis and principal component analysis for the spatial distribution of PM2. *Sustainable Cities and Society, 5.*

Zheng, R., Li, Z., & Na, S. (2022). How customer engagement in the live-streaming affects purchase intention and customer acquisition, E-tailer's perspective. *Journal of Retailing and Consumer Services*, *68*, 103015. doi:10.1016/j.jretconser.2022.103015

Zheng, W., Kark, R., & Meister, A. L. (2018). Paradox versus dilemma mindset: A theory of how women leaders navigate the tensions between agency and communion. *The Leadership Quarterly*, *29*(5), 584–596. doi:10.1016/j.leaqua.2018.04.001

Zhu, G., So, K. K. F., & Hudson, S. (2017). Inside the sharing economy: Understanding consumer motivations behind the adoption of mobile applications. *International Journal of Contemporary Hospitality Management*, *29*(9), 2218–2239. doi:10.1108/IJCHM-09-2016-0496

Zhu, Q., Liu, J., & Lai, K. (2016). Corporate social responsibility practices and performance improvement among Chinese national state-owned enterprises. *International Journal of Production Economics*, *171*, 417–426. doi:10.1016/j.ijpe.2015.08.005

Zhu, Y., Zhang, J. H., Au, W., & Yates, G. (2020). University students' online learning attitudes and continuous intention to undertake online courses: A self-regulated learning perspective. *Educational Technology Research and Development, 68*(3), 1485–1519. doi:10.100711423-020-09753-w

Zilber, S., Monken, S., & Quevedo-Silva, F. (2019). Adoption of Social Media by Small- and Medium-Sized Healthcare Enterprises. *BBR. Brazilian Business Review, 16*(5), 453–469. doi:10.15728/bbr.2019.16.5.3

Ziyae, B., Sadeghi, H., Shahamat Nejad, M., & Tajpour, M. (2021). A framework of urban entrepreneurship for women breadwinners. *Foresight, 23*(5), 597–609. doi:10.1108/FS-12-2020-0137

Zmiyak, S. S., Ugnich, E. A., & Taranov, P. M. (2020). Development of a Regional Innovation Ecosystem: The Role of a Pillar University. In *Growth Poles of the Global Economy: Emergence, Changes and Future Perspectives* (pp. 567–576). Springer. doi:10.1007/978-3-030-15160-7_57

Zollo, M., Reuer, J. J., & Singh, H. (2002). Interorganizational routines and performance in strategic alliances. *Organization Science, 13*(6), 701–713. doi:10.1287/orsc.13.6.701.503

Zoric, J. (2011). Connecting business models with service platform designs: Exploiting potential of scenario modeling. *Telematics and Informatics, 28*(1), 40–54. doi:10.1016/j.tele.2010.05.008

Zott, C., Amit, R., & Massa, L. (2011). The business model: Recent developments and future research. *Journal of Management, 37*(4), 1019–1042. doi:10.1177/0149206311406265

Zwanka, R. J., & Buff, C. (2020). COVID-19 Generation: A Conceptual Framework of the Consumer Behavioral Shifts to Be Caused by the COVID-19 Pandemic. *International Consumer Marketing, 33*(1), 58–67. doi:10.1080/08961530.2020.1771646

# About the Contributors

**Mihir Joshi** is working as Assistant Professor of Marketing with Banasthali Vidyapith University. He has completed his PhD in Emotional Intelligence and Consumer Decision making. He received prestigious ICSSR doctoral fellowship in 2016. His background includes bachelors in engineering and technology and Masters in Business Management. He has patent on AI and publications on entrepreneurship, IOT, Employee engagement in Scopus index journals. His wide area of interest includes Mindfulness, Workforce diversity and Entrepreneurial education. Besides Academia he has several years of industrial experience.

**Mohsen Brahmi** has received his PhD Dissertation in Economics ICT Management, researcher and teaching at Faculty Sciences and Business Institute Lecturer. He has supervised research in the Management Economics (Licenses L1 to L3). He is teaching Master Pro in Sustainable development and Industry corporate social responsibility and the Licenses Pro degree in Human Resource Management and Finance SME. His fields of research and publications are industry innovation economics and management in sustainable development, firm corporate social responsibility, policy and management of human resources, social and organisational supervision, and assessment of firm global performance. He is an Associate Editor for Scopus journal and he has several published research articles and international conference papers.

**Luigi Aldieri** is Full Professor of Economics at the Department of Economic and Statistical Sciences of University of Salerno. He holds a PhD in Sciences Economiques et de gestion at the Solvay Business School of Economics and Management (SBS-EM) of Université Libre de Bruxelles (ULB). His research interests embrace Applied Econometrics, the measurement of knowledge, geographic spillovers and economic performance of large international firms, as well as the empirical analysis of the effects of educational level on fertility in developed countries. In the 2% Top cited scientists in the world in Economics, Environmental Sciences, Economics & Business (Stanford University, Elsevier).

**Concetto Paolo Vinci** is Full Professor in Economic Policy, University of Salerno, Faculty of "Scienze Politiche". First degree: University of Naples Federico II; PhD in Development Economics, University of Naples Federico II; Research Activity, Department d'economie Appliquee–Economie du Travail et de l'Emploi (DULBEA-ETE) de l'Universitè Libre de Bruxelles. Main research interests: Efficiency wages and Dual Economies, Economics of Migration, Working Hours and Capital Operating Time, Innovation Economics.

* * *

**Abolghasem Arabiun** is an associate Professor in faculty of Entrepreneurship, University of Tehran, Iran. His research area is about technological entrepreneurship. Also, he has several publications in international journals and participated in several conferences in some countries.

**Amit Banerji** has approximately nine years of corporate experience. Nineteen years of teaching experience. Currently working as a Professor in the Department of Management Studies, Maulana Azad National Institute of Technology, Bhopal, India.

**Amal Ben Cheikh** has a PhD in Management Sciences specialized in Marketing and affiliated to the Applied Research in Business Relationships and Economics (ARBRE) Laboratory at the High Institute of Management (Institut Supérieur de Gestion (ISG, Tunis)), University of Tunis, Tunisia. Her research interests include tourism services, sustainable development, Energy policies, social acceptance of industrial projects and particularly the renewable energy projects, and landscape changes. She has already contributed with her research papers in different national and international conferences added to publishing in some relevant journals in the field. She aims to apply her knowledge in the field of promoting the deployment of renewable energy projects, and to improve citizens' life based on the research on human wellbeing and sustainable development.

**Abdelhabib Bourouis** received his ''Ingénieur'' degree in Computer Science from the University of Constantine (Algeria) in 1999, his ''Magister'' and ''Doctorat en Sciences'' degrees in Computer Science in 2003 and 2011, respectively, both from the University of Batna (Algeria). He obtained his ''HDR'' degree from the University of Biskra in 2015. He is a full professor at the University of Oum El Bouaghi (Algeria) since 2003. His research interests include artificial intelligence, model-driven engineering, cryptology, performance evaluation, and parallel and distributed simulation.

**Mohsen Brahmi** has received his PhD Dissertation in Economics ICT Management, researcher and teaching at Faculty Sciences and Business Institute Lecturer. He has supervised research in the Management Economics (Licenses L1 to L3). He is teaching Master Pro in Sustainable development and Industry corporate social responsibility and the Licenses Pro degree in Human Resource Management and Finance SME. His fields of research and publications are industry innovation economics and management in sustainable development, firm corporate social responsibility, policy and management of human resources, social and organisational supervision, and assessment of firm global performance. He is an Associate Editor for Scopus journal and he has several published research articles and international conference papers.

**Luca Esposito** is a PhD student at the Department of Economics and Statistics of the University of Salerno (Italy).

**Ghada Ferchichi** is a positive, passionate and hardworking person, who always strives to achieve the highest standard possible, at any given task. Possess good communication skills and have the ability to relate to a wide range of people. Always eager to learn, enjoys overcoming challenges and has a genuine interest in Non-Profit sector, Social Entrepreneurship and Digital Marketing. Currently working as the Europe Regional Manager at the Hult Prize Foundation, an organization that challenges people around the world to solve the planet's most pressing challenges through social entrepreneurship, every year the winner gets $1M in funding to make their idea a reality.

**Hajer Hadj Salem** is a doctor in management sciences specialized in Marketing. She's a professor at the Higher Institute of Technological Studies (ISET) of Nabeul, Tunisia, and a researcher affiliated to the Applied Research in Business Relationships and Economics Laboratory (ARBRE)Tunisia. Her research interests include societal marketing, consumer empowerment and sustainable development. She has been the organizer member for the International Congress of Engineering &Sustainable Development ''ICESD'' in Tunisia. She has national and international conference communications and she has some papers published in well recognized journals.

**Basma Hamrouni** is a doctor of university of Kasdi Merbah Ouargla at Algeria. Her work focuses specifically on decision support systems using the Artificial Intelligence techniques. She has been interested in the domain of decision making and Knowledge Management since her engineer studies. She had the opportunity to research about balanced scorecard, KPI, dashboard and Business Intelligence tools. In addition, she has already had the opportunity to apply them while working in many of companies.

**Elahe Hosseini** is a Ph.D. in Organizational Behavior and Human Resource Management, Yazd University, Yazd, Iran. Her research interest is about knowledge employees' voice, social media platforms, digital startups, sustainable development, industry 4 and social and entrepreneurship activities to develop entrepreneurship in developing countries. Also, she has several publications in international journals and participated in several conferences in some countries. The title of her doctoral thesis was about Designing A Multi-Level Process Pattern of Knowledge Employee Voice with the Genealogical Approach in Iran. She serves as an editor, a member of the editorial board in a series of distinguished journals such as the Iranian Journal of Management Studies and International Journal of Management and Enterprise Development. Also, she serves as a reviewer a series of distinguished international journals such as: Sustainability, Journal of Transnational Corporations Review, Journal of Sage Open, and Psychology Research and Behavior Management.

**Ahmed Korichi** is a full professor at the University of Kasdi Merbah Ouargla (Algeria). His research interests include artificial intelligence, vehicular Ad-Hoc Network VANET), Internet of vehicles (IOV), and parallel and distributed simulation.

**Rambabu Lavuri** is faculty in the Department of Marketing at Indian institute of Management, Jammu. He holds a Ph.D. from the Department of Business Management at Osmania University. Articles authored by him have been published in reputed international journals, such as the International Journal of Retail & Distribution Management, Journal of Cleaner Production, Journal of Environmental Management, Asia Pacific Journal of Marketing and Logistics, Journal of Promotion Management, International Journal of Emerging Markets, International Journal of Quality and Service Sciences, Journal of Environmental Planning and Management, Society and Business Review, Sustainable Development and so on.

**Pankaj Madan** is currently a Professor in the Faculty of Management Studies, Gurukula Kangri (Deemed to be University), Haridwar and Dean in Faculty of Engineering & Technology. He is Visiting Professor to Universities in China, Europe and Latin America. His research area includes operation management and data analytics. His literary contributions in Emerald, Taylor and Francis publications can be seen on researchgate.net or Google Scholar. He has authored more than ten books and conducted more than 500 workshops and training sessions.

**Nirbhay Mahor** completed MBA in 2017. Has approximately three years of college teaching experience. Currently enrolled as Ph.D. scholar under co-author

**Tania Mittal** is a Research Scholar in the Faculty of Management Studies, Gurukula Kangri (deemed to be university), Haridwar. She obtained her BCom(hons) and MCom (Finance) from the Delhi University and Panjab University respectively. She has also qualified NET in commerce in year 2019.

**Alireza Rajabipoor Meybodi** is an Associate Professor in Faculty of Economics, Management & Accounting, Yazd University. His research area is about organization behavior and human resource management. Also, he has several publications in international journals and participated in several conferences in some countries.

**Abhineet Saxena** is an incisive professional with 12 years of experience spanning diversified areas such as Corporate Training, Research, and Teaching. He received an MBA degree in Finance and Marketing from Rajasthan technical university, in 2010 and a Ph.D. degree in Microfinance from the University of Rajasthan in 2016. He is NET qualified and currently working as an Assistant professor (AP-3) at the Amity Business School, Amity University Rajasthan. Currently, he is also in charge of Yunus social business Centre – AUR Jaipur. His current research interests include Banking and Finance, corporate finance, Impact assessment of social security schemes, and Holistic rural development. He also received a post-Doctorate fellowship and award from ICSSR New Delhi in the year 2017. He is an experienced professional and has been guiding individuals and Research scholars in eminent educational Institutions. He has worked in various capacities such as Research Project Principal investigator, Educational Consultant, Data analytics Trainer, Examiner, etc., and has honed his professional training and management skills working with globally reputed organizations.

**Priti Saxena** is a faculty for Marketing in Welingkar Institute of Management & Research. She is an astute professional with over 20 years of work experience in corporate, research and academics. She is a PhD in Management and her research areas include sustainability, green marketing, green wash, green trust, CSR and its impact on financial performance of organizations etc.

**Sabrina Schneider** is a professor for strategy and innovation at the MCI in Innsbruck, Austria. Her research focusses on the impact of digital technologies on strategy and work.

**Garima Sharma** in her capacity as Associate Dean - IIC & Research, WeSchool Mumbai contributes to Institutional Innovation, Entrepreneurship, Intellectual Property awareness as also Research and Publication. She has been Co investigator for funded Research Projects in management and related areas Subjects taught by her over her teaching stint years include • Business Research Methods • Business

Statistics, • Perspectives of Management, • Competency Based HRM and Performance Management, • Social Marketing Marketing Research She has also been involved in training and consulting with corporates across Industries such as manufacturing, automobile, Steel, advertising, packaging etc. Her industry exposure spans more than a decade conducting MDPs as well as industry research and consultancy assignments.

**Kirti Sharma** is an assistant professor at Chandigarh University, Punjab, Chandigarh, India and did her PhD from management Studies, Gurukula Kangri (Deemed to be University), Haridwar. She was an ICSSR Fellow. Her one research paper was published in Scopus-index journal and one in UGC-CARE listed journal. She obtained her BCom and MCom (Finance) from the HNB Garhwal University and Diploma of PGDBA from the Symbiosis, Pune. She also holds a National Certificate of Business Professional Programmer by doing 'O' level from NIELIT, formerly named as DOEACC Society.

**Mehdi Tajpour** has Ph.D. Corporate Entrepreneurship at University of Tehran. Also, He is Postdoc in Faculty of Management and lecturer at University of Tehran. His main areas of interest are: Innovation Management, Higher Education, Entrepreneurship, Social Media, Entrepreneurial University, Academic Spin-Offs, Internationalization of University, Human Resources Management and Tourism. He had published several academic manuscripts in international journals and contributed to some national and international conferences. Also, he serves as a reviewer and editor series of distinguished international journals such as: Iranian Journal of Management Studies, International Journal of Environmental Research and Public Health, Sustainability journal, Kybernetes Journal, World Journal of Entrepreneurship Management and Sustainable Development, International Journal of Business and Globalisation, Cogent Business and Management Journal, Journal of Management Information and Decision Sciences, Journal of Entrepreneurship and Public Policy, Journal of Family Business Management and Innovation & Management Review.

**Jahangir Yadollahi Farsi** is Associate Professor in faculty of Entrepreneurship at University of Tehran. His main areas of interest are: Innovation Management, Entrepreneurship, Entrepreneurial University and Opportunity recognition. He had published several academic manuscripts in international journals and contributed to some national and international conferences. Also, he serves as a reviewer and editor series of distinguished journals.

# Index

## T



## U



## V

www.ingramcontent.com/pod-product-compliance
Lightning Source LLC
LaVergne TN
LVHW062115300926
849161LV00010B/2465
* 9 7 8 1 6 6 8 4 6 7 6 6 4 *